D1827595

SAN FRANCISCO GUIDE

YOUR PASSPORT TO GREAT TRAVEL!

CRITICAL ACCLAIM FOR
OPEN ROAD TRAVEL GUIDES!

*Whether you're going abroad or planning a trip in the United States, take Open Road along on your journey. Our books have been praised by **Travel & Leisure, The Los Angeles Times, Newsday, Booklist, US News & World Report, Endless Vacation, American Bookseller, Coast to Coast**, and many other magazines and newspapers!*

Don't just see the world – experience it with Open Road!

ABOUT THE AUTHOR

Stephanie Gold is a professional travel writer living in San Francisco. She is also the author of Open Road Publishing's *Israel Guide*.

ACKNOWLEDGMENTS

There are a lot of people who helped out in all sorts of ways. Eric went on excursions with me to check out restaurants and sights, and put up with my tiresome daily page count; he helped with a phenomenal amount of proofreading, and was supportive of the effort in every way imaginable.

Friends helped, too. Mary Roach, Steve Carr, and Beth Zimmers helped me research restaurants and clubs, and were understanding when I became a slave to the project, answering all invitations with "Can't, I'm working on my book." I truly appreciate Kitty Brody's offer to help with the proofreading, and the integrity of the guide is much improved thanks to her careful editing. I'd also like to thank Betty Borden, who worked through each page of the manuscript, reading with a diligent and discerning eye, weeding out glitches and contradictions as she went, and of course my publisher Jonathan Stein, who believed in me, guided me, and made it all possible.

Too many other people helped out for me to ever list them all. Restaurant, hotel, club, park, and museum staff fielded endless questions, took me on tours, and were generally kind and gracious. One of the pleasures of doing this book was discovering just how many great people work in my city.

HIT THE OPEN ROAD -
WITH OPEN ROAD PUBLISHING!

Open Road Publishing now has guide books to exciting, fun destinations on four continents. As veteran travelers, our goal is to bring you the best travel guides available anywhere! Here's what we offer:

• All Open Road travel guides are written by authors with a distinct, opinionated point of view – not some sterile committee or team of writers. Our authors are experts in the areas covered and are polished writers.

• Our guides are geared to people who want great vacations, great value, and great tips for both standard tourist sights *and* fun, unique alternatives.

• We're strong on the basics, but we also provide terrific choices for those looking to get off the beaten path and *experience* the country or city – not just *see* it or pass through it.

• We give you the best, but we also tell you about the worst and what to avoid. Nobody should waste their time and money on their hard-earned vacation because of bad or inadequate travel advice.

• Our guides assume nothing. We tell you everything you need to know to have the trip of a lifetime – presented in a fun, literate, no-nonsense style.

• And, above all, we welcome your input, ideas, and suggestions to help us put out the best travel guides possible.

SAN FRANCISCO GUIDE

YOUR PASSPORT TO GREAT TRAVEL!

STEPHANIE GOLD

OPEN ROAD PUBLISHING

1st Edition

To My Husband, Eric

Front and back cover photos by Ken Glaser, Jr. Inside photos: page 22, courtesy of San Francisco Convention and Visitors Bureau; page 72, courtesy of Sherman House; page 74, courtesy of Huntington Hotel; page 75, courtesy of Westin St. Francis Hotel; page 77, courtesy of Hotel Monaco; page 78, courtesy of Archbishop's Mansion.

Maps by Rob Perry.

TABLE OF CONTENTS

Contents

Contents

Contents

Contents

MAPS

San Francisco   16-17
BART System   86
Downtown   280-281
Golden Gate Park   291
SoMa   319
Bay Area   389
Marin Headlands   399
Point Reyes   404

SIDEBARS

Things Change!   19
San Fransisco's Population   30
Picking Names in the Bay   32
Nikolai & Concepcion   34
Two Years Before the Mast   34
The Story of Market Street   36
Naming the Golden Gate   37
Forty-Niner Inflation   38
The Birth of Levi's Blue Jeans   39
Tom Sawyer   40
Presidential Death in the Palace Hotel   41
Cable Cars   43
Pacific Heights   44
Emperor Norton   45
1906 Earthquake Survivors   47
The Palace of Fine Arts   48
Bridge Designs   50
Bridges Fact Box   51
Liberty Ships   52
Tolerance in San Francisco   54
Temperature Chart   59
Sales Tax   61
Area Codes   62
The History of Leander Sherman   73
Huntington History   74
Money "Laundering" at the St. Francis   76
Hotel Monaco History   78
The Archbishop Connection   79
Muni Malaise   86
The Mansions Museum Tour   118

Contents

1. INTRODUCTION

When the sky is blue and the sun shines, the city glints with beauty, the Victorian houses bask, and every rise rewards you with a view of the sloping city and the bay. Streets fill with shorts-clad sun-seekers, folks picnic in the parks, and the city feels as though it's opened its doors and its arms to everyone. But when the fog swims in, San Francisco attains a different aura, elusive and romantic, and lovely in a misty sort of way. Locals bundle up in sweaters and seek out their favorite cafes, to sip latte or wine, meet with friends, and watch the fog tendrils float by.

But San Francisco is not a closed club. Outsiders become insiders with ease, and they're soon regulars at their own favorite spots. I wrote this guide to help facilitate the process, to let visitors in on the same pleasures and past-times enjoyed by those who live here. It's not a big city, but it's large enough to absorb as many visitors as care to come. When you're here, you become a part of San Francisco. Progressive and trend-setting, but with a conservative society core, The City is known for its diversity, sophistication, and open-minded tolerance; anyone can fit in.

Few cities are as much in love with themselves, as head-over-heels, thrilled-to-pieces with themselves as San Francisco. Then again, few cities have as many fine reasons to feel so smug. It's a hospitality town, packed with hotels, restaurants, and music. It's a sight-seeing center, with scads of museums to peruse and neighborhoods to stroll. And San Francisco is the hub of the Bay Area, plus the vast expanses of natural beauty to the east, north, and south, full of trails to hike, beaches to loll on, and country roads on which to toodle along. In short, there's a lot to do, see, and eat here, and this guide was designed to help steer you to the best of whatever it is you like to do.

Over thirteen million people visit San Francisco yearly and fall in love with the bay and parks, the hill-top views and mild weather, pretty streets and brightly painted Victorian houses, the swinging nightlife, and the sensational food. Being smitten by San Francisco is just part of the experience. Gene Fowler said: "Every man should be allowed to love two cities, his own and San Francisco" – so you won't be cheating on your home town when you leave your heart here.

2. EXCITING SAN FRANCISCO! - OVERVIEW

William Saroyan said "No city invites the heart to come to life as San Francisco does ... There are no end of ways of enduring time in San Francisco, pleasantly, beautifully, and with the romance of living in everything."

The city Saroyan loved is still terrific, still diverse, and still filled to capacity with charm, sights, entertainment, and hospitality (as for romance, you're on your own). The three facets that are most distinctly, appealingly San Francisco, however, are the neighborhoods, the sweeping views, and the food.

ORIENTATION

San Francisco is a small city, just 46 square miles, located on a squarish tip of a peninsula roughly a third of the way down California's Pacific coast. To the west is the Pacific Ocean, to the east is the San Francisco Bay, north is the strip of the Bay known as the Golden Gate Strait (it's the strait of water connecting the Pacific through the Golden Gate to the Bay), and south is the base of the peninsula, San Francisco's only land border.

The roads south are the only ones that don't involve water. You can drive along the coast on Route 1 to Half Moon Bay, Big Basin Redwoods State Park, and Santa Cruz, though Route 101 (east of Route 1) along the south Bay is faster, straighter, and less scenic. You could take 101 south to Palo Alto (home of Stanford University), and onwards to San Jose if you were so inclined, and Route 280 will go there as well.

To the north, the Golden Gate Bridge leads to Marin County, with Route 1 winding up the beautiful, craggy coast toward Stinson Beach and Point Reyes, and Route 101 heading northeast to Santa Rosa and Wine Country. The Bay Bridge takes you east to Oakland, Berkeley, and Route 80, which will take you to Sacramento, and on eastward to New Jersey if you just keep on driving.

Within San Francisco's 46 square miles are 43 hills, plus some valleys, beaches, lakes, dunes, and wharves. There are also roughly 43 neighborhoods, though their definitions seem to change a bit each year, and the southern districts are rarely a part of a tourist itinerary.

In the northeastern corner is the Embarcadero, a series of shopping complexes and wharves that span that section of the Bay. From the Embarcadero, Market Street heads southwest, cutting a diagonal swathe through the financial and commercial districts. Just north of Market is the Financial District, full of sky-scraping high-rise office buildings, and dominated by the Transamerica Pyramid Building and the Bank of America tower. Just a bit north through the Chinatown Gate on Bush and Grant lies Chinatown, the largest Chinese community outside Asia. Spanning about eight blocks around Portsmouth Square (once the central plaza of old San Francisco), its main arteries are Grant Avenue, Stockton and Kearny Streets. Bordering and merging with Chinatown is North Beach, a district of Italian restaurants and cafes, with Washington Square and the Cathedral of Saints Peter and Paul at its heart, and Columbus Avenue forming its main boulevard.

Telegraph Hill, the location of the first western telegraph station, rises east of North Beach, and is crowned with Coit Tower up top. Further north and west along Taylor is Fisherman's Wharf, once a commercial fishing port established by 19th-century Italian immigrants, but now a heavily touristed row of restaurants, souvenir shops, and motels. Nearby to the west, The Cannery and Ghirardelli Square, once fruit canning and chocolate plants respectively, now house specialty shops, restaurants, and art galleries. And in the San Francisco Bay just off the Wharf is the former federal prison, Alcatraz.

Back on Market but a bit southwest you'll find Powell Street and the main cable car turnaround. Up Powell a couple blocks is Union Square, the ever-popular shopping district, and home to most of San Francisco's hotels and theaters. Further up the Powell slope is Nob Hill, an old posh neighborhood with some of the swellest San Francisco hotels, as well as Grace Cathedral and the cable car lines. North from Nob Hill, there's a minor dip, followed by Russian Hill, which peaks on Jones Street and overlooks North Beach to the east and Aquatic Park to the north.

Head west from Union Square and you go through the Tenderloin, a depressed neighborhood of recent Asian immigrants, cheap housing, prostitutes and drug dealers, and good, inexpensive ethnic restaurants. And west of that there's the Civic Center, home to the dome-capped city hall, the beautiful new Main Library, the opera, and symphony. Near Civic Center to the west of the main thoroughfare of Van Ness Avenue (the city street that connects to Route 101 north and south), Hayes Valley is the chic place to be, with its excellent restaurants, galleries, and boutiques.

On the western border of Hayes Valley is the Western Addition, a residential neighborhood of beautiful Victorian buildings from an older era when the area was better off than it is today, without the crime and dereliction that now plagues the neighborhood. West some more and you come to the Richmond, dubbed New Chinatown by some. It's a thriving residential community with shops and homes and some of the best restaurants in the city, representing every type of Asian cuisine.

North of Western Addition is Pacific Heights, the swankest neighborhood in San Francisco, where the old money built the biggest mansions with the best views of the Bay. And down the northern slope are Cow Hollow and the Marina, relatively flat neighborhoods built on landfill, with Fort Mason Center and the Marina Green and Harbor, and bordered by the Bay. Populated by young urban professionals, fine dining, and clever boutiques, the area is rich in the cafe culture, but poor in seismic stability. The Presidio, which was once the military bastion of San Francisco but is now a new and gloriously pine-filled park, is just west of these neighborhoods. Bakers Beach (San Francisco's nicest) is just west of the Presidio, followed by the beautiful and mansion-filled district called Seacliff. Keep going west through the Richmond and you come to Lincoln Park with the Legion of Honor, followed by Land's End and the Pacific Ocean.

And to the south, there's Golden Gate Park, bordered by Fulton Street, Stanyan, Lincoln Way, and the Pacific. In Golden Gate Park, as well as the famous Japanese Tea Garden, there are several museums, including the Asian Art Museum (regarded as the best collection of Asian art in the United States), the M. H. de Young Memorial Museum (with an important collection of American art), and the California Academy of Sciences. There are also miles in which to stroll through, picnic on, and practice your roller blading.

To the south of the park is the Sunset, a quiet, residential district of small houses that stretches for miles from Ocean Beach east to Haight Ashbury, where the hippies proclaimed the Summer of Love in 1967. Thirty years later, the Haight and the more easterly Lower Haight still attract the young, the tattooed, the drug-happy, and the nose-pierced. Heading south from Haight Ashbury, you pass through the lovely, hilly, residential districts of Ashbury Heights, Buena Vista, and further up still to the lofty Twin Peaks. Go south down the hill, past Market, and there's the Castro, the heart of the gay and lesbian community. Blending to the east is Noe Valley, a sunny residential district that leans a bit left of center, with lots of music stores, co-op groceries, pony-tailed men, and young families.

Directly east of Noe Valley is the Mission. Signs are in English and Spanish, taquerias are on every street corner, and the flavor of the neighborhood is heavily influenced by its mostly Latino residents. Valencia Street is the new center for trendy, excellent restaurants and clubs, though Mission, the next street over, is the traditional main thoroughfare of the district. Follow Mission Street north and it'll take you to the heart of the South of Market neighborhood. Also known as SoMa, what was once a dreary lot of warehouses is now a hotbed of nightclubs, top-notch restaurants, lofts, museums, and the new Center for the Arts complex.

There are other neighborhoods in the southern segment of San Francisco, but visitors rarely find a reason to go there. People might go south of the Sunset district to visit the zoo in Parkside, the shopping mall in Stonestown, or San Francisco State University in Park Merced, but otherwise they are just a bunch of unremarkable residential streets. Bernal Heights south of the Mission is a popular place for young couples to find semi-affordable houses, but there's little incentive for visitors. And while Giants games in Candlestick Park draw people into the mostly black Bayview neighborhood, the region is economically depressed and offers little to tourists.

NEIGHBORHOODS

There are over 40 different neighborhoods in the 46 square miles of San Francisco, and each as its own tone and flavor and identifying characteristics. The boundaries aren't engraved in stone (different maps represent them differently), and as you move from one neighborhood to another, it's not a sudden change that occurs when you cross the street; it's a gradual but perceptible shift in terrain, ethnicity, style, and wealth. Even the climates change, depending on how much protection they get from the fog and coastal breezes.

The neighborhoods represent the wealth of cultures here. In the Mission, store signs are in Spanish and English, Latino music seeps out of homes and cars, and the aroma of Mexican cooking fills the streets. There's lots more in the Mission, including generally warm, sunny weather, some very avant-garde theaters, and some of the finest, most popular clubs and restaurants in the city, but it's the Latino culture that shapes the neighborhood as a whole. Go west just a bit and you're in the Castro, an equally warm valley where the tone is set more by the predominantly gay culture than by any ethnicity. You're most likely to see men holding hands (though straights are allowed, too), and the history of the neighborhood is a testimony to the humanistic, tolerant attitude and politics of the city.

Chinatown is delirious with people, souvenir shops, vegetable stands and fish markets, places to eat, and music, while North Beach just next door keeps the Italian traditions with an outpouring of Italian restaurants, cafes, and warmth. Up the steep incline is Nob Hill, lofty in height and

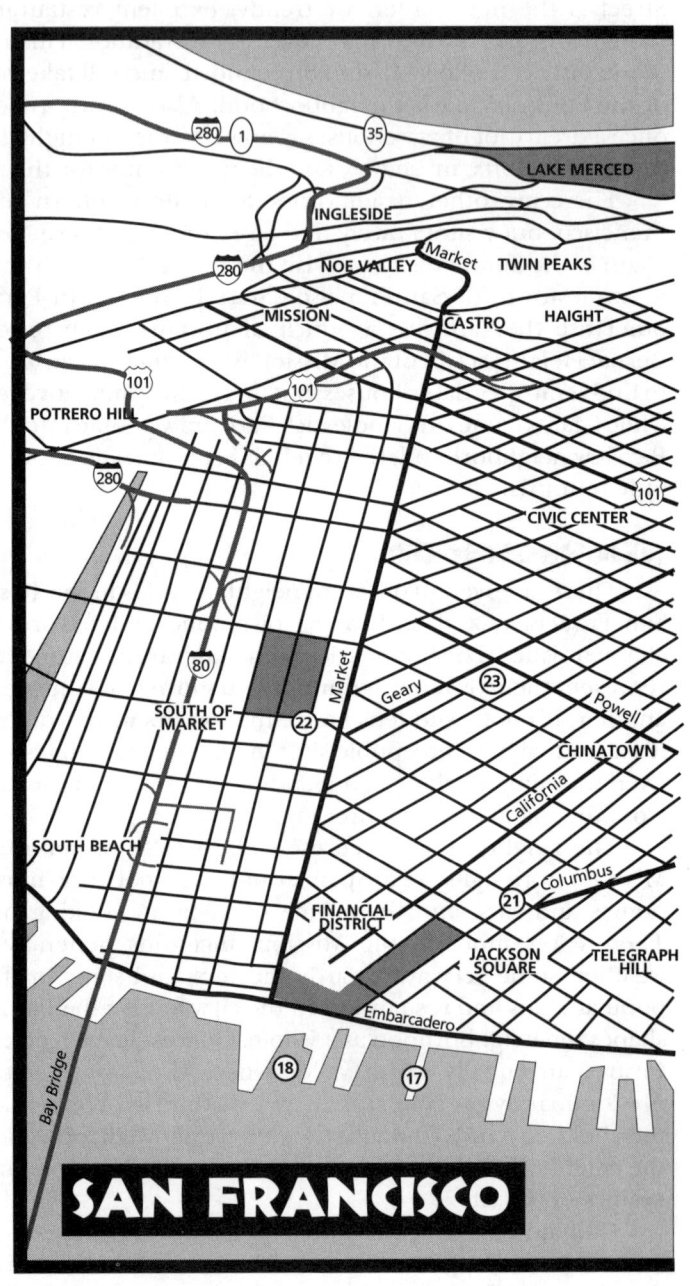

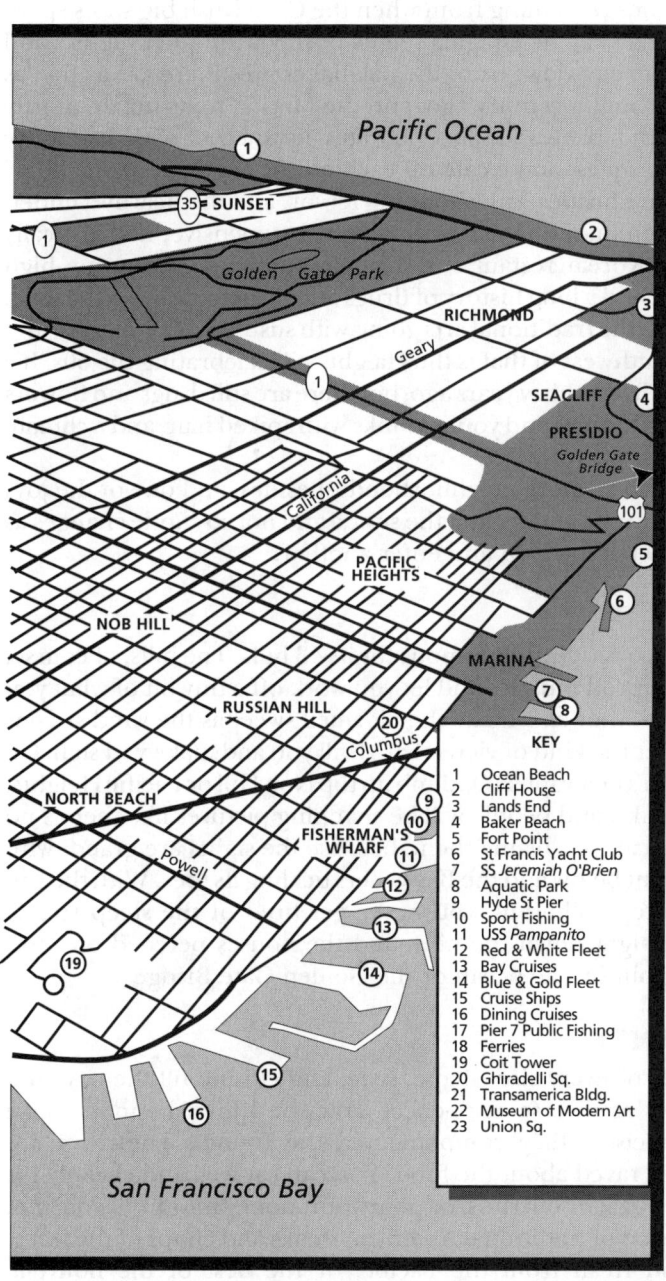

Pacific Ocean

SUNSET

Golden Gate Park

RICHMOND

Geary

SEACLIFF

PRESIDIO

Golden Gate Bridge

California

PACIFIC HEIGHTS

NOB HILL

MARINA

RUSSIAN HILL

Columbus

NORTH BEACH

FISHERMAN'S WHARF

Powell

KEY

1 Ocean Beach
2 Cliff House
3 Lands End
4 Baker Beach
5 Fort Point
6 St Francis Yacht Club
7 SS *Jeremiah O'Brien*
8 Aquatic Park
9 Hyde St Pier
10 Sport Fishing
11 USS *Pampanito*
12 Red & White Fleet
13 Bay Cruises
14 Blue & Gold Fleet
15 Cruise Ships
16 Dining Cruises
17 Pier 7 Public Fishing
18 Ferries
19 Coit Tower
20 Ghiradelli Sq.
21 Transamerica Bldg.
22 Museum of Modern Art
23 Union Sq.

San Francisco Bay

attitude, a bastion of traditional San Francisco society and luxury hotels, with fine mansions remaining from when the Gold Rush big shots spent their money there. Pacific Heights reigns poshly with quiet dignity and elegance, and the bay views from the palatial estates there are as fine as when they were built a century ago, and the Marina to its north, mostly white, young, and professional, celebrates its success with laudatory restaurants, boutiques, and a cafe on each block.

Union Square bustles with shopping fervor, and the nearby Tenderloin, now predominantly Asian and rich in inexpensive, authentically Vietnamese and Korean restaurants, struggles with a poor economy, high unemployment, and a long history of drugs and prostitution. To the west, Japantown keeps the traditional arts going with sushi, udon, hot tubs, and fine arts, and southwest of that is the Haight, still celebrating the 60s. It's a bit dirtier than it was thirty years ago, but there are still drugs and flowers in the hair, aging hippies and young punks with spiked hair, and a climate of anything goes.

There are plenty more neighborhoods, besides, and one of the joys is in exploring the city and feeling the subtle and not so subtle changes as you leave one neighborhood and enter another.

VIEWS

San Francisco is rightfully famous for its 43 hills. The hills, of course, are great for your calf muscles and let you work off a tiny bit of what you ate last night, but they also make the air smell sweet as the wind sweeps by, and they offer the kind of views that thrill you and make you sigh. Go to Coit Tower on Telegraph Hill, climb up top Nob Hill or Pacific Heights, ascend Twin Peaks, and people will be snapping pictures like there's no tomorrow. Nor can you blame them, because the sights are grand, with the city spread out below and the Bay waters tickling its toes. With the sun shining or the fog rolling in, you never get tired of the steep streets plummeting straight down the hills, and the houses perched on their slopes, looking out on the ocean or the Golden Gate Bridge.

RESTAURANTS

Restaurants of every size, shape, style, and cuisine fill the city, and when celebrities as diverse as Spencer Tracy and John Lennon spoke about San Francisco, they complimented the friendly nature of the people, but they raved about the food. You can eat well and cheaply for $5 on burgers, pizza, or burritos, or pour your money into $100 gourmet dinners composed of traditional American steaks and chops of the finest quality, seafood fresh from the Pacific, or the best of the nouvelle California cuisine, as dished up by the nation's best chefs, like Alice Waters, Wolfgang Puck, Julian Serrano, or Anne Sommerville.

And then there are the cuisines brought here by San Francisco's many immigrants. There's Chinese, Vietnamese, Japanese, Cambodian, Singaporean, Filipino, Korean, and Thai, there's Italian, French, German, Spanish, British, and Irish, there's Mexican, Salvadorian, Nicaraguan, Peruvian, Brazilian, and Caribbean, there's Middle Eastern, Greek, Jewish, and Mediterranean, there's even Tibetan, Indian, Russian, and Ethiopian. There are, unfortunately, the bad along with the good, and rip-offs as well as great values, so while experimentation is part of the fun of a vacation, I've revewed more than 285 establishments to steer you in the right direction.

THINGS CHANGE!

Long known as a restaurant town, there are over 4,000 restaurants in the city, and the competition is fierce. Old restaurants disappear and new ones pop up; they change hands and chefs and menus like a party girl changes clothes. In this guide we represent the restaurant scene of today, but there are no guarantees; winds shift and restaurants change just like that. The same is definitely true of nightclubs, and to a lesser extent hotels (they don't change hands very frequently, but rooms rates will vary). We hope the place (restaurant, club, or hotel) you had your heart set on is just as we described it, but we ask your flexibility in case the establishment has changed or entirely disappeared.

PARKS

The parks are as outstanding as they are plentiful, and Golden Gate Park is San Francisco's finest. Over 1,000 acres of meadows, lakes, gardens, and dells stretch three miles long to the ocean's edge, and museums of all sorts add science and culture to the natural beauty. You can row a boat, practice fly casting, ride a horse or bike, learn to roller blade, or just walk and walk and walk. They just don't come any better, and it's very safe, at least by day. And to the north, Lincoln Park looks out over the Pacific Ocean, with magnificent wind-swept vistas, and the stunning renovated California Palace of the Legion of Honor, too. Small parks and squares brighten up the various neighborhoods, providing sunbathing, frisbee, and picnic sites for all the communities.

But while Lafayette Park in Pacific Heights, Washington Square in North Beach, and Buena Vista Park above the Haight are lovely if you're in the neighborhood, San Francisco's only other park worth going out of your way for is the brand new Presidio Park – 1,752 acres of beautiful land given to the Golden Gate National Recreation Area (GGNRA) in 1994 when the US Sixth Army moved out. Full of trails, eucalyptus, and pine trees, there are plans to let some of the land revert to wetlands, which will be a boon to birds and bird-watchers alike. And of course outside of San

Francisco, there are miles and miles of GGNRA parks, including Angel Island in the Bay, the nearby Marin Headlands, Mt. Tamalpais in Mill Valley, and beautiful Point Reyes up north.

ACTIVITIES

All these park lands lend themselves to some great outdoor activities, and hiking ranks number one. The equipment isn't expensive (just some good boots or hiking sandals), you can have as much solitude or company as you want, and the setting is more beautiful than words can say. In summer the hills are golden brown, in spring they're freshly, brightly green, and the wild flowers - purple orchids, orange poppies, yellow buttercups, and blue lupines - make sober adults squeal with joy. Hawks soar and terns skitter, and bird-watchers say "look over there."

City walking is also recommended. The city is small enough and the parking bad enough that cars are often more bother than they're worth, and it's fun poking along quiet streets like Jackson in Pacific Heights or busy commercial centers like Clement in the Inner Richmond. What the hills demand in sweat and screaming muscle they give back in views without compare. You're puffing along, you crest the rise, and suddenly the blue bay, the bridges, and everything is there before you. It's a great excuse to pause and catch your breath.

Another way to enjoy the hills that's just as swell, far less strenuous, and absolutely the most popular activity in San Francisco is via cable car. Especially after a long walk, there's nothing like the pleasure of boarding a little tram and letting it pull you up the hills. Whether you nab a seat on a bench or stand on the running boards and hold on tight, the bells clang clang like a Rice-a-Roni commercial, the car chugs up the steep grade like the little engine that could, and lurches around corners giving you a deeper appreciation of what it means to leave your heart in San Francisco. Standing in line for the ride is a drag, however, and waiting for one to stop, only to have it whiz on by because it's full is even worse. And while during the day the California line is often less busy, the very best is to ride up Powell in the early morning or late night, with the car nearly empty and the fog muting the street lamps. This is how the city gets under your skin - or maybe it's just the night chill.

Aside from walking, cabling, and sight seeing, there are all sorts of other outdoor pursuits. Golden Gate Park is great for cycling, skate boarding, and rollerblading, and experienced cyclists take their bikes across the Bridge to puff up and whiz down the hills in Sausalito or the Marin Headlands. You can rent kayaks and sailboards in Sausalito's Richmond Bay, or row a boat in Golden Gate Park. In addition, there's horseback riding, fishing, rock climbing, surfing, and even swimming (indoors, generally, unless you're a member of the polar bear club).

For the less active, or as a rest from a day's hike, hot tubs are one of the more relaxing activities, and there are plenty of options, from traditional Japanese to casual California laid-back. Sitting in a cafe drinking latte and watching other people dash about is another popular activity, and one highly recommended.

There are all sorts of night-time activities, too. There's dancing and club-hopping, ballet and the symphony, and all sorts of bars to explore. San Francisco has the reputation of being sophisticated and wicked and pandering to all the pleasures, and while you can live it up in any style you want here, most of the city turns off its lights around 11pm. There are a few places that stay open all night if you're hungry or want to dance, but you'll find most night establishments locked up by 2am.

MUSEUMS

San Francisco is a great museum city. It has top-notch museums of fine arts, and some of the best science museums around, but there are also smaller museums celebrating the ethnic diversity of the city, and they're worth visiting as well. The de Young in Golden Gate Park and the California Palace of the Legion of Honor in Lincoln Park are the best for western art, but there's also a great Asian Art Museum, a grand new Museum of Modern Art downtown, and smaller museums with Mexican, African American, Italian, and Jewish exhibits. There's a Cartoon Art museum, the Musée Mecanique with ancient arcade games, and even an antique vibrator museum.

The science museums are excellent. The Exploratorium is one-of-a-kind, and the Academy of Science is also very good. There's a planetarium, an aquarium, and a new Underwater World, plus the Randall Museum, a nice kids' museum with animals to pet. And of course there's the zoo, which is excellent, and worth a visit with or without kids. There's a cable car museum showing the huge wheels winding the steel cables, and some cheesy museums down at Fisherman's Wharf, like the Wax Museum, the Haunted Gold Mine Fun House, and Medieval Dungeon. All kinds of people live here, and there are museums for all kinds of visitors.

EXCURSIONS

Swell as the City is, one of its qualities is its proximity to other great places. Berkeley is just across the Bay, the beaches and trails of Marin start just half an hour away, and the pleasures of the Napa and Sonoma Wine Country are not far north. If you want pampering and a good time, fine wines, fabulous foods, and some hot mud to draw out any remaining iota of tension, Calistoga is just an hour and a half from San Francisco.

LANDMARKS

The icons of San Francisco are firmly imbedded in people's minds. Travel halfway around the world and say San Francisco, and people who know just a few words of English will come back with "Golden Gate Bridge," Cable Cars and Fisherman's Wharf, Chinatown and sourdough bread, Summer of Love and earthquakes, such are the associations sparked by San Francisco. And while we can't promise you an earthquake, the others are easily enjoyed, and then there's the rest of the city to go out and explore.

Says Wilson Mizner, "Every port is my oyster but San Francisco is the coo-coo clam of them all," and that about sums it up.

LOMBARD STREET IN RUSSIAN HILL - "THE WORLD'S CROOKEDEST STREET"

RIVALRIES & NAME CALLING

Civic pride runs high; the local citizens want to take care of their museums and parks, their streets and neighborhoods, and they consistently vote the money to fund it. From "Baghdad-By-The-Bay" to the "City That Knows How," from Tony Bennett crooning about leaving his heart in San Francisco to Jeanette MacDonald singing "San Francisco," people can't help effusing about the place. Robert Kennedy said "I love this city. If I am elected I'll move the White House to San Francisco," and Rudyard Kipling wrote "San Francisco has only one drawback. 'Tis hard to leave."

San Francisco sees itself as the gem of the West Coast, and cherishes its sophisticated bon vivant image, notwithstanding that city some miles down the coast called Los Angeles. There are few pleasures San Franciscans love better than to trash L.A., via baseball, football, or witticism. And there's been a long-standing sibling sort of rivalry with New York, too, with residents of each complaining about the flaws of the other (the relative paucity of good bagels and pizza out here versus the weather and pace of life out there), and how unfortunate it is that the other is so blind to the truth that their city is undeniably the best, blah blah blah.

Few aspects of life reflect image and facilitate rivalries better than names, so it's not surprising how much annual ink gets spilled over just what you should and shouldn't call this city. It was known in these parts as The City when there were no other real cities for miles around, and the appellation stuck, but people still get their noses out of joint over it, taking it as spurious, uppity commentary on their own beloved homes. And then there is "Frisco," the name most San Franciscans love to loathe. To visitors, it carries a certain panache and swagger, but to San Francisco it's an outrage, and it ruffles the feathers and raises the hackles better than anything else.

3. SUGGESTED ITINERARIES

If you're overwhelmed by the options and want some help planning your visit, here are some suggestions for structuring your time. These structured days are packed very full, but you can always jettison some of the activities as your time, interest, and energy dictate.

ITINERARY ONE: THREE DAYS IN SAN FRANCISCO
Day One
From Union Square to Fisherman's Wharf, Coit Tower to Nob Hill, and back.

Get up early (by 9am, latest) and take the Powell-Mason cable car before the crowds make it a chore. Ride through Chinatown and get off at Mason and Vallejo. Walk down Vallejo to Columbus in North Beach and get some breakfast in Caffé Greco. Walk down Mason to Fisherman's Wharf. You may need just half an hour to feel like you've done it, or you may want to spend a few hours exploring the arcades, Underwater World, and shops. When you've had enough, walk the few blocks back to North Beach (or take bus 30 or 39).

Visit Washington Square Park, wander around the neighborhood, and consult the Where to Eat chapter to choose one of the many North Beach restaurants for lunch. To get to Coit Tower after lunch, you can walk up Filbert, or take bus 39 if your legs are flagging. After taking in the views and the murals, you need to evaluate your energy supply. You may want to head back to your hotel for a nap before dinner. If not, find some transport (feet, cable car, or taxi) to California and Mason on Nob Hill. Check out the mansions, fancy hotels, and Grace Cathedral, and take a breather in Huntington Park if the weather's nice. High Tea in one of the fine hotels is a very San Francisco afternoon diversion, but you should make reservations in advance, if you can.

Or, instead of Nob Hill, go explore the Center for the Arts at Third and Mission (the 30 bus will take you there from North Beach). The Yerba Buena Gardens are there, as is the San Francisco Museum of Modern Art.

Dine at whichever of the thousands of restaurants suits you best, and at night, take in a play, the symphony, go bar hopping, take in a jazz set, or cruise the clubs, as you prefer.

Day Two
The Marina, Fort Mason, and Alcatraz.

After breakfast, head to the Exploratorium. It's best first thing in the morning when it's still relatively empty. If you want the Tactile Dome to be part of your visit, you'll need to reserve it way in advance. Spend a few hours having fun inside, then wander around the grounds by the pond, and under the towering columns to let your brain rest. Get a bite to eat in the Marina, then head east to Fort Mason (or wait till you get to Fort Mason to eat if you want to experience Greens Restaurant). There are lots of little museums there, and you're right near the Yacht Harbor and Marina Green if you'd rather see boats than museums.

From Fort Mason, take the 42 bus to Fisherman's Wharf and hop a ferry to Alcatraz (you have to reserve it in advance, and the last boat leaves at 2:15pm - if that crowds your day too much you might skip Fort Mason). For the evening, do the same as last night: Eat well and have fun.

Day Three
Golden Gate Park, the museums, the Richmond, Cliff House and Ocean Beach, Lincoln Park, Japantown.

Eat breakfast, then go to Golden Gate Park, but first decide if you want to lunch in one of the Richmond restaurants or take a park picnic. You can walk the whole park if you feel like it, or just choose the few sites you want to see. The Japanese Tea Garden is very nice, as is the Shakespeare Garden, and the Conservatory of Flowers is very special. Have some lunch (either as a picnic, or walk out to Clement Street in the Richmond and choose a restaurant).

If you want to see the museums, head back into the park at Eighth, and both the de Young and the Academy of Sciences are right there. Otherwise, hop on a bus going westward, and get off at the Pacific Ocean. Visit the Cliff House, the Musée Mecanique, and the Camera Obscura. Then take a walk along Ocean Beach, or head up to Lincoln Park and the California Palace of the Legion of Honor.

To relax from the full day, have a hot tub and massage at Kabuki Hot Tubs in Japantown (make the reservations in advance). You can dine in Japantown, too, or anywhere else in the city.

ITINERARY TWO: FOUR DAYS IN SAN FRANCISCO

Days One Through Three
Follow the three days of Itinerary One.

Day Four
Marin County.
Rent a car, pack a picnic lunch, and head over the Golden Gate Bridge to Marin. Visit Sausalito in the morning, then drive out to either the Headlands, or Tennessee Valley for some scenery, a little hike, and a picnic. Or, alternatively, forego Sausalito and head directly to Point Reyes. Hike around, picnic, bird watch, and enjoy. Then come back to San Francisco, rest up, and plan your dinner and evening.

ITINERARY THREE: ONE WEEK IN SAN FRANCISCO

Days One & Two
Follow the first two days of Itinerary One.

Days Three Through Five
Wine Country.
Drive up to Wine Country. Make Calistoga your home base, and explore from there. Tour wineries, explore St. Helena and Napa, soak in mud baths and get massaged. And eat extremely well.

Days Six & Seven
Follow the last two days of Itinerary Two.

4. LAND & PEOPLE

THE LAND

Much of San Francisco's flavor comes from its unique geology and geography. Its location on an isolated peninsula, surrounded on three sides by bay and ocean waters, has certainly affected how San Francisco has developed, and its 43 hills (not the mere seven people sometimes claim, confusing San Francisco with Rome) can be felt in the city's choices of transportation (such as cable cars), its views, and your calf muscles.

Millions of years ago, California was ocean bed. Volcanic eruptions did their work, however, and the **Sierra Nevada** and **Coast Range** mountains were born. And San Francisco rose above the waters, as well as much of the land now covered by the bay. Over the years, waters running down from the Sierras to the sea carved out what's now **Raccoon Strait** between Angel Island and Tiburon, and carved more deeply still to form the channel that's now the Golden Gate. Ice ages and warmer times have caused the waters to rise, fall, and shift over the centuries, but around ten thousand years ago the waters rose to fill the bay and shaped the parameters of San Francisco as we know it.

San Francisco is built up now, a far cry from the sandy hills and dunes that once dominated the peninsula. But its geologic composition still plays a significant role in seismic safety and real estate value. Most of the city is built on sand, which is not the sturdiest of foundations in case of the ever-feared earthquake. When the tectonic plates shift and grind, sand wiggles about like Jello, and buildings fall. Safer than sand is the base of serpentine mineral that lies under a small segment of the city around Potrero Hill and Hunter's Point. And safest of all is the Franciscan bedrock that sits solidly under the hillier portions of San Francisco. The least secure, however, is the bay mud and landfill underlying close to 20% of the city, ringing San Francisco from the Presidio to Candlestick Park. If sand turns to Jello in an earthquake, the landfill turns to mush. So if you're looking for seismic security, the loftier the hill the more likely you're on bedrock, and the flatter the landscape, the more probable it is you're standing on sand or mud.

SAN ANDREAS FAULT

When the Earth's plates move and cause friction, the crust fractures to accommodate it, and this is known as faulting. The type of fault depends on the type and direction of how the plates move. The coastal Pacific plate and the American continental plate meet along the Western Pacific coast; the coastal moves northwest, the American moves southeast, and the result is a strike slip. And the best-known strike slip in the world, the **San Andreas Fault**, runs from near San Francisco down 250 miles to the hills behind Los Angeles.

It's been on the move almost continuously, a few centimeters a year for thousands of years, and hardly a day goes by without a tremor somewhere along its many branches and tributaries (so Los Angeles ought to reach San Francisco's latitude in about 10 million years). The last real Big Ones were here in 1906 and in Los Angeles in 1857, but the San Francisco quake of 1989 and the Los Angeles one in 1994 stopped the cities in their tracks well enough.

THE PEOPLE - BEFORE COLONIZATION

The first people to live here came five to ten thousand years ago, descendants from the Asian-Siberian rovers who crossed into Alaska from Siberia and kept on moving south. In the years before the Spanish came, California held as many as 53 major tribes and up to 90 different languages. In the Bay Area there lived four tribes: the Coast Miwoks, the Yokuts, the Wintun, and the Ohlone (called Costanoans or 'coast people' by the Spanish), and of them all, the Miwoks and Ohlone were the most numerous (when the **San Francisco Mission** and **Presidio** were founded in 1776, about 3,000 Miwoks and 10,000 Ohlone resided in the Bay Area). The Coast Miwoks lived in Marin and the North Bay (there's a beautiful hiking path in the Marin headlands called the Miwok Trail), and the Ohlone lived in the East Bay, the South Bay, and the sand dunes of San Francisco (there was water in Lake Merced and Mission Creek, and the Indians tended to live near these water sources).

Up until the Spanish colonization of San Francisco in 1776, the Miwoks and Ohlone lived simply, hunted and gathered, and used stone tools. They were a relatively short people, and the men wore decorated loincloths and plumed headdresses, and painted their bodies. Mostly they lived off the abundant wealth of fish, game, and edible plants, while acorns served as their diet staple. They had no knowledge of metal tools, wheels, or beasts of burden, but they lived well. The groups had defined and respected hunting territories, and the inter-tribal relations were peaceful and generous. There was plenty of land, food, and water, and harmonious relations were the rule.

When the Spanish arrived, life changed drastically. The peaceful, non-aggressive traits that had helped promote Bay Area harmony did not stand them in good stead against the colonizing, technologically advanced, arrogant Spaniards. The Mission used the locals to tend the farm, taught them Christianity and European morals, and gave them European diseases such as measles and syphilis. One hundred years after the Europeans arrived, the Indian population of California had dropped to 6% of what it had been, and the Bay Area Indians were pretty much wiped out.

THE LAST FEW CENTURIES

From the mid-1500s to the mid-1700s, the bulk of San Francisco's ethnic makeup was Native American, and then the Spanish ran the show till the Mexicans took over in 1821. However, as Europeans and US citizens alike were afflicted by itchy feet and empty pockets, men of English, Irish, Italian, German, Russian, and Chinese background set sail to explore the western frontier and attempt their fortunes. Then came the **Gold Rush** in 1849, and The City became swamped with every nationality and color. Some wandered on after the gold and silver mines ran dry, but many settled in San Francisco.

The next big boom was World War II. The war effort needed people, regardless of race or sex. People poured in from all over, especially blacks from the south. The shipyards put them to work for the duration of the war, adding a far more significant black presence to San Francisco's composition. What with the people who stayed, and the usual hodge-podge of immigrants a coastal port attracts, San Francisco has been a worldly amalgamation of ethnicities for a long time.

TODAY

Today, 768,300 people live in San Francisco proper (the larger metropolitan San Francisco area has 1,603,678 people). Of these, the largest ethnicity is white (44%), followed by Asian (32%), Latino (13%), and Black (10%). It is true that a hundred years back the dominant cultures (first Spanish and Mexican then Anglo-Saxon) ran the show, and immigrants were subjected to varying degrees of hardship, discrimination, and persecution (and it's also true that this still happens, though to a lesser extent, today).

But while San Francisco has not been spared the racism that afflicts the country as a whole, there is far more tolerance, respect, and cultural richness here than you'll find most anywhere else. San Francisco now is one of the most multi-cultural, diverse cities in the world, and its ethnic wealth is reflected in its educational curriculum, its politics, its museums, its theaters, and its restaurants.

SAN FRANCISCO'S POPULATION

Total Population (1990 census): 768,300

White:	*337,118*
Chinese:	*205,686*
Latino:	*100,717*
Black:	*76,343*
Filipino:	*29,100*
Japanese:	*10,800*
Other:	*8,536*

5. A SHORT HISTORY

EUROPEAN DISCOVERY & DEVELOPMENT

In the 1500s, San Francisco was just a stretch of sandy, wind-blown hills and dunes, and the magnificent San Francisco bay was shrouded from casual view by the frequently fog-bound peninsular arms of the Golden Gate, the narrow entrance from the Pacific Ocean to the bay. Spain was the dominant world power, and her imperial exploration was going strong, but it took a while for the San Francisco Bay to be "discovered," and historians debate just who found it first, but few debated the beauty of the area.

Father Pedro Font, who first set up the Mission on March 28, 1776, said: "Indeed, although in my travels I saw very good sites and beautiful country, I saw none which pleased me so much as this. And I think that if it could be well settled like Europe there would not be anything more beautiful in all the world, for it has the best advantages for founding in it a most beautiful city..." Once discovered by Europeans, the area developed rapidly.

In 1542, **Juan Rodríguez Cabrillo** sailed north from Mexico, the first European to explore the California coast and seek out some great harbors (since Spain took the Philippines in 1565, the trade ships needed safe ports). He found San Diego, Monterey and Point Reyes harbors, but the San Francisco Bay's narrow opening (the Golden Gate of repute) was not readily evident from safe sailing off the Pacific Coast. **Sir Francis Drake** is reputed to be the first European to enter the Golden Gate, but when in 1579 Sir Francis Drake sailed the Pacific coast in his *Golden Hinde*, weighted down with 30 tons of Spanish booty and in need of repairs, it's likely that he missed the Golden Gate as well and probably put in at a cove by Point Reyes (named Drakes Bay in 1792). He claimed the region for England and called it *Nova Albion*, but neither the name nor the nationality ever took.

In 1595, Point Reyes got another European visitor, and its present name. **Sebastián Cermeño**, a Portuguese captain doing reconnaissance for Spain, hit bad weather and put into Drakes Bay for repairs. The ship was sunk by another winter storm and the crew managed, amazingly, to make it back to the Philippines in a small launch, but before he left, Cermeño renamed the land (dubbed *Cabo de Piños* by Cabrillo) as *Punta de los Reyes* (King's Point), which has since been shortened and partially anglicized to **Point Reyes**. By the 1600s, the trade between Mexico and the Philippines was down to one ship a year, and Spain's empire was on the decline. They decided to focus on their South and Central American colonies and leave *Alta California* (San Diego and north) to the elements and the Indians.

By the 18th century, the Russians had done some exploration and colonization of their own in Alaska and northern California, sparking Spain's renewed interest (or fear) in California. It wasn't until 1769 that **Captain Gaspar de Portolá**, governor of Baja and Alta California, took another exploratory jaunt north, wasn't impressed with the large, open harbor off Monterey, and pushed on up north to what is now San Francisco. Part of his expedition was aimed at establishing reliable harbors, but another task commissioned by King Don Carlos III was to set up new Franciscan missions in Alta California (and replace the Baja Californian Jesuits with Franciscan friars). Since Portolá traveled by land, he and Sergeant **José Francisco de Ortega** were able to find the bay behind the Golden Gate, but he was disappointed anyway, because he had been looking for Drake's Bay, and the darned estuaries and inlets of San Francisco Bay kept interfering.

PICKING NAMES IN THE BAY

In August 1775, Lieutenant Juan Manuel de Ayala became the first European to sail through what is now the Golden Gate. He mapped the area and supplied numerous place names, such as Angel Island (Isla de Nuestra Senora de Los Angeles), Alcatraz (Isla de Los Alcatraces or Pelican Island), and Sausalito (Saucelito or Little Thicket of Willows). Isla de Los Alcatraces, incidentally, is what he named the island we now know as Yerba Buena, but an English map-maker in 1826 erred and tagged the name on the rocky outcrop we recognize today as Alcatraz. Names aside, Ayala's reports showed San Francisco Bay as a sheltered, large harbor, and put San Francisco on the map.

Scouting and mapping is just the research arm of colonization, and in September of 1775 **Captain Juan Bautista de Anza** responded to the English and Russian threat to Alta California with an overland party of 250 men and women, and the essential herd of cattle. They traveled north from Arizona and arrived in San Francisco March 28, 1776. They chose Fort Point (for its strategic bay views) for the military outpost (or Presidio) and Franciscan priest **Pedro Font** set up the Mission (now known as

Mission Dolores) in the more sheltered, fertile valley of today's Mission district by the stream they dubbed *Arroyo de Nuestra Senora de Los Dolores* (it being the Friday before Palm Sunday, *Viernes de Dolores* in Spanish) as a center for religion and trade. Three months later, Lieutenant **José Joaquin Moraga** (Anza's second-in-command) and Father **Junipero Serra** led the settlers in, and **Father Palou** celebrated the Mission's first Mass on June 29, 1776 (5 days before the signing of the Declaration of Independence some 3,000 miles to the east).

The missions controlled a lot of land, and, using Indian labor, they began to produce large quantities of cattle hides and tallow (the area's chief exports at the time), fruit and vegetables. The Indians living at the missions were forced to work hard and received few economic rewards; as recompense, they were given instruction in Christianity, and were taught some new skills. On the formal dedication day of **Mission San Francisco de Asis** on October 9th, the new settlers had a big party. Father Palou noted in his diary, "The day has been a joyful one for all. Only the savages did not enjoy themselves on this happy day."

Colonization and development inched along, with a ranch here, a saloon there, a more permanent chapel (it's still there today, dating from 1791), and a hide and tallow export business that kept the settlement afloat. The Spanish would have liked control of their settlements, but they refused to actually arm and man their presidios. In 1792 the English navigator **George Vancouver** laughed at San Francisco's paltry Presidio, manned by 35 soldiers and one brass cannon (the other having exploded recently during a practice firing). **Don Luis Antonio Arguello** was Presidio Commander from 1787-1806, and did the best he could considering the near total lack of Spanish material and financial support. Munitions were so low that in 1806 when a Russian ship visited and fired a friendly salute, the Presidio men had to row out to the Russians and borrow some powder so as to return the greeting.

By 1810, Mexico was fighting for independence, and Spain had her hands full without attending to her Alta California presidios, so San Francisco was really left to its own devices and decline. In 1812, the Russians established themselves at Fort Ross (up the northern coast, near the mouth of the Russian River), operating a trading and fur-trapping center, which they maintained until 1841. In 1821, Mexico won independence from Spain, and California (known as Alta California) became a province of the new Mexican nation (though they didn't get the good word till 1822). At that time about 3,500 Europeans had settled in Alta California, but the native Indian population was declining fast, thanks to Spanish enslavement, forced labor, measles, and general changes imposed on their traditional life-styles.

NIKOLAI & CONCEPCION

*Foreign seal hunters and whalers were welcomed, as was **Nikolai Petrovich Rezanov**, the Russian chamberlain. He persistently pursued Arguello's assistance (in the form of spare provisions for the Russian colony at Sitka) and the heart of Concepcion, Arguello's 15-year-old daughter. While his motivations (romantic, self-serving, or otherwise) aren't now known, the indisputable results were that Nikolai left San Francisco, laden with the supplies he came for, and Dona Concepcion's affections as well.*

The notorious affair sparked some literary endeavors. Gertrude Atherton wrote a novel and Bret Harte wrote a poem detailing their romance. They tell how Nikolai and Concepcion got engaged, but the marriage must wait for Nikolai to travel to Moscow and get the Czar's permission for him (a Russian Orthodox) to marry a Spanish Catholic. Forty years go by, the wilting Concepcion still has no word. Then, one night, Sir George Simpson of the Hudson's Bay Company visits for dinner. He tells a story he has heard of a Russian chamberlain who fell in love with a Catholic senorita, and in search of the Czar's nod, he rode across the Russian taiga, was thrown from his horse, and died. It made a swell dinner story, but was a painful way for Concepcion to learn of his tragic end.

In 1834, Mexico passed the Secularization Act. The Franciscans lost control of the missions and their enormous land holdings. The Indians, thus released from missionary control, returned to the wilderness or hired on as laborers at nearby ranchos. **Francisco de Haro** became the first *alcalde* (mayor) of **Yerba Buena**, the civilian pueblo that developed separate from the Presidio and Mission, the hide and tallow trade took off, and Yankee trade ships began anchoring regularly at Yerba Buena cove.

TWO YEARS BEFORE THE MAST

*In **Two Years Before the Mast**, Richard Dana describes San Francisco from the perspective of an approaching vessel. "Behind [the presidio] point is the little harbor, or bight, called Yerba Buena, in which trading vessels anchor, and, near it, the Mission of Dolores. There was no other habitation on the side of the bay, except a shanty of rough boards put up by a man named Richardson, who was doing a little trading between the vessels and the Indians." He later observed "If California ever becomes a prosperous country, this bay will be the center of its prosperity. The abundance of wood and water; the extreme fertility of its shores; the excellence of its climate which is as near to being perfect as any in the world; and its facilities for navigation, affording the best anchoring-grounds in the whole western coast of America—all fit it for a place of great importance."*

19TH CENTURY PROGRESS

The William A. Richardson noted by Dana in *Two Years Before the Mast* was in fact the first settler to build a permanent adobe dwelling on what's now Grant Avenue in 1836. Though British by birth, he put down San Francisco roots, took Mexican citizenship, and married the Presidio commandante's daughter. Other houses followed, and the town of Yerba Buena (named *good herb* by Richardson after an indigenous mint-flavored plant they used for tea) was on its way.

In the late 1830s, Francisco de Haro commissioned a survey of Yerba Buena, and the Swiss seaman **Jean Jacques Vioget** was hired to do a proper map and lay out some proper streets to replace the hodgepodge crisscross of paths that connected the Mission, Presidio, and Cove. At the time, the somnolent settlement of Yerba Buena was bound by today's Montgomery, Sacramento, Pacific, and Grant streets, an eight-block grid. Vioget planned the original streets very narrowly. Calle de la Fundacion (now Grant) was just 44 feet wide, and Kearny was just 45. Later they had to be widened to 75 feet, but the Chinatown stretch of Grant is still its original narrow width.

In 1841, the **Hudson's Bay Company** established a dry goods store which was purchased in 1845 by a very lucky **William D. M. Howard** following the juicy scandal involving the Hudson Bay's Company manager, the adulterous affair he was discovered in, and his subsequent suicide. Howard didn't know it at the time, but he'd just positioned himself to make a fortune from the gold rush. In 1845 the grid was expanded to include today's Stockton and Powell on the east, California, Pine, and Bush to the south, and Broadway and Vallejo in the North.

But in two years even these additions proved inadequate for the growing town. In 1847, **Jasper O'Farrell** was asked to widen the town's boundaries. The shallow waters just beyond the beach held promise, and O'Farrell extended the map grid right into the bay. Watery plots were snatched up, and new owners surveyed their properties in row boats. These lines eventually became wharves and streets, and much of what is now San Francisco is built on the subsequent landfill. This was the Yerba Buena of the 1840s, a small but growing mission town of around 500, run by a few dozen Mexican families who owned the huge inland ranchos (families such as Martinez, Moraga, and Vallejo who had towns named after them), and families like Noe and Guerrero who owned large tracts of the peninsula.

THE STORY OF MARKET STREET

Jasper O'Farrell added a 120-foot-wide boulevard that ran diagonally across the original Vioget plan for San Francisco. This turned into Market Street; it connected the existing plots with newly minted South of Market additions, bisected the town, and was twice as wide as existing streets. The locals were not very pleased with the enormous, land-hogging street, and there was talk of a lynching. As the mob and its hostile intentions grew, O'Farrell ran for North Beach and hopped a boat to Sausalito. He stayed there till the anger died down. His foresight was much more appreciated later, however, when the width of the street allowed for both cable car and regular traffic. O'Farrell was well-paid (with land) for his work, and he got lucky at the start of the gold rush as well. He retired in 1849 to a 60,000 acre ranch near Sebastopol in Sonoma County, and even got himself elected to the state Senate in 1858.

"FOREIGN" INTERESTS, THE BEAR FLAG REVOLT, & MEXICAN WAR

Mexico held Alta California, but foreign neighbors nosed about. At the time, the British were in Oregon (which was then part of British Columbia), and they looked south for trade and/or colonization. The Russians held a fort 70 miles north in Fort Ross, and the Americans were in the grip of expansionist, "manifest destiny" fever. **Pio Pico**, last Mexican governor of Alta California, said: "We find ourselves threatened by hordes of Yankee emigrants...whose progress we cannot arrest."

The US had tried to purchase the San Francisco peninsula from Mexico for $500,000 back in 1835, and Mexico's refusal did not lessen Yankee interest. President Polk sent **John C. Frémont** to California to map out the best overland routes, and he sent a secret message to Thomas O. Larkin (US Consul in Monterey) to "exert the greatest vigilance in discovering and defeating any attempt which may be made by foreign governments to acquire control" of California.

Tensions rose between the Californios and the American settlers, and Frémont was usually in the thick of it. Fueled by the concept of "Manifest Destiny" and land-lust, the Americans who reached California in the 1840s were not interested in assimilating to Mexican culture; they wanted to occupy. In 1846, an armed band of Americans betook themselves to the rancho of Vallejo. They accepted his hospitality of wine and *aguardiente*, made a very rough flag with a red star, a grizzly bear, and the words The Republic of California, and imprisoned the Vallejo family. Frémont resigned from the US army and joined the revolt. They captured the Mexican presidio at Sonoma. This short-lived event is known as the **Bear Flag Revolt**. San Francisco was peaceably taken, though three unarmed men were killed on the way, and the Bear Flag Revolt could have been well on its way were it not made moot by the Mexican War that was declared a month before on the Texas border (news of which did not reach San Francisco till after the revolt).

On July 7, 1846, Commodore **John D. Sloat** claimed California for the United States by raising the US. flag over Monterey, followed by the easy conquest of California by Commodore **Robert F. Stockton**, General **Stephen Watts Kearny**, and other US. soldiers. During the war, Yerba Buena was taken by US. troops under **Captain John B. Montgomery** of the *U.S.S. Portsmouth*, and renamed San Francisco. In 1848, the United States won the war with Mexico as well as possession of both Texas and California, under the auspices of **Treaty of Guadeloupe Hidalgo**.

NAMING THE GOLDEN GATE

Frémont was an active participant (some say the main instigator) of the Bear Flag Revolt, but he had a more lasting impact on the Bay Area as the man who named the Golden Gate. Whilst on an exploratory expedition to the West, he and some of his men rowed from Sausalito past the entrance to the bay. He christened the gap Chrysopylae, the Golden Gate, a name now irrevocably intertwined with San Francisco identity.

THE GOLD RUSH

In 1848, gold rocked the foundations of San Francisco even more dramatically than the change in nationality, the width of Market Street, or the earthquake that would follow 58 years later. The 1849 **California Gold Rush** and the 1859 **Comstock Lode** silver strike spurred the city's growth gigantically. Waves of immigrants arrived, and large Chinese, Italian, Filipino, and Japanese communities were established. By the late 1850s, San Francisco's population had jumped from 500 to more than 50,000. Hundreds of ships sailed into San Francisco's harbor, but they never sailed out. Captains and crew deserted to try their luck in the foothills of the Sierra Nevada Mountains, masts were torn down to serve as tent poles, ships became hotels, brothels, and laundries. When the city needed to expand her shores, about 400 ships (along with some sand and garbage) became landfill for what's now the Financial District.

It all started in 1847 some 133 miles away in the Sierra foothills. Gold was discovered at a sawmill under construction in Coloma, and the world came in droves. **John Augustus Sutter**, born in Switzerland, arrived in California in 1839, on the lam from a bad marriage and anxious creditors. He set up an adobe fort near the American River in what's now Sacramento, and built a ranch. Some years later, his millwright and carpenter, **James Marshall**, was sent off to set up a lumber mill to provide the growing San Francisco with wood, and he returned from Coloma in

January of 1848 with nuggets of gold. Sutter and Marshall swore one another to secrecy, with predictable results. Soon, all the mill workers were panning successfully for nuggets. The word hit San Francisco in March, but the townspeople were skeptical. It wasn't till May when charismatic **Sam Brannan** paraded his gold that San Francisco got a strong dose of gold fever. Brannan, who a year later was to found Calistoga as a hot springs spa, ran around Portsmouth Square carrying a gold-filled bottle aloft, crying "Gold! Gold! Gold from the American River!" Then, every able-bodied San Franciscan headed for the hills, after first stocking up with provisions from Brannan's hardware store.

In 1849, more than 100,000 launched themselves gold-ward. Nearly 800 ships left New York harbor alone, bound for San Francisco. In fact, the California gold rush spawned the greatest peacetime migration in modern history. Prospectors spread out from the lucrative Sierra foothills, and gold was eventually uncovered in 54 of California's 58 counties.

FORTY-NINER INFLATION

The forty-niners (those who came out in 1849 after gold) worked with pans and sluice-boxes, and often came away with $10-$15 a day, while their laborer brethren back east were averaging no more than a dollar. And as their incomes multiplied, the cost of life in San Francisco inflated to keep pace. A loaf of bread jumped from 4¢ to 50¢, a Portsmouth Square land plot that was valued in the spring of 1848 at $6,000 sold 6 months later at $23,000, and a property that cost $23,000 in 1848 resold at $300,000 in 1849.

San Francisco was one of the four counties without gold, but the city made its own fortune off the *Argonauts*, who needed supplies before they set out and entertainment on which to spend it when they returned laden with gold. The forty-niners were mostly bachelors or else they left their families behind. When in San Francisco, they needed places to stay, and they needed restaurants as well. In fact, San Francisco's reputation as a city rich in fine and ethnically diverse restaurants got its start during the gold rush. Shelter was at a premium and real estate prices soared - another tradition that started with the gold rush and is still in place today.

Drinking and gambling were the two favorite past-times, and both separated the miners from a good deal of their gold dust. Whiskey cost $30 a quart, but the demand was great, and the competing beer breweries were numerous. Gambling halls popped up everywhere, and soon there were hundreds of them. Prostitution was another popular diversion, and might have surpassed the other two, but for the lack of women. While booze and gambling halls proliferated with demand, the availability of the female sex was not as obliging. According to the state census of 1850, only 8% of the population was female, and few of them were unattached.

THE BIRTH OF LEVI'S BLUE JEANS

In 1853, the miners were flying high in the gold rush boom, but a problem persisted. They just couldn't get good, sturdy trousers. Levi Strauss (an immigrant from Germany) responded to his brother-in-law's call and to the needs of the miners. He came up with "waist-high overalls" made of cotton duck canvas, and a way of life was born. He resisted the term "jeans" which came from the cotton trousers worn by Genoese sailors, but he responded to the miners. Happy as they were with the new pants, their pockets kept ripping (if they were lucky) from gold nuggets. Nevada tailor Jacob Davis applied metal rivets to stress points (the fly bottom and the pocket corners), went into partnership with Strauss, and a legend was born. The 501 shrink-to-fit button fly design, now an American classic, was first advertised in the 1890s in catalog number 501, hence the name.

Strauss' factory dating from 1906 (the original one on Fremont was destroyed in the earthquake) is still there at 250 Valencia near 14th. There are free tours given every Wednesday at 10:30am and 1pm., but you can't buy blue jeans at the factory. You can call 415-565-9159 for more information or to make a reservation.

Mining continued for a long time in the Sierra foothills, but the first surge of productive gold-panning petered out fairly soon. After that, it required more labor and capital to get the remaining gold out of the hills than your average lone wolf miner could muster.

The effects, however, were felt in California for a long time. The sort of person lured out by the scent of gold was a dreamer and a risk-taker; he was independent and not always keen on rules. The Americans, Chinese, Australians, Europeans, and Latin Americans who eventually settled with or without their hoped-for fortunes radically changed the tenor of life in San Francisco.

THE FLAGRANT FIFTIES

The mining boom town that was San Francisco in the 1850s was a fire hazard waiting to be ignited, over and over again. The buildings were of wood and canvas, the lighting came from oil lamps, and water was not readily available. There were many fires; some were accidental but a good number were believed to be set by the Sydney Ducks, a mob of Australian ex-convicts who sailed into San Francisco on the winds of the gold rush, and looted the empty shops while the proprietors civic-mindedly fought the fires. The downtown area was pretty well destroyed. The May 1851 fire was terrible, the fifth in two years, and the citizens were fed up. Sam

Brannan and other leading property owners got together and formed the **First Committee of Vigilance**. They were far more successful than the local police force, and in their few months of operation four hoodlums were hung. Crime abated and the committee disbanded, but in 1856 the Second Committee of Vigilance responded to a renewed burst of lawlessness. A couple more murderers were hung, and relative peace reigned once again.

Hooliganism was not the only business to blossom in the boom years. The new gold capital and continued miner demands fueled the growth of cattle, agriculture, and lumber. Better transportation was also in demand, and stagecoach, freight, and steamship lines filled the need. **Wells Fargo** opened shop in San Francisco in 1852, and is still going strong as one of the leading bank chains. In fact, with all the gold dust flooding the streets, banking became a new and very lucrative San Francisco venture.

However, a town geared solely to the needs of one concern is asking for trouble, and it hit in the form of a financial depression in 1854 as mining activity began to wane. The city recovered, however, broadened its economic base, and continued to produce its new addition, the lucky, wealthy, elite. Mostly these were the merchants and bankers who profited from the gold rush second hand, and very few were actually miners. They took over Rincon Hill south of Market Street, chosen for its proximity to downtown and its fine weather. Nearby South Park, once an elegant extension of Rincon Hill, is just now making a come-back as a posh address for fine restaurants.

By 1859, San Francisco had replaced the canvas and flimsy wooden shacks with solid city buildings, and the port was alive with business. The old backwater town that **William Tecumseh Sherman** had termed a "horrid place" in 1847 was becoming a post-gold rush city settling into comfortable moderation when - bam - silver was discovered near Carson City, Nevada. And the rush was on again.

TOM SAWYER

The Transamerica pyramid now stands at 600 Montgomery, but in the 1800s there was a rooming house there instead that attracted the writers of that century, such as Bret Harte, Robert Louis Stevenson, and Mark Twain. Twain met a fireman one day in the public baths downstairs, and while the fireman is long since forgotten, his name, Tom Sawyer, lives on.

THE NEW BOOM

The **Comstock Lode** had churned out $22 million by the end of 1863, and another $300 million in the next 15 years. It was the richest discovery of silver ore ever, and San Francisco (along with a few individual speculators) was the main beneficiary. The city really burgeoned with the new influx of cash. The Bank of California was established by **William C. Ralston**. He also bought up the lumber rights around Lake Tahoe, and built the only rail line going to Virginia City (in Comstock Lode country). When a new, rich vein of silver was discovered in 1867, the Bank of California did magnificently and Ralston got filthy rich.

Ralston spread his money around San Francisco, seeding profitable ventures and cultural landmarks. He started a furniture factory and woolen mill, built the California Theater, and was the money and brains behind the Palace Hotel on Market Street, the ornate and impressive structure that was for the time (1875) the largest hotel in the United States, built where a few years earlier the wind swept uninhibited through the dunes.

PRESIDENTIAL DEATH IN THE PALACE HOTEL

President Warren Harding visited Alaska in the summer of '23, and on his way back he stopped for a little R&R in San Francisco. He stayed in the Palace Hotel and entertained himself, as was his wont, with a number of shapely ladies. He was found in the arms of one such, dead of a heart attack on August 2, 1923. A plaque in the hotel verifies that President Harding died there, though it neglects to tell in which room, or with whom.

A few others did nicely for themselves from the silver mines, notably the **Bonanza Kings**. They were a partnership of four poor Irishmen (**James Flood, William O'Brien, John Mackay**, and **James Fair**) who made a fortune on some shrewdly purchased mining stock. With this money they bought up lots of small claims, and patched them together into their one big Consolidated Virginia mine.

In 1873, miners struck the "Big Bonanza," a huge mass of silver worth more than $100 million. The four partners became the richest men in California. These men built elaborate, extravagant mansions on Nob Hill (short for Nabob Hill, the new posh neighborhood, once the cable cars were installed), and breathed the rarefied air of the very wealthy. The Flood Mansion, which was a luxury palace, burned down in the 1906 quake, but the Fairmont Hotel on Nob Hill today was built on land purchased by Fair, built by his daughters, and named in his honor.

Another famous foursome were the **Big Four**, and they changed the face of the west by providing the monetary muscle to push the western segment of the transcontinental railway. Ever since 1850 when California had joined the union, there had been talk of a railway linking east to west, but the slavery question had muddied the issue. Northern states wanted the railroad to go through the northern free states and end up in northern California, while the southern states, of course, wanted a southern, slave-holding route to southern California. So nothing got built. When, in 1861, the Civil War began and the southern states seceded, Congress was free to approve the Pacific Railroad Act, and was eager to do so in hopes of some Comstock silver to help fund the war effort.

The four merchants who coughed up the capital to found the Central Pacific Railroad (renamed the Southern Pacific in 1884) were **Charles Crocker, Mark Hopkins, Collis P. Huntington**, and **Leland Stanford**, names that are now an integral part of the Bay Area, with banks, hotels, and universities named after them. The first track work began in 1863, and six years, many sticks of dynamite, and lots of back-breaking labor later, the Union Pacific and Central Pacific lines met in Promontory, Utah, and the *golden spike* was driven to signify the link-up of east and west.

San Francisco cheered the event, and the Big Four were feted, but no one celebrated the contributions of the Chinese workers who were hired to inch laboriously through the Sierras. The Chinese immigrants had suffered discrimination and violence earlier in gold rush days, but the Chinese hiring preferences of Central Pacific really lit a fire in the bellies of those prone to immigration intolerance. The railroad company started off with Irish laborers, but found the Chinese worked harder and were more dependable. By the time the golden stake was driven, 85% of the workers were Chinese, and all were suddenly unemployed.

At first, San Francisco rejoiced in the completed rail line and the end of their isolation, but an economic depression soon doused their celebrations. The railway meant an end to San Francisco's inflated prices as cheaper goods were railroaded in, and a mass of unemployed flooded the city.

As usual, economic woes led to immigrant bashing, and the Chinese took the brunt of it. Of the 20,000 employed by the railroad, most made their way to San Francisco, as did thousands more Chinese still arriving from China. Unemployment was a terrible problem in the 1870s, and the Chinese were willing to work long hours for less; they became the convenient scapegoats for the violent frustration of the white majority.

The bigotry escalated, and Denis Kearney, a young Irish immigrant, fanned the flames. He organized his Workingman's Party with the motto "The Chinese Must Go!" and he turned crowds into mobs bent on looting and burning Chinese laundries and other businesses. His rhetoric struck a chord with the legislators, and some heavy-handed discriminatory laws were passed. The **Queue Ordinance**, passed in 1876 by the San Francisco Board of Supervisors, ruled that all Chinese who landed in the county jail had to have their braids cut off.

Other laws heavily taxed and restricted Chinese engaged in occupations such as agriculture and fishing that competed with whites. And in 1879, the state constitution was amended to prohibit Chinese from voting.

One result of all this racism was the creation of **Chinatown**. Since the Chinese were rejected by society, they formed their own businesses and restaurants that catered to their needs and wouldn't provoke white ire.

CABLE CARS

*In 1873, **Andrew S. Hallidie** changed the face of San Francisco with the addition of his cable cars, or Hallidie's Folly, as it was called by the skeptics. Based on the cable railway system he'd invented for mine ore transport, the cable car revolutionized transportation up the hills of San Francisco. It works like this: Thick steel cables run underground along the designated track, and are pulled along at the steady speed of 9.5 mph by massive wheels in the cable car barn. When the grip man lowers the pliers-like grip to grasp on to the cable, the cable car is set in motion; to stop the car, the grip man releases the grip and applies the brakes. The simple and effective design became hugely popular, and by the late 1800s San Francisco used nearly 500 cable cars and 103 miles of track on seven cable car lines. The system has been scaled down to the three lines that exist today, but the cable car barn which is also a museum is in the same brick building it's been in since it was built in 1907 following the earthquake.*

*The **Cable Car Barn Museum** (415-474-1887) at 1201 Mason is open daily from 10am-5pm November-March and 10am-6pm April-October, and admission is free.*

THE END OF THE NINETEENTH CENTURY & THE BARBARY COAST

The successful railroad and construction ventures of the Big Four (also known alternately as the robber barons or the railroad barons), gave them incredible wealth and power. They held a monopoly, that enormous concentration of power in one industry which later legislation outlawed. The word now conjures a family board game, but their transportation monopoly really held the screws to anyone wanting to ship freight in or out of California. Because there was no competition or regulation, they could charge whatever they felt like.

The rates became so extreme that it cost more to send something to San Francisco from Bakersfield than from Liverpool via New Orleans. The grip of the Big Four's empire was so tenacious and far-reaching, it was called "The Octopus." They all built magnificent mansions high on Nob Hill, and The Mark Hopkins, Huntington, and Stanford Court hotels there today still reflect some of their power.

PACIFIC HEIGHTS

The Pacific Heights of the late 1800s had a distinctly different flavor from the posh district today, owing in part to its flourishing hog farms at the northern end of Laguna and near the foot of Octavia. Hog calls mingled with fog calls till the 1891 ordinance that prohibited keeping swine or more than two cows north of Golden Gate Park.

The **Barbary Coast** is an evocative name, conjuring images of impish deviltry and San Francisco's charmingly wicked past. Named after the North African coastline, a strip once notorious for pirates and cut-throats, San Francisco's Barbary Coast was not in any way cute. The waterfront around Pacific and Broadway was a sordid, dangerous place, inhabited by a vast array of thieves, murderers, and derelicts. It was truly vile.

Starting with Sydney Town in the 1850s, the coast was on the edge of the bay, and the edge of social sanity, too. The Boar's Head was a typical dive featuring a woman having sex with a boar. The Fierce Grizzly bar had a live bear chained next to the door, and these were the established places. The seamy section grew, and swallowed up Chinatown and part of today's financial district. By 1885, 26 opium dens were counted open to the public. Other popular Barbary Coast amusements included gambling, drinking, and shanghaiing (or crimping, or otherwise forcing recruitment) of deckhands onto outbound ships. A conk on the head and you could wake up at sea with a long, unasked for sea voyage ahead, while the guy who supplied you was paid your first few months' wages for his crimping labor.

But the big business became prostitution. There were dance halls (places where men gathered to watch a sordid show, pretty girls served and encouraged the sale of whiskey, and would provide sexual service later on), there were cribs (jail-like collections of available female flesh with narrow stalls for fast sex at just 25-50 cents a pop), and there were parlor houses (up-scale brothels where gentlemen who could afford the $2-$10 fees could enjoy themselves surrounded by red velvet). Morton Street near Union Square (now daintily if ironically renamed Maiden Lane) was crammed with brothels.

The lowlife loved the waterfront, flocked to dives like the Bull Run on Pacific where the women drank booze to keep up with the men and enliven the festivities. Women who passed out were spread out on a mattress while the men queued up to have a go for anywhere from 25¢ to $1, depending on her looks. And, for an additional 25¢, a man could watch the guy before him go at it as well. But not everyone in the city approved. There were various attempts on the part of San Francisco citizens to clean up the waterfront, but nothing was strong enough or brutal enough to shake up the Barbary Coast till the earthquake of 1906.

GOLDEN GATE PARK

While the waterfront in 1868 was wallowing in vice, filth, and rats, the Board of Supervisors was looking westward for undeveloped land on which to map a major park for the growing city. They chose a long rectangular strip of barren sand dunes, three miles long and half a mile wide, stretching from Stanyan Street out to the Pacific Ocean. It was in a section of the city then known as the "Outside Lands," and only a few squatters lived there, so the land was cheap.

EMPEROR NORTON

Norton the First, Emperor of the United States and Defender of Mexico, was a well-loved San Francisco nut-case. He started life as Joshua Norton, but after a misguided attempt in 1853 to corner the rice market, during which he lost all his money and most of his sanity, he was "reincarnated" as the Emperor Norton that San Francisco knew and loved during the 1850s - 1870s. He put together an impressive uniform, complete with gold braid, epaulets, and a plethora of colorful ribbons on his chest, and he topped it all off with a high beaver hat decked with long ostrich feathers. He was a sight for sore eyes, with his regal bearing, and his many civic-minded edicts. He frequently wrote to Queen Victoria, Abraham Lincoln, the Czar, and the Kaiser with helpful tidbits of advice (much appreciated by them), and he ordered San Francisco to erect a lit Christmas tree in Union Square for the children. San Francisco, to its immeasurable credit, complied with alacrity.

The Emperor printed his own money (and the good San Francisco merchants honored it). He rode free (with dining car privileges) on all Central Pacific trains, and the California state legislature reserved him a seat in the Senate gallery. However, not all Emperor Norton tales are true. Some reporter wrote up a story linking him with the majestic canine mongrel companions, Bummer and Lazarus - a tale he denied vigorously, but to little avail. Most biographies adhere to the reporter's fabrication.

*When his imperial garb began to wear thin, the City generously granted him a $30 annual allowance to keep his outfit up to par. When Emperor Norton died in January of 1880, 20,000 mourners attended his funeral. He achieved a sort of immortality, however, thanks to Mark Twain, who based the King character in **Huck Finn** loosely on the Emperor.*

It wasn't easy to transform the windblown sands into the lush green oasis it is today, and many thought it an impossible fool's task. A newspaper editorial scoffed "a blade of grass cannot be raised without four posts to keep it from blowing away." With persistence and skill, however, the gardeners began to shape it into the "woodland park" the creators had in mind, with curving roads and rustic bridges to add to the bucolic flavor.

In the late 1800s, bicycle riding was extremely popular, and **Golden Gate Park** became the spot of choice for a bike ride, stroll, or picnic. And once the street cars were up and running, as many as 50,000 people a day took their leisure and recreation there.

In 1894, Golden Gate Park hosted the **Midwinter Exposition**, the first world's fair. M. H. de Young (then publisher of the *San Francisco Chronicle*) wanted to boost San Francisco out of a nationwide recession and show the world how balmy San Francisco's winters could be, and he promoted the idea energetically. The Exposition opened in January, closed in July, featured displays from 37 countries, and entertained more than 2.5 million people. There were foreign scenes, trained animal acts (a lion killed its trainer and really boosted the popularity of that show for a while), and the latest in technology: a Tower of Electricity that could be seen for miles.

Today's Conservatory of Flowers, the Music Concourse, and the Japanese Tea Garden were all built in the park's early days.

THE EARTHQUAKE OF 1906 & THE GREAT FIRE

San Francisco entered the twentieth century in style and confidence, proud to the point of smugness of their growing, gleaming metropolis. Six years later, however, they were reduced to ashes and rubble. April 18th at 5:12am, a tremor equivalent to 15 million tons of TNT went off under the San Andreas fault, which had been discovered and named just 13 years before. Had the Richter scale been in service then, it's estimated that the quake of 1906 would have been ranked around 8.3, more than thirty times more powerful than the 7.1 earthquake of October, 1989. Vibrations from the April quake were felt as far away as Birmingham, England.

Towns and cities along a two-hundred mile stretch north and south of the Point Reyes epicenter felt the impact and suffered serious loss; San Jose and Santa Rosa were hit hard, and a good bit of Stanford University in Palo Alto was destroyed. But San Francisco was the biggest city around, and sustained the most damage.

Witnesses reported seeing the ground undulate in waves two to three feet high. Sidewalks knuckled, fire hydrants were torn from the ground (causing the loss of valuable water), and hundreds of tombstones toppled eastward. Buildings shook, tilted, and crumbled too, especially those built on wobbly landfill, but though there were deaths caused by the earthquake proper, there were many more brought on by the fire.

1906 EARTHQUAKE SURVIVORS

Every year on April 18th at 5:12am, a group gathers at Lotta's Fountain at the intersection of Market, Kearny, and Post streets to celebrate San Francisco. The survivors of the big one are an ever-dwindling group, but some show up to reminisce. Other folks who can drag themselves out of bed that early without the aid of a giant temblor gather there as well to help sing "San Francisco."

The Great Fire

The earthquake lasted forty seconds, followed after 10 quiet seconds by an even stronger temblor 25 seconds long. The quiet after the quake was soon replaced with the sound of walls crumbling, people crying, and more ominous still, fire trucks responding to the first fires. Along with the wreckage, the earthquake severed gas mains, overturned stoves, spilled chemicals, and crossed electrical wires. It didn't take long for more than fifty separate fires to blossom among the ruins. To make matters worse, the main water pipes were busted as well, and when the fire fighters hooked up to the hydrants, precious little came out.

Communication between fire, police, and rescue units was impossible what with nearly all the telephone and telegraph wires out of service. One brave Postal Telegraph operator on Market Street was able to alert the world with a brief message before the fire sent him running. By early afternoon, the many little fires had joined forces into three main infernos. South of Market, north of Market near the waterfront, and Hayes Valley near City Hall were all up in flames. Eventually these fires devoured the intervening blocks of wood-frame houses and became one roaring furnace whose heat at times approached 2,700° fahrenheit. Glass and marble melted into pools, steel and iron twisted; the fire ate everything and could be seen 50 miles away.

Brigadier General Frederick Funston and the city's fire fighters actually tried to stand up to the blaze. They used every drop of water available, and dynamited buildings, but it was a hopeless case. For three days easterly winds fanned the conflagration, but on April 21st the fires had burned themselves out, the winds shifted to westerlies, and the flames subsided. A heavy rain fell, putting out any remaining embers and drenching the masses of homeless survivors.

Some of the survivors jumped aboard ferries to Oakland, but most set up shop in San Francisco's parks. Golden Gate Park was packed with tents and camping refugees. About 250,000 people, nearly two-thirds of the city's residents, were made homeless by the disaster, and they were the lucky ones. Somewhere near 3,000 are believed to have died. Even though the city was devastated, and most of it looked like Dresden after the bombing. Reconstruction began days after the fire was out to build massive refugee camps (the largest spanned 24 blocks in the Richmond) to temporarily house the homeless.

RECONSTRUCTION

Out of the earthquake's rubble grew the new San Francisco, but first came the clean-up. It's estimated that 15,000 horses died hauling off the crumbled stone and brick, most of which became new landfill in Mission Bay. Order was imposed on chaos, but not the order drafted by **Daniel Burnham**, the architect chosen to map out a glorious new city. He drew up a plan based on his beloved Paris, full of boulevards and plazas and brave new parks, but nothing ever came of it. Businesses wanted to be up and going *now*, and residents did not smile on plans that called for wiping out buildings that actually survived the flames, just to make way for Burnham's dreams. In three years, the city was pretty much rebuilt on its original lines.

The Panama Canal was instrumental in providing San Francisco with the impetus to replace its ruined City Hall, as San Francisco won the bid to host the grand **Panama Pacific International Exposition** of 1915. Okay, WWI had broken out, a few countries had withdrawn, and City Hall wasn't actually completed in time, but still it was a sensational celebration. The fair covered 635 acres of today's Marina, though at the time it was known as Harbor View and wasn't much developed (the Marina Green, once Washerwoman's Lagoon, is a by-product of the fair, but the region's Danish crab-catcher settlement known as Crabville-by-the-Bay had long since vacated the premises). The highlight was the 43-story Tower of Jewels, and its many thousands of colored, cut-glass beads shimmered and glinted from their high wires. The Exposition was a success in every way: boosting finances, lauding aesthetics, and rekindling the self-esteem of the city. The fair ran for 10 months, and when it closed in December of 1915, nearly 20 million people had attended.

THE PALACE OF FINE ARTS

The glorious Palace of Fine Arts on Lyon Street, which now houses the Exploratorium, was believed to have been the most beautiful of all the Exposition's many buildings, and is the sole remaining building that escaped razing. It was on Army land, so it escaped the bulldozer when the rest of the Exposition was cleared to pave the way for the new residential neighborhood.

ISLANDS & BRIDGES

Islands in the bay began to be put to use as society construed ever stricter notions of just who they wanted to mingle in their midst. **Alcatraz,** the same lump of rock mistakenly labeled *Isla de Los Alcatraces* (Pelican Island) in 1826, had been an Army fort with prison facilities since 1859, and during the Civil War it detained Confederate sympathizers, but in 1907 its function was revamped and it became a prison first and foremost. From 1907 to 1933 Alcatraz was a military prison, but in 1934 the army relinquished the island rights, and Alcatraz became a maximum security, minimum privilege, federal prison of notoriety.

For years, Alcatraz protected San Francisco society from the likes of Al Capone, "Machine Gun" Kelly, and Robert Stroud ("The Birdman of Alcatraz"), until it was closed by Attorney General Robert Kennedy in 1963 when it was determined that the cost of keeping an inmate in Alcatraz was equal to the cost of staying in the Waldorf Astoria. Native Americans occupied The Rock (more on this later) from 1969-1971, and in 1973 Alcatraz joined the **Golden Gate National Recreation Area** (GGNRA), and opened its prison gates to ferry-loads of tourists.

Not far from Alcatraz sits **Angel Island**, as lush with trees and wildlife as Alcatraz is barren. It, too, is now a valued part of the GGNRA, but in 1910 Angel Island became another means to San Francisco segregation. The 1906 fire may have cleansed San Francisco of its vile Barbary Coast, but its Chinese-bashing prejudices and discriminatory laws remained intact. The **Exclusion Act of 1882** that severely limited which Chinese could emigrate to the U.S. was tightened still further in the early 1900s; only those claiming a family to a U.S. resident need apply. In 1910 Angel Island was set up as an immigration and quarantine station, to carefully scrutinize the Chinese and their kinship claims. This was the catalyst for the "paper brides" and "paper children," the individuals without real ties who paid extravagantly for papers linking them to U.S. citizens. The system invited abuse, and many an illegal immigrant sold him or herself to years of slave labor in the U.S. for the special papers.

Plans had been afloat, as it were, since 1851 to connect San Francisco to her neighbors via an array of bridge designs. It wasn't till the 1920s, however, that the automobile intensified the need. The bay ferries had been doing admirable service since the city began, but by 1921 they were transporting more than 800,000 cars (along with pedestrian traffic, of course); by 1930 they were shuttling 6 million. The Dumbarton Bridge in the south bay opened in 1927, as did the Carquinez Bridge across Carquinez Strait, and the San Mateo Bridge was christened in 1929. The two big ones were to be next.

The **Golden Gate Bridge**, now an icon representing San Francisco world-wide, was by no means a foregone conclusion, at least to most. **Joseph Strauss**, of course, knew otherwise. This tiny man from Chicago who built more than 400 bridges in his life was adamant about his Golden Gate Bridge plans, and relentless about touting them. Others felt differently. There was the War Department (they owned the land on either side), the environmentalists (they didn't want the natural beauty spoiled), the Southern Pacific conglomerate (they owned the steam ship and ferry lines and weren't wild about the competition), and the problem of financing. Bonds had been approved, but in the 1930s the Depression was just getting worse, and only the $6 million bond guarantee of A. P. Giannini of Bank of America kept the project under way.

BRIDGE DESIGNS

San Francisco is lucky the bridge promotion took so long, and luckier still that Irving Morrow was Strauss' assistant. Strauss' initial design was hideously ugly. One critic described it as looking like "two grotesque steel beetles crawling out from either shore." Morrow came up with the seemlier, more elegant plan for the bridge we have in place today.

Construction was not easy, and entailed divers descending 100 feet in strong currents to blast 35-foot holes in bay bedrock for the steel piling foundation. It took four years to build, and the Golden Gate Bridge opened to great hoohah and fanfare May 27, 1937. It was beautiful, brilliantly engineered, bravely built (and all during the Depression); at completion it was the world's second-longest single-span bridge, measuring 4,200 feet (1,280 meters).

As is the case with a younger sibling tripping merrily down the path painfully forged by the elder, the **Bay Bridge** connecting San Francisco to Oakland had far less opposition. Financing bonds sailed through, and President Herbert Hoover, himself an engineer and Stanford graduate, took an active interest in the project and its federal approval. The bridge is actually two bridges: one connecting San Francisco's Rincon Hill to Yerba Buena Island, and the second connecting the island to Alameda in the East Bay. While public and political approval may have been easier, the actual work was much more difficult, since the span from San Francisco to Yerba Buena is twice as long as the mile suspension bridge span of the Golden Gate, and a tunnel had to be carved out of Yerba Buena Island to connect the two. It took more than three years, however, and on November 12, 1936, the 8.5 mile bridge was opened to traffic.

One more island of note came into its own in the 30s. **Treasure Island** was born of three years' worth of dredging, filling, and construction on the shoals of Yerba Buena, and it was built primarily to host the **Golden Gate International Exposition**, otherwise known as the 1939 **Worlds' Fair**. The Treasure Island name was made up by a creative press agent, based on the flimsy premise that the gold-rich Sierra streams that emptied into the bay loaded the dredged up island fill with precious metals; the notion was absurd, but the name stuck. The fair was held there as scheduled, but even though Count Basie and Benny Goodman performed, and Sally Rand the fan dancer drew scads of men to her Nude Ranch, the fair ended in the red. A few months after it opened, Hitler invaded Poland, and the fair closed in September 1940.

Treasure Island became the new west coast naval base after Pearl Harbor was bombed, and it will remain so till 1997 when the naval base shuts down. There have been a good number of suggestions as to what to do with the island next (including turning it into a big casino), but nothing's been decided so far.

BRIDGES FACTS

	Golden Gate Bridge	Bay Bridge
Length	nearly 1 mile	8.4 miles
Start to Finish	Jan. '33 to May '37	May '33 to Nov. '36
Cost in Dollars	$35 million	$77 million
Cost in Deaths	10 lives	27 lives
Types of Traffic	Car, Pedestrian, Bicycle	Car
Toll	$3 southbound	$1 westbound

WORLD WAR II

World War II did to twentieth century San Francisco what the discovery of gold did a century before: replaced its insular complacency with cosmopolitan sophistication, and replaced its homogeneous make-up with multicultural, ethnic diversity.

The Japanese bombed Pearl Harbor on December 7th, 1941, effectively demolishing the Hawaiian harbor, bringing the U.S. into the war, and focusing the U.S. military defense spotlight on its west coast. And San Francisco, a city that had until that moment felt ever so safe and removed, suddenly felt very, very vulnerable. The Presidio and Fort Mason, military relics from Spanish days, revved up into action, and new forts sprang up all around the bay. Treasure Island, the Alameda Naval Air Station, and Hunters Point Naval Shipyard in San Francisco were integral to Pacific naval operations, and the Oakland Army Base plus assorted Marin headlands defensive forts added to the intense war preparations. Enormous shipyards sprung up, employed over 100,000 men and women (three shifts a day, seven days a week) and battle ships were churned out. In 1944, the Bay Area was the world's shipbuilding leader.

San Francisco leapt out of the Depression into employment heaven. All the draftable men were gone, workers were needed, and all of a sudden women and minorities were being recruited from all across the nation. Latinos streamed north, and African Americans responded from the Deep South. When they arrived they were welcomed by an abundance of manufacturing and defense-related jobs, a welcome that was to wear thin when the jobs dried up. Local Chinese were now greeted warmly by employers, and women made up more than one-third of the shipyard builders. Since the days when the U.S. acquired California, San Francisco had turned into a predominantly white enclave, but the war effort sowed the seeds of today's rich diversity.

LIBERTY SHIPS

Liberty ships were the ship of choice. They were cargo vessels made to carry supplies (plasma, whiskey, medicine, munitions, and mail) to the troops overseas. Once the system was in place, Henry Kaiser's Richmond shipyard could assembly-line a 7,000 ton ship in just 42 days. Though the average assembly time was 6-8 weeks, Kaiser's yard once entered a competition with an Oregon shipyard, and actually produced a Liberty ship in 4 days (thereby winning the competition). By the end of the war, the Richmond yard had sent more than 500 ships out to sea, nearly 25% of all the ships built nationwide.

The one ethnicity not included in the universal welcome and war-effort employment was the Japanese. WWII ended August 14, 1945, and a delirious mass of happy humanity clogged downtown in riotous celebration. The **United Nations Charter** was signed here (as was the peace treaty with Japan in 1951) and the city continued to celebrate in the following weeks as it welcomed the men home.

Many of the returning soldiers stayed on in San Francisco, regardless of point of origin, and most of the civilians who'd responded to the call for help stayed on too. But while the faces and cultures of San Francisco reflected far greater diversity than in the relatively provincial pre-war years, the conformity of the '50s was strictly in vogue in what remained in many ways a fairly conservative, conventional city.

THE BEAT GENERATION

Americans were busy pursuing family, career, and material stability, and the uniform goals and expectations of the '50s were felt nationwide. Sensitive topics were not to be discussed blatantly in public, and ladies were to always don their hats and white gloves before going out. Appearances and denial ruled hand-in-hand.

It's not surprising that there were protests against what seemed to some a callous refusal to confront and deal with major problems like nuclear devastation and racism. A group of unconventional, bohemian writers in San Francisco's North Beach led the way articulately and doggedly, and people began to notice. **Jack Kerouac** said he belonged to the "beaten" generation, and he called them the **Beats**. And in October 1955, another North Beach denizen, **Allen Ginsberg**, gave his first public performance of *Howl*. **Lawrence Ferlinghetti** was part of the growing scene, and opened *City Lights*, a bookstore catering to poets and other literati, in 1952. It's now a North Beach landmark and a terrifically popular bookstore, and Ferlinghetti has a small North Beach alley named after him as well.

They and the other iconoclastic poets, jazz musicians, and artists challenged the norms in the face of society. Instead of the *de rigueur* jacket and tie, they began their own casual attire of beret and turtleneck, dark glasses and sandals. Coffee houses in North Beach and elsewhere were full of their black berets and passionate conversations, and **Herb Caen**, ceaseless *San Francisco Chronicle* writer who's still going strong with his column, didn't approve. Caen thought the Beats were "far out" in the same way that the Sputnik satellite was, and in 1957 he termed them "**Beatniks**," and so they have remained ever since.

By 1958, the Beatniks had full media coverage, and their North Beach scene was on all the organized San Francisco tours for a good gawk. By the early 1960s, however, the North Beach Beat scene was no more. Topless bars supplanted coffeehouses, and tourist inflation drove up the cheap rents. So many of the Beatniks found new lodgings in another neighborhood of inexpensive digs and youthful discontent: the Haight.

HAIGHT-ASHBURY

At the time, it was a forgotten neighborhood near the entrance to Golden Gate Park. The community was mostly black families and university students. San Francisco State University was there until 1952, when it moved to its present location on 19th Avenue, but the University feel and student residents remained. The Victorians were fairly rundown, and rent was cheap. The Beatniks felt right at home.

Pleased as the Beats were with the new neighborhood, they didn't feel that the youth of the Haight were quite as cool as themselves. They were junior cools, not quite hipsters, so they came up with a diminutive for them and called them **hippies**.

By the mid-60s, the Beats were history. The hippies reflected their influence in their political and philosophical alienation from society, but they expressed it quite differently. Red wine and poetry, jazz and Buddhism was all very well for the beatniks, but the hippies dug drugs, and an increasingly revolutionary music scene.

The **Haight-Ashbury Summer of Love** blossomed in 1967, but the distinctive hippie ambiance had begun shaping in '65 with funky coffee houses and funkier clothing. Ken Kesey and his Merry Pranksters hosted LSD parties, and advertised with flyers asking "Can You Pass the Acid Test?" Fledgling rock bands appeared as the general aura of the neighborhood took on an increasingly hippie flavor. Jefferson Airplane played its first gigs, and the Warlocks (soon to be the Grateful Dead), added their sounds to the mix. *Rolling Stone* magazine was launched as it covered the burgeoning Haight-Ashbury rock group activity.

The Summer of Love made Haight-Ashbury its home base, but the reverberations could be felt city-wide. The '60s revolution was by no means a uniquely San Francisco phenomenon, but its legacies changed the face of San Francisco more permanently than it did elsewhere. San Francisco's complacency was shaken to its conservative core, and the turbulence produced a far more tolerant, open-minded, eclectic society.

TOLERANCE IN SAN FRANCISCO

There is still an alarming abundance of racism, homophobia, and other hurtful forms of intolerance in San Francisco, but far less so than in most of the United States, not to mention the era of the '50s. But as the boundaries of acceptability continue to be pushed and challenged, the range that seems perfectly normal (or at least not terribly strange) keeps growing.

San Francisco stays on the cutting edge of strange and state of the art weird (it has a tradition to keep up, after all), and as new bizarre forms of self expression make their debuts, yesterday's oddities cease to turn heads. Respectable hotels that are at the heart of San Francisco conservative tradition (still a very strong presence) now hire male employees sporting earrings, San Francisco educators may be seen with purple or green coiffures, or with clean-shaven pates, and no one bats an eye.

THE LOMA PRIETA EARTHQUAKE OF 1989

Another shake-up for San Francisco, this time geological rather than cultural, came at 5:04pm of October 17, 1989. The biggest earthquake in the region since 1906, it registered 7.1 on the Richter Scale. The damage was extensive. The quake killed 67 people, injured over 3,000, destroyed more than $6 billion worth of property including over 100,000 buildings, and what was the worst blow of all to some, disrupted the 3rd game of the 1989 World Series between the Giants and the A's.

Power went down all around the city, and once again a terrible loss was caused by the fire that ensued. While City residents searched for battery-operated transistor radios to feed them news snips, people elsewhere across the country (including the worried relatives of San Francisco residents) saw hours of news specials featuring horrid scenes of the Marina in ruins and flames.

The epicenter was near Aptos, a small town close to Santa Cruz and Watsonville, both of which sustained terrible, devastating damage. Most of the deaths, however, were in the Bay Area. The Marina was the hardest hit district, thanks to its mushy underpinnings of landfill and mud. As the earthquake sent shivers through the bedrock of San Francisco's hills, it sent waves of destruction through the spongy foundations of the Marina, toppling buildings, tearing sidewalks, and once again severing gas lines that resulted in another awful conflagration.

The other site of devastation was Cypress ramp off of the Bay Bridge. The double decker structure collapsed, the top merged with the bottom, flattening cars and killing passengers. While it took months and months to refortify and rebuild (and re-tenant) the broken houses, the Bay Bridge was the priority, and it was back in operation four weeks later.

6. ARRIVALS & DEPARTURES

BY PLANE

San Francisco International Airport, *415-761-0800,* just 14 miles south of the city, is the fifth busiest airport in the US, and the seventh busiest in the world. Fifty major airlines connect here, and a new terminal will be completed by 1998. **Oakland Airport,** *510-577-4000 or 4010,* also handles some of the Bay Area air traffic, though most flights go to **SFO** (San Francisco International). To facilitate SFO-city transportation, a BART train connection is underway (but at a mindblowingly slow pace). In the meantime, there are a variety of ways to get to and from the airports.

Airport Shuttle vans are the best bargains. You share them with a few others (they generally take 3-7 people), they cost $10-$14 (depending on the company), and they will drop you off (or pick you up) anywhere in San Francisco. From the SFO airport, go out the main level exit, and cross the street to the van pick-up points. Super Shuttle is the largest company, but there are plenty of others to choose from, like Quake City, Bayporter, and Yellow Cab shuttles. You sometimes have to wait a bit for them to fill up, but you should be on your way in 5-10 minutes. Going to the airport, call a day in advance if you can (all the companies and phone numbers are in the yellow pages), and arrange a pick-up time. Most of these will go to and from Oakland airport, too.

The **SFO Airporter,** *415-495-8404,* is a bus service between the airport and the major downtown hotels. Buses run every 20 minutes from 5am-11pm, and the fare is $8.

Or, go by limo with **Airport Commuter Limo & Sedan Service,** *415-876-1777,* for 24-hour service to San Francisco, Oakland, and San Jose Airports. They work like the shuttles, and cost $10 per passenger to SFO.

Taxis are plentiful, cost around $30 to downtown, and take about 20 minutes from SFO. You can also share the cab with a few others, so long as the total destinations are no more than three.

If you want to go by car, there are countless **car rental** agencies at the airport.

A **SamTrans bus** is the cheapest and least convenient option. They run from a bit before 6am to a bit past midnight, between downtown San Francisco and the airport. The 7F is the express, it costs $2.50, and takes about half an hour; the 7B is the local, it costs $2, and takes an hour; the 3X costs just $1 and takes 20 minutes to shuttle you to the BART station in Colma where you transfer to take Bart to the city.

From the Oakland Airport, you can take **AIRBART** to save money. Take the AIRBART shuttle ($2) to the Oakland Coliseum BART station, and then transfer to a BART train to the city. They run every 15 minutes till 11pm.

BY TRAIN

Amtrak, *800-872-7245*, at the Ferry Building, Suite 140 (at the foot of Market) provides daily service to points north, south, and east. An Amtrak shuttle bus takes you over the bridge to the Oakland or Emeryville depot, where you board the actual train.

CalTrain, *800-660-4287*, at Fourth and Townsend, operates daily trains to destinations in the Southern Peninsula like Palo Alto for $3.50, and as far south as San Jose.

BART, *415-992-2278*, stands for **Bay Area Rapid Transit**, the 71-mile system that links eight San Francisco stations with Daly City in the south and 25 East Bay stations. The trains run Monday-Friday 4am-midnight, Saturday 6am-midnight, and Sunday 8am-midnight. Fares vary from 90 cents (within San Francisco) to $3.50 (from Fremont to Daly City).

BY BUS

Greyhound, *800-231-2222 or 415-495-1575*, in the Transbay Terminal on the first floor *(425 Mission and First)* has bus service to nearly everywhere in the continental US. From there you can take taxis or buses to any point in the city.

Green Tortoise, *415-821-0803*, has bus trips leaving from the Transbay Terminal, too. The Baja and Oregon trips are especially popular. Cross-country trips take 10 days by the northern route and 14 via the south. They're all sleeper coaches, and are a perfect way to travel for some (mostly those in the 20-40 category), but definitely not for others.

If you like mixing and mingling, if you're gregarious and mellow, Green Tortoise might be perfect. If you're a little introverted, and can't stand the thought of having to listen to other people's music, don't sign on. If you opt for the Tortoise, don't over pack but do bring slip-on shoes, and your favorite cassettes.

AC Transit, *510-817-1717*, in the Transbay Terminal at First and Mission runs buses between San Francisco and various East Bay communities like Berkeley, Oakland, and beyond.

Golden Gate Transit, *415-923-2000*, goes from the Transbay Terminal at First and Mission and links San Francisco to Marin and Sonoma counties. You can travel as far north as Santa Rosa for $4.50, and they leave every half hour.

SamTrans, *800-660-4287*, provides a bus link between San Francisco and Palo Alto for $2.50, with service to SFO airport and Peninsula communities.

BY FERRY

Blue & Gold Fleet, *415-705-5444*, at Pier 39 of Fisherman's Wharf has daily ferry service from San Francisco's Ferry Building and Pier 39 to Oakland's Jack London Waterfront, and Alameda's Main Street Terminal for $3.75 an adult, $2.10 a child, and $1.50 a senior. There is also transport to Vallejo (where Marine World Africa USA is located) for $7.50 an adult, $4 a child, and $6 a senior. All fares include AC Transit and Muni transfers.

Golden Gate Ferries, *415-923-2000, 415-332-6600*, at the Ferry Building by the foot of Market has ferries to Sausalito and Larkspur. The trip to Sausalito is $4.25 each way for adults, $3.20 for kids, and $2.10 for seniors. To Larkspur, the ferry is $2.50 for adults, $1.90 for children, and $1.25 for senior citizens.

The Red & White Fleet, *415-546-2896*, shuttles between Pier 43 1/2 in San Francisco and the docks in Sausalito and Tiburon for $5.50 each way for adults and seniors, and $2.75 for children. The ferry takes 20-40 minutes, and is usually more crowded than the less expensive Golden Gate boats.

7. PLANNING YOUR TRIP

CLIMATE

The weather in San Francisco is generally mild year-round. It's rarely hotter than 75° (24° C) or colder than 40° (5° C), and skies are clear more often than not. In the summer, the morning and evening fog rolls in off the Pacific (so it's thicker and cooler in neighborhoods near the ocean, and the fog sometimes doesn't even make it past the hills to the valleys of the Mission or South of Market districts), and it usually burns off during the day.

The annual rainfall averages 20 inches (508 mm), and most of it takes place from November-February. But even during winter, there are often days of warm, sunny tee shirt weather in between Pacific storms.

TEMPERATURE CHART		
Daily Mean in F°	High	Low
January	56	44
February	59	46
March	60	46
April	62	46
May	66	50
June	69	52
July	69	52
August	70	54
September	71	53
October	69	52
November	63	47
December	57	43

Though the averages help give a picture of San Francisco climate norms, the weather fluctuates too much from day to day for the averages to be that meaningful. When it's cloudy and rainy, the air is raw and chilly, and it doesn't vary much from morning to afternoon or valley to hill.

However, a sunny day plays havoc with your expectations. It can be 85° in the sun and out of the wind, but 65° in the shade or on top of a hill. And although in summer and early fall there are always a few heat waves with temperatures in the 90s and no breeze or fog in sight, there's no way of knowing when they'll start or when the soothing fog will slide in and cool the city down.

Summer Fog

The oft-quoted line "the coldest winter I ever spent was a summer in San Francisco" has been attributed to a host of wits (Mark Twain, Ambrose Bierce), and while San Franciscans bristle at any implied snub, there is more than a germ of wisdom in it. San Francisco is naturally air conditioned in summer by the banks of fog that, roiling along the Pacific Coast, find the break of the Golden Gate and wash on in. So forget for a moment your hot and sunny summer California notions.

On a typical Bay Area day in July, Berkeley will be simmering in 90° heat, but drive over the Bay Bridge and past the fog line, and you'll see people walking around in sweaters. Tourists know this, but it's hard when you're packing on a sweltering New York or Chicago day to ignore what your senses and years of Beach Boys songs tell you. More sweatshirts get sold as souvenirs than any other item, not just because of the cunning San Francisco designs, but because they're warm, snugly, and readily available when the fog rolls in and you begin to shiver in your shorts. So buy one by all means if you want, but pack smartly, too.

WHAT TO PACK

Whenever you visit, good footwear is vital. San Francisco is one of the loveliest cities to stroll about in, and also one of the hilliest. Waterproof, comfortable boots in the winter will greatly enhance your visit, and good walking shoes, sandals, or sneakers are essential when it's not raining. Your calf muscles will get a workout as it is; you don't need blisters.

In spring, summer, and fall, take along warm and cool weather clothes, and clothes that can be layered or fit into your day pack are especially convenient. A sweater that can fit under a jacket is all you'll need in the way of warmth. There are plenty of shorts days, but you can't count on them, and they may well turn chilly before long. Bring a bathing suit if you want, but be forewarned that the Bay waters are very, very cold. What you pack should also factor in how long you plan to stay in San Francisco and along the coast as compared to other, generally hotter, inland destinations like the wine country.

In winter, bring layered warmth. Tee shirts and turtlenecks, a sweater, raincoat, and collapsible umbrella should take care of you nicely. Mittens are rarely worn here, but a cozy scarf is a good idea.

The other consideration is style. You can eat and be entertained very well in San Francisco without ever venturing out of jeans or sweat pants, but they'll be out of place at the opera or the French Room of the Clift Hotel. You know your preferences and tastes; pack accordingly.

Banking
San Francisco is bank heaven. There are banks and ATM machines everywhere, stores and most restaurants take credit cards, and some stores are even accepting ATM cards. If you have the money in the bank, it should be easy for you to access it. Unless you don't have an ATM card, it's easier to travel with cash and credit cards than travelers checks – although travelers checks are probably safer than cash.

BUSINESS HOURS
Business hours vary. Government offices generally operate Monday-Friday 9am-5pm, but some have Saturday hours, and some stay open late one night. Department store hours also vary, but they won't differ much from Monday-Saturday 10am-8pm and Sunday 11am-7pm, except for Christmas time when most of the stores stay open longer. As for restaurants, most close at 10pm or 11pm, but there are some open till 2-3am, and a few open round the clock, too.
Major supermarkets like Safeway and Cala (with branches throughout the city) are open 24 hours a day.

SALES TAX
There's an 8.5% sales tax added on to all non-food purchases, unless you have the product shipped outside California.

PHONES, FAXES, & MAIL
Most of the hotel rooms have phones, and public phones can be found in lobbies of all the nicer hotels, as well as scattered about city street corners. Phone booths operate on 20 cents, but phone cards can also be used. Many hotel phones have data ports to accommodate a laptop computer or fax, but ask ahead of time. Hotel phones don't usually have fax facilities you can use. However, the better hotels have business centers with the full range of computer and fax equipment.
San Francisco has post office branches throughout the city (including one in the basement of Macy's in Union Square), and they are generally open Monday-Friday 9am-5:30pm, and Saturday 9am-1pm, though some branches differ by half an hour earlier or later. Page 15 in the San Francisco white pages lists all the branches so you can find the nearest and most convenient one.

AREA CODES

San Francisco: 415
East Bay, including Berkeley and Oakland: 510
North Bay plus Napa and Sonoma counties: 707
Don't forget to dial 1 before dialing another area code.

COST OF LIVING & TRAVEL

San Francisco has a reputation as the most expensive city in which to buy real estate, but if you're not shopping for town houses, you can get by on whatever feels comfortable. Accommodations range from $12-$1,200 a night, depending on your tastes and budget, and there is excellent food available at all levels. If finances are tight, you need to spend more time planning where to eat and how to get around, but so many of the most glorious sights in the city are free. How much you spend will have more to do with how much you want to pamper yourself.

For elegant and luxurious options, few cities come close. If you are so inclined, there are endless ways in which to spend your money and live it up. However, San Francisco also has a large immigrant and student population, so there's a lot of quality budget options, too.

If you're planning on moving here, it's another story. Buying a house in San Francisco really is exorbitant. $300,000-$1,000,000 will get you here what $50,000-$300,000 might get you elsewhere in the country. But renting is a much more reasonable option. Granted, it's more expensive than in small town America, but $1,000-$1,300 for a two bedroom apartment with a garage in a good neighborhood is what you could expect from the rental market.

However, if you're not really going to move here, you might as well daydream about the gorgeous mansions; a luxury fantasy doesn't cost any extra.

HEALTH CONCERNS

The most probable ailment from a vacation in San Francisco will likely come from over-eating; this city is generally not very hard on your well-being. But there are some other risks to be aware of. Colds are always more likely when you travel, since you're on the move, exposing yourself to new and interesting germs the likes of which you wouldn't meet at home.

Public transport is a good way to meet new people and their diseases, so washing hands after lots of Muni riding can help. Also, bring adequately warm clothes and remember to rest occasionally; your best defense is to keep your immune system happy.

STDs, including AIDS, are a serious risk not just in San Francisco, but throughout the world. If you're going to engage in sexual sport (be it gay or straight), make sure condoms are used to be safe.

The sun is a factor to be reckoned with here, even if the fog does cool the city down. Wearing sunscreen is especially recommended on those hazy days when the sun filters through but no one notices till later.

Another hidden danger of outdoor recreation is poison oak. Similar to the poison ivy of the east coast, poison oak lurks just off trails in lush vegetation. It's a climbing shrub with chemicals that can cause a nasty, terribly itchy skin rash. Usually identified by their clusters of three shiny leaflets, your best bet is to avoid them and stay on the path. However, if you do come in contact, the less you bruise the leaf the less the chemicals will be released, and a good washing with warm, soapy water can help dilute the effect. If you do develop a rash (and you'll know it by the shiny, aggravatingly itchy bumps that develop), cortisone cream does a good job of making it bearable (better than the old calamine lotion remedy), and it's available over-the-counter at any pharmacy. And while you're out of doors being careful, watch out for ticks, too. There have been some cases of Lyme's Disease traced to deer ticks in the Marin woods.

However, probably the biggest health complaint is blisters and sore leg muscles. There are some easy ways to mitigate both, without resorting to taxis everywhere. First, bring comfortable shoes (or sneakers or sandals) that are already broken in, and good socks, too. Put band-aides on *at the first hint* of rubbing, because it's so much easier to prevent blisters with band-aides than to deal with them after they have formed. And after a serious jaunt of hill-climbing, take some aspirin and do some leg stretches. Not only does this help for the next couple of hours, it actually prevents most of the tightening that would otherwise cause pain in days to come.

STAYING OUT OF TROUBLE

San Francisco is a friendly, welcoming city, but it *is* a city, with all a city's urban woes and correlated problems. All you have to do is corner a long-time resident to get an earful on how San Francisco isn't the way she *used* to be, crime's worse, the streets are dirtier, ad nauseam. And while a new mayoral administration is trying new tactics to improve the quality of life for all, problems still exist. There is poverty and homelessness, prostitution and drug-dealing, begging, mugging and violence.

Chances are that as a visitor, all you'll see are the panhandlers who gather around Market, Union Square, and North Beach, and all they'll do is ask for spare change. How you want to handle that request is up to you; your safety won't be in danger whether you give or keep on walking. There are some activities that are risky, however, and ways to maximize your well-being:

• Avoid driving while intoxicated. Local police will not hesitate to nab you on it, for one, and the hills and traffic are tricky enough without adding an extra handicap. Take buses and taxis if you're going out partying, and find some safe means of transportation if you're going wine tasting in Napa, as the local law there will ticket you in a second.

• Pedestrians have the right of way in San Francisco's crosswalks. If you're driving, make sure you stop for people crossing, and if you are the pedestrian, keep an eye out for crazy drivers who aren't looking. The same goes if you're cycling or roller-skating. You have the right of way, but they have the steel, so be cautious.

• Most of the city is safe to walk around in, but some neighborhoods have a high crime rate after dark, and you'd be better off not walking there, especially alone, at night. The Western Addition, the Tenderloin, and Hunter's Point fall into that category, as do the Mission and South of Market, though to a lesser degree. All of these neighborhoods have many charms and a lot to offer, but if you want to explore them, you're advised to get around by car, by cab, or in a group. The parks are dark at night, and you should save them for daylight.

TIME

San Francisco and the rest of California is on **Pacific Standard Time** (PST), which is three hours earlier than in New York, and eight hours earlier than Greenwich Mean Time (GMT) in London.

TIPPING

Customers usually tip restaurant waitstaff and taxi drivers 15%-20%, depending on the quality of the service. However, it's still up to you. Airport and hotel porters also get tipped, generally $1 per bag.

TRAFFIC REGULATIONS & PARKING

Driver's Licenses: A valid license from a Western nation will authorize you to drive in California for a year. Otherwise, you'll need a current International Driver License to drive here.

Curbing Wheels: You must leave your parked car with its wheels turned all the way towards the curb when facing downhill, and away from the curb when pointing uphill. Not only is this a safety precaution to prevent roll-away cars, it is required by law, regardless of the steepness of the incline.

Curb Colors: *Red* means no stopping or parking, ever; *yellow* is a loading and unloading spot for vehicles with commercial plates only; *white* is loading and unloading for passengers; *green* is for ten-minute limited-time parking; taxi zones are mixed *green, yellow, and black*; and *blue* zones are reserved for vehicles with a California issued disabled placard or plate.

Towaway Zones: Watch for signs prohibiting parking during certain hours, such as for street cleaning or during rush hour. Ticketing and towing will result in hefty fines and a lot of hassle. Parking in a bus stop won't result in towing, but the ticket is now more than $200.

Other Parking Rules: There are coin meters in most commercial districts, and many residential neighborhoods have two-hour parking limits unless you purchase a permit. If there are no signs indicating a time limit and no warning curb colors, you are in luck and can park. But parking is often quite tough to come by in some parts of town, such as Union Square, North Beach, the Mission, and the Inner Richmond. If you don't get lucky, check Chapter 21, *Practical Information*, for garages.

MORE INFORMATION, PLEASE!

History
A Short History of San Francisco, by Tom Cole
Norton I: Emperor of the United States, by William Drury
San Francisco Street Secrets, by David B. Eames
Strangers From a Different Short: A History of Asian Americans, by Ronald Takaki
The Haight-Ashbury: A History, by Charles Perry
The Mayor of Castro Street, by Randy Shilts
They saw the Elephant: Women in the California Gold Rush, by Jo Ann Levy

Local Color
A Fine Old Conflict, by Jessica Mitford
Baghdad-by-the-Bay, Only in San Francisco, or any others by Herb Caen (still a *Chronicle* columnist)
Isadora Speaks, by Isadora Duncan
The Shirley Letters, by Dame Shirley
Travels in San Francisco, by Herb Gold
Off the Road: My Years with Cassady, Kerouac and Ginsberg, by Carolyn Cassady

Novels Set in San Francisco
Desolation Angels, by Jack Kerouac
Edwin of the Iron Shoes, by Marcia Muller
San Francisco Stories: Great Writers on the City, edited by John Miller
Tales of the City, by Armstead Maupin (recently made into a PBS series)
The Joy Luck Club, by Amy Tan
The Maltese Falcon, by Dashiell Hammett
Trip Master Monkey, by Maxine Hong Kingston

8. SAN FRANCISCO WITH KIDS

It is both easy and enjoyable to travel in San Francisco with the kids along. Lots of hotels are well-stocked with all the paraphernalia you'd want for an infant, many have pools, and if they don't have baby-sitting services, they should be able to make a reliable reference. There are so many good restaurants it shouldn't be hard to find one with food that'll please everyone, and there are plenty of sights and entertainment geared especially towards children. As for expenses, hotels usually let kids stay with their parents for free, Muni transportation is very cheap for kids, and most museums have low children fees, too.

Not all the hotels are as well prepared for children as the Westin St. Francis and Clift, but the Ritz-Carlton, the Canterbury, the Andrews, the Juliana, and the Hotel Californian all have good family room set ups, and it's worth asking other hotels as well. Most are happy to oblige.

As for activities that kids would enjoy, it depends, of course, on the age and interests of your children, but here are a few that regularly go over well.

Fisherman's Wharf always goes over big with children and teens. There's a full video arcade plus bumper cars and lots of souvenir shops. The **San Francisco Zoo** is always great, and the **Exploratorium** is unusually wonderful and popular (especially if you can get reservations to the tactile dome), and the small **Randall Museum** is free and well-loved by kids. too. **Marine World Africa USA** *(707-643-6722)* in Vallejo is popular with kids. They have got killer whales, tigers, sharks, and more. **Q-Zar** *(415-775-6700)* at 2801 in the Cannery is an amazing laser game that most kids go nuts over.

Cyber Mind *(415-693-0348)* in the Embarcadero is a virtual reality center that teens love; and if your children like **sports**, there's the full line-up of ice-skating, hiking, bicycles, swimming, and even rock-climbing, and in April-September there are two local baseball teams (the San Francisco

Giants and the Oakland A's) to watch. There are **beaches** and **nature trails** and beautiful **parks**, and terrific **picnic** locations, and you can walk across **Golden Gate Bridge** if no one's too spooked by heights. For younger children, it's worth keeping the local libraries in mind. The schedules vary, but they all have **story-telling** hours, and they do a very nice job of it.

And there's always something else. Check the Kids Events page of the Sunday paper Pink Section for the special films, story-telling, plays, exhibitions, concerts, and happenings going on that week. Your kids may get worn out and tired (or maybe it's you who will), but it's unlikely that they'll get bored.

9. FOOD & DRINK

FOOD

The culinary arts of San Francisco could easily be its own book. There is every ethnic variety here from Japanese to Ethiopian to Vietnamese to Afghani, and every food style from traditional steak house to vegan to nouvelle California cuisine. You can pay anywhere from $4-$65 for a satisfying, delicious meal, and dine surrounded by grunge funk or French elegance. As for beverages, there are quite a few quality wines and beers produced in San Francisco or its environs.

Most of San Francisco's excellent food comes courtesy of the people who've immigrated here. Asians make up 32% of San Francisco's population, so it's no surprise that San Francisco is overflowing with Chinese, Thai, Vietnamese, Japanese, Filipino, and Korean restaurants. Dim sum is very popular for weekend brunch, and there are sushi bars throughout the city. And while Chinese food is no stranger to the rest of the United States, few cities have the abundance of Asian variety and quality that you'll find here.

Another major source of restaurant wealth comes from the Latino community, which represents 13% of the city. There are taquerias and burrito joints throughout the city, ranging in quality from humdrum to gourmet, but that's just the start. Mexican flavors show up in all the innovative gourmet restaurants. Traditional Mexican cuisine is available throughout the Mission neighborhood, where you can also find plenty of Salvadorian and Nicaraguan restaurants, and there are a number of Brazilian restaurants scattered about San Francisco, too. The rich variety of peppers and fruits and spices are readily available in city markets for any adventurous kitchen, and they appear frequently in nouvelle Californian cuisine.

Italian immigration has nearly petered out, but the Italian community is still very strong, making this is one of the premier spots in the country for superb Italian cooking of all sorts. And while San Francisco pizza does not enjoy the same sort of acclaim as say New York or Chicago, there are some very reputable pizzerias of both traditional and gourmet varieties. From peasant Tuscan fare served in cozy nooks with rustic warmth to superbly crafted Milano elegance, it doesn't get much better.

Tapas restaurants are very popular these days, offering Spanish cuisine in small, inexpensive portions, encouraging people to share and taste. There are a lot of very good Middle Eastern restaurants; a smattering of Indian and Russian restaurants are springing up in the Richmond where the new influx of Russian immigrants have been settling. But underneath all the trends, San Francisco retains a solid traditional streak, and the old steak houses and seafood bars never want for customers.

While carnivores will have no difficulty meeting their needs in San Francisco, this is a swell city for vegetarians. Vegetarians make up a sizable market here, and many restaurants cater to their tastes. But even among meat-eaters, meatless dishes are gaining popularity thanks to the rise of health-conscious eating, and the growing number of fine chefs turning out stunning vegetarian creations (Greens Restaurant in Fort Mason has been a guiding gourmet light for years, and their tasty, organic, innovative dishes are still winning awards).

While many restaurants offer strictly vegetarian (and in some cases, vegan) dishes, most feature all kinds, but with substantial vegetarian sections. Gone are the days, at least in San Francisco, where the menus are 99% fish, fowl, and red meat, with one mediocre vegetarian platter off in a corner. Chinese, Thai, Indian, and Middle Eastern restaurants generally have healthy vegetarian menus, and most of the Italian eateries have numerous vegetable-based selections as well.

There are many other types of ethic cuisines in abundance here, way out of proportion to the population, because new would-be restaurateurs are always looking for a new food niche, so there are Irish pubs and British fish and chips shops, German restaurants, and African eateries. You can find Creole cooking and Caribbean cuisine, down-home southern, Greek, and Tibetan. This is a restaurant town, and anything goes, at least for a while. There are over 4,000 restaurants in San Francisco (which is more than one for every ten residents), though they shut down as quickly as they spring up. It takes a combination of good food, location, and luck to make it work.

What with the thirteen million tourists and business people who visit each year, and the sophisticated dining palates of San Franciscans, the city attracts the best of the chefs, and they design some magnificent eateries. There are lots of excellent French restaurants, and places serving fine Continental cuisine, but the best in the culinary world here comes from the kitchens of the nouvelle Californian chefs, who follow in the footsteps of Alice Waters, using seasonal produce and flavors from the east and west in a mix of tradition and innovation. While not all innovative nouvelle cuisine combinations work (such is the nature of experimentation), the very best (Chez Panisse, Postrio, Masa's) turn out stupendously sublime creations.

DRINK

As for drink, the Bay Area is awash with the best that **Napa** and **Sonoma** valleys produce. San Francisco is full of wine connoisseurs, and while the wine shops are full of French, Italian, Spanish, Australian, German, and you name it, the bulk is from local California wineries, and they're very good. And any wine shop employee worth his or her cork can tell you all about them.

But you aren't limited to wine. Local breweries have been putting out some of the best beers in America for a long time. San Francisco's pride is the **Anchor Brewery** in Potrero Hill which has been making its Anchor Steam beer for just over a century. Anchor Steam beer is on tap at many bars, and you can certainly buy it in six-packs throughout the city. Sierra Nevada's Pale Ale from nearby Chico is another remarkably good beer that's a local favorite. Then there are the countless micro breweries in the area. If you want to conduct research on local beer, the **Brewery on Columbus** and **Twenty Tank Brewery** on Eleventh are good places to start. And if you go up to Napa Valley, you can compare them with the ales made by the **Calistoga Inn Brewery**.

Another Calistoga product is the **Calistoga sparkling water**, and there are lots of other flavored and unflavored sparkling and mineral waters available. What with fruit juices like **Odwalla** and flavored sodas like Calistoga, Koala, Crystal Geyser, and Snapple, there's no reason to settle for alcohol if you don't want it.

10. SAN FRANCISCO'S BEST HOTELS & INNS

San Francisco has many fine hotels and inns, but these are special. They are listed below from most to least expensive.

SHERMAN HOUSE, *2160 Green Street. 415-563-3600, 800-424-5777, fax 415-563-1882. Located in Pacific Heights, and just a block or so away from Cow Hollow and the Marina. It has eight luxurious rooms which rent for $200-$395 a night and six suites which cost $595-$825, each uniquely decorated and named.*

This was once the home of Leander Sherman, one of San Francisco's early arts patrons. He built this two-winged Baroque Italianate mansion in 1876, and for a while after his death the great house languished, but the Sherman House has finally been brought back to prominence and style in its new life as a small luxury hotel. All the rooms and suites in the main house are beautifully decorated with Jacobean and French Second Empire antiques as well as rich brocades, and they are amazing.

The Galleria is a beautiful room where guests can sit, chat, read, and whatnot. The Music Room, lit by an ornate leaded-glass skylight, is dominated by Sherman's grand piano, while Roman toga-clad busts, palm trees, and French tapestries add to the continental panache. And while the occasional pianist guest treats the place to a Mozart sonata, the room is more often filled by the twittering of finches who reside in the magnificent aviary chateau. From there, a grand mahogany staircase leads up to the east wing rooms. The hardwood floors are gorgeous (and among the oldest in the city), and there are 14 wood-burning fireplaces.

The Paderewski Suite is a fine example of what a suite can be. It was once Sherman's billiards room, and the dark wood wainscoting and wood-beam ceiling lend a very British feel. All is elegant and stylish, and done up in Jacobean Period finery. There's a stunning canopied bed surrounded by heavy brocade curtains, and the lovely, pillow-filled window seats look out over the garden. There's a bin of wood waiting by the fireplace, and the bathroom not only has its own jacuzzi, but a second fireplace, too.

The Leander Sherman Suite, however, takes the cake. Inside there's a four-poster canopied bed and brocade curtain that sets it apart from the sitting room, a marbled fireplace, and elegant writing desk. The bathroom is special, too, with its Roman style tub, but the big treat is the brick-laid terrace. The Leander Suite lets out onto one of the loveliest patios with the most sensational of bay views, while the wrought iron table and cushioned settee call out for a picnic lunch or sunset cocktail.

The Carriage House has a more contemporary feel, with silk floral fabrics, rattan, French country furnishings, and verdant garden views. One room has a refrigerator, wet bar, and game table, another is cool and airy with Chinese slate floors and walls of French-paned windows, while a third has a sunken living room plus a balcony that wraps round three sides and overlooks the bay, and their bathtubs are finished in teak.

All the rooms, of course, have phones and TVs, while some of the suites have stereo systems as well. The formal gardens in back of the house were designed by Thomas Church, and the walkways have been repaved with cobblestones from the Cable Car Restoration Project. There's also a replica of a Victorian greenhouse, brought from England, for hotel guests to enjoy. There are butlers to attend to the luggage and room service, and a first rate restaurant available to hotel guests only. And whatever room or suite you choose, you're bound to feel pampered by the sumptuous elegance of the house and the attention of the staff.

INSIDE SHERMAN HOUSE

THE HISTORY OF LEANDER SHERMAN

Leander S. Sherman arrived in San Francisco in 1861, a 14-year-old Bostonian kid with a lot of energy. Fairly rapidly he progressed from street-sweeper to clock repairman, but when Sherman was offered a job as a general clerk in A. A. Rosenberg's music store, he accepted immediately, because music was his great passion. By the time he was 23, Leander had saved enough to buy Rosenberg out. He let C. C. Clay become his partner, the music company became Sherman Clay & Company, and it's been operating under that title for over a hundred years. They sold the sheet music and instruments the growing San Francisco desired, and became the leading importer of Steinway pianos to the American West.

With his accumulating fortune he built the mansion on Green Street in 1876, and he and his family lived there till he died in 1926. He was very active in the world of music (he helped get the San Francisco Symphony going, and helped support the Opera, too), and for nearly three decades the world's great musicians performed in his grand recital hall. Lillian Russell came there, as did Enrico Caruso and Lotta Crabtree, among others. Ignace Jan Padarewski, the Polish pianist, was a good friend of Sherman's, and he played many a time on Leander's piano.

Now owned by Manouchehr Mobedshahi (an economist from Iran who fell in love with the Sherman House in 1981), the mansion continues Sherman's tradition of high standards and superb hospitality.

HUNTINGTON HOTEL, *1075 California* Street. *415-474-5400, 800-227-4683, fax 415-474-6227. Located between Mason and Taylor, it has 143 rooms. Doubles are $190-$240 (less $20 for singles), and the suites cost $290-$790.*

This is the least promoted but most lovely, refined, and elegant hotel on Nob Hill. Once inside the ivy-covered brick facade, the lobby sets the tone with its grandfather clock and crystal chandelier, soft lighting and oil paintings, and especially comfortable arm chairs, and it just gets better from there.

The rooms are stunningly elegant. The views are great, as are all Nob Hill vistas, but the furnishings and details surpass any others. The lighting is lovely, the furniture is distinguished *and* comfortable (a rare combo), and the design abounds in taste. There's a recessed bar, an unobtrusive TV and phone, and fine damasks. This is the real thing, quality that speaks for itself, the blue blood essence of Nob Hill San Francisco. The suites are all this and more. There are thick carpets, rare silks, and a fax-equipped antique desk. And in the enormous marble bathroom there's a separate shower stall as well as a marble bath, and a mini-TV. The bedroom has a grand four-poster bed, big mirrors, and the same swell view of the city.

THE HUNTINGTON HOTEL

This was once an apartment building (six permanent residents still live here), so all the rooms are a bit different, with their own style and personality, and regular guests all have their own favorites. The only drawback to this exclusive old hotel is that the walls aren't as soundproof as you find in newer, less tradition-soaked hotels.

The Big Four Restaurant is here, which provides exemplary room service to hotel guests. The traditional choice of old San Francisco money, the Huntington now attracts new money as well, or anyone who wants the Huntington's understated elegance and commitment to service.

HUNTINGTON HISTORY

In the late 1800s Nob Hill was the swankest address in town. The Railroad barons built their mansions there, as did the beneficiaries of the Comstock silver mines. And so did the Tobin family. Tobin, the founder of Hibernia Bank, built a large mansion in 1870 where the Huntington now stands. It didn't survive the earthquake and fire, however, and the building that stands there today was constructed in 1922 as residential apartments rented by the week and day. $2.5 million went into the making of it, and the result was an exclusive collection of apartments called "the last word in luxury" by the Daily Herald. In 1945, the building began its metamorphosis into the hotel it is today. Word spread, and the Huntington became a top choice for visiting royalty, dignitaries, and society's elite. Princess Grace stayed here, as did Claudette Colbert, the Vanderbilts, and the Rothschilds. Still known for its high standards and personal, discreet, gracious service, the Huntington still attracts today's royalty (Princess Micheal of Greece, Oscar de la Renta, Desmond Tutu, and Robin Williams) as well as Fortune 500 CEOs and others who pull the world's strings.

WESTIN ST. FRANCIS, *335 Powell Street. 415-397-7000, 800-228-3000, fax 415-774-0124. It has 1,200 rooms in new and old wings. Singles are $185-$275, doubles are $185-$305, and suites are $225-$550, though specials as low as $99 are sometimes offered.*

Directly on Union Square, as it has been since 1904, the historic building has been welcoming the world's finest for nearly a century. The Post Street entrance is the original one, its lobby is traditionally vast and marbled, and it has the Magneta Clock, which was a San Francisco rendezvous landmark for decades, but now just serves to decorate a portion of the lobby.

The main building (the original one) is beautiful, with airy high ceilings, wide hallways, and lovely chandeliers. The Standard rooms were originally built for accompanying servants, and they didn't do badly. Small but charming, they are quite nice, and they even have their own foyers. The Classics are larger and even nicer, and the Deluxe have all that plus they face the square.

The Tower is the new addition, and has one of those glassed-in elevators that show you the world as you ascend. It makes up for its lack of history with a wealth of modern amenities, and better soundproofing between rooms. The deluxe rooms are high up with great city and bay views. They have an attractive color scheme of burgundy and cream, plus a marble desk, a TV armoire, and all the amenities you could ask for like a hair dryer and iron. There are also business floors that cater to business needs.

HAVE TEA AT THE LOVELY COMPASS ROSE, WESTIN ST. FRANICS HOTEL

A very nice feature to this hotel is its attitude towards children. Not only do children under 19 stay free in their øparents' room, there's a Kids' Club as well. Children get age-specific gifts, and the welcome-pack includes a self-guided tour of the hotel and information on other activities and restaurants in the city that are specifically appealing to children.

The hotel also has all the paraphernalia (cribs, high chairs, potty seats, etc.) that traveling families might need. The staff is very friendly, and is happy to help with whatever arrangements you may need. The hotel also runs a number of dining and entertainment spots, such as the Compass Rose Room, above the lobby and magnificently decorated (serving lunch, High Tea, and dinner with evening dancing), and Club Oz, a nightclub.

MONEY LAUNDERING AT THE ST. FRANCIS

The St. Francis initiated coin-cleaning, the world's only legal money-laundering operation, in 1938, and no dirty dime has changed hands since. The custom was started for the ladies, and more specifically out of consideration for their white gloves which were being tainted by silver tarnish. And although the silver dollars which inspired the service are rarely seen at the hotel these days, quarters, dimes, nickels, and pennies still come in dirty and go out clean. They use lead shot and Boraxo soap, and as the machine rotates, the coins get cleaned and polished. Once clean, the coins are rinsed, separated from the shot, dried under 250-watt bulbs, counted, and repackaged. Along with the crisp fresh bills they stock to change greenback, the money going back to St. Francis guests is guaranteed clean and fresh. Known as "St. Francis money", the local shops can recognize who's staying at the St. Francis.

More than any other, Arnold Batliner was the main man of the coin washing operation. He was titled hotel coinwasher in 1962, and as such he reigned supreme for 31 years, finally retiring at the age of 88 April 26, 1993. During his tenure, he cleaned over 1,105,000 pounds of change worth an estimated $17 million. Arnold Batliner died November 18, 1995, at the age of 91, just a few months younger than the hotel itself. Not just anyone can fill Arnold's shoes, and while the search for the new coinwasher continues, the St. Francis marketing and accounting departments share the task and the honor.

HOTEL MONACO, *501 Geary Street. 415-292-0100, 800-214-4220, fax 415-292-0111. Located near Taylor, it has 201 rooms and 34 suites. The rooms cost $170-$210, and the suites are $235-$395. Seven rooms are equipped especially for the disabled. They're right in the theater district, and have the Grand Cafe next door.*

This lovely hotel just opened in Union Square in June 1995, and it's a masterpiece, a real gem. The faux-finish ochre and putty colors of the lobby evoke Monaco's sense of style, a Mediterranean presence, and a sense of humor as well. There's an enormous fireplace warming the lobby, and painted hot air balloons frolic on the ceiling. The potted plants and ferns are on a grand scale, as is the bronze filigree staircase (a 1910 original) that rises from the lobby. Off the lobby is the living room, and it's stunning with its fireplace, magnificent paintings, comfy sofas and chairs, pillars and plants. By day it's a lovely room for reading and hanging-out, and at night there's complimentary wine for hotel guests.

The rooms are especially appealing and delightful. The walls are pinstripe (charcoal and white or pistachio and yellow, depending on the room), the beds have a half-canopy, great pictures adorn the walls, and the enormous round mirror is both functional and stylish. The Canopy Queen is a little smaller but adorable, with lovely fabrics and a full canopy. It has more of a homey feel, is popular with single, female guests, and it costs the least, too. The double-paned windows cut the outside noise to nil, the phones all have data ports, and the state-of-the-art climate control lets you set the heat or air-conditioning as you like, and check on the weather outside to boot. The TV is gigantic, and it's equipped not just with cable and pay-per-view, but with Nintendo as well ($7.98 an hour).

ONE OF THE GORGEOUS ROOMS AT THE HOTEL MONACO

HOTEL MONACO HISTORY

Built in 1910 as the elegant Hotel Bellevue, it was getting a bit decrepit by the 1980s. A Japanese firm purchased it in 1988 and put $16 million into retrofitting before they bowed out in 1992, a consequence of a declining economic boom. Bill Kimpton (president of the Kimpton Group that owns 14 hotels in San Francisco alone) came along with his knack for being in the right place at the right time, sunk another $20 million in designers and soft goods, and the Hotel Monaco joined the San Francisco hotel scene.

All the usual luxury amenities are included, such as robes, hair dryer, bath phone, fridge, and mini-bar, but it's the extra touches of luxury and colorful fun that really make it. The moss plant is lovely, the marbled bath surfaces shine, and the fabrics and patterns are a delight. Then there is the luxury suite. It's a corner room very much like the others but with more toys like the VCR and CD player, a sitting area that is exquisite, and a stunning bathroom with a huge six-foot jacuzzi and separate shower.

Downstairs is a modern gym, a little massage room, and the spa with its saunas, stylish decor, and ten-person jacuzzi hot tub. Adjacent to the hotel, its restaurant the Grand Cafe is worth a visit for the artwork alone. It's not traditional San Francisco like the Nob Hill grande dames, but the Monaco gives its modern interpretation of the San Francisco tradition of luxury and comfort in great style. You can only be charmed by a stay here.

THE ARCHBISHOP'S MANSION, *1000 Fulton Avenue. 415-563-7872, 800-543-5820, fax 415-885-3193. Near Steiner on Alamo Square, this is an historic landmark, a restored 1904 home with 15 rooms. The rooms, each named after an opera, are $129-$189 and suites are $215-$385, depending on the floor, size, amenities, and time of week. Continental breakfast is included and is served in your room, and there's wine in the afternoon in the parlor.*

BATHE BY A COZY FIRE AT THE ARCHBISHOP'S MANSION!

Wow – it's amazing as soon as you enter the grand portals, and it just gets better from there. The Parlor is ever so elegant, in a cream-hued, peachy, French aristocratic way. The grand crystal chandelier sparkles, and long, heavy drapes swathe the windows.

Classical music swells in the background, glorious redwood pillars soar, and French antiques (such as were popular in the early 1900s) everywhere keep the magic alive. There is also an enormous mirror by the grand staircase, so expect to see your lovely morning visage as you begin your descent.

The Don Giovanni Suite is the top of the line, and it's exceptional. The ornately carved, canopied, four-poster bed stands on carved claw feet, and the bathroom is fully equipped with terry robes and the essential rubber ducky. And for your convenience, the shower stall and bath get separate rooms. The living room is decorated impressively too, though in a grand rather than a cozy fashion, with a massive fireplace and sensational views.

THE ARCHBISHOP CONNECTION

In 1904, the Great Cathedral of St. Mary's was completed, but the Archbishop Patrick Riordan didn't have a home. He chose Alamo Square, the fashionable address of the time, for his mansion. Fashions come and go, but bedrock is forever, and thanks to Alamo Square's granite foundations the buildings there didn't suffer the full brunt of the 1906 earthquake. The Archbishop opened his home, and it became a refugee center for the people camping out in Alamo Square. Archbishop Riordan died in 1909 (after playing a substantial role in helping San Francisco to build churches, schools, and hospitals - he had an enormous influence in the transformation from gold rush boom town to modern city) and the Mansion was occupied by succeeding Archbishops till 1945.

From 1945-1980 the house was neglected, but Jonathan Shannon and Jeffrey Ross bought the place and spent two years of intense restoration before opening its doors to the public. And now the Archbishop's Mansion is a luxury hotel that's also a designated historic landmark.

The Carmen is a suite like no other. The bedroom is beautiful, with white lacy spread, fireplace, and feather-stuffed sofa. The attached room, nearly as large, is more like an unusual parlor than a bathroom. At its center is an elegant, claw-footed tub, with a more modest glassed-in shower off to the side, and the commode is discreetly hidden behind an ornate silk screen. The room is popular with honeymooners and anniversary celebrants; the staff will happily set up a silver ice bucket with champagne to perch next to the sumptuous tub. At the opposite end of the price spectrum is La Bohème, a smaller, quainter, and cozier room, with French antiques and a large, luxurious bath (but no robes).

All the rooms come with private phones, TVs are available on request, the staff people are genuinely friendly and very helpful, and unlike many of the other grand renovated Victorian mansion hotels, the Archbishop actually has a working elevator.

HOTEL REX, *562 Sutter Street. 415-433-4434, 800-433-4434, fax 415-433-3695. Located between Powell and Mason, it has 96 rooms. Singles and doubles go from $115-$155, and suites are $225, with 10% off for seniors. There's morning coffee and newspapers in the lobby Monday-Friday, and guests can use Sheehan's pool and gym nearby for $4. Fax and secretarial services are available as well.*

Its standards remain, but everything else has just undergone a major overhaul, and for the better (though it was pretty nice before). What was the Orchard for 10 years is now the Rex, an artistic and sophisticated boutique hotel in Union Square. With club-like 1920s interiors and salon portraits, restored period furnishings and artistic touches, the hotel is dedicated to the artistic and literary traditions of San Francisco.

The lobby is attractive, appealing, and opulent. Quiet jazz tunes play on the sound system, and it's a place that makes you want to sit down and relax. The new carpet is a beautiful burnt orange with richly colored floral trim, and there's a gas fireplace, a bar serving complimentary wine and appetizers at 5pm nightly (or you can get a more sophisticated cocktail if you wish) and there are small cocktail tables at which to enjoy them. In addition, there are fine writing desks, quality leather chairs and sofas, and a bookshelf full of good books.

The renovated rooms are reminiscent of Bloomsbury in the 20s and 30s, with stripes and patterns, wide-check fabrics, dark woods, period furnishings and glazed yellow walls. The hand-painted lamp shades are fantastic and retro, but the comforts are all modern, including cable TV with remote, direct-dial phone (with data ports), and fully stocked mini-bar. The bathrooms are painted in muted pastels, have hair dryers, and unusually fun shower curtains, while the lofty ceilings reflect the hotel's 1904 origins.

The suites are even nicer, with a beautiful parlor, one and a half baths, and the essential bidet. Heat is individually controlled, and there are all the other extras like same day laundry and valet, concierge services, parking, and non-smoking floors. The Rex also has a useful, well-designed stack of destination cards, made of cheerfully colored construction paper, opening out into mini-guides to jazz, wine, chocolate, experimental theater, books, and beer. All in all, an old favorite has become a very cool new place.

HOTEL BOHÈME,*444 Columbus Avenue. 415-433-9111, fax 415-362-6292, email: HotelBoheme@MCIMail.com. Located near Vallejo, it has 15 rooms, all with private bath. Singles and doubles are $105-$120, depending on the room.*

This remodeled Victorian in North Beach used to be the Millefiori Inn, but with the change of name and ownership have come many other wonderful changes. The rooms are delightful, if a little small. Though it nods to the 90s (the rooms all have cable TV, remote control, and phones with data ports), the tone is one of another time, when Ginsberg and Kaufman, Ferlinghetti and Clifford, and Bowler and Kerouac were Beats supreme. The rooms have all the modern amenities, but the burnt orange paint, bistro tables, Matisse and Picasso paintings and Chinese parasol light shades infuse the rooms with bohemian charm.

This is not a Nob Hill luxury hotel, but the North Beach locale and retro look may be more appealing for folks who want to be in the thick of where things are happening. And while the inside rooms are quieter, the outside rooms (where Ginsberg stays when he visits) overlook more colorful street scenes.

There's not a lobby as such, but there is a welcoming desk in the evenings with a decanter of cream sherry and a tray of sherry glasses for you to help yourself to a nightcap, and a couple of stools to perch on. There's also a basket of menus from local restaurants to help you make your decisions. And it's right across from Caffe Greco for breakfast in the morning or dessert at night.

The hotel is not just situated in North Beach, it's awash with the aura of North Beach forty years ago, with lamp shades of sheet music collages, Ginsberg poetry, and newspapers from the 50s. In its brochure (a work of art by itself), Eileen Kaufman says, "Life was full of dancing, singing, poetry, parties, people, painting, music, sunshine, moonlight, rooftops, laughter, and love...These were times of plenty." This is the time the hotel lovingly honors. It's real triumph, however, is that it manages to cast its funky bebop bohemian flavor in such an updated, elegant fashion. In short, it's a truly delightful place to stay. And the new management is most attentive to all the nuances of comfort.

ALAMO SQUARE INN, *719 Scott Street. 415-922-2055, 800-345-9888, fax 415-931-1304. Located near Fulton, it has 12 rooms, no smoking and all with private bath, in two attached, restored 1890s Victorian mansions. Rooms are $85-$135, depending on the size and amenities of the room, while suites run $125-$275. A full American breakfast is included, as is free parking, but there is no elevator. All rooms have phones, but only the suites have TVs.*

The Alamo Square Inn is right on Alamo Square park, and it's composed of two differently styled but equally beautiful mansions, one a grand 1895 Queen Anne and the other a cozier 1896 Tudor Revival. They're connected by later additions such as the glorious solarium, and all facilities are easily accessible no matter in which room you stay. The solarium is lovely, full of flagstones, healthy, thriving plants, and the occasional smoker (as this is the only room where that activity is allowed), and it connects the Queen Anne to the second building. There's a beautiful garden in back, and classical music plays throughout.

The Queen Anne has been restored and furnished to reflect the splendor of its day, with the Parlor Room and Drawing Room (where afternoon wine is served) set up on its gorgeous wood floor in Victorian elegance, and decorated in sumptuous reds and peacock designs. The rooms are exceedingly lovely, bright, and beautiful with lots of authentic period details like wainscoting on the walls, and those terrific reading lamps with the dangling silk fringe. The suite is also beautiful, but far more contemporary and open. Its bath has a sunken jacuzzi, and the art deco living room has a TV and stereo, while other suites have kitchenettes or small sun decks, too.

Walk in the Tudor and the feeling is very different. The redwood paneling and lower ceilings provide a sense of warmth and family, while the built-in window seats make you want to trash your sight-seeing plans and hunker down for the day. There's even a corner game table set in a bay window alcove that's as good for playing Monopoly as for planning out the day's route. Oriental carpets are everywhere, and there's an enormous fireplace.

The rooms are pretty. The color scheme changes from room to room (there's the Green Room, the Brown Room, and so on), but all are decorated with satin spreads and curtains, double paned windows to keep out the street noise, and oriental carpets are standard throughout. The bathrooms are charming as well, and though most come with a shower stall instead of a bath, you can request a room with a bath.

It's hard to go wrong in the Alamo Square Inn if you like pampering the old way, with lots of Victorian charm. However, you need to let go of some of your modern ways. There are TVs only in the suites, and authentic to a fault – there's no elevator. Also, while the square across the street is very green and pretty during the day, and Postcard Row is just down the block, this isn't a neighborhood to stroll around at night.

THE AMSTERDAM, *749 Taylor Street. 415-673-3277, 800-637-3444, fax 415-673-0453. Located near Sutter, it is a small place with 34 rooms, all with private bath. Singles are $69-$79, doubles are $79-$89, deluxe rooms with jacuzzi are $89-$129, and continental breakfast is included.*

Built in 1909, the Amsterdam has a European air to it, with warmth, French Victorian antiques, and personal attention. It's on the slope from

Nob Hill down to Union Square, so the location couldn't be much better (unless you have a thing against slopes). Once inside, the lobby makes you feel part of a lovely, well-kept French aristocrat's home. There's a small library just inside the entrance with an interesting collection of old books, and you're free to borrow and read what you will during your visit. The sitting area has beautiful antique lamps, elegant sofas, and a refurbished antique radio.

A typical room comes with a four-poster bed, an arm chair and a table - all authentic antiques and all made of the same dark, dark Georgian wood. While full of antiques, the rooms are all fully, modernly equipped, with a cable TV, remote, direct-dial phone, and AM/FM radio. There are plants scattered about (some real and some fake), lamps are polished brass, and the windows are double-paned against the Taylor traffic for peace and quiet. The bathrooms have just been remodeled, and are now equipped with hair dryer and trimmed with marble, and the rooms downstairs have jacuzzi tubs, which makes for a nice way to end a day full of hiking and sightseeing. Some of the rooms have their own private decks, too.

There's a fax on the premises for guest use, and the downstairs breakfast room is simple and homey and equipped with a microwave and coffee maker. Outside there's a terrace, open all day, and a perfect spot for a quiet, sunny place to read or talk. With its combined charm, comfort, location, and price, this is one of the best deals in the city.

COMMODORE, *825 Sutter Street. 415-923-6800, 800-338-6848, fax 415-923-6804. Located near Leavenworth, this is one very hip hotel. There are six floors with 113 rooms that cost $69-$99 and suites for $109, with group and senior discounts available. The Titanic Cafe serves breakfasts and lunches in art deco diner splendor, and the Red Room is the city's newest bar.*

In an art deco class of its own, the lobby of this Union Square hotel has a very distinctive flavor of artsy San Francisco. The wavy painted map of the city looms behind the green leather couch, faced by very tall-backed mustard yellow velvet chairs. The whole lobby has an animation festival look, as though the lamps and tables want to jump up and do a little dance with the dish and the spoon. And near the front desk is the brightly painted Wheel of Fortune with nine different unique sites. The way it works is each day there'll be a San Francisco trivia question posted, and the first guest to answer the question accurately will get to spin the big wheel and win the prize represented by the site where it lands.

The rooms vary. Those on the 5th and 6th floors are classified Deluxe, and they're in keeping with the lobby style. The design is sophisticated and whimsical, and the accommodations are comfortable, and come with cable TV, phone with data port, and walk-in closet. The bathrooms are simple and functional. The standard rooms on the other floors, while perfectly adequate, have standard decor, are cheaper, and lack the panache. There is also a two-room suite (standard) with one large room (with bed and sitting area) and a small, child's alcove.

The major renovation that's just been completed transformed the wood-paneled elevator into an entertaining and colorful conveyance, and local artists have been commissioned to decorate each room with different paintings, photos, and caricatures of 113 different and little-known San Francisco gems (like the Exploratorium, the Castro Theater, and City Lights Books), with accompanying history, providing the rooms with their names and decor. Other services include a San Francisco Resource Library, and an "Insider's Daily Tip Sheet," put out daily with all the offbeat happenings that day.

The Commodore is geared to the urban adventurer who wants to see San Francisco through the eyes of the locals, and it has customized a number of guides that show the City that exists beyond Fisherman's Wharf. The Commodore has come a long way from its 1920s origins, when it provided $3 rooms to seamen; the new incarnation of this old hotel is fun, savvy, and dedicated to its guests.

In addition, the Commodore has just unveiled the Red Room Bar, a very artsy, very cool, very red place for a drink. Done in a funky New York style, the bar's red leather stools and crushed red velvet couch are bathed in a dim red glow. It's popular with San Francisco's art element, the 30ish crowd of designers, architects, et al who can afford the $5-$6 drinks, as well as with the hotel's guests.

11. GETTING AROUND TOWN

BY BUS

The **San Francisco Municipal Railway**, *415-673-6864*, better known as **Muni**, operates buses throughout the city. Their orange-and-white striped paint jobs with the MUNI logo (though a few are mostly covered with ads for milk or Phantom of the Opera), identify them, and they're all clearly marked with their route number and destination. Some are diesel powered, and others run on electricity (you'll see these buses connected by flexible poles that ride along the power lines up above), but regardless of power source, they behave the same; they stop at marked bus stops (some have bus shelters, some are merely marked by yellow paint on a pole or the street), and you pay your fare when you get on.

Most lines operate 6am-midnight, and a few lines operate an owl service from midnight-6am, too. The bus fare is $1 for any ride, and if you ask you'll get a transfer good for two more rides, within the allotted time as shown at the bottom of the transfer. To use the transfer, present it to the bus driver. For the first use, they'll tear off the top, and for the second time they'll keep the remaining part.

There are also **Muni passes** good for lots of Muni riding; you can buy them at Safeway and a variety of small corner groceries. The following passes are good for unlimited cable car, Muni bus, and metro riding: there's a one-day pass for $6, a three-day pass for $10, a seven-day pass for $15, and a month pass for $35. There's also a one-week pass that's different. It goes from Sunday-Saturday (unlike the seven-day pass that starts whenever you buy it), and it costs just $9, but when you ride the cable car you need to pay $1. There are also Muni tokens that cost $8 for a roll of ten.

There are very good **Muni Maps** available at most stores for $2, and they're worth having if you're going to stay a while. Not only do they show all the bus routes in the city, they describe the route of each line, and tell its hours of operation. Otherwise, most bus shelters have the maps under glass, and San Francisco people are usually glad to help out. And there's one more option, too. You can call the Muni **Information Line**, *415-673-6864*, daily from 9am-5pm, for bus and streetcar information of any sort, but expect to be on hold a long time.

MUNI MALAISE

San Francisco resident bus riders are disgruntled, and for good reasons (service is slower, graffiti and vandalism are up, as is violence on some lines, and buses are more crowded), however, compared to many another urban system, Muni works pretty well. It's fairly easy to get to where you want to go, the Muni maps are easy to follow, and the fares are reasonable. While the system could and should be better (and the city's administration is looking for solutions), the buses are adequate for most purposes. Policemen are now required to ride the lines at least once a day, and they're working on the rest of it.

BY METRO

The **Muni Metro** streetcars are part of the same **Municipal Railway** system as the buses. They run on tracks (sometimes underground and sometimes on street level), and the fares work exactly the same as on the buses. In fact, when the Metro streetcars stop running at 10pm, the lines resume on buses on equivalent street routes till 12:30am.

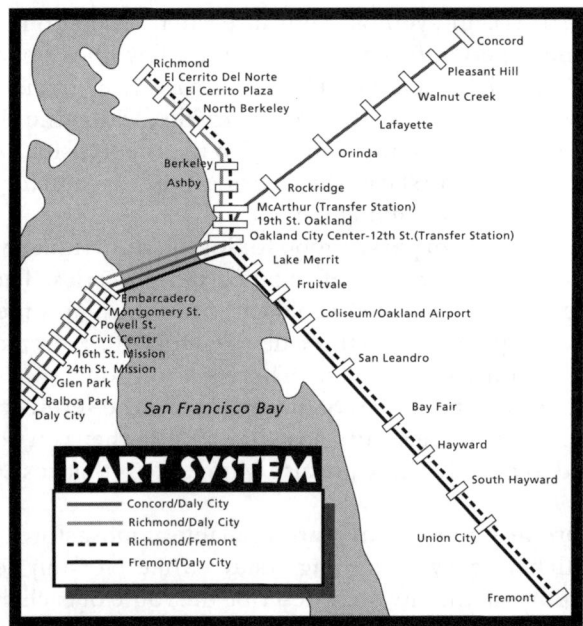

There are five Metro underground stations on Market (at Embarcadero, Montgomery, Powell, Civic Center, and Church), combined with the **BART** stations. You go down the same stairs as you would for BART by the blue BART signs marking the entrances, but the Muni Metro trains have separate turnstiles.

BY CABLE CAR

Cable cars run 6:30am-12:30am, and they're the best-known and most popular form of transportation in the city. To ride a cable car, you need $2 (the conductor can usually break a larger bill), and a lot of patience. There are three cable car lines to choose from. One goes from Powell at Market along Mason to Bay at Taylor, and these are marked saying Taylor or Mason. Another starts from the same place on Powell but goes along Hyde to Beach, and these are marked Hyde.

While both the Mason and the Hyde lines end up somewhat near Fisherman's Wharf (the Taylor depot is much closer), the California line doesn't come close - instead it goes from the foot of California west to California and Polk. So, if you just want the fun of a cable car ride, take the California line, because it's always less crowded. However, if it's Fisherman's Wharf or the trip back you're after, you may have to wait a long time.

You can queue up where the lines start, and watch the show when the cable car is manually turned, or you can wait anywhere along the route where a cable car sign indicates it'll stop. Be warned, however, that if the car is full, it won't stop. The very early and late cable cars usually have lots of room, however, and the morning or evening fog adds a pleasant San Francisco piquancy to the ride.

BY TAXI

Taxis are a good alternative. Because the city just isn't all that large, a cross-town cab rarely costs more than $10 (the fare starts at $1.70, and increases by 20 cent increments). The drivers generally know the city and are fairly good (though bad eggs exist in every city). You can hail a cab without much difficulty along Market Street or around Union Square and the major hotels, or call one to pick you up.

The main city companies are:
• **Yellow Cab**, *415-626-2345*
• **Veteran's**, *415-552-1300*
• **De Soto**, *415-673-1414*

You can also try **Luxor**, *415-282-4141*, **National**, *415-648-4444*, or **City**, *415-468-7200*.

BY CAR

Cars are certainly handy from time to time in the city, but more often they're a burden and a nuisance. Parking is usually a major hassle, and the hills can be daunting if you're not used to driving on them. The best rule of thumb is to try San Francisco without a car, first, and then rent one as you feel the need (a full list of rental companies are in the back of the Practical Information chapter). Then, if you do decide to rent a car, try the 800 number if there is one, because the national rate is often a bit cheaper than the local one.

BY FOOT

This is the best way to appreciate San Francisco, at least as long as it's enjoyable and you're not in great pain. There are side streets and alleys, there's browsing and exploring, and there are great views atop each hill.

The best plan is to choose a neighborhood or sight, get there by whatever means seems most convenient, and then stroll. There are also a number of good and free walking tours sponsored by the Friends of the Library, listed in Chapter 19, *Day Trips & Excursions*, in the GuidedTours section. But if you're not used to lots of hilly walking, make sure you wear good shoes that are not brand new, take band-aides, and remember to do some calf muscle stretches *after* you've done some major walking.

BY BICYCLE

It's a lot of fun to ride a bike around San Francisco, so long as you map a route along the relatively flat parts. There are a number of bike rental shops near Fisherman's Wharf, and the coastal routes from there are the prettiest and least hilly. Riding through Golden Gate Park is beautiful, and the Marina Green has some bike paths, too.

However, this is a city without nearly enough bike lanes, and street riding is a dangerous occupation. Plenty of people ride daily and are fine, but some do get hurt. So, ride defensively and have a little healthy fear of traffic when you're not in a protected path or lane.

12. WHERE TO STAY

San Francisco offers a tremendous variety of places to stay, many of which are terrific. I've included more than 175 hotels and inns to give you the biggest choice available when you're planning your visit here. I've also warned you about some of the clunkers that you're better off avoiding.

The hotels listed here take all major credit cards unless otherwise noted. The hotels are sorted by alphabetically-listed neighborhoods, and they're arranged from most to least expensive within each neighborhood section.

CASTRO & UPPER MARKET

ANNA'S THREE BEARS, *114 Divisidero Street. 415-255-3167, 800-428-8559, fax 415-552-2959. Located near Duboce, there are three suites (otherwise known as Baby Bear, Mama Bear, and Pap a Bear, ascending with the floor levels) which cost $225, $275, and $295, respectively. The rates assume double occupancy (add $25 per additional person), and there are weekly rates as well, ranging from $1,250-$1,650.*

This is a lovely old Edwardian building on a quiet, residential street, with leaded glass windows and a wrought iron gate. Inside, the suites are just as lovely. These suites are actually flats that run the floor's length, completely furnished with every conceivable comfort and accessory. They are all no-smoking, two of which have two bedrooms, while the top penthouse has three. In addition to the bedrooms (done up with canopied beds, lace curtains, antique furniture, and lots of charm), each flat has a full kitchen, dining and living rooms, working fireplaces, decks, and sensational views of the city.

There are cable TVs, of course, plus private phones, and fax machines are available if you need one. All the rooms are decorated beautifully and stylishly, to provide you with a comfortable, private place to stay in San Francisco, with all the informational services you may want, but none of the hotel clutter and bother.

THE VILLA, *379 Collingwood. 415-282-1367, 800-358-0123, fax 415-821-3995. The Villa is up in the Castro hills above (and parallel to) Castro, on the corner of 21st. It has 12 rooms and suites (not all right here) which rent for $95 (for the rooms with shared bath), $130 for most of the suites, while the larger suites with kitchen all go for $150-$200 (with discounts for long-term stays), continental breakfast included.*

The Villa is an apt name as the place features many levels with an outdoor heated kidney-shaped pool, deck, and barbecue grills. The real thrills, however, come from the luxurious comfort and modern deco style, plus the magnificent panoramic city views you get on the decks and from some of the suites as well. The front garden is beautifully landscaped, the deck is gorgeous and full of flowers, and the shared kitchen and living room are just lovely. Rooms come with TV and VCR, phone and answering machine, some have a private entrance or stereo, and all are superbly, artfully decorated, and the staff is especially attentive to your comfort. They also rent a couple of apartments nearby of the same quality and standards, but with two bedrooms, a kitchen, and in one of them, a jacuzzi as well.

INN ON CASTRO, *321 Castro. 415-861-0321. Near 17th on the north side of Market, there are eight rooms (most of which have baths) which range from $80-$150, but most are $120. On the low end you get a tiny room with shared bath, while $150 gets you a suite with sun deck and sitting area, but full breakfast is included for all.*

These rooms on the other side of Market are homey and comfortable, they all have phones, and if they don't have a TV, you can get one just by asking. There's a nice small deck in back with a view of the city, and though the kitchen is not for general use, the common sitting area is comfortable and lovely at the same time, with an abundance of fine art and healthy greenery. From outside, you wouldn't know this was an inn; it just looks like a brightly painted, lovely old Edwardian with purple and blue trim, but if you look closer you'll see the name is on the door and you're at the right place.

It's a fine piece of history, dating back to somewhere between 1898-1902 (the stories vary, but they know it's from before the quake) and it's been lovingly restored by the interior decorator owner. It's especially popular with the professional middle-to-older gay market, though that's by no means all who come to stay. It's a good choice if you want to be near the Castro but not smack in the middle of it.

WILLOWS INN, *710 14th Street. 415-431-4770, fax 415-431-5295. Near Market, there are 11 rooms, all with shared baths. Singles are $70-$88, doubles are $78-$96, the two-bedroom suite is $105 for two people, plus $10 for each additional guest, and a large, lovely, extended continental breakfast served in your room is included.*

The rooms here in this 1904 Edwardian hotel are quite pretty, with hand-crafted willow furnishings, plantation shutters, and country antique extras. All rooms come with phone, clock radio, and sink, and great kimono bathrobes are provided to ease the shared-bath trip, and some have a fridge as well. They give a lot of service and comfort for their reasonable rates, providing good quality soaps and towels, the morning paper with breakfast, cheese in the evening, and sherry with chocolate at night.

There's a lovely common room with big-backed willow seats, lots of fine artwork, trees and plants flourish everywhere, and there's a shared kitchen area with microwave and fridge, too. The toilets and showers are all immaculate and as charming as shared facilities get, and there's parking available at $8 a day. The folks who run the Willows are very nice and friendly, and while the inn caters to the gay community, all are welcome.

BLACK STALLION, *635 Castro. 415-863-0131, fax 415-863-0165, but call first to arrange a fax. Located between 19th and 20th Sreets, this is a three-story Victorian with 8 rooms (all shared bath). Singles are $80-$95, doubles are $95-$110, and include a large continental breakfast.*

Right in the thick of the Castro, the rooms are simple and all in black; the paint is black, the sheets are black, and when possible the furniture is black, too. Most rooms have working fireplaces, and nice Victorian decor. There's a common lounge, and a lovely redwood deck and backyard garden. It's a friendly place, with attentive staff who occasionally do extras like summer barbecues. They are geared toward the gay male population, especially those into leather and Levi's, though anyone is welcome. Be forewarned, however, that clothing in the house may be considered optional.

DOLORES PARK, *3641 17th Street. 415-861-9335, 415-621-0482. Located between Church and Dolores, the Dolores Park includes 5 rooms with shared bath. Singles go for $60-$85, doubles are $90-$95, there's a suite with a bedroom, a kitchen, sitting room, marble bathroom, and big sun deck for $155-$165, plus a carriage house which can hold up to four people with kitchen, fireplace, and jacuzzi for $275 (this is where Tom Cruise stayed). An extended continental breakfast (pretty much everything but meat) is included for all, as well as afternoon coffee, tea, or wine. They are a non-smoking establishment, have a two-night minimum, and welcome children 12 and older.*

This 1874 Edwardian, very different in tone from the Stallion, is a preserved treasure, and inside it is just beautiful. There are murals on the walls, all the rooms are decorated with antiques, with floor to ceiling velvet drapes in some rooms and golden damask drapes in the dining room. The rooms all have cable TV, clock radio, and phone, and lovely antiques (one room sports an enormous headboard, while another has a four-poster bed instead). Breakfasts are served on the sunny patio, weather permitting, and in the elegant dining room on inclement days. They take their history and elegance seriously, and while they're sometimes a little disorganized, their site has a distinctive vintage San Francisco flavor that is very special.

TWENTY FOUR HENRY, *24 Henry Street. 415- 864-5686, 800-900-5686, fax 415-864-5686, and email: WalteRian@aol.com. Located between Sanchez and Noe (north of Market) and offering 5 units in an old Victorian (circa 1880s), one of which has a private bathroom, while the rest do not, plus apartment suites nearby. Single room rates range from $55-$80, doubles are $75-$90, suite apartments are $95 (for single or double occupancy), and an extensive continental breakfast buffet from 8-11am is included for all.*

Set on a pretty, quiet, tree-lined street that's right near but not in the middle of all the action, a rainbow flag marks the house, but there's no B&B sign in sight. This is one lovely, well-maintained place (happily unscathed by the earthquake and fire of 1906), and the beautiful, homey parlor with its crystal chandelier and velvet sofas is just the start. Classical music plays softly on the stereo, and plants, flowers, books, magazines, and Tiffany-style lamps abound.

All the rooms have their own phone line with data port and answering machine, from the cute little single room with its view of Henry Street to the master bedroom with its private bath and windows overlooking the garden patio, and all are nicely decorated and comfortable. The shared bathrooms are also pleasant, even if they are down the hall. The suites are swell, too, though they're a few blocks away. They all have private phones and answering machines, parlor areas separate from the bedroom, refrigerators, and large cable TVs, and one has a fully equipped kitchen plus a VCR as well. Super nice people (Rian and Walter) own and run this guest house, maintaining a sense of beauty, style, homey comfort, and personal warmth.

It's no surprise this place is especially popular (though not exclusively so) with the gay and lesbian community, and that scores of locals choose them to put up their visiting parents or other out-of-town guests. They are equally well adapted to vacationers and business guests, and extend their genuine hospitality to all.

PENSIONE SAN FRANCISCO, *1668 Market. 415-864-1271, fax 415-861-8116. Located between Van Ness and Haight, there are 36 rooms. Singles are $42-$45, doubles are $52-$55, and there are 16 hall baths.*

Equidistant from the Castro and Civic Center, there is no central lobby, though each floor has its own little sitting area with comfy chairs, fireplace, and stuffed deer head. An old, restored cage lift takes you up in style, but the rooms themselves are quite simple. There's a good bed, a good dresser and closet, a phone, a picture, and not much else. Built sometime shortly after the 1906 earthquake, the Pensione has a few country rustic touches here and there, but it doesn't go all out in the decor department. The end result is a centrally located budget deal somewhere between cute and plain.

CHINATOWN

GRANT PLAZA, *465 Grant Avenue. 415-434-3883, 800-472-6899, fax 415-434-3866. Located on the corner at Pine, there are 72 rooms for $39-$55 a single and $47-$63 a double. It's just inside Chinatown near Union Square and the Chinatown public library branch.*

The staff speaks fluent Chinese and so-so English, and will win no friendliness awards. The rooms won't be earning any rave reviews, either. They're adequate but boring, with private bath, TV, phone, and lots of street noise. Don't bother.

YMCA CHINATOWN, *855 Sacramento. 415-982-4412. Located near Stockton, this YMCA is for men only, and none of the rooms has private bathrooms. Singles are $29-$31 (depending on size), doubles are $37.40, and if you pay for six nights you get the seventh night free. There's full access to gym and pool, but no breakfast, continental or otherwise.*

The staff here is quite friendly, but the place is quite unpleasant. Up the dirty metal stairs to the hallways, plywood covers the doors, aiding security but adding to the depressing tone. The dismal rooms have a bit of old, worn furniture (narrow bed, desk, cabinet), grimy carpeting, and little outside light, and the small single is not for the claustrophobic. The only saving grace here is the gym access, but it may not be worth it. If you want to be able to use a gym, check out the YMCA on Golden Gate, where the rooms are much nicer.

CIVIC CENTER

INN AT THE OPERA, *333 Fulton. 415-863-8400, 800-325-2708, fax 415-861-0821. Located near Franklin, the Inn has 48 rooms. Singles are $125-$175, and doubles are $140-$185 (depending on the type of room), and suites cost $200-$260, continental breakfast included.*

Awash in fine silks, classical music, and good manners, you walk off the noisy, windy street into a piece of heaven. All the rooms here come with minibar, microwave, small cable TV, terry robes, and phone, and they're all decked out in French country ambiance, too. The Standard is a tiny lunch box of a room, and the Moderate is cute and cozy, but not large, while the Jr. Suite is lovely and pretty and quaint and all good things. French doors separate the bedroom from the sitting room (which has a couch that folds out into a bed). But whichever room you stay in, the wainscoted halls and pale pastels, pretty lobby and lovely flowers will enhance your stay, and the staff are just as gracious and helpful as can be.

Built originally for the ballet and opera to house their singers and dancers, lots of ballet principals and symphony conductors still pass through. They can also provide secretarial services, as well as obtain tickets to performances of the opera, symphony, and ballet.

CATHEDRAL HILL HOTEL, *1101 Van Ness Avenue. 415-776-8200, 800-622-0855, fax 415-441-2841. The hotel is located near Geary and is just across the street from the Richelieu. They have 400 rooms and 12 suites, costing $109-$129 a single, $129-$149 a double, and $250-$450 a suite, depending on how booked they are when you make your reservations. They also have discount rates for AAA, groups, frequent travelers, seniors, government and military, and almost any other justifiable reason you can concoct.*

They are very big on architecture, but not so big on service, and are as different from the Inn at the Opera as they could be. They cater to conferences and tour groups; they certainly don't cater to the individual traveler, and you'd be lucky to find a bellhop to help with your luggage or a staff member available to show you a room, and the staff you can find seem poorly trained. The rooms are large, and decorated in hotel bland. They do have safe parking, and offer access to a nearby health club ($10 a day), but you can find these amenities at plenty of other, nicer hotels, and you'd be much better off.

RICHELIEU, *1050 Van Ness Avnue. 415-673-4711, 800-295-7424, fax 415-673-9362. Located near Geary, there are 151 rooms, costing $99-$159, depending on whether you get the deluxe, the jr. king suite, or the full king suite, but there are plenty of discounts (AAA, for one) available.*

Built in 1908, they retain the grand ceilings, stained glass, and crystal chandeliers in the lobby. The elevator, however, could drive you nuts with its many-faceted mirror paneling that fractures your reflection like a fun house horror. The rooms are pretty big, especially the suites, and the furnishings are the standard hotel floral with a few Victorian touches, while the views are all of ugly Van Ness Avenue. All the rooms have cable TV, safe, coffee maker, and hair dryer, and the hotel provides a morning limousine, an executive gym, and an afternoon tea and cookies hospitality hour. They think very highly of themselves here, but while they're a cut above Cathedral Hill, they aren't really all that special, mirrors and crystal notwithstanding.

ALBION HOUSE, *135 Gough. 415-621-0896, fax 415-621-3811. Located near Oak, there are 9 rooms that go for $85-$135, depending on size of room and amenities. They provide a full, gourmet breakfast, as well as complimentary afternoon brandy.*

The living room in this 1906 relic is great. It's got a big, central fireplace, a grand piano, and lots of comfy sofas. Beautiful music issues from the speakers, and there are flowers everywhere. What more could you want? The rooms are lovely too, though small, and they're comfortably, pleasantly furnished. Though it's not what you'd call fancy, the Albion gives you charm without luxury.

ABIGAIL, *246 McAllister. 415-861-9728, 800-243-6510, fax 415-861-5848. Located near Larkin, it has six floors with 60 rooms and one suite (all with bath) and is run by the same folks who own the Phoenix. Rooms run $69-$84, the suite is $129, and weekly rates start at $375.*

The Abigal was built in 1925 as the Glenburn Hotel to accommodate the celebrities performing at the Fox Theater, and it's still popular with singers, dancers, and musicians who perform at the nearby opera, symphony, and ballet. The original cage lift is nicely renovated, and the rooms are smallish but artistically Victorian, with interesting fabric designs, antique furniture, big closets, down comforters, phone, and modern TV with remote. The deluxe rooms have more design touches than the regular rooms, but they're all extremely pleasant, and the hotel carries an artistic cachet. In addition, there's parking for $7.50 a day, and access to a nearby health club as well.

DAYS INN, *465 Grove. 415-864-4040. Located near the Civic Center, it has 40 rooms which cost $55-$60 a single, and doubles are $60-$65.*

The rooms are stale and boring, though they're adequate if you don't care about style or San Francisco flavor. They have TV, microwave, and coffee makers, and they're clean. The staff verges on rude, and the neighborhood is a bit questionable. Any way you look at it, this isn't your best bet.

DOWNTOWN - FINANCIAL, MARKET, & SOUTH OF MARKET DISTRICTS

MANDARIN ORIENTAL, *222 Sansome Street. 415-885-0999, 800-622-0404, fax 415-433-0289. It has 154 rooms and four suites. Singles and doubles are $285-$330 (depending on the size of the bed) and suites are $405-$1,400.*

Right in the thick of the financial district, the Mandarin is geared towards business, but the lobby, with its inlaid marble and cut crystal, is suitable for business and pleasure. Soft jazz plays in the background, and a regal, carpeted staircase climbs up to Silks, their fine Pacific Rim restaurant. The building host many business floors, but the hotel occupies just the ground floor and floors 38-48. The Mandarin emphasizes service and those extra touches. The glassed-in sky bridge connects the hotel's two towers, and supplies stunning Bay Bridge views as well.

The attractive rooms all have doorbells, as well as magnificent views (the lowest rooms are 38 floors up), individually controlled heating and air conditioning, minibar, fridge, two phones (and a third in the bathroom) and high quality materials. The bathrooms are loaded with Italian marble, as well as two robes (terry and cotton), clock, and slippers. The decor is tasteful, with oriental touches and green potted plants, and the amenities have been upgraded to include voice mail, big TVs, fine linens, hair dryers, and your choice of terry or thin cotton robes. The bedrooms are large, and the Mandarin king corner room gives you a smashing view from the marble tub. They have a business center open 7am-7pm with PC work stations, fax and photocopying facilities and secretarial services, a new fitness center, and Silks, their award-winning Asian restaurant.

SHERATON PALACE, *2 New Montgomery Street. 415-92-8600, 800-325-3535, fax 415-543-0671. Located off Market Street, it has 550 rooms. Rooms cost $285-$355 depending on room size, location, and decor, with specials discounted as low as $139.*

The hotel prides itself on its grandeur and history, but the stained glass dome and ornate chandeliers fit awkwardly in the busy Market Street setting. Built in 1875 as a uniquely grand luxury hotel, and rebuilt in 1909 after the earthquake fire, the hotel does a good job of retaining a feel for how the swells did it up in days gone by. The spacious, scented rooms feature dark wood and period pieces, but they look more authentic than appealing. The stately feeling is there, but the Palace caters now to the business visitors, and the Conference Center is more popular than the historic ballroom. They have added nice features like a big indoor lap pool and health club, but the staff ranges from brusque to rude, and the service doesn't match the rates. If you're looking for proximity to Moscone Center, but with a touch of old, elegant San Francisco, this is your hotel. But if you want comfort, charm, and personal attention, look elsewhere.

HYATT REGENCY, *5 Embarcadero Center. 415-788-1234, 800-233-1234, fax 415-398-2567. It has 805 rooms. Weekday rates are $205-$255 and weekend rates are $159-$205, depending on availability. They also have special romance and epicurean packages from time to time. They have a small fitness room, but also sell day passes ($8 for Club One and $12 for YMCA) to fuller facility gyms.*

This Hyatt is enormous. It soars and sprawls. The reception desk is nowhere near the ground level entrance, but if you can follow the signs up the escalators you'll get there eventually in the largest atrium lobby in the world (it's even in the Guinness Book of World Records). The glass elevator capsules skitter up and down building sides like water bugs. The intricate tiered architecture creates a vast and busy feel while you wait on line for the next not-so-friendly attendant to check you in. The rooms all are identical, and all come equipped with hair dryer, iron, board, cable TV, two phones with data ports and voice mail, and separate vanity, while fridges are available if you ask. Half the rooms have little balconies, and all the hallways look down over the lobby floor. The rooms themselves are nice and comfortable, with an easy chair, attractive artwork, and a warm tone from the cherry wood. The Hyatt boasts the only revolving rooftop in Northern California, and while a drink in the Equinox can be a kick, you don't need to stay here to enjoy it. This hotel is convention heaven, but tourist hell, despite its proximity to all the Embarcadero shopping. There are much more personable places to stay for the money.

HOTEL GRIFFON, *155 Steuart. 415-495-2100, 800-321-2201, fax 415-495-3522. Located just south of Market and across from Rincon Center, it is a small, personable hotel with 64 rooms. The Snug (and it is) is $155, it's $165 for the Standard, $185 for the Bay View, and $250 for the Penthouse Suite, continental breakfast included, as is free access to the spanking new YMCA across the street.*

Brick walls and marble counters and floors set a tone of warmth and class, and the rooms follow through. It's been a hotel since 1905, but it's come up in the world since its sailor flop origins. The Bay View rooms do, in fact, have lovely vistas, but all the rooms have coffee maker and iron, hair dryer and phones with voice mail and data port, plus room service from Roti, their wonderful restaurant (it's in their lobby and is described in detail in the *Where to Eat* chapter). It's a shame the windows don't open, but they make up for it with nicely furnished rooms, brick tones, vanity, mini-bar, and sitting area. They cater to business folk and couples looking for a weekend escape, and as such, the halls rarely ring with children's chirping, which is a plus if you're looking to get away from it all.

HARBOR COURT HOTEL, *165 Steuart. 415-882-1300, 800-346-0555, fax 882-1313. It has 131 rooms. Singles and doubles are $160-$175 depending on bay or courtyard view, the Penthouse Suite is $295, and weekend rates are available. Complimentary coffee and tea is in the lobby all day, wine is offered in the evening, and use of the YMCA across the street is free. And there's complimentary limousine service each weekday morning to the financial district.*

Another Kimpton hotel, the staff upholds the Kimpton standards with their friendly, professional, polite service. The lobby is comfortable and informal, pleasant but not grand. A gas fire burns behind the grate, and a big TV is on, but the volume is dimmed. The building dates back to 1906, but features have been upgraded, like the double-paned windows to keep out the noise. The Deluxe rooms are the interior ones, small and cute and looking over a small courtyard. The Bay Views, not surprisingly, look out over the Embarcadero and the water, and are a bit larger. The baths are simple, the beds half-canopy, and all the rooms have honor bar, cable TV, movies, and phone with data port. And the penthouse is beautiful with lots of glass. Harry Denton's Restaurant and Night Club is off the lobby, and they play jazz in the evenings.

MARRIOTT, *55 4th Street. 415-896-1600, 800-228-9290, fax 415-896-6177. Located near Market, there are 1,498 rooms and 39 floors. The rooms are priced on availability (that is to say, the fuller they are the more they charge), and* *they fluctuate with the winds. Right now, the rates range from $139-$185 for a standard double, depending on day of week, and view.*

It's just one block from Moscone Convention Center, and it's geared mostly to the business and convention trade. To see a room you first need to go through the Sales office, so one of their friendly staff can show you around. Though unusual, seeing a room is not hard. The rooms are pleasant without being sensational, but they are equipped for convenience. All the rooms have climate control, huge TV, phone with message light and modem outlet, an iron with board, and the higher up you go the better the view and the loftier the price.

Getting a clear answer on prices, however, is less easy than seeing a room. The hotel also has a large health club with indoor pool, whirlpools, fitness classes: the works. What the location lacks in charm it makes up in convenience. Just a block or two away from Moscone, Union Square, the new Yerba Buena Arts Center, and a bunch of museums, if you stay at the Marriott you'll be right in the thick of the city.

MOSSER'S VICTORIAN, *54 4th Street. 415-986-4400, 800-227-3804, fax 415-495-7653. Located between Market and Mission, it has 165 rooms, some with bath and some without. Budget rooms that share baths are $39 for a single and $49 a double, while rooms with private facilities cost $89-$119, and the suites are $159. All rates include continental breakfast, and there are often winter specials, group discounts, and other promotional rates available.*

Just across the street from the Marriott, but with Victorian charm and personal appeal, the Mosser's lobby sets the tone with fine marble floors, oriental rugs, artwork, and antiques. It was built for the 1915 Pan American Exposition, and the Mossers have restored it to its original luster. Upstairs, the halls are beautifully wainscoted, and they lead to pretty rooms featuring lots of wicker and ecru. Along with the small cable TV, and voice mail phone with data port, there are modified bay windows, and pleasant furnishings.

Though the rooms are very nice, Mosser's charm has more to do with the friendly staff (most of whom have been with the Mosser family since they opened the hotel in 1980), and the style set by the Mossers themselves. Charles Mosser is a playwright and composer (he wrote four musicals, and thousands of country and romantic ballads), and his continued devotion to the arts is apparent in the jazz they host in Annabelle's (their attached bar-bistro), and the works of local artists they display. His wife (the Annabelle of note) has left her mark as well. Her great interest in antiques can be seen in the lobby furnishings, and her Filipina origins can be felt in the bistro's decor. But beyond all that, they are a gracious, amiable family, and their warmth permeates the hotel.

TEMPLE, *469 Pine Street. 415-781-2565. Located between Kearny and Montgomery, it has 5 floors and 85 rooms, half with bath. Without baths, singles* *are $30 and doubles are $35; add $10 for private baths, and if you stay longer than 3 days there are discounts available.*

Right in the middle of the financial district, if you're doing business here, chances are your company will put you up somewhere snazzier. If you're on a tight budget, however, this is probably the cheapest suitable hotel in the district. Built in 1910, the original cage lift is nicely painted, and the rooms are adequate for the money, with bed, small TV, sink, and bureau. There's no phone and no attempt at decor, but it's clean and freshly vacuumed.

AIDA, *1087 Market. 415-863-4141, 800-863-2432, fax 415-863-5151. Located near 7th, it has 6 floors with 186 rooms (100 with bath and 86 without) that were remodeled in 1994. Run by the same man who own the Albergo Verona, the rates are the same and include the same donut breakfasts and round-the-clock coffee and tea. Singles are $28 without bath and $33 with, doubles are $33 without bath and $44 with, and donuts with coffee or tea are available in the lobby for breakfast. There's also a dorm with beds for $15.*

Awful carpets line the elevator, and the rooms are nothing special, with a bed, TV, phone, and old chest of drawers, but improvements are in the offing for the Aida. Renovations are under way, it's just a matter of time. For now, it's a budget hotel with clean bathrooms and meager towels, steam heat and little attempt at decor, but big plans for a parking garage, a new lobby (one that will take advantage of the marble underneath), and new furnishings.

GLOBE HOSTEL, *10 Hallam Place. 415-431-0540, fax 415-431-3286. Located near Folsom and Harrison, between 7th and 8th Streets in SoMa. Also known as Interclub, they have three floors and 142 beds (each room has 5-6 beds plus a toilet, shower, and fridge). They charge $15 a night, though in the off season they often charge $10 for the first night and $15 thereafter.*

The rooms are quite basic, with little storage space and no frills. There's no shared kitchen, though there is one very overcrowded common fridge, and they provide a big breakfast for just $2-$4. There's no curfew, and the reception is open 24 hours a day. They have a sun deck, a laundry room, and a common room with TV and pool table, plus free coffee and lemonade (powdered) after 11am. This is a rather smoky, uninspiring place, nowhere nearly as nice as the Green Tortoise. Reservations can be made by sending a check for the first night to Interclub Globe Hostel, 10 Hallam Place, San Francisco, CA 94103.

INTERNATIONAL STUDENT CENTER, *1188 Folsom. 415-255-8800, fax 415-938-0113. Located between 7th and 8th, it is another low budget alternative. They cater to international visitors, but it's not a hard and fast rule. If there are a number of beds free, you'll probably be welcomed even if you're American. They charge $13 a night for a bed, and $84 for the week, though winter discounts sometimes apply.*

There are no private rooms, but the dorms hold 3-4 beds at most, and they're spare, clean, and small, with a sink in each room. There's no laundry, but they do have a kitchen, and a comfy, quiet living room with a great chess board. The exposed brick walls add a lot of character and texture, the smell of stale beer wafts up from the bar downstairs, while the odor of cigarettes seems to come with the territory. There's no curfew, and while luxury it is not, it's a friendly sort of place.

EUROPEAN GUEST HOUSE, *76 Minna Street. 415-861-6634. Located between 8th and 9th Streets south of Mission, it has a number of dorm options. It costs $10 to stay in the dorm room that holds 15 beds, $12 for the 4-person room, and $14 to stay in a 2-person room (with student discounts of $1 per night).*

The rooms are tiny, with no nooks, crannies, or places to store things, though near the kitchen there are lockers you can rent for $1 a night. They cater to European travelers (but anyone's welcome), and while they provide a communal kitchen (not the cleanest) with microwave, a TV room, laundry facilities, and a roof garden, there are no sofas or bits of comfort and warmth.

FISHERMAN'S WHARF

All hotels here are constrained by the 5-story limit (otherwise they'd be soaring skyscrapers, still trying to outdo one another for the view), and the terrain here is flat, resulting in few bay views.

For more spectacular vistas, you'll need to check into one of the many hillier neighborhoods. Some of the hotels here in tourist central take advantage of the high volume of those wanting to stay as close as possible to Pier 39. It's called "rates based on availability" and it means that the fewer rooms available the more they'll charge you, because they can. If you want to stay at one of the hotels that charges according to such guidelines, the earlier you make reservations, the lower will be your rate.

HYATT FISHERMAN'S WHARF, *555 North Point. 415-563-1234, 800-233-1234, fax 415-563-2218. Located near Taylor, it has 313 rooms. In high season singles and doubles range from $184-$214, while in low they span $139-$169, depending on availability. They frequently have special packages including breakfast or parking, so it's worth asking. They also have Business Plan rooms (plus $15 a night) that include free local access calls and continental breakfast.*

For your money you get a few touches of class that are lacking in most of the other hotels down here. The lower lobby has a fountain and fireplace, and the rooms come with a dark-wood armoire containing shelves and TVs. It's upscale from the Marriott, but it still isn't what you'd call elegant. Though some rooms have a small slice of a good view (crane your head and you can make out the bay), most look out on the housing projects or other hotel facades. They do provide a heated pool, hot tub, and workout facility, and parking is $16 a night.

MARRIOTT-FISHERMAN'S WHARF, *1250 Columbus. 415-775-7555, 800-228-9290, fax 415-474-2099. It has 256 rooms. Singles and doubles are $129-$209, depending on season and availability (lower rates are possible for government employees).*

The halls here smell vaguely of locker rooms, and the rooms are adequate but not at all lovely. They come with desk, phone, TV, mini-bar, and hair-dryer, but lack pizzazz. Parking is $17 a day, and the service is perfunctory and not the best; the staff seems to know its job but doesn't seem to care.

RAMADA HOTEL, *590 Bay Street. 415-885-4700, 800-228-8408, fax 415-771-8945. Located near Jones, it has 233 rooms. In high season the rate is $175 and in low it's $150, but there are often discounts that go as low as $109 and $99, respectively.*

Compared to the other big chains down here, the rooms are fairly nice. The soft rose carpet is warm and welcoming, the phone, cable TV and desk see to your entertainment and business needs, and the small table and chairs are attractive. Clint Eastwood thought so too, and generally stayed here while filming his Dirty Harry films. There's also 24-hour parking available for $8 a day.

HOLIDAY INN, *1300 Columbus. 415-771-9000, 800-750-9094, fax 415-771-7006. Located near North Point, it has 585 rooms. In high season, rates are $130-$180 and in low they're $69-$140, depending on availability.*

Parking for guests is $9 a day (it's $20 a day for the public), there is a swimming pool, and a business center. The lobby isn't much, the halls smell of eau de motel, and the rooms, on the drab side, are even mustier.

SHERATON AT FISHERMAN'S WHARF, *2500 Mason. 415-362-5500, 800-325-3535, fax 415-956-5275. Located near Beach, it has 525 rooms. High season rates are $119-$189 (single or double), the low season range is $99-$169, and none of it is worthwhile.*

The lobby has the required sofas and marble, but there's no touch of sophistication or warmth, just a boring beige theme that is consistent throughout the hotel. The rooms (more beige) are completely clean, devoid of any dirt, personality, or charm, and the card keys are finicky. A lot of their business comes from corporations, and perhaps that affects the tone. They have a full business center, underground parking, a heated pool and health club, as well as all the usual big hotel amenities. But when asked what's so special about the Sheraton, they said it's the big name, and that pretty much says it all.

TUSCAN INN, *425 Northpoint. 415-561-1100, 800-648-4626, fax 415-561-1199. Located near Mason, it has 220 rooms and suites. Singles and doubles are $108-$178, following the same availability policy as the Marriott.*

This Kimpton Group hotel was built five years ago and is the newest addition to the Fisherman's Wharf hotel scene. It's also the most appealing. Unlike some of the big name hotels (like the Sheraton, for example), the lobby feels welcoming, with warm tones, comfy chairs, and a working fireplace. It makes a peaceful change from the noisy, echoing chaos of the Sheraton.

The rooms are quite pleasant, with homey colors and a few classical touches (nicely shaped arches, and real keys instead of those impossible cards). Mornings in the lobby feature coffee, tea, and biscotti, and in the afternoons they have a wine service as well. They sell $7 day passes to the 24-hour Nautilus across the street, and valet service is available for $13 a day. Despite their proximity to the tourist-clogged pier, they aim for a touch of Italian pensione. The interior design coupled with the personal attentions of the staff make this the nicest hotel this close to the wharf.

THE WHARF INN, *2601 Mason. 415-673-7411, 800-548-9918, fax 415-776-2181. Located near Beach, it has 50 rooms and 1 penthouse suite. The rates vary by season and room type (with AAA discounts), but they don't shift according to how many rooms are available. In the high season (June-October), the regular rooms cost $108-$138, and in low season (November-May) the rates range from $73-$93.*

Though its facade is not impressive (it's of the '60s motel genre, and there's nothing the innovative manager can do to change that), the rooms themselves are cozy and comfortable. The penthouse, done in warm rose tones, has a deck and great view of the bay, 2 bedrooms, and a pleasant kitchenette. It's not elegant, but it's cheerful and nice. The Wharf Inn is the only independently-owned hotel in the Fisherman's Wharf area, and after 35 years in the business, it's also the oldest (see architecture note above). Not only is parking free, you can get to your car whenever you want without dealing with tokens or valets. Most of the rooms are sound-proofed to cut the traffic noise, and they're roomier than the Tuscan Inn. The prices are generally lower than other Wharf options, and the staff usually goes out of its way to be friendly and helpful.

TRAVELODGE AT THE WHARF, *250 Beach. 415-392-6700, 800-255-3050, fax 415-986-7853. It has 250 rooms. Standard rooms rates for singles and doubles are $105-$170, depending on the view. There are also discount rates ranging from $69-$99, subject to availability.*

They get the occasional high school or senior citizen group, but the lodge is generally full of traveling Europeans. The rooms are just a tad nicer than mediocre, they come with TV, air-conditioning, and Mr. Coffee machines, and some have balconies looking out over the bay. The halls all come equipped with the standard machines for soda and ice, the keys are one-time insertion cards, so you don't want to blow it. This wharf-side accommodation, however, is more than just a place with rooms; they take up a whole block. There's an outdoor heated pool, novelty shops and fast food restaurants, and free parking in their lot. It's not a stylish place, but they are geared towards tourists, and set up both Grayline and Tower tours as well.

SAN REMO, *2237 Mason. 415-776-8688, 800-352-7366, fax 415-776-2811. Located between Francisco and Chestnut, it is an Italianate Victorian with 62 rooms. Except for the penthouse apartment, all the rooms have shared baths. Singles cost $35-$55 and doubles are $55-$75, but they'll take 10% off when you show your Open Road Guide.*

Between North Beach and Fisherman's Wharf, it's the only hotel anywhere near the wharf with this much charm and personality; it's one of San Francisco's gems, and certainly the most reasonably priced. Each room, though small, is uniquely furnished with brass or iron beds, lace curtains, and antique wicker furniture. Some rooms have sinks, some have views of Coit Tower or the bay, but all are inviting. Some folks are turned off by the thought of shared baths, but even the commodes here are special. All the hall facilities are in individual rooms (you still get privacy), and in addition, all the facilities (blindingly clean) have been selected and installed with the same attention to antique charm as the room furnishings.

The claw-footed tubs and brass pull-chain toilet mechanisms are straight out of the hotel's Victorian origins. The penthouse is the one room with its own bath. Perched atop the hotel like a pilot house on a ship, the views from the smallish penthouse are magnificent. The San Remo was originally built in 1906 by A.P. Giannini (he started Bank of America as well) after the earthquake. The current owners bought the old hotel in 1970 and have been restoring it to its present health and beauty ever since. Thanks to their efforts, it's imbued with the warmth of a European pensione as well as the authentic touch of San Francisco's history.

HAIGHT ASHBURY

STANYAN PARK, *750 Stanyan. 415-751-1000, fax 415-668-5454. Located near Waller, it has 36 rooms, all with bath. Singles and doubles are $85-$105 and suites are $130-$185, with continental breakfast included.*

Across the street from Kezar Stadium and Golden Gate Park, the Stanyan Park Hotel is a world away from the jeans and nose ring culture of nearby Haight Street. It's a remnant from the turn of the century when the Haight's park-side, resort value was just coming of age. This old restored 1905 Victorian has kept the period decor and nuances to go along with the bay windows. The rooms are pretty and pleasant, with subtle wall paper and poster beds. Some are in the back and quiet, others have bay window views of the park across the street, but all have clean bathrooms, phone, TV, and remote. And in the afternoon the dining room is set up with coffee, tea, and cookies for a little mid-day snack.

RED VICTORIAN INN, *1665 Haight Street. 415-864-1978, fax 415-863-3293. Located near Cole, with its 18 idiosyncratically decorated theme rooms, it is a product of Sami Sunchild's creative mind and peace-loving world view. Each room has its own name and motif, and the prices differ depending on amenities, size, private versus shared bathroom, and how long you're staying. Singles for one night with shared bath start at $59 in the Butterfly Room and go to $88 in the Cat's Cradle, while doubles in the same two rooms run $76-$110. Only three of the rooms have private bathrooms, and they are $94-$110 per single and $120-$126 a double. Then there's the Peacock Suite, with living room and stained glass windows at $134 for one and $200 for two people. The rooms all have phones but no TV, there is no elevator, and all prices include continental breakfast. In addition, there are discounts for longer stays.*

The Inn was started in 1977 by Sami, when she began to renovate and decorate the 1904 Victorian she'd bought the year before. Each room differs greatly from the rest, but here are some examples. The Sunshine Room is full of yellows and oranges. Even the sink is painted with a smiling cheery-cheeked sun radiating from the bottom. The Butterfly Room sports nets and gauze and soft-colored lights, while the Rose Garden is a bit more open, airy, and noisy from its Haight Street window. There's a fake rose on the window table, bejeweled with fake dew. Artistic with a Haight Ashbury flavor, this is a friendly and casual establishment. And downstairs in the Peace Center, moon-eyed staff will book talks with the Insight Counselor, sell life-affirming gifts, and donate all profits to peace.

CARL HOTEL, *198 Carl. 415-661-5679, fax 415-661-0661. Located near Stanyan, this is the cheapest and most basic of the Haight area hotels. They have 28 rooms, most of which share baths. For a single without bath, the price is $39, and it's $49 with bath; doubles are $59-$69 with shared bath and $79 for private.*

They claim to be a "home away from home," but this may be true only if your home isn't all that spiffy. It's okay for the money, though, and clean enough with homey touches. The rooms all have a small TV with remote, a phone, and a small fridge. There are laundry facilities handy, and a nice garden patio out back.

CARL STREET UNICORN HOUSE, *156 Carl. 415-753-5194. Located between Stanyan and Cole, it is a beautiful 1895 Victorian with two rooms on the first floor for guests. They charge $40 for a single, $50 for a double (the bath is shared), with a continental breakfast included. Weekend stays should be for at least two nights, one night stays are $5 extra, there's a 10% discount for stays of 7 days, there's no smoking, and children over six are welcome.*

The rooms are pretty, with hardwood floors, laces and wall quilts, textures and interesting photos. The first floor, with its bathroom, small kitchen, dining room, and living room (replete with comfortable sofas and beautiful stained glass windows) is open for B&B guests, and there's a little garden out back, too.

Miriam Weber has lived here for 40 years, and she opened her downstairs to guests 17 years ago. She runs a lovely inn with a home-like air, decorated with her impressive antique collection of 300 ethnic dolls. It's located on a quiet street above Haight Ashbury right near Golden Gate Park, without a sign or notice that would indicate the big house behind the gate is anything more than a beautiful, well-kept home.

MARINA & COW HOLLOW

ART CENTER, *1902 Filbert. 415-566-1526. Located near Laguna, it has four rooms, three of which cost $95, while the suite is $125, with a buffet breakfast included.*

This is a most unusual place to stay, and it will be heaven for some and anathema to others. The building itself was constructed in 1857, and it's a grand old piece of history, but most of the personality and character here come from the woman who runs it. All the rooms are decorated with her original paintings, so along with the usual furniture, you might find snorting horses and contemplative clowns in colorful oil paintings on the walls. The rooms are all different, with names like The Gaviota and Captain Nemo's Focsle, and the decor features bamboo canopy beds, and homey sitting areas. One has a fireplace and another has a writing room, but most have kitchenettes and private entrances.

You'll know the proprietor when you see her, she's the one with Damien the Macaw on her shoulder. She's very fond of him, and she'll happily keep on talking to you about the history of Cow Hollow and the rest of the City (and she knows a lot), never minding him pooping on her shoulder or the schedule you're anxious to keep. So, if you want a homey place with kitchen facilities and private entrances, if you like to be surrounded by art this may be the place for you. On the other hand, if you want reliable service, and someone to always be there with an efficient response when you have a question or need, you ought to find a place that's a little less laid back.

BED & BREAKFAST INN, *4 Charlton Court. 415-921-9784. Located off Union between Laguna and Buchanan, it has 11 rooms, four of which are shared bath pensione rooms for $70-$90, while the five with private bath are $115-$140. They also have two penthouse suites which cost $190 and $275, and a light breakfast comes with all the rooms.*

Located on a winsome lane off Union, the building itself is cute as a button, with ornate lettering marking the entrance. The rooms have sofas and chairs (decorated with a fruit and flower design), frilly lace, and a tiny cable TV. The bathrooms are cheery (some sinks are painted with happy pictures), with a shower stall instead of a bath. The suites have larger TVs, wicker furnished sitting rooms, and quaintness everywhere. The bathrooms are pretty crowded, however, and the carpets lean towards the ugly. It is a charming little house, but it may be a bit too quaint and boutique-like for some.

DAYS INN, *2358 Lombard. 415-922-2010, 800-556-2667. Located between Pierce and Scott, it has 22 rooms with bath, cable TV, and free parking. A room with queen bed is $78, a king is $88, two beds are $98, and continental breakfast is included.*

This is a fairly nice place, for a motel. There's a cabinet with cable TV, the beds have headboards, the rooms have armchairs, desks, and phones, and the bathrooms are well-cleaned. However, you can easily hear the noise of Lombard Street, though it isn't abominable, and the smoking rooms really retain their cigarette odor. Still, it has a nicer style than most, and you're just down the block from The Home Plate if you want to top off your continental breakfast with good, wholesome food.

EDWARD II, *3155 Scott. 415-922-3000, 800-473-2846, fax 415-931-5784. Located near Lombard, it has three floors with 29 rooms. Rooms without baths start at $69, rooms with baths start at $89, and the suites start at $160. The rates include a nicely done continental breakfast, and a sherry in the hotel pub in the afternoon. For parking ($9 a day), make sure to reserve in advance.*

The staff here is friendly and personable, and the rooms are quite appealing, with their wicker furnishings and country shutters. The love seats are very comfortable, as are the beds, the pin-stripe wallpaper is distinctive, and while all the rooms come with cable TV and phone, some have pleasant kitchens, too. The bathrooms are all clean, and some are attractively done in terra cotta tiles. The suites are quite nice, too, with extra touches of lace and comfort, plus canopied beds and whirlpool baths. Noise from Lombard, however, does filter in, especially if the windows are open. There's no elevator, but the well-maintained, 1915 white-banister staircase under the stained glass skylight has plenty of character, and the morning repast is served in an airy, pleasant, British-style breakfast room. All in all, this is an attractive, moderately priced place to stay.

COW HOLLOW MOTOR INN, *2190 Lombard. 415-921-5800, fax 415-922-8515. Located near Steiner, it has three floors with 117 rooms and 12 suites. Singles are $73, doubles are $78-$86, rooms with two beds for three-four people are $$85-$100 (though they may be going up two dollars come summer), and the suites with fireplace and kitchen are $175-$225 a night. There are weekly and monthly rates, but for the suites only, and the parking is indoors and free.*

There is no real lobby here, just an office with lots of signs saying "No Pets Allowed," but for a motor inn, this place is one of the best. The rooms are big and airy, with your standard sort of furnishing, cable TV, and phone. The bay windows are a nice touch, and the windows over Lombard are double-paned against the noise. The bathrooms are big, too, and are equipped with hairdryers. The suites are very nice indeed, with antique furniture, fully equipped small kitchens, working fireplace, and four-poster bed complete with fringed canopy. Some of the suites have two bedrooms with two baths, which make them convenient for families, and they're equipped with what the manager jocularly referred to as mother-in-law closets, and they are truly nearly big enough for a regular room. The whole place is well-maintained and recently renovated, and it's a cut above your average motor inn.

COVENTRY MOTOR INN, *1901 Lombard. 415-567-1200, 415-921-8745. It has 69 rooms at $73 a single and $78 a double.*

There is no reason to stay here. The rooms are no better than anywhere else on the Lombard strip, and the staff can be rude and unpleasant. Go elsewhere; there's no dearth of nicer places.

MARINA INN, *3110 Octavia. 415-928-1000, 800-274-1420, fax 415-928-5909. Located at Lombard, it has 40 rooms, and the rates vary according to the season. In summer, weekday rates are $65-$85 and on the weekend $75-$95, while winter rates run $55-$75, and there are further discounts for seniors and AAA. Continental breakfast is included in the morning, there's sherry in the afternoon, and an evening turn-down service that includes chocolates on your pillow.*

In the Inn's favor and disfavor, it's directly on Lombard, with all its convenience and easy access to the freeway, as well as its traffic and noise. Given that, the rooms here are pretty nice. After the grand marble entrance, a modern, efficient, charmless elevator takes you up to rooms with appealing green carpet, big wood-frame, two-poster beds, pine furnishings, and sprightly floral wallpaper. The small bathroom has shower, tub, toilet, and tile floor, with a sink/vanity alcove off the bedroom. All the rooms have a phone, fan, and cable TV, and while they're not real big on service, there is a nail salon just next door.

PLANTATION INN, *3100 Webster. 415-921-5520, fax 415-931-4137. Located near Greenwich, it has a connecting driveway from Lombard, as well. It has 56 rooms that go for $50-$65 depending on number of beds, and there are adjoining rooms for $80.* This is your standard motel structure, with two tiers of rooms surrounding the parking lot and pool. The rooms are pretty standard too, with cable TV and phone, small, clean bathroom with shower, a big closet, and Gideon's Bible by the bed.

The staff, however, is especially nice, the small pool is heated and has a few Roman statue busts scattered about for that extra touch, there is an exercise room and sauna, and its location off the main street makes for a much quieter stay.

VAN NESS MOTEL, *2850 Van Ness. 415-415-776-3220. Located near Chestnut, this motel has 42 rooms with bath. The rooms can be $50, but it depends on when you ask; the rate seems to fluctuate a bit.*

There's coffee in the rooms, and donuts in the office, but it's not enough to make this a worthwhile place to stay. The Van Ness is a good example of how unsavory the average motel is; it's the sort that, by comparison, makes most of the others listed here look good. The rooms are decorated in motel tacky, with old TVs and radios. The fact that they advertise their phones as push-button says volumes about their concept of state of the art electronics. And, to top it all off, it's staffed by cold, unpleasant workers who would rather not be bothered. So don't bother them.

THE SAN FRANCISCO MOTOR INN, *1750 Lombard. 415-921-1842. They have 20 rooms, with rates ranging from $35-$70, depending on the month.*

They, too, have depressingly dreary rooms, despite the TV and phone, and another manager trained to be miserly with information and help.

SAN FRANCISCO INTERNATIONAL YOUTH HOSTEL, *Building 240 at Fort Mason. 415-771-7277, 800-444-6111. It is open 24 hours daily, has 21 rooms with 127 beds (4-20 a room), charges $15 in summer and $13 in winter, and membership isn't required. Reservations can be made by phone with a credit card, but payment must be made in cash or travelers' checks.*

Perched on a hill overlooking the bay, the hostel is way at the back of Fort Mason, but it's not hard to get there. Plenty of buses (the 42, 47, and 30) can take you to Northpoint and Van Ness, and from there it's a simple case of following the signs up the hill. And when you get there, the setting is lovely; the air smells of fresh grass, and the hostel itself (or Building 240, as its friends call it) sprawls across the pinnacle. The rooms are pleasant enough, with solid pine bunks, and a few (but not enough) cubbyholes in some of the rooms. The sitting room is very nice, with very comfortable sofas, light music, and a central wood-burning stove to gather about.

There's an excellent information bulletin board listing discounts, other hostels, and events, and a pile of *Bay Guardian* newspapers will keep you up-to-date on politics and nightlife. The facilities include a communal kitchen, laundry, a cafe, and a small patio out back. But while a few of the toilets have that certain outhouse odor, the location makes up for a few rough spots. It's right by the Marina Green, which is a real plus if you like jogging, cycling, or frisbee, and the whole Fort Mason complex of theaters and small museums is just a stone's throw away.

NOB HILL & LOWER NOB HILL

RITZ-CARLTON, *600 Stockton. 415-296-7465, 800-241-3333, fax 415-291-0288. Located near California, it has 336 rooms. Singles are $255-$375 and doubles are $275-$395, depending on location. The Club rooms are $450, and the suites are $575-$675.*

Slightly lower on Nob than the other noble hotels, the Ritz-Carlton makes it up with opulence and polish. Flashier than the Stanford Court, the lobby is replete with marble halls and oriental carpets, and just drips with crystal. Even the elevators come with elegant oriental carpets. As for the rooms, the higher the better and pricier. The rooms are elegant, with plenty of mahogany wood, three phones, and marble in the bathrooms. The business club floor is cozy and lovely, with generous spreads of complimentary food. They also do High Tea in the lobby, and have a Teddy Bear Tea with hot chocolate for kids during the winter holidays. Their Sunday Jazz brunch ($32 per person) is lavish, and enhanced by the lovely brick courtyard where tables are set up in fine weather.

The suites are nice as well, but the Ritz people pride themselves most on the service. They have won 5-star and 5-diamond ratings, and it's the attentive, personal service that's done it. The hotel didn't open till 1991, but they did a good job of instilling a 19th century feel, with antiques and paintings and columns.

STOUFFER STANFORD COURT HOTEL, *905 California. 415-989-3500, 800-227-4736, fax 415-391-0513. Located near Powell, it has 402 rooms. The listed rates for singles and doubles are $215-$345, but there are often special discounts available. There are also suites, ranging from $475 on up to $2,000 for the two bedroom Presidential.*

Uniformed doormen and bellboys, dark walls and recessed lights set the formal tone. The lobby is quiet with none of the flash and fanfare of the Fairmont. A hokey sepia-toned mural (painted 5 years ago) under a stained glass dome connects the hotel to San Francisco's (and Leland Stanford's) railroad and gold mining past, while the marble tables and leather-upholstered chairs show the Stanford's continued commitment to tradition.

The hallways are elegant, but the rooms are unremarkable as far as style and decor. They are certainly designed for comfort and convenience, however. The bathrooms have heated towel racks, telephones, and even a 4 inch TV by the sink. Some rooms look out on the street, but the inside rooms are quieter and look over the courtyard. The hotel displays a lot of lovely Japanese art, and some interesting antiques such as a noble-looking grandfather clock given by Napoleon to a general. More importantly, however, the service here is unparalleled. The wake-up call accompanied by a tray of coffee or tea left unobtrusively by your door is just one example of the discreet attention and care the staff (many of whom have worked here since day 1) devote to their guests. In addition to the hotel comforts, Stanford Court is blessed with a remarkably fine restaurant, Fournou's Ovens, described in more detail in the next chapter.

FAIRMONT HOTEL AND TOWER, *950 Mason. 415-772-5000, 800-527-4727, fax 415-772-5013. It has 596 rooms. Singles are $199-$309 and doubles are $229-$339.*

Towering atop Nob Hill, the Fairmont doesn't do things by halves. The establishment takes up a whole city block, and it's all on a grand scale. The lobby is regal and glitzy, nothing subdued about it. A bold carpet of swirling pink on black, vast marble pillars and gobs of gilt, plus red plush chairs all combine for a look that says fancy and proud of it. The rooms have a variety of categories (deluxe, superior, etc.) and views, but they all come equipped with fax machines and modem lines.

The rooms in the hotel proper (the original rooms built in 1907) are lovely. There are enormous closets with vanity table, big enough for the giant trunks people traveled with in days of yore, and big, lovely bathrooms with terry robes and the works. The deluxe rooms are tastefully decorated, and the views are magnificent (the inside standard rooms are similar but without the views). The Tower was added in 1961, and it rises 24 floors. The Tower room furnishings are less special and the bathrooms are smaller, but the views are sensational (and are the reason for the loftier prices - most guests request Tower rooms). One side has city views and the other looks out over the Bay. Both are terrific, just specify your preference when you reserve. The Fairmont does suites as well, and they are truly luxurious. The Versailles Suite, for example, seems to go on forever. The bed is canopied, and the sitting room has majestic furnishings.

MARK HOPKINS INTER-CONTINENTAL, *999 California. 415-392-3434, 800-327-0200, fax 415-421-3302. It has 393 rooms. Singles and doubles are $190-$270, depending on the view, the suites run $375-$575, and the luxury suites start at $900. Discounts and special packages are, however, often available depending on season and occupancy.*

Just across the street from the Fairmont, the Hopkins is more like its stately older brother. The lobby says understated elegance; it's far quieter and more sedate than the Fairmont gala. The rooms are styled more attractively than the Fairmont's as well, with dark mahogany furniture and marble bathrooms. The quality and elegance is reliable and omnipresent. The Business Club floor gives extra services for the extra price, and its set up with computers and fax to go with the complimentary club food and drink. All the views are magnificent, so just state your preference for Golden Gate or Bay Bridge when you reserve. The suites in the Mark Hopkins are sensational and varied. The Garden and the Jacuzzi suites have lovely outdoor terraces; the Cyril Magnin Suite is most impressive.

Cyril lived there for the last years of his life, and his custom touches (Japanese painting, mirror walls, enormous closets, and unique canvas shades) set the rooms apart. The step up, glassed-in terrace has incredible views of the whole city.

The Mark Hopkins has other fine features as well. Nineteen floors up is the Top of the Mark, known around the world for its 360° views of the city, evening cocktails, and impressive Sunday brunches ($36 for the buffet, $42 with California bubbly, and $44 with French Champagne). It's a festive spot now, quite different from its Weepers' Corner history when women watched mournfully as their men sailed off to war.

HUNTINGTON HOTEL, *1075 California. 415-474-5400, 800-227-4683, fax 415-474-6227. Located between Mason and Taylor, it has 143 rooms. Doubles are $190-$240 (less $20 for singles), and the suites charge $290-$790.*

This is the least promoted but most lovely, refined, and elegant hotel on Nob Hill. Once inside the ivy-covered brick facade, the lobby sets the tone with crystal chandelier, soft lighting, oil paintings, and especially comfortable arm chairs, and it just gets better from there. The rooms are stunning. The views are great, as are all Nob Hill vistas, but the furnishings and details surpass any others. The lighting is lovely, the furniture is distinguished *and* comfortable (a rare combo), and the design abounds in taste.

This is the real thing, quality that speaks for itself, the blue blood essence of Nob Hill San Francisco. The suites are all this and more. There are thick carpets, rare silks, a fax-equipped antique desk, and enormous marble bathroom with separate shower stall and mini-TV. All the rooms are different, with their own style and personality, and regular guests all find their own favorites. The only drawback to this exclusive old hotel is that the walls aren't as soundproof as you get in newer, less tradition-soaked hotels. The hotel also has the Big Four Restaurant, (described in more detail in Where to Eat) which provides exemplary room service to hotel guests. The traditional choice of old San Francisco money, the Huntington now attracts new money as well, or anyone who wants the Huntington's understated elegance and commitment to service.

THE WHITE SWAN, *845 Bush. 415-928-6000, fax 415-775-5717. Located next to the Huntington Hotel, between Mason and Taylor, with 27 rooms. Done up in Hunting English style, the inn is otherwise similar to the Auberge and is replete with working fireplaces and stuffed teddy bears. The rooms range from $145-$165, and the suites are $195-$250, full buffet breakfast and afternoon tea included.*

All the rooms come with fireplace, TV, bath, and more blasted teddy bears, while the Romance Suite has a full-canopied bed, champagne, and bubble bath. Downstairs is a little patio with fountain, another fireplace, and more bears. Valet parking is $19 with in and out privileges. The staff is a bit stand-offish, and while this perhaps is in keeping with the Traditional English motif, it isn't as courteous as a small inn should be.

NOB HILL LAMBOURNE, *725 Pine. 415-433-2287. Located near Stockton, its 20 rooms have kitchenettes. Rooms and suites cost $145-$225, including TV and VCR, stereo, computer, fax, and continental breakfast.*

The modest entrance midway between Dashiell Hammet Street and the Joice Streets steps welcomes you to a friendly inn lobby of warm rose tones. The bedrooms dress up comfort and convenience with pretty style. The comforters and pillows are goose-down, and the modern electronics (TV, stereo, IBM-compatible computer, and fax in every room) more than make up for the lack of view. The suites are pretty as well, with satin spreads, but even the regular rooms come with lovely touches like fresh flowers and elegant pillows, and all the rooms have small kitchenettes. The rooms use real keys instead of cards, and there's a sense of serenity throughout. There are spa services as well offering massage, yoga, facials, manicures, and waxings at competitive rates (and exercycles in some rooms); the Lambourne caters to business people but is geared for comfort.

VINTAGE COURT, *650 Bush. 415-392-4666, 800-654-1100, fax 415-433-4065. Located near Powell, with 106 rooms. Singles and doubles are $129-$159, including continental breakfast, afternoon wine, and coffee or tea available all day long.*

The lobby is cozy with its hearth and sofas, the hallways elegant, but the rooms are unusual and a bit cheesy – a shame because the staff is quite friendly and the hotel is otherwise very nice. It also has the advantage of hosting Masa's, San Francisco's best and most exclusive French restaurant, and hotel guests get preferential reservation treatment.

LA PETITE AUBERGE, *863 Bush. 415-928-6000, fax 415-775-5717. Located between Mason and Taylor, it has 26 rooms. Singles and doubles are $110-$160, and suites are $220, full buffet breakfast and afternoon wine and hors d'oeuvres included.*

Fires burn warmly in all the hearths, and the French country decor is punctuated everywhere with stuffed teddy bears. The rooms are cozy with bears, fireplaces, and lace curtains, while the Petite Suite is extra charming. It has its own entrance, deck, and spa tub, along with comfy swivel chairs by the hearth and a homey feel. The staff here is a bit warmer than the White Swan's.

NOB HILL INN, *1000 Pine. 415-673-6080. Located near Taylor with 21 lovely rooms with varying rates. The tiny studio is $71, the larger one is $99; a 1 bedroom is $135, $159 with kitchenette, and $200 for the 2 bedroom with kitchenette, and the rates include continental breakfast and afternoon sherry or tea.*

Built in 1907, the inn's wainscoted walls, Victorian furnishings, and antique (but functional) cage lift maintain old-fashioned charm, while the rooftop open air jacuzzi add a touch of modern luxury. The rooms are attractive and cheerful if not enormous, but you can hear the street traffic below. Large groups are discouraged, but otherwise the staff is personable and helpful. If you're interested, they can also tell you how to own piece of the action and buy into the Nob Hill time-share.

CORNELL, *715 Bush. 415-421-3154, 800-232-9698, fax 415-399-1442. Located near Stockton, the Cornell is a delightful French hotel with 55 rooms, only 27 of which are available for day-to-day rental (more on this later), but all of which are non-smoking. Singles are $70-$85, doubles are $75-$100, junior suites cost $105-$115, and breakfast is included. There's also a weekly special of $475 (single) and $595 (double) which includes seven breakfasts and five dinners at the mediocre French restaurant downstairs.*

This is a special and unique hotel. The building dates from 1915, and the Edwardian feel has been maintained beautifully, down to the antique cage lift that they brought back to life. The hotel is run by a French couple, and the French tone is much more a part of this hotel than La Petite Auberge, which purports to be a French style inn. The Cornell is the real thing, or as real as French gets in San Francisco, and they run the disappointing French restaurant, Jeanne D'Arc, downstairs, as well.

The rooms are not fancy but are done nicely in French provincial decor, and all have phone, bath, and cable TV. And there's great artwork on all the walls. If you want Nob Hill but don't want the fanfare or costs of the big hotels, the Cornell is a good choice. Unfortunately, they are involved in a protracted and complicated battle with the city. The powers that be want the hotel to become a residential hotel, and the current compromise allows them to rent just half their rooms day-to-day (plus 25% more in summer). The weekly special lets them sidestep the regulations a bit, and it's also an exceptionally fine deal.

SAN FRANCISCO RESIDENCE CLUB, *851 California. 415-421-2220, fax 415-421-2335. Located near Powell, it has five floors with 83 rooms that rent by day for $38-$95 a single and $58-$95 a double, depending on the size of the room, and whether you share a bath, have a half bath (your own toilet, use the hall shower), or have the full private bathroom. But most people stay longer, and there are weekly rates ($235-$600) and monthly rates ($695-$1600) as well, all including full breakfast and dinner. No credit cards accepted.*

This is a hidden gem of reasonable Nob Hill lodging, quietly sandwiched in among the big-name luxury hotels. Built in 1910 as apartments, in WWII it was rented out to those working for the war effort, and was quite the rough house. For the past 40 years, however, it's been the Residence Club, a European-style pensione providing friendly, comfortable housing to foreign students, new residents, and visiting tourists.

There are nice Victorian details, and while it isn't fancy, it definitely has character. The rooms vary a lot by size, view, and bath facilities, but even the small rooms are cute and homey, and the shared baths are shared within the wing only. The whole place has a familial, homelike feel, with den mother Elizabeth Blatz buzzing about greeting people, solving problems, and exuding warmth. There are laundry facilities, and the meals, while not gourmet, provide hearty sustenance. You can stay for just a night or two, but some folks stay on for fifteen years. Vacancies don't last long, but you can reserve a room with a $100 deposit (you can get a refund with two weeks notice).

GOLDEN GATE, *775 Bush. 415-392-3702. Located between Stockton and Grant, this is a restored 1913 Edwardian with 23 rooms. Singles and doubles without baths cost $59, rooms with baths are $89, and continental breakfast plus afternoon tea is included.*

A great antique lift harking back to 1913 takes you up to the attractive rooms. They're not big, but they are cozy, with wicker and drapes, and a small TV. The toilets and claw-footed tubs are antique and meticulously maintained. The rooms without their own bath facilities are smaller still, but quaint and homey and a very reasonable rate for the city. The manager of this small, family-run hotel is friendly, and so is Nemo, the hotel cat.

GRANT, *753 Bush. 415-421-7540, 800-522-0979, fax 415-989-7719. Located near Powell, this is an old run-down hotel with 76 rooms, all of which come with bath, phone, and color TV. A single costs $45, a double is $49, and 10% off in winter.*

Gems exist, but sometimes you get just what you pay for. The Grant elevator stinks of Play-doh, and their rooms are ugly, ugly, ugly. The furniture is cheap, the halls aren't much better, and the walls need a fresh coat of paint. You're better off elsewhere as the Grant is a depressing place.

NORTH BEACH & TELEGRAPH HILL

HOTEL BOHÈME, *444 Columbus. 415-433-9111, fax 415-362-6292, email: HotelBoheme@MCIMail.com. Located near Vallejo, there are 15 rooms, all with private bath. Singles and doubles are $105-$120, depending on the room.*

This remodeled Victorian used to be the Millefiori Inn, but with the change of name and ownership has come many other wonderful changes. The rooms are delightful. Though it nods to the 90s (the rooms all have cable TV, remote control, and phones with modem jacks), the tone is one of another time, when Ginsberg, Ferlinghetti, and Kerouac were Beats supreme. The rooms have all the modern amenities, but the burnt orange paint, bistro tables, Matisse and Picasso paintings and Chinese parasol light shades infuse the rooms with bohemian charm. The inside rooms are quieter, but the outside rooms overlook more colorful street scenes. The hotel is not just situated in North Beach, it's awash with the aura of North Beach forty years ago, with lamp shades of sheet music collages, Ginsberg poetry, and newspapers from the '50s.

In its brochure (a work of art by itself), Eileen Kaufman says "Life was full of dancing, singing, poetry, parties, people, painting, music, sunshine, moonlight, rooftops, laughter, and love ... These were times of plenty." This is the time the hotel lovingly honors. It's real triumph, however, is that it manages to cast its funky bebop bohemian flavor in such a luxurious, elegant fashion. In short, it's a truly delightful place to stay. And the new management is most attentive to all the nuances of comfort.

WASHINGTON SQUARE INN, *1660 Stockton. 415-981-4220. Located on Washington Square, it has 15 rooms. Singles and doubles with shared bath are $85-$95, and rooms with bath are $95-$180, depending on size of room, distance from street, view, and other such amenities. An extended continental breakfast is included (in the lobby or in your room), as is an afternoon tea service with hors d'oeuvres and wine, for guests and their visitors. There's complimentary newspaper, fresh flowers in your room, and also valet parking available ($17 a day).*

This old Victorian across from Washington Square Park was rebuilt on its original foundations after the 1906 quake, served as flats and then a doctor's office and pharmacy, but it's been an inn for the past 17 years. The rooms all have their own touches and personalities, and they're all non-smoking. It's pleasant, quaint, and clean, but not really elegant or sophisticated. The staff take good care of you, however, and the afternoon tea (4-7pm) is a good example. It's not just the complimentary tea (4 kinds) and wine, the cheeses and pates, cucumber sandwiches and cakes; the atmosphere is cozy and relaxed, and you feel pampered. Whether you've had a long day of sight-seeing or business meetings, you'll welcome a late afternoon chance to snack and read the paper or chat with other guests in the cozy lobby. And if you're lucky, it'll be chilly enough for them to put their fireplace to use.

EUROPA, *310 Columbus. 415-391-5779. Located near Broadway, it has 76 rooms and hall baths. Singles are $25, doubles are $30, and the weekly rates are $90-$140. The front street rooms are the more expensive, though the back rooms are quieter.*

This hotel may or may not have seen better days, but now it's certainly fairly seedy and run-down. Above the Condor (now transformed from a strip joint to an up-scale pub) on a noisy corner of Columbus, it's not run by the most hospitable of folks, and most of the guests here are long-term residents. No children are allowed, and it's just as well.

GREEN TORTOISE HOSTEL, *490 Broadway. 415-834-1000. Located near Kearny, the Green Tortoise is perched on a hill in North Beach. They have 40 rooms (mostly 2-4 beds per room), and for a dorm bed in their rather charming* *old Victorian home they charge $15 in summer and for now $12 in winter (but the winter rate may be abolished soon). Private rooms are $19.99 for a single, $35 a double, and there's no curfew. Just finished is a cute little house around the corner with 4 rooms for couples who want a little more privacy and quiet. It has its own kitchen, and a deck with a great view, and it's the same $35 for a double. All rates include continental breakfast, free coffee and tea throughout the day, as well as access to a newly built communal kitchen, laundry room, and a sauna (open 24 hours daily).*

There are too many lovely touches and fine points to include, but this is the best hostel in the city. The dorm rooms are cheery, with good carpentry, comfortable wood bunks, and homey touches. The private rooms are nice as well. The crystal chandeliers and wall sconces, fresh paint and elegant staircases mesh somehow with the youth hostel demeanor of young folk bopping about in cut-offs. The hostel's been in business since January of '94, but the building has a long North Beach history.

Built in the early 1900s, one of the three buildings that are now combined used to be the Swiss American Hotel. Rumor has it that one building was a brothel at one time, and their renovations are uncovering some remarkable rococo murals and decorations. The owners and managers are always adding and improving, with guest comfort in mind. There's a meditation room, a sitting (and smoking) room with old sofas. Green Tortoise's travel office is there (see Arrivals & Departures for more information on their bus tours), and the shared bath rooms are individual, not large communal affairs. Reservations can be made by sending a check in advance to Green Tortoise Hostel (494 Broadway, San Francisco, CA 94133).

THE BASQUE HOTEL, *15 Romolo Place. 415-788-9404. Located near Broadway and Columbus, it is a small place with weekly rates only from $90-$140, depending on occupancy and room size. To find Romolo Place, walk down Broadway. One block from Columbus is the small lane. Turn up the hill by Columbus Books and the colorful Gold Mountain wall mural, and the Basque Hotel and Restaurant is on your left. After 5pm the double doors are open; otherwise knock at the single door.*

The rooms are small, clean, and very charming. The folks who run the place are friendly and sincere, and the hotel is very quiet. The Basque Restaurant serves family style French country dinners for $13 ($9 for children), and it's a lot of food. It's open Tuesday-Saturday 5-10pm.

PACIFIC HEIGHTS & LOWER PACIFIC HEIGHTS

SHERMAN HOUSE, *2160 Green. 415-563-3600, 800-424-5777, fax 415-563-1882. Located in Pacific Heights, and just a block or so away from Cow Hollow and the Marina. They have eight luxurious rooms which run $200-$395* *a night and six suites which cost $595-$825, each uniquely decorated and named, and there are attentive butlers round-the-clock at your service.*

This was once the home of Leander Sherman, one of San Francisco's early arts patrons, and he built this French-Italianate mansion in 1876. Now a small luxury hotel, all the amazing rooms and suites in the main house are beautifully decorated with English and French antiques as well as lovely brocades. The Galleria is a gorgeous setting for guests to sit, chat, read, and whatnot, while the Music Room is dominated by Sherman's grand piano, with palm trees, plaster busts, and French tapestries adding to the continental panache. And while the occasional pianist guest treats the place to a Mozart sonata, the room is more often filled by the twittering of finches who abide in the magnificent birdy chateau.

The Padarewski Suite is a fine example of what a suite can be. It was once Sherman's billiards room, and the dark wood wainscoting and wood-beam ceiling lend a very British feel. There's a stunning canopied bed surrounded by heavy brocade curtains, and the lovely, pillowy window seats look out over the garden. A bin of wood waits by the fireplace, and the bathroom not only has its own jacuzzi, but a second fireplace, too. The Leander Sherman Suite, however, takes the cake. Inside there's the four-poster canopied bed and brocade curtain that set it apart from the sitting room, and the bathroom is special, too, with its Roman style tub, but the big treat is the brick-laid terrace. The Leander Suite lets out onto one of the loveliest patios with the most sensational of bay views, while the wrought iron table and cushioned settee call out for a picnic lunch or sunset cocktail. The Carriage House in back has a more contemporary feel, and all the rooms, of course, have phones and TVs, while some of the suites have stereo systems as well. And whatever room or suite you choose, you're bound to feel pampered by the sumptuous elegance of the house and the attention of the staff.

THE MANSIONS HOTEL, *2220 Sacramento. 415-929-9444, fax 415-567-9391. Located between Buchanan and Laguna, it has 21 rooms and suites. Rooms are $129-$189, suites are $200-$350, and the rates include both a full breakfast and the evening Magic Performance (which otherwise costs $15, unless you order dinner from the $23-$32 menu).*

Equal parts opulent hotel, museum, and haunted house, the Mansions is a very bizarre establishment. It was built 1887 by Utah Senator Richard Craig Chambers, one of the richest men of the time. He moved to San Francisco and indulged his wealth with the enormous, twin-turreted Queen Anne Victorian mansion that was converted to a hotel. But it's his daughter Claudia who's responsible for most of the atmosphere here. She played the piano, she was an obsessive porkaphile (loving pigs, that is, not their meat), and it's her ghost that is said to haunt the Mansions. Whether you believe in ghosts or not, her presence is certainly felt in the decor, thanks to the hundreds of pig replicas, statues, paintings, and stuffed animals that fill every nook and cranny. Fact or gimmick, the haunting issue is also the force behind the evening magic shows where a human head on a platter reads your mind, and other ghost-like activities.

THE MANSIONS MUSEUM TOUR

The reception foyer, lit by an elaborate crystal chandelier, is full of murals, and signatures (Barbra Streisand, Joe Montana, etc.) of their celebrity guests. The rooms downstairs are open to the curious general public, and are unlike any you might find at other hotels. There's the Music Room, with Claudia's piano covered with pigs, then there's the Billiard Room, with Tiffany-style lamps, the oversized doll house from Edward Albee's Tiny Alice set, a stained glass nickelodeon player piano, and a glass case full of piggy figurines. And then, further on, is the Pig Museum. Claudia had a pet pig, and hundreds of pig artifacts and porkabilia honor her fondness for the creatures. On the other side of the foyer, past the celebrity hallway, it the Historic Documents Parlor, with authentic signatures from Abraham Lincoln, John Hancock, Houdini, and more. There is, of course, a mural depicting pigs playing pool, as well as some lovely antiques and a marble Beniamino Bufano sculpture.

More Bufano pieces, the largest collection anywhere, can be seen in the Dining Gallery. Past this gallery is another Dining Room with what is thought to be the largest continuous scene of stained glass ever. It's called "Garden in Heaven," and was brought from a Spanish villa in Barcelona. And behind the stained glass is the rear sculpture garden, including Bufano's grand relief. On the right hand side of the Christ figure's out-stretched arm, a finger is missing. This is not an oversight. It is in remembrance of Bufano's own act of protest, wherein he chopped off his own finger and sent it to Franklin Delano Roosevelt in a plea to end the war.

The rooms and suites are all decorated differently, though all contain at least one pig reminder. While the building is Victorian, the decor is a mix of Asian, modern, and Victorian antique. The Emperor Norton room has a small but nice bathroom, lovely lamps and furnishings, plus a loud mural of Norton himself taking up most of one wall. The themes don't all go together (Norton, pigs, Victorian, Asian), but it certainly isn't boring.

The suites all have fireplaces, but are otherwise quite different. The Celebrity has its own garden entrance, while the Josephine (where Streisand stayed) has its own deck, is French, and very opulent. And then there's the Presidential suite with separate bedroom and parlor, two fireplaces, two bathrooms, a canopied bed, deck, and a library of over 2,000 books.

While the meandering mansion is lovely, the pig and haunted house business can get on some people's nerves - quiet elegance is not the tone here. And while the theatrics and museum pieces are unique and amazing, the young staff is not well-trained, and isn't as attentive as they should be. Still, if you want fun and dazzle with sumptuous furnishings, this could be the haunted mansion for you.

JACKSON COURT, *2190 Jackson. 415-929-7670, 800-738-7477, fax 415-861-0954. Located near Buchanan in Pacific Heights, it has 10 rooms, all with bath, and all no smoking. The room rates are $125-$180, with a large continental breakfast included and afternoon tea with cookies in the parlor as well, but no elevator. Street parking is restricted except on weekends, but there's a nearby garage that costs $10 for overnight.*

This grand house was built in 1900, with all the care, fine details, and dark woods that used to be lavished on fine homes. A solarium foyer greets you with an abundance of green plants on a flagstone floor, and the interior proper is even lovelier, with a graciously elegant parlor of mahogany beams, a cheery fire in the enormous hearth, and a Tiffany-style lamp shedding its muted glow. Sit there for a moment and feel the weight of the world evaporate - a sensation that's worth the price all by itself. Each room is decorated differently, but they all adhere to the same good standards of charm and comfort, and all come with private phone, cable TV, a combination of antique and contemporary furnishings, and fresh flowers.

On the low end, the rooms are cozy and beautifully decorated. One has a fireplace, another handsome antique furniture, and the Corner Room has window seats overlooking the street. The largest room, the Executive, has an impressive marble fireplace, and a nice sitting area that's separate from the brass bed, while the Garden Court (it was once the dining room and is now the most expensive room here) is big and handsome with its dark wood paneling, and is blessed with a private garden patio. All the rooms feel spacious, the staff are as helpful and nice as can be, and the quiet, tree-lined residential neighborhood is a pleasure to stroll.

THE QUEEN ANNE, *1590 Sutter. 415-441-2828, 800-227-3970, fax 415-775-5212. Located near Octavia, it has four floors and 49 rooms that go for $99-$150, depending on room size and amenities (fireplace and fridge), and the suites are $175-$275. Children under 12 are free, and all rooms come with continental breakfast and morning paper, plus sherry and cookies in the afternoon.*

The parlor sitting room with a fire burning warmly in back sets the Victorian tone, with a collection of antiques (English and American), and authentic period touches, reflecting its history as one of the first large houses built in this area back in 1890 by Senator James G. Fair (one of the

Comstock Lode silver kings). The rooms are attractive, and all have cable TV, room phone, bathroom phone, and hair dryer, plus bay windows and more Victorian details.

The suites are all different, and are decorated with luxury and fun in mind. The Garden Suite, for example, has a small fountain (the water turns on and off with a switch), double fireplaces, loads of draping ivy, a luxurious bed, and pink blossoms everywhere. The staff is kind and pleasant, and the hotel offers a limousine shuttle to the financial district.

QUEEN ANNE'S HISTORY

Built by Senator James G. Fair (one of the Comstock Lode silver kings) in 1890, this was no senatorial mansion. Rather, the Queen Anne started as Miss Mary Lake's School for Girls, an institution to train young upper class ladies for their upcoming society roles. It narrowly escaped the destructive fire and quake in 1906 (they were just three blocks from the firewall), so the Queen Anne still features many of its original details. After the school closed in 1899, the building had a brief stint as Cosmos, an exclusive gentleman's club that was a far cry from the original, prim clientele, then landed in the hands of the Episcopal Diocese. They brought the building back to women, but not the society girls who used to practice posture and conversation. The Episcopalians opened the Girls Friendly Society Lodge, a home and haven for the working woman.

Following World War II, the Diocese sold the Lodge, and the property went through several owners who operated the building as a ho It got run down, and boarded up, till the K.R. VI Company purchased it in 1980, and began work renovating and restoring to meet modern safety codes while salvaging the original ambiance, and the Queen Anne opened as a luxury guest house in 1981. The rooms still sport the original door knobs, a rediscovered safe from its Girls Lodge days is on display in the lobby, and a Lodge flyer (with a picture of the Lodge at that time) hangs in what was previously the confessional booth, but has been renovated for phones. The hotel continues to honor its century-old history while updating its modern amenities for a comfortable combination of luxury and lore.

LAUREL MOTOR INN, *444 Presidio, on the corner of Presidio and California. 415-567-8467, 800-552-8735, fax 415-928-1866. It has 49 rooms, 18 of which have kitchenettes, and 2/3 of which are non-smoking, and you can bring a pet if you don't leave it alone. Singles are $75, doubles are $82, those with kitchenettes are $10-$17 more (depending on the view), and continental breakfasts are included.*

This lodging doesn't fit the usual categories; it's not a motel or a big hotel, nor is it boutique hotel. It's just a comfortable place to stay that doesn't cost an arm and a leg, and has been run by the same owner since it was built in 1962. The rooms are pleasant, if not deluxe, with typical furniture and framed artwork above the beds, heat lamps in the bathrooms (most have showers, but you can ask for one of the few with a tub), and all the rooms have cable TV, phone, and radio, and you can rent a VCR for just $5 a day. The little kitchenettes are well-equipped, and microwaves are available on request.

Many of the rooms look out over Presidio, giving your average street view, but for a slighter higher rate, you can have a quieter room with a sensational view of the city, which even includes a small glimpse of the bay. The guest list is mixed, and many are affiliated with the nearby hospitals (either as doctors or as visitors of those in the hospital). The people who stay here are nice people, as are the folks who run the place. There's no better place in this neighborhood for the money.

MONTE CRISTO, *600 Presidio. 415-931-1875, fax 415-931-6005. Located near Pine, it has 14 rooms full of charm and antiques. Rooms with shared-bath are $63-$73, rooms with private baths are $78-$98, and deluxe rooms are $108. Stays of more than five nights are 10% off, and there's an extended continental breakfast included.*

The Monte Cristo was built in 1875, and the whole inn is imbued with an antique style and wallpaper harking back to earlier times. At one time this building served as a bordello and a speak-easy, but now the rooms are very lovely, with antiques and charm. They are spacious and appealing, and very quaint. A small color TV (no cable) makes its nod to modernity, but there are no phones in the rooms. Unfortunately, the grumpy, taciturn staff puts a quash on the elegance, and takes much of the shine of its appeal.

POLK GULCH   √

LELAND HOTEL, *1315 Polk. 415-441-5141, 800-258-4458, fax 415-441-1449. Located near Bush, this is a friendly place with 104 rooms, at $40 a single and $48 a double without bath, $48 a single and $55 a double with bath, and $58 a double for a studio apartment. You can also rent by the week for $220.*

This is not fancy city, but they have a nice way about them, and some nice touches, too. The hotel was built in 1906 right after the earthquake, so the ceilings and stairs and such are imbued with turn-of-the-century style. The lobby is especially great, with an alcove set by a full wall mural, all in burgundy and pale white, with tropical birds etched under a romantic moon, and there are plenty of flourishing trees everywhere. The rooms are fine but not deluxe, the marble-topped dressers have some style, the bathrooms are old but clean, and the kitchens in the studios are well-stocked. All the rooms have color TVs and phones, and you can rent a VCR and movies ($6.51-$9.77 a day or $24.93 a week) from the front desk. While 90% of their guests are gay, anyone is welcome, and there's a friendly, family style among the staff, including Mr. Cat, an enormous fatso of a feline who parades at will. They welcome vacationers, but they also have a number of guests in transition, who've moved to the city and staying there till they get a permanent abode, so long-term rates are available, too. And, as a special bonus, they're right across the street from Aladdin Restaurant and their delicious, cheap Middle Eastern meals.

RICHMOND

CASA ARGUELLO, *225 Arguello. 415-752-9482, fax 415-681-1400. Located between California and Sacramento, it has four rooms for $55-$79, depending on whether you share or have a private bath, plus a suite for $85. A large continental breakfast is included, but all rates assume a two night stay; it'll cost an extra $10 for just one night. There is street parking for free or nearby lot parking for $10, and there's no smoking. Located near Golden Gate Park, USF, and the commercial, restaurant-laden Clement Street, this is the one place to stay in the neighborhood.*

Two of the rooms shared a bath, and the other three have private facilities, all the rooms have a small TV and one has a small fridge, but none of them have phones. The rooms have a grandma's guest room feel, with carpeting, and lots of silk flowers. The common living room is pleasant, with more fake flowers, some sofas and chairs, a TV, and a comfy, homey feel.

SFO AIRPORT

HOTEL SOFITEL-SAN FRANCISCO, *223 Twin Dolphin Drive, Redwood City. 415-598-9000, 800-763-4835, fax 415-598-0459, it has 319 rooms, 28 suites. Generally speaking, rooms are $185-$205 and the suites are $215-$245, but on weekends they often have special rates of $95 for the regular room and $125-$155 for the suites, and they have special discounts (based on availability) starting as low as $93 a single and $98 a double. Reservations a couple of weeks in advance is recommended, and they have a parking garage, plus free airport shuttle.*

This is a big, modern structure on the water, with all the amenities. The rooms are quite passable and comfortable, though not particularly attractive, and they all have two phones with voice mail, cable TV with remote, mini-bar, and hair dryer, and there are extras like an evening turndown service with a fresh rose and a chocolate truffle. There's a restaurant and French bakery, and a lobby bar and lounge overlooking the waterfront, with live music and complimentary hors d'oeuvres. There's an outdoor heated pool overlooking the lagoon, a exercise facility with Universal weight equipment that's open day and night, and a spa that does facials, body treatments, and massage. There's also a nice jogging path that takes you through a park and children's play area.

WESTIN HOTEL, *1 Old Bayshore Highway, Millbrae. 415-692-3500, 800-228-3000, fax 415-872-8104, it has 338 rooms. The rooms are $175 for a single and $195 for a double, while the Guest Office rooms are $195 a single and $215 a double. There's an airport shuttle service, and they have a United ticket and check-in counter, too.*

Just two minutes from the airport, out front are palms, a fountain, and the bay, and inside is the Westin's usual attention to detail and service. They have various dining options and a lobby lounge for drinks. The rooms are pleasant enough, if not breath-taking, and they all come with coffee maker, two phones with voice mail and data port, and cable TV. And the Guest Office rooms have a fax machine, modem, and printer, too. The hotel has a fully equipped fitness center, an indoor pool, sauna, and jacuzzi, and there's a six-mile jogging trail in the Bayfront Park.

EMBASSY SUITES, *150 Anza Boulevard, Burlingame. 415-342-4600, 800-433-4600, fax 415-343-8137, it has 339 suites. The suites cost $123-$200 on weekdays and $109-$200 on weekends, depending on availability (which means the busier they get the more they'll charge). They provide free shuttle service to the airport, and a full breakfast with complimentary newspaper is included.*

It's set right on the water, with palm trees out front, and they have a stunning new atrium full of palms and ferns and other flourishing greenery where the breakfast is served. In the evening, there's a Manager's Reception in the central courtyard, a pleasant place with streams and waterfalls. The suites are made up of two rooms, with a either a king-sized or two double beds, two dual-line phones with data port and voice mail, and two cable TVs with remote. The living room has a dining/work table, a sleeper sofa, a refrigerator, microwave, wet bar, and coffee maker. The hotel has a heated indoor pool, a whirlpool, sauna, and steam room, and a free shuttle to a nearby full service health club. They're also near a golf course, and paths for walking, biking, and jogging.

SAN FRANCISCO AIRPORT HILTON, *in the San Francisco International Airport. 415-589-0770, 800-445-8667, fax 415-589-4696. It has 529 rooms. Singles are $149-$169 and doubles are $169-$189 on weekdays and on weekends (Thursday-Sunday) they're $99, based on availability, and they have parking as well as a shuttle to the airport.*

The only hotel actually at the airport, the bucolic garden courtyard is really lovely and it gives you a break from the airport bustle. The rooms are attractive, and they all have refreshment center and coffee maker, iron and board, two-line phones with voice mail, and cable TV with remote, and many of the rooms have balconies overlooking the pool or garden courtyard. The hotel is fully equipped, with formal and informal dining options, a lobby bar with big screen TV, piano, and pool table (plus karaoke on weekends). They have a Business Center with PC workstations, modem, fax, photocopying, and secretarial services, and for relaxing, there's a fitness center, outdoor heated swimming pool, and whirl-pool spa, and they have also got a shoe shine stand and an airline arrival and departure information terminal.

AIRPORT MARRIOTT, *1800 Old Bayshore Highway, Burlingame. 415-692-9100, 800-228-9290, fax 415-692-6861. It has 684 rooms. Singles and doubles are $89-$159, pets are welcome, and there's free parking and an airport shuttle.*

This is a full-service hotel with a very pleasant atmosphere. The rooms are just fine, with cable TV, phones with voice mail, and either king-sized or two double beds. There's a writing desk, and a sitting chair with ottoman, while the bathrooms have tubs and hair dryers. The staff is friendly, and there's a beautiful out-door promenade that overlooks the bay and the end of the runway. They have round the clock room service, plus laundry facilities, a concierge, and valet service. They have two restaurants and a bar lounge with entertainment, as well as a pool, exercise room, sauna, whirlpool, and a jogging trail.

CLARION HOTEL, *401 Millbrae Avenue, Millbrae. 415-692-6363, 800-223-7111, fax 415-697-8735. It has 435 rooms. In general, room rates are $109-$129 a single, and $119-$149 a double depending on availability, but they have a bunch of discounts like Triple A and the Entertainment Card, and there's a free airport shuttle.*

There are six floors in the tower, with two floors forming the rest of the hotel. They have a fitness center, whirlpool, and outdoor heated pool, and there's a garden as well. The rooms are ordinary, with cable TV and phone, but the garden is nice.

RED ROOF INN, *777 Airport Boulevard, Burlingame. 415-342-7772, 800-325-2525, 415-342-2635. It has 200 rooms. Their rates for are singles $77-$87 and for doubles it's $88-$98. They have a restaurant and pool, and pets are accepted.*

The rooms are nothing special, with cable TV and phone, but they are a slightly less-expensive alternative if you need to stay by the airport.

LA QUINTA MOTOR INN, *20 Airport Boulevard, South San Francisco. 415-583-2223, 800-531-5900, fax 415-589-6770. It has 174 rooms. Singles are $75-$81, doubles are $85-$91, continental breakfast is included, there's free parking, and airport shuttle service is provided. There are also discounts available.*

Coffee is served 24 hours a day in the lobby, and they have a 24 hour restaurant with room service as well. The rooms and bathrooms have all just been remodeled and redecorated, and all come with phones with data ports and large 25-inch TVs with cable, movies, and Nintendo. There's a washer and dryer, a pool and jacuzzi, and an exercise fitness room, too. There are lots of flowers out front, and the staff is very nice.

SUNSET

HILL POINT GUEST HOUSES, *15 Hillpoint Avenue. 415-753-0393. Located near Parnassus and Irving, they offer 20 furnished rooms and apartments to students and UCSF visitors. Singles with shared bath and kitchen cost $45-$60, standard rooms with bath are $67-$75, and suites cost $89-$195, with Austrian continental breakfast.*

Hillpoint is in a charming cul de sac, with the rooms scattered throughout the pretty houses at the end. Unfortunately, the insides aren't as nice as the facades promise. The main house (#15) has a little fountain outside and lots of plants and flowers, while inside the lobby is all a clutter with stuffed teddy bears and cuckoo clocks, knickknacks and shaggy, flopping Shiatsu dogs. The rooms themselves are adequate and comfortable without being especially lovely or elegant. They have fabulous views of the city, the park, and the Marin hills, but the carpets are drab and the bathrooms are unappealing. The low-end single is small and poorly furnished, while the suites have large sitting areas, small kitchenettes, and smaller bedrooms. Most of the rooms have a large TV and private phone, though the lower-priced student rooms have neither. If you need to be near UC and want a suite, Hillpoint is well-located; otherwise the other two Inner Sunset inns are nicer.

MOFFAT HOUSE, *431 Hugo Street. 415-753-9279, fax 415-564-2480. Located near 5th and Irving, it is one of three houses run by the Moffats, with four rooms each. Most are shared-bath though a few have private baths, and they cost $39-$79, depending on room size and bathroom situation. A large continental breakfast is included, and they offer a unique exercise discount whereby 25 cents per mile you walk or jog gets deducted from your bill (as per the honor system). In fact, a log book in the front foyer records moving testimony of many miles trekked by countless guests.*

The house is a 1910 Edwardian, and the rooms themselves are very simply but pleasantly decorated, with a small TV and the people who run Moffat are warm, down-to-earth, friendly folk. The shared bathrooms and toilets are nicely tiled and appealing, and some of the rooms have their own deck. Right near the park, on a quiet street, and close to the commercial avenue, too, this is a very likable place.

BOCK'S, *1448 Willard. 415-664-6842, fax 415-664-1109. Located up from Parnassus, it is a small 1906 Edwardian inn with 3 rooms to offer, costing $40-$65 a single and $60-$75 a double, with an expanded continental breakfast included. A two day minimum stay is required, weekly 10% discounts, and there's no smoking.*

In a little blue house on Willard, this is a lovely home run by warm, knowledgeable Laura Bock, a native San Franciscan and a fine, welcoming host. The house is nicely restored 1906 Edwardian, with typical Edwardian features like redwood paneling and banister, oak floors, and diamond-patterned front windows. This is not, however, a mansion full of antiques. It feels like a home, and is decorated pleasantly and comfortably. One of the rooms has a private bath and deck, and all come with phone, TV, and coffee/tea service, and they also all have handmade quilts on the beds, books strewn about, and small sitting areas.

There's a communal living room, dining room, and a deck with a tremendous view, and while it's off on a quiet street, it's near UCSF, Golden Gate Park, and the Inner Sunset shops and restaurants. Bock's business has been booming for 17 years; this is a swell place.

TENDERLOIN

THE PHOENIX HOTEL, *601 Eddy. 415-776-1380, 800-248-9466, fax 415-885-3109. Located near Larkin (right next to Pearl's Jam House), it has 44 rooms with bath. Regular rooms are $99, and suites are $129-$139, and all include continental breakfast. Discounts are often available as well.*

The place looks like the archetypal motel, with two levels of rooms all grouped about a small pool courtyard. The "lobby" is just a place to check in and out of, and while there's some interesting sculpture about the pool area, the views are mostly of the tall buildings nearby. The rooms are nicer than your average motel, with palm trees and bamboo furniture as well as cable TV, remote, and an in-house movie channel. They even have bamboo xylophones, which should really be standard for every motel room. The pool is heated and the parking is free. It's a place that's far more appealing on warm, sunny days than in the cold and wet.

EMBASSY, *610 Polk Street. 415-673-1404. Located near Turk, it has 84 rooms ($40 a single and $50 a double), all with bath, TV, and phone, and there's free parking, too.*

There's no real lobby to speak of, and a no-nonsense reception lady who means what she says. When she says "follow me," she's talking to *you.* The rooms are nice enough, with enormous walk-in closets. They all have private facilities, but some have baths and others come with shower stalls. The Embassy is a hotel with old-time sensibilities, and rather than afternoon teas and such fluff, they provide the important amenities: free parking, a barber shop that'll style both men and women, and an archetypal cocktail lounge that is great in a dim, red, slightly sleazy way.

ALBERGO-VERONA, *317 Leavenworth. 415-771-4242, 800-422-3646, fax 415-771-3355. Located near Eddy, it has 6 floors with 65 rooms, and parking. Singles are $28 without bath and $33 with, doubles are $33 without bath and $44 with, and donuts with coffee or tea are available in the lobby for breakfast. There's also one 15-person dorm with beds for $15, and the parking (usually $5) is free if you show them your Open Road guide.*

The pleasant lobby is a nice change from yucky Leavenworth. The 1908 ceiling is beautifully restored, and the fireplace, rocking chair, and antiques impart warmth. Still, this is a low budget hotel, and the rooms have minimal decor. There's the bed, the TV and phone, the towels, soap, and shampoo, and not much more. There are some nice touches, however, like the original cage elevator, and a friendly owner. There are vending machines for soda and candy, and while they don't have laundry facilities, you can make an arrangement with the maid if you need some clothes washed.

YMCA CENTRAL BRANCH, *220 Golden Gate Avenue. 415-885-0460. Located near Leavenworth, it has nine floors of 109 rooms for men and women. Dorm beds are $15 (with valid IYH ID), singles are $26 (+ two dollars for a TV), and doubles are $36, shared bath. There are just two singles with bath and TV for $37.50, and no such doubles. They do, however, have triples with bath and TV for $58.50. While not all the rates include TV or bath, they do include a slight continental breakfast, and use of the excellent gym facilities (membership isn't required), as well as access to the laundry room.*

The staff is friendly, and the weight room, swimming pool, sauna, and aerobics classes may make up for the sterile aura of the rooms. They are plain but cozy, and the dorms have desks and lockers. All feels safe and clean, though not brimming with quaintness or charm. To make reservations, mail them a money order for the first night's stay to the address above, zip 94102, but no reservations are possible for the dorm beds.

UNION SQUARE

FOUR SEASONS CLIFT, *495 Geary. 415-775-4700, 800-652-5438, fax 415-931-7417. Located near Taylor, it has 17 floors with 329 rooms. Singles are $225-$340, doubles are $225-$370 (depending on room type) and suites are $375-$1,050. The art-deco Redwood Room lounge is an elegant spot for a martini or High Tea. Special weekend and package rates are often available.*

A San Francisco landmark with a tradition to match its posh interior, the Clift has been an exclusive San Francisco Hotel since 1915, when it was the grande dame of its time. The rich pine paneling of the lobby reflects the light cast by French crystal chandeliers. A door man stands at the ready outside, classical music plays within, and the tone is set. The rooms are roomy and have some nice amenities. The desk is in its own little alcove, the exceedingly comfortable beds come with down pillows and duvets (unless you prefer otherwise), and the new TVs have videos on command. The bathroom comes with marble and robes, phone and hair dryer, and the decor is semi-Victorian. The deluxes are even roomier than the moderates, and have their own little sitting area, while the suites are very tasteful and exclusive. The suite bathrooms are something else, but glass unfortunately tops the tables and desks, casting a jarring note in an otherwise elegant setting.

The Clift's services are exemplary. What with personal butler service, same-day laundry and dry-cleaning, complimentary shoeshine, exercise room, and valet parking, they take care of their guests quite attentively. They even have a Young Travelers Program that includes all the baby-care items (bottles, diapers, baby bathtub, etc.) parents might need. There are babysitting services, Nintendo on the tube, board games like Monopoly and Junior Trivial Pursuit, Dr. Suess books, and videos like Lion King. The Clift accepts pets as well, and is one of few hotels with dog walking, vets on call, and litter boxes.

The rooms and services are nice, but the Clift is even better known for its Redwood Room. Built in 1933 out of a single 2,000 year-old redwood tree, the style is art deco at its most posh and romantic. It's been the watering hole of choice for San Francisco ladies and gentlemen for half a century, and its style and class still permeate the darkly atmospheric and glorious room. The martinis are notoriously fine, and there's still a cigar corner (and cigars are still sold at the bar), but there's a no-smoking section as well. Jazz starts at 7pm nightly, and while the drinks are no bargain here, that's not why one comes to the Clift. They also serve High Tea here in the afternoon, and it's one of the nicest settings in the city. In addition to the Redwood Room, the hotel's French Room is known for its original French crystal chandeliers and Louis XV decor and for its deluxe French cuisine. It's a fine place to go for a special celebration meal. See the *Where to Eat* chapter for more details.

THE CLIFT'S GHOST

The Spanish Suite way atop the 15th floor has some very stunning views, and it's not hard to comprehend why Robert Odell, the man who made the Clift the swankest hotel of its day, chose the suite as his living quarters. He came to a sticky end there, and for the past 20 years employees have claimed ghostly sightings. They say he's a bit playful at times, and is not a malevolent ghost.

THE GRAND HYATT, *345 Stockton. 415-398-1234, 800-233-1234, fax 415-391-1780. It is immense, and you can easily get lost among its 36 levels and meandering hallways, wandering down carpeted catwalks amid marble and objets d'art. There are 693 rooms and 24 suites, with rates from $225-$275 for standard and view rooms, while suites run $350-$850. There are weekend specials, however, for $169-$204, and a Romance Special for $219.*

The rooms are all pretty standard, what fluctuates is the view depending on how high up is your room. Full of browns, golds, and black, the rooms are adequate without being spectacular. The Hyatt really caters to business travelers, and there are a number of business club floors with exclusive privileges, comforts, and facilities. The Regency Club offers top floor rooms and suites with private lounge for an extra $35, or there's the Business Plan for a mere $15. There's a full fitness center and Club 36, way up top with jazz, cocktails, and splendid view.

WESTIN ST. FRANCIS, *335 Powell. 415-397-7000, 800-228-3000, fax 415-774-0124. It has 1,200 rooms in new and old wings. Singles are $185-$275, doubles are $185-$305, and suites are $225-$550, though specials as low as $99 are sometimes offered.*

Directly on Union Square, as it has been since 1904, the historic building has been welcoming the world's finest for nearly a century, while the newer tower makes up for its lack of history with a wealth of modern amenities, and better soundproofing between rooms. The Post Street entrance is the original one, its lobby is traditionally vast and marbled, and it has the Magneta Clock, a San Francisco rendezvous landmark for decades. The main building (the original one) has airy high ceilings, wide hallways, and lovely chandeliers.

The Standard rooms, originally built for accompanying servants, are still quite nice. Small but charming, they even have their own foyers. The Classics are larger, and the Deluxe face the square. The Tower is the new addition, and has one of those glassed-in elevators that show you the world as you ascend. The deluxe rooms are high up with great city and bay views, an attractive color scheme of burgundy and cream, marble desk, TV armoire, and all the amenities like hair dryer and iron. There are also business floors that cater to business needs.

A very nice feature to this hotel is their attitude towards children. Not only do children under 19 stay free in the parents' room, there's a Kids' Club as well. Children get age-specific gifts, and the welcome-pack includes a self-guided tour of the hotel and other activities and restaurants in the city that are specifically appealing to children. The hotel also has all the paraphernalia (cribs, high chairs, potty seats, etc.) that traveling families might need. The staff is very friendly, and is happy to help with whatever arrangements you may need. The hotel also boasts a number of dining and entertainment spots, such as the Compass Rose Room (serving lunch, High Tea, and evening dancing) and Club Oz, their nightclub, which are described more in the dining and nightlife chapters.

HOTEL NIKKO, *222 Mason. 415-394-1111, 800-645-5687, fax 415-421-0455. Located near O'Farrell, it has 522 rooms including 22 suites, and the rates run $195-$285 a single, $225-$305 a double, and $385-$1300 for the suites. There are weekend packages available that include parking and use of the Fitness Center (which is $11 a day, otherwise), and children under 18 staying in the room with the adults are free of charge.*

The lobby is sharp and sleek, with tall ferns, taller ceilings, and lots of marble and glass. It's much more likable and special than the Hilton, with exquisite flowers and impeccable service, and it's comfortable, too. The rooms, for the most part, are far less spectacular than the lobby. The Standard is aptly named. Despite the phone in the bathroom and mini-bar, the decor doesn't match the level set by the lobby.

The top three floors are the Nikko floors, and the Nikko rooms (at the upper range of the room tariffs) feature extra amenities like CD player, three phones, coffee maker, bathrobes, continental breakfasts, and incredible views, but the room decor is as drab as the Standard rooms below. The Tatami Suite ($975), on the other hand, is everything the lobby made you expect. The sitting room is lovely, and in the day time the tatami bedroom has a low-riding Japanese table with cushions; the futons aren't rolled out till night. The Japanese bathroom is wonderful, with a deep tub to soak in and a wood-floored scrub room to thoroughly cleanse yourself before immersion. The Nikko has a lot going for it, including its renowned Cafe 222 and atrium-style glass-enclosed pool, but it does Japanese design a lot better than it does American.

HOTEL MONACO, *501 Geary. 415-292-0100, 800-214-4220, fax 415-292-0111. Located near Taylor, it has 201 rooms and 34 suites. The rooms cost $170-$210, and the suites are $235-$395. Seven rooms are equipped especially for the disabled. They're right in the theater district, and have the Grand Cafe next door.*

Just opened in June 1995, this is a real gem. The faux-finish ochre and putty colors of the lobby evoke Monaco's sense of style, a Mediterranean presence, and a sense of humor as well. There's an enormous fireplace, and overhead hot air balloons frolic on the ceiling. The potted plants and ferns are on a grand scale, as is the bronze filigree staircase (a 1910 original) that rises from the lobby. Off the lobby is the living room, and it's stunning with its fireplace, magnificent paintings, comfy sofas and chairs, pillars and plants. By day it's a lovely room for reading and hanging-out, and at night there's complimentary wine for hotel guests.

The rooms are especially appealing and delightful, with pinstripe wallpaper, and great textures, fabrics, and style. The double-paned windows cut the outside noise to nil, the phones all have data ports, and the climate control lets you set the heat or air-conditioning, and check on the weather outside. The TV is gigantic, and it's equipped not just with cable and pay-per-view, but with Nintendo as well ($7.98 an hour). All the amenities are included, such as robes, hair dryer, bath phone, fridge, and mini-bar, but it's the extra touches of luxury and colorful fun that really make it. Then there is the luxury suite. It's a corner room very much like the others but with more toys like a VCR and CD player, a sitting area that is gorgeous, and a stunning bathroom with a huge six-foot jacuzzi and separate shower.

Downstairs is a modern gym, a little massage room, and the spa with its saunas, stylish decor, and ten-person jacuzzi hot tub. Adjacent to the hotel, their restaurant, the Grand Cafe, is worth a visit for the artwork alone (see the *Where To Eat* chapter for a full review). It's not traditional San Francisco like the Nob Hill grande dames, but the Monaco gives its modern interpretation of the San Francisco tradition of luxury and comfort in great style. You can only be charmed by a stay here.

CAMPTON PLACE, *340 Stockton. 415-781-5555, 800-235-4300, fax 415-955-5536. Located next to Anjou Restaurant, it has 126 rooms. A single is $170, a double is $220, king rooms range from $220-$330, and suites are $420-$960.*

Campton Place is a small deluxe independently run hotel. The lobby is nice and intimate, with cream walls, crystal chandeliers, flowers, very comfortable sofas, and classical music in the background. There are also mirrors on the ceiling if you want to see what you look like from on high. The innovative architecture of this hotel really stands out. Even the hallways are graceful and interesting, and the rooftop garden is very special. The rooms are swell, too. The Deluxe really is, with beautifully combined fabrics and colors, all impeccably maintained. The bathrooms sport terry robes, marble counters, and French milled soaps, and a phone - what more does one need? And the Superior rooms are very lovely as well. The rooms are cheerful but not loud, sunny but not hot. There is lots of original art throughout, oriental and otherwise, and quality details everywhere. The hotel also has the renowned Campton Place Restaurant, which provides room service to hotel guests.

HILTON, *333 O'Farrell. 415-771-1400, 800-445-8667. It has 1900 rooms costing $155-$235 a single and $155-$255 a double, depending on the elevation of your room.*

Taking up a whole city block and composed of three buildings, this monolith of a hotel is vast and impersonal. The lobby looks important, with crystal and marble and leather club chairs, but it feels like Grand Central Station with folks coming and going and rushing this way and that. The rooms are nice with some sense of style and all the amenities, and the bathrooms are full of mirror and marble. Upstairs is a health club and pool, and they have a few restaurants. It's probably a good choice for large business groups, but it's not very intimate for individual travelers.

PARC FIFTY FIVE HOTEL, *55 Cyril Magnin. 415-392-4734, 800-338-1338, fax 415-403-6602. It has 32 stories and 1,008 rooms and suites. The regular rooms cost $155-$195 (based on availability), Club rates are $275, the suites are $1,200, and packages are often available. The whole hotel is wheelchair accessible, but some rooms are specially outfitted to accommodate the handicapped, including strobe light alerts for the hearing-impaired.*

Now an addition to the Crowne Plaza collection of hotels, the Parc has lots of pluses and minuses. The lobby doesn't speak well of the hotel for all its marble and enormous mirrors; it's cavernous and scattered, and the reception desk is equipped with roped aisles to structure the hotel guest queues. The Parc has, however, just undergone a major renovation and face lift, and the rooms have benefited. The rooms are comfortable with a touch of class as well as conveniences like irons and boards. The desks are granite-topped, the bathrooms are large, marbled, and phone-equipped, and the look is light and airy. The Executive Club is very nice, combining comfort with a smashing view of the bridge, and some of the suites have decks. In addition to the restaurants and hotel pub, there is also a fully equipped health club with exercise rooms, sauna, and massage area.

PRESCOTT HOTEL, *545 Post. 415-563-0303, 800-283-7322, fax 415-563-6831. Located near Stockton, it has 7 floors and 165 rooms, half of which are Deluxe (their regular rooms) and the other half Club (the exclusive top floors). Deluxe are $185, Club are $215, suites are $235-$255 (Deluxe and Club), and the penthouse is $700. There is limo service to the financial district, valet service ($21 a day), and health club access at the Press Club next door for $12. But the biggest plus of all is Postrio, Wolfgang Puck's celebrated restaurant.*

The Prescott is a true marriage of old San Francisco (the winding staircase with its white banisters speaks of the building's 1917 beginnings) with today's sense of style and top-notch comfort. Off the lobby is the living room, a truly beautiful, warm, welcoming room with a giant of a brick fireplace and plenty of arm chairs and sofas, for reading and taking it easy during the day or wine and cheese in the evening.

The suite is state of the art, with two TVs and a VCR, a new fax, granite-topped desks and vanity, honor bar - the works. The bathrooms are huge and lovely, with jacuzzi tub, robes and hair dryer, and special shaving mirror. The decor of the Prescott rooms is neo-classical, à la Ralph Lauren, with lots of hunter greens, taupes, and deep burgundies and silk wall paper. You can tell that the hotel caters more to corporate travelers (who make up about 80% of the guests) than the leisure trade. The Deluxe room is just as fine as the suite. The bathroom is a tad less large, but the room is furnished in the same style with the same care.

The Club level is in another section completely, and to get there you stroll through a mahogany cat-walk that leads straight to the Club lounge, a perk that makes it worth the extra price. Continental breakfast is served here in the morning, and from 5-7pm Club guests are invited to a cocktail reception (full-bar) with hors d'houevres provided by Postrio. The lounge is everything you'd want it to be; it's smoke-free, with dark woods and green walls, sofas and arm chairs in which to relax, mingle, read, or snack.

One of the Prescott's main attractions, however, is their restaurant, Postrio. Prescott guests can get Postrio's finest delivered as room service, and enjoy some of the most exquisite cuisine in the state.

HOLIDAY INN AT UNION SQUARE, *480 Sutter. 415-398-8900, 800-243-1135, fax 415-989-8823. It has 400 rooms. Standard rates for singles are $175-$185, doubles are $190-$205, and suites are $195-$750, but large discounts exist depending on season and occupancy.*

The escalator isn't always on, but the elevator not only works but speaks to you as well. This is another Union Square skyscraper, and the closer you get to the 29th floor, the more fantastic the views become. The rooms don't vary, however, and what you get is a desk of dark wood, arm chair and bedspread of floral print, a TV, small bathroom, iron, and hair dryer.

GALLERIA PARK, *191 Sutter. 415-781-3060, 800-792-9639, fax 415-951-951-9611. Located near Kearny, it has 162 rooms and 15 suites. Singles and doubles are $170-$190, and suites are $215-$355, with weekends substantially less expensive.*

This building from 1911 has a pretty lobby in a unique bluish shade of green, its original skylight, and a warm, welcoming nouveau-sculpted fireplace. The rooms use real keys, they're attractive with a homey feel, and the windows are double-paned for added quiet. They all have plants, pay-per-view cable TV, mini bar, air-conditioning, phone with data port, and hair dryer, and the suites have a stereo as well. The hotel also has a small fitness room, and Perry's Downtown Grill, a friendly and very popular sports bar and lunch spot next door. There's complimentary morning coffee and evening wine, a rooftop garden and jogging track, and there is valet parking, $21 a day.

DONATELLO, *501 Post. 415-441-7100, 800-227-3184, fax 415-885-8842. Located on the corner at Mason, it has 94 available hotel rooms as well as 45 time-share properties. Their rooms are $155-$195, while the suites start at $250.*

The rooms have all just been renovated, so they're spanking new, elegant, and are very nice indeed. Good and spacious, they have marble-topped dressers, fine TV and phone, clock radio, a couple of arm chairs, and a little table with leather-encased ice bucket, glasses, sparkling water, and a jar of candies. The bathrooms are fully equipped with marble sink, hair dryer, phone, and plenty of toiletries. The lowest rooms have gorgeous patios with chairs and flowers, while the others make up for the lack with wonderful views (the suites on the highest floors have the best views). The south side rooms are quieter, while the street side is livelier - take your pick. The whole building is peaceful and well put together. The lobby is very pleasant, with a grand piano and classical music in the background. There's a fitness center with jacuzzi and sauna, a club lounge, and a wealth of tapestries, antiques, and original works of Starlie Sokol-Hohne's art. And it's just a block from Union Square, but well away from the hullabaloo.

SIR FRANCIS DRAKE, *450 Powell. 415-392-7755, 800-227-5480, fax 415-677-9341. It has 417 rooms. Singles and doubles are $139-$199 depending on bed type, junior suites run $189-$229, suites are $350-$650, and discounts are often available.*

Not to be confused with the Westin St. Francis, the 1928-built Drake is back to big and grand, vast arced mirrors, marble pillars, and crystal. Even the plants are big, and so are the colors. The Presidential Suite (named so, though no presidents have actually stayed there) has a lovely patio and is very big, but it's not in the same class as the Huntington or St. Francis. The regular rooms are pretty small, and under all the flash and swagger, the seams show and the furnishings look a little cheap by Nob Hill standards. It is, however, less expensive, and they do have doormen in fancy-dress uniforms, which one supposes can be a real plus.

RAMADA INN, *345 Taylor. 415-673-2332, 800-272-6232, fax 415-398-0733. Located between Ellis and O'Farrell, it has 120 rooms. Their rack rate is $150, but, special prices almost always apply, such as $89-$109 a room in winter and $95-$110 in summer, depending on bed size.*

For close to 80 years this was the Mark Twain Hotel, till they sold all to Ramada. The rooms now are pleasant enough, with private bath, safe, fridge, and coffee-maker, and muted florals cover the bedspread and chairs. The hotel has a rooftop sun deck, and parking is $15-$17 a day.

INN AT UNION SQUARE, *440 Post. 415-97-3510, 800-288-4364, fax 415-989-0529. Located near Stockton, it has six floors and 30 rooms, all no smoking. Singles and doubles are $130-$190, depending on room size and type, the suites are $180-$300, and the rate includes a large continental breakfast served in the lobby or your room.*

Owned by the same folks who operate the Washington Square Inn, this building goes back to 1916, when it first opened as a hotel. Unlike at the Amsterdam, the hallway books here are painted, but the Inn's other amenities are very real. The stand of umbrellas in the lobby is a fine example of thoughtful attention; the umbrellas (long, full ones, not the travel affairs that get inverted by every gust of wind) are there for your use in case inclement weather should strike during your visit. Each floor has its own sitting lobby with phone and fireplace, and the elegant hallways have sconces, white walls, and mirrors. The rooms are attractive and comfortable, all are different, with different charms, and the larger ones have full canopied bed and mini-lounge area. They are pleasant, and the brass lion knocker is a nice touch.

The bathrooms are fine, with hair dryer and robes, though a few have shower only. The suites are done very nicely. They're well-maintained with a slightly old-fashioned flair. The lobby is a comfortable place, with daily newspaper. In the afternoon there's a tea service, and in the evening they offer complimentary wine.

THE JULIANA, *590 Bush. 415-392-2540, 800-328-3880, fax 415-391-8447. Located at the corner of Stockton, just above the Stockton steps, it is a beautiful, warm, friendly hotel with 106 rooms and suites. Regular rooms cost $135-$155, family rooms are $155-$165, and the suites cost $165-$195, including coffee and tea in the lobby all day, and wine by the lobby fireplace in the late afternoon. The prices depend on availability, and there are usually a number of special promotional packages going on, like the Cupid's Cure Package for $149 that gives you a room plus chilled champagne, chocolates, and continental breakfast in bed.*

The lobby is full of warm colors, comfy sofas and chairs, and a rack of newspapers, both local and out-of-state. Beautiful fresh flowers are on each table and the fireplace is most appealing. The rooms are just as nice. The salmon tones are easy on the eye, the chairs are comfortable, and the amenities are up to date with cable TV and remote, pay-per-view, a mini-bar, ironing board and iron, air-conditioning and hairdryers, and the phones all have voice mail and modem jacks.

The Executive Suites are just right, with two phones and a room apart from the bedroom for small meetings or interviews, and the Family Rooms, with their master bedroom and small kid's room (each with phone and TV), are perfect for a couple traveling with a child. The hallways are pleasant, and show off the hotel's 1905 origins with classic wall sconces and soft light, there's a City Park Garage just a block up Bush that charges $15 a 24-hour day, and Physis (a nearby fitness club with lap pool) offers unlimited all-day privileges for $10 a day. The prices are moderate, the location is nicely set between Union Square and Nob Hill, the staff couldn't be friendlier, and the atmosphere of the whole place is warm and lovely.

HANDLERY UNION SQUARE, *351 Geary. 415-781-7800, 800-843-4343, fax 415-781-0269. Located between Powell and Mason, it has eight floors with 377 rooms. Singles are $120-$150, doubles are $130-$169, suites are $135-$320, and they have a small heated outdoor pool. The main building dates back to 1908, but the Club section was added in 1963, and this accounts for the different styles and prices in the two wings.*

The standard rooms in the main section are pretty and comfortable, with nice little bathrooms (some just have showers). All rooms have safes, air-conditioning, new TV with cable, remote, and Nintendo, plus coffee maker and make-up mirror. Pinks and blues are the hotel colors, in rooms and hallways alike. The Club section is different. For one, there's the pool (no life guard, however), and many of the rooms have little balconies overlooking it. These rooms are a little cozier with plusher fabrics and decor, and extra amenities like terry robes, electric shoe polishers, and vanity sections by the bathrooms. Along with the pool, the Handlery also has a sauna, valet parking, barber shop and baby-sitting services.

CARTWRIGHT, *425 Sutter. 415-421-2865, 800-227-3844, fax 415-983-6244. Located near Powell, it has 114 rooms. Singles are $120, doubles are $139-$149, morning coffee and afternoon tea included (and specials sometimes available). There are other perks as well, such as fresh flowers, terry robes, and plenty of antiques.*

Dignified and pleasant, the place was built in 1915, and it feels like it, in a very nice way. They have pretty little rooms, with little bathrooms and little desks, and big walk-in closets as per the era in which they were built. Along with the old-time feel, they also have all the useful modern items such as cable TV, clock radio, and phone. Old-world charm with modern amenities is their motto, and it fits. The antique furnishings lend distinction, and the library is very lovely and peaceful.

HOTEL REX, *562 Sutter. 415-433-4434, 800-433-4434, fax 415-433-3695. Lcoated between Powell and Mason, it has 96 rooms. Singles and doubles go from $115-$155, and suites are $225, with 10% off for seniors. There's morning coffee and newspapers in the lobby Monday-Friday, complimentary hors d'oeuvres and wine in the lobby Tuesday-Saturday, and guests can use Sheehan's pool and gym nearby for $4. They have fax and secretarial services as well.*

Their standards remain, but everything else has just undergone a major overhaul, and for the better (though it was pretty nice before). What was the Orchard for 10 years is now the Rex, an artistic and sophisticated boutique hotel. The lobby is attractive and opulent, with quiet jazz tunes, a beautiful burnt orange carpet with richly colored floral trim, a gas fireplace, bar and cocktail tables, fine writing desks, quality leather chairs and sofas, and a bookshelf full of good books.

The renovated rooms are reminiscent of Bloomsbury in the '20s and '30s, with stripes and patterns, wide-check fabrics, dark woods, restored period furnishings and glazed yellow walls. The hand-painted lamp shades are fantastic and retro, but the comforts are all modern, including TV, direct-dial phone (with data ports), and mini-bar. The bathrooms are painted in muted pastels, have hair dryers, and resonate with the new image, while the lofty ceilings reflect the hotel's 1904 origins. The suites are even nicer, with a beautiful parlor, one and a half baths, and the essential bidet. The Rex also has a useful, well-designed stack of destination cards, made of colored construction paper, opening out into mini-guides to jazz, wine, chocolate, experimental theater, books, and beer. All in all, an old favorite has become a very cool new place.

HOTEL TRITON, *342 Grant. 415-394-0500, 800-433-6611, fax 415-394-0555. Located near Bush just by the ornate entrance gate to Chinatown, it has 140 rooms (including 7 suites and 24 EcoRooms) for $105-$175 a room and $195-$285 a suite.*

This trendy, avante garde spot is not just another Union Square hotel. The lobby welcomes you to an alternative world of music (from hip-hop dance to jazz, depending on the hour), magnificently bizarre furniture, hand-crafted lamps, gold leaf columns, and a little fireplace in the corner. Then there are the rooms. Equipped with luxurious feather comforter, honor bar (with trademark rubber ducky, which no proper honor bar should be without), cable TV with remote, movies, and Nintendo, a vanity with hair dryer, and a closet complete with umbrella, iron and board, the rooms are flush with all the newest amenities but it's the decor that makes them special.

The colors and designs are snazzy, artsy, and unique. The walls are painted with interesting designs, the fabrics, lamps, and etceteras are all put together with a good eye and a light heart. Even the bathrooms, while small, are attractive with perky blue and white tiles. The EcoFloor is all this and more. On the EcoFloor, everything is recycled, energy efficient, biodegradable, and pure. The cotton is special organic cotton, the air is filtered and ionized, and the soap and shampoo (all hypoallergenic) is pumped from reusable dispensers that save on landfill. And the suites should be experienced as well. The Jerry Garcia Suite was designed by the man himself, including the fabrics, the walls, and the Jerry Garcia ties. The suites all have CD players and VCRs, and the bathrooms are big, lovely, and sport Triton terry robes.

The hallways are lined with intriguing black and white photos and hung on hand-painted walls. There is a little art gallery with changing exhibits of local artists, and there's a small and colorful fitness room as well. Cool staff sport pony-tails and black caps, and the guests are mostly a diverse and groovy crowd of Germans and French, artists and rock bands, the young and hip, and parents visiting their kids in the city. The Triton is not for everyone, but if you've an eye for design it's a fun place to stay.

DIVA, *440 Geary. 415-885-0200, 800-553-1900, 415-346-6613. Located between Mason and Taylor, it has 110 rooms. The room rates are $119-$139 and suites are $300, and include breakfast in your room along with the newspaper. Rates are often lower in winter, and other discounts sometimes apply.*

The rooms are contemporary and pleasant, with a few stylish touches. Full of artwork, the rooms are also supplied with all the electronic niceties like TV and remote, VCR and pay-per-view, and phones with modem jack. Few rooms actually front the street, however, and views are not part of the hotel's perks. Each floor has an apple room (a little sitting area with a big bowl of complimentary apples, you know - an apple room), there's a business center with fax machines, and they have a small but pleasant fitness room as well.

As popular with the corporate crowd as the L.A. designer clique, it's right across from the Geary Theater and not far from Union Square.

KENSINGTON PARK, *450 Post. 415-788-6400. Located between Powell and Stockton, it has 86 rooms. Singles and doubles are $115, with views of Nob Hill and Union Square from some corner rooms, and the royal suite is $350. Coffee and croissants are provided in the morning, as are tea, sherry and snacks in the afternoon.*

Snazzier, more elegant, and more interesting than the Inn next door, you feel it as soon as you walk in. Marble statues (one holding hammer and chisel, the other strumming a lyre) flank the entrance, colorful designs, beams, and mini-frescos decorate the towering ceiling, and velvety sofas, and a lacquered Oriental screen, marble floor, and an elaborate crystal chandelier round out the tone. It was built in 1923 as an Elks Lodge, which no doubt accounts for the gothic atmosphere and enigmatic designs, and the Elks still own the place, and congregate on the 3rd floor. The 2nd floor houses Theater on the Square, but the rest is dedicated to the hotel.

The rooms themselves are large and airy, the bathrooms are full of marble facing, brass fixtures, and modern amenities such as hair dryer and phone. Mahogany armoires (with modern TV) and desks (topped with green writer's lamp), Queen Anne style, and fine views of Union Square or Nob Hill add to the appeal. It's not a cozy sort of place, but the Kensington is unique and wonderful, cares deeply about their guests' comfort, and is a genuine Union Square bargain.

YORK, *940 Sutter. 415-885-6800, 800-808-9675, fax 415-885-2115. Located between Hyde and Leavenworth, it has 96 rooms. Singles are $106-$114, doubles are $112-$122, suites are $210, and they all come with continental breakfast and newspaper in the morning and some wine in the afternoon. Book a month ahead and you may get a discount.*

The York was built in 1922, which accounts for its high ceilings and sound architecture. Rooms are nicely appointed; they are comfortable and cheerful. Each room comes with a huge walk-in closet, safe and minibar, cable TV, voice mail and data port on the phone, and coffee maker, plus a separate mirrored vanity alcove. There's a nice but small fitness room downstairs, parking ($16 for valet, $14 on your own) and morning limo service to Fisherman's Wharf. In addition, they have the Plush Room, a cabaret-style entertainment venue next door, and hotel guests get 50% off the show. All in all, this is a pleasant and considerate place, a bit further from Union Square than most, but the only hotel that can truthfully claim that Hitchcock's *Vertigo* was filmed there.

CHANCELLOR, *433 Powell. 415-362-2004, 800-428-4748, fax 415-362-1403, email: chnclrhtl@aol.com. Located near Union Square, it has 137 rooms. Singles are $105, doubles are $125, and a suite costs $225.*

Across the street from the Sir Francis, the Chancellor has much less pomp and fuss. There are no flashy doormen, and no crystal, though above the elevator there are clocks from major cities around the world.

The rooms, pleasant enough but with small baths, are neither outstandingly good nor bad.

KING GEORGE, *334 Mason. 415-781-5050, 800-288-6005, fax 415-391-6976. Located between Geary and O'Farrell, it has 150 rooms. Officially, singles are $115 and doubles are $125, but discounts are usually in effect offering rooms for $79-$99.*

The friendly British lobby is airy and comfortable, and sets the tone just right for this engaging, warm hotel, and the desk staff are warm and helpful. The rooms are lovely - clean and pretty without being fancy. They sport Victorian patterns and charm, all mauve and cream; there's an old-fashioned flavor brought up-to-date with modern amenities like TV, phone, and closet safe. The King George has been in business since 1914, and it still retains an old San Franciscan aura, with hall sconces and antique desks. The hotel also does a High Tea in the afternoon, with different tea, crumpet, sandwich, and sweets options at reasonable rates.

HOTEL BEDFORD, *761 Post. 415-673-6040, 800-227-5642, fax 415-563-6739. Located near Leavenworth, it has 151 rooms and suites. Rooms cost $109-$129 depending on size and view, and the suites are $175. Children under 14 stay free (when with adults), and special rates are sometimes available for weekends or during the winter.*

Built in 1928, the lovely lobby is light and airy, with fresh white paint highlighting the elaborate carvings. A clanky, clunky elevator takes you to the rooms, and they're nicer than just adequate, but not very special. They do come with fridge and coffee maker, TV and VCR, and phone. The suite is appealing, though the furnishings aren't on a par with the grand lobby. They have all the same amenities as the regular room, plus an extra TV and VCR in the bedroom.

SAVOY HOTEL, *580 Geary. 415-441-2700, 800-227-4223, fax 415-441-2700 ext. 297. Located near Jones, it has 83 rooms and suites. The Superior and Deluxe rooms are $105-$125, while the suites run $185-$195.*

The Savoy is a pretty place with a lot of nice antique touches, especially the lamps. The rooms are fine if not spectacular, and the same goes for the white-tiled bath. The rooms come with French inn decor, down-filled mattresses, TV and remote, phone and minibar, and a bit of street noise. The hotel has Victorianesque wall paper and lights, a twisting stair case, and the Savoy Brasserie is attached. As an added plus for fans of blues dives, the Blue Lamp is just across the street.

RAPHAEL, *386 Geary Boulevard. 415-986-2000, 800-821-5343, fax 415-397-2447. Located between Powell and Mason, it has 152 rooms. Singles are $99-$129, doubles are $109-$139, and the suites are $160-$225, morning coffee included. There are plenty of specials and promotional rates, too.*

The pleasant little lobby is a nice respite from the Geary street noise, with artful touches in the Victorian chairs, antiques, and Italian oil painting. The rooms go from small and cute in the quiet back of the building to quite spacious with a couch (that folds out) and sitting area. Regardless of size, all rooms have lovely hand-painted doors, cable TV with remote and pay-per-view, vanity alcove and hair dryer, two phones per room, ice in every ice bucket, and evening turndown services. The staff is friendly, happy, and of good cheer, the rooms are well-priced for the charm, space, and amenities they provide. And check out the fascinating chandelier, above the little bookshelf of obscure but borrowable books off the lobby.

WARWICK REGIS, *490 Geary Boulevard. 415-928-7900, 800-827-3447, fax 415-441-8788. Lcoated near Taylor, it has 80 rooms. Singles are $95-$130, doubles are $105-$140, the suites range from $145-$205, and continental breakfast plus the morning newspaper are included.*

Built in 1913 and done up in the French boutique style with lots of antiques, canopies, and fireplaces, the rooms have very high beds, cable TV with the all-important remote (and pay-per-view as well), lacy curtains, and mirrored armoires. The windows are double-paned to cut the street noise, and the bathrooms have marble-topped vanities (some inside and some separate from the bathroom). There's an interesting little lobby with an unusual central sofa which defies description that they call the Pouf Chair. The olive velvet seats are back to back, and very comfortable as well as unique.

HOTEL UNION SQUARE, *114 Powell. 415-397-3000, 800-553-1900, fax 415-399-1874. Lcoated near Ellis, it has 131 rooms. Singles and doubles are $99, junior suites are $129, continental breakfast is included each morning as is afternoon coffee and tea.*

Location is this hotel's best and worst feature. It's right there on Powell Street by Union Square, but then again it's right there on Powell Street by Union Square. And if that's where you want to be, this is an attractive place with cheery rooms. The rooms vary a bit in size, some look out over the street, and the nicest have brick walls. It's not sparkling new, but it's a likable place.

SHANNON COURT, *550 Geary Boulevard. 415-775-5000, 800-821-0493, fax 415-928-6813. Located between Taylor and Jones, it has 177 rooms. Singles and doubles are $95- $120, and suites are $115-$275, including morning and afternoon coffee and tea (plus cookies) in the lobby.* The Deluxe room is nice and spacious, with a soft carpet, big mirror, cable TV, phone, and a bathroom with a noisy fan. Done in a Spanish art deco style in 1929, there is not, unfortunately, much style left anymore. It's well located - just next to Harolds International Newsstand and across from the Blue Lamp - but it's lacking a good reason to chose it above the rest.

CANTERBURY HOTEL, *750 Sutter. 415-474-6464, fax 415-474-5856. Located between Taylor and Jones, it has 250 rooms. Singles and doubles range* *between $95-$119, with suites for $99-$150, and great family plans. As many as three kids 18 and under stay free in parents' room, and there are senior discounts as well.*

This hotel, long a bastion of English tradition, is renovating for a warmer, more contemporary look. The fireplaces remain, but the suit of armor is off to the auctioneer, and the wing chairs have been replaced by comfortable new sofas and love seats. The rooms are bright and colorful, if not beautiful or special. The furnishings are not deluxe, but the rooms come with all the amenities (air-conditioning, coffee maker, cable TV with pay-per-view and remote control, small fridge, phone with voice mail), and the staff is friendly.

The Canterbury is also the site of Lehr's Greenhouse Restaurant, a plant and flower bestrewn San Francisco landmark that has received its own small face-lift. The beautiful glassed-in garden in back has been brought up-to-date, and the ivy-choked dining room has been pruned a bit for a roomier, more open look. Also new is the cigar room, which is all the rage among smokers, but glassed off from non-smokers. Up front they have a very pleasant new bistro ($6-$15), with huge windows, Mediterranean colors, and so many spirits in the bar they need a library ladder to reach them all. The Canterbury Hotel was built in 1928 and has been attending to San Francisco visitors for a long time, but remodeling and renovations add a welcome fresh touch.

MARINES MEMORIAL CLUB, *609 Sutter Street. 415-673-6604, 800-562-7463, fax 415-441-3649, and email: MarineClub@aol.com. Located near Mason, it has 137 rooms. Non-military guests can stay here for $95-$105 on weekdays and $100-$110 on weekends; there are major rate reductions for military personnel starting at $65 a single and $70 a double, but it depends on your duty status. There are also suites that range from $110-$195.*

The rooms are richly colored, simply decorated, and comfortable. Most are quite roomy (especially the deluxe corner rooms), and the staff is friendly. This place was established in 1946 as a memorial to Marines who died in the Pacific during World War II, and the non-profit club membership is open to members of all branches of the US military. They have a full pool and health club downstairs, and the Marine Memorial Theater just off the lobby is host to some of the best plays in San Francisco.

ANDREWS, *624 Post. 415-563-6877. Located near Taylor, it has 7 floors and 48 rooms with private bath. Rooms are $86-$109, and the suites are $119, including continental breakfast and an evening glass of wine.*

The hotel, built in 1905 before the great quake and fire, is clearly a warm, lovely, cozy place from the moment you step inside the lobby, whose English feel, grandfather clock, well-stocked bookshelves, and clubby chairs have a welcoming feel. The fully automated and restored original cage lift is one way to get to your rooms, the beautifully maintained stairway with its white banisters is another. But however you ascend, the rooms are extremely likable, pleasant, and homey. The beds sport iron head-railings (painted white), the curtains are lace, and the arm chairs are invitingly soft and comfortable, with old-fashioned floor lamps.

The modern amenities, however, have not been lost amid Victorian charm. There's a small TV with remote, a phone and clock radio, and the overhead chandelier is on a dimmer switch. The small bath is attractive, and the big walk-in closet has a full-length mirror. The suites are lovely, too. They are decorated in the same style, but have a sitting room as well, and a larger bathroom with a tub and separate shower. While the sofa doesn't turn into a bed, the hotel gladly provides rollaways or cribs for visiting families. The little breakfast delivered to your door each morning is very nice, and despite the street noise that filters in, this is a delightful place that gives a lot for its moderate rates.

ANDREWS HOTEL - A HISTORY

Back in 1905, construction began for the Sultan Turkish Baths, a gentleman's bath and relaxation establishment. It was a Class A structure, meaning a steel frame that was state-of-the-art for the time. It was a good move on the part of the architects, because some months later in 1906 the big quake struck the city. Though the fire that followed left its mark, the Baths frame was hardly damaged by the earthquake, and repairs didn't take long. The Sultan Baths, which finally opened in 1907, was a full service affair, with a tiled hot room, a rubbing room, a restaurant, bar, barber, and chiropodist. Bedrooms could be rented as well, and the place had a steamy reputation that didn't arise from the sauna.

In 1928, the Sultan Baths catered to its last gentleman, and a hotel opened in its place. During the next decades, 624 Post was an office building, a youth hostel, and a number of restaurants (including The China Doll, which had an aquarium spanning most of a wall). In 1981 Harry Andrews acquired the property, renovated it to its original Victorian splendor, and named it after his grandfather, under whose name it flourishes today.

BERESFORD ARMS, *701 Post. 415-673-2600, 800-533-6533, fax 474-0449, email: beresfordsfo@delphi.com. Located near Jones, it has 96 rooms. Singles are $89, doubles are $99, the Jacuzzi suites are $115-$150 (equipped with bidet and your choice of wet bar or kitchen), and there are senior and AARP discounts available. There's morning coffee and donuts in the lobby, and tea, wine, and snacks in the afternoon.*

The Arms was built in 1912 as a luxury apartment building (though it wasn't fully completed till 1922, due to the interruption of World War I), and original attention to detail and elegance is still evident today. The

lobby is full of crystal, and there's a grand, old-fashione
throughout. The rooms have mahogany headboards and arm
mirrors and high, Victorian ceilings. They also have TV wit ,
phone, and a small fridge. The suites are the same but more ɔo. The
bathrooms come with a jacuzzi tub and a bidet, the parlor has a Murphy
bed, and the kitchen is fully stocked. The Beresford, while not a luxury
hotel, still retains a touch of elegance. The crystal sparkles, and the Arms
echoes some of the best of old San Francisco.

    *HOTEL BERESFORD, 635 Sutter. 415-673-9900, 800-533-6533, fax
415-533-5349, email: beresfordsfo@delphi.com. Located near Mason, it has 112
rooms. Singles are $89, doubles are $99, (plus 10% discounts for seniors and
AAA), and a continental buffet breakfast is included.*

    Across the street from the Sheehan, the Beresford is a friendly, family-
run place. Built as a hotel in 1912, the small rooms, steam radiators, and
Victorian style wall paper combine to create a homey, Victorian feel, but
they have modern amenities too, and the small bathrooms have jacuzzi
tubs. It's a good mid-range choice, and has the big plus of The White
Horse Taverne next door.

    *HOTEL CALIFORNIAN, 405 Taylor. Tel 415-885-2500, 800-227-
3346, fax 415-673-5784. Located near O'Farrell, it has 17 floors and 250 rooms.
Singles are $85, doubles are $95, suites are $159, and children under 12 are free.*

    Built by the Glide family (of Glide Memorial Church fame) in 1927,
the Californian retains old-world charm and flavor. The lobby sets the
tone with its high ceilings, chandeliers, and pillars; it's very San Francisco.
The rooms are very cozy, all done up in an old style, reminiscent of a visit
to grandma's house. The pristine white chenille bedspreads are homey
and quaint, and the lamps, furniture, and decor all follow suit. The Queen
corner rooms are the nicest, thanks to their extra windows and light, so
you might want to ask for one when you reserve. Eleanor Roosevelt used
to stay here when the U.N. resided in the building across the street, and
Bing Crosby was another frequent guest, thanks to the radio station
nearby. Nowadays, however, most of the hotel's business comes from
Japanese and German travelers and groups.

    *COMMODORE, 825 Sutter. 415-923-6800, 800-338-6848, fax 415-923-
6804. Located near Leavenworth, it is one very hip ho They have six floors of 113
rooms that cost $69-$99 and suites for $109, with group and senior discounts
available. Their Titanic Cafe serves breakfasts and lunches in art deco diner
splendor, and the Red Room is the city's newest bar.*

    In an art deco class of its own, the lobby has the very distinctive flavor
of artsy San Francisco. The lobby is very artistic and funky - an architect's
dream – but the rooms vary. Those on the 5th and 6th floors, classified
deluxe, are in keeping with the lobby style. The design is sophisticated and
whimsical, they're comfortable, and come with cable TV, phone with data

port, and walk-in closet, while the bathrooms are simple and functional. The standard rooms on the other floors, while perfectly adequate, have standard decor and lack the panache. There is also a two-room suite (standard) with one large room (with bed and sitting area) and a small, child's alcove. And major artistic renovations have just been completed on the elevator, and local artists have been commissioned to decorate the rooms focusing on 113 different and little-known San Francisco gems (like the Exploratorium, the Castro Theater, and City Lights Books), with accompanying history.

In addition, the Commodore has just unveiled the Red Room Bar, a very artsy, very cool, very red place for a drink, and other services include a San Francisco Resource Library, and an "Insider's Daily Tip Sheet" they put out daily with all the off-beat happenings of the day.

UNION SQUARE PLAZA, *432 Geary. 415-776-7585, 800-841-3135, fax 415-776-4749. Located near Mason, it has 72 rooms, all with bath. Singles are $75, and each additional person is $10 extra, but there are big winter discounts, and other packages are often available.*

Built circa 1910, the hotel really isn't up to the elegant tradition promised by the crystal chandeliers and grand staircase. There's no real decor in the rooms beyond the colorful drapes and spread, and the TV and phone go back a few years. It's all clean if a bit scuffed, and you could stay here if you're on a budget and love Union Square and the theater district, but otherwise I wouldn't.

POWELL, *28 Cyril Magnin. 415-398-3200, 800-368-0700, fax 415-398-3654. Located near Powell, it has 140 rooms. Room rates are usually $75 a single and $85 a double, but in winter they can go as low as $59 and $69.*

The rooms are fine (some spacious and some less so), if not first class, with TVs and phones that function but are not brand new, carpet and paint a bit worn, mini sitting areas, and small but clean bathrooms. The lobby is peaceful, with a colonial look of trees and high wood ceilings. They are right near Market and the Powell cable car turn-around, which is a busy corner, both convenient and a bit hectic.

HOTEL DAVID, *474 Geary Boulevard. 415-771-1600, 800-524-1888, fax 415-931-5442. Located between Mason and Taylor, it has 50 rooms with bath. Singles are $69-$79, doubles are $89-$99, and they come with a full breakfast at David's Deli next door, as well as 15% off for other meals. There's also free transport from the airport with a two-night stay.*

How can you not like a room with a framed painting of a quizzical shoemaker holding a red boot above the red-spreaded bed? It's not deluxe, but it's clean and affordable, right in the middle of the theater district, and directly next to the best Jewish deli in the city, run by the same David of David's Hotel (more on David's Deli in the restaurant chapter). The rooms all have phone and cable TV, flowers you could hardly tell are fake, and a touch of luxury in the tiled bathrooms in the form of towel-racks providing towels perfectly heated for your drying pleasure. There's not much more to the rooms, but the Kali Weinerowska *Shoemaker* copies may be incentive enough, and your host, the sardonically affable David who built this enterprise 43 years ago, will be happy to provide the rest. He adds a great touch of personal reality in what can become an impersonal, anonymous city. Besides, the complimentary breakfasts combine quality and quantity for perhaps the best deal in town.

BREAKFAST AT DAVID'S DELI

Breakfast starts out with fresh fruit and fruit juices, followed by a full selection of eggs (including lox and scrambled eggs, franks and eggs, and pastrami omelet) and pancakes. They even serve matzobrei (a traditional and mouth-watering matzo and eggs concoction). Or you can go with French toast, potato pancakes, or their rightfully famous blintzes. David's kosher corned beef croquettes topped with poached eggs is yet one more fantastic, filling breakfast entree. There are tons of side orders from bagel to bacon to pickled herring, and sweet pastries as well. The breakfast rule is you eat what you want, and it's all on the house. Just don't forget to tip the waiters, and don't make yourself ill stuffing yourself with too much of a good thing.

THE AMSTERDAM, *749 Taylor. 415-673-3277, 800-637-3444, fax 415-673-0453. Located near Sutter, it is a small place with 34 rooms, all with private bath. Singles are $69-$79, doubles are $79-$89, deluxe rooms with jacuzzi are $89-$129, and continental breakfast is included.*

Built in 1909, the Amsterdam has a European air to it, with warmth, French Victorian antiques, and personal attention. The mini-library just inside the entrance welcomes you with its store of old books (yours to borrow while you visit), and the lobby is full of antiques like the beautiful lamps and the ancient radio.

A typical room has a four-poster bed, armchair and table - all authentic antiques and all in dark, dark Georgian wood. They are fully, modernly equipped, however, with cable TV, remote, phone, and radio. There are plants scattered about (some real and some fake), the windows are double-paned for quiet, and the lamps are brass. The bathrooms have just been remodeled with hair dryer and marble, and the rooms down-stairs have jacuzzi tubs. There's a fax on the premises for guest use, and the downstairs breakfast room, simple and homey, has a microwave and coffee maker. Outside is a terrace, open all day for a quiet, sunny place to read or talk. Some rooms have private decks, as well. With its combined charm, comfort, location, and price, this is one of the best deals in the city.

POWELL WEST, *111 Mason. 415-771-1200, 800-771-1200, fax 415-346-3196. Located near Eddy, it has 65 rooms. Singles are $69, doubles are $79, and senior citizens get a 10% discount.*

This hotel is changing hands, and the new manager has big plans in store. For now it's pretty standard, with a plastic shower curtain (light blue) and plastic cups by the plastic ice bucket. All the furniture is painted pink, with a few nicks here and there. However, new carpets, curtains, and wallpaper have just been installed, and further renovations are underway. It's conveniently near Market and Powell, but the street section is a bit seedy, and Chez Paree, the live nude girls theater half a block up, doesn't do much to add class or distinction.

FITZGERALD, *620 Post. 415-775-8100, 800-334-6835, fax 415-775-1278. Located near Taylor, it has 6 floors and 47 rooms, all with private bath. Singles are $59-$79, doubles are $69-$99, and suites are $95-$115, depending on the day of week, continental breakfast included. Summer rates are a bit higher, and rates can be negotiated for stays longer than 3 days. In addition, there's access to a large indoor heated pool and small gym nearby, and a pub. The weekends usually get filled up, so a reservation a week or so in advance is advised.*

A narrow little cage lift (you close the metal screen yourself) takes you up to some unimpressive rooms. The front ones are roomy and noisier than the back rooms, and somewhat spiffier than the nearby Dakota Hotel. They come with small, adequate baths, phone, old TV, pictures on the wall, and a better grade of carpet, but not what you'd call lovely. And the halls smell faintly of curry.

LOTUS, *580 O'Farrell. 415-885-8008, 800-827-7287, fax 415-885-8008. Located near Leavenworth, it has 70 rooms. Singles are $55-$78, and doubles are $65-$98, depending on whether the bath is private or shared.*

The building is 70 years old and could be lovely if it were cared for, but such is not the case. The elevator is scungy, and the rooms are uninspired and drab.

SHEEHAN, *620 Sutter. 415-775-6500, 800-848-1529, fax 415-775-3271. Located near Mason, it was once a YWCA but is now a hotel with 71 rooms. Rooms without baths are $45 a single and $55 a double; with baths, singles are $55-$75 and doubles are $70-$85, continental breakfast included. There are also larger family rooms as well.*

Built in 1917, the Sheehan's been a hotel for 8 years now, and attracts a lot of European and Australian guests. The rooms themselves are just okay. The furniture isn't exactly ragged, but neither does it sparkle. The economy rooms use the hall share facilities, but the rest have their own toilets and a tub or shower. They all have cable TV, and the larger rooms have large tiled baths to go with them. The big plus though, is in the basement. Hotel guests get to use the enormous heated (80°) pool and less-than-enormous fitness room down there, relics of the YWCA days.

Non-guests can use the facilities too, for a mere $4 a day or $45 for a 15-use pass.

ANSONIA-CAMBRIDGE, *711 Post Street. 415-673-2670, 800-221-6470, fax 415-673-9217. Located near Jones, it is a B&B with 123 rooms. Singles are $44-$56, doubles are $54-$69 (depending on bathroom arrangement), and suites are $27.50 per person (min. 3-4).*

The gum-ball dispenser on the reception desk seems like a good sign, and the guardsman chairs (old black leather with five foot tall backs) are distinctive. Unfortunately, they're the best things in the whole hotel. The rooms are depressing. The TVs and phones are old, the pictures on the wall of one room were half out of their frames, there's a lot of street noise, and all the doors creak.

Some rooms have private bathrooms, some are without, in which case you use the awful hall facilities. And some rooms are connected by a bath. This arrangement is called a share bath if you're strangers, and a suite if you're a group, but it's suite in name only, as the rooms are just as grody as anything else in this over-rated hotel.

BERESFORD MANOR, *860 Sutter. 415-673-3330, 800-533-6533, fax 415-474-0449. Located between Jones and Leavenworth, it has 89 rooms. Singles with shared bath are $45-$50, doubles are $55-$60, private baths are $60 and $70, respectively, and rates include breakfast and dinner Monday through Saturday and continental breakfast on Sundays. There are weekly rates as well, with $180 for shared facilities and $300 for private.*

The rooms are likable, not fancy and the paint's peeling on the radiator, but the curtains are lace, as well as nice old-fashioned touches like a sink in the room, and a big claw-foot tub in the bathroom. The building dates back to 1925, and was state of the art at the time. The Manor has the mandatory TV and phone along with the antique furnishings, and there are laundry facilities as well. The lounge is homey, and the wainscoted elevator is quite nice. The Manor tends to attract a student crowd, the desk staff is both friendly and helpful, and for the price, it's nicer than any place else near Union Square.

MARY ELIZABETH INN, *1040 Bush. 415-673-6768, fax 441-7451. Located near Jones. For women only, rooms are $45 a single and $60 a double, with weekly rates as well.*

Two meals a day are included, and they have a library and laundry on the premises.

DAKOTA HOTEL, *606 Post. 415-931-7475, fax 931-7486. Located near Taylor, it has 42 rooms that cost $45 a night and $190 a week.*

This is not a first-class hotel; it's not even second-class. But the building has some personality, the rooms aren't foul or disgusting, and the prices are pretty low. Some rooms are nicer, some a little tackier, but all have TV, comfortable bed and chairs, and private bath, but no phone.

There are stains and scratches on the wall and street noise, plus the original cage lift and Victorian winding stairs.

THE BERESFORD NAME

Lord Beresford was the younger son of the aristocratic Beresford family in England, but he was a bit of a black sheep, and didn't fit in with the family image. So, in 1895, the family dealt with him as families with black sheep did in those days; they put him on retainer and shipped him far away, in this case off to New Mexico. He became quite a guy there, went into cattle ranching (and is said to have started the cattle industry in Canada), and there are places named for him scattered about the country, such as the Lord Beresford Park in San Mateo. In 1905, however, there was a massive train wreck, and he was on it. After his death, some lurid details of his life surfaced. Apparently, he'd had TB and had been attended to by a mulatto nurse, one Lady Lu. That he'd been grateful to or fond of her was made clear by the number of properties Beresford left to her. Needless to say, the family back home was neither pleased nor amused, and they sailed over pretty damn quick to deal with the matter. The result saw Lady Lu settling for lifetime occupancy in a house in New Mexico, which is now a museum.

OLYMPIC, *140 Mason Street. 415-982-5010. Located near Ellis and across the street from the Powell West, the Olympic has 85 rooms that go for $30-$60 depending on single or double occupancy and bathroom status.*

The Olympic is centrally located in that it's near both Market Street and Union Square, but it's not worth it. The front desk is extraordinarily disorganized. A simple request for a brochure set off a flurry of searching behavior, with no positive result. The lobby is upstairs, beneath five tiers of rooms and a sky-light. It's most unfortunate. The chairs are plastic and gross, the carpet's a garish red, and the signs of neglect are everywhere, from the plain, bare rooms on up. It's a shame because this old San Francisco structure could really shine if someone were to devote a lot of money and TLC.

GEARY, *610 Geary Boulevard. 415-673-9221, 800-227-3352, fax 928-2434. Located between Jones and Leavenworth, it has 120 rooms. Singles are $36; doubles are $45, triples and quads are available, and there are occasional winter discounts as well.*

The hotel is run by the Dharma Realm Buddhist Association, and the Chun Kang vegetarian restaurant, affiliated with the same group, is next door. Renovations are going on bit by bit from the top floor down, but even the renovated rooms are not exactly swank. Old blue vinyl curtains cut the window light, the spread is generic hotel ugly, and the chairs (one orange weave and one of red vinyl) really add that extra touch. The elevator gets stuck sometimes which can be unnerving, and the smell of incense (loved by some and loathed by others) permeates throughout. The Six Guidelines of the hotel (No fighting, No greed, No seeking, No selfishness, No self-benefiting, No lying) are fine guidelines to have, but other than that, the hotel doesn't really have much to recommend itself unless you are interested in the Buddhist facet.

ADELAIDE INN, *5 Isadora Duncan Lane. 415-441-2261, fax 415-441-0161. It has 16 rooms and is at the end of the small alley off Taylor between Post and Geary. Singles are $32-$38 and doubles are $42-$48, and continental breakfast is included.*

The inn has an old, homey, budget feel, and the rooms are small (with a sink, mirror, couple of pictures, a dresser, a tiny TV, and no phone). Beloved by many, especially by visiting Europeans who sense a kindred spirit, the Adelaide tends to fill up quickly.

PACIFIC BAY INN, *520 Jones Street. 415-673-0224. Located near O'Farrell, it has 84 rooms, all with bath. A single is $199 a week, a double is $225-$299 (depending on bed types and whether the room has a microwave), and there are no daily rates.*

Just next door to some good budget restaurants (Dottie's True Blue Cafe and Shalimar), and on the cusp between Union Square and the Tenderloin, the Pacific Bay Inn is neither awful nor deluxe. The bedspreads are cheap and flowery, the smell is of roach spray, but the paint looks clean and relatively fresh. The rooms come with phone and TV, toilet and shower, but the street noise comes through. Look elsewhere.

ALEXANDER INN, *415 O' Farrell. 415-928-6800, 800-843-8709, fax 415-928-3354. Located near Taylor, it has 62 rooms. Rooms with shared bath are $28-$35 and those with private facilities are $64-$72, continental breakfast included.*

Built circa 1930s, the Alexander rooms are plain with a touch of the pleasant. They're all equipped with coffee makers, safes, phones, and TV, the bathrooms have cheerful yellow tiles, and the curtains are pink. Some carpets are stained, however. Popular with families, budget travelers (there are suite and triple arrangements that can accommodate 3-4 people), and Trek America groups, there's a vending machine room with a microwave, and a laundry room with coin-operated washer and dryer as well.

STRATFORD, *242 Powell. 415-788-3207. Located near Geary, it has 105 rooms, all with TV. Singles or doubles without baths cost $24.95 and with bath they go for $34.95, with 12% off for students.*

This hotel is cheap, in all senses of the word. A room with bath also has a horrid carpet, chintzy dresser, worn chairs, tired bed, insect spray smell, and intense street noise. The red plastic ashtray is a nice touch. Only the best for Stratford guests.

THE SWEDEN HOUSE HOTEL, *570 O'Farrell. 415-885-9773. Basically residential, the rates are $85-$95 a week, and none of the 30 rooms have private baths.*
The rooms are quite basic. The shag carpet is awful though the room itself is clean. There's a sink and bureau, a closet, and you can rent a TV. This is only for those on the strictest budgets who want to stay a while.
DOWNTOWN (UNION SQUARE) HOSTEL, *312 Mason. 415-788-5604. Located near Geary, it charges $14-$16 for members, $17-$19 for non-members, on a first come first served basis. There are 150 beds, with 2-6 beds a room, no curfew, and the reception's open 24-hours a day. They provide a communal kitchen and TV room, and are right by Union Square.*
There are no rooms with private bath, and all the rooms are very, very basic. They do have a kitchen, free nightly movies, and free bag storage at check-in, and they take credit cards. For more charm and better conveniences, however, I'd go to the Green Tortoise in North Beach.

WESTERN ADDITION, JAPANTOWN, & THE FILLMORE

THE ARCHBISHOP'S MANSION, *1000 Fulton. 415-563-7872, 800-543-5820, fax 415-885-3193. Located near Steiner on Alamo Square, it is an historic landmark, a restored 1904 home with 15 rooms. The rooms, each named after an opera, are $129-$189 and suites are $215-$385, depending on the floor, size, amenities, and time of week. Continental breakfast is included and is served in your room in the morning, and there's wine in the afternoon in the parlor.*
Wow. This place is amazing from the moment you enter the grand portals, and it just gets better from there. The Parlor is ever so elegant, in a cream-hued, peachy, French aristocratic way. The grand crystal chandelier sparkles, and long, heavy drapes swathe the windows. Classical music swells in the background, glorious redwood pillars soar, and French antiques (such as were popular in the early 1900s) everywhere keep the magic alive. There is also an enormous mirror by the grand staircase, so beware your image as you begin your morning descent.
The Don Giovanni Suite is the top of the line, and it's exceptional. The ornately carved, canopied, four-poster bed stands on carved claw feet, and the bathroom is fully equipped with terry robes and the essential rubber ducky. And for your convenience, the shower stall and bath get separate rooms. The living room is decorated impressively too, though in a grand rather than a cozy fashion, with a massive fireplace and sensational views.
The Carmen is a suite like no other. The bedroom is beautiful, with white lacy spread, fireplace, and feather-stuffed sofa. The attached room, nearly as large, is more like an unusual parlor than a bathroom. At its center is an elegant, claw-footed tub, with a more modest glassed-in shower off to

the side, and the commode is daintily hidden behind an ornate silk screen. Popular with honeymooners and anniversary celebrants, the staff will happily set up a silver ice bucket with champagne to perch next to the sumptuous tub.

At the opposite end of the price spectrum is La Bohème room, smaller, quainter, and cozier, with French antiques and a large, luxurious bath (but no robes). All the rooms come with private phone lines, TVs are available on request, the staff people are genuinely friendly and very helpful, and unlike many of the other grand mansion hotels, the Archbishop actually has a working elevator.

RADISSON MIYAKO HOTEL, *1625 Post. 415-922-3200, 800-333-3333, fax 415-921-0417. Located between Webster and Laguna in Japan Center, it has 218 rooms. Singles cost $139-$179, doubles are $159-$199, and the suites go for $279-$299, with full breakfasts included, and no cost levied on children 12 and under who stay in their parents' room.*

The hotel blends east and west, Japanese and American, and it works well. The exterior of the hotel is traditional Japanese, with intricate roof lines, wide overhangs, and Koi fish ponds, and the landscaped garden out back beautifully represents Japan's heritage as well. The interior combines Japanese design with contemporary American for a spare, streamlined look, and six million dollars worth of Japanese antique art adds to the style. Some of the rooms have western-style furnishings, with thick carpets, conventional beds, and bentwood chairs, while the hand-painted, lacquered *fusuma* screens add an Asian touch. The bathroom also caters to both cultures, with Japanese style sunken tubs and wash-up taps and buckets, but providing shower stalls as well.

The Garden Wing, however, offers the full Japanese treatment, with *tatami* mats on the floors, sleeping futons with down comforters, and *shoji* screens that open to reveal lovely rock gardens. The Japanese suites are even more sensational, with marbled *o-furo* bath, shrine garden, redwood saunas, and low tables. There are also Club floors that more fully attend to business travelers, and executive suites that take Japanese comfort and beauty to yet a higher level.

All the rooms come with phones, cable TV, and minibar, as do most hotels, but they also make shiatsu massage room-visits as well. Right next to the Kabuki movie theater, they get packed out during the Asian Film Festival every spring and the International Film Festival held every May. They also have an exercise room downstairs, and a highly rated restaurant (see Yoyo Tsumami Bistro) that continues their East/West blend.

MAJESTIC HOTEL, *1500 Sutter. 415-441-1100, 800-869-8966, fax 415-673-7331. Located near Gough, it is just down the street from the Queen Anne, and has five stories with 51 rooms and suites. Room rates run $125-$160; suites are $250; and all include morning newspaper and afternoon sherry.*

The name says it all, or most of it, anyway. The lobby greets you with amazing chandeliers, velvety down-filled sofas, French and English antiques, and long, silk-tasseled brocade drapes, oozing sumptuous grandeur as it did in 1902 when the Majestic first was built. The rooms are all different, but all are done up to reflect their Edwardian beginnings, with tall, imposing beds and nice turn-of-the-century touches in the bathroom, plus modern conveniences like cable TV, hair dryer, terry robes, and phone. Some of the more deluxe rooms have a fireplace, claw-foot tub, and fridge as well, and the suites are just afloat with marble, antiques, and the good life.

ALAMO SQUARE INN, *719 Scott. 415-922-2055, 800-345-9888, fax 415-931-1304. Located near Fulton, it has 12 rooms, no smoking and all with private bath, in two attached, restored 1890s Victorian mansions. Rooms are $85-$135, depending on the size and amenities of the room, while suites run $125-$275. A full American breakfast in included, as is free parking, but there is no elevator. All rooms have phones, but only the suites have TVs.*

The Alamo Square Inn is composed of two differently styled but equally beautiful mansions, one a grand 1895 Queen Anne and the other a cozier 1896 Tudor Revival. They're connected by later additions such as the glorious solarium, and all facilities are easily accessible no matter in which room you stay. The Queen Anne has been restored and furnished to reflect the splendor of its day, with the Parlor Room and Drawing Room (where afternoon wine is served) set up on its gorgeous wood floor in Victorian elegance, and decorated in sumptuous reds and peacock designs. The rooms are exceedingly lovely, bright, and beautiful with lots of authentic period details like wainscoting on the walls, and those terrific reading lamps with the dangling fringe. The suite is also beautiful, but far more contemporary and open. The bath has a sunken jacuzzi, and the art deco living room has a TV and stereo, while other suites have kitchenettes or small sun decks, too.

The solarium is lovely, full of flagstones, healthy, thriving plants, and the occasional smoker (as this is the only room where that activity is allowed), and it connects the Queen Anne to the second building. Walk in the Tudor and the feeling is very different. The redwood paneling and lower ceilings provide a sense of warmth and family, while the built-in window seats make you want to trash your sight-seeing plans and hunker down for the day. The rooms are pretty, and while the color schemes change from room to room, the satin spreads and curtains, double-paned windows to keep out the street noise, and oriental carpets are standard throughout. The bathrooms are charming as well, and though most come with a shower stall instead of a bath, you can request one that has a bath if that's a concern. There's an enormous fireplace, oriental carpets everywhere, and a pretty garden out back.

CHATEAU TIVOLI, *1057 Steiner. 415-776-5462, 800-228-1647, fax 415-776-0505. Located near Golden Gate, it has 7 rooms in this renovated 1892 mansion. Those with shared bath are $80 Sunday-Thursday and $100 Friday-Saturday, rooms with private bath are $100 mid-week and $125 on weekends, and the elaborate suites with parlor and jacuzzi are $160 and $200. The rooms are all named after famous period personalities (Isadora Duncan, Jack London, etc.) and are filled to the brim with antiques. All rooms come with phones, and an extended continental breakfast with quiche and yogurt as well as the muffins and fruit.*

Once you get past the heavy, locked front gate and make your grand entrance, you're inundated with the Tivoli experience. The foyer is filled with flowers and their scent, and the parlor is replete with sofas and chairs and knickknacks and pictures and statues and lamps, and a piano to boot. It's fascinating, with tons to look at and discover, but it's not very restful or soothing.

TIVOLI HISTORY

The history of the mansion is pretty interesting. It was built by the renowned architect William Armitage in 1892 for the Oregon lumber baron Daniel B. Jackson, together with three adjoining apartments to the west, and Jackson and his wife lived there in what was then known as the "Seattle Block" till 1898. The second owner was Mrs. Ernestine Kreling, widow of not one but two Kreling brothers, and operating owner of the famous Tivoli Opera House. She lived in this Alamo Square chateau till 1917, when the site was taken over by various Jewish organizations housing orphaned girls and the Yiddish Cultural Center. It was run by Yiddish intelligentsia who fled Russia following the 1917 revolution, and they started up a Yiddish Literary and Dramatic Society plus a Yiddish school, staying in this mansion for 31 years.

The building served as a rooming house from 1961 to 1975, at which time Jack Painter, Ph.D., purchased and renovated it into a center for the New Age Movement in psychology, and called it the Center for Release and Integration. The house was filled with lotus flower murals, Tibetan bells, a hot tub full of nude students, and Pelvic Release classes, culminating in a watery live birth that was filmed for educational TV. The current owners took over in 1985, set about restoring the mansion to its former Victorian townhouse splendor, re-dedicated the house to the promotion of art and music, and reopened as a luxury bed & breakfast.

Upstairs, the doors are massive and the rooms are decorated on the same opulent scale. There are huge four-poster beds, vibrant stuffed peacocks, pictures and beautiful lamp shades and all that is colorful and Victorian. The suites are lush and plush and heady, with a boggling array of sofas and chairs (seven in all), plus a four-poster canopied bed so high you really need to climb up into it, and a marble bath. And if you ascend up the winding stairs to the very top floor (there's no elevator), you'll see the stained glass sky lights, and the beautiful shared bathrooms with the claw-foot tub under the magnificently mounted swordfish. The staff here is a bit fussy, and there are lots of rules regarding charges for extra beds, lost keys, etc. This is a fascinating place, and if it's too busy for your hotel tastes, it's well worth trying for a guided tour.

METRO, *319 Divisadero. 415-861-1271, fax 415-863-1970. Located between Oak and Page, it has 25 rooms, all with private shower, cable TV, and phone. Rooms cost $50-$60, suites are $74-$94, and there's free over-night parking.*

The Metro rooms are smallish but cute, undecorated but clean, and with a home-like feel. The plywood doors don't do much to add appeal, but lots of plants spruce up the hallways. They attract an eclectic clientele, with gays, international tourists, and parents visiting their adult kids equally represented. For the price, it's not a bad deal.

B&B REFERRALS

American Family Inn Bed & Breakfast San Francisco, *PO Box 42009, San Francisco, CA 94142. 415-497-1913.* They reserve B&Bs in private homes from basic to deluxe for $55-$155, depending.

Bed & Breakfast International, *PO Box 28291, San Francisco, CA 94128. 415-696-1690.* They reserve private rooms in the Bay Area as well as other parts of the US. Rooms start at $55 and go up to $100 or more.

HOME EXCHANGE

International Home Exchange Association, *41 Sutter St., Suite 1090, San Francisco, CA 94104. 415-673-0347, 800-788-2489.* They can provide more information. In addition you can list your home in a number of directories, and for a price can purchase them and scan other listings.

Homelink International, *Box 650, Key West, FL 33041. 800-638-3841.* Has four annual directories and thousands of domestic and foreign listings. Membership is $50.

Intervac International, *Box 590504, San Francisco, CA 94159. 415-435-3497.* Has three annual directories and membership is $62.

Loan-a-Home, *2 Park Lane, Apt. 6E, Mount Vernon, NY 10552. 914-664-7640.* Deals with long-term exchanges, and a directory that costs $35.

HOTELS BY DOLLAR CATEGORY

For your convenience, hotels are listed below by price, starting with luxury and working through to hostels. Within each category, the hotels are listed alphabetically by neighborhood.

The dollar signs translate to:

$$$$ (more than $160 a double)
$$$ ($100-$160 a double)
$$ ($50-$99 a double)
$ (less than $50 a double)

$$$$
Anna's Three Bears, Castro
Dolores Park (suite), Castro
Griffon, Downtown
Harbor Court, Downtown
Hyatt Regency, Downtown
Mandarin Oriental, Downtown
Sheraton Palace, Downtown
Hyatt Fisherman's Wharf, Fisherman's Wharf
Ramada Inn, Fisherman's Wharf
Fairmont Hotel and Tower, Nob Hill
Huntington Hotel, Nob Hill
Mark Hopkins Inter-Continental, Nob Hill
Ritz-Carlton San Francisco, Nob Hill
Stouffer Stanford Court Hotel, Nob Hill
Sherman House, Pacific Heights
Hotel Sofitel-San Francisco, SFO Airport
Westin Hotel, SFO Airport
Campton Place, Union Square
— **Donatello**, Union Square
Four Seasons Clift, Union Square
Galleria Park, Union Square
Grand Hyatt, Union Square
Hilton, Union Square
Holiday Inn, Union Square
Hotel Monaco, Union Square
Hotel Nikko, Union Square
Parc Fifty Five Hotel, Union Square
Prescott, Union Square
Westin St. Francis, Union Square
The Archbishop's Mansion (suites), Western Addition
Chateau Tivoli (suites), Western Addition

$$$
Inn On Castro, Castro
➤ **The Villa**, Castro
Albion House, Civic Center
Cathedral Hill Hotel, Civic Center
Inn at the Opera, Civic Center
Richelieu, Civic Center
Marriott, Downtown
Holiday Inn, Fisherman's Wharf
San Francisco Marriott, Fisherman's Wharf
Travelodge at the Wharf, Fisherman's Wharf
Tuscan Inn, Fisherman's Wharf
Wharf Inn, Fisherman's Wharf
Bed & Breakfast Inn, Marina
La Petite Auberge, Nob Hill
Nob Hill Inn, Nob Hill
Nob Hill Lambourne, Nob Hill
Vintage Court, Nob Hill
White Swan, Nob Hill
Hotel Bohème, North Beach
Washington Square Inn (with bath), North Beach
Jackson Court, Pacific Heights
The Queen Anne, Pacific Heights
The Mansions, Pacific Heights
Airport Marriott, SFO Airport
Clarion, SFO Airport
Embassy Suites, SFO Airport
San Francisco Airport Hilton, SFO Airport
Canterbury Hotel, Union Square
Cartwright, Union Square
Chancellor, Union Square
Diva, Union Square
Holiday Inn, Union Square
Hotel Rex, Union Square
Inn at Union Square, Union Square
➤ **Juliana**, Union Square
Kensington Park, Union Square
King George, Union Square
Marines Memorial Club, Union Square
Prescott Hotel, Union Square
Ramada Inn, Union Square
Raphael, Union Square
Savoy, Union Square

Shannon Court, Union Square
Sir Francis Drake, Union Square
Triton, Union Square
Warwick Regis, Union Square
York, Union Square
Alamo Square Inn, Western Addition
The Archbishop's Mansion, Western Addition
Chateau Tivoli, Western Addition
Majestic Hotel, Western Addition
Miyako Hotel, Western Addition

$$
Black Stallion, Castro
Dolores Park, Castro
Pensione San Francisco, Castro
Twenty Four Henry, Castro
Willows Inn, Castro
Abigail, Civic Center
Days Inn, Civic Center
San Remo, Fisherman's Wharf
Carl Hotel, Haight Ashbury
Carl Street Unicorn House, Haight Ashbury
Red Victorian Inn, Haight Ashbury
Stanyan Park, Haight Ashbury
Art Center, Marina
Coventry Motor Inn, Marina
Cow Hollow Motor Inn, Marina
Days Inn, Marina
Edward II, Marina
Marina Inn, Marina
Plantation Inn, Marina
Van Ness Motel, Marina
Cornell, Nob Hill
Golden Gate, Nob Hill
San Francisco Residence Club, Nob Hill
Washington Square Inn (without bath), North Beach
Laurel Motor Inn, Pacific Heights
Monte Cristo, Pacific Heights
Pacific Heights Inn, Pacific Heights
Casa Arguello, Richmond
La Quinta, SFO Airport
Red Roof Inn, SFO Airport
Mosser's Victorian, SoMa

Bock's, Sunset
The Phoenix, Tenderloin
Alexander Inn (with bath), Union Square
The Amsterdam, Union Square
Andrews, Union Square
Ansonia-Cambridge, Union Square
Beresford, Union Square
Beresford Arms, Union Square
Beresford Manor, Union Square
Californian, Union Square
− **Commodore Hotel**, Union Square
Fitzgerald, Union Square
Handlery Union Square, Union Square
Hotel David, Union Square
Lotus, Union Square
Mary Elizabeth Inn, Union Square
Powell, Union Square
Powell West, Union Square
Sheehan, Union Square
Union Square, Union Square
Union Square Plaza, Union Square
Metro, Western Addition

$

YMCA Chinatown, Chinatown
Grant Plaza, Chinatown
Aida, Downtown
European Guest House, Downtown
Globe Hostel, Downtown
International Student Center, Downtown
Temple, Downtown
San Francisco International Youth Hostel, Marina
San Francisco Motor Inn, Marina
Grant, Nob Hill
The Basque Hotel, North Beach
Europa, North Beach
Green Tortoise Hostel, North Beach
− **Leland Hotel**, Polk Gulch
Hill Point Guest Houses, Sunset
Moffat House, Sunset
Albergo-Verona, Tenderloin
Embassy, Tenderloin
James Court, Tenderloin

YMCA Central Branch, Tenderloin
Adelaide Inn, Union Square
Alexander Inn (without bath), Union Square
Dakota Hotel, Union Square
Downtown Hostel , Union Square
Geary, Union Square
Olympic, Union Square
Pacific Bay Inn, Union Square
Stratford, Union Square

13. WHERE TO EAT

In this chapter, the neighborhoods are arranged alphabetically, and within each neighborhood the restaurants are listed from splurge (more than $20 an entree) to expensive ($15-$20 an entree) to moderate ($8 to $15 per entree) to inexpensive (less than $8 for most entrees) – *and all restaurants accept major credit cards unless otherwise noted.*

Within the price categories, the restaurants are listed alphabetically by cuisine as follows: Afghani, African, American, Asian, Cajun, Caribbean, Chinese, Filipino, German, Irish, International, Italian, Japanese, Jewish, Mediterranean, Mexican, Middle Eastern, Nouvelle California Cuisine, Sandwiches and Salads and Picnic Supplies, Seafood, Singaporean, Spanish Tapas, Thai, Tibetan, Vegetarian, and Vietnamese.

CASTRO

MODERATE

American

THE PATIO CAFE, *531 Castro. 415-621-4640. Located near 18th, the Patio Cafe has been drawing crowds to their unusual dining room for over 20 years. They're open Monday-Saturday 8am-10:30pm and Sunday 8:30am-10:30pm, and they serve a mix of American and international cuisines.*

What's special is the dining room. It's a patio setting on a big, sprawling wood deck, with tiffany style lamps and hanging plants everywhere. Covered by sky lights that give natural lighting year round, they have heating fixtures as well that allow you to enjoy the outdoor feel even on the chilliest of days. They do some fancy drinks that mean business at their indoor bar, and serve breakfast, lunch, and dinner in the back. Breakfasts ($3.50-$8) include all your usual egg-pancake-French toast options, as well as biscuits and gravy, corned beef hash, and cheese blintzes. Lunch type dishes are available morning and afternoon, too, for $5-$9. They have hamburgers, vegi-burgers, and turkey burgers, variously flavored grilled chicken sandwiches, a meatloaf plate, and a good selection of salads and pastas. It's a very casual atmosphere, comfortable for a quick meal or hanging out for a while with friends.

Italian

THE SAUSAGE FACTORY, *517 Castro. 415-626-1250. Located just down the street from the Patio, this is an Italian restaurant and pizzeria that is open daily from 11:30am-1am.* The interior is beautiful, in a woody, dim, cozy way. Warm and amiable, there are colored glass lamps and red vinyl booths, big glass windows if you want to be seen, and private nooks if you don't, and great big platters of good food on every table for $6-$13. Sandwiches (Italian sausage, meatball, hamburger, and more) all come with spaghetti, pizzas come with the usual round-up of toppings, there are big plates of spaghetti, ravioli, and lasagna dishes, plus the more expensive specials like saltimbocca, veal scaloppini, and chicken cacciatore. Whatever you get, the warm atmosphere remains the same, and you won't leave hungry.

CAFFE LUNA PIENA, *558 Castro. 415-621-2566. Located near 18th, Caffe Luna Piena is a fairly new and well-liked cafe. They're open for lunch Monday-Friday 11am-3pm, for brunch Saturday-Sunday 9am-3pm, and dinner Tuesday-Sunday 5:30-10:30pm.*

Inside they have nice wood, fine artwork, and an open grill, plus a beautiful deck in back with plenty of tables, open to the sun or sheltered, as you prefer. Gary Chen's Italian dishes ($6-$10.50 during lunch and $9-$15 for dinner) include foccacia sandwiches, grilled pork chop with mashed potato, spinach, and mustard sauce, and penne pasta with red chard, tomatoes, and house-made sausage. They also do brunch, offering eggs (with roasted potatoes and biscuits), frittatas, smoked salmon with polenta and poached eggs, buttermilk waffles with apple currant compote, and more.

Mexican

LETICIA'S, *2247 Market. 415-621-0441. Located near Sanchez, Leticia's is open Sunday-Thursday 11am-11pm and Friday-Saturday 11am-midnight, with happy hour 3-5:30pm. The interior is a big wide open dining room with a Roman cellar motif.*

The walls look like they're carved out of vault stone, and Roman statues cavort in back, but the food is all Mexican. Main dishes ($7.25-$11) cover the usual enchiladas, flautas, chimichangas, tostadas, and burrito, but the experience is much more atmospheric than your average taco stand, and the food is all of the best quality. They also do steaks and burgers for a change of pace, and they have a lunch-time special for $5.25.

Spanish Tapas

PACHÁ, *544 Castro. 415-431-7622. Located next to Luna Piena, tapas are served Sunday-Thursday 11am-10pm and Friday-Saturday 11am-11pm, and accepts no credit cards.*

It's artistic and colorful inside, with red brick floors, blue walls, great art, and wonderful lanterns, plus fine Andalusion music pouring out the speakers. Outside is a lovely patio of brick and wood and greenery, with colorful placemats and bizarre yet comfortable artsy chairs. This is a very pleasant setting in which to enjoy the tasty Spanish food, all of which is fresh and homemade. It's not gourmet or cutting edge, but you can taste the fine quality of the ingredients, and the care that went into the cooking.

PACHÁ'S TAPAS STORY

Legend has it that in a small drinking bodega in southern Spain, a barman named Don Julio Dominguez came upon a way to make his bar more popular. He figured if he kept his customers thirsty they'd drink more, so he began to place a salty treat or two in a dish atop their drinks (thereby keeping the flies out, too). The little dishes (and by extension, their contents) were dubbed "tapas" (from the Spanish verb 'tapar' which means 'to cover'), and the rest is culinary history.

Tapas, salads, and sandwiches are priced $4.25-$7.25; main dishes run $8.50-$10.50. The grilled, spiced chicken breast sandwich is popular, as is tostada de ceviche, pollo al ajillo (chicken sautéed in olive oil and lots of garlic), the pollo a la Yucateca (in achiote sauce with peppers, onions, black beans, and orange relish), and the Pacha paella is another favorite.

INEXPENSIVE
American
   SLIDERS DINER, *449 Castro. 415-431-3288. Located near Market, it is open Sunday-Thursday 11am-midnight, but stays open till 2 or 2:30am on weekends. This Sliders is very much like the diner on Sutter and Polk, with the same low $3.25-$5.50 prices.*
   The burgers have an excellent rep, and they are, in fact, decent though not superb. You can get six or eight ounces of beef grilled as rare or well-done as you like, and you can heap it high with salad fixings. There are also low-fat and vegetarian burgers, various chicken, steak, and tuna sandwiches, fried chicken, and an assortment of dogs round out the diner menu. It's a diner like diners used to be, big on the chrome and black vinyl, low on service and comfort. It plays the nostalgia market and turns out reliably adequate food.
   ORPHAN ANDY'S, *3991 17th Street. 415-864-9795. Located on the corner with Market (and just down the street from Castro), it has been around serving diner fare for 18 years, but its real claim to fame is that they stay open 24 hours a day, 7 days a week.*
   The only days they ever close are Thanksgiving and Christmas, and even then, they might just open up anyway. It's a real hole-in-the-wall with

the formica counter and vinyl booths, dishing basic diner grub for $4-$7, for the most part, though the steak and shrimp dishes inch up closer to $9. There are eggs (any style) plus a host of omelets, hot cakes and pork chops and homefries. There are loads of sandwiches, from the lowly fried egg or grilled cheese to burgers to club sandwiches and chicken breast. They even have throwbacks like tuna melts, and coronary disasters like chicken fried steak with country gravy. It's not exactly a diet haven here, but it is always open, and everyone needs a greasy burger now and again, anyway.

Mexican

POZOLE, *2337 Market. 415-626-2666. Located between Castro and Noe and open Monday-Friday 4pm-midnight and Saturday-Sunday noon-midnight.*

This is a burrito joint of another color, and lots of it. It's the Mexican death theme here, with skeleton figures, lots of elaborately melted candles, eerie colorful aura and Santeria cult decor. There's Madonna with a half-eaten apple and an angel with a beer bottle, basking in candlelight. The Mexican cuisine is as unusual as the decor, and most main dishes are $6-$8. There are the Pozole Classic items such as quesadillas filled with cactus and rock shrimp, and pollo con mole with chicken in a fruity, spicy mole sauce, plus black beans and rice, but the new thing here is the low-fat menu (on the flip side of the full fat Classics).

Featured dishes include chicken burrito with roasted peppers in lime-tomatillo sauce, and tacos de pescado with lime-marinated red snapper and grilled red onions, and all with just one or two grams of fat. It's very small here, thick with color and atmosphere; the food and aura makes this a popular spot, quite different from your usual neighborhood taqueria.

Middle Eastern

LA MEDITERRANEE, *288 Noe Street. 415-431-7210. Located near Market and open Tuesday-Sunday from 11am-10pm.*

They serve tasty Middle Eastern dishes like hummus, baba ghanoush, levant sandwiches, and filo dough pies for $6-$7.50 a meal, from the same good menu used in their Fillmore branch. The setting is pleasant enough, though not stunning. They have tables inside and a couple out on the sidewalk as well (though it's a fairly busy corner), and while the decor isn't drop-dead gorgeous, it's perfectly adequate, and the food is good.

Sandwiches, Salads, & Picnic Supplies

CALIFORNIA HARVEST RANCH MARKET, *2285 Market. 415-626-0805. Located near Sanchez and open daily from 10am-11pm.*

This is a market, not a restaurant, but they have some of the best fresh gourmet take-out food around, for a picnic or a quick bite on the go. They have freshly made soups ($2.85 a cup), a beautiful salad bar that includes sushi and fantastic pasta salads ($4.29 a lb.), fabulous breads, wrapped sandwiches ($4.25-$5.35), muffins and biscotti and cookies and more. Once you go in, it's hard to drag yourself away; there are benches outside where you can sit and eat without having to wait another moment.

CHINATOWN

INEXPENSIVE

Chinese

GREAT EASTERN, *649 Jackson. 415-986-2500. Located near Grant and open daily 11am-1am.*

They serve a variety of Chinese fare, but their specialty is seafood. Check out the huge fish tanks in back, select your dish from the board menu, and give your nod to the fish, brought flopping to your table for approval like a bottle of wine at a French restaurant. Non-seafood dishes are $7-$9, and the seafood meals are more.

HOUSE OF NANKING, *919 Kearny. 415-421-1429. Located near Jackson, this is a yuppie trap that doesn't deserve its fine, glowing reputation.*

This place is open 11am-10pm Monday-Saturday, 4-10pm on Sunday, and around dinner time you'll see the line of people outside who could eat really good Chinese food if only they would go somewhere else. The waitstaff are not what you would call friendly. Impatient and brusque, they're off and away before you finish your order; the dishes are slopped down minutes later, shortly followed by the check.

A TRIBUTE TO KONG'S

Before House of Nanking began doing business at 919 Kearny, one of San Francisco's finest Chinese eateries, Kong's Cafe, was knocking 'em dead at the same location. Kong's had incredible food and friendly service. Tragically, Kong's has gone the way of Ambrose Bierce and Jimmy Hoffa.

The food was so good that just the anticipation of it could replace years of psychoanalysis. No matter what black clouds were snaking tendrils into your heart, the first sip of hot-and-sour soup would begin to dissipate them. By the end of the bowl, you were generally smiling broadly. Any residual unhappiness that may have been left after the soup would unfailingly be vanquished by the shredded pork with hot garlic sauce. One bite of this would have you feeling wonderful. Two bites would have you feeling more wonderful, and so on, until, by the end of the plate, you were shining brightly with a geniality unmatched by anything in the world outside of Kong's, a geniality made possible only by eating something so hot that it is painful but so delicious that it is irresistible.

By Eric Brody

As for the food ($3.30-$5.25 for non-seafood entrees), it tastes okay, but that's it. Neither exceptionally good nor exceptionally bad, it's mediocre Shanghai cuisine that is definitely not worth a wait or a repeat visit (or a first visit). The ingredients seem fresh, but the spicy isn't even mildly hot, and there's much better Chinese food readily available. Only waiting in line for an hour or so and getting really hungry could make this food taste at all special.

TAIWAN, *289 Columbus. 415-989-6789. Located near Broadway, Taiwan is run by the same folks who operate Taiwan Restaurant in the Richmond, and they're open daily 11am-3:30pm and 5pm-midnight.*

The menu spans the full range, but they sell a lot of pot stickers, pork tripe soup, steamed dumplings, and crispy chicken ($4.50-$8). They claim their pot stickers, steamed dumplings, and crispy chicken are the best, and while that's a bit of an overstatement, the food is pretty good. It's not worth going out of your way, but they are reliable for a good and inexpensive meal.

HANG AH TEA ROOM, *1 Hang Ah Street. 415-982-5686. Located off Sacramento near Stockton it's open 10am-9pm Tuesday-Sunday and 10am-3pm on Monday, serving dim sum and other Chinese dishes for $4-$7.*

They proudly proclaim they are the oldest tea room in San Francisco, in business since 1920. But history aside, it's the food that matters, and the Hang Ah score is mixed. I'd stay far away from their deep-fried wontons and egg rolls unless you're a glutton for oil, but their barbecued pork rolls (pork how) are the best in Chinatown, really. Other steamed dim sum are okay; it depends what you get. But they are more than just a dim sum parlor, and have an extensive menu. The barbecued spare ribs are very good, the fried rice is okay, and the fortune cookies are crisp and tasty.

The restaurant has a cute alley entrance, but the actual room is fluorescent-lit and drab, with little attempt at decor. During a typical lunch, 98% of the faces you see will be Caucasian, though the diners will range from solo eater with newspaper to a party of corporate associates, and the dress will range from sweat pants to business suits. They have lunch specials ($4.50 for a plate of dim sum and a dish of fried rice), but unless you have a tremendous appetite, I'd just order off the menu so you can avoid the greasy items and just get what is good.

FORTUNE WOK, *1358 Mason. 415-392-9656. Located near Pacific, open Thursday-Tuesday 11:30am-9:30pm, and they deliver for free.*

This is it, the real thing: the illusive, cheap Chinese hole-in-the-wall with fantastic food of your dreams. It looks like any other: the plain formica tables, the absence of warmth, the big fish tank. But the food is way better than average, the prices way lower ($4-$7 for entrees), and the ingredients clearly fresh and of good quality. The Fortune Wok Chicken is excellent, as is the Szechwan Pork, though the Hot & Sour soup is just

DIM SUM

Pronounced "deem sum," the style of cuisine dates back nearly 1,000 years ago to the Imperial Court of the Sung Dynasty. When the Emperor fled the Mongols, he took the dim sum concept with him, and by 1900 it was a well-established culinary tradition in Canton. It literally means "to touch the heart," with harmonious combinations of flavors in small bite-sized treats. There are many sorts and tastes, from deep-fried to barbecued to steamed to baked, using seafood or pork, duck or chicken or vegetables, and it's fun to pile your table with small dishes and try a bunch of them.

Chinatown

J&J, *615 Jackson. 415-981-7308. Located near Kearny and open daily from 9am-2:30pm and 5-10pm and it's one of the best. The flavored dumplings are especially good, as is the bean curd skin and the seafood.*

Dol Ho Restaurant, *808 Pacific. 415-392-2828. Located near Columbus, this is a smaller, more intimate dim sum cafe, open daily 7am-5pm. The atmosphere is nothing special, but if you don't like the football stadium vastness of many dim sum halls, the Dol Ho is a good option. They serve a variety of small plate dishes for $1.50, medium plates for $2, and large entrees for $2.40 each. And the food's pretty good, too.*

Royal Jade, *675 Jackson. 415-392-2929. Located near Grant, open daily 9:30am-11pm, it looks like your basic, bland dining room, but the dim sum is anything but basic and bland. Creative and delicious, the stuffed mushroom caps are just one example of their unusually fine food.*

Hang Ah Tea Room, *1 Hang Ah. 415-982-5686. Located off Sacramento near Stockton, it is open 10am-9pm Tuesday-Sunday and 10am-3pm on Monday, serving dim sum and other Chinese dishes for $4-$7. They say they are the oldest tea room in San Francisco, going back to 1920, but you wouldn't know it without being told. Some of the dim sum (like the pork how) is quite good, but the deep fried stuff is mighty greasy.*

Downtown

Yank Sing, *427 Battery. 415-781-1111. Located near Clay and open Monday-Friday 11am-3pm and Saturday-Sunday 10am-4pm for lunch. They do gourmet dim sum using fresh ingredients, and they have a very wide selection. In addition, the restaurant is attractive and airy, and reservations are a good idea.*

Wu Kong, *101 Spear in 1 Rincon Center. 415-957-9300. It is open for lunch and dim sum weekdays 11am-2:30pm and on weekends 10:30am-2:30pm, dinner is served daily 5:30-9:30pm, and parking in the basement garage is free. They serve dim sum (and lots of other dishes) from Shanghai* *and Canton in an elegant dining room full of crystal and fresh linen. They have a wide variety of dim sum ($2-$3.50 a plate) including vegetable shui mai, pot stickers, and baked red bean cake, plus mango pudding, pan-fried shrimp roll, and baked barbecue pork puff.*

Canton, *655 Folsom. 415-495-3064. Located near Third, open Monday-Friday 11am-10pm, Saturday 10am-10pm, and Sunday 10am-9pm, and does a high quality dim sum. Their chicken thighs, dumplings and bok choy in oyster sauce are all well worth ordering.*

Richmond

Ton Kiang, *5821 Geary. 415-387-8273. Located near 22nd, open 10:30am-10pm Sunday-Thursday and 10:30am-10:30pm Friday-Saturday, and serving great steamed dumplings, fried spring rolls, barbecued pork, and seaweed salad.*

okay. They have a varied menu with a large vegetarian selection, and it is the best restaurant of it's kind that we've found in the North Beach-Chinatown area. They also have a Budget Delivery special of three entrees (your choice) plus appetizers and soup for just $15. They used to have a wonderful sign outside, a not-quite-clear-on-the-concept special, claiming "Our food will definitely make you leave your appetite in San Francisco." Alas, the sign's there no longer, but the good food remains.

Thai
   PARADISE, *923 Pacific. 415-391-1666. Located between Powell and Mason, Paradise serves some very tasty Thai food every day from 11am-3pm and 5-11pm. They also deliver for orders of $10 or more.*

   All the food is good, but some are truly magnificent, such as the Spicy Beef Salad and the Pharam Puk (spinach, carrots, and green beans in a spiced peanut sauce). They have soups and curries, Pad Thai (Thai noodles) and spicy wontons, seafood specials, vegetarian dishes, and a garlic section as well. The dishes are mostly $6 or $7, which is a small price to pay for a bowl of paradise. They definitely have some of the best Thai food in the neighborhood.

CIVIC CENTER & UPPER MARKET
EXPENSIVE
Nouvelle Cuisine
   STARS RESTAURANT, *555 Golden Gate. 415-861-7827. Located near Van Ness, this is one of the most renowned restaurants in San Francisco thanks to chef Jeremiah Tower, and serves its American nouvelle cuisine for lunch*

weekdays from 11:30am and nightly for dinner from 5:30pm. They do a prix fixe lunch for $20 or you can order off the a la carte menu ($7-$ 14 an entree), and dinner is all a la carte, with main dish prices $20-$26.
Inside it's not daunting at all, despite the fame and clientele. Huge green trees set a friendly, casual tone, and the staff are just as accommodating as can be. It's a show here, and everything's on stage, including the food prep in the big open kitchen. The menu changes daily, but items such as butternut squash soup with bourbon cream, wood oven gnocchi gratin with smoked chicken and garlic cream, and mahi-mahi with pasilla chili tartare sauce should give a sense of Tower's culinary style.

Though its sheen and quality have dimmed a bit, and the prices have gone sky high, it's still a swell place to see who there is to be seen, and to be seen by same. Or you can try the food for less of an investment at Stars Cafe around the corner.

MODERATE
Cajun
FLOOGIES, *1686 Market. 415-864-3700. Located near Gough, just down the street from Zuni, this is a self-proclaimed swamp cafe serving Louisiana and Gulf Coast cuisine. They're open Monday-Friday 11am-2:30pm, Tuesday-Thursday 5:30-10pm, and Friday-Saturday 5:30-11pm, offering Floogies food for $6-$10.*

The walls are painted all the nicest swamp colors (mango, peach, moss, and bayou black). Pristine white linen covers the tables, and brown paper covers the linen (helping it stay pristine); they look like tables ready for some serious food. You can take your pick from a wide assortment of po-boys (such as oysters, catfish, or vegetarian), gumbo, jambalaya, red beans 'n 'rice, and a bayou catfish, griddled or fried up in a cornmeal crust. The bread basket comes full of yummy corn bread and the Blackened Voodoo beer is quite good, but unfortunately, the gumbo, jambalaya, and beans with rice are mediocre. Catfish fingers are excellent, and not greasy at all, but it's a pity about the ranch dressing flavored sauce.

If you know your po-boy from your beignet and are looking to re-experience the magnificence of New Orleans cuisine, Floogies will probably let you down, though it's perfectly adequate for a change of pace if your expectations aren't too high. It's too bad, because much of what Floogies offers is good, but it all verges on disappointment. The music is good, but a shade too loud, the swamp theme is cute, but comes close to tacky, and the service lets its rough edges show; for example, if you order a plate to share (and the portions are huge - one appetizer and entree can easily feed two), they grudgingly plop an empty plate in front of one of you and let you do the splitting. So be forewarned; there are good finds here, but you'll need to do some careful wading.

Italian

CAFE DELLE STELLE, *395 Hayes. 415-252-1110. Located near Gough (down the street from its previous location), this is just as lovely and rustic in its new habitat, and is open for lunch Monday-Friday 11:30am-2:30pm, for dinner Monday-Friday 5:30-9:30pm and 5:30-10:30pm on Saturday.*

The big corner windows let in all the sunlight, and give a great view of all the sidewalk and street traffic. Lots of potted plants clearly thrive in the sunny setting, while the white stucco walls with mint trim put you in mind of a Mediterranean village. There are tables out on the sidewalk, too, for use in good weather. The food is as homey and rustic and warm as the decor, and ranges from $8-$11 an entree.

There are pasta dishes like pappardelle with homemade sausage, shiitake, and tomatoes or cheese ravioli in a lemon and cream sauce, meat dishes like grilled garlic rosemary chicken or braciole (grilled pork chops in a zesty tomato, olives, and capers sauce). There are a number of good vegetarian options as well. They have maintained a strong following thanks to their easy-going warmth and good food, and they are continuing the tradition in their new location.

INCONTRO, *41 Franklin. 415-252-1110. Located between Page and Oak, it's open for lunch Monday-Friday 11am-2:30pm, for dinner 5-10pm week nights, and till 11pm Friday and Saturday. Actually, they stay open during the off hours of 2:30-5pm, but only for coffee, salads, and starters.*

The name means "encounter" or "rendezvous", depending on your preferred language, but linguistics aside, it's a swell place to get together. Just opened in February of '96 by Ted Zuur and Joe Aries, this small, pretty restaurant has exquisitely lovely blue lights over each white linen-swathed table, along with flowers in cobalt blue vases and warm terra cotta floor tiles which are enhanced by little blue designs. White trim surrounds the big, beautiful windows (you can see the world go by and they can see you, so don't make it *that* kind of encounter). This new Italian restaurant serves moderately priced pasta, risotto, polenta and antipasti ($6-$13), as cooked by Andreas Maniscalco, former chef from Sausalito's Spinnaker.

The sfincioni (a fresh foccacia starter with anchovies and a tomato ragu) and bruschetta pomodoro (garlic toast with tomato, basil, and walnut pesto) are especially recommended to start with, and they take great care with all the salads, using the freshest produce. The pasta main dishes are excellent, too.

Vegetarian versions can be made of most of them, and the waiters are happy to take your special orders. Incontro is a fine addition to the Civic Center scene, and its open, airy ambiance welcomes instantly.

Mediterranean
   ZUNI CAFE, *1658 Market. 415-552-2522. Located near Gough, it's open Tuesday to Sunday 7:30am-midnight, serving innovative Mediterranean fare to one of the coolest crowd of patrons in the city.*

There are oysters and excellent burgers, interesting salads and pizzas, tasty piccolo fritto, and chicken roasted in a wood oven, and complex platters such as grilled duck breast with spiced prunes, red cabbage, polenta, and watercress; while the food ($9-$20) is quite good, people go there for the scene.

Inside the decor is exposed brick and distressed wood, white linen cloth covered by white butcher paper, great art on the walls, a long copper bar, and big, wonderful windows giving you a view of all market Street. Of course, everyone else gets a view of you, too - that's part of the Zuni experience - so dress your coolest to blend with the beautiful people. There's a fun buzz of energy, a happy mix of diners, and terrific people-watching, especially from the seats upstairs. Reservations are a good idea, though you can always hang out at the bar and socialize while you wait for a table to clear.

Nouvelle Cuisine
   STARS CAFE, *500 Van Ness. 415-861-4344. Located near McAllister, it's open for lunch daily 11:30am-2pm, and they have a bar menu for 2-5:30pm; dinner starts at 5:30pm and goes till 9:30pm Tuesday-Thursday, till 10:30pm Friday-Saturday, and till 8pm Sunday-Monday (and every day the late supper menu kicks in for an hour past when dinner is over).*

The lower-priced cousin of Jeremiah Tower's Stars Restaurant, the cafe sports a classic bistro look that's classy and casual, with lots of green plants, and big windows looking out over busy Van Ness. The staff is friendly and professional, and the food has Tower's stamp of eclectic nouvelle cuisine. There's a fixed price lunch ($14.75) Monday-Saturday, or you can order off the regular menu at $9-$17 for a platter with wood oven roasted chicken with okra, black eye peas, Andouille sausage and spicy onion rings, or ancho-cumin marinated pork loin with coriander-sage couscous. They also do fabulous pizzas with toppings like comice pear, fontina cheese, and smoked prosciutto, or shiitake mushroom, roasted onions, and Gruyere.

   CALIFORNIA CULINARY ACADEMY, *625 Polk. 415-771-3500, ext. 229. Located near Turk, it has two dining options, the more formal Napa Room upstairs, and the more casual Sonoma Grill downstairs.*

Because the Academy is primarily a chef-training school, the dining room hours are more abbreviated than most restaurants, but on the other hand, you get a sensational bargain of quality food and service for the price.

The Napa Room *is open for lunch Monday-Thursday from noon-1:30pm and for dinner Monday-Friday 6-8pm, and reservations are recommended.* They serve modern continental, eclectic cuisine ($11-$17 an entree) such as truffled risotto with artichoke hearts and fava beans, roast duck breast in orange bigarade sauce, and braised pheasant in Riesling, green cabbage, bacon, apples, and juniper berries. Their a la carte menu is in place Monday-Wednesday, while Thursdays and Fridays they do their incredible buffets ($20 for lunch and $26.50-$30 for dinner).

The Sonoma Grill *is open Monday-Friday 11:30am-1:30pm for lunch and 6-9pm for dinner (it's all a la carte at $10-$12 an entree, except for Friday night when they do their famous prime rib buffet for $14).* Everything is good here, but the stir fry of shrimp, scallops, and vegetables is especially wonderful, as is the marinated chicken breast in chile lime butter. The bar has a wide range of interesting beers on tap, and the dessert buffet is a sensational treat not to be missed.

Vegetarian

MILLENNIUM, *246 McAllister. 415-487-9800. Located near Larkin, it is a relatively new vegetarian restaurant attached to the Abigail hotel. They're open for lunch Tuesday-Friday 11:30am-2:30pm, and for dinner Tuesday-Saturday 5-9:30pm.*

The menu leans in a Mediterranean direction, and uses all organic, low-fat, dairy-free ingredients, resulting in vegan* meals that for the most part have fewer than three grams of fat per serving (and in some cases, no fat at all) for $10.25-$15.25 an entree. Their concept, and it's a good one, is a healthy, vegetarian, gourmet, stylish dining experience. Unfortunately, they only manage to pull off some of that ambitious slate. The look is the part that works best. Set in the 72-year-old Abigail Hotel's carriage house, if you're in just the right place you can see bits of the lush garden out back.

Jazzy music tinkles in the background, and the downstairs dining room is set with simple elegance, with white linen topped by cobalt blue glasses and candles. Colorful artwork dots the walls, and black and white tiles snazz up the floor. The food is as low-fat and sodium-free as promised, and unmarred by eggs, butter, or any other dairy product (though milk is available on request for your coffee, as is goat cheese for your polenta), and gourmet ingredients like portobello mushrooms, saffron, and wild rice are used liberally in dishes like the Millennium Steak (made of seitan in a marsala sauce), polenta torte, and the winter filo purse filled with a medley of winter vegetables.

What's lacking is flavor. Though the occasional dish (like the filo purse) is actually tasty, most are not. The bread spread is just palatable, and even a relatively simple dish like warm spinach salad is ruined, drowning in its vinegar and oil dressing with no rescue in sight, while the tempting grilled smoked portobello mushroom on garlic toast need salt in a bad way. As for the seitan (a wheat gluten substance), don't get it unless you already know you like it. It's a shame. You can have a lovely evening here, drink fine wine and dine by candle light, and easily drop $50-$70 on a dinner for two, but for that kind of money you should leave happier. Nothing tastes bad, but it doesn't actually taste good, either.

The menu promises that their vegan cuisine will leave your taste buds singing, but it left ours whining instead. They claim to be a cut above Greens (the vegetarian restaurant in Fort Mason), but the sad truth is they don't even come close. To their credit, they are a healthy alternative, and if you are strictly vegan, you'll find more elegance, diversity and innovation here than anywhere else in the city, but otherwise you'd do better choosing another spot to dine.

*Vegan cuisine follows dietary laws that forbid all meat and dairy ingredients, including eggs and butter.

INEXPENSIVE
American
JUDY MAY'S M&L MARKET, *691 14th Street. 415-431-7044. It is open Monday-Saturday 11:30am-5:30pm.*

This is a small old-style counter deli with old-style quality hot pastrami at old-style prices ($3.79). Forget trendy cactus and pottery, the soup here is served in a styrofoam cup for $1.89. But the corn chowder is everything you'd hope for from nearby up-scale eateries, and they have a loyal, local following.

Chinese
ELIZA'S, *205 Oak Street. 415-621-4819. Located near Gough, it is open for lunch Monday-Friday 11am-3pm and dinner Monday-Saturday 5-9pm, serving fine, reasonably priced Hunan and Mandarin cuisine, just like the branch in Potrero Hill.*

Lunches cost just $4.50-$5.15 while dinner entrees might climb as high as $7-$9. They have all the standard dishes, and a good selection of vegetarian dishes as well. There are weird and wonderful glass vases along the high shelves, and pink cloth under glass on the tables. Colorful contemporary murals decorate, and the atmosphere is festive.

Italian
SPUNTINO, *524 Van Ness. 415-861-7772. Located between McAllister and Golden Gate, it is open Monday-Friday 7am-9pm and Saturday-Sunday 10am-9pm, though if it's a show night (ballet, symphony, or opera) they stay open later for a post-entertainment snack.*

They are a little-known civic center gem, modern and relaxed, with tables big enough to spread out your newspaper as you sip your cappuccino or get together with friends for lunch. The sharp black trim and huge windows have a streamlined style, and the food is pretty good, too. The panini sandwiches, pizzas, and pastas run $5-$9, and make for a satisfying lunch, snack, or dinner. They have a fine selection of desserts, too.

Mexican

LAS ESTRELLAS, *330 Gough. 415-552-1312. Located between Linden and Fell, Las Estrellas serves healthy Mexican food daily 11:30am-9pm.*

The walls are pale yellow and aqua blue, adorned with little stars and birds, and the cheerful tables are stained red, blue, green, and yellow. Festive and airy and welcoming, the food is tasty, light, and low-fat, a new California version of Mexican cuisine. They have the usual assortment of tacos, burritos, quesadillas and such ($2.45-$6), filled with lardless whole beans, fresh vegetables, and a nice, spicy taste. The dishes are styrofoam and the forks are plastic, but you can't get better food for less, especially in this neighborhood.

FINANCIAL DISTRICT, DOWNTOWN, & EMBARCADERO

SPLURGE

Japanese

KYO-YA, *2 New Montgomery. 415-392-8600. Located in the Sheraton Palace Hotel, it is the toniest Japanese restaurant in San Francisco, and it's open for lunch Tuesday-Friday 11:30am-2pm and for dinner Monday-Saturday 6-10pm.*

The sashimi is as fresh as can be, and the toro (fatty tuna) is melt-in-your-mouth succulent. They also have cooked Japanese meals that don't involve raw seafood, such as shabu-shabu. Full dinners range from $31-$60, and are exquisite. The dining room is divided into five little sections, separated by silk curtains, creating intimate dining for up to 86 guests, but there's also a sushi bar if you want to see the action. The decor is very contemporary, and it goes nicely with the traditional Japanese cuisine.

Mediterranean

RUBICON, *558 Sacramento. 415-434-4100. Located near Montgomery, it is the star-studded dream child of Francis Ford Coppola, Robin Williams, and Robert DeNiro, serving California Mediterranean cuisine for weekday lunches 11:45am-2pm and dinners Monday-Saturday 5:30-10pm. Lunch entrees cost $12-$15 and dinner is a la carte at $20-$26 an entree or $32 for prix fixe.*

This is a place to see and be seen, but it's also for dining very well in pleasing surroundings. The attractive dining room rambles around corners and upstairs, creating intimate, cozy nooks and alcoves in a two-level dining room that seats many. The food is excellent and interesting. There are lunch dishes like crispy chicken on warm bacon, potato and spinach salad, roasted pork loin sandwich with apple and onion chutney, or portobello mushroom sandwich with aioli and grilled red onions. For dinner they serve wonderful plates like roast loin of venison with spätzle and butternut squash, or seared tuna with a chick pea pancake and tomato confit.

The menu changes by the season to take advantage of what's fresh, but you're just about guaranteed that it'll be great, and the pretty woods, open, airy feel, and Italian earth tones all help make this a suavely relaxed, subtly elegant place to dine.

Seafood

AQUA, *252 California. 415-956-9662. Located near Battery, it does lunch during the week 11am-2pm and dinner Monday-Saturday, 5:30-10:30pm, and reservations are necessary unless you get really lucky.*

This creative seafood restaurant next door to the Tadich Grill's bastion of tradition opened in 1991 under chef Michael Mina, preparing seafood sensations for $14-$16 during lunch time and $26-$38 for dinner. Here you'll find tartare of Ahi tuna and carpaccio of Hawaiian swordfish for starters, along with more standard crab cakes and smoked salmon with caviar. There's ginger glazed salmon with horseradish potato gratin in spiced orange marmalade, and pan roasted scallops with fettuccine, stewed artichokes, and smoked lobster broth. Inside, it's sleekly designed, with flagstone floors and marble table tops, enormous mirrors and mottled faux finished pillars. It's elegant, slightly noisy, upscale, and popular (though not quite as "in" as it used to be), creating a contemporary setting for innovative seafood arrangements.

EXPENSIVE
American

MAXFIELD'S RESTAURANT, *at Market and New Montgomery in the Sheraton Palace Hotel. 415-392-8600. It serves lunch daily 11:30am-2pm, with dinner 6-10pm, and a bar menu is available in the Pied Piper bar after that.*

The atmosphere is warm and clubby, with dark green palm trees, and superbly matching soft leather booths so tall and wide you wish you were taller and wider to take advantage of the space. The room is splendid, with a tile floor to die for, a patterned stained glass ceiling that's really lovely, all paneled in rich, dark wood. The food is traditional American at its finest, for $11-$17 an entree. Using the best quality ingredients and seasonal delicacies, Maxfield's turns beef medallions and grilled halibut into sensational, flavorful, perfectly seasoned dishes. Winter sees the addition of succulent mushrooms like chanterelles, oyster, and even the little-known lobster mushroom, and other months sport whatever is in season. Their crab cakes are the crabbiest you will ever have the pleasure of tearing into, the salads are delicious too, and the wine list is quality. And there's jazz ('40s swing) 7-10pm Thursdays and Fridays in the bar. The Maxfield Parrish mural in the Pied Piper supplies color and class, as well as names for both the restaurant and bar.

MORE ON MAXFIELD'S

*The Palace Hotel was originally built in 1875 as what was then the largest hotel in the world. The area now occupied by the Pied Piper Bar started as a barber shop, then metamorphosed into the Happy Valley Bar (after the neighborhood which was known as Happy Valley at the time - a name that disappeared with the quake and fire of 1906, when for a while the valley stopped seeming so benevolent). In the bar is the Maxfield Parrish mural, **The Pied Piper of Hamlin**, commissioned by the owners for $20,000 in 1909 after they saw his Old King Cole painting in New York. Now valued closer to $2.5 million, the mural was lent to the M. H. de Young Museum during the Palace's 1990 restoration.*

Many of the fine details in the bar and restaurant (the stained glass ceilings, the mosaic tile floors) were part of the loving and all-out 1990 renovation that cost 180 million dollars in the effort to restore the hotel to its former magnificence. The tiles were discovered under wall-to-wall carpet that had hidden their glory for 30 years, the new floor was reconstructed according to the original pattern, and the finished product is classier than any carpet could dream of being.

Mediterranean
   ROTI, *155 Steuart. 415-495-6500. Located in the Hotel Griffon south of Market and across the street from Rincon Center, it is a pleasantly casual restaurant with delicious food, open Monday-Friday 11am-10pm, and weekends 5-11pm.*
   Brick walls and big French windows (opened on hot days), nicely linened tables, and colorful European posters on the walls set the tone for a good time. They claim to have the best Manhattans in San Francisco, but they're better known for the big brick hearth fire above which skewered chickens merrily roast. And further back is a seafood bar, with oysters, prawns, etc. chilling on ice. They have tasty starters ($4-$9) like sourdough goat cheese toasts with smoked hazelnuts, and red curry mussels with roasted garlic croutons, and they may be the only place around to get smoky venison chili. Entrees ($12-$24) include the spit-roasted chicken, seared dayboat scallops with black pepper linguini, and stuffed quail with chili maple glaze on wild rice. And the service is always good.

Seafood

TADICH GRILL, *240 California. 415-391-1849. It is open Monday-Friday 11am-9pm and Saturday 11:30am-9pm. Tadich is traditional and wonderful, and very busy at lunch time, serving large platters of seafood for $11-$20.*

Walk in any afternoon and you'll find all the seats at the long wood bar taken, the terrific semi-private booth enclaves full, and lines of people waiting patiently for lobster and crab, oysters and scallops, and a full selection of fish. Once you get a seat, there are sauteed prawns and swordfish steak, grilled trout, and broiled sea bass to choose from, plus traditional seafood dishes like hangtown fry (with oysters, bacon and egg) and cioppino, as well as veal cutlets, ravioli, bacon and eggs with hash browns, burgers, steaks, and chops. There is one vegetarian plate and a number of salads, but this is, by and large, a fish and meat kind of place. Dark wood, oak floors, and white linen form an appealing milieu, the food is very good, and the loyal regulars are numerous, as they have been for 148 years.

TADICH HISTORY

The grill started in 1849 as a Gold Rush coffee stand run by three Croatian immigrants down by Long Wharf (which is now Commercial Street). As the city grew, the location shifted a few times, so that in 1871 when John Tadich arrived from Croatia and joined the restaurant business it was The New World Coffee Stand on Kearny. Tadich stayed, but the name changed in 1882, thanks to the irritating and arrogant election campaign of one Alexander Badlam, Jr., who ran under the slogan "It's A Cold Day When I Get Left." Badlam was a New World regular, and when San Francisco resoundingly defeated him, he went to the New World to drown his sorrows.

San Francisco, however, didn't let him lick his wounds in peace. They dumped a wagon load of ice at his doorstep, and the papers took advantage of the particularly chill November to make numerous references to The Cold Day. That day was so linked in people's minds with the restaurant, it became The Cold Day Restaurant, and remained so till 1912, when Tadich (who had become restaurant proprietor in 1887) split with his partner, who took the Cold Day for his new restaurant. Tadich needed a new name, and he came up with Tadich's Grill, The Original Cold Day Restaurant, which over the years became plain old Tadich Grill. The restaurant finally found a permanent home at 240 California in 1967. It's run now by the Buiches, a Croatian family Tadich sold to 1961, making this a rare family enterprise that's been under Croatian ownership since 1849, and the oldest restaurant to be in continuous operation in California.

MODERATE
American
   BRICKS BAR & GRILL, *298 Pacific. 415-788-2222. Located near Battery, it's open Monday-Friday 8am-9pm, and they sometimes stay open as late as 10pm.*

The old brick building lends a lot of character and warmth along with its name, and it's been there a long time. It was built in 1907 after the earthquake demolished The Old Ship Saloon, the earlier version of Bricks. The Old Ship Saloon was, in fact, an old ship, *The Arkansas,* which ran aground on the rocks of Alcatraz in 1849. The passengers and crew lit out for Gold Country, and the ship was left stranded. The ship became landlocked in 1851 when landfill extended the city into the bay, and with a little fixing up, Joseph Anthony was able to open it as a saloon. Henry Klee built the brick building and he built it to last.

Inside, it's very comfortable and affable, with a wonderful pub-like, roll-up-your-sleeves-and-dig-in feeling. It's casual and welcoming and very well-liked. They have a bar that does a terrific martini where smokers can eat, and lots of stools and tables, and they all get filled up during lunch. Yet another place claiming "best burger in the City," they also have popular blue plate daily specials. Meals here run $5-$9, and they're great. You can get a variety of burgers (all with your choice of fries, salad, or cottage cheese), old-fashioned sandwiches like the BLT, the classic club, a grilled ham and cheese, or a Louisiana hot link on a French roll. They have an assortment of salads, a couple of steaks, and Julie's blue plate special as chalked up on the board. They have swell breakfasts, too, and a lot of genuine geniality.

   JACK'S, *615 Sacramento. 415-986-9854. Located between Kearny and Montgomery, it is open 11:30am-2:30pm Monday-Friday for lunch and 5-9:30pm Monday-Saturday for dinner.*

This is an American Grill with roots going back to 1864, when Jack's set the San Francisco standard. Past the heavy yellow curtains you'll find the grill decor of dark wood, bentwood chairs, white walls and brass hooks that can be found in grills nationwide, but which started here. The tables are set with white linen, and the experienced staff are ready to show you some serious dining.

Meals ($8.50-$20) generally include a lot of meat and seafood, done the American way, and that old grill ambiance. There are old favorites like broiled calf's liver with bacon and onions, good lamb or mutton chops, broiled sweetbreads, and a fine selection of oysters, cracked crab, and Continental appetizers.

Chinese

WU KONG, *101 Spear in 1 Rincon Center. 415-957-9300. It is open for lunch and dim sum weekdays 11am-2:30pm and on weekends 10:30am-2:30pm, dinner is served daily 5:30-9:30pm, and parking in the basement garage is free.*

Wu Kong serves sumptuous Shanghai and Cantonese cuisine in a crystal and fine art bedecked dining room; it's a peaceful place, with white linen and tasteful elegance. They have a wide variety of dim sum ($2-$3.50 a plate) including Shanghai specialties like vegetable shui mai, pot stickers, and baked red bean cake, plus Cantonese items like mango pudding, pan-fried shrimp roll, and baked barbecue pork puff. But they have a full and intriguing menu of entrees ($7-$16), too. There are lots of shark's fin dishes, excellent seafood, and tasty vegetarian selections as well. The Drunken squab and vegetarian goose are wonderful, as are the pan-fried noodles and crystal prawns. This is fine Chinese dining that is a cut above the rest.

YANK SING, *427 Battery. 415-781-1111. Located near Clay, it is open for lunch only Monday-Friday 11am-3pm and Saturday-Sunday 10am-4pm.*

This is a dim sum restaurant with a difference: the food is exquisitely prepared, and the ambiance is pleasant. Like other dim sum restaurants you select small dishes from the traveling carts of goodies pushed past your table, your guest check gets stamped for each item, and you pay up when you can eat no more. But unlike other such places, the setting is bright and open, but with attractive room dividers and small alcoves that create the feeling of intimate dining, though the restaurant holds hundreds, and the aisles are good and wide for the dim sum carts to show their wares.

The tables are elegantly set, and the clear infusion tea pots are unusual and pretty. They actually manage that rare dim sum treat: pleasant atmosphere with excellent food. On any given day they'll have 80 different items on their carts ($2-$5 per), offering such treats as snow pea leaf dumplings, silver-wrapped chicken, and curry chicken turnovers, and the barbecued pork buns, tea-smoked duck, and minced squab are especially fine.

French

LE CENTRAL BISTRO, *453 Bush. 415-391-2233. Located near Montgomery, it is open Monday-Saturday 11:30am-10:30pm.*

They serve traditional French bistro fare in a very casual Parisian bistro atmosphere, with lots of brick walls and art, white linen, fresh flowers, and stained glass sky lights. They have all the standards like onion soup, escargots, and paté, and their entrees ($12-$21) include a lot of fish, steak, and rack of lamb. They also have a few daily pasta dishes, and some French specials like boudin noir and cassoulet (which is terrific).

CAFE CLAUDE, *7 Claude Lane. 415-392-3505. Located between Kearny & Grant and Bush & Sutter, and it's open Monday-Thursday 8am-10pm, Friday 8am-11pm, and Saturday 10am-11pm, and there's live jazz Thursday-Saturday at night.*

This is a very likable, very French place, though at night it can get too loud, especially when they have jazz playing. Just a half block down from Le Central and a little more moderately priced, it's on a small lane away from the heavy flow of traffic. Inside are lots of informal tables, booths, and banquettes, outside are tables with umbrellas, and the attractive young waiters with thick French accents are everywhere.

They offer lunch items like onion soup, baguette sandwiches, pizza, focaccia, salads, and grilled croque monsieur or madame sandwiches for $4-$8. Their dinner menu offers many of the same items, plus heartier entrees ($9-$12) like cassoulet, couscous Merguez, and poussin rôti. It's all quite good, and if the ambiance isn't too boisterous for you, it's a great choice for a casual meal out.

Italian

IL FORNAIO, *1265 Battery. 415-986-0100. Located at Levi Plaza, and open Sunday-Thursday 7am-11pm and Friday-Saturday 9am-midnight (but during the week they don't serve food 10:30-11:30am).*

The name means "the baker" in Italian, and the company started as a baking school outside Milan in 1971. They taught students how to bake with traditional recipes gathered from throughout Italy, and there are now over 1500 Il Fornaios in Italy. In 1981 they brought their show to the US, offering breads plus Italian food in 12 locations along the northwest coast. In their San Francisco location, they have a beautiful restaurant as well as a take-out fast food counter.

The restaurant itself is lovely – all glass enclosed and contemporary Italian decor, looking out over Levi Plaza, and the glassed in patio is just as attractive, looking over the gardens and toward the fountain. They offer a full range of Italian dishes, with antipasti, soups and salads, pizzas, pasta, and daily specials, with entrees ranging $7.50-$14. They have great sandwiches at lunch time, and their bread is excellent. You can get fried calamari, carpaccio, or fresh mozzarella with tomatoes and basil for a starter, or a fine salad of arugula (with red onion, ricotta, and yellow tomatoes) or spinach (with walnuts, mushrooms, pancetta, and gorgonzola dressing), for example. Pizza toppings are fresh and interesting, and pastas combine top quality olive oil with fine ingredients like roasted garlic, sun-dried tomatoes, shiitake mushrooms, Italian sausage, or fresh vegetables. There are also chicken, fish, and steak dishes, and each month they feature a different region of Italy. This is a place where you're just about guaranteed great food and a pleasant experience.

The take-out counter, open daily 6:30am-10pm, has coffee, cookies, wine, and their good bread, plus good sandwiches, green salads, and pasta salads for $3.25-$5.75. And a series of gardens, fountains, and plazas are right nearby for a picnic.

Nouvelle Cuisine

FOG CITY DINER, *1300 Battery. 415-982-2000. Located just down the street from Il Fornaio, this is a San Francisco experience of a very different nature, though of equally fine quality, and they're open daily 11:30am-11pm.*

Fog City is long and narrow like a diner should be, casually classy with marble topped bar and dark woods as befits a Financial District eatery, with original tile floors and formica tables for that small-town retro feel, and stunningly excellent food because this is San Francisco, after all, with main dishes for $7-$16. There are lots of booths with diner windows, as well as table and counter seating; it's a good place to watch the traffic, watch other diners, and be watched right back.

There is an amiable good humor feeling throughout, from the signs that announce their motto, "No crybabies," to the warm, witty, welcoming staff, this place retains its style and good humor while other fashionable places stick their noses in the air and go down the tubes. The waitstaff is not snooty in the least, and is always happy to assist, explain, and advise. But they could be as genial as all get out, and it wouldn't maintain its edge were the food not so unflaggingly good. They have small plates that can be combined for a swell meal, such as the crabcakes (which are superb), the Nantucket scallop ceviche, onion rings, quesadilla with chili peppers and hazelnuts, and mu-shu pork burritos (all $4.50-$8), and the salads are very good, as are the sandwiches. The large plates offer equally tasty nouvelle American cuisine, pork chops in lemon apple sauce with garlic mashed potatoes, barbecue roast quail with pecan cornbread stuffing, and flatiron pot roast with horseradish potato pancake.

They do change the menu from time to time, so don't get too attached to any one item (the garlic custards, for example, have gone by the wayside, which is a great personal tragedy). And leave room for the desserts, which are incredibly good.

Spanish Tapas

SOL Y LUNA, *475 Sacramento. 415-296-8696. Located near Battery, it serves spicy tapas in a chic, industrial style for lunch Monday-Friday 11:30am-2:30pm, dinner Monday-Saturday 5:30-9:30pm, and dancing Wednesday-Saturday 10pm-2am.*

Sol y Luna is ultra-sleek and techno curvy inside the big plate glass windows. The dishes cooked up by Argentinean chef Gustavo Navarro cost $2.50-$8.50 for his soups, salads, and tapas, and $10-$12 for the larger lunch platters, and it all sounds fantastic. There's gazpacho, there's corn salad, there are crab cakes with mango and black bean salsa, empanadas, and sunwraps (burrito-like items full of interesting stuffings, along the lines of World Wrapps), plus various fish dishes. Unfortunately the fresh flavors touted by the menu aren't quite as fabulous as expected. Nothing is bad, but the food just isn't quite as interesting as it promises.

BELDEN PLACE

This short lane between Pine & Bush and Kearny & Montgomery is the new restaurant row. The pavement is crowded with rows of outdoor tables and umbrellas, and your dining choices include French, Italian, American Pub, Mediterranean, and Mexican, with interior decors to match their culinary themes. And if none of that suits you, there's always the Burger King and Mrs. Fields cookies at the end of the lane.

CAFE BASTILLE, 22 Belden. 415-986-5673. It is open Monday-Thursday 10am-10pm and Friday-Saturday 10am-11pm, with live jazz Thursday-Saturday. This is the French portion of Belden, with choices of crepes, croque monsieur and madam sandwiches, andouille sausage with sautéed onions, grilled Ahi tuna with pesto, and quiche ($7-$12). They also have salads and onion soup, plus French country entrees like pork loin with prune sauce or roasted chicken Basquaise with couscous and ratatouille. The food is pretty good, and the jazz at night is a nice plus.

CAFE TIRAMISU, 28 Belden. 415-986-5673. It is open Monday-Friday for lunch 11:30am-3pm, and for dinner Monday-Saturday 5:30-10:30pm. Chef Pino Spinoso from Basilicata does a menu of varied Italian cuisine, drawing on the flavors he grew up on in southern Italy as well as more commonly known Italian dishes. The pastas and entrees ($8-$15) include lots of eggplant, tomato, and sharp cheeses, plus caper sauces, lamb chops, and pan-roasted salmon on a bed of cannellini beans, artichokes, and radicchio. This is one of the better options among the Belden restaurants.

VIC'S PLACE, 44 Belden. 415-981-5222. It is a saloon with typical American pub-style food, open 10-10 Monday-Friday. They have a vast array of burgers, some salads, and daily specials, all for $4.50-$10.25.

CAFE 52, 52 Belden. 415-433-5200. Mediterranean cuisine is served for lunch Monday-Friday 11am-3pm, and dinner 5-10pm Wednesday-Friday. They have Middle Eastern appetizers such as baba ganoush and hummus, big salads from classic Greek to Caesar to chicken salad, and a Mediterranean array of entrees ($8-$12) that includes shish kebab, tortellini Alfredo, pizza, risotto alla Milanese, and crab quesadilla.

LITTLE FIESTA TAQUERIA, 56 Belden. 415-989-9750. It's open Monday-Friday 11am-3pm for lunch. The usual selection of burritos, tostadas, nachos, and tacos ($3.60-$7), but the quality isn't very good.

INEXPENSIVE
Mediterranean

CAFE DE STIJL, *1 Union Street. 415-291-0808. Located near Levi Plaza, this is a small, artistic cafe with a chic design and a changing menu. Entrees cost $4.50-$7, is open Monday-Friday 7am-5pm, and Saturday 8:30am-3:30pm.*

Pronounced "de shteel" after the early 1900s Netherlandic school of art that favored rectangular shapes and primary colors, their artful tables and chairs are not plentiful in the tiny space, but on nice days there's additional seating at tables on the sidewalk. The food varies, but there are always salads and pastas, and pizzettas and polenta too. There's a Middle Eastern and Mediterranean cast to the food, so the grilled chicken sandwich might have a zatar and garlic labne sauce, spicy lemon chicken kebabs come with Persian rice pilaf, and the turkey sandwich is accented with provolone, pesto, and roasted peppers.

Sandwiches, Salads, & Picnic Supplies

LA NOUVELLE PATISSERIE, *895 Market. 415-979-0553. It's near Fourth, on the ground level of the San Francisco Shopping Center, and they're open Monday-Saturday 9:30am-8pm, and Sunday 9:30am-6pm.*

If you've been shopping and shopping and are close to dropping if you don't eat something soon, the Patisserie is handy and good. Along with a full range of coffees and exquisite fruit tarts, pastries, and cakes (delicious but not overly rich or sweet), they have some very tasty panini sandwiches, quiche, and tortellini salad for just $3.25-$7 a dish.

PICKLE, PEPPER & ROMAINE, INC., *200 Pine. 415-433-9904. Located near Battery and open Monday-Friday 7am-4pm while the other branch at 95 Fremont, 415-243-9088, near Mission, is open Monday-Friday 10am-3pm.*

Neither are big on decor or atmosphere, but they are both places to get quick, inexpensive deli. They have a vast array of fresh sandwich makings and a good number of ready-to-go salads too, all for $2.75-$4. There aren't many places where you can eat for money like that.

Thai

MITAPAB, *124 Columbus. 415-296-8330. Located near Pacific and open Monday-Friday 11am-10pm and Saturday 5-10pm, serving excellent Thai food in their upstairs maroon-hued dining room, or by delivery, for $5-$8 an entree.*

There are wonderful curries and Thai salads, lots of vegetarian dishes, fried rice noodle meals, and spicy soups. They don't get a lot of notice, but Mitapab has some of the best and certainly the most undiscovered Thai food in the city. And for dessert, there's fried bananas with coconut ice cream, which is always fine, and when the season allows, the more traditional mango with sticky rice.

Vietnamese
TÚ LAN, *8 Sixth Street. 415-626-0927. Located near Market, this is a magnificent Vietnamese hole-in-the-wall that's open Monday-Saturday 11am-9pm.*

They're proud to list Julia Child as one of their fans, and she visits for good reasons. It's smoky from the grill, the tables are a bit sticky, and the decor is all sleaze street drab, but the fantastic food for just $3.75-$6 makes it worth enduring the linoleum and florescent lights. Their soups are legendary, and big enough to easily feed two, and the salads, grilled items, noodle and rice dishes are equally good. It's not worth planning your day around, but it's a great place to know about if you're down on Market Street when you get hungry.

FISHERMAN'S WHARF
EXPENSIVE
French
CHEZ MICHEL, *804 North Point. 415-775-7036. Located near Hyde, French style dinners are served Tuesday-Sunday 5:30-10:30pm.*

The contemporary elegance of the dining room (with its blond wood, plantation shutters, spacious tables, and white linen) is inviting, and the food sounds good, too. Entrees ($13-$23) run the gamut from the vegetarian plat du jour to marinated venison with pink pepper sauce, yams, and chestnut puree. There are some very good fish dishes (Ahi Tuna in coriander sauce or scallops in rich mustard) plus a fine pheasant dish with duck mousse. It's all served in the bright and soothing room by a gracious staff for a stylish, leisurely dining experience.

MODERATE
French
ZAX, *2330 Taylor. 415-563-6266. Zax is located between Columbus and Francisco and serves nouvelle French cuisine in a cozy yet formal dining room not far from Fisherman's Wharf, towards North Beach. They're open for dinner only, Tuesday-Saturday from 5:30-10pm.*

The menus change a bit from month to month, but certain favorites are standard. The goat cheese soufflé starter ($5.50) is delectable, and the salads are very well done, too. Entrees ($13.50-$17) include roast rabbit (with artichokes, braised garlic, chanterelles, and prosciutto), oven roasted ono, risotto of rock shrimp, and steelhead salmon wrapped in bacon with lentils, roasted winter vegetables, and thyme. At Zax they put great care into their cooking and their service as well. It's a lovely place for a special meal.

INEXPENSIVE
Mexican
TAQUERIA SAN JOSÉ, *2257 Mason. 415-749-0826. Located near Francisco, just a block up from Bay, it's open 9am-9pm daily with the best Mexican available in the Wharf or North Beach, and the prices are low ($2-$5.50).*

This taqueria serves Mexican breakfasts, filling and tasty burritos (the chicken is especially good), and full dinners served with beans and soup featuring Mexican specialties like menudo (weekends only) and enchiladas verdes. They have delicious, refreshing agua fresca (fresh fruit drinks of melon, lemon, or horchata) for just $1. The jukebox is awful, however, and the interior has that fast food aura to it. If you're hungry, you like authentic Mexican cuisine, and want a quick meal in or a great picnic to go (neither the piers at the wharf nor Washington Square Park in North Beach are more than a few minutes away), this new place is a great addition to the neighborhood.

HAIGHT ASHBURY & LOWER HAIGHT
MODERATE
Caribbean
CHA CHA CHA, *1801 Haight. 415-386-5758. Located near Shrader, it is pure delight with excellent Caribbean style tapas and main dishes. Open daily 11:30am-4pm and 5-11pm (till 11:30pm Friday and Saturday), they take neither credit cards nor reservations.*

Dinner time almost always entails a wait, but they do have a bar area to start on sangria and gaze at the gold-sprayed cupids hanging from the ceiling in the meantime, or you can put your name on the list and take a stroll. Through the door and you're among a lively, colorful group of little tables (covered with blue and green plastic depicting bountiful fruit baskets), weird, enigmatic shrines up on the walls, welcoming brick walls, green palms, and nifty music. Fun as the energy is here, the food is even better. People mostly share tapas ($4.50-$7), though the main dishes ($10.25-$12.50) are no slouches. The shrimp sautéed in Cajun spices is very good, and the grilled chicken pailliard with mustard sauce is incredible, as is the fried plantains with black beans and sour cream. You need to not mind close crowds and noise to enjoy, but if you like an up-beat atmosphere, you'll like the lively pace and great food here.

Thai
THEP PHANOM, *400 Waller. 415-431-2526. Located near Fillmore, it serves some the best Thai food in San Francisco nightly from 5:30-10:30pm for $6-$10 an entree, and reservations are a good idea.*

This is a pretty restaurant with Victorian appeal, and the coconut chicken soup is sensational, and the beef salad and the curries are pretty great, too. The service is impeccable, and the meal won't disappoint.

INEXPENSIVE
African
   MASSAWA RESTAURANT, *1538 Haight. 415-621-4129. Located near Ashbury, it is open 11:30am-10pm on weekdays and 11:30am-11pm on weekends, serving delicious East African Eritrean food, with the spongy injera bread under mounds of stewed meats, lentils, spinach, and yogurt.*

Massawa has both meat and vegetarian dishes, lined with injera and piled with chickpeas, lentils, spinach, and salad, for $7-$10, but two can easily split one plate for a lunch or light meal.
   AXUM CAFE, *698 Haight. 415-252-7912. Located near Pierce, it serves truly delicious and inexpensive Ethiopian food daily from 10am-10:30pm.*

An Ethiopian breakfast starts the day like no other, with shehan foul or fitfit breakfast (one with fava beans, tomatoes, jalapeno pepper, sour cream, and garlic all topped with Ethiopian spices and served with a French roll, the other made of French bread cut in pieces and topped with Ethiopian sauce and yogurt, for $3.50-$3.75, though there are traditional American breakfasts ($4) as well. The main dishes, both meat and vegetarian, are excellent too; they're swell for lunch or dinner, and cost a mere $4-$6.

What you get is a big plate, lined with injera (the thin, spongy, crepe-like bread that keeps your fingers clean as you scoop and mop up all the goodness), and topped with the dish of your choice. The dinner-for-two plate is exceptionally beautiful, and comes topped with beautiful piles of all five vegetarian stews. They're all great, but if you need to chose just a few, the spinach (*hamli*), mushroom (*kintishara*), and lentils (*tumtumo*) are especially fine. You don't need (or get) utensils. You just tear into the injera, scoop up a mound of spicy ragout, pop it in your mouth, and you're on your way.

This is a low-budget venture in all sorts of ways. The tables and chairs are your basic formica and vinyl, the decor consists mostly of an amateur-but-colorful Ethiopian mural on one wall, and the staff consists of two people working hard in the kitchen and on the floor. But a fine aroma fills the small room, and the food, while inexpensive, is finely cooked and lovingly arranged. And there's a wide variety of drinks (good beers on tap, coffee or chocolate drinks, steamed milk specials, and fruit drinks) to wash it all down.

Mexican
   ZONA ROSA, *1797 Haight. 415-668-7717. Located near Shrader, they make excellent burritos as well as other Mexican dishes 11am-10:30pm daily, and they're healthy, too.*

Everything except the tortillas are made from scratch, the beans and sauces are cooked without lard, and no preservatives, tenderizers, or artificial coloring taints the food. In the burritos ($3.75-$4.45) you get your choice of whole bean or refried, and a half of one makes a pretty filling meal. They also carry enchiladas, tacos, tamales, quesadillas, and fajitas, but it's the burritos that most customers come back for. When I've been stranded on a foreign long-distance bus, starving and without a rest-stop in sight, it's the Zona Rosa burritos that have tortured my imagination and added to my hunger.

Middle Eastern

KAN ZAMAN, *1793 Haight. 415-751-9656. Located near Stanyan, it serves Middle Eastern cuisine Tuesday-Sunday noon-midnight and Monday 4:30pm-midnight, no credit cards accepted.*

Through the beaded entrance is the Middle Eastern emporium of hummus and dolma, dim lights, desert colors of sands and burnt orange, and hubble bubble hookahs to boot. Started a few years ago as a place to hang and be welcome, eat well without breaking the bank, and relax in the traditional leisurely pace of the Middle East, there are traditional seatings in little nooks with lots of fabric and pillows, plus regular western tables with chairs.

Hot and cold maza appetizers ($2.50-$4) like hummus, baba ganoush, meat or spinach pies, and foul mudamas (which isn't foul at all, but the name for fava beans in a garlic lemon sauce) are delicious, and perfect for a nibble or a meal. Main dishes ($6.50-$8) run from the simple but tasty Imjadare (a rice, lentil, onion, and yogurt mix) to various shish kebabs. In the Levant, after a full meal one lazes back with an Arabic coffee and a toke on the water pipe (called *Argeelah* in Israel and Palestine, *Shee Sha* in Egypt, and *Hubble Bubble* by tourists). This pleasure is only available to men in the Middle East, but for a mere $7 Kan Zaman brings you a pipe, loaded with one of their aromatic tobaccos ($2 a refill), regardless of gender or any other factor. Or forget the smoke and just relax with coffee or tea.

HAYES VALLEY

EXPENSIVE

Italian

VIVANDE RISTORANTE, *670 Golden Gate. 415-673-9245. Located near Franklin, it is a grand and lovely Italian restaurant in Opera Plaza, open daily 11:30am-11pm.*

It's very Mediterranean inside Vivande, with all those popular ambers and ochres and terra cottas, creating a serene ambiance, with great lamps, and designs etched on the wall. Carlo Middione's fine and rustic cuisine is prepared in the open kitchen for $12.50-$22.50. The risottos are especially good, and the lunch pizzas are quite nice, too, but don't fill up on pasta or pizza because the chocolate earthquake cake still awaits.

Seafood
HAYES STREET GRILL, *320 Hayes. 415-863-5545. Located near Franklin, it serves lunch weekdays 11:30am-2pm and dinner Monday-Thursday 5:30-930pm, Friday-Saturday till 10:30pm, and Sunday till 8:30pm.*

Inside their basic formal dining room (white linen, pristine setting), all looks very nice, but the tables are a bit close together. Their specialty is seafood, and their fish dishes ($11.50-$18.50) typically are very fresh with simple sauces. There's Yellowfin and Sea Bass, Swordfish and Ono, all with your choice of sauce on the side. The shellfish dishes are excellent, too, and the creme brulee is a popular way to polish off the meal.

MODERATE
German
SUPPENKÜCHE, *601 Hayes. 415-252-9289. Located near Laguna and serving the best German food in town, with a beer list to match, and they're open nightly for dinner 5-10pm and for brunch on the weekend 10am-3pm.*

The best of German hospitality and peasant simplicity awaits you within. Raw pine wood tables bear steins of flowers, the plain white walls are trimmed with forest green, and a few strands of ivy loop about the specials black board. The atmosphere is both pleasant and festive, and while you wait for your meal ($9.50-$14.50 a main dish) you can amuse yourselves with good beer and attempts at pronouncing your dishes in German. Jägerschnitzel mit Spätzle, Champigionsauce und gemishtem Salat is nearly as much of a mouthful as the pork loin with mushroom cream sauce, dumplings, and mixed salad itself. The food is delicious, for example the potato pancakes, heavenly Spätzle in cheese and onion sauce, wonderful German ravioli, and tasty schnitzel, too.

There's plenty of pork on the menu, but there's also some chicken and fish, and a few vegetarian items as well. The brunches ($5-$8.50) are heart-warming and belly-filling too, with light standards like muesli, potato pancakes, and Kaiserschmarrn mit Apfel und Pflaumenmus (Emperor's pancake with apple and plum compote) and heavier fare like grilled pork sausages with sauerkraut and mashed potatoes that should send you home for a solid afternoon nap.

JAPANTOWN & WESTERN ADDITION
EXPENSIVE
Japanese
YOYO TSUMAMI BISTRO, *1611 Post. 415-922-7788. Located near Laguna, this is an East-West restaurant serving very interesting and tasty meals*

for breakfast, lunch, and dinner daily from 6:30-11am, 11:30am-2:30pm, and 5:30-10pm, while the bar is open and serves food daily 11:30am-11pm. The restaurant melds French and Japanese cooking, resulting in a successful new approach, thanks to chef Michael Leviton. Downstairs you'll find contemporary design with white linen, candles, flatware and chopsticks. Japanese-style windows look out over Post Street, while western style chairs provide the seating. Appealing colors of burnt orange, green, and mauve brighten up the walls, and appealing modern music plays softly in the background. Upstairs in the bar area it's more informal, but equally pleasant. The light fixtures are artistic, lovely, and interesting, and they cast just the right tone.

The dinner entrees change from time to time, range from $15-$19, and feature such culinary treats as roasted halibut with green papaya in coconut broth with cilantro pesto, a crisp skinned salmon with green lentils, Bhutanese red rice and garlic cream, and red curry melted duck with sautéed greens, bacon, and ginger tomato confit. They also have a sumami menu (little dishes like tapas) that includes red curry spiced beef with green papaya salad and coconut creme fraiche or sesame spinach salad that can be ordered separately ($3-$5) or in a tower of four ($15) or tower of six ($22), with bento boxes of goodies stacked one above another.

This is a great place for a long and leisurely meal or a short snack before or after a Kabuki movie.

MODERATE
French
CHEZ MOUSTACHE, *803 Fillmore. 415-922-8607. Located near Grove, it is open for dinner Tuesday-Saturday 5:30-10pm, with live weekend entertainment (such as a French ballad guitarist or a classical flutist) starting around 5:30 or 6pm.*

It's a charming little box of a room, done up nicely in salmons and peaches with blue trim. The tables are covered with white linen and paper, nice candles add a warm glow, and the entrees cost $9-$16. The kitchen is right off the dining room, and a festive atmosphere often develops, with chef Alex Longardino calling out and interacting with the diners. They offer traditional hors d'oeuvres like escargot, onion soup, and pate de foie de canard, the pasta is homemade and excellent, and the beef Bourguignonne and coq au vin are popular too.

All in all, the Moustache is a fine addition to the area. If you aren't driving, however, you might want to take a taxi, since the neighborhood can get a bit dicy at night.

Japanese
ISOBUNE SUSHI, *1737 Post. 415-563-1030. Located near Buchanan in Japan Center, better known as the Sushi Boat place, it is open 11:30am-10pm daily.*

They may not have the very best sushi in the world, nor the largest selection, but it's a very entertaining way to dine on sushi. What they have is a circular counter around a channel of water, on which boats topped with sushi dishes float by. You have to think fast, because by time you decide you want a particular item, it may be way down stream if you don't adroitly grab the dish of your dreams while it's still in front of you. Have a few jars of sake and see if that improves your aim. You just take what you like and pile the empty dishes by your side (that's how they'll figure the bill when it's time to pay), though you can also ask the waiter for items you don't see on the sushi stream.

The plates range in price from $1.20-$2.50, and typically hold two pieces of sushi, so your ultimate bill depends on how big your appetite is and how expensive your taste. The sushi is pretty good, if not spectacular, and it makes for a fun night out.

INEXPENSIVE
Japanese
TAMPOPO, *1740 Buchanan. 415-346-7132. Located on the pedestrian walkway between Post and Sutter, they serve their glorious bowls of ramen 11:30am-2:30pm and 5:30-11pm, though their day off has not yet been decided. At press time there was no visible sign with the restaurant's name, but it's right under the Video CD People Rental and across from Neo Town House Living.*

Clean and airy, stylish and spacious, and very new. For years they operated out of a little hole-in-the-wall upstairs in the Japan Center's Peace Plaza, and when the doors shut and the lights went out, loyal fans from all over San Francisco mourned. So it was grounds for great rejoicing when it became clear that they had in fact just moved across the street to a spiffier space, with a long green bar and plenty of tables not too close together. The menu remains the same, and if the absurdly low prices have been jacked up a dollar, the food is well worth it.

My favorite is Ramen Noodle With Wonton and Roasted Pork, but it is the homemade broth that lifts the meal out of the ordinary. It is a soup the truck-driver in the movie *Tampopo* (their namesake) would have approved of heartily. The soup bowls are enormous (one could easily feed two people), and still inexpensive. They range from $4.50-$6.75, and they're all good. There are other dishes as well, such as pan-fried noodles, curry rice and pot stickers (no treat), but ramen is the focus here.

MARINA & COW HOLLOW
EXPENSIVE
American

IZZY'S STEAK & CHOP HOUSE, *3345 Steiner. 415-563-0487. Located near Lombard, it is open daily for dinner from 5:30pm-10:30 on weeknights, 5pm-10pm on Sunday, and 5:30-11pm on the weekend.*

Steaks here will cost you $20 a plate, and it's a fine celebration of the steak house tradition (the New York sirloin with creamed spinach and fries is an especially swell, meaty meal). Unlike many of the other steak houses in San Francisco, Izzy's is casual inside, with a saloon atmosphere and lots of San Francisco and Izzy memorabilia on the wall. It's named after Izzy, a Portuguese immigrant who ran a speakeasy downtown during prohibition. His place on Pacific featured steak and booze from when he opened in 1910 to when he died in 1944, and today's Izzy's is not only named in his honor, it carries on the tradition.

Mediterranean

PLUMP JACK CAFE, *3127 Fillmore. 415-563-4755. Located near Filbert, it offers innovative Mediterranean cuisine and excellent wine options weekdays for lunch 11:30am-2pm and Monday-Saturday for dinner 5:30-10:30pm, at $14-$20 a dish.*

Taupe walls and chairs pair up with white linen and fresh, artful flowers for an unusual, appealing look, while interesting, metallic touches add a unique, new San Francisco feel. They also have a private room in back which can be reserved at no extra charge. The menu changes daily, but you can count on the Caesar salad, the duck confit with brandied apple compote, and while the risotto is always good, the ingredients might be artichokes, lemon, chevre, and leeks one week and something else the next, and the grilled pork loin with cipolline onions, rhubarb, mustard greens, and sweet potato puree will change with the season.

While the food is excellent, they are also well known for their wine. The list changes all the time as new harvests come in, and they're brought to you with just a nominal mark-up. With over 60 wines on the list, 25 or more of which can be ordered by the glass as well, wine mavens will be in heaven. And, the knowledgeable, friendly staff will be happy to assist the rest of us.

MODERATE
Asian

BETELNUT, *2030 Union. 415-929-8855. Located near Buchanan, it is open Sunday-Thursday from 11:30am-11pm and Friday-Saturday from 11:30am-midnight. It's an exciting new Asian restaurant that mixes innovation, style, and some very good food.*

You're advised to try this place out during the day or on a week night, because it gets so jam-packed on a Saturday night that the unfortunates who didn't plan ahead with reservations end up waiting 45 minutes or more, and the bar area gets more crowded than a rush hour bus, and just as pleasant. Asian accents decorate in a spare sort of way, the counter is candy red, and synchronized bamboo fans over the bar help keep the air circulating.

Wade past the bar scene, however, and the dining room is a beautiful, calm oasis, free from the mob scene up front, with spacious, comfy booths and tables, and magnificent aromas. The rooms just keeps on going back and around, full of deep wood tones, tile floors, and a gentle, quiet patter of dishes and conversations. And the food is as tasty as it is varied. Ranging from $5-$15, their selections include curried beef samosas with papaya chutney, chicken salad with red pepper dressing, oven smoked sea bass with ginger cucumber nanasu, tea smoked duck, and Singapore chili crab. And if you forget to make reservations, the Dragonfly Lounge has a panoply of deluxe drinks, from the Jade Empress to the Taiwan On to entertain you while you wait.

British

LIVERPOOL LIL'S, *2942 Lyon. 415-921-6664. It is near Lombard and across from the Presidio gate, and they're open Monday-Friday 11am-2am and weekends 10am-2am.*

Liverpool Lil's claims to have one of the best burgers in San Francisco, but their menu offers much more than standard pub grub, most of which is available for reasonable $7-$13 prices. Their burgers are, in fact, magnificent. They get an A+ in burgerdom – tasty and meaty, and topped with good quality cheese and grilled onions, though the accompanying shoestring fries are way too dry.

But along with the fish and chips, and the steak and kidney pie, they prepare appetizers like escargot, mussels marinara, and baked brie, and their dinner menu includes a good number of steaks, chops, chicken Dijonaise, and bouillabaisse. In addition, they are a good alternative to Mel's for a late-night snack. Out front under the festive lights is a nice patio with tables, but the main restaurant dining room is inside, in back, past the bar. Smoke-free, pub-like, and very appealing, there's grillwork and colored glass, tablecloths under glass, and lots of happily dining families and couples. The bar section, also friendly, is a bit smokier. There are your basic stools at the bar, booth banquettes, a couple of big sports screens, and a wall plastered with sports photos, plus one secluded nook by the window with two stools, a little shelf for drinks, and the best views of the house. Lil's is a very happening place on a weekend afternoon, with the dining room and patio (in good weather) packed with brunches and lunchers, and the bar full of early revelers. With brick floors and dark wood, all of Lil's has a warm, congenial air, and good food, too.

French

BAKER STREET BISTRO, *2953 Baker. 415-931-1475. Located between Greenwich and Lombard, it serves wonderful, moderately-priced French food Tuesday-Saturday 5:30-10:30pm and Sunday 5-9:30pm for dinner and 10am-2pm Tuesday-Sunday for lunch.*

Cozy, charming, candlelit, and all other fine descriptions beginning with "c," this is a delightful little spot in which to enjoy Patrick Garnier's fine French cuisine, and the attached cafe next door is where they serve lunch. The romantic atmosphere is enhanced by the tile floor and the local artwork hanging on their walls. Luscious fruit paintings add warmth and color now, but the displays change every few months. The quality of the food, however, remains constant. A la carte dishes ($4.75-$6.25 for lunch and $8.75-$9.75 for dinner) include croque monsieur, goat cheese salad, chicken breast in ginger sauce, and rabbit in mustard, or take the best deal in town, their four-course dinner for $14.50.

Italian

PANE E VINO, *3011 Steiner. 415-346-2111. Located near Union, it is a cozy trattoria serving Northern Italian standards Monday-Saturday 11:30-2:30 for lunch and for dinner 5-9:30pm on Sunday, 5-10pm Monday-Thursday, and 5-10:30pm Friday-Saturday.*

Classic Italian decor of brick and plaster sets the tone, and the smell of fresh, warm bread fills the air. The tables are awfully close together, however, and it gets a bit noisy when the room is full. The food is generally tasty, and priced at $8-$18 an entree, depending on whether you go for pasta or lamb chops. The polenta is reliably good, as is the whole grilled fish, and the gnocchi with roasted rabbit. And this must be the one Italian restaurant in the city that serves butter instead of olive oil with their bread.

LA PERGOLA, *2060 Chestnut. 415-563-4500. Located near Steiner, they're open 5:30-10:30pm week nights and till 11pm on weekends.*

Done up nicely inside with linen tables and roses, low track lighting, and lovely pictures on the wall – but the tables are pretty close together, and you are bound for disappointment if you require candlelight with your dinner. The food is, of course, Italian, with a little of everything. Starters ($5.50-$8) include standard sautéed mushrooms on polenta, calamari in a spicy tomato and garlic sauce, and carpaccio, while the pasta ($9.50-$12.50) feature risotto and gnocchi daily, plus a ravioli filled with ricotta and spinach in lemon cream sauce, and pasta hats stuffed with chicken and sausage. Then there are the meat entrees ($15.50) of lamb, veal, prawns, pork, and rabbit. Owned by the same man who runs

Mangiafuoca in the Mission, La Pergola has been serving good quality food to Marina locals for ten years.

Mexican

CAFE MARIMBA, *2317 Chestnut. 415-776-1506. Located near Scott, it's open 11:30am-11pm week days (except Monday afternoons, when they're closed) and 11:30am-midnight on weekends.*

Another Reed Hearon and Louise Clement special, this Mexican restaurant is as popular as Lulu's, their Mediterranean place in SoMa. Colorful Mexican folk art rules the interior, delicious Oaxaca cuisine fills the tables, and the Marina crowds love it. What is pleasantly lively most of the time turns unpleasantly loud and crowded when it gets packed, like Saturday night, when the waiting line is long and boisterous. Tons of weird little figurines stand along the ledge, and up above is a humongous orange papiermache being with horns, bulging eyes, and a wild protruding tongue. There are bright colors everywhere, and good smells as well. If you're really lucky, you can nab one of the window tables, and watch the scenes inside and out. With entrees priced $6-$14, the moles are especially good, and the enchiladas are too.

Mediterranean

CAFFE CENTRO, *3340 Steiner. 415-202-0100, fax 415-202-0153. It is open Tuesday-Saturday 5-11pm, and Sunday 10am-3pm for brunch and 5:30-9:30pm for dinner.*

The brunch selection includes an eclectic mix of items, from Huevos Centros to house-made granola with fruit and yogurt, Nicoise salad to a Moroccan chicken sandwich ($4.50-$9). The dinners have the same eclectic flair (minus the granola), and offers some very interesting pastas (including pumpkin ravioli), some wonderful salads like warm baby spinach with pear, walnut, and gorgonzola, and some fine meaty entrees of duck, chicken, salmon, or lamb for $7.50-$14. In addition to good food and a friendly, with-it aura, Centro has patio dining, microbrews on tap, and live jazz every Wednesday and Sunday night.

Spanish Tapas

ALEGRIAS, *2018 Lombard. 415-929-8888. Located near Webster. Serves Spanish tapas Wednesday-Sunday 11:30am-2:30pm, and daily 5:30-11pm. In addition, Thursday-Saturday a flamenco guitarist strums traditional Spanish tunes from 7:30ish till 10pm.*

Alegrias offers robust, family-style Spanish cuisine of tapas and entrees in a friendly, appealing setting for $9.50-$13.50 an entree and $3-$6 for tapas. They opened in the latter part of '95, and chef-owner Cesar Faedi does a fine job cooking up his inherited family recipes, served in pleasant surroundings at tables spaced for privacy; the dining rooms manage airy, light, cozy, and warm all at the same time. The white walls are hung with ivy and hand-painted dishes, the tables are set with white linen and candles, and the Spanish guitar music is a perfect touch.

Interesting tapas include mussels in garlic and wine, brandy-flamed cheese, stewed tripe, garlicky shrimp, and crepes filled with tuna, apple, and hearts of palm. The entrees are also terrific, like the crispy garlic chicken, and zarzuela de mariscos. The desserts, too, are unusually good. *Alegrias* means joy, and it's expressed delightfully in both the delicious food and the warm atmosphere.

Tibetan

LHASA MOON, *2420 Lombard. 415-674-9898. Located near Scott, this is yet another restaurant in restaurant-glutted Marina, but it's the only one in the city serving Tibetan cuisine. They just opened in 1996, and they serve their momos and high plateau pasta Tuesday-Friday 11:30am-2:30pm, and Tuesday-Sunday 4:30-10pm for $7.50-$9.50 an entree.*

Walk in and you enter a soothing, special world, less frenetic than traffic-clogged Lombard or the hip and happening Chestnut scene. The colors are peaceful, and Tibetan folk music provides pleasant and interesting background ambiance. Gyatso, the Tibet-born owner, makes sure everything runs smoothly, while the chef, also from Tibet, cooks his heart out. They both left in 1959 when the Chinese invaded, and what they recreate here is the cuisine of Lhasa before the invasion, the way they remember it from the 40s and 50s. It's a complex and tasty cuisine, well worth preserving.

Momos, the national mainstay of Tibet, are dumplings (steamed or fried) not unlike Chinese pork buns, with a doughy shell wrapping delicious fillings of chopped meat or vegetables nicely spiced and flavored. The curries also are popular; they're lighter than Indian curries, less spicy, and very good. There are quite a few vegetarian dishes, such as Himalayan corn and tofu soup, mung bean cake flavored with spicy soy vinegar, garlic, and chili, and hearty pastas as well. Not only is it unusual, it's tasty too, and worth a visit.

Vegetarian

GREENS, *Fort Mason's Building A. 415-771-6222. It is open for lunch Tuesday-Thursday 11:30am-2pm and Friday-Saturday 11:30am-2:30pm, while on Sunday they serve brunch 10am-2pm. A la carte dinners are served Monday-Friday 5:30-9pm, and Saturday is the one evening they do their prix fixe dinner. Reservations are needed way in advance for a prix fixe meal, and are usually necessary for the other meals as well. However, Greens now has a Greens to Go counter that's open to all Monday-Friday 8am-9:30pm, Saturday 8am-4:30pm,* *and Sunday 9am-3:30pm, and you can take your soups, sandwiches and salads ($2.25-$4) to enjoy in their dining room from 8-10:30am and 2:30-5pm, when the lunches aren't in progress.*

Greens is best known for its sensational vegetarian food, organic produce, and gourmet combinations, but what comes to mind next is the view. One whole wall of windows in this converted warehouse looks out over the marina harbor, sailboats bobble in the tide. The Golden Gate Bridge connects the lumpy hills of the Marin headlands, and the Pacific Ocean stretches out toward the horizon. Views just don't get any better.

But if you can tear your eyes from the waves, the menu is pretty spectacular, too. Lunch ($5-$10) offers items like Moroccan carrot soup with spiced yogurt and cilantro or black bean chili with jack cheese and creme fraiche, wilted spinach and frisee salad with onions, feta, olives, garlic, and mint, or a pizza with peppers, onions, chipotle chilies, cilantro, cheddar, plus smoked and dry jack cheeses. Dinner entrees ($10.25-$13) are similar, though the menu is always a bit different. They have their famous pizzas but with different toppings, their mesquite grilled vegetable brochettes, risotto, and enchiladas, and more. And the brunch menu ($5.50-$10.50) is similarly fresh and intriguing.

THE STORY BEHIND GREENS

*The **Zen Center** in the sixties consisted of the San Francisco branch on Page Street and their Tassajara Zen Mountain monastery near Carmel. So popular was the Tassajara monastery summer guest season, that in 1972 the Zen Center responded to Bay Area requests and acquired Green Gulch Farm in Marin. To sell produce from the farm they opened the Green Gulch Green Grocer near the Page Street center, and they founded the Tassajara Bread Bakery to provide more of their fine baked goods to their insatiable fans. Greens restaurant started similarly in 1979. Tassajara summer guests wanted the same high quality vegetarian food in the Bay area, and Greens was the result.*

The Zen Center sold the Green Grocer in 1989 and the bakery in 1992; Greens remains their sole (but highly profitable) business. They get as many of their ingredients as possible from the Green Gulch Farm, which insures freshness and organic health. And Annie Somerville, the executive chef who got her start in cooking from her interest in Zen Buddhism, gets inspiration from the farm as well. She often visits the farm to see what's growing, and she plans her changing menus accordingly.

For all these meals, the plain, unassuming wood tables don't steal the food's thunder, while color-happy modern art paintings and interesting sculpture decorates the room. On Saturday night, however, the tables are covered with linen, the price for dinner becomes $38, and you get a feast.

There are unusual breads, like a pumpkin seed hearth loaf, plus a couple of magnificent salads, a soup, entree, and dessert. Whatever the menu, you can count on the salads and pizzas to be superb. There's no healthier, tastier way to treat yourself in the city.

INEXPENSIVE
American

HOME PLATE, *2274 Lombard. 415-922-4663. Located near Pierce, it is open for breakfast daily 7am-4pm. Reservations are taken on week days only, and on weekends there's a sign-up clipboard list outside, and a long wait.*

Inside the small, plain, white-walled room are a bunch of white formica tables with blue paper place mats, and happy brunchers digging into plates of goodness. The breakfast plates ($3.75-$7) run the gamut from egg dishes of all sorts to homemade granola with fresh fruit to cheese blintzes to pancakes, waffles, and French toast.

Their scones are legendary, and are served with each breakfast, and when you order your pancakes (or waffles or French toast) with the fresh fruit topping, there are few breakfasts anywhere that could look or taste more appealing. They do, however, serve less breakfasty items, too. They have a whole menu's worth of pasta dishes, soups and salads, sandwiches (including burgers, roasted chicken, and Andouille sausage), plus sautéed chicken dishes, and all for the same low prices.

PLUTO'S, *3258 Scott. 415-775-8867. Located near Chestnut, it is great for healthy comfort food 11:30am-10pm Monday-Thursday, 11:30am-11pm Friday, 9:30am-11pm Saturday, and 9:30am-10pm Sunday.*

Billed as "Fresh Food For A Hungry Universe," they are certainly a worthwhile and inexpensive option when your own little corner of the universe is hungry. It's a bit calmer and less frenzied than Marimba and World Wrapp's, though the music can be just a bit loud here, too. It's easy on the eyes; instead of wild colors and thingamajigs there are soothing blond wood tables, pastel accents and earth tones. One wall is filled with teaser words just barely visible, like "Steaming Hot Rich Chunky Warm" and "Creamy Smooth Luscious Tart." There are also great big plates of very tasty, healthy, cheap food ($3-$6) matching those descriptions. To partake, go to the counter and take a menu/guest check. They mark it for all that you order, bring the food to your table, and you just pay your total when you're ready to leave.

There are big and beautiful and delicious salads, there's roasted poultry and freshly grilled meats ready for the carving, eggplant sandwiches, garlic potato rings, freshly sautéed vegetables, and more. It's a friendly place, and they deliver what they promise.

International

WORLD WRAPPS, *2257 Chestnut. 415-563-9727. Located between Scott and Pierce, it serves international burritos daily 10am-11pm (and smoothies from 8am) for $3.20-$7 a meal.*

This is healthy, tasty, fast food to go, or you can eat there as well if you don't mind knocking knees with the person across the table and talking over somewhat loud music. It's cheerful and friendly in the very small walk-in, with colorfully painted tables, counters, stools, and napkin holders. Popular with the local crowd, the counter wrappers keep pretty busy. It's great for take-out, they have a good vegetarian and low-fat selection, and it's a good option for families with kids, too.

An alternative to traditional fast food, they put gourmet, fresh ingredients in tortillas made from whole wheat, tomato, or spinach. The traditional Mexican burrito is a bit boring, but the Thai chicken, teriyaki chicken, and grilled veggies with goat cheese wraps are delicious, and there are lots more (mango snapper, Mandarin stir-fry, the Bombay) that sound great. And the smoothies are sensational. Made of juice, fruit, and yogurt or sorbet, they are refreshing, fruity, and delicious. We can vouch for the Real Raspberry and the Tropical Storm, but they all look wonderful.

Italian

PASTA POMODORO, *2027 Chestnut. 415-474-3400. Located near Fillmore, open Monday-Saturday 11am-11pm, and Sunday noon-11pm, and no checks or credit cards accepted.*

This is a much smaller eatery than their North Beach branch; in fact there is just one regular table, with the rest of the seating spread out along the kitchen and window counters. Not surprisingly, there's a wait list white board outside, with a big tomato-red marker with which to sign up. But if the space is smaller, the food's just as good, mostly $4-$6 a dish, and take-out, prepared quickly, is an option, too. The cappellini pomodoro (their namesake) is very popular, and both the pesto linguini and the conchiglie gorgonzola are very fine. They also have healthy pastas prepared without oil, butter, or cheese, that are very tasty and a big selection of salads served in half or full portions, as well.

Sandwiches, Salads, & Picnic Supplies

S.F. GOURMET, *2128 Chestnut. 415-441-4800. Located between Pierce and Steiner, this is a gourmet take-out shop that's open daily 11am-10pm.*

They make interesting, fresh meals to go for $3-$5 an item. They have shelves of fancy soups like carrot ginger orange or broccoli leek, a panoply of salads, and entrees as well, like polenta. They also have a mean array of desserts, and snack foods like cheese, chips, and such. Everything is ready to go for a picnic, and they have a microwave if you want your food warmed up.

MISSION
EXPENSIVE
Nouvelle Cuisine
   FLYING SAUCER, *1000 Guerrero. 415-641-9955. Located near 22nd, it serves California eclectic for dinner Tuesday-Saturday 5:30-9:30pm for $17-$24 an entree.*
   It's a design-fest in there. Under low lights, bas relief folk art covers the walls and art objects abound. There are seats upstairs and down, in the back room or by the window, but wherever you sit, it'll be with a trendy crowd who keeps the place packed till late at night. The menu, though it changes often, is filled with items like crisp skinned salmon and roasted tomato mash in warm shiitake and chive sauce, duck confit with potato pecan pie, or a broccoli leek custard with cranberry chutney. It has a trendy, designer-type following, and a long wait for a reservation.

MODERATE
American
   WOODWARD'S GARDEN, *1700 Mission. 415-621-7122. Located near Duboce, it is a tiny and adorable restaurant with an open kitchen, serving excellent American food for dinner Wednesday-Sunday with seatings at 6, 6:30, 8, and 8:30pm. They take reservations (but no credit cards), and you need to reconfirm your reservation on the day you plan to eat at one of their nine tables.*
   The menu changes weekly, but prices are usually $14-$17, and items like fennel-stuffed pork chop with mashed potato, smoked salmon on potato-scallion latkes, and duck breast on lentils are an example of the sort of wonderful cuisine they prepare. And aside from the food, dining at Woodward's is a warm and lovely experience.

Caribbean/Latin American
   BOOGALOOS, *3296 22nd. 415-824-3211. Located near Valencia, it's open Monday-Friday 8am-3pm, Saturday-Sunday 9am-4pm, Tuesday-Thursday 5-10pm, and Friday-Saturday 5-11pm, and they take neither reservations nor credit cards. Boogaloos is an American diner experience by day with Latin American accents, while at night the Latin American specials take over. Tapas run $4.25-$6, and dinner plates are $7-$11.*
   True, there are a lot of tapas spots cropping up all over the Mission, but Boogaloos has some special dishes you won't find elsewhere, like the chicken mole chalupa, the zarzuela seafood in almond saffron broth over rice, and a mixed vegetable pancake in miso ginger dressing. Owned by the same man who runs Cha Cha Cha in the Haight, with chef Peter Hood

(who started Spaghetti Western), they have the food down but the decor is still in a transitional mode. There are splatter paintings, tile mosaics, and a patch-work effect of kooky things that scream their colors at the top of their lungs. They have a strong following in the neighborhood, however, and brunch is a really happening time, especially in summer when the sidewalk tables fill up first, with lots of people waiting and milling about outside.

Indian

RASOI, *1037 Valencia. 415-695-0599. They're open for lunch (an all-you-can-eat buffet) Monday-Friday 11am-2:30pm and for dinner daily 5:30-10:30pm.*

The food here treads lightly with the oil, with their array of tandoori chicken, lamb, and prawns, their curries and seafood platters, and a good selection of vegetarian dishes, too. Dinner entrees range from $8.50-$13, while the lunch time buffet is just $6. Their motto is "Indian food with a new Attitude," and the interior decor is certainly a lovely change from the usual. It is truly beautiful in there, with wood floors, stained glass, comfortable cushioned chairs, Indian murals on the walls, and candles on the tables. It is interesting and cozy and romantic and hip, and a swell place to sample north Indian cuisine.

International

THE ROOSTER, *1101 Valencia. 415-824-1222. Located near 22nd, it is open Sunday-Thursday 5:30-10pm, Friday-Saturday till 11pm, serving up hearty country concoctions from around the world for $10-$13 an entree.*

The Rooster's delicious food and mellow atmosphere make you want to linger over your dinner, and slowly drink in the earth tones, design details, savory dishes, and relaxing cordiality. The service is prompt, efficient, friendly, and knowledgeable, but it's not a place for chowing down and bolting out the door; it's much nicer to dawdle over the peasanty wood tables and enjoy.

The husband-and-wife chefs, Jean-Paul Billaut and Shaw-Na Lee, meld their international culinary expertise into an intriguingly eclectic menu, using subtle flavors that blend well, and taste very good in a light, clean way. You can start with Papa Lee's North China vegetable dumplings (tasty pot sticker crescents) or the ginger sautéed mussels, before moving on to the main dish. There's beef Bourgignon and Moroccan lamb stew, Mama Lee's Chinese braised salmon, and pasta orecchiette with wild mushrooms, roasted walnuts, broccoli, aged parmesan, and sage, and plenty available for vegetarians to choose from, as well. Jazz zings in the background, adding an upbeat feel, while little candles flicker on the tables. Strings of dried peppers and gourds hang off the pillars and wall, and the room curves round and back like an underground cavern, but the light fixtures defy easy description. Made with artistic combinations of crystal, rusted iron, wire mesh, and green glass, they provide just enough light to enhance the rustic tone. Good for a family, a friendly gathering, or a romantic date, with hearty, fresh food, and genial warmth.

Italian

MANGIAFUOCA, *1001 Guerrero. 415-206-9881. Located near 22nd, it serves dinner nightly, 5:30-10pm on weeknights and till 11pm on weekends.*

They opened four years ago, an informal and rustic, cozy version of their more classical La Pergola that's been in business since 1988 in the Marina. It's charming inside. They play a little jazz, and a little Italian music on the CD, and have a warm and homey fireplace, and little lamps strung on little wire tracks light up the room. The floors are wood, the tables are splashed with muted colors and designs, palm trees are scattered about, and cheerful colors coat the walls, decorated with beautiful artwork.

But this isn't a museum, it's a place to eat. Their Northern Italian cuisine ($9.50-$14.50) has a touch of California to it, and it's very good. Antipasti offer sautéed mushroom and zucchini on soft polenta, and spinach salad with gorgonzola in mustard dressing. For an entree, you can choose from their home-made pasta (such as the risotto and the gnocchi of the day, tagliolini with seafood and sundried tomato, and pasta filled with salmon mousse in a saffron-like sauce), or from the meat and seafood dishes done on the wood burning grill. All in all, the combination of good food and friendly Italian warmth has made this a new favorite in the Mission, and for good reason.

Japanese

WE BE SUSHI, *1071 Valencia. 415-826-0607. Located near 21st, it is on restaurant row (they also have branches in the Richmond and the Sunset). They're open for lunch Monday-Friday 11:30am-2:30pm and for dinner Monday-Saturday 5-10pm.*

This is a tiny restaurant, but it's very pleasant and casual nonetheless, and a reliably nice place to go for sushi. Their sushi items range from $1.50-$3, and are always fresh and tasty. There's an upbeat, slightly tongue-in-cheek attitude about the place, and they have an amusing story on the back of their menu about how their first name (McSushi) was contested by McDonald's, and how they came to get the name they now use, but the big draw is the good, reasonably priced food.

Mediterranean

BRUNO'S, *2389 Mission. 415-550-7455. Located near 20th, this is one of the most happening Mission restaurants of the moment, and they're open for* *dinner Tuesday-Sunday 6:30pm-1am (and the lounge is open nightly from 6pm-2am).* First opened in the 1930s, last year Bruno's came back big time with a stylish supper club look and '50s era jazz in the bar. The dining room is a bit more formal than the lounge, with white linen and luxurious, high, curved, red wrap-around booths for cozy dining with a view. Entrees here cost $10-$16, with items such as quail salad, steamed mussels in orange saffron broth, Moroccan duck leg with Israeli couscous, and red wine braised oxtails with parsnip mashed potatoes going like expensive hot cakes.

Middle Eastern
ARABIAN NIGHTS, *811 Valencia Street. 415-821-9747. Located near 19th, it is open for dinner Tuesday-Saturday 6pm-midnight, and they have got wonderful belly dancing shows, too.*

Arabian Nights is full of Middle Eastern atmosphere, from the kilims and low but comfortable cushion seats with etched brass trays and tacky red candles to the scarves and copper teapots dangling about. There's even a fake stone wall with water trickling down into a little pool. The meze starter dishes ($3.25-$6) are terrific, and the entrees ($9.50-$15) of kebabs, rack of lamb, and the like are also done well. It is, however, a bit of an odd crowd who hangs out here, further imbuing the place with an authentically foreign feel that's part fancy and part sleaze.

Nouvelle Cuisine
VAL 21, *995 Valencia. 415-821-6622. Located at 21st (hence the name), it is open for dinner Sunday-Thursday 5:30-10pm and Friday-Saturday 5:30-11pm, and for brunch on the weekend 10:00am-1:30pm, and there's free (validated) parking at the garage across the street.*

Chef Collin Smith's eclectic California cuisine include main dishes ($12-$16) like southwestern blackened free-range chicken, which comes with chipotle-lime aioli, brown rice, orange scented black beans, and fried plantains, while the grilled salmon in coconut curry sauce incorporates Asian influences. Their Caesar salad is a frequently requested starter, and the chocolate pudding dessert also enjoys a loyal following. Inside, it's artfully designed and decorated, with lots of colors, dim lights and candles, an airy ambiance, and an appealing, casual feel.

THE SLOW CLUB, *2501 Mariposa. 415-241-9390. Located near Hampshire, The Slow Club is open for lunch Monday-Friday 11:30am-3pm, dinner Tuesday 6:30-10pm, and Wednesday-Saturday 6:30-11pm, and reservations aren't accepted.*

This area is now called North Mission (the new triangle of hip restaurants and clubs), and the film noir, industrial, spare hi-tech look helps make this the place to be. Designed by award-winning Praxis architects as a lounge, the dimly-lit bar draws the locals as a favored hang-out; all you have to do is walk inside to know this is where the cool people go to eat and relax. The kitchen prepares California cuisine at about $5.50-$12 a dish; the menu changes daily but the food is always terrific.

They often feature tamales, pizza, lasagna, pork loin, polenta, and pasta, done exquisitely with innovative combinations of the freshest ingredients. The antipasto plate of fresh roasted vegetables and cheese is great, and the pasta is excellent, too. One night's menu had braised lamb shanks on creamy polenta, and desserts like fresh poached figs with candied walnuts and creme fraiche and chocolate pot de creme with candied pecans.

Spanish Tapas

TIMO'S, *842 Valencia. 415-647-0558. This is yet another tapas restaurant, this one is open nights only from 5pm till 10:30 Sunday-Wednesday and till 11:30pm Thursday-Saturday, serving small plates for $4-$10. Live flamenco music Thursday nights; other location near Ghirardelli Square.*

Timo's serves various soups and salads, many of which feature garlic and/or anchovies, plus a wide assortment of room temperature tapas plates like the three-layer frittata of tomato, gruyere cheese, and spinach, the spicy pork tenderloin in Romesco sauce, the steamed mussels in garlic and white wine, and Peruvian rock shrimp and squid ceviche. The hot dishes are no less interesting, with frogs legs in garlic, New York steak on black beans with chipotle sauce, and Catalan spinach with pine nuts, raisins, and apricots.

INEXPENSIVE
Crepes

TI COUZ, *3108 16th Street. 415-252-7373. Located near Valencia, not far from Picaro and across from the Roxie Theater, this is a little bit of France that's gotten very popular, a Crêperie bretonne. Monday-Friday 11am-11pm, Saturday 10am-11pm, and Sunday 10am-10pm they flip pancake-like crêpes, fill them with a host of stuffings from savory to sweet for $2-$6.25, and call them krampouz.*

The savory crêpes use buckwheat flour (*blé noir*), and are filled with fine foods like egg, cheese, ratatouille, smoked salmon, or sausage. The dessert crêpes, made from wheat flour (*froment*) get filled with various butters, chocolates, and fruit, and ice cream spreads are topped with crême fraîche & chantilly (not the lace). While they don't take reservations, they do accept credit cards. The village decor is pleasant, the food is tasty, and the scene is fun. They have an attitude about food-to-go amounting to their recent New Year's resolution not to participate in it, and a little rant on their menu explaining that ("What is food-to-go anyway? Well-prepared dishes that sit too long in sauces and dressing; food that gets cold and mushy") and their related commitment to sparing the environment tons of throw-away containers. Of course, their crepes do get mushy when they sit around, so it's probably just as well.

Mexican

LA CUMBRE, *515 Valencia. 415-863-8205. Located near 16th, it has set the Mission burrito standard for 28 years. Open Monday-Saturday 11am-10pm and Sunday 11am-9pm.*

Join a long line of assorted hungry burrito-eaters and push a tray till you're asked what you want (and you'd better have made your mind up by then) plus the follow-up questions (hot sauce? tomatoes? for here or to go?). Down the line you can order drinks, and when you get to the cash register you pay for your meal ($2.75-$5.25) and whisk it off to one of the wooden table and stool sets, or off for a picnic elsewhere. The carnitas (grilled steak) is excellent, but everything else is pretty good, too. And the agua frescas (fresh fruit drinks) are wonderful.

PANCHO VILLA TAQUERIA, *3071 16th. 415-864-8840. It is just around the corner from La Cumbre between Mission and Valencia, and it's open daily 10am-midnight.*

This is another long-time neighborhood favorite, with excellent food and huge portions. You can get a very basic beans and rice burrito for about $2, and enormous super burrito will cost you $4.85, and $8 will buy a full plate with entree, beans, rice, and salad. The carne asada is especially good here, as are the agua frescas, but you're not going to go wrong here no matter what you get.

LA TAQUERIA, *2889 Mission. 415-285-7117. Located near 25th, it has been turning out good burritos and tacos for 22 years, and it's open 11am-9pm Monday-Saturday and 11am-8pm on Sunday.*

Their carnitas is especially good, and the fruit drinks (agua frescas) are deliciously refreshing. You'll pay $2.25-$3.75 a meal, and credit cards are not accepted.

Middle Eastern

AMIRA, *590 Valencia. 415-621-6213. Located near 17th, it is open for dinner Tuesday, Thursday, Sunday 5-10pm, Wednesday 5-11pm, and Friday-Saturday 5pm-midnight. They serve delicious, inexpensive Middle Eastern food, and they have live entertainment, too. The belly dancing takes place every night around 8:30pm, additional shows Wednesday, Friday, and Saturday at 10pm, plus weekend live music.*

The aura is all Arabian here, with cushions and the full array of Middle Eastern decor. It's atmospheric and entertaining, but the best part is the food. You can easily and happily fill up on their appetizers ($3.50-$7), ordering plates of hummus, baba ganoush, tomato in tahini sauce, dolmas, falafel, and tabouli. Lots of people just dip and share their way to a filling meal without spending more than $7 a head, and never making it to the entrees. However, if you want more meat on your plate, there are plenty of chicken and lamb based dishes ($8-$11) with couscous and kebabs, plus more specialty items like Damascene apricot chicken or Libyan chicken in lemon and spices. There are also a few vegetarian entrees, like kushari, Turkish eggplant, and a vegetarian couscous. And afterwards, a pot of Turkish coffee or mint tea is a sensational way to finish the meal. All in all, you'll eat very well at Amira, and the belly dancing is a lot of fun, too.

CAFE ISTANBUL, *525 Valencia. 415-863-8854. It's located between 16th and 17th and is still a tiny, cute place with cheap Middle Eastern food, though the quality seems to have gone down a bit recently.*

There are a few tables with etched brass tray tops on your way to the counter, and a few low tray tables with settee cushions that aren't quite as soft and wonderful as they look on a raised mezzanine. Beaded lanterns, rugs, and such add the Middle Eastern color, and the Fat Chance Belly Dancers are truly wonderful. They perform Saturdays at 8:30 and 9:30pm, but you'll need to get there a good bit in advance if you hope to snag a seat. They manage to combine exceptional traditional dancing and ululations with a very hip attitude. They're very cool.

The food at one time was terrific, and it's worth checking out because it may have just hit a rough patch. They have got all the usual dips to go with pita, like hummus and baba ganoush, they have dolma (not very good) and falafel, tabouli, and spinach or meat pies sandwiches for $1.50-$3.75, and $4.50-$7 for a big combo plate. They also have a whole host of teas (Arabic, mint, apple, sage, and more) by the pot, and other hot drinks (coffee and non) plus a bunch of Arabic fruity drinks.

TRULY MEDITERRANEAN, *3109 16th Street. 415-252-7482. Located near Valencia, it is open Monday-Saturday 11am-midnight and Sunday 1pm-10pm, and provides another Mission walk-in with very tasty, very cheap Middle Eastern fare.*

They have your basic falafel, shwarma (with lamb or chicken), kebabs (broiled chunks of lamb) and kebobs (ground, seasoned, grilled lamb), as well as the salads (hummus, baba ganoush, tabouli), and feta pitas. They're all fresh and tasty (in fact, they occasionally close early if they run out of food), and cost a mere $3.25-$5, tax included. To wash it all down, there are your standard soft drinks, freshly squeezed carrot or orange juices, and a refreshing garlic mint yogurt drink.

There's not much here in the way of atmosphere or decoration, but the food is very good.

Spanish Tapas
ESPERPENTO, *3295 22nd Street. 415-282-8867. Located near Valencia, it does tapas in Spanish style daily from 11:30am-3pm, and 5-10pm or so, and they don't take credit cards.*

Esperpento is bright, fun, and lively inside, and a bit noisy, too. There are lots of colors, plus fans, Spanish shawls, and pictures on the walls. With dining upstairs and down, inside and out, you've lots of options, and that's before you get to the menu. They have tons of choices, both hot and cold, including items such as cured, grilled squid, sautéed spinach in béchamel, chicken in garlic sauce, shrimp in salsa, and spicy potatoes for $3.75-$7 a plate (except for a couple pricier numbers). They also do paella ($26 for 2 people), combination platters ($5.75 for lunch and $7.50 for dinner) and various seafood and vegetarian specialties like snapper & clam in Spanish sauce.

PICARO, *3120 16th Street. 415-431-4089. Located between Valencia and Guerrero, Picaro is a fun and lively place for tapas, salads and chocolate mousse, and is open daily from 11am-3pm and 5-11pm, reservations accepted but not credit cards.*

They have live flamenco (music and dance) Thursday and Sunday nights 8-10pm (but the Sunday show is better and more passionate). To get a seat with a view on those nights, you'd be best off coming around 7pm, or making a reservation. Even without the flamenco, Picaro is a cheerful place, with great colors — orange and amber — on the walls, bizarre art work, and an interesting, vibrant crowd. The food shares the same menu and fine preparation as Esperpento, since they're owned by the same people. It's a swell place to dine, alone, with a friend, or with a group.

NOB HILL
SPLURGE
French
FLEUR DE LYS, *777 Sutter. 415-673-7779. Located near Taylor, it has been called one of the best and most romantic French restaurants, and it's open for dinner Monday-Thursday 6:30-10pm, Friday-Saturday 5:30-10pm.*

Elegant and lovely and richly sensuous within, red cloth billows down from the ceiling like an opulent tent top, the lighting is appropriately dim, and the green-rimmed china all have delicate flower patterned centers. There are a la carte menus ($27-$36 an entree), and prix fixe ($52 for vegetarian or $65 with meat), and the food is sophisticated and gourmet. The menus change all the time, but if there's no boneless quail stuffed with swiss chard and pine nuts, enhanced by foie gras, or herb crusted lamb rack on roasted shallots with olive *jus*, there'll be something else just as sublime. Wines from their wonderfully worn, leather-bound wine lists are top notch and top dollar. You can spend anywhere from $42 for a California Chardonnay to $1,450 for a Chateau Mouton Rothschild 1961, and top it all off with their amazing desserts for a very special meal.

Nouvelle Cuisine

THE DINING ROOM, *600 Stockton. 415-296-7465. Located in the Ritz-Carlton near California. The dining room turns out California French cuisine for dinner Monday-Saturday 6-9:30pm.*

The decor is elegantly, classically beautiful, with marble and fine linen, polished silver and sparkling crystal, low lights and long windows looking out over Nob Hill. The prices are fixed ($45-$59, depending on number of courses) and the food is sensational. This is a chef who believes in the best quality ingredients, and as always that philosophy adds a luster of excellence to otherwise good cuisine. The menu changes, but if you visit in the winter, you might see something like glazed oysters with leek fondue and Osetra caviar or warm quail salad with fennel pepper relish, polenta, and wild mushroom for starters, roast lobster with blood orange and tarragon or duck leg confit with pear ginger chutney for an entree. Whatever you get, it'll be delicious, and the service is in keeping with the Ritz' usual flawless, genuinely friendly style.

What's new here is the bar arrangement. It's as classy as it always has been, and it still has the largest single malt Scotch collection in the country, but the smoking policy has been undergoing some refinements. It's been a cigar-smokers' haven for some years now, but the bar entrance was open, and not all the diners appreciated the pungent aroma. When cigar smoke was banned, those used to the 'pleasure' were not thrilled. The compromise came with some reconstruction. The bar is now enclosed with a lovely beveled glass door addition, and the smoke stays in. Also of note to cigar-smokers, personal humidors can now be rented by the year. This new arrangement seems to be to everyone's liking, and the bar's clubby elegance can still be appreciated by smokers and non-smokers alike.

MASA'S, *648 Bush. 415-989-7154. Located near Powell (off the Vintage Court Hotel), it is open for dinner Tuesday-Saturday 6-9:30pm, serving one of the most exclusive and extraordinary French meals this side of the Mississippi.*

Julian Serrano's foie gras with truffle Madeira sauce and other creations make you temporarily forget the pain of the $70 (four courses) or $75 (seven courses) fixed prices. Reservations are pretty well a must, and the elegant setting nicely complements the food. It's a small dining room, draped with richly colored, silk tasseled heavy brocade. Vibrantly colored impressionistic pictures decorate the walls, adding to the opulent aura. The items change all the time, but the prix fixe menu offers lots of choices. If warm quail salad with artichokes and pine nuts doesn't thrill you, there might be oysters poached in vermouth sauce and garnished with osetra caviar for a starter. If you don't like lamb noisettes with green peppercorns in Zinfandel sauce, perhaps medallions of wild striped bass with roasted fennel will be on the menu. You may not know what your choices will be, but you do know what you'll be paying, and that you'll get a sublime meal for your money.

EXPENSIVE
American
THE BIG FOUR RESTAURANT, *1075 California. 415-474-5400. Located off the Huntington Hotel lobby, it is open Monday-Friday 7-10am, 11:30am-3pm, 5:30-10:30pm, and Saturday-Sunday 7-11am, and 5:30-10:30pm.*

The front lounge has leather club chairs, a warm fire, is set for drinks or a bar menu snack, and there's piano entertainment daily from 5-11:30pm. Past the bar is the restaurant proper, and the tables are all in white linen. Dark wood, rich leather, and tasteful lighting set a more formal tone, and antiques, beveled glass, and a remarkable collection of San Francisco memorabilia bring to mind the days of the Big Four, the railroad tycoons who made their fortunes in 1869. The food is top-notch contemporary American, and this is the place to go if you want to treat yourself while surrounded with the feel of old elite San Francisco. Dinner entrees range from $13.50 (dungeness crab cakes or wild mushroom risotto) to $26.50 (grilled Sonoma lamb chops with potato-goat cheese galette) while the lunch menu goes from sandwiches ($9.50) to chicken pot pie ($10) to a fresh crab meat salad ($14.50). And the quiet, club atmosphere comes with it all.

Mediterranean
FOURNOU'S OVEN, *905 California. 415-989-1910. Located in the Stanford Court Hotel at Powell, it serves Ercolino Crugnale's superb contemporary American cuisine daily from 6:30am-2:30pm, week nights 5:30-10pm and weekends 5:30-10:30pm.*

Breakfast and lunch are served in the outer wing, full of light and air and palms, with large conservatory-style windows looking out over Nob Hill, while dinner is enhanced by the Mediterranean design of the formal dining room, with its rich dark wood, intricate wrought iron grillwork, and prominent ovens which are beautifully faced with hand-painted Portuguese tiles. There are nooks, crannies, and special rooms to suit any need, and the genteel, quiet feel matches the hotel mood. The special reserved woody wine bins of regular patrons just add to the classy aura.

Atmosphere is all well and good, but Crugnale's food is sensational. Starters run $7-$13, and they're wonderful. The tortilla soup may sound odd but it is, in fact, excellent and very popular, and the fritto misto of artichokes and calamari with lemon aioli is succulent and light and deeply delicious, and the roasted portobello mushroom with polenta, a winter special, is also done just right. Among the entrees ($15-$28), their lamb, is quite good, but then so is the risotto, the salmon, and the oreccheitte pasta with rock shrimp. After which, the sorbets are always flavorful and refreshing, though the flavors themselves change with the seasons, and the chocolate hazelnut cake is intensely magnificent.

The service is impeccable, and the high quality is consistent. If the prices give you pause, there's a twilight supper special (5:30-6:30pm) of $21 for two courses or $26 for three, but whenever you go, you're guaranteed Crugnale's stellar cooking and a fine dining experience.

MODERATE
American
THE WHITE HORSE TAVERNE, *635 Sutter. 415-673-9900. It serves American and Continental cuisine in a charmingly pubby atmosphere just next to the Beresford Hotel. They're open daily from 7am-2pm (lunch starts at 10am but breakfast continues till 2pm) and they serve dinner Tuesday-Saturday 5:30-10:30pm.*

Breakfasts cover the usual egg offerings, as well as hot cakes, eggs Benedict, steak and eggs, and corned beef hash ($4-$7). The lunch menu lists a fine hamburger, plus still more substantial pub grub like lasagna, lamb stew, or corned beef with cabbage, as well as a variety of sandwiches ($4.50-$7). Dinner focuses on meat as well (despite the one vegetarian special), with fish, prawns, chicken, pork or lamb chop, T-bone steak, and on Fridays and Saturdays only, prime rib ($10-$15). If you want cuisine that's hearty rather than nouvelle, and a place that emphasizes good, filling food without a lot of folderol, the White Horse is your tavern. And they make a mean Irish coffee, too.

INEXPENSIVE
Mexican
EL NOPALITO TAQUERIA, *885 Bush. 415-931-3130. Located near Taylor, it has inexpensive, delicious, authentic Mexican fast food to go from 10am-10pm seven days a week.*

It's a hole-in-the-wall and there's no place to sit down, but if you want a fast snack or a filling meal, and like authentic Mexican food, you won't find anything better in the neighborhood. There are tacos, burritos, nachos, tamale and chili relleno plates, quesadillas, and tostadas for $2.80-$4.85, combination plates for $5.25, and a la carte tamales and enchiladas for $1.50. Their spicy actually has some kick to it, and a lot of good flavor as well. Two blocks north, Huntington Park on top of Nob Hill would make a lofty perch for a down-to-earth picnic.

Middle Eastern
ALADDIN MEDITERRANEAN RESTAURANT, *1300 Polk Street. 415-441-2212. Located on the corner of Bush in Lower Nob Hill on the way toward the Tenderloin, it's open Sunday-Thursday 11am-11pm and Friday-Saturday 11am-midnight.*

This is a bright, clean, new establishment that just happens to have the best falafel in San Francisco. This is the closest you're ever going to get to the real stuff, with a full open Mediterranean salad bar, without hopping a plane for Israel. The Palestinian owner knows quality, and offers it at reasonable rates. A pita of falafel (with all the salad bar fixings you care to add) costs $3.59, a shwarma or kabob is $4.59, and a for a full plate (instead of just the pita sandwich) add $2. The hummus is very good, and the portions are generous. If you're in the neighborhood and hungry, you couldn't do better.

NOE VALLEY
MODERATE
Japanese
IZUMI SUSHI, *317 Sanchez. 415-552-8070. Located near 16th, it is open Wednesday-Monday 5:30-10pm, and if you're in the neighborhood, they have got excellent Japanese food at reasonable prices.*

Izumi Sushi is a small place with lots of sushi and lots of vegetable dish appetizers. Sushi a la carte runs from $2.25-$3, though there's also a combination plate (including tea, miso soup, and appetizer) for $11.50. The vegetable specials change according to what's fresh and in season, but they usually have green beans in ginger sauce, gomae (spinach in sesame sauce), and a wonderful baked eggplant creation. The miso soup is made fresh each day, and the staff is delightful.

MATSUYA, *3856 24th Street. 415-282-7989. Located near Church, it is open for dinner Monday-Saturday 4:30-10:45 (though they're sometimes closed Mondays if someone's sick or has an appointment - it's that sort of place).*

Inside it's small and casual, with five tables and a sushi bar, and inexpensive, good food. Sushi is the focus here, and you can get a la carte dishes for $5 or sushi combination dinners for $10-$16. There are other options, too. The donburi is just $5.50-$7, and there's teriyaki steak or salmon for $11.50. Fusae Ponne, who's run this 20-seat place for more than 40 years, has not raised the prices in the last seven, the quality is tops, and you get their endearing personalities as an added bonus.

Nouvelle Cuisine
FIREFLY, *4288 24th Street. 415-821-7652. Located near Douglass, it is open daily 5:30-9:30, serving their own brand of eclectic, international home cooking.*

The Firefly is cute and cozy - just the right setting for their country cuisine. The appetizers ($5.50-$6.75) are very interesting. The shrimp and scallop pot stickers are a beloved specialty, but they have lots of other swell items, like shiitake mushroom stirfry on crisp scallion pancakes, and roasted gold beet soup with sorrel creme fraiche. Among the main courses ($9.75-$15.25), they have good braised beef, grilled salmon with sesame glazed yams and soba noodle salad, country-style pork ribs, and excellent vegetarian dishes that change with the seasons.

INEXPENSIVE
Chinese
ERIC'S CHINESE RESTAURANT, *1500 Church. 415-282-0919. Located near 27th, it is an excellent and inexpensive place, and they're open Sunday 12:30-9:15pm, Monday-Thursday 11:30am-9:15pm, and Friday-Saturday 11:30am-9:50pm.*

The lunch plates are $4, while dinner dishes range from $4.75 (for Eric's chow mein) to $8.50 (for the fresh clams with black bean sauce). The cuisine here is Hunan and Mandarin, with spicy dishes like spicy smoked pork, orange beef, and Eric's prawn salad, and more moderately spiced items like walnut prawns, ocean garden, and string beans with bean curd. There's a good vegetarian selection, interesting seafood, and wonderful specials.

NORTH BEACH
EXPENSIVE
American
ALFRED'S, *886 Broadway. 415-781-7058. Located near Mason, it has been attending to the neighborhood's steak needs since 1928. They're open for lunch only on Thursday from 11:30am-2:30pm, and for dinner nightly 5:30-11pm.*

Alfred's has the traditional steak house look, with the booths, the red walls and crystal chandeliers, the long bar, and the meat. If you're looking for good quality beef, and lots of it, Alfred's got it, with selections ranging from minute steak ($15) to Alfred's New York steak ($21.45) to their 60 ounce double porterhouse ($50). There's also chicken, lobster tail, and lamb chop, but this is a steak house first and foremost, whose motto is "Real Martini, Real Steak, Real San Francisco."

Italian
MOOSE'S, *1652 Stockton. 415-989-7800. Overlooking Washington Square Park, Moose's serves lunch and dinner daily with jazz piano from 8pm, and Sunday brunch with jazz piano 10am-2:30am, plus there's valet parking.*

The restaurant is divvied up into the formal dining room with lots of white linen, an open kitchen, and a big window looking out over the square. The bar lounge sports dark wood, a big sports screen, and a lively pre-dinner clique. The bronze moose dripping water from his antlers is the warmest greeting you'll get unless you're a known big-name, as the staff is a little full of itself.

This is a see-and-be-seen sort of place among San Francisco's social and political circles, and very big with the cocktail crowd who sling back the Electric Blue Mooses and Sam's Royal Fizzes with gusto. The lunch and dinner menus are nearly identical, differing mainly in the extra dollar or two per item in the evening. Dinners include such dishes as roasted clams with spicy garlic sausage or wild mushroom strudel starters, braised rabbit risotto or toasted garlic Bolognese gnocchi pastas, and entrees ($15-$24) of veal, pork, steak, chicken, and fish. Lunch entrees include a few sandwiches and are more in the $8-$14 range. Though the attitude needs a little work, the food is top quality, and very tasty.

Nouvelle Cuisine

CYPRESS CLUB, *500 Jackson. 415-296-8555, fax 415-296-9250. This is an unusual restaurant serving contemporary cuisine from a menu that changes daily. The bar menu opens at 4:30pm, and dinner goes from 5:30pm till closing (depending on the night).*

The Cypress prides itself on fresh seasonal ingredients, daring combinations, and their one-of-a-kind decor, which is teeming with brass and copper archways and lavish curvy velvet chairs. The restaurant is also known for its sumptuous desserts, extensive wine cellar, and dedicated service. Though still good and popular, some of the dishes have suffered of late, and the Cypress is no longer as "in" a spot as Postrio, for example.

MODERATE

Afghani

HELMAND, *430 Broadway. 415-362-0641. Located near Montgomery, it is just up the street from Enrico's but entirely different. They serve Afghani cuisine here nightly from 5-10pm Sunday-Thursday and 5-11pm Friday-Saturday.*

The dining room is a crisply pleasant, full of white linen, fresh flowers, and formally attired, attentive waiters. Entrees ($9-$15) include lots of lamb, and the pumpkin-stuffed ravioli are excellent.

American

WASHINGTON SQUARE BAR & GRILL, *1707 Powell. 415-982-8123. It's open for lunch Monday-Friday 11:30-3 and a weekend brunch Saturday-Sunday from 10am-3pm. They're open daily for dinner 5-10:30pm, and till 11:30pm on weekends, and valet parking is always available.*

Known familiarly as the Washbag, it's been a San Francisco tradition since 1973, and the building that houses it has been around even longer, since the early 1900s. There's a woody bonhomie and clubby congeniality inside, plus a little snootiness that comes from its many years as the "in" place for reporters, politicos, and the North Beach cognoscenti.

And the food's quite good as well, in a traditional sort of way. Starters include traditional favorites like oysters Rockefeller, carpaccio, and truffle & cognac pate ($7-$10), while entrees feature lots of meat, with veal Marsala, smoked game hen, the classic New York steak sandwich, and shrimp scampi (mostly $11-$17). The noise can begin to bounce a bit at peak dinner times, but it's a fine lunch or dinner San Francisco tradition that has kept its quality up.

French

CAFE JACQUELINE, *1454 Grant. 415-981-5565. Located near Union, it's open for dinner Wednesday-Sunday 5:30-11pm, and reservations are a good idea.*

They serve soufflés and only soufflés, and from the moment you walk in to this cozy, romantic restaurant, your senses are ruled by the fabulous smells that emanate from the tiny kitchen in back. That's where Jacqueline herself stands in full chef regalia, cracking eggs and whipping up the best soufflés in San Francisco. Jacqueline grew up in the south of France and learned her culinary magic at the Cordon Bleu school there, but she's lived in this country since 1958. And despite the many opinions that a soufflé cafe in North Beach was a foolhardy notion, she opened shop in 1979, and it was enthusiastically successful from the first day. Given the charm of the place and the wonderful food, this isn't a big surprise.

There are just ten tables in the intimate, dimly lit dining room, with sage green baseboards topped by cream walls, and amber-shaded lamps lighting the tables. The menu is simple. Aside from onion soup and salads, there are soufflés. Each soufflé serves two, and they cost $20-$25, depending on whether you get the simple gruyere soufflé, or have other ingredients added, such as spinach or garlic, leek or shiitake, asparagus or Roquefort. And while you're at it, you might as well share a dessert soufflé, too. They cost $25-$30, feed two-four, and are decadently magnificent. You can opt for chocolate, lemon, or white chocolate and be very well pleased, but the chocolate with Grand Marnier is just amazing.

Irish

O'REILLY'S IRISH PUB AND RESTAURANT, *622 Green. 415-989-6222. Located near Columbus, O'Reilly's serves Irish dishes 11:30-9pm Monday-Wednesday, 11:30am-10pm Thursday-Friday, 10:30-10pm Saturday and 10:30am-9pm Sunday.*

Brunch on the weekends features the traditional Irish breakfast (available weekdays, too, with eggs, rashers, sausages, black & white pudding, chips, and grilled tomato for $9), plus items from the regular menu such as the wonderful Irish Toasties (sandwiches of corn beef with Swiss, or sausage and mushroom, for example, pressed in the toaster machine for $6-$7). The dinners are Irish, too.

Particularly popular among the starters ($4-$8) is the smoked salmon on boxty (a potato pancake), and of the entrees ($6-$12), the lamb stew and cottage pie are hearty and heartily recommended by the owner. There's also traditional Irish lamb stew, corned beef and cabbage, and steak and kidney pie to chose from. The dining room is attractively done in greens and creams, white linen drapes the tables, and the Irish street lamp twined with ivy (and transplanted from the streets of Dublin) sets the tone nicely. There's Irish music Wednesday, Thursday, and Sunday nights from 9:30pm-12:30am or so, and on Tuesday there's live rock and roll, at least for now (the schedule is still in flux). They are also trying to get Irish set dancing going on Sunday afternoons from 4pm on, and you don't need to know what you're doing to join in, because people there will instruct.

Italian

COLUMBUS ITALIAN FOOD RESTAURANT, *611 Broadway. 415-781-2939. Located near Columbus it's open Monday-Saturday from 11:30am-9pm, serving up outstanding Italian food as it has for 25 years.*

May DiTano (chef and owner) may cut corners on decor and ambiance, but she takes no shortcuts on the quality and preparation of her dishes, and it shows. The entrees cost $8-$15, and they can compete with the finest in San Francisco. She's known especially for the calamari, and it is truly outstanding. Also special are the sautéed vegetables, sweat breads, and polenta, and the saltimboca is fine as well. While the exceptionally tasty food is reason enough to visit, it would be worthwhile just for the experience alone. Authentic doesn't begin to do justice to this hole-in-the-wall cafe. The sign outside is upside down (placed that way on purpose by May, to catch your eye and to let the world know that she's still there), and inside are four tables against the wall and a long counter lined with green vinyl swivel chairs, behind which the vociferous, opinionated, and lovable proprietress cooks up a storm, dishing political observations and general advice along with the calamari and pasta. As an added bonus, a surrealistic gnomish waiter refills your water while you enjoy a really terrific Italian meal.

ENRICO'S, *504 Broadway. 415-982-6223. Located near Kearny, it's open daily from noon till closing (which is 11pm on week nights and midnight on the weekend).*

Enrico's serves Mediterranean dishes ($12-$17), but the menu changes weekly. They always have pizzas, pastas, burgers, tapas, and sea bass done up in some interesting fashion. They have live jazz nightly which starts at 7pm on Sunday, 8pm Monday-Thursday, and 9pm Friday-Saturday, but it generally just provides some chic background music for your dining or hanging out. But the biggest appeal to Enrico's is its heated patio. Get a table out there and you've got the best seat in the house for watching the Broadway hullabaloo pass by while you sip your cappuccino. Smoking is permitted on the porch, which may be an incentive for you to get an outdoor table, or motivation to dine in the contemporary Italian room inside.

FIGARO, *414 Columbus. 415-398-1300. Located between Vallejo and Green, this is a new Italian restaurant/cafe on the Columbus strip, and a very welcome one. Open daily from 10:30am-midnight, Luigi serves up Tuscan, Roman, and Southern Italian cuisine.*

The specialty here is the gnocchi, made fresh daily, and really something special, and there's pasta, calzone, pizza, and carne dishes as well, most of which cost $6-$9. You start out with good bread and olive oil, set on marble table tops. The lighting is soft, the linen napkins are soft, and the ceiling is covered with faux Italian fresco. The windows angle out over Columbus, and the room stretches way back.

The food varies; some is exceptionally good, and other dishes miss the boat. The fusilli with sausage is delicious, but the carpaccio could easily be skipped, as could the calzone. And the gnocchi is spectacular. It seems to dissolve in your mouth, with none of the gumminess that sometimes mars this dish - just satisfying, soothing tastiness. Stick with what's good, and you'll get a great, reasonably priced meal in a charming setting. They serve breakfast as well, and in good weather, the outdoor back patio is a nice break from busy Columbus.

RISTORANTE FIOR D'ITALIA, *601 Union. 415-986-1886. Located near Stockton, it's far more successful in its advertising schemes than in its kitchen.*

Yes, it was established in 1886 and the location is right, unfortunately the food is wrong. It attracts the ignorant and unwary with a massive coupon campaign, but once burned, they don't come back for seconds. Don't buy the image; there are too many really good restaurants in this neighborhood to spend your money here.

LITTLE CITY ANTIPASTI BAR, *673 Union. 415-434-2900. Located between Powell and Columbus, lunch and dinner is served daily 11:30-11pm (and till midnight Thursday through Saturday), with brunch Sunday from 11am-4pm, but it's best known for its antipasti.*

Little City has been here for 15 years, and they have a pretty loyal following. It's informal and woody inside, with flowers and artwork, a touch of brick, and great big picture windows. It's a pleasant place to have a snack and a glass of wine, and watch the busy world storm by. The antipasti are the main draw, and people often forgo an entree and dine on antipasti alone. Most are $6-$7.25 a plate, and 3-4 make a fine shared meal.

The baked brie and roasted garlic bulb is a steady favorite, as is the quesadilla with smoked duck, Swiss cheese, and roasted bell pepper salsa, and the pear and cheese caramelized with Roquefort and black pepper gastrique (a relatively new addition) has also been getting rave reviews. Entrees include lots of interesting Italian pasta dishes, paella, lamb, chicken, and seafood, and the salads are excellent.

MICHELANGELO CAFE, *579 Columbus. 415-986-4058. Located near Union and open Monday-Saturday 5-11pm and Sunday 3-10pm. They don't take reservations or credit cards, but that doesn't stop folks from waiting patiently in the long line outside.*

First there's the wait – no sign-up list or any such thing, just the line that stretches toward the corner, even late on a Sunday night, making you feel a little foolish, and wondering if it'll be worth it. Well, it is. People brave the wait and keep coming back, not because others are doing it, but because the food is great, and the atmosphere is the kind you come to North Beach for. Run by a lively, no-nonsense Italian family since 1987, the atmosphere inside is festive and warm. Tables are covered with Romanesque-Italianate frescos (cupids, fleshy women, men in togas), the walls are loaded with paintings of all sorts, faux brick and pillars line the mantels, and great stained-glass lamps hang everywhere. A little plate of olives welcomes you, and they are exceptional. As for the wine, it's worth it to get a bottle or pitcher if for no other reason than you get to drink it out of hand-painted Biordi ceramic goblets. The salad, unfortunately, is swimming in dressing, but everything else here is swell.

The main dishes (mostly $9, on up to $15) are tasty and hefty. Their gnocchi are good (nearly as good as Figaro's), and the calamari sauté are just as tender and delicious as can be. Their tomato sauce and cream sauce are both fabulous and seasoned just right, and the accompanying vegetables are perfect. There's a family-style atmosphere here, from the huge bowl of parmesan you dip into to sprinkle on your pasta, to the salads bowls of gummi bears and amaretto cookies plopped down in front of you after your meal so you can help yourself to some dessert. You may not care to stand in line in order to eat, but if you do join the queue, at least you know a bountiful good meal awaits you.

ROSE PISTOLA, *532 Columbus. 415-399-0499. Located between Union and Green, this is a new Italian addition to the Columbus strip. This new Reed Hearon restaurant is open Sunday-Thursday 11:30am-midnight, and Friday-Saturday 11:30am-1am, and reservations are advised.*

The interior (which stretches all the way back to Stockton Street) is beautiful, with warm woods, white linen, and tiny colored floor tiles that give a country-style welcome. The prime Columbus location affords great views, and the atmosphere is somewhere between chic and kitchen-friendly. The food ($6.50-$10.50 for pasta, focaccia, and pizza, $3.50-$5.50 for antipasti and vegetable dishes, and $10-$17.50 for seafood, meat, and fowl) is all Italian. There's a big selection of small dish items for the tapas crowd, but there are plenty of platters heaped with gnocchi or spaghetti, and bowls full of cioppino, too. The salads are great, the ricotta stuffed peppers are wonderful, and good focaccia bread is served with all meals. And if you're just looking for dessert, you should be aware that there's a hazelnut chocolate tort with espresso pudding waiting for you on the sweets menu.

THE STINKING ROSE, *253 Columbus. 415-781-7673.*

This is a gimmicky place. The use of garlic is nothing new in North Beach, and better food can be found elsewhere.

U.S. RESTAURANT, *431 Columbus. 415-362-6251. Taking up the corner of Columbus and Stockton, it is open Tuesday-Saturday 6am-9pm, and no credit cards accepted.*

The current owners have been serving up good old Italian American food for 32 years, but they're wet behind the ears compared to the restaurant's starting date of 1906. For years the U.S. Restaurant has had the reputation of providing large portions of good, hearty food, and this is one well-founded reputation. The formica tables and florescent lights are reminiscent of old American diners, and so are the matronly wait-resses, and so is the food. If you want relaxed dining that smacks of yesteryear, and big portions of grub, if you're not in the mood for raddicio and goat cheese and yearn for a plate of pot roast, head here.

The breakfasts are substantial, with Italian sausage as well as all the usual eggs, hotcakes, and omelet options, but with none of the frills, and run $3.25-$5 for most items and $5.50-$8 for omelets. Most of their renown, however, comes from their portions of meat. Pot roast and pork chops, burgers and cutlets, and daily specials like osso buco, veal scaloppini, and short rib of beef form the U.S. staples. Pasta comes with the entrees, and the ravioli is really great, but skip the sandwiches. A dinner entree costs around $7-$9, and you won't leave hungry.

Spanish Tapas

LA BODEGA, *1337 Grant. 415-433-0439. It's open Sunday-Thursday from 5-11pm and Friday-Saturday 5pm-1am, serving up mediocre tapas and hoky Flamenco entertainment.*

A Spanish party mood exists: the owners will let you drink from their wine skins, making you feel special and part of the club. After you've been limbered up a bit with red wine, the Flamenco dancers come on, and enjoin the customers to form a dancing chain that winds its way though both dining rooms.

This is a good place if you want to get drunk and act silly while no one from back home can see, but for quality Spanish dining, try Alegrias in the Marina.

INEXPENSIVE
American

MO'S, *1322 Grant. 415-788-3779. Located between Green and Vallejo, it is open Sunday-Thursday 11:30am-10:30pm and Friday-Saturday 11:30am-11:30pm.*

Rarely found by tourists but beloved by neighborhood locals, Mo's serves some of the very best burgers ($4.75-$7.25) in town, as well as superb spicy chicken breast sandwiches ($6.75), lamb burgers ($5.75), and vegetarian fajitas and sandwiches ($5.75-$6.75). Their fries (they come with the sandwiches) are fantastic, and the servings will keep you well-fueled for hours. Even if you do manage to have extra room, however, the shakes are a disappointment. The decor, however, is a down-home delight. It's tongue-in-cheek 50s, with chrome trim, 3 Stooges and Marilyn Monroe pictures, and a huge papiermache cow rear end sticking out from the wall near a pensive papiermache head. It's clean and clever, but it's the food that keeps the locals coming back.

Chinese

BRANDY HO, *217 Columbus. 415-788-7527. Located near Pacific, it is perhaps the only Chinese restaurant to combine excellent food with nice decor and atmosphere, and they're open daily 11:30am-11pm (and till midnight Friday-Saturday).*

The dividers and plants help give a sense of privacy (though the tables feel quite close and noisy when the place is hopping), and the hanging Chinese lanterns with their triple red pepper motif are a pleasant change from the usual over-bright fluorescent lights. We come here regularly, however, because the food is so good. Their hot and sour soup is one of the world's best (and can be made vegetarian if you ask), and the chicken salad with spicy peanut sauce and noodles is another favorite. They have especially good chow mein, mu shoo pork, hot and sour beef, and so on. Prices are fair, mostly $5-$6 an entree, and the restaurant's dependable for good food, fresh ingredients, and a swell meal.

Indian

KAMAL PALACE, *641 Vallejo. 415-421-1132. Located near Columbus, it is a new ethnic addition to the North Beach restaurant line-up, and they're open*

daily 10am-11pm. Their regular menu ranges from $8-$16, but their all-you-can-eat lunch buffet from 11:30am-3:30pm is a great deal at just $6 per person.
Indian music plays in the background, and the air is rich with spicy smells. The green-clothed tables are nicely spaced to give you lots of room and privacy, while mirrored walls add to the spacious feel. There are flowers everywhere, which are festive if not real. The buffet offers a good selection of tandoori chicken, rice, a variety of sauces, deep-fried samosa, and plenty of Indian breads. And on your way out, make sure to take a spoonful of the coconut and anise mix in the bowl on the bar to finish the meal off with a taste of sweet and spice.

Italian
PASTA POMODORO, *655 Union Street. 415-399-0300. Located near Powell, it's open Monday-Friday 11am-11pm, Saturday noon-midnight, and Sunday noon-11pm. No checks or credit cards.*
It's strange but true. In an area jam-packed with Italian restaurants, it's hard to find better than mediocre Italian food. But Pomodoro, a newcomer to a traditional neighborhood, is a great find. They prepare superlative Italian food at unusually reasonable prices. You can eat in the cheery dining room or take it out; the food's prepared quickly so you can be done and on your way if that's what you need, or you can linger over your pasta in the festive atmosphere of the restaurant, look out the big windows, and watch the busy North Beach hustle. The Cappellini Pomodoro (their namesake) is very popular and only $3.95, and the Conchiglie Gorgonzola ($4.75) is outstanding. They also have healthy pastas prepared without oil, butter, or cheese, and a big selection of salads served in half or full portions, $3-$5.50.
L'OSTERIA DEL FORNO, *519 Columbus. 415-982-1124. Located between Union and Green, it's open Monday, Wednesday, Thursday from 11:30am-10pm, Friday, Saturday 11:30am-10:30pm, and Sunday 1-10pm.*
Small, friendly, and very reasonably priced, they dish up some extremely tasty northern Italian cuisine. An *osteria* in Italy is a place to get together for some wine, beer, and a light bite to eat, and the *forno* (oven) is how they prepare most of their meals (though they do have a small burner for boiling the occasional water). Their focaccia sandwiches ($4.75-$5.75) are delicious, and light (especially compared to the equally tasty but much heavier sandwiches produced by Mario's down the street). They do a roast of the day for $7.45 (the pork roast is especially popular), and they produce fine pizzas as well (by the slice or pies serving 2-4 for $10-$17). Their salads are popular, their special pumpkin raviolis are delicious (assuming a taste for pumpkin), the speck (smoked prosciutto) graces a number of plates, and the affogata al caffe (vanilla ice cream in espresso, $3.25) is a magnificent way to top off a wonderful meal. The dining room

is small (just 11 tables), and no reservations are taken, so get there early on a weekend to avoid the line. Children are welcome, but they don't have any highchairs.

TOMMASO'S, *1042 Kearny. 415-398-9696. Located near Broadway, it's open Tuesday-Saturday 5-10:45pm and Sunday 4-9:45pm.*

Tommaso's is an authentic true North Beach treasure. It's a genuine pizza parlor with history, charm, personality, and the best Italian pizza in San Francisco. They serve pastas, chicken, veal, eggplant, and seafood (the Coo Coo clam appetizer ($9) is legendary) and the cannoli ($3) is terrific, but it's the pizzas and calzones ($11-$15 to feed two) that made Tommaso's reputation, and it's what we come back for again and again. Of course, the festive pitchers of house red wine ($6.50 for small and $9 for large) add to the appeal, as do the cozy semi-private booths under the wonderfully cheesy murals of Italian sea and castle scenes.

Amber lanterns cast a warm, complimentary glow, the waiters and waitresses are all part of a big, friendly family of owners, a happy hubbub fills the restaurant along with the amazing smells emanating from the kitchen, and the booths (worth the wait rather than sitting at the central table) are conducive to family dining and romantic trysts. There are usually lines for Friday and Saturday dinners, but it's less likely if you get there early.

CAFFE FREDDY'S EATERY, *901 Columbus. 415-922-0151. On the corner at Lombard, it's open Monday-Thursday 11am-10pm, Friday-Saturday 9:30am-10:30pm, and Sunday 9:30am-10pm, and usually the street parking isn't bad.*

This is a casual, friendly, neighborhood place with pretty good food and very reasonable prices. Inside are diner-like booths and cheery crayon drawings on the walls, but the outside tables are most popular when the sun shines. Freddy's is a personal favorite for Sunday brunch because the Tuscan Eggs ($4.95) dish is so fine, though the breakfast pizzettas and salads are also good. It's a nice place for a lunch or dinner as well. The focaccia sandwiches ($3.45-$5.95) are tasty, though the salmon serving isn't very filling. Their salads (10 options at $3-$6) are beautiful, their thin-crusted, creative pizzettas ($4.95-$7.45) are good, as are the polentas. They also serve fish and steak specials ($4.45-$7.45), soups, pastas, and calzones.

GIRA POLLI, *659 Union. 415-434-4472. Located near Columbus, it's open daily 4:30-9:30pm for the best roasted chicken in San Francisco.*

They are a tiny restaurant with an enormous wood-fired rotisserie (capable of doing 126 chickens at one time), and they all emerge sensationally crispy, with rosemary and sage seasonings, moist meat, and delectable skin. They have pastas as well (manicotti, ravioli, tortellini), and roast lamb too, but the chicken is their primary focus. Each portion comes with full servings of potatoes and vegetables (delicious) and bread (not the best) to make a simple and wonderful meal. If you eat in, the prices are $7 a chicken quarter and $10 a half, but take out is $6 a quarter, $9 a half, and $13 a whole.

The restaurant itself has a doll-sized dining room that's done up warmly and beautifully with lots of crisp linen and fresh flowers. Or, you can get your chicken to go.

MARIO'S BOHEMIAN CIGAR STORE CAFE, *566 Columbus. 415-362-0536. Located across from Washington Square Park on Union, this is maybe the best cafe in North Beach, and perhaps the world, and they're open Monday-Saturday 10am-midnight, and Sunday 10am-11pm.*

Narrow and small, with a counter/bar and a few tables along the windows that look out to the park, just a few items are served here, and they're done very, very well. You couldn't ask for a better cappuccino or espresso, and you could sit over it for hours reading the paper, arguing politics or flirting with your sweetie, and no one would ever give you the nudge (not that they wouldn't want to - during the busy hours a free table at Mario's is a precious prize).

This is a very friendly sort of place, and the counter is a good place to sit if you feel like meeting people. But plenty come here just for the food, and it's certainly worth a special trip. Their hot focaccia sandwiches are good beyond belief. The meatball sandwich is legendary, but there are veggie, eggplant, frittata, and sausage sandwich es to choose from as well, all on their excellent bread and pulled hot from the oven up front for just $5.75-$6.25 an enormous sandwich. Along with the sandwiches, they also serve cannelloni, polenta with sausage, and pizza for $8.50, and they're good, too.

But even though the food is wonderful, it's the atmosphere that is most special, that is the epitome of North Beach culture. This has been Mario's since 1971, but it had been the bohemian cigar store a long time before that, back when cigars were the focus. After Mario bought it food became more important and they phased the cigars out, but now sell them again. As for the bohemian part, that's a tradition that's never wavered.

LIGURIA BAKERY, *1700 Stockton. 415-421-3786. Located near Filbert, it is open for business Monday-Friday 8am-4pm, Saturday 7am-4pm, and Sunday 7am-noon, unless they run out of focaccia early.*

Focaccia is what they do here, and they do it exceptionally well. You can get a big sheet of pizza flavored or raisin focaccia for $2.20 and onion or plain for $2, and for an extra five cents they'll slice it up for you. Liguria is an old-time piece of Italian North Beach, a bakery with focus that supplies its neighborhood with its one, tremendous item. And it makes for a fine picnic in Washington Square park, too.

Vietnamese

VIETNAM RESTAURANT, *620 Broadway. 415-788-7034. Located between Stockton and Grant, it's open daily from 8am-3am serving steaming bowls of Vietnamese goodness for just $3.80, and there are grilled, rice, and noodle dishes for not much more.*

This is just a narrow walk-in with a counter and a few dingy tables, but they're open late and the food is fine, if not quite as superlative as Tu Lan. They were, however, the only North Beach restaurant to remain open on the evening following the 1989 quake, serving heartening bowls of soup by candlelight.

NORTH BEACH CAFES

Caffe Trieste, 601 Vallejo. 415-392-6739. Located between Columbus and Grant and open 7am-11pm weekdays and till 12:30am weekends. With warm colors of amber and red, an odd Italianate fresco on the back wall, and tables inside and out, the ambiance is flavored by opera on the jukebox, and the happy burble of a roomful of North Beach denizens. Every coffee and espresso drink imaginable is served, as well as tea, soda, and wine, plus cakes, focaccia, quiche, and pizza. It's the sort of place where people come to talk, read, work on their laptops, or play Scrabble, and it all fits in.

Caffe Greco, 423 Columbus. 415-397-6261. Located between Vallejo and Green, it is open daily 7am-midnight, as it has been since 1988. This is definitely the busiest of North Beach cafes, and an open table during peak cafe time is a rare find. This is the place to come for a latte and a big slice of delectable dessert, and to see and be seen. There are small cafe tables inside amid the huge and colorful vintage European posters and cheerful clamor, or out on the sidewalk the better to enjoy the sunshine and the Columbus Street traffic. And as with all the North Beach cafes, you're as welcome to sit with a group as to sit alone with a good book, nursing your cappuccino. There are breakfast and lunch items on sale here that are just fine, but most people come here for the various coffee drinks, the wonderful tiramisu and cake and pie, and the lively scene.

Cafe Puccini, 411 Columbus. 415-989-7033. Located just next door to Caffe Greco, it is open 6am-11:30pm Sunday-Thursday and 6am-1am on weekends. They have been in business since 1977, with the traditional coffee drinks and rich desserts, and a jukebox full of opera arias for your listening pleasure. They also have a fine window through which to view the Columbus traffic, and it's usually not as hectic as next door at Greco. They get the spill over when the tables are full at Greco's, or if people want a slightly quieter milieu.

PACIFIC HEIGHTS
EXPENSIVE
French

THE HEIGHTS, *3235 Sacramento. 415-474-8890. Located near Presidio, it's open for dinner Tuesday-Sunday with seatings from 5:30-9:30pm.*

Contemporary French is the cuisine, set in three lovely dining rooms overlooking gardens and Sacramento that feel like home, but more elegant. The menu changes weekly depending on what's fresh and in season, but typical entrees ($22-$25) might be vegetable pot au feu, lobster with haricot vert and Italian pancetta, or rack of farm lamb with asparagus, carrots, and pearl onions in lamb jus. Or, you can chose the tasting menu of six dishes ($60 for the food, or $80 with a wine for each dish).

The rooms manage to be both lovely and intimate at the same time, with terra cotta tiled floor, white linen swathing the tables to match the pristine white walls, plus handsome candlesticks and gorgeous fresh flowers in milky glass vases. The rooms make you feel pampered before you even take a look at the menu.

Nouvelle Cuisine

CAFE KATI, *1963 Sutter Street. 415-775-7313. Located at Fillmore, it is open for dinner Tuesday-Sunday 5:30-10pm, and while you can leave a reservation request on the answering machine, you need to speak to a real live person to confirm it (actual people are available to answer the phone after 2pm on days they're open). They're just a block from the Kabuki theater, and they'll validate parking at either the Kabuki or Japan Center garage.*

It's lovely and very appealing inside, with pale banana-colored walls with orange trim, and white linen on the tables. And there's a pretty back room, too, that looks out on a wee garden. Light classical music plays on the stereo, and the walls are hung with a changing gallery of local artists' paintings (and they're for sale, too). They serve California cuisine ($15-$19) that is a blend of east and west, with innovative combinations and equally artful shapes.

The towering Caesar salad that rears up from your plate is one of their signature dishes. They also have some great crabmeat pot stickers, and Vietnamese style (not fried) mango spring rolls. Most of the entrees change monthly, but some examples are the walnut crusted chicken breast with Gorgonzola, and Asian marinated Chilean sea bass in a wild mushroom ragu, with parsnip chips. They always have some vegetarian platters, too.

MODERATE
American
ELLA'S, *500 Presidio. 415-441-5669. Located near California, Ella's dishes up neo-classical American food with flare Monday-Friday 7am-9pm, and for weekend brunch 9am-2pm. The brunch line often starts forming at 8:30am, and reservations are taken only for 8 or more (you must be called back for confirmation).*

Amiable and open, the artwork was chosen with a good eye for style. There are plenty of plants and flowers, and the big windows look out over the busy traffic of California and Presidio. Ella's is especially known for its breakfasts, but the lunch and dinners are quite good, too. The menu changes daily ($6-$11), but on a given day you may find items such as curried cream of chicken soup, duck and grapefruit salad in a mint vinaigrette, macaroni and cheese, and stuffed peppers in spicy tomato sauce.

They make good salads, and always have burgers, hot dogs, chicken pot pie, fresh fish, and lots of desserts.

Italian
VIVANDE PORTA VIA, *2125 Fillmore. 415-346-4430. Located between California and Sacramento, it's a terrific neighborhood Italian restaurant, open daily from 10am-10pm for take-out and 11:30am-10pm for sit down, offering two distinct dining options.*

First, there's the take-out deli, and the food in the long glass case is amazing. There are luscious cheeses, top quality meats, wonderful patés, chicken or mushroom pies, eggplant sandwiches, onion cheese tarts, frittata, and oodles of swell salads for around $3-$6 an item.

Then there are the linen-clad sit-down tables of the cafe. The floor is composed of big tiles, and a red brick wall makes for a warm, textured background for the colorfully hand-painted ceramic dishes. Lunch dishes ($9-$14) include salads, tarts, and pot pies from the deli, as well as other wonderful cold and hot creations. There are Milanese tortas, frittata, chicken galantina (rolled, boneless chicken with veal, juniper berries, and pistachio nuts inside), an assortment of pasta dishes, boscaiola (a sauté of sausages, potato, mushrooms, onion, wine, and garlic), and wonderful sausage or oyster sandwiches.

For dinner, the prices are a little higher at $14-$17, and include dishes such as risotto, beef tenderloin, and pork loin in a wonderful sauce. The choices change from time to time, but their excellent reputation remains, due to their dedication to quality ingredients and fine dining.

JACKSON FILLMORE, *2506 Fillmore. 415-346-5288. Located near Jackson, it is open daily for dinner, Sunday 5-10pm, Monday 5:30-10pm, Tuesday-Thursday 5:30-10:30pm, and 5:30-11pm on Friday-Saturday. To make* *a reservation (taken for groups of three or more), you need to speak to a real person instead of leaving it as a message on their machine.*

Inside this trattoria it's a bit stark, with white walls, a black counter, and an artwork gallery adding a bit of life. Entrees ($8.50-$16) like gnocchi and pasta are popular (especially those with truffles), and the spicy fish dish is good, too. But this place isn't quite as exceptional as it once was.

INEXPENSIVE
Middle Eastern

LA MEDITERRANEE, *2210 Fillmore. 415-921-2956. Located near Sacramento and open 11am-10pm Tuesday-Sunday, no reservations accepted.*

La Mediterranee serves tasty Middle Eastern dishes like hummus, baba ganoush, levant sandwiches, and filo dough pies for $6-$7.50 a meal. They also have slightly less common dishes like chicken pomegranate and lule kebab (a ground lamb dish) for the same reasonable prices. The food is of the same good quality as is served in their Noe branch, but the atmosphere is a bit more charming. It's a long, narrow restaurant with small tables (and one table outside, too), a festive, cozy air, and funky, artistic decor like the large fish banners and the wire-made hanging caged man. And on weekend nights there's often a list and a wait.

Sandwiches, Salads, & Picnic Supplies

S.F. GOURMET, *2066 Fillmore. 415-441-3800. Located near California, this is a gourmet take-out shop that's open daily 11am-10pm.*

Relatively new, a sister-store to their branch in the Marina, they are a welcome addition, with meals to eat in or to go for $3-$5 an item. They have shelves of fancy soups like carrot ginger orange or broccoli leek, a panoply of salads, and swell sandwiches they make up fresh behind the deli counter.

They also have some heartier entrees, and a good selection of desserts. Everything is ready to go for a picnic, but they also have cheery tables if you want to sit down and enjoy a good, fast, inexpensive meal here.

POLK GULCH
EXPENSIVE
Italian

ACQUERELLO, *1722 Sacramento. 415-567-5432. Located near Polk, modern Italian dinners are served Tuesday-Saturday 5:30-10:30pm.*

This restaurant is small and intimate with pretty tables and a romantic feel, and the menu has a lot of appealing items for $10-$12 a pasta and $19-$23 an entree. The cuisine is clearly Italian, but the innovations add a California touch. There is ridged pasta (homemade and wonderful) with foie gras and black truffles or parsnip-potato gnocchi over wild boar ragu, there's filet of lamb crusted with basil-pine nut crumbs over white Italian beans, and a rolled Calabrian braciole of beef stuffed with spinach and parmesan that's very special.

The menu changes to take advantage of the fresh, seasonal offerings, but you can count on the food being interesting and very good.

MODERATE
Seafood
SWAN OYSTER DEPOT, *1517 Polk. 415-673-1101. Located near California, it is open 8am-5:30pm Monday-Saturday, and doesn't accept reservations or credit cards.*

First opened in 1912, the Swan Oyster Depot has an old-time feel. Folks still pull one of 20 stools up to their beautiful marble-topped counter and order bowls of steaming chowder, plates of iced oysters, and a pint of cold Anchor Steam beer to wash it down. Even if the food ($5.75-$12) were lousy it would be a fun place to lunch in, but the food happens to be exceedingly fresh and tasty as well.

The workers who man the crab and clams are great - friendly and funny and personable. It's tough to find a seat during the lunch-time rush, but a mid-afternoon seafood snack is perfect here. It's the friendliest, most character-filled seafood establishment in the city, and our favorite.

INEXPENSIVE
American
SLIDERS DINER, *1202 Sutter. 415-885-3288. Located near Polk and open daily 11am-midnight.*

The self-styled home of the do it yourself burger, Sliders actually grills the burgers for you. You just help yourself to the salad bar and accessorize to your tastes. These burgers have been touted as god's gift to the burger-eating world, and while they aren't spectacular, Sliders does an okay burger for a better-than-okay price. $3.25 gets you six ounces and $3.75 gets you eight ounces of beef grilled as rare or well-done as you like, and you can heap it high with salad fixings.

For the same money there are also low-fat and vegetarian burgers, various chicken, steak, and tuna sandwiches, fried chicken, and an assortment of hot dogs round out the diner menu. The decor is straight from the diners of yore, with chairs of black vinyl and chrome, stools around the L-shaped counter looking out onto Sutter, and a self-service, low-budget appeal.

POTRERO HILL

MODERATE

Italian

APERTO, *1434 18th Street. 415-252-1625. Located near Connecticut, they serve great Italian food Monday-Friday 11am-2:30pm and 5:30-10pm, Saturday 9am-3pm and 5:30-10pm, and Sunday 9am-30pm and 5:30-9pm.*

The entrees here run $9-$13 for dinner, but just $5-$7.50 for lunch or brunch. The focaccia is house-made, and it forms the base for a fine selection of daytime sandwiches with roasted vegetables and mozzarella, roast pork with peppers, mozzarella, and pesto, or roast chicken with tomato, lettuce, and hot pepper aioli. The pastas are good, too, with penne in a mushroom (porcini, shiitake, and field), garlic, tomato, white wine, and cream sauce, or tagliolini with arugula, smoked bacon, jalapeno, garlic, and grana cheese as examples. And at night, along with the pastas, there are roast chicken, meat, and fresh fish dishes that change daily.

INEXPENSIVE

Chinese

ELIZA'S, *1457 18th Street. 415-648-9999. Located near Connecticut, it's open Monday-Friday 11am-3pm and 5-10pm or so, depending on business, and Saturday-Sunday they stay open all day 11am-10pm.*

Run by Ping and Jan Sung, the Chinese California cuisine is served to a colorful Matisse theme, with Italian pottery and Wedgwood demitasse cups. The entrees cost $6.50-$9, and include such lovelies as mango with prawns, asparagus with salmon, and sesame chicken. They also have an outlet near the Civic Center.

RICHMOND

EXPENSIVE

French

ALAIN RONDELLI, *126 Clement. 415-387-0408. Located near Second, it does California French for dinner Tuesday-Sunday 5:30-10:30pm.*

Cozy but formal, and very popular, there are lots of olive greens and browns and muted tones inside, with highly unusual mirror placemats. The food is creative French, with entrees $16-$19. The fig-stuffed foie gras, pear and Roquefort gastric, and the lamb pot au feu are especially fine, but there are other interesting items as well, like the brie and cumin tart, mussel soup with orange, saffron, and fennel, and monkfish broiled in caraway and honey. They have been winning awards and rave reviews non-stop, and they're the most gourmet French place in the Richmond.

Seafood
CLIFF HOUSE, *1090 Point Lobos Avenue. 415-386-3330, it is way out on the beach where Geary dead-ends at the ocean.*

The food is just fine at the Cliff House Restaurant, but people really come here for the view over the Pacific, and for the history as well. For good reason, the place gets jam-packed as the sun goes down, and if you manage to get a window table at sunset, there's no nicer place in the city to sip a cocktail and feel like the world is your oyster. The menu itself is big on fish. In the salad department they have calamari ($6.45), shrimp or crab Louis ($15 or $17), and seared ahi tuna ($15), while their entrees (mostly seafood) are $15-$20. Once the sun goes down, you lose the impact of the view, so you might just leave the dining to elsewhere.

CLIFF HOUSE STORY

Built in 1863, the first Cliff House was modest by today's standards, and was surrounded by dunes. Society's upper crust would drive out to Ocean Beach for horse racing and would dine after. Prominent San Francisco families like the Stanfords, Crockers, and Hearsts made a habit of it, and the guest register notes three U. S. presidents. In 1881, Adolph Sutro bought the place, and he built a little railroad so the carriageless general public could get there as well. On Christmas of 1894, however, the Cliff House was destroyed by fire. Sutro built a new one in 1896, and it was something else.

Styled after a French chateau, it had 8 stories, spires, and an observation tower 200 feet above sea level. It was the spot for dining, dancing, and entertainment, but while it survived the earthquake of 1906, it ended in fire, like its forerunner, the following year. The Cliff House that exists today was built in 1909 by Emma, Sutro's daughter, according to neoclassic designs. The Sutro family sold the Cliff House in 1952 to George Whitney, and in 1977 the National Park Service acquired it. The Cliff House today is preserved by the Golden Gate Recreation Area as one of San Francisco's historic landmarks.

MODERATE
Cambodian
ANGKOR WAT, *4217 Geary. 415-221-7887. Located near 6th, a Cambodian restaurant of the highest magnitude, is open Monday-Saturday 11am-2:30pm and daily 5-10pm, and Friday and Saturday at 7:30 and 9pm they stage performances of Cambodian Royal Ballet.*

From Geary, you enter a different world. Plink-planking Cambodian music plays lightly and soothingly in the background, and bas relief topless Cambodian dancers in ceremonial headdresses grace the walls. The front room near the entrance has a traditional seating arrangement of low tables and cushions, while the inner room features chairs and tables, set beautifully with white linen, brass candlesticks, a rose, and the white napkins folded just so and sticking jauntily out of the water glasses like horns. At the far end is a glassed-in terrarium, an inside garden with dragon, pagoda, and loads of plants. Before this is the stage on which the Cambodian Royal Ballet troupe struts their stuff every Friday and Saturday nights at 7:30 and 9pm.

But far and away the best reason to come to Angkor Wat is the food. Sensationally presented and subtly spiced, everything seems great, and the waiters are happy to advise. The Nuom Am Bang (Cambodian Style Crepe) filled with prawn, chicken, vegetables, and delicate peanut-lime sauce ($4.95) is excellent, and the Trorb Trung Kor (eggplant with ground pork, black tiger prawn, and garlic sauce, $10.95) is unbelievably good. Our waiter was adamant that the eggplant dish needed rice, and of course he was right. The curries are very tasty (spiced but not at all hot), and the only disappointment is that eventually you've got to stop eating.

Chinese
HONG KONG FLOWER LOUNGE RESTAURANT, *5322 Geary. 415-668-8998. Located near 17th, it is open for lunch Monday-Friday 11am-2:30 and 10am-2:30pm on weekends, but they're open for dinner nightly 5-9:30pm.*

This is an elegant Chinese restaurant, where the most selective and wealthiest Hong Kong transplants dine. Their entrees go from $7.50-$28, though most are in the $8-$12 range. Here you can get shark fin soup (that's what costs $28), as well as lots of other good seafood (steamed oysters, clams with black bean sauce, wok-charred crab). The shrimp are excellent, and the smoked black cod is sensational. There's also Peking duck, kung po chicken, braised tofu, Mongolian beef, and Fook Ken style fried rice, to name just a few dishes from their selection of 75.

French
CAFE MAISONNETTE, *315 8th Avenue. 415-387-7992. Located between Clement and Geary, it's a homey French cafe open Tuesday-Sunday for dinner 5:30-9pm (and till 10pm Friday and Saturday).*

It's small (just nine tables), adorable (with white latticed ceiling, blue wainscoting, flowers and candles on white tablecloths, and lace curtains) and they serve good, simple French food. The appetizers (just $4.50-$5.50) include brie-stuffed ravioli in garlic vegetable broth, goat cheese with mixed greens, raisins, and orange slices, and escargot, while the entrees ($13-$18) feature items like roast duckling with sweet potato pancakes or pan-roasted pork loin with vegetable in a peppercorn mustard sauce. And though it's close and a bit boxy inside, the setting is great for romance, and chef and owner Ronald Tseng will take good care of you.

Filipino

PHILIPPINE RESTAURANT, *3619 Balboa. 415-752-8657. It's open Wednesday-Saturday 3-10pm and Sunday 3:30-9:30pm.*

This small off-the-beaten-track restaurant has a fiercely loyal neighborhood following, and a slowly spreading city reputation for very good Filipino cuisine at relatively low prices ($4-$16 for a la carte and $6-$15 for the combination plates, with the seafood dishes costing the most, as usual), and they have quite a large menu as well. There are appetizers such as the standard lumpia, as well as less-well-known dishes.

There are noodle dishes with appealing names like lug-lug, and appealing flavors as well, and rice plates ranging from the simple garlic fried rice to Arroz Valenciana, the chef's special. They serve lots of seafood dishes and curries, and there are also special entrees like asado, dinuguan (a garlicky pork stew), and roasted suckling pig (with reservations only), and while they do prepare vegetarian fare, you have to ask for it specially. This is a good place to sample a new cuisine, or further enjoy old favorites.

Italian

MESCOLANZA, *2221 Clement. 415-668-2221. Located near 23rd Avenue, offering Italian cuisine for dinner nightly 5-10pm.*

Rustic and pretty, with blue & white checked oil cloth on the tables, bent wood chairs, and white linen napkins adding to the cozy appeal, while the walls are decorated with a sense of fun - cows, impressionistic carrots and peppers, copper pots and pans. They serve pasta, gnocchi, thin-crust pizza, and meat for $8-$13, making this a popular neighborhood spot. There's linguine in garlicky clam sauce, the old standard of Fettuccine Alfredo (otherwise known as heart-attack on a plate), and ravioli filled with Swiss chard and leek in an olive oil and garlic and butter sauce. They also have a good selection of veal dishes (Marsala, piccata, pizzaiola) as well as shrimp and the fish of the day.

Japanese

MURASAKI, *211 Clement. 415-668-7317. Located near Fourth, this is a small and very likable sushi spot that's open for dinner nightly 5pm-midnight.*

The fish is fresh, the rice is nice, and the atmosphere is pleasant, if not exceptional. The dishes ($5-$20) offer sushi, sake-cured salmon, and especially fine deep-fried soft-shelled crab. They also have tempura, teriyaki, donburi, and udon, and while the decoration isn't special, the food is pretty good.

WE BE SUSHI, *3226 Geary. 415-221-9960. Located near Parker (they also have branches in the Sunset and Mission). They're open for lunch Monday-Friday 11:30am-2:30pm and for dinner Monday-Saturday 5-10pm.*
The restaurant is small, but it's very pleasant nonetheless, and a reliably nice place to go for sushi. Their sushi items range from $1.50-$3, and are always fresh and tasty. There's an upbeat, slightly tongue-in-cheek attitude about the place, and they have an amusing story on the back of their menu about how their first name (McSushi) was contested by McDonald's, and how they came to get the name they now use, but the big draw is the good, reasonably priced food.

Mediterranean

TUBA GARDEN, *3634 Sacramento. 415-921-8822. Located between Locust and Spruce, it is open Monday-Friday from 11am-2:30pm, Saturday 10:30-2:30, and Sunday 10am-2:30pm.*
Inside it's all very lovely, like someone's elegant Victorian home, with oriental carpets and wrought-iron, marble-topped cafe tables, while the garden seating out back is gorgeous, with a fountain and lots of plants. And in back of that is the carriage house, built in the 1800s, which can be reserved for private parties.
The food is very good, and presented beautifully, with entrees ranging $8-$12. They have lots of beautiful salads (Caesar, spinach, Greek, Oriental chicken), plus a popular poached salmon, and there are good sandwiches and hot entrees (pasta, quiche, polenta with saffron and sausage) as well. The Tuba Garden is elegant and very Pacific Heights lovely. They have been going strong for 21 years, and the homemade desserts are legendary in the neighborhood.

Russian

KATIA'S, *600 Fifth Avenue. 415-668-9292. Located near Balboa, it serves its fortifying Russian cuisine Tuesday-Sunday 11:30am-2:30pm and 5-9pm, and till 10pm Friday and Saturday.*
Going strong for two years now, with live Russian accordion and guitar music nightly (and looking for a balalaika player), this is one pleasant place. The small 11-table dining room is cozy and open and pleasant, and very welcoming, just like Katia, the warm and friendly proprietor. Starters (soups, salads, and zakuski, going for $2-$4.50) include a fine beet borsch and piroshki (baked instead of deep-fried, and a far cry from the dreck you get microwaved at the corner store), eggplant, caviar, smoked salmon, and good, dark house rye bread to go with all. Entrees ($6-$11) feature the soothingly delicious pel'meni (ground pork dumplings in chicken soup), beef stroganoff, good chicken cutlets, and shashlik. The house tea continues the warming trend, the service is

friendly, and the blini (wheat crepes dripping with butter) can be ordered with smoked salmon, herring, or black Russian caviar for a special treat.

Seafood

BLUE POINT, *2415 Clement. 415-379-9726. Located near 26th, this is a stylish neighborhood seafood restaurant open Tuesday-Sunday 5-10pm.* Given the food quality, this restaurant is a bargain, with pasta dishes $7.50-$9, and meat or seafood entrees $10-$14. Tony Batchon's Mediterranean seafood place is a charmer. It's small and cozy, but airy and not at all claustrophobic. The pale yellow walls, deep mahogany trim, artistic black chairs, and gleaming oak floor come together to make an open, pretty, classy decor that's fashionable but not slick, and warm but not stuffy. With the down-to-earth and friendly service, it makes a swell setting for a dinner out. There's sautéed clams over linguine with prosciutto and peas in a sherry cream sauce, there's crab ravioli with crab legs in rosemary cream, or mostaccioli with Italian sausage and roasted garlic in a portobello mushroom sauce.

Or, if you want to skip the pastas, you can choose from a spectacular cioppino, a fine rib-eye steak, or an equally fine roast chicken with sautéed sausage, peppers, and onions. And every night there's a changing menu of fresh fish dishes, with the cilantro grilled swordfish winning many fans. But while the entrees are as good as they sound, the neighborhood folk keep coming back for the starters, choosing among the pan-seared shrimp with goat cheese, sun-dried tomatoes, and basil, the salmon carpaccio, the hummus and baba ganoush, and the clam chowder. From the rosemary flavored olive oil on every table to the great desserts (tiramisu, and a chocolate torte with white chocolate and dark chocolate sauce, plus raspberries, for example), all the details are just right.

Singaporean

STRAITS CAFE, *3300 Geary. 415-668-1783. Located near Parker, it's open Sunday-Thursday 11:30am-10pm, and Friday-Saturday 11:30am-11pm. They do Singaporean cuisine here for $7.50-$14 during dinner, but $5-$9 during lunch.* There are excellent salads (their version of chicken salad is wonderful, as is the gado-gado), the fried rice or noodle dishes (nasi or mee goreng), the staples from that region, are very tasty and nicely spiced, and then there are the more involved curries and banana leaf packets of trout or spicy salmon pate. They have a good selection of vegetarian dishes, plus plenty of fish and meat, and while the dishes taste authentic, they make use of the local fresh produce. It's a very likable place, with ceiling fans and central columns done up like palm trees. There are mango-colored walls and sea-green plates spruced up with white linen, and the wait staff is well-trained, friendly, and efficient. There's a tropical island aura without it being kitsch or gimmicky, and it's a pleasant place in which to eat, hang out with friends, and wile away an hour or two.

Vietnamese
JASMINE HOUSE RESTAURANT, *2301 Clement. Located near 24th. it's open Sunday-Thursday 11am-10pm and Friday-Saturday 11am-11pm.*

The food is all Vietnamese here, and very fine, but the prices vary quite a bit depending on what you order. You can get noodle soups (beef or chicken stock), wonderful lunch rice plate specials, and fine chicken, beef, pork, or vegetarian dinners for $4-$7, while Chef Nhan Nguyen's House roast crab and barbecued catfish, arguably the best in San Francisco, will cost you $16-$17.

There's a large selection of wonderful, less expensive seafood dishes as well (clay pot catfish, deep fried trout, salmon curry), plus lots of stir fry, salads, tofu dishes, and fine garlic noodles. Inside, there are white walls, white linen, glass on the tables, and plants all around. It's pleasant enough, pretty but not spectacular, but the food makes it special.

INEXPENSIVE
American
BILL'S PLACE, *2315 Clement. 415-221-5262. Located near 24th, this is one of the best places in the city for a burger. They're open Sunday-Thursday 11am-10pm and on weekends 11am-11pm, but they don't take credit cards.*

They have been a San Francisco tradition for 38 years, and their good reputation is bolstered with down-to-earth, old-fashioned American food that costs just $3.25-$7. The inside has varnished tables and a counter by the grill, but in good weather you can sit out back in the garden, a bucolic setting with tables, plants, and flowers. They have eight standard burgers (including a veggie burger, chiliburger, steak burger, and diet plate), plus 20 celebrity burgers, named after personalities such as Carol Doda (she introduced topless dancing to the City), David Letterman, and Beverly Sills.

There is also a variety of hot dogs and sandwiches (from the lowly tuna melt to the exalted reuben), a bunch of chicken burgers, a welcome addition of a kids' menu with burgers and sandwiches, and a fine selection of fries, onion rings, and assorted other side dishes. There are breakfast items served till 1pm daily, and a wonderful menu of fountain specialties to wash your burger down in the cold froth of a milk shake or a handsome plate of pie a la mode.

Chinese

TAIWAN, *445 Clement. 415-387-1789. Located near Sixth, it looks unremarkable but dishes up good Taiwanese food Monday-Friday 11am-10pm and weekends 10am-midnight for $4-$8.*

Taiwan is often crowded (though they do take reservations), and they claim their pot stickers, steamed dumplings, and crispy chicken are the best. It's your basic interior with pink walls and glass over formica table tops, but it's pleasant enough. While their "best of" claim is a bit of an overstatement, the food does taste pretty good. It's not worth making a special trip for or going out of your way, but if you're in the inner Richmond, are hungry, and like Chinese food, Taiwan will feed you well without greatly depleting your wallet.

TSING TAO, *3107 Clement. 415-387-2344. Located near 32nd, this is a good Chinese restaurant, despite the uninspired, Chinese restaurant atmosphere, and it's open Sunday-Thursday 11am-9:30pm and weekends 'till 10pm.*

The oilcloth-covered tables and paper placemats don't lessen the quality of the Mandarin and Szechuan food, which cost mostly $5-$7 an entree, and $4 for luncheons. The shrimp in garlic sauce is very good, and the mu shu pork is reliably good, too. The hot and sour soup is hit or miss, but when it's a hit, it's sublime.

TON KIANG, *5821 Geary. 415-386-8530. Located near 22nd, it's open daily 10:30am-10pm, and they serve Hakka Chinese cuisine and dim sum all day long.*

The dining room is a quiet blend of traditional Chinese and more contemporary touches, with white linen table clothes, round central tables and inset booths, and pretty, blue-rimmed china. The staff is formal and efficient, and the food ($5-$12, not counting the $18 Peking duck) is very good. The Shanghai dumplings are special here, as is the salt-baked chicken (a Hakka specialty), and the clay pot dishes.

They also have spicy dishes like Mongolian beef and spicy Szechuan chicken with red chili peppers, and a good selection of squid, prawn, and crab dishes, too. They are also renowned for their dim sum, with barbecued pork buns, shrimp-stuffed crab claws, egg custard tarts, and foil-wrapped chicken just starting the list. It's not usually en route to anywhere, but it may be worth the effort if you're in the general neighborhood and want good dim sum.

Mediterranean

GRECO ROMANA, *2448 Clement. 415-387-0626. Located between 25th and 26th, it is open Tuesday-Thursday noon-10pm, Friday-Saturday noon-11pm, and Sunday noon-10pm.*

They make some Greek specialties like gyro plates and Greek salads, plus Italian dishes like linguine in clam sauce and fettuccine bolognese for

$5-$8, but their specialty, the item that won first place at the San Francisco Fair, is the pizza. The ingredients are all very fresh and good, they have a full line of toppings you can choose from, and the Genova (with pesto, pine nuts, and sundried tomatoes) is exceptional.

Mexican

GORDO TAQUERIA, *2252 Clement. 415-387-4484. Local near 24th, it is open daily 10am-10pm.*

This Mexican place makes excellent burritos that are filling, tasty, fresh, and cheap (just $3-$4).

Singaporean

SINGAPORE MALAYSIAN RESTAURANT, *836 Clement Street. 415-750-9518. Located between 9th and 10th. it's open Monday, Wednesday, Thursday, and Friday 11:30am-3pm and 5-10pm, while Tuesday, Saturday, and Sunday they're open 11:30-10pm.*

Their name tells the kind of cuisine they serve, and it's reliably delicious. The dining room is not special, and glass covers all the linen, but the dishes are tasty and cheap. There are plenty of noodle soups with a variety of vegetable, prawn, or pork ingredients in well-spiced broths, and the entrees ($4-$9) range from curried coconut chicken to sautéed prawns with mint leaves, lemon grass, and coconut, to fried noodles with tofu, bean sprouts, and potato in a great tomato sauce. The gado-gado is good, as is everything else. And for adventure, choose a plum or lychee drink instead of the soda.

Thai

SIAMESE GARDEN, *3751 Geary. 415-668-8763. Located near 2nd Avenue, it is open daily 11am-11pm, serving good Thai food in pleasant enough if unspectacular surroundings.*

There's a varied menu of soups, salads, and entrees featuring poultry, beef, pork, seafood, and vegetables for $5-$10, but the best dishes are the curries. The rice is served out of those ornate tin tureens, then topped with any number of curries in spicy (from mild to hot), rich, coconut milk broths. Other dishes are especially good, too, such as the tom kar gai soup and the pad thai, but it's hard to go wrong.

Vietnamese

LE SOLEIL, *133 Clement. 415-668-4848. Located near 2nd, it serves Vietnamese food daily 11am-10pm.*

The dining room is unremarkable, with a fish tank up front and tables with linen under glass. The food is good, however, and the prices fairly low. Lunch dishes average about $5, while dinner entrees are closer to $8, and the servings are generous. You can get all sorts of noodle soups, plus nicely spiced rice and noodle dishes. There's sautéed prawns with coconut and curry, there's the clay pot special with stir fried chicken, Chinese sausage, and gingered mushroom, there's barbecued pork, and plenty of vegetarian dishes, too, like eggplant in garlic sauce or bean curd with vegetables.

RUSSIAN HILL

EXPENSIVE

American

HARRIS', *2100 Van Ness. 415-673-1888. Located near Pacific, it lays claim to being the best steak house in the city. Clubby and dark, they're open for dinner daily. Monday-Friday the bar opens at 5:30 and dinners go 6-9:30pm or so, while on weekends dinner is available 5-9:30 or so.*

Mrs. Harris opened this place in 1984 after completely revamping what had been a steakhouse for 50 years. It was built originally in 1906 (after the earthquake) as a showroom for the fancy and now-forgotten Marmon Car, and the windows which once displayed the Rolls-Royce of the time now showcase the Rolls-Royce of meat-hanging beef loins aged for 21 days in 33° dry storage (they neither freeze nor deteriorate) to perfect and ripen their flavor.

They have got just about every style of steak you can think of ($24-$31), but their specialty, the Harris Steak, is a New York cut with the bone in, and Mrs. Harris herself recommends it for flavor. They also, however, carry prime rib, chicken, lamb, fresh fish, one token vegetarian dish, and lots of seafood appetizers, plus American classics like grilled liver with onions and bacon, Maine lobster with steamed clams and a baked potato, and calf's brain in brown butter, lemon, and capers. Harris' other specialty to set the tone for the perfect steak is the perfect martini - served individually in its own carafe and chilled in a tub of ice, these martinis will gladden the heart of martini connoisseurs everywhere.

MODERATE

Italian

RISTORANTE MILANO, *1448 Pacific. 415-673-2961. Located between Jones and Leavenworth, it is open Tuesday-Saturday from 5:30-10:30pm, and Sunday 5-10pm, and reservations are usually needed.*

This is a reliably outstanding Italian restaurant, with good food and attentive service. It's popular and is full during peak dining hours, but it doesn't have the same overly-packed, unappealing party atmosphere I Fratelli sometimes gets. The pasta dishes ($10-$11.25) are homemade and delicious, with a creamy risotto of the day, gnocchi in gorgonzola or tomato basil sauce, spinach and ricotta ravioli with butter and sage, and tonnarelli in light cream sauce with porcini mushrooms and Italian sausage, among others. There are also fish and meat dishes (grilled lamb chops with rosemary and garlic, saltimboca with chicken) that cost $12-$16. The design inside is contemporary Italian, with simple lines and colors. It's warm but not boisterous inside, and you can count on getting a fine meal.

I FRATELLI, *1896 Hyde. 415-474-8240. Located near Green, it's open daily 5-10:15pm, serving their excellent Italian fare to the ever-loyal hordes. Reservations are almost always a good idea, especially for the weekend, when folks waiting for tables overflow the bar onto Hyde Street.*

It's a pleasant restaurant, at least when it isn't too jam-packed and noisy, but even then the good food keeps people coming back. Blue checked tablecloths, candles, and pitchers of house wine set an appealing tone. The starters ($3.25-$6) include an addictive garlic bread, and the carpaccio is pretty good, too. Among the pasta ($10-$12) and the meat/fish dishes ($12-$15), the fettuccine compleanno (with andouille sausage, tasso ham, chicken, shrimp, and spicy cream sauce) stands out as a winner, very rich and very delicious, and the scaloppini di vitello alla saltimboca is another good choice, but then the menu is full of them.

It's a real scene on the weekends, though the scene is pretty homogeneously young professionals, and the busy throng aspect attracts some as it turns others away. If you don't like the action, however, you can always try them during the week when the food's just as good and the dining room's a bit quieter.

Spanish Tapas

ZARZUELA, *2000 Hyde. 415-346-0800. Located by Union, it serves tapas Monday-Saturday noon-10:30pm.*

The menu offers a full selection of hot and cold tapas ($2.75-$5.50 per small plate) and full-sized regional specials (including paella, which takes at least 30 minutes to prepare) for $9-$14. The warm, friendly atmosphere with rough wood and brick accents blends nicely with the traditional Spanish decor, crisp white linen settings, and soft candlelight. They have good sangria, and some very tasty tapas (mussels or shrimp in garlic and white wine is excellent) and very fine paella, but too many of the tapas aren't up to speed. Either they're cutting corners on ingredients, or just getting sloppy, but the overall general quality has declined since they first opened.

Though the quality isn't quite as top-notch as it was, Zarzuela still sets a fine tapas spread and attracts a strong local following (so expect a wait on weekend nights, since they don't take reservations).

INEXPENSIVE
International
   WORLD WRAPPS, *2227 Polk Street. 415-931-9727. Located near Vallejo, just opened in April of 1996 thanks to the vast popularity of their Marina location, it serves international burritos daily 10am-11pm (and smoothies from 8am) for $3.20-$7 a meal.*

Eat in or take it to go, either way it's good, healthy food, and the Russian Hill spot is a bit roomier and more comfortable than in the Marina. An alternative to traditional fast food, they wrap fresh, gourmet ingredients in tortillas (whole wheat, roma tomato, or spinach), with a variety of international flavors to choose from. The traditional Mexican burrito is a bit boring, but the Thai chicken, teriyaki chicken, and grilled veggies with goat cheese are delicious, and plenty more (mango snapper, Mandarin stir-fry, the Bombay) sound interesting. And the smoothies are sensational. Made of juice, fruit, and yogurt or sorbet, they are refreshing, fruity, and delicious. We can vouch for the Real Raspberry and the Tropical Storm, but they all look wonderful.

Italian
   MARIO'S BOHEMIAN CIGAR STORE, *2209 Polk. 415-776-8226. Located near Vallejo, it serves the same fine food as the original branch down in North Beach, and they're open daily 10am-midnight.*

Their hot focaccia sandwiches are just as good as those in their North Beach store, and they serve the same meatball, veggie, eggplant, frittata, and sausage sandwiches for $5.75-$6.25, an enormous sandwich. Along with the sandwiches, they do the same cannelloni, polenta with sausage, and pizza for $8.50 as in North Beach, and in fact this is where it all gets cooked (the Columbus cafe doesn't have a kitchen). Since this is a larger space, with a real kitchen, they can have a somewhat expanded menu, with Caesar salads and specials, such as they can't do in North Beach. But while the food is just as good and the atmosphere is convivial, it's just not the same as the original.

Mexican
   ¡WA-HA-KA!, *2141 Polk. 415-775-1055. Located near Broadway, this is a Oaxaca Mexican Grill open Monday-Friday noon-11pm and weekends 11am-10pm.*

They make unusual and unusually good burritos, with very fresh ingredients and lots of vegetables (peppers, carrots, mushrooms, and onions) in their vegetarian burrito. There are other options, however. There are tacos and tacones, quesadillas and nachos, tostadas and fajitas. For $3-$6 you can get a filling and delicious entree, and a dollar more gets you the full combination with rice, beans, and salad. It's pleasant to eat on the distressed wood tables that blend with the southwestern decor, but it also makes for good take-out fare.

Sandwiches, Salads, & Picnic Supplies

REAL FOOD DELI, *2164 Polk. 415-775-2805. Located near Vallejo, it's open daily 8am-8pm.*

They prepare a variety of salads, sandwiches, and desserts that are trés California, generally good for you, and very delicious. The selection changes from day to day, but they usually have a great orzo and feta salad, Chinese noodles, and outstanding chicken salads, whose prices range from $2.20-$9.90 lb. Their chicken pot pies ($3.75) are unusually good, and the sandwiches ($4.75) are fine as well. There are tables inside and out, or you can get takeout for a picnic.

SOUTH OF MARKET (SOMA)

EXPENSIVE

Nouvelle California Cuisine

HAWTHORNE LANE, *22 Hawthorne. 415-777-9779. Located off Howard between Second and Third, it was opened by David and Anne Gingrass when they left Postrio. They do lunch Monday-Friday 11:30am-2pm and dinner 5:30-10pm daily, serving their nouvelle California cuisine in a stylish setting.*

The design is stunning. They took an old warehouse and turned it into a knock-out. The space is open and airy, but set off with curvy lines, wavy shapes, and exquisite details like the door handles fashioned from wrought-iron to look like tree twigs. Beautiful modern art graces the walls, the brightly varnished cherry wood bar occupies the center, or choose between the enticing circular booths by the wall or the settee booths by the enormous windows that look out on Second Street. Wherever you sit, the mood is one of happy good cheer, and the food is delicious. Dinner entrees range from $19-$24 (or $10-$14 during lunch), and some specialties include shrimp pulled live from the tank, maple-glazed quail, and rare seared yellowfin tuna with fried green beans and garlic chips. They also have a host of deluxe cocktails to enjoy at their gorgeous bar, and it's quite the scene when work begins to let out.

42 DEGREES, *235 16th Street. 415-777-5558. Located off Third behind the Esprit outlet, it's a new chic jazz supper club with excellent food that's open Monday-Friday 11:30am-3pm and dinner Wednesday-Saturday 7pm-midnight. Reservations are taken for dinner, smoking is permitted on the patio only, and there's classic dinner jazz nightly from 8-11pm, with no cover charge.*

Set in the industrial district by the old Southern Pacific tracks, it's run by the same folks who are enjoying such success with the Slow Club, but with a fancier menu. Inside there are booths on the mezzanine, informal seating below, and outside seating that's sheltered from the wind. Lunch items ($5.50-$7) feature pizzetas, chicken pot pie, and sandwiches of grilled eggplant or homemade chicken and apple sausage. Dinner ($14-$21) is heftier on the plate and the wallet, with Niman-Schell rib-eye steak, saffron risotto with asparagus and pine nuts, and grilled sea bass with garlic roasted eggplant and rich cream infused lentils as examples of the hearty and succulent meals they dish up to go with the jazz.

MODERATE
American
FLY TRAP RESTAURANT, *606 Folsom. 415-243-0580. This is a transplanted San Francisco tradition that's open Monday-Thursday 11:30am-10pm, Friday 11:30am-10:30pm, and Saturday 5:30-10:30pm.*

The Fly Trap is a continental sort of place, serving traditional dishes from France, Germany, Italy, and the USA. Their menu features items like Chicken Jerusalem (in a cream and artichoke sauce), Hangtown Fry (an oyster and bacon frittata) and Veal Picatta, as well as Calf Brains and Sautéed Sweetbreads specials. They also do fine pastas, and a number of seafood appetizers and salads. The starters are mostly around $7, and entree prices range from $9.50-$16.75. The interior is pleasant though unremarkable, with white linen tablecloths and napkins, and waiters in formal black.

THE FLY TRAP HISTORY
The name has an interesting origin. In the late 1800s, when this restaurant got its start, it was located on Market Street, it was called Louie's, and the streetcars that plied Market were pulled by horses. The streetcars brought Louie customers, and the horses brought Louie flies. Louie responded with a square of fly paper per table, and the G.I.s of 1898 responded with the clever nickname of "fly trap." Louie was not amused, and eventually ditched both the restaurant and San Francisco, and returned to Italy. The restaurant lived on, however, as did the new name, which became official when the place was reopened after the 1906 fire. Owners and locations have changed, and the flies of yore are no longer, but the Fly Trap Restaurant remains a popular San Francisco venue.

CAFFE CENTRO, *102 South Park. 415-882-1500, fax 415-882-1502. Located on the corner of Jack London, it's open Monday-Friday 7:30am-7:30pm, and Saturday 9am-5:30pm.*

This is a cute cafe with artwork on the walls, music at just the right volume, and very tasty food for $3-$6. You can order your sandwiches, salads, soups, and grilled fare at the counter if you want to stay, or at the outside counter around the corner for take-out. There are little green tables and chairs on the South Park sidewalk as well as tables inside, and the staff is very friendly.

Caribbean

CARIBBEAN ZONE, *55 Natoma. 415-541-9465. Located near Mission and between First and Second, it's open for lunch Monday-Friday 11:30am-2:30pm and for dinner Monday-Thursday 5-10pm and Friday-Saturday 5-11pm. They also are starting club entertainment nights, with Latin orchestras (9-11 pieces) playing Thursday evening 10pm-1:30am for $8 cover, or only $3 if you dine there earlier (the kitchen will still close at 10pm, but there'll be tacos available for the hungry.*

Wildly colorful, festively verdant – this is a funky tropical South of Market restaurant. Amid palms and bright paint, they serve big platters ($11-$17) of spicy Caribbean fare like chili pork loin roast with smoked garlic, candied yams and braised greens, or pecan catfish, roasted in pecan butter with spicy saffron rice and okra ratatouille. Reggae music adds to the lively air.

French

LE CHARM, *315 Fifth. 415-546-6128. Located near Folsom, it serves delicious and low-priced French lunch Monday-Friday 11:30am-2:30pm, and dinner Tuesday-Saturday 6-9:30pm (till 10 on weekends).*

Small and boxy inside, with the golden-orange walls favored so by SoMa restaurants, and a small patio in back that's open in nice weather, it's pleasant but a bit noisy, and reservations are a good idea because it fills right up.

Lunch entrees run $5.50-$8.50, including items like grilled lemon chicken sausage, roasted salmon on mashed potatoes, and that old French standby, the cheeseburger with French fries. The three-course dinners are $18, and this cute-industrial bistro turns out some serious coq au vin, duck salad, and tarte tatin.

SOUTH PARK CAFE, *108 South Park. 415-495-7275. Located just next door to Caffe Centro, it's open Monday-Friday 7:30am-10pm, Saturday 6-10pm.*

The cafe really hums at lunch time; in fact it gets quite noisy. The cream walls and green plants are soothing on the eye, but the action is busy, making it a good place to people-watch but a bad choice for a quiet tete-a-tete. This is a popular French restaurant, with a well-established reputation. If there are no tables available, patrons gladly pull up a stool and eat at the bar.

There are traditional French sandwiches like Croque Monsieur, and entrees that range from steamed mussels to couscous to boudin noir ($7.50-$10 for lunch, $10-$15 for dinner). The salads are beautiful, and the food is nothing to sneeze at, but the service, while professional, is a bit full of itself. While the torn white butcher paper on the tables seems to convey informal dining, there's a definite snootiness in the air.

SOUTH PARK

This strip of green off 2nd between Bryant and Brannan is a peaceful change to the surrounding urban downtown. There's a tiny playground for children, a bunch of picnic tables, and a collection of fine restaurants. You wouldn't know it to look at it, but South Park has a lot of history as well.

In the 1850s, South Park and nearby Rincon Hill were the flashiest parts of town, the neighborhood of choice for the merchants, bankers, and the few rare miners who made fortunes off the gold rush. By the 1870s, however, the new wealthy elite such as the Bonanza Kings chose Nob Hill as the site for their opulent mansions, and South Park lost its snob appeal. A Japanese settlement was located here for a while, but the 1906 earthquake and fire reduced the place to charred rubble. By the 1960s, the area was far more popular with junkies than with the affluent. In the 70s, however, investors began redeveloping, and today South Park is clean and pretty and fairly upscale.

Italian

RISTORANTE ECCO, *101 South Park. 415-495-3291. Located across the street from South Park Cafe, and owned by them as well, but it's a much more pleasant place, and it's open weekdays 11:30am-10pm, and 5:30-10pm on Saturdays.*

The dining room is peaceful and lovely, with white linen covered by paper. The walls are in earth tones, cream and dark brick, and the tall windows look out over the park. The menu ($10-$16 an entree) offers starters such as fritti misti and carpaccio, while the main dishes range from linguine all'Ecco (with pears, pecans, and gorgonzola) to grilled salmon in a lemon, fennel, almond vinaigrette.

RUBY'S, *489 Third. 415-541-0795. Located near Bryant, it is a small place known for their terrific and unusual pizza, though they have got lots of other good food to offer as well. They're open for lunch Monday-Friday 11:30am-2:30pm, and for dinner Tuesday-Thursday 5-10pm, Friday-Sunday 6-10pm (they may close as late as 10:30, depending on business).*

Ruby's is a great source for delivered dinners, but it's a lovely place to eat in. Small and welcoming, warm Mediterranean tones color the walls, white linens embrace the tables, and a heavenly aroma fills the air. The pizzas use a dense, cornbread crust, and they are not only delicious, they are unusually filling (grown men can rarely eat more than two slices).

They have three standard pizzas, and three specials that change daily and are worth looking into. They cost $3-$4 a slice, $16-$20 per whole pie, and generally speaking the pizzas with garlic are very good.

But there is more to Ruby's than pizza alone. They make two tasty sandwiches, grilled chicken and grilled eggplant on focaccia, both with interesting extra ingredients ($7.25) and a host of salads, pasta plates, and appetizers for $5-$14. They use fresh ingredients, most of their innovative combos work well, and they deliver after 5pm.

BIZOU, *598 Fourth Street. 415-543-2222. Located near Brannan, it serves Mediterranean lunches during the week 11:30am-2:30pm and dinner Monday-Saturday 5:30-10 or 10:30pm.*

Pronounced "bee zoo," this popular restaurant is very nice inside, with mustard-colored, antiquified wall, wood chairs, and French chanteuse music on the stereo. Their rustic French/Italian menu ($10.50-$16.50 an entree and $4.50-$10 for salads and starters) has some real winners like tempura-fried green beans, apple and frisee salad with goat cheese, lamb shanks with mint pesto, braised beef cheeks, and sizzling shrimp. Their crisp Italian flatbread is very good, too.

Mediterranean

LULU, *816 Folsom. 415-495-5775. Located near Fourth, it's open Monday-Friday for breakfast (in the cafe) 7-11am, and the restaurant proper is open Sunday-Thursday 11:30am-10:45pm and till 11:45 on Friday and Saturday.*

Reed Hearon's first sensation, the cuisine is Mediterranean and runs $7-$18 for items such as their rosemary roast chicken (from the wood-fired rotisserie in back), and fritto misto with artichokes, and specials like roast suckling pig with dandelion or squab salad with quince, fennel, and roasted chestnuts. The place is madly popular with many, though not all dishes work so well, and some feel the place is carried more by its momentum than by actual quality.

Inside, it's expansive and colorful, with varnished wood tables set simply with festive yellow and blue dishes and white linen napkins. The feel is open, the better to see and be seen, under the uniquely arching, slatted ceiling, designed to let in just the right amount of natural light. It strikes the balance of not too loud and not too bright, with just the busy rumble of a roomful of diners and efficient waitpersons. In the back is the brick oven with chickens roasting over an open fire, and the brick pizza oven just next to it. Even the lovely, blue-tiled bathrooms keep the style going. Next door is the cafe, with the same lunch and dinner menus, but open for breakfast, too. It's smaller, quieter, and more sedate, with a little store of LuLu jarred goods, books, and dishes on sale.

Nouvelle California Cuisine
FRINGALE, *570 Fourth Street. 415-543-0573. Located near Bryant, it is a cozy, modern brasserie serving California cuisine with Basque overtones weekdays for lunch 11:30am-3pm and Monday-Saturday 5:30-10pm for dinner.* Chef and owner Gerald Hirigoyen creates some truly delicious meals ($11-$16, a little less for lunch) like foie gras medallions in duck broth, pork tenderloin confit, steamed mussels with fried garlic, and Roquefort ravioli. The blond wood and cream walls, colorful paintings and bright windows make for a stylish haven from the frenzied Fourth Street traffic. Soft jazz plays in the background, and white linen picks up the window trim. The staff doesn't ooze warmth, but the food is magnificent, and more than justifies the restaurant's great popularity.

INEXPENSIVE
American
HAMBURGER MARY'S, *1582 Folsom. 415-626-1985. Located near 12th, it is open daily Monday-Friday 11:30am-12:15am, and weekends 10am-1:15am. There are also plenty of specials like happy hour Monday-Friday 4-7pm, Melrose Monday night (to watch the show with free food and discount shooters), and Sunday Unplugged, when they invite local bands to perform.*

This is a real slice of San Francisco funk, going on its 24th year. It's busy and bustling, the walls are cluttered with pictures and mirrors at odd angles, antique lamps hang from the red ceiling, and loud, thumping music fills the air. And wherever you look, folks are busy gorging on burgers and fries ($6-$8 for most platters). They also have a bang-up Bloody Mary, too. The aura may be a bit much for some, but if you thrive on the sounds of clattering plates and rock & roll, this is a fun and historic place to have a burger.

Mexican
¡WA-HA-KA!, *1489 Folsom. 415-861-1410. Located near 14th, it's open Sunday-Thursday 11:30am-10pm, Friday 11:30am-12:30am, and Saturday 11:30-1am and serves the same fine Mexican Oaxaca fare here as they do in their Russian Hill and Marina outlets.*

Inside, there's their trademark southwestern style tinted tables and chairs, plus some nifty exposed brick to add to the atmosphere. Take it to go or eat here (upstairs or down), either way the burritos and such are made with fresh ingredients, and they turn out reliably tasty meals for just $3-$6. The vegetarian burrito is especially good, with lots more vegetables than you usually find in a burrito, and the tacos, quesadillas, tostadas, and fajitas are good, too.

SUNSET-INNER

EXPENSIVE
Seafood

PJ'S OYSTER BED, *737 Irving. 415-566-7775. Located near 9th, it serves lunch Monday-Friday 11:30am-2:30pm, and brunch on the weekend 11:30am-3pm. Dinner is Sunday 4-10, Monday-Thursday 5-10, and Friday-Saturday 5-11pm.*

PJ's is open in the hours between lunch and dinner, but they just serve cold items off the oyster bar. This is a very popular, frequently crowded, over-rated place, with entrees costing $14-$19, and appetizers from $5-$16. The oyster bar is quite good, but some of the cooked dishes tend toward heavy sauces. They have gumbo and chowder and bisque, jambalaya and grilled alligator and Cajun chops with prawns, and a lot of attitude.

MODERATE
French

ZAZIE, *941 Cole. 415-564-5332. Located near Parnassus, it's up a few blocks from Haight Street in what's usually referred to as Cole Valley. It's a small, cute place that's open daily 8am-2:30pm and 6-9:30pm (till 10pm on weekends). They take reservations, but only for parties of six or more, and not for after 7pm.*

Zazie's serves great breakfasts ($3-$7) with pancakes, French toast, Irish oatmeal, granola with fresh fruit, eggs done a variety of ways, and wonderful gingerbread pancakes. Their lunches ($7-$10) and dinners ($9-$12) are country French, with roast trout Provencal, various couscous dishes, roast chicken and pork, and pasta Provencal. This is a lovely neighborhood place with fine, fresh food and a charming ambiance.

Italian

BAMBINO'S PIZZA RESTAURANT, *945 Cole. 415-731-1343. Located near Parnassus. Open Sunday-Thursday 11:30am-11pm, and till midnight Friday and Saturday.*

This small, 17-table establishment has been serving pizzas and pastas ($7-$13) to the neighborhood for 14 years, and while it's not worth a special trip, they're a viable option if you're in the neighborhood. Their pizzas and calzones are good, but they serve lots of other dishes as well. There are sandwiches (burgers, grilled chicken, grilled eggplant with artichokes and roasted red peppers), lots of good salads (Caesar, Greek, spinach, and mixed greens with pear, pecans, and brie cheese), pastas including lasagna (meat or vegetarian), ravioli, angel hair with sun-dried tomatoes, fresh vegetables, roasted garlic and olive oil, and linguine with fresh clams, and entrees with chicken breast, fresh vegetables, or seafood specials. All in all, there's something for everyone, and at a decent price.

PASQUALE'S PIZZERIA, *700 Irving. 415-661-2140. Located near 8th, it is open noon-midnight on weekdays and noon-1:30am on weekends.*

The pizza and such is okay here, a tad better than mediocre. The pizzas start at $7.30 for a small cheese, while the sandwiches and pasta dishes (with chicken, veal, or shrimp) run $4.80-$15. This isn't fine or fancy dining, but it's perfectly acceptable if you're hungry, nearby, and want Italian.

Japanese

WE BE SUSHI, *94 Judah. 415-681-4010. Located near Eighth. They also have branches in the Richmond and Mission. They're open for lunch Monday-Friday 11:30am-2:30pm and for dinner Monday-Saturday 5-10pm.*

The restaurant is small, but it's very pleasant nonetheless, and a reliably nice place to go for sushi. Their sushi items range from $1.50-$3, and are always fresh and tasty. There's an upbeat, slightly tongue-in-cheek attitude about the place, and they have an amusing story on the back of their menu about how their first name (McSushi) was contested by McDonald's, and how they came to get the name they now use, but the big draw is the good, reasonably priced food.

GOEMON, *1524 Irving. 415-664-2288. Located between 16th and 17th. Open every evening but Tuesday from 5:30-9:30pm, though they often stay open on weekends till 10pm.*

Goemon has traditional Japanese decor and reliably good sushi.

EBISU, *1283 9th Avenue. 415-566-1770. It is open for lunch Monday-Friday 11:30am-2pm, and for dinner Monday-Wednesday 5-10pm, and till midnight Friday-Saturday.*

A very popular restaurant, they don't take reservations and the line to get in can take forever. Inside there is western-style seating at tables in a lackluster room, sushi bar counter seats, and wonderful low-style Japanese tables behind shoji screens (for which the wait is the longest). There is sushi a la carte at $2-$5 a small plate, sushi platters ($10-$14), or tempura, teriyaki, sashimi meals for $8-$16. The food is reliably good, but it may not be worth the wait.

Middle Eastern

YAYA, *1220 Ninth Avenue. 415-566-6966. Located between Lincoln and Irving, this is an upscale Middle Eastern restaurant serving lunch Tuesday-Saturday 11:30-2pm, and dinner Tuesday-Sunday 5:30-9pm for $11-$14.50.*

There are a number of interesting dishes here, like the ravioli stuffed with cardamom and dates, the Japanese eggplant stuffed with lamb and tamarind, and the filo creations. The atmosphere, though decorated with some wonderful Mesopotamian art, is a bit sterile somehow, missing that festive air that brings a restaurant to life.

STOYANOF'S, *1240 9th. 415-664-3664. Located between Lincoln and Irving, it's open Tuesday-Thursday 10am-9:30pm, Friday-Saturday 10am-10pm, and 4:30-9pm on Sunday.*

This is not a place to idle away the afternoon, but it's good for a quick Middle Eastern meal, and the food is very good. They have meze items ($3-$5) like hummus, dolma, tabouli, and tzatziki, plus spanikopita and other stuffed filo pastries. There are also entrees ($9-$14) with lots of seafood specials (Greek fisherman's stew, grilled salmon with cilantro garlic butter, swordfish shish kebab), plus other dishes like moussaka, roast lamb, and spiced kofte kebabs.

Thai

MAE-THIP, *524 Irving. 415-664-3664. Located between 6th and 7th, it's open daily 5-10pm, and their dishes cost $6-$9.*

They have a good green salad with tofu and egg, great soups (especially the *tom ka talay* seafood soup). The curries are all very good, with the yellow and red curries a bit milder than the green. They also have good vegetarian dishes, an excellent peanut sauce, and an entree called *mieng kum* with spinach and shrimp and peanuts that's exceptional.

MARNEE THAI, *2225 Irving. 415-665-9500. Located between 23rd and 24th, it is open 11:30am-10pm every day but Tuesday, when they're closed. They have lunch specials for $4.75, and during dinner, entrees range from $6-$8.50, depending on whether you're ordering vegetarian, meat, or seafood.*

There's the usual assortment of soups like *tom ka* and *tom yum* (one with coconut milk, lemon grass, ginger, and chicken or prawns, the other a hot and sour base with mushrooms, tomatoes, and lemon grass), noodle dishes like *pad thai*, and vegetarian dishes like spinach sautéed in garlic and soy bean sauce or *praram phak*, vegetables in a peanut curry sauce. They have also plenty of chicken, seafood, and pork-based meals as well. The food is reliably good, and the dishes are authentic Thai.

SUKHO THAI, *1319 9th. 415-564-7722. Located between Irving and Judah, it's open daily 11am-10pm. They serve very good Thai food for $6-$10, with lots of vegetarian and lots of seafood specials.*

Sukho Thai features many curries, with roast duck, prawn, chicken and beef, but the spicy salmon curry is especially popular. The seafood hot plate is another favorite, and the soups are good, too. There's a good vegetarian selection, with sautéed spinach and tofu in peanut sauce, sautéed eggplant with bean sauce, garlic, chili and basil, and a good coconut milk-based vegetable soup. There are the usual pan-fried noodle (pad thai) dishes, noodle salads, and a number of inexpensive lunch specials, too.

INEXPENSIVE
Chinese
SHANGRI-LA CHINESE VEGETARIAN RESTAURANT, *2026 Irving. 415-731-2548. Located between 21st and 22nd, it's open daily 11:30am-9:30pm.*

This vegetarian Chinese restauratn offers a lunch special for $4.25 including main dish, soup, and the works, but usually the entrees cost $4-$7. With dishes like Peking special sauce noodles, mustard green with bean curd skin, and vegetarian tempura, the food is excellent. Especially good are the eggplant in hot sauce, hot and sour soup, sweet and sour walnuts, and ta-ta noodles, and they have fried bananas with ice cream for dessert – but avoid the crispy vegetable ball and mushroom appetizer.

Mexican
GORDO TAQUERIA, *1233 9th. 415-566-6011. Near Lincoln, it is open daily 10am-10pm.*

Like their branch in the Richmond, this Gordo has very good burritos for $3-$4 that just hit the spot.

TELEGRAPH HILL
EXPENSIVE
Italian
JULIUS' CASTLE, *1541 Montgomery. 415-392-2222. Located near Union, it's up a hill no matter where your starting point, and it's open nightly 5-10pm.*

You can't miss it - it's the pink-shingled, turreted chateau with the amazing views that was built in 1922. Up 18 steps to the dining room, inside it's swell in a baroque sort of way, with gilt-edged chandeliers and moldings, white linen and dark woods, and windows that afford some of the best bay and bridge views around. There are nooks and cozy side corners, bay windows and dark wine-colored fabrics, silver plate dinner ware and gilt rails, and entree prices from $9-$28. A glass of wine will cost $6.25-$12, while a bottle is $25-$460.

The food is gourmet, there's no denying it, but it's not as sensational as they make it out to be. You can dine relatively inexpensively on pasta (these are the $9 dishes), such as gnocchi in a meat ragout, vegetable-filled ravioli, and porcini mushroom risotto. Then there are the secondi platti, which start at $19. These are ample and elaborate dishes like grilled free range veal loin wrapped in pancetta with stewed leeks, Yukon mashed potatoes and roasted garlic sauce, or sautéed gulf shrimp, Maine scallops and Mediterranean mussels with fire roasted bell peppers, tomato, and curried basmati rice. But people mostly come here for the splendor of the pink castle and the magnificence of the view.

INEXPENSIVE
Chinese
   HUNAN, *924 Sansome. 415-956-7727. Located between Broadway and Vallejo, it serves delicious Chinese food daily 11am-9:30pm for $4.50-$9.*
   Hunan has some exceedingly tasty dishes, and this is no secret, hence the mobs that descend around lunch time. Some known gems are their onion cakes, Diana's Special Meat Pie (even though it may not sound like great Chinese food, it is), the Chicken Salad, Beef with Bean Curd (exceptional), Eggplant with Meat Sauce, and on and on and on, excepting only the stewed beef dishes which are a bit foul. The decor is nothing to write home about, but it isn't unpleasant, and some attempts (nice plants, good bar) have been made to create atmosphere. The food is especially fine, however, and is a treat not to be missed.

TENDERLOIN
INEXPENSIVE
Vietnamese
   SAIGON, *560 Larkin. 415-474-5698. It's open Monday to Saturday 7am-6pm and Sunday 8am-4pm.*
   Just a small Vietnamese cafe with no atmosphere to speak of, but they serve great ready-made baguette sandwiches for $1.50-$2. The barbecued pork is very good, but they also have chicken and meatball sandwhiches.

UNION SQUARE
SPLURGE
French
   THE FRENCH ROOM, *495 Geary. 415-775-4700, ask for the French Room. Located near Taylor, it is a formal and stunning room in the impressive Clift Hotel.*
   Not surprisingly, the cuisine here is traditional French, expertly prepared and served. Breakfast is served Monday-Friday 6:30-11am Monday-Saturday, Sunday brunch is 10am-2pm, and dinner is served Tuesday-Sunday 5:30-10pm (lunch and Monday dinner are served in the Clift's Redwood Room). The dinner menu has traditional French appetizers ($6-$15) like Sonoma foie gras, escargot with sweetbreads, lobster, and a cognac cream sauce, and a Normandy Brie soup. Entrees ($19-$36) include prime certified Angus beef, lobster cioppino, Petaluma duck, and peppered rare ahi tuna. This is not a prime place for vegetarians, but fans of top-notch meat prepared with French skill should love it.
   The decor, however, is for anyone with an eye for class and beauty. The French Room ceiling drips antique French crystal, the tables sparkle with starched linen, lovely china, and polished silver, and the decor is all Louis XV. The food, service, ambiance, and overall elegance attain the

heights of fine dining. This is a special place in which to celebrate a special event. You won't be disappointed.

Nouvelle Cuisine

POSTRIO, *545 Post. 415-776-7825. Located near Taylor and connected to the Prescott Hotel, this is the birthplace of California's nouvelle cuisine, led by the talented and innovative chef, Wolfgang Puck. They serve breakfast Monday-Friday 7-10am, and lunch is 11:30am-2pm, brunch Saturday-Sunday is 9am-2pm, and dinner is served nightly 5:30-10pm. The cafe section remains open on a first-come-first-served basis till 11pm or so. Reservations are usually a must, unless you are staying as a guest at the Prescott, in which case you can order room service from Postrio.*

Wolfgang Puck's style combines western dishes with Asian flavors, and he comes up with the best of both worlds. Appetizers ($10-$14) include exquisite items like stir fried garlic lamb with fresh chili and mint, sautéed foie gras with cranberry Szechuan glaze and tangerine ver jus, and giant blini of smoked salmon, dill creme fraiche and whitefish caviar. The main courses ($19-$28) get even better. The Chinese style duck with spicy mango sauce and crispy fried lotus root is a Wolfgang Puck signature, but then the grilled squab with sweet potato foie gras spring roll and candied rhubarb is pretty impressive too. And the grilled rare tuna with sweet and sour eggplant, wilted greens and red pepper sauce is addictive (though it's a pricy habit to support). The menus change a bit from season to season, but some dishes (like the duck) are never cut. The pastas, breads, and pastries are made on the premises daily, and they even have their own butcher shop where they make their own sausages (perhaps this is the secret to Puck's famous pepperoni pizza). The desserts are works of art as well, and the creme brulee is unlike any you've ever had.

While not all nouvelle cuisine works (in the wrong hands the quirky combos can be truly horrid), Puck and the two head chefs who trained under him (Mitchell and Steven Rosenthal) are masters, and the dishes as a whole transcend the individual ingredients they combine. If you want to splash out for a special meal, you won't get better quality than at Postrio. As added bargain, Postrio is a very cool and hip place to be, and you can see and be seen while you dine in style.

EXPENSIVE
American

THE REDWOOD ROOM, *495 Geary. 415-775-4700, ask for the Redwood Room. Located in the Clift Hotel, near Taylor, it's open daily 11am-11pm, though the mid-afternoon hours of 3-5pm are taken up with High Tea.*

This darkly romantic room was carved out a single 2,000 year-old redwood tree in 1933 (before old-growth trees were considered a national treasure). The art deco style and classy tone have attracted San Francisco society for years, and if you don't mind spending more for a sandwich than you usually spend on three, lunch in the Redwood Room is real experience.

There are soups like clam chowder or French onion, and salads like gorgonzola or baby Napa greens ($6-$10) for starters. The Clift burger ($11) comes with bacon and Swiss cheese, and the open face roast leg of lamb sandwich on onion flatbread ($13) is magnificently filling and delicious. There are also lobster or smoked turkey club sandwiches, lamb chops, prime rib, or blackened swordfish dishes ($12-$17). Jazz starts at 7pm nightly, and you can go with just cocktails (expect to drop $6 or so per drink), or dine here as well. Either way, you'll spend a bit but reap a lot in atmosphere and style.

Nouvelle Cuisine

CAMPTON PLACE, *340 Stockton. 415-955-5555. Located just up from Union Square, the chefs here prepare some of the most exclusive meals in San Francisco. Breakfast is served Monday-Friday 7-10:30am, Saturday 8-11am, Sun 8-10am, and Sunday brunch is 10am-2pm. Lunch is Monday-Friday 11:30am-2pm, and Sat noon-2pm, and dinner is Monday-Thursday 6-10pm, 5:30-10:30pm Friday-Saturday, and 6-9:30pm on Sunday.*

Just off Campton Place Hotel, luncheons includes selections such as foie gras terrine with pears and endive starters ($6.50) and entrees that run the gamut from pasta al ceppo with venison Bolognese ($9.50) to a smoked salmon and caviar club sandwich ($14.50). For dinner, you might start with a lobster bisque ($6.50) or spinach and goat cheese salad ($6) followed by a meal of beef short ribs in truffle sauce ($26) or lobster and monkfish in Indian spices ($28). There's also a special Wednesday night bargain of a set $25 three-course dinner to go with the Wednesday night jazz. Whatever you get, you can be sure the service will be attentive, and the setting lovely.

PLAZA RESTAURANT, *345 Stockton. 415-403-4854. Located in the Grand Hyatt, it's an elegant and soothing respite from the hectic activities of Union Square, and it's open daily 6:30am-10pm, with Sunday champagne brunch from 10am-2pm.*

The rattan furniture and lush palm trees take you far away, while the immense picture windows let you watch all the hustle-bustle of Union Square from the peace of your rattan chair, as water from the fountain splashes placidly. There are no free lunches, however, and you pay for your surroundings. Starters like crab cakes or quesadillas run $8-$10, sandwiches like a burger, hot pastrami or grilled chicken are $9.25. Dinner entrees showcase fish, pasta, and red meat plates ($16-$22). They have a wealth of salads and healthful dishes that combine fresh ingredients for a lot of flavor without the fat. The Plaza also serves a prix-fixe dinner menu ($28) featuring a bounty of seafood.

MODERATE
American
PERRY'S, *185 Sutter. 415-989-6895. Located near Kearny, it's open Monday-Saturday 11am-9pm. Known for its clam chowder ($6), burgers ($8), and potato skins ($6.25), this cafe/sports bar is very popular, and rightly so.*

Perry's is friendly and relaxed, and while the many TVs feature sporting events, the volume is muted so all you hear is the happy din of customers relaxing and talking. The chowder is better than average (it's good without being superb), the pints of beer are refreshing, and if you're in Union Square and hanker after a burger, this is the place to go. They also offer more unusual meals like chicken breast on walnut focaccia or grilled ahi tuna along with the standard chili, burger, and onion rings. The cloth napkins and butcher paper over blue check table cloths add some charm, and the atmosphere is full of geniality.

French
ANJOU, *44 Campton. 415-392-5373. Located off Stockton in an alley half a block up from Union Square, it is open Tuesday-Saturday 11:30am-2:30pm and 5:30-10pm.*

This charming French restaurant has a small dining room with intimate seating (despite the close proximity of the tables, most of which are downstairs, with a few on an upstairs balcony). Lots of brick gives the room warmth, the tables are set brightly with starched white linen and fresh flowers, and the framed paintings of fruit are a perfect touch. All interior decorating aside, the food is sensational.

For lunch, you have a choice of the a la carte menu ($12-$15 for entrees) or a prix fixe Express menu for $11 which includes a cup of soup or small green salad plus one of a number of entrees, while most dinner entrees run $9-$15. And it's all worth it. The warm eggplant salad with Montrachet goat cheese is sensational, as is the roasted quail stuffed with dried cranberries and served with house-made sausage, and there are plenty of other intriguing dishes we haven't tried. It's a gem of a place that serves up deluxe French cuisine at fair prices, without an attitude problem, and in Union Square to boot.

PLANET HOLLYWOOD

2 Stockton. 415-421-7827. Located near Market, open daily from 11am-1am.

This is the place to go if you're stimuli-starved, say if you've been in one of those sensory deprivation chambers for too long. Here you will find abundant stimulation for all your senses, unending entertainment for easily bored children, and plenty of conversation starters for that awkward first date. The placemat all by itself is a winner, with its dozens of yearbook photos of now famous stars. The names are supplied, but on the periphery. It provides hours of fun trying to match them up, but only if you can tear your eyes away from the walls and displays. You find yourself awash in sights and sounds, with studio memorabilia hanging off the rafters and movie soundtracks, punctuated by cinema previews to go with the big video screens, filling the endless dining room. Not an inch isn't filled with items, like the bronze casting of Gloria Swanson's forearms, the teddy bear from Sleepless in Seattle, Don Johnson's pastel yellow pants from Miami Vice, the loaded gamblers dice used by Robert Redford in Indecent Proposal, and tons more. And in the spaces not taken up by old yearbooks, film props, and lip prints from the likes of Tom Cruise, Michelle Pfeiffer, and Brooke Shields, there are video images, zebra patterns, wild paintings, and a sparkling blue night sky ceiling.

And then there's the food. The main entrees range in price from $8-$15, and subtle isn't part of their culinary vocabulary, nor are they familiar with the concepts of low-fat or light. Chicken Crunch is one of their starters, made of chicken strips breaded with Cap'n Crunch (yes, really), and deep fried. It doesn't exactly taste like the cereal, it's more like an up-scale version of McNuggets, but there's an unpleasantly sweet aftertaste that can only come from the Cap'n, and we'll not dwell on their version of Texas Nachos, made with deep fried dough as its base. The portions are enormous; one bowl of pasta could easily satisfy two average diners. While the salads, pastas, burgers, and pizzas are all palatable, they don't exactly lead the city in excellence, though if you like ribs, their barbecue is fairly good. Then, if you haven't quite had your fill of artery cloggers, there are the desserts. Go with the White Chocolate Bread Pudding if you dare, the Caramel Crunch Pie (made with real Snickers bars) if you want chewy, but the Hollywood Mousse Pie is the most popular. Made of Oreo cookies, sweetened whipped cream (that tastes like Oreo filling), ice cream, and more Oreo crumble, this cloyingly sweet dessert has enough calories to tip the scale by itself, but lacks the good taste to make it worthwhile.

And, after filling your ears with movie music, your eyes with decoration overkill, and your mouth with a lot of fattening food, a trip to the bathroom will finish the sensory overload with an assault on your nose from an overwhelming array of perfumes lining the sink counter ("It's for fun," says the attendant, "help yourself"). If you didn't come from one, a trip to the sensory deprivation suite begins to sound pretty good after a visit to the universe of Planet Hollywood.

Italian

SCALA'S BISTRO, *432 Powell. 415-395-8555. Located near Sutter (attached to the Sir Francis Drake though it's entrance is from Sutter), this is a* *superb and very stylish Italian restaurant open daily 11:30am-midnight for lunch and dinner with entrees for $9-$16.*

Just two years old and in one of the most restaurant-saturated neighborhoods in town, they already have a very loyal local clientele; you absolutely need reservations for the pre-show rush. There are some fine starters ($6-$8). The calamari on fennel is crispy like it should be, the Anchor Steam mussels are excellent, the grilled portobellos with sautéed greens, toasted garlic, and onion rings are great, and the booths are the perfect place to eat them.

The clam linguini is a winner, as is the seared salmon and the grilled double-cut pork chop. And their Bostini Cream Pie has a following all its own. The rooms are quite appealing, open and airy with nice lighting and jazz playing softly. The look is that of a Tuscan villa, with lofty ceilings, formal waiters, and an open kitchen in back. Though lots of diners here are dressed up for a night out, there's no dress code. They just want you to be comfortable and enjoy the excellent Neapolitan food.

Japanese

SUSHI MAN, *731 Bush Street. 415-981-1313. Located near Powell, it is open for dinners only Monday-Saturday from 5:30-11pm.*

It's all sleek and contemporary inside - no bamboo in sight - with lots of gray, black, and pink. The sushi ($2.50-$4.50 for 2-6 pieces) is excellently prepared and extremely tasty. They do the standard maki and nigiri, but the spicy tuna is special. It is delicious, addictive, and well worth the visit. If, however, you don't want to dine completely on raw fish, there are cooked entrees as well ($9.50-$14), such as grilled chicken, salmon steak, and tempura prawns. Also on the menu is a bit of Japanese folklore: "Japanese proverb says that if you have the pleasant experience of eating something you have not tasted before, your life will be lengthen (sic) by 75 days." There's no nicer way to extend your life than by sampling Sushi Man's special concoctions.

NANBAN-TEI OF TOKYO, *101 Cyril Magnin. 415-421-2101. Located on a short street off O'Farrell and Market between Powell and Mason, it is an exemplary sushi and yakitori restaurant, full of the graciousness, service, and exquisitely prepared dishes you'd find in a posh place in Japan. It's open for lunch Monday-Friday 11:30am-2pm, and daily for dinner 6-11:30pm.*

Located on the second floor (making the bathroom a bit of a trek, but allowing views of the peons below), as soon as you make your way past the entrance curtains, you're greeted by a minimum of three hearty Japanese renditions of *irasshaimase* (welcome to their place), and the experience begins. The atmosphere is Tokyo modern and cozy at the same time, and the food is delicious. They have a full sushi menu. It's all very fresh and it's done very well, but the California rolls and unagi (cooked eel) are especially fine. Along with sushi ($3.50-$5.50 for two to four pieces) however, is a large and innovative yakitori menu. Yakitori means cooked meat, and what you get are thin bamboo skewers of grilled foods, ranging from asparagus wrapped in pork to quail eggs to mushrooms stuffed with chicken. For $3.25-$5 you get two sticks' worth. You can make a meal of them, or of the sushi, or our preferred meal of some of both. Despite their proximity to Union Square they are not on the usual tourist circuit, and you can always count on high quality food and attention.

Jewish

DAVID'S DELI, *474 Geary. 415-771-1600. Located near Taylor, it is open daily 7am-midnight.*

David's is the best Jewish delicatessen in San Francisco, and while the competition isn't stiff, the food still stands up to the memories and comparisons of East Coast snobs and Eastern European experts. It's authentic, it's delicious, it's dripping with cholesterol and worth every bite. Take the cheese blintz, for example. For $9.95 you get a plate swarming with two large blintzes, swimming in sour cream and jam, swooning with the kind of cheese flavor you remember from your childhood.

They have lots of other Jewish favorites as well. There's borsht and matzo ball soup ($4), meat loaf, stuffed cabbage, roast chicken ($8-$10), boiled chicken (if you must, $10), potato pancakes ($7), and a cavalcade of towering deli sandwiches for $5-$13. David's Deli is perfect for a pre- or post- theater snack, a satisfying lunch, or any old meal where the flavor outweighs the aura and the consequences. And the deserts need to be tried, because mere words won't do them justice.

Nouvelle Cuisine

GRAND CAFE, *501 Geary. 415-292-0101. Located near Taylor, it is part of Hotel Monaco, is open daily 7-10:30am, 11:30am-2:30pm, and 5:30-10pm (till 11pm Saturdays and Sundays), and dinner reservations are usually needed, especially before and after the theater.*

The name sums it up: it's grand and how. The statues grab you first. Bronze male figures with tall rabbit ears gamble and frolic, do hand stands and peer down from above. A bronze bloodhound sits droopily near the entrance by the feet of a couple of bronze recliners sitting with martinis. And the longer you sit at your table, the more fun and whimsical touches you discover, with textures and artwork and more. The fabulous Beaux Arts pillars and soaringly splendid roof seem lifted from a European ballroom, but it's the chandeliers that really stand out, like immense three-tiered cheese wheels of diminishing size, like an upside-down wedding cake, shedding a warm amber glow throughout.

But you can't just sit and ogle; there's a menu before you. The appetizers are magnificent, especially the creamy onion soup. Very rich and oniony, it may be the best onion soup in the world. The entrees are good too, though somehow not quite as sumptuous as the starters and artwork promise. Top it all off with a bourbon apple pecan cake in raspberry sauce and creme fraiche, and you'll leave a very happy customer.

The entrees feature lots of seafood, plus chicken, steak, lamb and such, and generally run $9-$16. The fine acoustic balance has been mastered here, so there's the hum and clatter reminiscent of a Parisian cafe, but you can talk intimately without having to raise your voice. And when you don't feel like talking, there are more fun details to discover.

RUMPUS ROOM, *One Tillman Place. 415-421-2300, fax 415-421-2316. It is parallel to Campton Place, off Grant. A relatively new Union Square addition, there is lively eclectic art (fish, Dick Tracy, etc.) on the walls, white linen and yellow daisies on the table, a nice menu, and they're open 11:30am-2:30pm Monday-Saturday, 5:30-10pm Sunday-Thursday, and 5:30-11pm Friday and Saturday.*

Lunches range from $6 (the Rumpus Burger) to $16 (the New York steak), and the turkey salad, ahi tuna salad, and vegetarian burrito are especially good. Dinners range from $11 (penne with tomato, arugula, and spicy fennel sausage) to $17 (the New York steak again), and the Dungeness crab ravioli, Rumpus Caesar salad, pan roasted garlic chicken, and lobster risotto are well worth having. The chocolate brioche cake is a fine way to top it off, and the wine list is quite extensive. All in all, it's a good, up-beat, upscale Union Square alternative.

Thai

THAI STICK, *698 Post. 415-928-7730. Located near Jones, it serves good Thai food Sunday-Thursday 11am-3pm and 5-10pm, Friday-Saturday 11am-3pm and 5-11pm.*

The Thai Stick is a few blocks off the beaten Union Square path, but if you're looking for Thai food, it's not far to go. The dining room is airy and light, with lots of windows, light wood, blue walls, and Thai decorations. They have been open since 1988, and the quality is dependably good. Their Tom Ka soup is very good, but then so is most everything.

They have a good range of poultry, pork, beef, seafood, and vegetarian dishes, and the prices are generally $6-$9, not counting the seafood and specials. And if you save room, the fried banana with coconut ice cream is a terrific way to end a meal.

INEXPENSIVE
American

DOTTIE'S TRUE BLUE CAFE, *522 Jones. 415-885-2767. Open Wednesday-Monday from 7:30am-2pm, Dottie's specializes in breakfast.*

They have been in business six years, during which time they have garnered a pretty sizable San Francisco following. The True Blue Plate (two eggs, bacon or ham or sausage, home fries, and toast or muffin for $6.25) is standard fare, and other plates add pancakes or French toast, andouille sausage, or fresh fruit salad, plus there's a daily frittata ($6.75). They also have a lunch menu (starting at 11am), with soup, black bean chili, salads, burgers, and sandwiches for $3.50-$6.75. Dottie's is really a modern diner with the feel and personal approach of an older time. Named after a woman (Dottie) who owned a diner in Brooklyn and for whom the original owner once worked (end of Dottie connection), the True Blue Cafe uses fresh ingredients, has curtains of lace and great home fries, and is a beloved breakfast establishment.

LEFTY O'DOUL'S, *333 Geary. 415-982-8900. Located between Powell and Mason, it serves hof brau type food daily 7am-midnight.*

There's a long counter of steaming, hearty grub, yours to pile on your tray and eat at long tables in the back. Hearty sandwiches are $5 and dinner plates are $7.75, and there are daily specials of such items as meat loaf, short ribs, breast of lamb, and corned beef and cabbage ($4-$7). The interior, with its bar and piano (for evening entertainment), and old San Francisco memorabilia, hasn't changed much since it first opened in 1958, and they're still serving the same stomach-warming, soul-satisfying American plates.

LORI'S DINER, *336 Mason. 415-392-8646. Located near Geary, it is open seven days a week, 24 hours a day.*

This is not the best food in the world, but it's certainly adequate, and if you're there, hungry, and don't want a big production or bill, Lori's is a viable option. Served in true diner atmosphere and style, you can get the full range of breakfast items (eggs, hash browns, omelets, sausages) any time, day or night, but they have burgers, sandwiches, and a few vegetarian dishes, too, and generally cost $4.50-$7 an item (though a few pricier dishes like grilled salmon or pork chops are available as well). It's not gourmet, but it is a place to get standard American food at an easily affordable price. There are two other locations in the Union Square area as well. The branch at *500 Sutter near Powell (981-1950)* is open daily 6am-10pm (and till 11pm Friday and Saturday), and the *149 Powell branch near O'Farrell (677-9999)* is open daily 7am-10pm (and till 11pm on weekends). But while the hours vary from branch to branch, the menu remains the same.

Indian

SHALIMAR RESTAURANT, *532 Jones. 415-928-0333. Located near Geary, it's a fast-food Indian restaurant open daily 11:30am-3pm and 5pm-midnight. No credit cards accepted.*

The food is delicious and fresh, there is no atmosphere to speak of unless you count the plastic blue & white checked tablecloths – but the prices are rock bottom. There are Tandoori barbecues ($2.50-$6.50), tasty curries ($3-$4), vegetables, and Indian breads ($1-$2.50). Eat in if you must, or take out if you have a place to go (you're just a few blocks from Union Square). Either way, the food is excellent.

Indonesian

INDONESIA RESTAURANT & CAFETERIA, *678-680 Post. 415-474-4026. Located between Jones and Taylor, it is open daily 11:30-10pm.*

In a two-block radius with three Indonesian restaurants, this is the best, though its food isn't quite as reliably good as the Thai food served by the nearby Thai Stick. Their appetizers ($1.50-$6) feature deep fried tongue-twisters like empek-empek palembang (hard boiled egg and deep fried fish cake in hot and sour sauce) and martabak telor (deep fried beef, onion, and eggs wrapped in crispy dough).

Entrees ($4.50-$7) include Indonesian standards like gado-gado (vegetables in spicy peanut sauce) and mie goreng (fried noodles with vegetables and meat) as well as various curries, fried rice dishes, and soups. They also do a rijstafel, an Indonesian spread of goodies for $17 per person (for a minimum of two). It's not the height of Indonesian cuisine, but it's a good place to sample a different and delicious style of Asian cooking.

Japanese

KANTARO SUSHI, *124 Ellis. 415-986-2339. Located near Powell, it serves good Japanese food like sushi and donburi, though it is neither as superb nor as expensive as Nanban-Tei. They're open daily 11am-11pm, but their lunch menu is more extensive and cheaper.*

During lunch for $5.50-$8, you can get combination specials (complete with soup, salad, rice, and green tea) such as tempura chicken teriyaki, barbecue beef, maguro sashimi, or a variety of sushi combinations. They also have big bowls of hot and cold noodles (udon or soba), plus a selection of donburi dishes that are delicious and filling. Dinner is mostly a sushi menu, and you can always order sushi a la carte. Inside it's pleasant, with traditional Japanese decor and small tables. It does get quite busy during lunch, and they only take reservations for dinner, but the crowd moves quickly, and you rarely have to wait long.

BRUNCH ROUND-UP

THE FRENCH ROOM, *495 Geary. 415-775-4700.*

Located in the Clift Hotel near Taylor, it serves what may be the best, most elegant brunch in all of San Francisco on Sundays from 10am-2pm for $35 per person. You enter through the Redwood Room to a world where daily cares and the quick city life succumb to the soothing strains of live harp music (unobtrusively present enough to mask the chatter of other brunchers' talk). Green palms, gilt mirrors, soaring ceilings, and exquisitely set tables with fine china and fresh posies take you to the aristocratic France of Louis XV; all you have to do is slow down, enjoy the cordial yet refined service, and have the brunch of your life.

It starts with Mumm Cuvee in a tall champagne flute and a glass of freshly squeezed orange juice by its side. There is an immense buffet of tables throughout the French Room and spilling over into the Redwood Room. The finest table by far is the one with the ice sculpture of a soaring eagle (that slowly melts into a snub-nosed, dripping bird of prey as the morning wears on), looking on over a bounty of seafood treats. The lox and smoked whitefish are superb, surprisingly so for a room that is as unlike a Jewish deli as a room can be (don't hunt for the bagels - they'll be brought to your table in a little basket). The tables are laden with more goodies than you know what to do with: there's prosciutto and melon, scallops and fresh jumbo shrimp, salads and chicken and muffins and more. In the Redwood Room a man stands at the ready to carve you some roast beef, or scoop your dish full of breakfast extras like bacon, sausages, or Belgian waffles.

But don't fill up on shrimp and lox, because these are all just starters. There's still the entree to come. There are traditional brunch items like eggs benedict (with ham or with spinach instead), pancakes and the like. Then there are the dishes for serious eaters. You can get blackened swordfish, grilled ahi tuna swimming in wasabi butter and garnished with roe, or garlic roasted prime rib of beef, before heading to the dessert table to dip some strawberries in molten chocolate, nibble on a raspberry, or top it off with a chocolate cookie to satisfy the most jaded chocoholics.

Kids get the VIP treatment with balloons (soon to be seen floating on the lofty ceiling) and a box of animal crackers. And for the final grace note, the chairs are exceptionally comfortable. The room, ambiance, staff, and food are just as lovely, cordial, delicious, and elegant as could be. It's what other places try for, cut corners, and miss.

TOP OF THE MARK, *1 Nob Hill. 415-392-3434.*

Located at the intersection of Mason and California, it has a lavish spread Sundays 10am-2pm for $32 per brunch with juice and coffee, $36 for a Bouvet sparkling wine brunch, and $42 for Piper Heidsieck Cuvée. The brunch is elegant and the buffet tables are laden with a profusion of hot and cold treats, but the quality of the food isn't quite as sensational as at the French Room. The hot items in their chafing dishes get a bit steamy after a while, and the canapés begin to lose their luster. The freshly carved roast beef is rare and just right, and the dessert table won't leave you with an iota of room to spare, but it's the views that are the real smash appeal. Towering high above Nob Hill, the windows go on and on, providing a stellar 360° view of the entire city. If the panoramic view is your goal, the Top of the Mark is the brunch for you, but if elegant atmosphere, service, and food quality are of greater importance, check out the French Room or the Ritz.

THE RITZ-CARLTON TERRACE, *600 Stockton. 415-296-7465. Located near California, it serves a magnificent brunch Sundays 11am-2:30pm for $42 (and half for children under 12). The price includes all the fabulous food you can eat, plus juices (fresh squeezed, including grapefruit as well as orange) and coffee, and though the drinks are separate, traditional brunch cocktails like the gin fizz or Bloody Mary are very popular. It's as hard to know where to begin describing as it is to know what to start eating: there's the food, the room, and the service, and all are extraordinary.*

The room inside is elegant, with lighting and crystal to match the champagne, oysters, and the jazz, which is pleasant and unobtrusive, with just enough swing to give it some kick. In the summer, however, brunch rises a step from wonderful to sublime, because in the summer brunch is served out on the terrace. The brick-laid courtyard with fountains and flowers and wrought-iron tables is absolutely gorgeous in the morning sunlight, and the hedges shield you from the wind and the noise. Ken Muir's winter trio grows to a quintet in summer, and plays al fresco. However, the sun can't always shine, and the winter brunch is pretty swell too. While the room isn't as aristocratically fine as the French Room, it's a little more relaxed and convivial sort of elegant. The white iris in the cobalt blue vase on each table is just one of many lovely touches, and fresh roses adorn the buffet selections.

Decor aside, the food is sensational. To start with, the seafood is fresh and plentiful. Under the ice-sculpted deer, fresh oysters and shrimp are piled high (and frequently replenished). There are three types of caviar, all superbly rich, with blini to put them on, as well as very fine smoked whitefish and sturgeon, house-smoked salmon, and a fantastic assortment of sushi. And then there are the chafing dish entrees. The Peking Duck is tasty if not crisp, and the breakfast sausages are good too. There are eggs benedict, seafood pilafs, and more. Of all the main dishes, however, the freshly carved Beef Wellington stands out. Succulent and delicious, it's so tender it doesn't feel too heavy for breakfast. And, if you've been prudent in your gorging, the dessert table is laden with items rich in calories and joy. The chocolate raspberry mousse is as wonderful as it sounds, and the twenty other options are fine too. There's also a bountiful fruit platter, a bit lighter than the tiramisu or cheesecake, and very refreshing.

The waitstaff is more than attentive; they're genuinely friendly as well. They clear your dirty plate so you can dirty another one, and refold your napkin every time you leave the table. And life feels very, very good. The fountain burbles, the jazz tootles, and it couldn't be lovelier.

TEAS AROUND TOWN

THE COMPASS ROSE, *in the Saint Francis Westin Hotel. 415-774-0167. This is a very lovely tea setting, full of style, atmosphere, and history. The Complete Tea Service (scone, tea sandwiches, berries with Grand Marnier cream, petits fours, and tea) is $14.50, the Royal Tea (with champagne too) is $19.75, and there are a la carte options that let you tailor your tea to include just what you want.*

The food is very good, though the service is sometimes a bit chilly. The room, however, is an integral part of the experience. There's a gold leaf bible screen from the 16th century and a bamboo screen from 18th century China that was once a backdrop for a Chinese minstrel show, there are 19th century Korean cloisonné vases, bronze cobra lamps from the 1920 art deco period, a mosaic marble table from Victorian England, and so much more. The eclectic collection of fabulous pieces from various centuries and civilizations makes for a fun and fantastic setting for an elegant tea.

When the St. Francis opened in 1904, The Cafe was its dining room, with lovely fluted columns, ornate ceilings, crystal lamps an colorful orchids, much as it is today. In 1913 the hotel expanded, 4,000 books streamed in, and The Cafe became the library, beloved hangout of Mark Twain, Ernest Hemingway, and their ilk. Then, in 1939, Templeton Crocker (one of the owners) got the bug to design the cocktail lounge to end all cocktail lounges. The staff argued against a modern bar in the St. Francis, epitome of traditional elegance. Crocker paid not a jot of attention, and the Patent Leather Bar was born, as full of chrome, leather, and glass as a Cadillac and just as sleek. The black patent leather walls added a certain tone, and soon the room was nicknamed "Bar Sinister" and "Coffin Corner." From 1958-1979, The Terrace Room took over, and all the staff were done up in elegant Oriental outfits. The St. Francis decided, however, that the suave modernity didn't match the old elegance of the rest of the hotel, and in 1982 The Compass Rose came to be, after Italian wood carvers, equipped with photos of the original Cafe, did their best to recreate its style and glory.

GARDEN COURT OF SHERATON PALACE, *Market and New Montgomery. 415-546-5000. It serves tea Wednesday-Saturday 2-4:30pm in Garden Court, including fruit tarts, scones, pastries, and tea sandwiches. The*

Princess Tea ($13) is for children 12 or younger, and includes just the sweets without the sandwiches (but with the all-important scepter and crown), the Authentic Tea is $17 and includes sandwiches, and the Royal Tea ($21) has champagne as well. Reservations are a good idea, and people generally dress up.

The Garden Court High Tea is an experience and a half, though the aura and style exceeds the actual quality of the food. A woman plays harp in the center of the vast room, and little girls preen under their silvery princess tiaras (called crowns, and an integral part of the Princess Tea). Families sit at long tables with comfy sofas, but a table for two is adorable in its petiteness, elegant with its green marble and wrought-iron, and set to a tee with linen jacquard miniature place mats, gold-rimmed china, and heavy, polished silver. But anyone can set a nice table. The Garden Court flavor comes more from what's overhead. The ceiling is magnificent, opulent, spectacular. The muted light through the stained-glass is soft and refined, and diffused by 1,000 pounds of crystal divvied up among 10 gorgeous chandeliers.

Everything comes to the table at once: the tea and the 3-tiered china food caddie. The tea is meticulously poured through the silver strainer, and you are left to enjoy. Unfortunately the tea is tepid and weak, though at our request the elegant tea staff replaced the pot with hotter weak tea. The goodies are all good, but the portions are meager, at least as far as the tea sandwiches are concerned. There are plenty of sweets, with clotted cream, lemon curd, and an overly-perfumed rose petal marmalade condiments on the side. The chocolate-coated strawberries are pale and unripe, and when we left, the sugar high didn't make us feel like we got our money's worth. The Garden Court tea is coasting on its laurels a bit, and doesn't really deliver the quality the crystal and polish promise.

THE REDWOOD ROOM, *495 Geary. 415-775-4700. Located in the Clift Hotel near Taylor, it serves high tea Tuesday-Saturday 3-5pm for $15 (but be aware the tea is served in the lounge area during the winter holiday season).*

The Redwood Room is one of the most charming, comfortable, historic rooms in the city. A silver tiered tray brings the goodies, which include tea sandwiches of smoked salmon with cream cheese and watercress on pumpernickel bread, chicken mango salad with a touch of curry on toast, and pinwheels of papaya and dill mousse with bay shrimp. There are petit fours, scones, chocolate-dipped strawberries, and pastries. And while the quality of food is a touch higher than say the Palace, it's the room itself which makes a difference.

It's not so grand and elegant as the Palace Hotel's Garden Court, nor so stately as the Ritz. The Redwood Room is warmer and clubbier. The deep redwood tones, comfortable chairs, and art deco touches make this a place you can easily hang out in for hours, talking and enjoying and taking it all in. It's easy to be at ease in the Redwood Room, where high society goes when it wants to relax and enjoy. And the tea time pampering and goodies are just icing on the cake.

RITZ-CARLTON, *600 Stockton. 415-296-7465. Located near California, it has a variety of teas from light to royal ($14-$22), but the full tea ($18), complete with sandwiches and the works, is the most popular.*

Tea is done very nicely, and the food is excellent. The room is very pretty, just right for an afternoon tea. There's the de rigour crystal chandeliers, the beautiful wall hangings and paintings, and lovely, comfortable sofas and chairs. A woman strums a harp in the corner, and the high ceiling, stately lines, and tall, curtained windows bespeak aristocracy and leisure. It's the extras, however, that go the distance.

The teas on the menu are clearly labeled for caffeine content, the tea pots are equipped with built-in strainers that ease the process, and the three-tiered brass server comes laden with top-notch goodies that transcend your average tea sandwich and cookie. You get smoked salmon and caviar on dark rye, prosciutto and asparagus tips, and the usual cucumber sandwich is perked up with Roquefort and walnuts. There's a scone with Devonshire cream and lemon curd, and the sweets (shortbread, fresh fruit tartlette, madeleines, and cakes) don't leave you feeling like you ate the sugar bowl.

The service is perfect (attentive and friendly, not at all intrusive), and the atmosphere lends itself to a family treat, friendly chat, or business meeting. So popular have the business teas become, that the Ritz now offers a Tea Etiquette class (to teach the niceties of how to pour, what gets eaten with fingers, and what requires the fork) so you don't end up with lemon curd on your face. The classes keep getting filled up, and the High Teas get booked around the winter holidays, so reserve well ahead.

Other Tea Options
STOUFFER STANFORD COURT HOTEL, *905 California. 415-989-3500.*

Located near Powell, from 2:30-5pm light tea is served at $10.50 per person with scones, petite pastries, fruit tartlettes, cookies and tea, or full tea for $14.50, offering the same plus a variety of sandwiches like chicken with Italian cheese, and salmon with creme fraiche.

MARK HOPKINS, *999 California. 415-392-3434.*

Located near Mason, Tea in the Nob Hill Terrace is served from 2:30-5:30pm with five different sandwiches, followed by scones, cakes, and pastries for $12.95.

RESTAURANTS BY CUISINE

Afghani
Helmond, North Beach

African
Axum Cafe, Lower Haight
Massawa Restaurant, Haight Ashbury

American
Alfred's, North Beach
Bricks Bar & Grill, Financial District
Dottie's True Blue Cafe, Union Square
Ella's, Pacific Heights
Firefly, Noe
Fly Trap, SoMa
Hamburger Mary's, SoMa
Harris', Russian Hill
Homeplate, Marina
Izzy's Steak & Chop House, Marina
Jack's, Financial District
Judy May's M&L Market, Upper Market
Lefty O'Doul's, Union Square
Lori's Diner, Union Square
Maxfield, Downtown
Mo's, North Beach
Orphan Andy's, Castro
Patio Cafe, Castro
Perry's, Union Square
Pluto's, Marina
Redwood Room, Union Square
Sliders Diner, Castro
Sliders Diner, Polk Gulch
Tadich Grill, Financial District
The Big Four, Nob Hill
Vic's Place, Financial District
Washington Square Bar & Grill, North Beach
Whitehorse Taverne, Nob Hill
Woodward Gardens, Mission

Asian
Betelnut, Marina
Yoyo Tsumami, Japan Town

Brunch
Caffe Freddy's Eatery, North Beach
Homeplate, Marina
The French Room, Union Square
The Ritz-Carlton Terrace, Nob Hill
Top of the Mark, Nob Hill

Burgers
Bill's Place, Richmond
Bricks, Financial District
Hamburger Mary's, SoMa
Liverpool Lil's, Marina
Mo's, North Beach
Perry's, Financial District
Sliders, Castro
Sliders, Polk Gulch

British
Liverpool Lil's, Marina

Cajun
Floogies, Civic Center

Cambodian
Angkor Wat, Richmond

Caribbean
Boogaloos, Mission
Caribbean Zone, SoMa
Cha Cha Cha, Haight

Chinese
Brandy Ho, North Beach
Eliza's, Civic Center
Eliza's, Potrero Hill
Eric's, Noe Valley
Great Eastern, Chinatown
Fortune Wok, Chinatown
Hang Ah Tea Room, Chinatown
Hong Kong Flower Lounge, Richmond
House of Nanking, Chinatown
Hunan, Telegraph Hill
Shangri-la Chinese Vegetarian Restaurant, Sunset

Taiwan, Chinatown
Taiwan, Richmond
Ton Kiang, Richmond
Tsing Tao, Richmond
Wu Kong, Downtown
Yank Sing, Financial District

Crepes
Ti Couz, Mission

Dim Sum
Canton, SoMa
Dol Ho Restaurant, Chinatown
Hang Ah Tea Room, Chinatown
J&J, Chinatown
Royal Jade, Chinatown
Ton Kiang, Richmond
Wu Kong, Downtown
Yank Sing, Financial District

Filipino
Philippine Restaurant, Richmond

French
Alain Rondelli, Richmond
Anjou, Union Square
Baker Street Bistro, Marina
Cafe Bastille, Financial District
Cafe Claude, Financial District
Cafe Jacqueline, North Beach
Cafe Maisonnette, Richmond
Chez Michel, Fisherman's Wharf
Chez Moustache, Western Addition
Cliff House, Richmond
The Dining Room, Nob Hill
The French Room, Union Square
The Heights, Pacific Heights
Fleur de Lys, Nob Hill
French Room, Union Square
Le Central, Financial District
Le Charm, SoMa
South Park Cafe, SoMa

Ti Couz, Mission
Zax, Fisherman's Wharf
Zazie, Haight Ashbury

German
Suppenkuche, Civic Center

High Tea
Compass Rose, Union Square
Garden Court, Market
Mark Hopkins, Nob Hill
Redwood Room, Nob Hill
Ritz-Carlton, Nob Hill
Stouffer Stanford Court, Nob Hill

Indian
Kamal Palace, North Beach
Pasand, Marina
Rasoi, Mission
Shalimar, Lower Nob Hill

Indonesian
Indonesia Restaurant, Nob Hill

International
Planet Hollywood, Union Square
Rooster, Mission
World Wrapps, Marina
World Wrapps, Russian Hill

Irish
O'Reilly's, North Beach

Italian
Acquerello, Polk Gulch
Aperto, Potrero Hill
Bambino's, Sunset
Bizou, SoMa
Cafe Delle Stelle, Civic Center
Cafe Tiramisu, Financial District
Caffe Freddy's Eatery, North Beach
Caffe Luna Piena, Castro
Columbus Italian Food Restaurant, North Beach

Enrico's, North Beach
Figaro, North Beach
Fior D'Italia, North Beach
Gira Polli, North Beach
I Fratelli, Russian Hill
Il Fornaio, Embarcadero (Levi Plaza)
Incontro, Civic Center
Jackson Fillmore, Pacific Heights
Julius' Castle, Telegraph Hill
Liguria Bakery, North Beach
Little City Antipasti, North Beach
L'Osteria del Forno, North Beach
Mangiafuoca, Mission
Mario's Bohemian Cigar Store Cafe, North Beach
Mario's Bohemian Cigar Store Cafe, Russian Hill
Mescolanza, Richmond
Michelangelo Cafe, North Beach
Moose's, North Beach
Pane e Vino, Marina
Pasquale's Pizzeria, Sunset
Pasta Pomodoro, Marina
Pasta Pomodoro, North Beach
Ristorante Ecco, SoMa
Ristorante Milano, Russian Hill
Rose Pistola, North Beach
Ruby's, South of Market
Sausage Factory, Castro
Scala's Bistro, Union Square
Spuntino, Civic Center
The Stinking Rose, North Beach
Tommaso Pizzeria, North Beach
U.S. Restaurant, North Beach
Vivande Porta Via, Pacific Heights
Vivande Ristorante, Civic Center

Japanese/Sushi
Ebisu, Inner Sunset
Kyo-ya, Downtown
Goemon, Sunset
Isobune Sushi, Japan Town
Izumi Sushi, Noe Valley
Kantaro Sushi, Union Square
Sushi Man, Union Square

Matsuya, Noe Valley
Murasaki, Richmond
Nanban-Tei, Union Square
Tampopo, Japan Town
We Be Sushi, Mission
We Be Sushi, Richmond
We Be Sushi, Sunset
Yoyo Tsumami Bistro, Japan Town

Jewish Food
David's Deli, Union Square

Malaysian
Singapore Malaysian Restaurant, Inner Richmond

Mediterranean
Bizou, SoMa
Bruno's, Mission
Cafe de Stijl, Embarcadero
Cafe 52, Financial District
Caffe Centro, Marina
Caffe Centro, South of Market
Enrico's, North Beach
Fournou's Oven, Nob Hill
42 Degrees, SoMa
Greco Romana, Richmond
LuLu, SoMa
Plump Jack Cafe, Pacific Heights
Roti, Downtown
Rubicon, Financial District
Tuba Garden, Richmond
Zuni Cafe, Civic Center

Mexican
Cafe Marimba, Marina
El Nopalito Taqueria, Lower Nob Hill
Gordo Taqueria, Richmond
Gordo Taqueria, Sunset
La Cumbre, Mission
Las Estrellas, Civic Center
La Taqueria, Mission
Leticia's, Castro
Little Fiesta, Financial District

Pancho Villa Taqueria, Mission
Pozole, Castro
Taqueria San Jose, Fisherman's Wharf
Wa-ha-ka, Russian Hill
Wa-ha-ka, SoMa
Zona Rosa, Haight

Middle Eastern
Aladdin, Nob Hill
Amira, Mission
Arabian Nights, Mission
Cafe Istanbul, Mission
Kan Zaman, Haight
La Mediterranee, Castro
La Mediterranee, Pacific Heights
Stoyanof's, Sunset
Truly Mediterranean, Mission
Yaya, Sunset

Nouvelle California Cuisine
Cafe Kati, Pacific Heights
California Culinary Academy, Civic Center
Campton Place, Union Square
Cypress Club, North Beach
Firefly, Noe Valley
Flying Saucer, Mission
Fog City Diner, Embarcadero
Fringale, SoMa
42 Degrees, SoMa
Hawthorne Lane, SoMa
Grand Cafe, Union Square
Masa's, Nob Hill
Plaza Restaurant, Union Square
Postrio, Union Square
Rumpus Room, Union Square
Stars Cafe, Civic Center
Stars Restaurant, Civic Center
The Dining Room, Nob Hill
The Slow Club, Mission
Val 21, Mission
Woodward's Garden, Mission

Russian
Katia's, Richmond

Sandwiches, Salads, & Picnic Supplies
California Harvest Ranch Market, Castro
La Patisserie, Downtown
Pickle, Pepper & Romaine, Inc., Financial District
Real Foods Deli, Russian Hill
S.F. Gourmet, Marina
S.F. Gourmet, Pacific Heights

Seafood
Aqua, Financial District
Blue Point, Richmond
Cliff House, Richmond
Hayes Street Grill, Civic Center
Pacific Cafe, Richmond
PJ's Oyster Bed, Sunset
Swan Oyster Depot, Polk Gulch
Tadich Grill, Financial District

Singaporean
Singapore Malaysian Restaurant, Richmond
Straits Cafe, Richmond

Steakhouse
Alfred's, North beach
Izzy's Steak and Chop House, Marina
Harris', Russian Hill

Spanish Tapas
Alegrias, Marina
Esperpento, Mission
La Bodega, North Beach
Pacha, Castro
Picaro, Mission
Sol y Luna, Financial District
Timo's, Mission
Zarzuela, Russian Hill

Thai
Mae-Thip, Sunset
Marnee Thai, Sunset

Midapab, Financial District
Paradise, Chinatown
Siamese Garden, Richmond
Sukhothai, Sunset
Thep Phanom, Lower Haight
Thai Stick, Nob Hill

Tibetan
Lhasa Moon, Marina

Vegetarian
Greens, Marina
Millenium, Civic Center
Shangri-la Chinese Vegetarian Restaurant, Sunset

Vietnamese
Jasmine House Restaurant, Richmond
Le Soleil, Richmond
Saigon, Tenderloin
Tu Lan, Downtown
Vietnam Restaurant, North Beach

14. SEEING THE SIGHTS

San Francisco is a city of neighborhoods, and they have distinctly different histories, auras and charms. The City is relatively small, but there are over 40 neighborhoods, and part of the fun is seeing how dramatically the tone changes as you pass from one to another. One of the great pleasures of San Francisco is strolling about, wandering and poking your head in places, and exploring.

The most frequently visited neighborhoods are listed below in alphabetical order, with all their attractions and sites.

CASTRO

Occupying Eureka Valley southeast of Twin Peaks, the Castro is the warm and sunny center of San Francisco's gay and lesbian community. It was named Castro Village in 1890 after Castro Street, which was itself named after the Mexican general José Castro. Spreading south from Market, the area lies roughly between Noe Valley, Diamond Heights, the Mission, and Twin Peaks.

Once a Scandinavian neighborhood, and later a bastion of Irish and Italian residents till they sold their old Victorians and moved to the suburbs, the Castro has been the hub of the gay and lesbian community since the 1970s, when it reveled in gay liberation, partied in the streets, and renounced the closet. Still proudly gay, though saddened by the dismal advent of AIDS, it's now a gregariously open neighborhood overflowing with good restaurants, interesting shops, gay bars, and geniality.

The favored activities in the Castro are hanging out in sunny restaurant back gardens or strolling the streets, just wandering about. **Harvey Milk Plaza** (named after the assassinated Supervisor) is at the happening corner where Castro, Market, and 17th Street intersect, it's the heart of the district, and just across the way on Castro is the **Castro Theater**, *415-621-6120*. Built in 1922, this is the grandest of San Francisco's old movie palaces. Baroquely ornate inside, the real crowd-pleaser is the

Wurlitzer pipe organ, which plays nightly before each film. Along with the **Gay and Lesbian Film Festival**, which is held each June, the theater runs a great selection of films all year long. They run various themes, such as film noirs, Bette Davis series, musicals, etc., changing films every couple of days. They show films you may never see anywhere else, and always to enthusiastic audiences.

A SHORT HISTORY OF GAYS & LESBIANS IN SAN FRANCISCO

There's been a homosexual presence in San Francisco for a long time. Alice B. Toklas, who was later to become Gertrude Stein's "companion," was born here in 1877, and in 1896 Robert Allan Nicol wrote to Edward Carpenter (British reformer championing homosexual rights) that "really you have quite a following in San Francisco alone." In 1908, Edward Stevenson published **Intersexes: A History of Similisexualism as a Problem in Social Life**, *noting that the Presidio was "a garrison noted for its homosexual contingent ... especially during the time of the sudden Spanish American War," and by the 1930s North Beach had The Black Cat (a gay bar), Mona's (a lesbian bar), and downtown there was Jack's Turkish Baths, San Francisco's first homosexual bathhouse.*

In 1961, the League for Civil Education organized a "gay vote," and the same year José Sarria, a drag queen known as the Dowager Widow of the Emperor Norton, Empress of San Francisco and Protectress of Mexico, became the first openly gay man to run for Supervisor. The gay and lesbian community lobbied for civil rights and protection from police brutality, and in the '70s, what with a "gay-in" in Golden Gate Park and the 1972 Board of Supervisors ban on gay discrimination in municipal employment, gay rights began to blossom. The city went on to host its first Gay Day Parade in 1972, and in 1977 San Francisco held its first Gay Film Festival, the oldest continuing lesbian and gay film festival in the world. But it was the 1977 election of openly gay Harvey Milk to the San Francisco Board of Supervisors that moved the city's gay history into a new sphere.

By this time the Castro was enthusiastically gay, and Milk was known as the Mayor of Castro Street, as noted in Randy Shilts' Milk biography of the same name. In March of 1978 the San Francisco Board of Supervisors passed "the most stringent gay rights law in [the] country," and Dan White was the only supervisor to vote against it. Eight months later, Dan White assassinated Supervisor Harvey Milk and Mayor George Moscone. White was found guilty of voluntary manslaughter rather than murder, thanks to the notorious Twinky Defense (the claim that over-abundance of sugar made him temporarily lose his mind), and White Night riots followed, ending in violent confrontations between police and gays on Castro Street.

> *The first cases of AIDS were reported in San Francisco in 1981, and in 1986 the Names Project AIDS Memorial Quilt was founded by Cleve Jones to commemorate his best friend, Mark Feldman. On February 14, 1991, over 275 lesbian and gay couples registered at City Hall as Domestic Partners, and later that year the Eureka Theater saw the world premiere of Tony Kushner's Pulitzer Prize-winning Angels in America: A Gay Fantasia on National Themes.*
>
> *But milestones and important dates aside, the gay and lesbian community is an integral part of the San Francisco community as a whole. It has its political facets, its arts and literary contributors, its members who mix and mingle with the larger straight community, and its more flamboyant individuals. The community still deals with the horror of AIDS, nasty incidents of gay-bashing, and the fluctuating political tide, with a continuing message of tolerance and respect.*

The **Names Project**, *2362 Market Street*, is the public workshop for this over 25,000 paneled quilt that's hand-stitched and decorated as a memorial to those who have died of AIDS. It's more than beautiful; it's a moving experience to view the pieces worked on by the friends and family of those who are gone.

Up above the hubbub of Castro rises Corona Heights, a steep granite rock of a hill with beautiful houses that enjoy fantastic views. Just put one foot in front of the other up 14th Street and you can have the same views. Keep on going to Roosevelt Way (and then on to Museum Way) along the twisty, turny streets to get to one of the best children's museums in the city, the **Randall Junior Museum**, *199 Museum Way, 415-554-9600*. It's open Tuesday-Saturday 10am-5pm, and the Animal Room is open 10:30am-1pm and 2-5pm. Admission is free, and while the museum focuses on the arts, sciences, and natural environment, the highlight is the petting corral where your kids get to stroke the raccoon, feel the scaly tail of the possum, and learn a lot in a manner that's about as hands-on as it gets. The staff are very friendly and knowledgeable, and the hill behind the museum has a great trail leading up to the top for the prize view of the city.

CHINATOWN

San Francisco, as a populous city, was born in 1849, thanks to the Gold Rush and the ensuing vast immigration. Chinatown dates back to then. They came, almost without exception, from Canton, and set up shop all along Sacramento, which by 1880 was already known as Little China. Even today, old timers still occasionally call Sacramento by the old name, *Tong Yan Gai*, or "Chinese Street." The first known Chinese resident, however, arrived in February of 1848 under a labor contract to one

Charles Gillespie who lived on Dupont and Clay (just a block north of Sacramento), and the first Chinese restaurant opened late in 1848 at Jackson and Kearny.

It was there at the Canton Restaurant that the first meeting of California Chinese was held in December 10, 1849 to discuss mutual problems and goals. In those early days, this section of town was shared by the French Quarter, but when the French abandoned their Gold Rush niche, the Chinese remained. In 1877, caught up in the swirl of anti-Chinese sentiment, a mob tried to burn Chinatown down. They failed, but the 1906 earthquake and fire didn't and Chinatown was leveled.

Following that catastrophe, there was much talk of relocating the neighborhood to a less central sector, such as Hunter's Point or San Mateo, where it would serve as a sort of exotic theme park, but Chinatown rebuilt quickly before the talk could become reality. Many of the pagoda roofs and Chinese railings built at that time were part of a deliberate attempt to stamp the neighborhood with Chinese character, the idea being that tourist popularity and indelible Asian flavor would help spare the neighborhood from further displacement plans.

Chinatown has drawn visitors since its beginnings. Rudyard Kipling in 1889 was hot to visit the "Chinese quarter," calling it "a ward of the city of Canton set down in the most eligible business quarter of the place." And before that, Oscar Wilde came visiting in 1882, and said "San Francisco is a really beautiful city. China Town, peopled by Chinese laborers, is the most artistic town I have ever come across ... in the Chinese restaurant, where these navies meet to have supper in the evening, I found them drinking teas out of china cups as delicate as the petals of a rose-leaf, whereas at the gaudy hotels I was supplied with a delft cup an inch and a half thick. Then the Chinese bill was presented - it was made out on rice paper, the account being done in Indian ink as fantastically as if an artist had been etching little birds on a fan."

Chinatown's fancy green-tiled entrance, the **Dragon's Gate**, *is just up from Union Square where Grant Avenue meets Bush*. Through the gate and you're in one of the largest Chinese communities outside of China, 24 blocks of markets, restaurants, temples, museums, shlock shops, and culture. It's a horror to drive through (Grant, once named Dupont when it was the first street in San Francisco, retains its narrow dimensions and is often jammed with no-go traffic, while Stockton, the market street, is generally clogged with unloading trucks), but it's great (if noisy and crowded) to explore by foot. If possible, avoid the area altogether during rush hour and weekend mornings, as the commuting and shopping frenzies make it all just a bit too much. The boundaries aren't carved in stone (the neighborhoods expand and shrink, merge and usurp over time), but Bush, Kearny, Powell, and Broadway form a rough perimeter.

Grant and Stockton are by far the most crowded, and also by far the most visited by tourists. Stray a bit afield, however, and you can wander the more genuine Chinatown with less chaos and tumult. Aside from the restaurants, there are herb shops, fortune cookie factories, bakeries, intricate architecture, and myriad interesting stores and alleys to explore.

Portsmouth Square, *at Clay and Kearny*, was once the central plaza of old Yerba Buena back in the 18th and 19th centuries, and it's where Montgomery first hoisted the American flag in 1846. Back then it was the border from which Chinatown sprang, but now it's firmly within Chinatown lines, and serves as the central meeting spot for Chinatown. Folks meet here to play chess, practice tai chi, gossip, and hang out.

Not far down the street, the **Chinese Culture Center**, *750 Kearny, 415-986-1822*, on the third floor of the Chinatown Holiday Inn, is open Tuesday-Saturday 10am-4pm, and admission is free. They have lots of art shows, art galleries, and occasional films as well. The **Chinese Historical Society**, *650 Commercial near Kearny, 415-391-1188*, has artifacts tracing Chinese Immigration. It's open Tuesday-Saturday noon-4pm, and admission is free. It's a small museum with interesting history and good photos of Chinese immigration to California, their early culture here, and the discriminatory laws and attitudes they faced.

The area is full of intriguing Chinese-style buildings and associations (groups started in the nineteenth century that serve as temple-clubs). The **Old Chinese Telephone Exchange**, *743 Washington*, a part of the Pacific Telephone and Telegraph Company, is in a colorful three-tiered pagoda. It's just a bank, now, but it was the first Chinese-style building that went up after the 1906 fire, and it's where California's first newspaper was printed by Sam Brannan, Mormon entrepreneur, from 1847-1849.

On Waverly Place (parallel to Grant between Sacramento and Washington) are a number of associations, and you're welcome to visit their temples, though a donation is usually requested. The **Sue Hing Benevolent Association**, *123-9 Waverly*, was built in 1911, and the **Tien Hau Temple** (founded in 1852) is on its top floor. It's open daily 10am-5pm, and is dedicated to Tien Hau, Goddess of Heaven and Sea, protector of sailors and fishermen, prostitutes, performers, and wanderers. Another one nearby is **Norras Temple**, *109-11 Waverly*, in the Lee Family Association building. The temple's on the third floor, and is open daily 9am-4pm.

For more temple viewing, go to **Buddha's Universal Church**, *720 Washington, 415-982-6116*. Its five stories are full of murals and tile mosaics, but it's only open the second and fourth Sunday of each month from 1-3pm, except from January to March, when it presents bilingual costume plays on the weekends to welcome the Chinese New Year.

Old St. Mary's Church, *600 California near Grant*, represents a distinctly Irish Catholic religious presence. Built in 1854 with handsome red brick brought round the horn from Boston on a foundation of granite quarried in China, this was the city's main Catholic cathedral until 1891, and the first constructed on the West Coast. Nowadays it's best know for its fine (and free) Tuesday 12:30pm chamber music concerts, and the Beniamino Bufano statue of Dr. Sun Yat Sen (who spent some of his exiled years in San Francisco) in St. Mary's Square across the way.

To see a less religious side of the culture, visit **The Great China Herb Company**, *857 Washington (just around the corner from Tien Hau)*, one of the larger of many wonderful herb shops throughout Chinatown. They have tree roots, bark, flowers, and leaves, all measured out on hand scales and tallied up on an old abacus, and sold for ailments ranging from headache to sinusitis to impotence. And over in **Ross Alley**, *parallel to Grant and Stockton, between Jackson and Washington*, is a small factory that churns out more than 200,000 fortune cookies a year.

The Cable Car Barn Museum, *1201 Mason, 415-474-1887*, is open daily from 10am-5pm November-March and 10am-6pm April-October, admission is free, and it's just up from the bustle of Chinatown. In 1873, Andrew S. Hallidie took the cable-run mine ore transportation system and devised a city version. San Francisco sneered and called it Hallidie's Folly, but the cable cars of San Francisco are now the number one tourist draw, and a very civilized way to get about town. The museum itself is pretty interesting, even though it's free. You not only learn how the cable cars work, you actually see the massive wheels winding the 11 miles of thick steel cable that pull the cars up the steep hills, as they have been doing in this brick building since 1907. It won't absorb a major part of a day, but the museum does make for worthwhile hour if you're in the neighborhood.

CIVIC CENTER

Officially named the **James Rolph, Jr. Civic Center**, but known simply as the Civic Center to all and sundry, the main municipal buildings were built on the rubble of the previous city hall left by the 1906 earthquake and fire. Sandwiched *between Market Street, and the downtrodden, crime-ridden districts of the Tenderloin and the Western Addition*, Civic Center is an area more than it is a neighborhood.

Despite its grungy neighbors, the Civic Center keeps growing, keeps trying to upgrade itself and its surroundings. The district includes a lot more than mere municipal halls. Along with City Hall and United Nations Plaza, there's the Opera House, Davies Hall, and the glowing new gem, the lovely brand new Main Library, a joy inside and out. The old building which the library outgrew is being readied to become the new Asian Museum, to provide more room for the exhibits that had been housed in Golden Gate Park next to the de Young Museum. There are lots of fine restaurants to accommodate the symphony, opera, and City Hall crowd, a trendy crop of galleries and restaurants in nearby Hayes Valley, and a homeless contingent that remains a political and ethical thorn. The last administration attempted to drive them away, earning criticism for not curing the problem, just redistributing it where the mayor couldn't see it. The homeless problem continues, providing a somber counterpoint to the glorious buildings and fashionable eateries.

City Hall was finished in 1915, pretty much in time for the city party of the Pacific International Exposition celebrating the city's resurrection. Order was imposed on chaos, but not the order drafted by Daniel Burnham, the architect chosen to map out a glorious new city. Burnham said "Make no little plans. They have no magic to stir men's blood, and probably of themselves will not be realized. Make big plans." He drew up a plan (nice and big) based on his beloved Paris, full of boulevards and plazas and brave new parks, but nothing ever came of it. Businesses wanted to be up and going and *now* and residents did not smile on plans that called for wiping out buildings that actually survived the flames, just to make way for Burnham's dreams. In three years, the city was pretty much rebuilt along original lines, but the Civic Center is one section that reflects Burnham's big thoughts.

City Hall itself takes up two square blocks between Polk and Van Ness, Grove and McAllister. Ground was broken April 5, 1913, nearly $4 million was spent, and opening ceremonies were held in December, 1915. One of the finest examples of French Renaissance architecture in America, it's made of granite from the foothills of the High Sierra on the outside, with marble within, and it's patterned after the Capitol in Washington, but with a higher dome. The 1989 earthquake did a passel of damage, and it's currently closed for repair and seismic retrofitting.

Across from City Hall is the spanking new **Library Main Branch**, *McAllister and Larkin, 415-557-4400,* which opened April 1996, and was built on the site of the original gold-domed city hall that was destroyed in the 1906 fire. It's beautiful inside and out, graceful and glorious and full of everything slick and new. With 300 computer terminals and 500 laptop outlets, the library takes a giant leap into the technological age. There are African-American, Gay & Lesbian, environmental, Filipino, and San Francisco history centers, a Children's Center with a garden terrace, a center for music and art, a cafe, plus multimedia facilities to blend the sounds, sights, and texts. There are also books, of course, with space for the many that were hidden away on inaccessible stacks in the old site, plus lovely skylights that just put an extra glow on it all.

Across the street, the old main library site is being readied to receive Asian art pieces from the old site in Golden Gate Park. The new **Asian Art Museum** should be ready to open its doors to the public by the year 2000.

Up the street from City Hall on the Van Ness side is the **Louise B. Davies Symphony Hall**, *210 Van Ness near Grove, 415-431-5400*. Louise B. Davies donated $31 million towards this symphony hall, and it was completed in 1981. Built of glass and granite, its modern structure is at odds with the other buildings, but inside the composition allows for continued fiddling to get the sound just right. There are tours available Wednesdays 1:30 and 2:30pm and Saturdays 12:30 and 1:30pm.

The **War Memorial Opera House**, *301 Van Ness, 415-621-6600*, is just a block away. Similar in style to City Hall, the interior is rich with marble, old-world detailing, and comfort. It opened in 1932, and once the seismic retrofitting is finished the San Francisco ballet will resume performances here as well as the opera.

Continuing up the street is the **Veterans Building**, *401 Van Ness*, where the Museum of Modern Art used to be before it moved South of Market. It still houses the Herbst Theater on the first floor, and is a popular place for lectures, readings, and performances. It was also just recently the site of U.N. celebrations, marking the 50th anniversary of the United Nations Charter which was signed in the theater here.

Also nearby is the **San Francisco Performing Arts Library and Museum**, *399 Grove near Gough, 415-255-4800*. It's open Tuesday-Friday 10am-5pm and Saturday noon-4pm, and admission is free. Also known as PALM, it houses the largest West Coast collection of performance photographs, news clips, manuscripts, and other such documentation.

Just a block south of Grove is Hayes Street. The freeway ramp that used to dominate this locale was demolished after the 1989 earthquake, and the result was a rebirth. **Hayes Valley** is full of wonderful restaurants, plus interesting galleries and boutiques. Be aware, however, that it borders rather closely on a fairly rough section of the Western Addition neighborhood, and after dark it's not a good idea to stroll around on your own if there are no people about.

DOWNTOWN

The vast, vague sprawl loosely referred to as "Downtown" is actually made up of a few areas: the Financial District, Jackson Square, the Embarcadero, and Market Street. It's where the business of the city gets done, and while each sector has its own history and aura, the boundaries lose their meaning in day-to-day conversation.

The **Financial District**, the fiscal heart of San Francisco, goes way back to the city's beginnings. Originally centered along Montgomery (otherwise known as Wall Street West), the area is generally bounded by Clay, Drumm, Main, Mission, Third, and Kearny. In the 1800s, Montgomery was as far east as you could go without getting your feet wet, and it's where Sam Brannan came in 1848 to announce the discovery of gold on

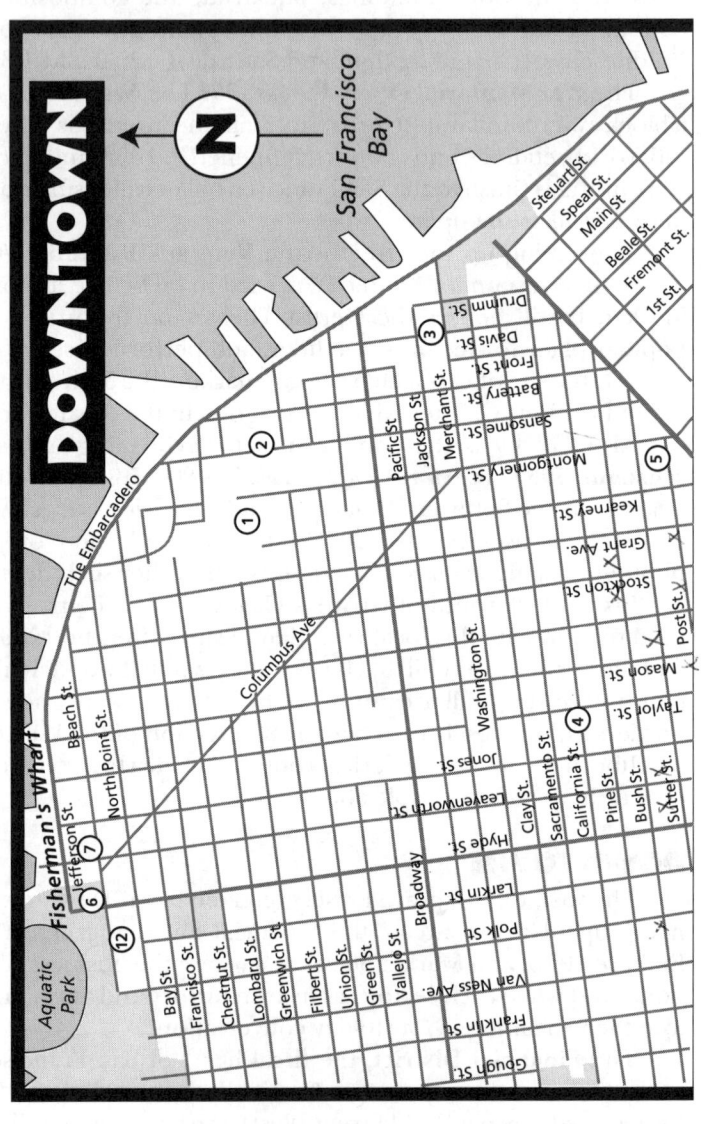

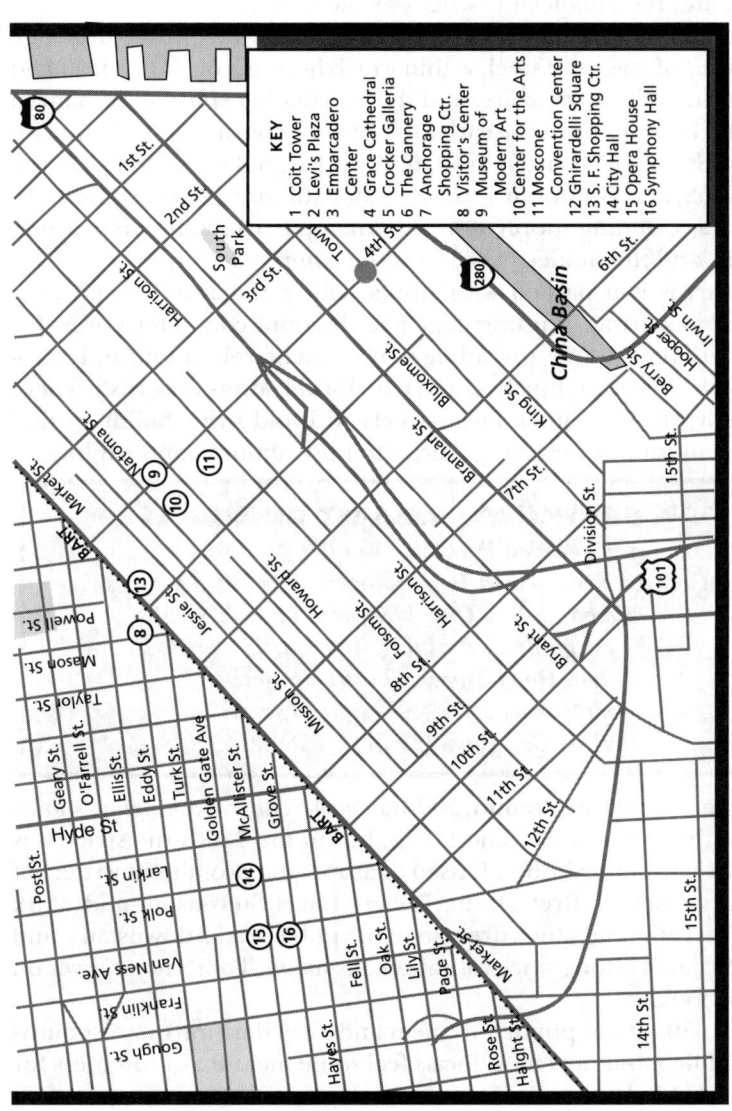

KEY

1 Coit Tower
2 Levi's Plaza
3 Embarcadero Center
4 Grace Cathedral
5 Crocker Galleria
6 The Cannery
7 Anchorage Shopping Ctr.
8 Visitor's Center
9 Museum of Modern Art
10 Center for the Arts
11 Moscone Convention Center
12 Ghirardelli Square
13 S. F. Shopping Ctr.
14 City Hall
15 Opera House
16 Symphony Hall

the American River. Hundreds abandoned ship and went a-prospecting, and them that found gold brought it on back to the big city to whoop it up, spend, and invest. Big money poured in, what with the gold rush, the silver rush, and the train barons. Money was the pulse of old San Francisco, and the Financial District was the heart.

Nowadays the district forms the skyscraper skyline, with tall, gleaming structures of glass and steel, within which business deals get dealt and financial transactions transpire, and the speculating spirit and financial acumen still lives. Some of the early rush-inspired businesses still flourish today. Levi Strauss got started in 1850, Wells Fargo Bank in 1835, Shreve & Co. in 1852, and Gumps in 1861, and they still rule the roost today. In gold rush days, mining supply stores sprang up to capitalize on prospectors' needs, and the modern version is the computer store.

The area is jam packed with stores selling Macintoshes and PCs, hardware and software, cutting edge and discount computer wares. It's also alive with restaurants, providing nourishment, relaxation, and attentive venues for business lunches, and bars for the after-work rush. There are also, surprisingly, quiet small streets with old brick buildings and interesting antique stores and galleries to nose about in and explore.

SAN FRANCISCO'S TALLEST BUILDINGS

Transamerica Pyramid, 853 feet/48 stories
Bank of America World Headquarters, 779 feet/52 stories
Embarcadero One, 569 feet/45 stories
Wells Fargo Bank Building, 561 feet/43 stories
Hilton Hotel Tower, 493 feet/46 stories
333 Market Street, 474 feet/33 stories
Russ Building, 435 feet/31 stories

The **Transamerica Pyramid**, *600 Montgomery near Washington*, stands tall and distinctive as it has since 1975, but in the 1800s the space was occupied by a rooming house. It used to attract the prominent writers of that century, such as Bret Harte, Robert Louis Stevenson, and Mark Twain. One day Twain met a fireman in the public baths downstairs, and while the fireman is long since forgotten, his name, Tom Sawyer, lives on in Twain's books.

In the 1970s, it was popular to sneer and heap derision on the pointy-topped building, but now most locals feel some measure of fondness for the unmistakable landmark. There's an observation area open for free Monday-Friday on the 27th floor, and there's a nice green square (Redwood Park) behind it which offers a fine picnic spot, plus noon-time concerts in the summer, but the best way to appreciate the building is to see it from a distance.

Down the street a block is the **Wells Fargo History Museum**, *420 Montgomery near Sacramento, 415-396-2619*. It's open Monday-Friday 9am-5pm, and admission is free. A fully restored 1865 Concord stagecoach sets the tone, and the display goes on to detail the history of the rugged old transport service that delivered mail, merchandise and people from 1852 on. There's a good collection of Gold Rush artifacts (including some fine gold nuggets), and an interesting section devoted to women's involvement in business.

The **Bank of America Building**, *555 California*, the second tallest in San Francisco, takes up a major chunk of land bounded by California, Pine, Montgomery, and Kearny. Built in 1969 of marble and polished red granite, there are outdoor plazas with modern sculptures, and up 52 floors you'll find the Carnelian Room, *415-433-7500*, open to the public at night for expensive dinners, weekend brunches, and sunset cocktails. It's no longer actually owned by BofA (it leases from another company now - go figure), but it still makes a contribution to banking culture with the abstract black granite sculpture in its front plaza. Designed by Japanese artist Masayuki who called it "Transcendence," local wits redubbed it "Banker's Heart" and smirk en route to meetings.

The **Pacific Coast Stock Exchange**, *301 Pine near Sansome, 415-393-4000*, buzzes inside the hulking 1915 building and is generally closed to the public, but you can arrange a tour if you call two weeks in advance. The **Stock Exchange Tower** *around the corner at 155 Sansome*, the exchange's original building, now houses the City Club of San Francisco, a private concern. When this Miller and Pfleuger building with its black marble-walled entry and Art Deco gold ceiling was remodeled in 1930, **Diego Rivera** was hired to paint some murals inside, while his wife, Frida Kahlo, hung out on the scaffolds to keep him company. To gain admission and see the Rivera murals, you need to set up an appointment through the Mexican Museum by calling *415-441-0404*.

Another notable structure in the district is the **Hallidie Building** (named after Andrew Hallidie, the inventor of the cable car), *130 Sutter between Kearny and Montgomery*. It's believed to be the world's first all-glass curtain-wall building, and the reflective structure is hard to pass by unnoticed.

Nearby, the **Mills Building and Tower**, *220 Montgomery*, was erected in 1891 according to a Burnham and Root design of white marble and brick. It survived the 1906 fire pretty well, and the 22-story tower was added in 1931. In 1927, the **Russ Building**, *235 Montgomery*, across the street from the Mills Building and Tower, was called "the skyscraper," and it remained San Francisco's tallest till the 1960s.

One more notable site is a small concrete island with a towering cast iron column at the corner of Market, Kearny, and Geary. Known as

Lotta's Fountain, it was donated to the city in 1875 by Lotta Crabtree, a popular entertainer, and it really was a fountain, once. There was a small riot at its dedication, thanks to a disappointed group of rowdies who expected the fountain to pump beer (due to their association with Lotta's entertaining days), but the site is better known as a meeting spot after the 1906 earthquake. Each year on April 18th a rapidly diminishing group of quake survivors gather here to mourn friends, lay wreaths, and observe a moment of silence.

Jackson Square was the historic heart of the Barbary Coast, the rollicking, unsavory, crime-ridden, rat infested, bordello-filled wharf area that was unstoppable and untamable till the earthquake and fire of 1906 brought it down. There's not really a square there, but the area involved is within the Pacific, Sansome, Washington, Columbus Street perimeter north of the Financial District. The area near Jackson and Battery contains the oldest surviving neighborhood in San Francisco, one of the few within the fire zone that made it through 1906. There are brick buildings dating from the Gold Rush (filled now mostly with antique stores and art galleries).

The **Ghiradelli Chocolate Factory** was located for nearly 40 years (1857-1894) at 415 Jackson before the operation was transferred to its present location near Fisherman's Wharf. Nearby Balance Street (named for an abandoned ship, not for weight measures) and Gold Street are appealing alleys, but Hotaling Street, another such lane, has been immortalized in San Francisco history.

The **Hotaling Building**, *429 Jackson on the corner with Hotaling Street*, used to be a whisky warehouse, the largest on the West Coast. The 1906 fire threatened the area, but the building was saved by Navy Lieutenant Frederick Newton and his men, who ran a hose from Pier 43 (over Telegraph Hill) all the way down to Jackson Square. The wondrous rescue of the warehouse sparked the pen of Charles Field, who wrote: *If, as they say, God spanked the town for being over frisky, Why did He burn the churches down and save Hotaling's whisky?*

Nearby is the **Golden Era Building**, *732 Montgomery*, where a literary periodical was published containing the works of Mark Twain and Bret Harte, to name just two.

The **Embarcadero** merges with the Financial District where the waterfront wraps around the curve in the bay, spanning the area from Pier 39 to China Basin. The name is Spanish for "landing" or "quay" and it refers to the region created by filling the bay in behind the Seawall from the 1860s to 1900s. Much of it used to be obscured by the Embarcadero Freeway, a ramp off the Bay Bridge planned to span the whole waterfront to the Golden Gate Bridge. It was only allowed as far as Broadway, and the 1989 earthquake put an end to it. It was closed and eventually torn down, to the delight of those championing the rebirth of the waterfront (and the despair of anxious commuters), but the net result is a wide open swath of bay view that's now popular for walks, bike rides, and potential development.

To the northeast beneath Telegraph Hill at the foot of Filbert is **Levi's Plaza**, a small, pleasant park with a fountain surrounded by lots of Levi Strauss-owned office buildings, including their world headquarters, and the old red brick Ice House (which was once an actual ice repository). There are two great restaurants here: Il Fornaio and Fog City Diner.

Walk south along Battery toward Sacramento and you'll hit the **Embarcadero Center**, an enormous ten-acre, eight-block complex with a couple of hotels, a multi-screen cinema, parking garages, and five tall buildings (endearingly named Embarcadero One, Two, Three, Four, and Five), the first four of which are all shopping mall, and the last being the Hyatt. Built in the 1970s, there are over 125 shops (like Ann Taylor, The Limited, and Banana Republic) and restaurants (such as Splendido and Pizzeria Uno).

For entertainment outside of shopping, there's the new **Embarcadero Center Cinema**, *415-325-0810*, there are quite a few **modern sculptures** scattered about (and you can get a pamphlet from the Hyatt Regency in Embarcadero Five describing in detail a walking tour of 20 such Embarcadero sculptures), and there's **Cyber Mind**, *415-693-0348*, a virtual reality center. Open Monday-Thursday 10am-8pm, Friday-Saturday 10am-11pm, and Sunday 11am-7pm, this is a wild and highly entertaining place. In virtual reality, you play with or against other people (friends, family, corporate colleagues, etc.) to blow them away, shoot 'em up, or play pool where you are the cue ball.

Just south of Embarcadero Center near the waterfront is **Justin Herman Plaza**. It's a busy place on a sunny weekend day, with kite flying, skateboarding, sunbathing, et cetera. It's often the site for arts and crafts shows, mimes, and summer noontime concerts, too. It's home to the Vaillancourt Fountain (built in 1971) - yet another controversial decoration about which San Franciscans love to air their opinions.

Follow the Plaza along the water to the foot of Market Street and you'll be at the **Ferry Building**, dating back to 1896 and modeled on the Cathedral Tower of Seville by architect Arthur Page Brown. It's a slender, lovely landmark, a clocktower 230 feet tall that welcomed ferry commuters for decades. The tower survived the 1906 quake (though the four clock faces all read 5:17 for a year after), and it now is the site of the Port Commission, the World Trade Center, and more importantly for most, an open-air Saturday **farmer's market**.

An unusually pleasant stroll can be had along **Herb Caen Way** (recently so named in honor of the *San Francisco Chronicle* columnist

renowned for his 60 years of local scuttlebutt and San Francisco adora-
tion), a wide pedestrian path that follows the Embarcadero south of the
Ferry Building. You can watch the waves slap the industrial wharves, and
see the city shoreline without the hordes that crowd Pier 39.

There are a few other notable landmarks to be found along Market
Street downtown. At the corner of Market and Battery is the **Donahue
Monument**. Designed by Douglas Tilden in honor of the waterfront, a
plaque marks this spot as the old San Francisco Bay shoreline in 1848.

Market Street is not only an important boulevard used to divide the
city into north and south, its bisecting, angled design has posed architects
with a challenge since Jasper O'Farrell was hired in 1847 to fix the city
survey and plot new streets. The buildings at *333 Market* (a modern
building designed by Skidmore, Owings, and Merrill), *540-548 Market*
(the classic **Flatiron Building** designed by Charles Haven), and *582 Market*
(Willis Polk's stunning **Hobart Building**) show three different answers to
the conundrum.

On the south side of Market at New Montgomery is the august
Sheraton Palace Hotel, which opened in 1875, and was restored after the
devastation wrought by the 1906 fire. Along with its elegant restaurants,
there's an original Maxfield Parrish painting on the wall in the Pied Piper
bar. Described in more detail in the hotel and restaurant chapters, there's
also a Tuesday tour led by the Friends of the Library.

And down Steuart Street a block south of Market is **Rincon Center**.
This used to be one of the poshest addresses in town in the early 1800s,
back when it was Rincon Hill, but when Nob Hill became accessible to
cable car traffic, Rincon Hill's residential popularity waned. The hill was
cut down to act as anchorage for the Bay Bridge, and Rincon Center now
finds itself in the midst of the Financial District, a shopping complex that
spans two blocks. There are lots of shops, some very good restaurants, a
History Room with artifacts and a mural by Anton Refregier containing
27 panels of California life from Native American times to WWI, and a
lobby with an unusual fountain that pours from the atrium ceiling down
to the pool below in a constant shower.

Keep heading south on Steuart till Harrison and you'll hit the **Hills
Brothers Coffee Factory**. Its brick facade bespeaks its origins, and the
lobby has wonderful old photos from days gone by, but now it's just
another office complex. And right next door is the **Gordon Biersh
Brewing Company**, *2 Harrison*, a micro brewery that makes its beer on the
premises and serves it up with lunch and dinner at their restaurant. The
beer itself is a bit disappointing and is not worth a special trip.

FISHERMAN'S WHARF

Once known as Bilge-Water Bay, **Fisherman's Wharf** now is 1% fish processing center and 99% tourist central. Bounded by Hyde, Bay, the Embarcadero, and the San Francisco Bay, most of the action happens on Jefferson. It is a real wharf and port, it's been the commercial fishing center since 1900, and a few real fishing boats still exist, but now it's mostly a conglomeration of a zillion hokey and cheesy tourist trap sights, T-shirt stands, and mediocre restaurants. Indelibly (and inexplicably) linked in people's minds with San Francisco, there are some fun things to do there and it's popular with kids, but it is by no means the be-all and end-all of San Francisco. It was, in fact, the original mission of this guide book to inform you of your sight-seeing and eating options beyond the confines of the glutted Wharf.

Over ten million people a year come to visit Fisherman's Wharf, and the majority of them do so on sunny weekends. If you want to see the sights but avoid the heaviest crowds, a weekday morning will be less thronged. However, and especially if you have kids, the crowd may be part of the draw. There is a validated parking garage at Pier 39, and some highly sought-after street parking, but public transport is advised. The Taylor cable car takes you very close, as do bus lines 19, 30, 39, 32, 15, 47, 49, and 42. Most San Franciscans won't come anywhere near the place (unless friends from out-of-town insist), but it's the top destination for Bay Area teens. Once the final school bell clangs, kids around the city make a bee-line for the Wharf.

The top attraction for them is **Pier 39**. Built in 1977 and open daily 10:30am-8:30pm, at least, there are T-shirts, key chains, kites, very popular sweatshirts (because the fog often catches shorts-clad tourists unawares), and hundreds of other souvenirs, as well as food stalls and cafes of all sorts. Street performers here mug and mime, juggle and joke, and pass the hat, and the whole pier has the air of a commercial amusement center.

But of all the diversions, the most popular with kids is the **arcade**, with its carousel, bumper cars, Namco Cyber Station, and video games. The newest attraction on the pier, however, is **Underwater World**, *415-623-5300*, a 40 million dollar state-of-the-art aquarium that opened in April, 1996. It's already popular, and you can (and should) reserve dive times in advance. It's open daily 10am-8pm, costs $13.50 per adult and $6.75 for children and seniors, taking you on a one-hour guided tour that replicates an underwater dive with moving sidewalks taking you through a 400 foot see-through acrylic underwater tunnel, showing the indigenous fish and natural habitat of the San Francisco Bay.

There is some other nearby entertainment as well. **Ripley's Believe It Or Not Museum**, *175 Jefferson near Taylor, 415-771-6188*, is open

Sunday-Thursday 10am-10pm, Friday-Saturday 10am-midnight, and the cost is $8 for adults, $6.75 for teens, seniors, and students, and $5 for children 5-12.

The **Wax Museum**, *145 Jefferson near Taylor, 415-885-4975*, is just down the street and is open Sunday-Thursday 9am-11pm, and till midnight Friday-Saturday. The entrance fee is $9.95 for adults, $7.95 for teens aged 13-17, $4.95 for children 6-12, $6.95 for seniors, and free for kids younger than six. They suggest you give yourself an hour to see all the over 250 wax celebrities in all their glory. In the complex they also feature the **Haunted Gold Mine Fun House and Medieval Dungeon**, and you can get a discount gold pass to see all three for $18.95 for adults, $14.95 for teens, $9.45 for kids 6-12, and $13.45 for seniors.

And for those interested in boats, the **Historic Ships on Hyde Street Pier**, *415-556-3002*, is open daily 10am-6pm April-September and 9:30am-5pm October-March. Admission costs $3 per adult and $1 per youth aged 12-17. There's also the *USS Pamanito, Pier 45, 415-929-0202*, a WWII submarine, open for public viewing daily from 9am-6pm for $4 per adult, $2 per senior and youth, and $1 per child ages 6-12. And the **National Maritime Museum**, *Aquatic Park at the foot of Polk, 415-556-3002*, shows ship models, maps, and maritime history artifacts. It's open daily 10am-5pm, and admission is free.

Across Beach Street from Aquatic Park is **Ghiradelli Square**. Now it's a shopping complex with more than 70 shops (mostly clothing and jewelry stores), restaurants, and a few interesting craft galleries (such as the Xanadu Gallery, Folk Art International, Creative Spirit Gallery, and the California Crafts Museum). Back in 1860, however, this was a woolen factory making uniforms for Union soldiers during the Civil War. In 1893 the Ghiradelli family took over and created the famous chocolate business, and the Gothic clocktower was added in 1916. The chocolate is now produced in the East Bay (as it has been since 1960), but the **Ghiradelli Chocolate Manufactory**, a candy shop and ice cream parlor on the ground floor, sells all the chocolates you're likely to desire (as does **Cost Plus** *at 2552 Taylor* for considerably less).

The **Cannery**, *Jefferson and Leavenworth*, (just east of the Hyde Street Pier) is another historic factory-turned-mall. It was built in 1894 out of red brick, and in 1906 Del Monte put it to use canning peaches. In 1968, The Cannery was opened as a shopping complex, and it now hosts more shops, galleries, and restaurants, plus the new **Museum of the City of San Francisco**, *on the third floor, 415-928-0289*. Open Wednesday-Sunday 10am-4pm, admission is free, though a $2 donation is suggested. Along with the eight-ton head of the Goddess of Progress statue that toppled off City Hall just before the 1906 quake, there's a fine collection of historical maps, photos, and other assorted San Francisco artifacts.

And if you need to shop a little more, the **Anchorage Mall** is just across the street.

There is another attraction out at the Wharf, and it's free of charge: the **sea lions**. They have been hanging out off the piers since 1990, and they put on a great show. They weigh up to 1,000 pounds, and they heave themselves about out of water with much flopping and slapping, but in the water they're sleek swimming machines. They are not, however, paid entertainment, and they follow no set schedule. When they do show up, however, they sunbathe and slobber, gamble like pups and snore like grumpy old men, and their barking calls surge over the waterfront like the fog.

If you want to be out on the water, too, there's a wide range of **cruises**. **Red & White Fleet**, *415-546-2628* and Blue & Gold, *415-705-5444*, offers trips to Alcatraz, Angel Island, and Sausalito are detailed in the *Day Trips & Excursions* chapter, and both are located near Pier 39. The **Hornblower**, *415-788-8866* and **Pacific Marine Yachts**, *415-788-9100*, offer brunch cruises that are described in the *Day Trips & Excursions* chapter as well.

There are a good number of **fishing charters** that leave Fisherman's Wharf, coordinated by Jacky Douglas, *415-586-9800*. They take 15-25 passengers, cost about $45 per person, and go for salmon, bass, sturgeon, halibut, or shark. It's a lot of fun, though if you don't live here, there's the question of what you're going to do with all the fish you catch.

The **Oceanic Society**, *415-474-3385*, offers a different kind of trip, out to the Farallon Islands to see the whales, dolphins, sea turtles and birds. It costs $48 for the January-April six-hour whale watching trips, and $62 for the June-November eight-hour Farallon Island natural history expeditions. They leave every Saturday-Sunday, and some Fridays, and passengers must be at least 10 years old. While the trip can get rough, especially in winter, they'll send you a complete preparatory package including what to take and do to avoid sea sickness. Qualified naturalists lead all the trips, and you usually see whales during winter and summer. Make reservations a few weeks in advance, at least, and ask about youth rates (if applicable), because they're trying to add some discounts.

And a final word about the food. Fisherman's Wharf is crawling with restaurants, cafes, seafood snack stalls, and fast-food outlets, but very little of it is haute cuisine. With over 10 million annual visitors, they don't have to try very hard to get customers, so most of them don't. A few good options are described in the Fisherman's Wharf food chapter, but most of the fancy fish restaurants here are over-priced and mediocre. This is not the neighborhood to go for the best in fish. What to do when you get hungry at the Wharf? Lower your standards and eat wherever, or walk up the few blocks to North Beach and eat better for less.

GOLDEN GATE PARK

In 1868, the Board of Supervisors was trying to establish a title to the four square leagues called the Outside Lands that were granted to San Francisco under Mexican law. The public was clamoring for a municipal park, and efforts were united. They chose a long rectangular strip of barren sand dunes, three miles long and half a mile wide, stretching from Stanyan Street out to the Pacific Ocean, and reached a compromise settlement with the squatters.

It wasn't easy to transform the 1,013 acres of windblown sands into the lush green oasis it is today, and many thought it an impossible fool's task. A newspaper editorial scoffed "a blade of grass cannot be raised without four posts to keep it from blowing away." With persistence, luck, and skill, however, the gardeners began to shape it into the "woodland park" the creators had in mind, with curving roads and rustic bridges to add to the bucolic flavor.

In the late 1800s, bicycle riding was extremely popular, and Golden Gate Park became the spot of choice for a bike ride, stroll, or picnic. And once the Geary, Park, & Ocean Railroad (aka the Steam Dummy) was up and running in 1881, as many as 50,000 people a day took their leisure and recreation there.

The success of Golden Gate Park was due mostly to two men, **John McLaren** and **William Hammond Hall**. McLaren left Scotland in the late 1860s after studying at Edinburgh's Botanical Gardens. He was appointed Assistant Superintendent of Golden Gate Park in 1887, and became Superintendent three years later. He once said "Always work with Nature, never against it. Never interfere with the beauty the Creator has given us," and under his leadership, the Park was developed according to that rule of thumb. Known as "the man who lived to plant a million trees," he was allowed to continue as superintendent until his death in 1943, instead of being made to retire at the standard age of 70 in 1916. McLaren also helped set up the refugee camps in the park following the 1906 quake. The warm welcome afforded by the park helped endear Golden Gate Park to San Franciscans even more than the early days of leisure.

Hall designed the Park, and was its first superintendent from 1871-1876. He was the man responsible for building the roads, planting trees, and designing the Children's Playground. Hall was instrumental in discovering that barley and lupine could take root and turn the sand into green fields (following an accidental barley spill that then took root). It was Hall who put McLaren in as Assistant Superintendent, and Hall also was responsible for designing the park roads and paths full of bends and curves to discourage fast drivers and to shelter visitors from the wind. Lovely and practical as the curvy roads are, however, they can also easily

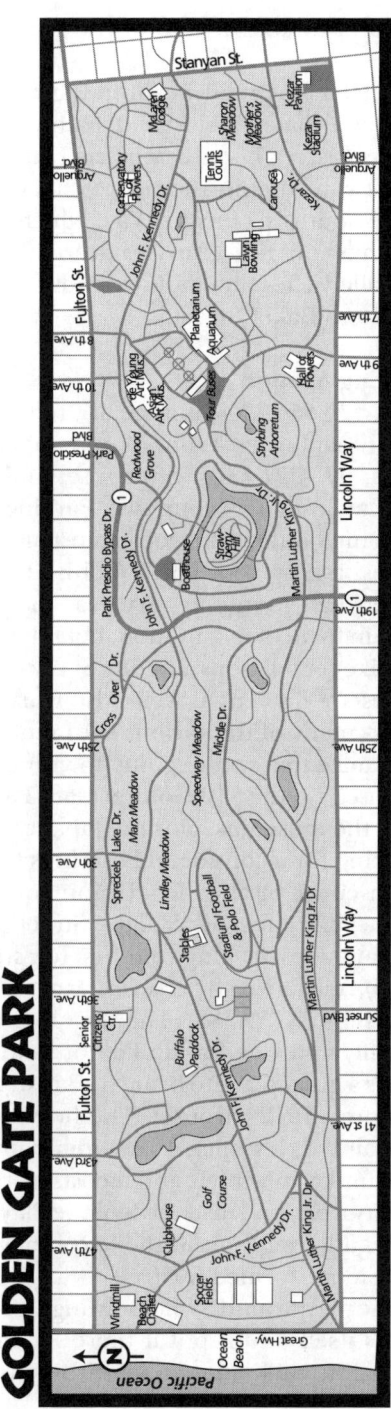

disorient you. It's helpful to keep a map of the park handy for a park excursion.

The Park today is well-maintained, beautifully green, full of museums and activities as well as isolated fields and paths, and very popular. Stanyan Street forms its eastern boundary in the Haight Ashbury neighborhood, Fulton Street runs the northern stretch all through the Richmond, and half a mile south is Lincoln Way, which forms the Sunset boundary from Stanyan on out to Ocean Beach and the Pacific. And one narrow strip of green called The Panhandle extends from the park proper east through the Haight to Baker Street.

Getting There & Getting Around

Golden Gate Park, *415-666-7200,* is large; it's full of things to do and see, and it's well worth exploring. From May-October, the **Friends of Recreation and Parks**, *415-221-1311*, offer free guided walking tours each weekend, or you can just go on your own. Parking is difficult within the Park (and off limits on Sunday), but you can usually find easy parking along Fulton. Bus access is easy, too. The 5, 7, 18, 21, 28, 29, 33, 44, 71, and N Judah Muni Metro all go into or very near the park. Once there, walking is really the main form of locomotion, but biking is another good option, and there are bike rental shops all along Stanyan. And, for the deft and brave, roller blades are for rent as well. Also worth knowing before you head into the park, many of the various sites require entrance fees, and if you know in advance that you're going to visit them all, it may be worth your while to purchase the $10 **Golden Gate Park Cultural Pass**, which gets you into all the museums, plus the Japanese Tea Garden and the Conservatory, making for a considerable savings for adults. You can buy it at any of the museums, or at TIX in Union Square.

From the east, the entrance off Haight Street is usually full of homeless and hippie wannabes, making your first few steps a bit unsavory (though not dangerous), but it's worth persevering to reach the **Children's Playground** and **Carousel**, *415-759-5884*. The Mary B. Connolly Children's Playground is open daily and free for all. Full of sandpits, slides, forts, swings, and seesaws, it's a great place to bring the kids. And, it's right next to the beautifully restored 1912 carousel. The horse and other carved animals are festively painted, it's open 10am-5pm daily in summer and 10am-4pm Thursday-Sunday in winter, and it costs just $1 for adults and 25¢ per child for a jaunty ride. And just north of the Playground is **Hippie Hill**, a popular hippie gathering spot in the late 1960s and early 1970s, where the Grateful Dead performed for free.

Further north of the playground along Bowling Green Drive (past the **bowling lawn**, which is itself a fun spot if there's a bowling match on, watching the serious, white-clad old men and women carefully concentrate on the small lawn balls), and on past the tennis courts, the path takes you to John F. Kennedy Drive and the **Conservatory of Flowers**, *415-362-0808*. It's open daily 9am-6pm in summer, and 9am-5pm in winter, or will be once the repairs have been completed. Call first to see if it's open before making any plans. Once it's back in operation, admission will be $1.50 for adults, 75¢ for seniors and children, and free for all during the last half hour.

The greenhouse was built in 1879, based on London's Kew Gardens, and it's stunningly beautiful, with its graceful Victorian lines, and white window panes. Built originally in England and shipped around Cape Horn for the James Lick estate in San Jose, it was purchased by a citizens group led by Leland Stanford and Charles Crocker (since Lick died before the Conservatory arrived) and they donated it to the park. Inside the dome, tropical palms loom, delicate orchids bloom, and warm mugginess reigns supreme. Unfortunately, the winter of 1995 blew an especially nasty storm into San Francisco, and trees smashed down right, left, and through the conservatory. The Conservatory is currently closed and under repair (after a desperate effort to raise funds saved the greenhouse from the garbage heap), but it's expected to open its doors sometime in 1997. And even if you can't go in, the sweeping lawns in front of the Conservatory are beautiful in their own right, with flowered gardens used to spell out welcoming messages, and gentle slopes perfect for reading, napping, or picnicking.

West along JFK Drive will take you to the **M. H. de Young Memorial Museum**, *415-863-3330*. You can enter from 10th Avenue off Fulton, and the 44 bus goes right there. It's open Wednesday-Sunday 10am-4:45pm, and admission is $6 for adults, $4 for seniors, $3 for youths, free for kids under 12, and free for everyone the first Wednesday of each month when the museum remains open till 8:45pm. Your entrance ticket is also good for admission to the Asian Art Museum next door and the Legion of Honor Museum in Lincoln Park if you go the same day.

The museum got its start in 1894 following the California Midwinter International Exposition – thanks to Michael de Young (editor of the *Chronicle* at the time) and his determination to get a fine arts museum going in San Francisco. It took a good while for the quality of exhibitions to come up to snuff, but they now house a respectable collection of art from the Americas, including work by Grant Wood, George Caleb Bingham, Georgia O'Keeffe, and Winslow Homer, and a fine collection of American art donated by Mr. and Mrs. John D. Rockefeller III in 1979. They have a good African Art collection as well, plus an unusual collection of Albert Bierstadt works. There are also special exhibits that can be quite spectacular, and it's worth calling or checking the paper for their current shows. They also have a fine cafe that stays open till 4pm.

Asian Art Museum, *415-668-8921*, is in the wing just next door to the de Young, and it, too, is open Wednesday-Sunday 10am-4:45pm, and admission is $6 for adults, $4 for seniors, $3 for youths, free for kids under 12, and free for everyone the first Wednesday of each month when the museum remains open till 8:45pm. Your entrance ticket is also good for same-day admission to the de Young next door, and the Legion of Honor in Lincoln Park.

They have a great collection of art from throughout Asia, the largest of its kind outside Asia. They have paintings and tapestry, bronzes and ceramics and jades from forty Asian nations, thanks in large part to the Avery Brundage Collection. Brundage, a persnickety Chicago million-aire, donated his collection to San Francisco on the condition they build a special museum to house it, and a wing was added to the de Young in 1966. There's a fine collection of Chinese art, a small but excellent Japanese collection, and some very good Korean and Indian collections as well. The treasures require more room than the wing has to offer, however, and in the year 2000 a move is in store. The old Main Branch of the Library in Civic Center just vacated its beautiful building for a more spacious new branch building across the street on McAllister. Money has been approved, and by 2000 the Asian Art Museum will be ready to showcase its collection in its own grand home.

Across the way from the art museums in the Music Concourse is the **California Academy of Sciences**, *415-750-7145*. It's open daily 10am-5pm for most of the year and until 7pm from July 4th till Labor Day. Admission is $7 for adults, $4 for seniors, and youth aged 12-17, and $1.50 for children 6-11, and it's free (and crowded) the first Wednesday of every month. Considered one of the top five natural history museums in the country, it's got both the **Steinhart Aquarium** and the **Morrison Planetarium**. It's a great place, and you could easily spend hours and hours exploring their permanent exhibits, not to mention the special shows. Founded in 1853 to study the Californian natural world, the Academy started with weekly meetings of naturalists. Then, in 1891 millionaire James Lick (the same who had ordered the Conservatory from England) gave the Academy a grand building on Market Street. The building didn't survive the 1906 fire, and in 1916 they moved into their new Golden Gate Park home. They remain there now, though the building's been enlarged a number of times since 1916.

In the museum, there are well-constructed, interactive displays ex-ploring the history of evolution, Arctic dioramas, Australian aboriginal culture, and the African Safari, with life-size reproductions of the animals in their natural habitats. The Aquarium is well worth a visit too, and they're all in favor of the new Underwater World opening up at Pier 39, considering it as complementary rather than competition. They have a huge 100,000 gallon Fish Roundabout containing 14,000 critters, and a coral reef with tropical sharks, fish, and clams, while the Space and Earth Hall has an "earthquake floor" that allows visitors to thrill to the sensations of an earthquake without fearing for their lives. The Far Side display of Gary Larson cartoons, however, is always the one guaranteed to please and entertain. The Discovery Room for Children is a hands-on playroom where kids 4-11 years of age can touch everything, and can even make some displays of their own.

The **Morrison Planetarium**, *415-750-7141*, right in the middle of the Academy of Sciences, charges an additional $2.50 for adults, and $1.25 for seniors and students (call for the schedule) for their wonderful astronomy shows. With a live narrator, 150 projectors, and a triad sound system, they show and tell the story of the planets and stars. **The Laserium**, *415-750-7138*, also has shows (different nights and hours) with laser lights and loud music (from the ever popular Pink Floyd *Dark Side of the Moon* to the Beatles and Nine Inch Nails) blasting your senses.

The **Music Concourse**, *415-666-7035*, is a destination in and of itself in summer, for the free band concerts held Sunday and holiday afternoons at 1pm.

Just behind (south of) the Academy of Sciences is the **Shakespeare Garden**. It's not nearly as well-touristed as other spots in the park, it's free, and it's a lovely little gem. Flowers are planted all around, and labeled with Shakespeare quotes referring to the flower in question. In addition, especially during the spring when the sun is warm but the wind often brings a chill, the protective hedge provides a warm, secluded glade. There are two hundred flowers here that can be cross-referenced in your Complete Shakespeare, as well as locked doors protecting Shakespeare's bust (it's a copy of his actual death mask), and the doors only get opened once a year, on his birthday.

The next big park attraction, heading west, is the **Japanese Tea Garden**, *415-752-1171*. It's open daily 9am-6pm in summer and 8:30am-6pm in winter, and it costs $2 for adults and children 13-17 and $1 for seniors and children 6-12. It's just down the street from the Asian Art Museum, and it's a real change of pace. This four-acre garden was created by G. T. Marsh in 1894 for the Mid-Winter Exposition, with ponds, streams, peaceful landscaping, and an arched wood moon bridge. There's also the Tea House with little cups of tea and small cookies, and the place is especially lovely and busy in spring when the cherry blossoms are in full bloom.

The **Strybing Arboretum and Botanical Gardens**, *415-661-1316*, is open 9am-4pm on weekdays, and 10am-5pm weekends, and admission is free. Close to 9th and Lincoln, the Arboretum's 70 acres form a glorious tribute to Bay Area indigenous plants, as well as to plants from other nations, so long as they can thrive in our clime. All told there are over 6,000 plant varieties, plus a nice little pond that attracts ducks, swans, and herons. The Succulent Garden and Garden of Fragrance are extremely popular, but the California Collection of Native Plants, and Nobel Conifer Garden are quite fine, too. Whether you're a gardening expert or just want to stretch your legs in pleasing surroundings, it's hard to find a nicer place to walk.

There's one more oft-visited site that's just a bit west of the Arboretum and Japanese Tea Garden, and that's **Stow Lake**, *415-752-0347*. It forms a placid ring around Strawberry Hill island (on which the Chinese Pavilion was assembled in 1981 after having been shipped from Taipei in 6,000 pieces), and you can walk around, sit and gaze from the convenient benches, or hire one of the rowboats or paddleboats. It's a favorite weekend destination for locals, especially on nice weekends.

While these sites all lie in the eastern half of the park, if you keep strolling (or cycling or roller blading, or whatever) two miles west towards the ocean, you'll pass all sorts of nice meadows and pools. Notable among them is **Buffalo Paddock**, with real live American bison happily grazing away. Buffalo were first purchased for the park in 1891, though Wyoming buffalo are being imported these days to replenish the herd. **Golden Gate Stables**, *415-668-7360,* are in the center of the park, and they're available for lessons and rentals. The **fly-casting pool**, *415-386-2630*, is also nearby (roughly near Sunset Blvd.), and there's model yacht sailing on **Spreckels Lake** near 36th.

Golden Gate Park Golf Course, *415-751-8987*, is a nine-hole course further west near 45th, and at the very end are the two **windmills**, the Murphy Windmill and the Dutch Windmill (which was constructed by Alpheus Bull in 1902, and was able to pump 30,000 gallons of water an hour). Around the Dutch is the **Wilhelmina Tulip Gardens**, which is at its finest in early spring. And then you're at Ocean Beach.

HAIGHT ASHBURY

The Haight-Ashbury **Summer of Love** flowered in 1967, but the distinctive hippie ambiance that still colors this neighborhood began taking shape in '65 with funky coffee houses and funkier clothing. Ken Kesey and his Merry Pranksters hosted LSD parties, advertised with flyers asking "Can You Pass the Acid Test?" and fledgling rock bands were attracted to the new hip district. *Jefferson Airplane* played its first gigs (they lived at 130 Delmar), and the *Warlocks* (soon to be the *Grateful Dead*, they stayed at 710 Ashbury), added their sounds to the mix. *Rolling Stone* magazine was launched as it covered the burgeoning Haight-Ashbury rock group activity, and gonzo journalist Hunter S. Thompson partied with the Hell's Angels at 318 Parnassus.

In the 1860s, the Haight area was slated to be a part of the Golden Gate Park. Squatters and speculators' claims complicated the matter, though, and in the end the eastern park section was narrowed to one long band called the Panhandle, sticking out as a gaunt extension from the park proper. By the 1890s, the Haight-Ashbury district was a fashionable resort area, and San Francisco's wealthy built country homes. Even more development followed the 1906 quake and fire, and since the fire hadn't reached this far, no rubble needed to be cleared. The depression of the 30s hit the neighborhood hard, however, and the decline lasted a long time. The old, lovely Victorians fell on poor times as mortgages weren't met. The district got a new life and a new set of residents in the 40s and 50s as blacks who'd immigrated to San Francisco to work in defense plants looked for housing. This was a residential, family neighborhood when the Beatniks found it in the early 60s, before the hippie revolution.

The Summer of Love made Haight-Ashbury its home base, and while the 60s revolution was by no means a uniquely San Francisco phenomenon, its legacies altered the tone of the Haight Ashbury district more permanently than they did elsewhere. A walk down Haight Street today is not so very different in some ways from what it was 30 years ago. Bare-footed, long-haired idlers still hang out, plaiting ribbons in their locks, but the tone has changed.

In the '70s, the Haight got mean and nasty. Flower Power and Free Love were replaced by junkies and slime bags; the Summer of Love devolved into a decade of discontent. Haight-Ashbury today is successful but not much cleaner; the neighborhood has kept many of its long-time residents but continues to attract the youthful malcontent from across the nation, and the stores capitalize on its notoriety. Rent in the area is no longer cheap, and the neighborhood is again made up of mostly middle class denizens, some young professionals, and burgeoning families. Graying old hippies, teenybopper hippie-wannabes, and the homeless still clog the sidewalks, panhandling, smoking a variety of substances, and hanging out, and punks, derelicts, residents, and tourists all mingle in a noisy, colorful tangle.

The Haight generally is thought to encompass the area between Buena Vista Park and Golden Gate Park, with Oak, Central, Frederick, and Stanyan the streets on its perimeter. How long you want to spend there probably depends on your age and your tolerance for chaos, but Haight Street is not just an interesting and colorful place to gawk. There are some excellent vintage clothing shops, a couple very good new clothing shops, a fine book store, and some good eating. The cafe scene is very much in evidence, and it's right near the park entrance, and the Inner Sunset. Buena Vista Park on the hill above Haight and Lyon is a pleasant green break from it all. Folks lie out in the sun on nice days, and at night it's a popular gay cruising scene. Walk up Buena Vista West and there are some pretty houses to look at, like the **Spreckels Mansion** *at 737 Buena Vista,* built for sugar baron Richard Spreckels in 1887, and lived in later by Jack London and Ambrose Bierce.

LOWER HAIGHT

Within the area framed by Fell, Steiner, Waller, and Webster, the Lower Haight in the 1980s was the grunge capital, the hip center of the drug, rock, cafe, Generation X scene. It is still that to some extent, thought the scepter has been passed to Valencia Street in the Mission according to most. There are some good, cheap eateries, some popular nightclubs, and some rundown old Victorians. Not the safest place to wander around at night, it's not the most dangerous either, and Mad Dog in the Fog and Nickie's BBQ still draw big crowds.

THE MARINA, FORT MASON, & THE PRESIDIO

Bordered roughly by Laguna, Lombard, Van Ness, and the Bay waters, this upscale neighborhood was first known by the charming name of the Marina-Vanderbilt Tract, but the name changed a number of times before ending up as **The Marina.** Created from the bay out of landfill in 1915 to form the site for the grand Panama Pacific International Exposition (the fair covered 635 acres of today's Marina), before the marsh was made into solid earth, it was known as Harbor View and wasn't developed. The Marina Green (once Washerwoman's Lagoon and Gaslight Cove) is a by-product of the fair, but the **Palace of Fine Arts** on Lyon Street that now houses the **Exploratorium** was believed to have been the most beautiful of all the Exposition's creations, and it's the only building that escaped the bulldozer. It was on Army land, so it was allowed to remain when the rest of the Exposition was razed to pave the way for the new residential neighborhood.

Along with **Cow Hollow** (the northern slopes of Pacific Heights that stretches from Greenwich to Vallejo, it was named in the 1870s after the many local dairy farms, and which is very much a part of the Marina community), the Marina has grown into a yuppie paradise of fine residential apartments, restaurants, bars, and boutiques. The 1989 earthquake did serious damage to this neighborhood (thanks to its landfill base, which turns to wiggly mush when the earth shifts), and the ensuing fire was even worse. Humans have an uncanny ability to forget pain and ignore distressing thoughts, however, and the neighborhood's popularity rebounded quickly. The cafe culture is strong here, with coffee shops on every block, and a sunny Sunday morning will find the Union Street sidewalks jammed with window shoppers, cappuccino quaffers, brunch browsers, and other assortments of idle relaxers in shorts and sunglasses. Be forewarned that the parking situation here is often abysmal, and take a bus or taxi if you can.

The **Marina Green** stretches out along Marina Boulevard, and it's a cheery green strip, full of joggers and kites, kids and leisure-seekers. Its flat terrain invites skaters and cyclists, and anyone who wants to sit out on a fine day and enjoy the people, bay, and boat views. To the west of the Green, the **Yacht Harbor** bobs with pretty boats, and off on the opposite spit of land are the St. Francis Yacht Club and the Golden Gate Yacht Club. On a nice weekend day the bay will be full of sail boats, and it's always a lovely sight. But aside from the Green, and the shops and cafes along Union and Chestnut, the best reason to visit the Marina is still the Exploratorium.

The Exploratorium, *3601 Lyon near Jefferson in the Marina (near the water and near the Golden Gate Bridge), 415-561-0360 for recorded information, 415-561-0362 for Tactile Dome reservations, is in the Palace of Fine Arts building.* There's parking (often full), or you can get there by bus #30 (from Fisherman's Wharf or downtown), or by #22, 28, 41, 43, or 45 from elsewhere. In summer, the museum is open daily 10am-6pm, and till 9:30pm on Wednesdays; in winter the museum hours are Tuesday-Sunday 10am-5pm, and till 9:30pm on Wednesdays (they're closed Mondays except for holidays). Adult admission is $9, it's $7 for students (with ID), $5 for youth ages 6-17, $2.50 for children 3-5, $5 for those with disabilities, and $7 for seniors. Admission is free the first Wednesday of each month, but be forewarned that on those days the museum is packed and far less enjoyable. Tactile Dome admission is different. You need reservations in advance, and you pay $12 which includes the Dome and the museum. They also have a cafe with sandwiches, salads, soups, and snacks.

The Exploratorium's been described in so many different ways: a scientific playland, the most original museum of science in the world, and as weird and wonderful as the inside of founder Frank Oppenheimer's brain (Frank, brother of J. Robert, was a physicist like his older brother and worked on the bomb with him in the 40s, but took to elementary and high school teaching after the war). Frank's stance, that "no one ever flunked a museum," was the starting point for the museum. It's meant to be fun, so much fun you don't realize how much you're learning. You're just looking at strange and fascinating things, playing and making stuff happen.

Of course, you can always read the card explaining the scientific principals involved if you're so inclined. Basically, the Exploratorium is a vast hall of hands-on, manipulative activities and exhibits, bunched loosely by thirteen broad subject areas marked by overhead signs, including weather, color, electricity, motion, life sciences, language, vision, and touch, as well as special exhibits that change every few months. This is not a place where you ever need to tell your kids "no, no, don't touch." Everything is for touching and doing, and kids love it.

AT PLAY IN THE EXPLORATORIUM

Children adore the Bicycle Wheel Gyro Seat, and it's rarely empty. There's an internet section set up, with orange-jacketed guides at the ready to lead you into the world on-line (the guides, usually high school kids who've found a new calling in life, are very helpful and can be found throughout the museum). There's a row of squeeze and sniff bottles filled with different scents for you to try to identify (potato, popcorn, coffee, and more). And the cow's eye dissection never has an empty seat. Kids throng around and say "oh, yuck" and "oh, gross" and "can I touch it" (the answer is always "yes") as the patient guide tells what each part does and why some animal eyes shine green in the night while human eyes don't.

In the language section there's a pitch switch that takes your voice from soprano to bass (gales of laughter always seem to erupt from the pitch switch alcove). Learn how dice-rolling probabilities work, see if you're color blind, track your genetic recessive genes on a computer (can you curl your tongue?, do you have dimples?), twiddle knobs all over the place and see, hear, and feel what happens.

If you go to just one museum or activity in the city, you should go here, with kids or without. If you can, come on a weekday, because it's more fun if you don't have to wait for the crowds to give you a turn. Most people stay a couple of hours, after which the fun turns to sensory overload, and your brain sponge just can't absorb any more.

And the **Tactile Dome** is absolutely worth it, if you have the foresight to reserve in advance (though you can always try on a last minute basis - you might get lucky). It's pitch black, and you crawl, slide, slither, and climb your way through the amazing pathways of textures and fun. It's fine for anyone seven and up and not about to give birth. We won't tell you more because part of the fun is experiencing it yourself, but it shouldn't be missed. And one more thing: The Exploratorium Museum Shop is one of the best in the city for anyone with kids, a love of science, or both.

To the east of the Marina Green is **Fort Mason**. Sandwiched between Aquatic Park and the Marina Green, its history goes back to World War II when it was a depot shipping supplies to the Pacific. It was converted into a cultural center in 1977, and the long warehouses (labeled picturesquely Building A, B, C, D, and E) are now filled to capacity with wonderful small museums, theaters, and shops. And even if you don't feel like poking around, Greens Restaurant is reason enough to go there. And up above the Fort Mason complex is the **Fort Mason Golden Gate National Recreation Area**, a beautiful swath of rolling green land with sensational views of Marin and the Bay, winding paths, and a youth hostel.

WHY THE PALACE OF FINE ARTS STILL STANDS

It was meant to be rubble, but the Palace of Fine Arts stands tall and magnificent thanks to public demand, which sometimes insists on just the right things. It was back in December of 1915, and the grand Panama-Pacific International Exposition (a world's fair to celebrate the rebirth of San Francisco following the catastrophic earthquake and fire of 1906) was coming to a close. The Palace of Fine Arts was just one of many amazing structures on the mile-long stretch of San Francisco Bay where the Exposition was built, but it was by far the people's favorite, and they got together to preserve the Palace when the Exposition came to an end. It was all well and good not to demolish the structure, but there were other problems. The colonnades and rotunda and such had been built to last just a few months, and extensive preservation was in order.

In 1962, funds had been collected for restoration by demolition. The rotunda and columns were smashed, and concrete, solid reconstruction began. By 1968, the Palace was complete again, but to what purpose? Dr. Frank Oppenheimer came up with the answer. After working with his brother J. Robert Oppenheimer building and testing the first atomic bomb in Los Alamos, NM in the 1940s, he became the father of a museum for science, art, and human perception in 1969, and the gallery of the Palace of Fine Arts has ever since been the site of San Francisco's Exploratorium.

Mexican Museum, *Building D of Fort Mason, 415-441-0404*, is open Wednesday-Sunday noon-5pm. Admission costs $3 for adults, $2 for seniors and students, and children under 12 enter free. However, on the first Wednesday of each month, the museum hours are noon-7pm, and everyone enters free of charge. It's been in Fort Mason for some time now, but plans have been afoot for a lovely, new space to be built that will be five times the present size near the corner of Third and Mission, just across from the Center for the Arts. Funds and plans keep getting delayed and subjected to political detours, but the information as of now says the new museum doors will be open by late in 1998. For now, the museum exhibits in Fort Mason change every three months, and it takes around 45 minutes to an hour to see it all. Also, there's a store, La Tienda, which is open during gallery hours and sells Mexican folk art, books, tapes, and jewelry.

African American Museum, *Building C of Fort Mason across from the Museo ItaloAmericano, 415-441-0640*, is open Tuesday-Sunday 11am-5pm, and costs $3 for adults and $2 for children (though the fees may be going up in summer to $5 and $3), and it includes a recorded tour. The exhibits are made possible by the African American Historical and Cultural Society; it takes about half an hour to see what they have, and it's all very interesting - a must if you're interested in African American history, and worth seeing for anyone who's just traipsing through Fort Mason.

The newest exhibit which is becoming part of their permanent collection is "Portraits in Black," and it focuses on the **Buffalo Soldiers**, a group of African-American soldiers and cowboys who fought for America from the 1860s-1920s (they were so named by American Indians for their courage and decency as warriors). They were recruited to fight in the Indian Wars, the Spanish American War (and charged with Teddy Roosevelt up San Juan Hill), on up through WWI. The photos of these African American soldiers and their families are from the private collection of author-historian Anthony L. Powell, whose grandfather took the pictures from the late 1880s to the late 1920s, providing rare and wonderful documentation of a hitherto neglected group.

Museo ItaloAmericano, *Building C of Fort Mason, 415-673-2200*, is open Wednesday-Sunday noon-5pm, and admission is $2 for adults and $1 for students and seniors. It's right across the hall from the African American Museum, and the appealing artwork should make for an interesting and pleasant 15-30 minutes. It's not necessarily worth making a special detour to visit, but it is worth looking through if you're wandering about in the Fort Mason complex, and they have a small but intriguing gift shop, too.

On the western side of the Marina is the **Presidio**, *framed by Lyon Street in the Marina, Pacific and Lake Streets to the south, the Pacific Ocean to the west, and the San Francisco Bay to the north*. It's vast and lovely, and unlike most of San Francisco, the Presidio is best explored by car, though bus lines 28, 29, 43, and 76 do go through. Spanish for *garrison*, the Presidio was the military outpost set up on Fort Point by Captain Juan Bautista de Anza in 1776. De Anza chose Fort Point for its strategic bay views, and the valuable land remained under military control from 1776-1994, though the national flag changed a few times (when Mexico gained independence from Spain in 1822, the Presidio became a Mexican fort, and it passed to United States hands when American troops usurped possession in 1846).

The fortifications were never required to defend the city from foreign attack; as is often the case, the blow came from within. Across the country, the US government has been closing military bases that are no longer deemed necessary for the country's defenses, and the Presidio was right up there on that list. So in 1994, the US. Sixth Army was out, and the Golden Gate National Recreation Area (GGNRA) acquired all 1,752 acres of beautiful land. Three years later it's all still in transition, as commissions listen to all the interest groups, and try to decide who and what will get to set up shop in the 1776 adobe Officers' Club. The Gorbachov Foundation already has an office there, a youth hostel idea is being bounced around, and all sorts of other tenants are being considered, as well as innovative concepts like instituting a water taxi system and restoring Lobos Creek.

NEW MUSEUM AGREEMENT

Just negotiated with the Presidio and the Fort Mason complex is an agreement to build a new museum space, large enough to accommodate big exhibits. The first to arrive will be from the Smithsonian Institution in Washington, and there are more lined up to follow. Call the Visitor's Information Center for pertinent details like new name, address, and phone number.

While the Presidio Project holds meetings, the park itself is open to the public, and there's lots of it. The bulk of the park is wild woodland, with acres and acres of pine trees and well-tended paths, perfect for a long hike or bike ride (one and a half miles of the 400 hundred mile Bay Area Ridge Trail are in the Presidio, and it's just been upgraded). Many just come for the natural scenery, but there are a few more structured sites, too. **The Presidio Visitor's Information Center**, *Building 102 on Montgomery Street (within the Presidio, not the street that runs through the Financial District), 415-561-4323*, is open daily 10am-5pm, and they can give you maps, advice, and show you their Presidio pictures.

Nearby is the **Presidio Museum**, *at Lincoln and Funston by the cannon, 415-561-4331*, which is open Wednesday-Sunday 10am-4pm, and admission is free. Built in 1857 as the military hospital, they have dioramas and exhibits on the early history of the Presidio (both archaeological and military), and they also have two Earthquake Huts out back, good examples of the temporary housing (numbering in the thousands) that went up all over the city to shelter the refugees of the 1906 quake (one of the photos shows rows and rows of these huts as they stood in Golden Gate Park and the Presidio).

The Fort Point National Historic Site, *at the base of Golden Gate Bridge, 415-556-1693*, is open Sunday-Wednesday 10am-5pm, and admission is free. It's a brick fortress that was completed in 1861 (against possible Confederate attack), and you can explore on your own, or join a ranger-led tour starting 11am and 3pm on weekends, and at 3pm only on weekdays. And while you're there, if you brought warm clothes you might take a walk across the bridge, too. The view from the middle of the span is mighty impressive, with San Francisco on one side, Marin on the other, water roiling below, and the fog billowing in.

Crissy Field is a beach and dune area along the northeast bay shore of the Presidio that's undergoing major renovations. It used to be the site for vast Independence Day celebrations, but for the new Presidio plan, 47 buildings have been razed, pavement has been removed, and while the final picture has not been decided on, lots of public access is guaranteed, and wetlands attracting heron and other water fowl (as it used to be before the landfill) is a serious possibility.

And on Crissy Field Avenue and McDowell Road (near the stables) is the **Pet Cemetery**. Behind the white picket fence lie the remains of many a cat, dog, and parakeet, buried under the evergreens. Around the point to the west of the bridge is **Baker's Beach**. Less readily accessible than Ocean Beach, it is by far the cleanest, prettiest beach this side of Marin. To get there, you need to drive along Lincoln Boulevard in the Presidio, looking carefully for Battery Chamberlin Road. Turn north toward the water, park the car in the lot, walk the path to the beach, apply sunscreen, and enjoy.

PRESIDIO GOLF COURSE

The Arnold Palmer Presidio Golf Course, 415-561-4653, is now open, for the first time ever, to the public. It was built in 1895, and is the second oldest course west of the Mississippi. The views of city and ocean are unbeatable, and the course itself is beautiful, with 160 acres full of cypress and eucalyptus and green, rolling hills. The course has just been renovated, and a new club house has just been built. It's a good idea to call and reserve, and the 18-hole green rates are $25 on weekdays, and $35 on the weekend. To get there by car, drive down Arguello, into the Presidio, to the golf course.

THE MISSION

The Mission now is alive with Latino culture and avant-garde artists, the cool club scene and a sizable homeless contingent, an unhealthy crime beat, and some of the best restaurants in San Francisco. It's history goes back to before colonization in the Bay Area, and it's changed its tune many times since then.

Chutchue was an Indian village west of what used to be Dolores Lagoon, inhabited by the area's Ohlone Indians. Then the Spanish arrived. Franciscan priest Pedro Font set up the Mission (now known as Mission Dolores) in March of 1776 in this sheltered, fertile valley by the stream they called *Arroyo de Nuestra Señora de Los Dolores* (it being the Friday before Palm Sunday, *Viernes de Dolores* in Spanish) as a center for religion and trade. Three months later Father Father Junipero Serra led the settlers in, and Father Palou celebrated the Mission's first Mass on June 29, 1776 (five days before the signing of the Declaration of Independence some 3,000 miles to the east). The mission controlled a lot of land,

and the forced labor of Native Americans (under the banner of teaching them religion and civilized ways) tended to the crops. In later years a Mexican farm, *Las Camaritas* (meaning The Cabins), was built up between Mission Dolores, Erie Creek, and Dolores Lagoon (what's now 16th Street, Folsom, 18th, and Mission). In the late 1800s and early 1900s, this was a sunny, rural neighborhood, filled with Irish and German settlers, and the site of **Woodward's Gardens**, *13th and Mission*, a verdant botanical garden with playground and zoo. Now one of the most densely populated districts, the neighborhood has returned to the Latinos, and the warm, sunny weather (the valley is protected from most of the city's fog) and abundance of palm trees add to the temperate tone.

Mission Street is the main artery, filled with buses and cars, two BART stations, taquerias and shops, disaffected youth sporting multiple body piercings, mothers with their children, and produce stores bursting with mangos, avocados, and chile peppers. Parallel and one block west, Valencia is the new hip location. Called New Bohemia by columnist Herb Caen, every time you turn around there's a new restaurant or club opening up, and it's already got the highest density of artists, neighborhood bars, coffee houses, avant-garde theaters, and book stores in the city. Many of the restaurants are top quality, and with prices a little lower than you might find elsewhere, and at night the music scene includes swing jazz, fusion eclectic jazz, blues, punk rock, and just about everything else.

Mission Dolores, *Dolores and 16th Street, 415-621-8203*, is open daily from 9am-4pm, and admission is $1. This is the place founded by Fathers Font, Serra, andPalou, the sixth of Serra's string of 21 missions. Originally called *Mission San Francisco de Assisi*, work on the adobe construction began in 1782 and was completed in 1791 by a team of unhappy Native Americans. The roof tiles and adobe bricks were all made on site, and no nails were used to secure the beams (pegs and leather thongs were used instead), but many of the decorations came from Spain via Mexico. They have a small museum, and a cemetery of more than 5,000 Native Americans (many of the deaths were a result of measles that decimated the slave-laborers). One of two remaining early cemeteries (all but this one and the Presidio's were removed in 1914), it's an interesting place to see some history, including the graves of those lynched in the mid-1800s by the Committee of Vigilance.

Next door is the 1913 **Basilica of San Francisco**, where most of the masses are held. Done in ornate Spanish Colonial style, it forms quite a contrast with the quieter, more modest Mission.

Latino art is booming in the Mission. **Galeria de la Raza**, *2855 24th Street, 415-826-80019*, exhibits lots of local and international artists, and the **Studio 24 Galeria** shop sells Latin American crafts. They specialize in the *Dia de los Muertos* masks and figures around Halloween time, but they are open and interesting year round. There's also a lot of street art, murals, and lovely blue sidewalk tiles adding to the color of the neighborhood. The **Precita Eyes Mural Arts Center**, *348 Precita, 415-285-2287*, gives guided walks of the Mission's murals every Saturday at 1:30pm for $3 per adult and $1 for students under 18.

FEMINIST VALENCIA

There's a decidedly radical, feminist (both lesbian and straight) tone to the neighborhood, with a fine alternative movie theater, **The Roxie**, *3117 16th Street, 415-863-1087, and a number of good fringe theaters.* **Modern Times Bookstore**, *888 Valencia, 415-282-9246, has a well-stocked leftist selection, and* **Old Wives' Tales Bookstore**, *1009 Valencia, 415-821-4675, is a feminist Mecca.* **Good Vibrations**, *1210 Valencia, 415-974-8980, is a feminist sex store with an antique vibrator museum, and the* **Women's Building of the Bay Area**, *3543 18th Street, 415-974-8980, hosts workshops, conferences, and readings by writers such as Alice Walker and Angela Davis.* **The Bearded Lady Women's Cafe**, *485 14th Street near Valencia, 415-626-2805, will put the espresso spark back in your blood after you have relaxed at* **Osento**, *955 Valencia, 415-282-6333, a women's bathhouse with steam rooms, hot tubs, and massage.*

NOB HILL

Shortened from "Nabob Hill" after the newly rich gold rush **Big Four** who built their mansions and townhouses here. It should have been named after Andrew Hallidie, though, because it was his invention of the cable car that made the 376 foot hill accessible in 1873. Charles Crocker, Mark Hopkins, Leland Stanford, and Collis Huntington deserted the previously popular Rincon Hill area south of Market, and bought up lots at the peak of the hill, where California intersects Taylor by what's now Huntington Park. Those men are long gone, but their names still rule the hill, gracing the poshest of hotels. As popular as this hill once was as an address for those with money, Nob Hill has retained its cachet as the king of the San Francisco traditional luxury hotel.

The hotels remain, but the original buildings, for the most part, were reduced to cinders by the 1906 earthquake and fire. The shell of one survived, and James Flood spent $1.5 million to rebuild the Flood mansion, *1000 California Street*. The **Pacific Union Club** bought it in 1909, and it is still, today, an exclusive club for the wealthy.

Grace Cathedral, *1051 Taylor and California, 415-776-6611*, dominates the hill grandly, but it doesn't date back any further than 1964. It's endowed with historic touches, however, like the main doors, cast from Ghilberti's original "Doors of Paradise" in Florence. Built on the site of the Crocker mansion, it took 53 years to complete.

THE MONEY THAT POURED INTO NOB HILL

*The **Bonanza Kings** were a partnership of four poor Irishmen: James Flood, William O'Brien, John Mackay, and James Fair. They made a fortune on some shrewdly purchased mining stock. With this money they bought up lots of small claims, and patched them together into their one big Consolidated Virginia mine. In 1873 miners struck the "Big Bonanza," a huge mass of silver worth more than $100 million. The four partners became the richest men in California. These men built elaborate, extravagant mansions on Nob Hill, and breathed the rarefied air of the very wealthy. The Fairmont Hotel went up on land purchased by Fair, built by his daughters, and named in his honor, and the Flood Mansion is now the Pacific Union Club.*

*Another famous foursome were the **Big Four**. The transcontinental railway changed the face of the west, and the four merchants who coughed up the capital to found the Central Pacific Railroad (renamed the Southern Pacific in 1884) were **Charles Crocker, Mark Hopkins, Collis P. Huntington**, and **Leland Stanford**, names that are now an integral part of the Bay Area, with banks, hotels, and universities named after them. The first track work began in 1863, and six years, many sticks of dynamite, and lots of back-breaking labor later, the Union Pacific and Central Pacific lines met in Promontory, Utah, and the golden spike was driven to signify the link-up of east and west.*

The top of the hill at Mason is quite the intersection, with the **Mark Hopkins Hotel** at Mason and California to the south, the **Fairmont** to the west, and a private apartment building where Alfred Hitchcock filmed *Vertigo* in 1958 (across the street from the Fairmont at Sacramento).

NOE VALLEY

A sunny, pretty community that carries over some of the progressive vibes from the nearby Castro and Mission, without the sexual preference of the one or the ethnic preponderance of the other. It was settled in the late 1800s by successful working class folk, taking over the slopes that were once grazing land for a herd of goats, back when the place was known as Nanny Goat Hill. Named after José de Jesus Noé, the last Mexican alcalde in 1846, the neighborhood is west of the Mission, north of Diamond Heights, east of the Castro, and south of Eureka Valley, and the major thoroughfares are 24th Street, Noe, and Sanchez.

Baby boomer couples and small families flock to the small one and two family Victorian houses built years ago, and for a while the rents weren't that high since it's a neighborhood without a single bay view. It's a very residential community, full of good restaurants, cafes, easy-wear clothing boutiques, music shops, and book stores (such as the Mystery Bookstore, *746 Diamond*), the sorts of enterprises valued by the small working families who live there.

This is a place to visit if you feel like wandering. No tour buses come through here, and the air is casual, genial, a little self-congratulating, but very pleasant.

NORTH BEACH

North Beach is truly one of the most delightful, cosmopolitan neighborhoods in San Francisco. It's got everything you could desire - superb restaurants, cafes, book stores, night life, public transport, and streets that call out to be explored. The one thing it doesn't have is an abundance of parking spots, and that's because its appeal is no hidden gem. San Franciscans visit, East Bay suburbanites visit, Europeans and Asians visit, and Americans from across the country visit. It's a joy to sit at one of the many fine cafes sipping cappuccino, watching the crowds swish by, and listening to Italian, English, Chinese, German, Russian, Spanish, and French music and language at the same time.

North Beach started as an Italian enclave of fishermen in the 1800s, and the Italian flavor is still very much present in the endless Italian restaurants, the Italian coffee and pastries available at every cafe, the Italian delis selling provolone and prosciutto and homemade sausage and ravioli, and the older Italian generation passing the day in the old gathering spots, still speaking Italian. However, the character of the neighborhood is also deeply entwined with a bohemian, artistic image.

In the 1800s, Mark Twain and Bret Harte hung out here, followed by the Beatniks of the 1950s, who called North Beach their home (such as Allan Ginsberg who read *Howl* for the first time in 1956, resulting in a circus of an obscenity trial). Early comedy houses (like the Hungry i, which has now turned to sex shows) hosted Lenny Bruce and a young, terrified Woody Allen, and these days it's not uncommon to see writers furiously pounding away at laptop computers in the local cafes. Bookstores, poets, and coffee house intellectuals are nearly as plentiful as the cannoli, and alleys all over the neighborhood (such as Ferlinghetti Way, Turk Murphy, Kerouac) have been renamed to honor the writers, artists, and musicians who've lived here. There was a time when rents in North Beach were very, very low - a time that invited poor Beatniks to pitch camp. That time is long gone, however, and today's bohemian needs a sizable bankroll or a good job to afford the inflated rents.

The third major element in North Beach is good old-fashioned sleaze. Carol Doda started the striptease here with her big silicon bosom in 1964 at the Condor Club (now an upscale bistro with nothing more racy than a painted outline of her famous piano that used to go up and down while dancers strutted their stuff on it - even the neon sign outside that announced the Condor Club with flashing red nipples is gone). Broadway was and is still the main drag for girlie peep-shows (sailors from around the world throng the bars during Fleet Week), and signs promising "Live Nude Girls" flash on either side of the avenue.

Despite all this, North Beach continues to be a place where women can walk comfortably at night. There are usually people around, and the air doesn't feel menacing. Poetry rooms, jazz clubs, and elegant restaurants coexist peacefully with the skin dives, and no one gets too worked up over it. People get more upset about the throngs of panhandling homeless people than about the sex shows.

NORTH BEACH ROOTS

Back in the 1800s, the northeastern point of land was at North Point, roughly at the intersection of today's North Point and Grant. As early as the 1850s, people were thinking the city would grow in this direction; Alderman Meiggs put in a road around the eastern bend of Telegraph Hill, filled in some of the marsh, and built a 1,600-foot wharf off Powell and Francisco (where the bay started back then). Meiggs ran into some financial difficulties, forged his way through it, and took off to Peru when his creative financing came to light, but the wharf stayed for a while. A precursor to Fisherman's Wharf, it was a combination dock, restaurant, bar, and amusement park. Abe Warner ran the Cobweb Palace, a bar decorated with tropical parrots, wild monkeys, and cobwebs that, out of superstition, Warner wouldn't clean.

Nearby was an educated pig who'd play cards with customers, and a seafood joint serving unlimited crab legs with a nickel's worth of beer. The fishermen, however, were all in North Beach, hauling fish off the Green, Union, and Filbert wharves. By the 1880s, a powerful Fishermen's Association had grown from the handful of Italian fisherman who started out 30 years before. Round about 50,000 pounds of fish were being sold daily in San Francisco from the docksides in "Italy Harbor," while small double-ended feluccas with lateen-rigged sails plied the waters. Crabbing was also fruitful; as early as 1887 they were pulling in close to 300,000 crabs. In 1900, however, the state Fish and Game Commission ordered the fishermen to move to what's now Fisherman's Wharf. The pescatori were not very happy, since the new harbor offered not nearly as much shelter; not till 1926 when the Hyde Street Pier and Pier 45 were completed did the situation improve.

*To learn more North Beach history, try the **North Beach Museum**, 1435 Stockton, on the mezzanine of the Eureka Bank. It's open Monday-Friday 9am-4pm, and admission is free.*

Washington Square at Union and Columbus is at the heart of North Beach in the same way that piazzas are central in Italian towns. It was given to the city in 1852 by Mayor John White Geary when he returned to his native Pennsylvania, but it wasn't a very nice place at the time (it was used as a dump, and later as a graveyard). But when Columbus Avenue was cut through the grid in 1872, the graves had been moved and the place cleaned up a bit. They planted some greenery, put a white fence picket around it, and made it part of the community (in a different way than a dump or a graveyard is).

Dr. Henry Cogswell donated the Benjamin Franklin statue and water fountain in 1904, as part of his well-meant but doomed-to-failure attempt to construct at least one water fountain for every hundred bars in San Francisco. The other statue, from Lillie Hitchcock Coit to the firefighters of San Francisco, is more in keeping with the spirit of North Beach. Mornings now in Washington Square find scores of senior citizens practicing tai chi, while sunny afternoons see clusters of properly dressed Italian gentlemen sitting on benches discussing the world, and legions of sun-worshippers, reading or taking a nap under the shadow of the **Cathedral of Saints Peter and Paul**. Built in 1924, the 191 foot twin white spires of the Romanesque church add to the European feel, and most of the masses are still said in Italian, though a Sunday mass is in Chinese for the local Chinese contingent.

Not far away, there's another church, **Saint Francis of Assisi**, *610 Vallejo at Columbus*. It closed a few years ago and is no longer open to the public, but this was the first San Francisco parish church named after the city's patron saint. It was established in 1849, but the wood church burned down in the 1906 earthquake, and the new structure was built up shortly thereafter.

Most of what there is to do in North Beach involves eating, drinking, or being entertained. It's a place to hang out, walk, mosey around, poke about, and think about eating again. The *Where to Eat* chapter describes many, many North Beach restaurants, and ditto the *Nightlife* chapter for music venues. Daytime activities (aside from eating - don't forget to eat) center more on the cafes and book stores. **City Lights**, *261 Columbus*, opened by Ferlinghetti in 1953 is still a haven for the literati, with poetry readings, and shelves and shelves of books.

Vesuvio's next door is another swell place that also happens to have a long history, and you're as welcome here to read a book or play chess while you drink as you are to make small talk at the bar. **Columbus** is the main commercial avenue, slanting across from Fisherman's Wharf towards the Financial District. **Grant Avenue**, two blocks east of Washington Square is the oldest street in San Francisco (it used to be called Dupont), and it's great to walk down, looking at the boutiques and restaurants. And then there's Broadway, sleaze-city, but with a fine used book store, **Columbus Books**, *540 Broadway*.

PACIFIC HEIGHTS

The highest point in Pacific Heights, 378 feet at the top of **Lafayette Park**, bordered by Laguna, Sacramento, Washington, and Gough streets, commands a fabulous view of the Bay. This goes a long way towards explaining the exclusiveness of the address and the prices asked by the great mansions with their widows walks, and the sumptuously refurbished Victorian town houses. The northern and southern slopes are equally posh, however, with fine dining and chic shops. All told, the neighborhood goes from Vallejo in the north to California in the south, Van Ness in the east to Presidio in the west, with the elite still maintaining distinctions between the Heights and Lower Pacific Heights.

The city's wealthy divide their addresses between Pacific Heights and Seacliff. Former California Governor Jerry Brown lives in Pacific Heights, as does former San Francisco mayor Frank Jordan, Gordon and Ann Getty, romance writer Danielle Steele, and singer Linda Rondstadt. Robin Williams and his family, on the other hand, reside in a Seacliff mansion.

The Pacific Heights of the late 1800s had a distinctly different flavor from the posh district today, owing in part to its flourishing hog farms at the northern end of Laguna and near the foot of Octavia. Hog calls mingled with fog calls until an 1891 ordinance prohibited keeping swine or more than two cows north of Golden Gate Park. The area grew more attractive to the rich after the livestock moved off, but the 1906 quake and fire really helped raise the value of Pacific Heights real estate. The fire that surged westward from downtown halted at Van Ness. To help maintain the fire line, Commander Funston dynamited the luxurious homes all along Van Ness. The fire stayed put and died down though thanks more, historians believe, to a shift in the wind than to the demolitions. Regardless of who was right, the rich still needed to find new homes, and they moved westward to the char-free hill above the Bay.

Even if you're not in the market for a seaview mansion, Pacific Heights is lovely to walk around, window shopping for grand houses and fashionable clothes. Broadway, Jackson, Washington, and Laguna make

PACIFIC HEIGHTS STEPS

The Pacific Heights hill begins its descent to the Marina at Broadway. Broadway to Vallejo to Green is quite a steep hill, and the steps from Vallejo to Green, built into the sidewalk in 1915 for the Exposition, number 197.

for great residence ogling, while Fillmore from Pacific to California (known as Lower Pacific Heights) is the street for shops and restaurants. At *2222 Broadway* is a mansion built by **James Flood**, Comstock lode millionaire, and at *2080 Washington on Lafayette Park* is the **Spreckels Mansion**. Alma Spreckels was so pleased with the job done by George Applegarth that she had him design the California Palace of the Legion of Honor in Lincoln Park, too. Applegarth's work testify to his artistic skill, but Alma is commemorated too; she's the model for the bronze figure on the Victory Monument in Union Square.

A couple blocks away is the **Haas-Lilienthal Victorian**, *2007 Franklin*, which was built in 1886 for $18,000, and you can have a tour for $4 per adult and $2 per senior and child. The **Octagon House**, *2645 Gough near Union, 415-441-7512*, is an unusual, eight-sided home (it was thought to bring good luck) built in the mid-1800s. Full of excellently preserved antique furniture, it's open February-December on the second Sunday and second and fourth Thursday of each month from noon-3pm, and admission is free.

You can tour these as well as the rest the great houses of Pacific Heights by contacting **Pacific Heights Tours**, *415-441-3004*. They cost $3 per adult, and $1 per senior and child, while the Haas-Lilienthal house charges its own admission

RICHMOND

South of the Presidio and north of Golden Gate Park, the Richmond extends all the way west from Arguello to the ocean. It used to be known as The Great Sand Waste, but nowadays it's more a new and busy Chinatown than a waste of any sort. Divided into Inner and Outer Richmond, with the fuzzy dividing line somewhere around 14th Avenue. This neighborhood is unlike most of San Francisco. The land is mostly flat (it was dunes once, remember), and most of the streets are laid out in an orderly, easily learned grid.

From Arguello in the east, the avenues (not to be confused with the numerical streets south of Market) progress numerically from 1-48 out near the Pacific, while the streets running north-south are named alphabetically, starting with Anza and progressing up to Yorba in the Sunset. It's a large residential sprawl, with one and two family homes more easily affordable than in, say, Pacific Heights or Russian Hill, and the area is full of families, predominantly of Asian descent, though there's a growing pocket of Russian immigrants putting down roots around Balboa.

The fog is the major drawback. Without hills to impede its progress, when the fog moves in off the coast, it quickly blankets the whole neighborhood, so summer in the Richmond can be a bit bleak if you like the sun. With all the great restaurants and cafes on Clement Street, however, you might not even notice. There's Chinese and Vietnamese, Japanese and Thai, Malaysian and Singaporean, French and Italian, Russian and American. It's a great neighborhood for eating. And they have one of the best used book stores in the city, the **Green Apple**, *506 Clement near 6th, 415-387-2272.*

About eight blocks northeast is **Temple Emanu-El**, *Arguello and Lake, 415-751-2535,* San Francisco's oldest and largest synagogue, and it's open to visitors Monday-Friday 3-5pm, free of charge. The congregation itself dates from 1851, but this cream-colored, red-domed Roman-Byzantine temple (the congregation's third) was designed by Bakewell & Brown in 1925. Inside, there are classrooms and courtyards, and decoration rich in Jewish symbolism.

While Clement Street in the Inner Richmond is great for walking and browsing and dining, most of the sights are out by the ocean.

Adolph Sutro, mayor from 1895-1897, added a lot to San Francisco in the way of elegance, beauty, and recreation. A German immigrant who made his fortune at Comstock with his superior drainage tunnels, he invested heavily in Ocean Beach property. He was thought a fool to pour good money into a mound of sand, but his engineering skills and far-seeing visions turned his sandlot into one of the grandest spots in San Francisco. He built himself a home overlooking the dunes and sea, and installed life-size copies of Greek and Roman statues throughout his property. He also built a magnificent **Cliff House**, patterned after the castles of his childhood. It survived the quake and fires of 1906, but burned in its own, separate fire in 1907.

There were Cliff Houses before and after, but the **Sutro Baths** were unique. They opened in 1896 at a time when public bathhouses were popular, and they were the largest of the kind in the world. Sutro designed seven swimming pools (six salt water and one fresh water), and had 500 dressing rooms. All in all, with its multiple levels, galleries, promenades, and two-acre roof of 100,000 panes of glass, the glorious complex could accommodate more than 20,000 people at a time.

A narrow gauge train trundled visitors to the baths, and they were very popular. But times changed, and by 1954 the low attendance didn't justify the required repairs, and it closed. In 1966, the building was demolished, and a fire polished it off. All that remains now are the foundations out by Point Lobos, and the still-popular Sutro Bath picture depicting the interior full of swimmers and spectators. There is a Cliff House now where Sutro's once stood. It's a pricy restaurant with okay food and sensational views, but for a lot of people it serves mostly as a landmark.

Musée Mécanique, *1090 Point Lobos beneath the Cliff House, 415-386-1170*, is open Monday-Friday 11am-7pm and Saturday-Sunday 10am-

8pm. Admission is free, but the many magnificent antique toys, player pianos, and assorted other mechanisms operate on quarters and dimes (don't worry, there's a modern machine there that gives change). It's one of my favorite amusement spots in the city, and its beautiful setting overlooking the Pacific and Seal Rock is just gravy.

Inside this tiny museum is a vast collection of all manner of coin-operated historic pleasures, from the six-foot, red-haired "Laughing Sal" who bellows gales of laughter on your two quarters to old pin-ball foosball games. Fortune-teller machines rate your sex-quotient or type out your fortune, strongman devices test (and belittle) your strength, the Mechanical Carnival sets hundreds of little figures into motion, and the cheerfully tinny sounds of player piano, snare drums, flutes, and xylophones fill the room. There are modern video games in the back and they always have a flock of young devotees uninterested in yesteryear's versions. There is even one of the city's three remaining black-and-white instant photo booths, which delivers a strip of four pictures for just $2. It's a fun place to come with or without kids.

Across from the Musée is a **GGNRA Visitors Center**, *415-556-8642*, which is open daily 10am-4:30pm. They have a good selection of books on local flora and fauna (especially the birds and the seals), and an interesting collection of pictures showing the Cliff House and area through the years.

Also on the same level is the **Camera Obscura**, *415-750-0415*. Open daily (unless fog or rain ruins the view) 11am-sundown and costing $1, this giant eye on the world is far more enjoyable than you might think. Constructed in the 1800s, a panoramic view of the ever-changing, ever-fascinating warp and weave of the ocean is portrayed (using a mirror and two lenses, magnified seven times) on a 5-foot curved table in a dark room. The effect is quite spectacular.

Lincoln Park begins on its eastern side where 33rd Avenue meets the Pacific, and curves around the point to the west where Anza reaches water. Lincoln Park has glorious vistas, wind and fog and a public golf course, and the magnificent California Palace of the Legion of Honor. The 270-acre park is a wonderful place to hike, and take in the power of the Pacific. There are paths all over but wear good shoes if you choose to go out on the point, because some of the paths have a lot of loose gravel.

Up past the Cliff House is **Lands End**, a prominent headlands bluff in Lincoln Park. Named in 1827 after the well-known English headlands, it's had other names as well. The Spanish called it Punta Angel de la Guarda (Guardian Angel Point), and it was also known Point Lobos, but that name is now reserved just for the point itself. Lands End Beach (also called Miles Rock) is to the west of Lands End. In the 19th century it was a picnic spot, but it's now a clothing-optional beach.

The California Palace of the Legion of Honor, *Lincoln Park at 34th and Clement. 415-863-3330.* Open Tuesday-Sunday 10am-4:45pm and admission is $6 for adults, $4 for seniors, and $3 for youth. The museum stays open the first Saturday of the month till 8:45, and admission is free the second Wednesday of the month. Also, same-day admission is good at the Asian Art Museum and the de Young Museum with your ticket stub, and you can visit the Legion of Honor if you've already paid admission to the other museums.

It was closed from 1992-1995 for seismic renovations, but it re-opened to great fanfare, and is now a great jewel of a museum, with lighting and new paint that perfectly complement the exhibits. Modeled after the 18th century Parisian Legion of Honor, its location couldn't be more striking as it sits up on the cliffs overlooking the ocean and bridge. The museum is a result of Alma Spreckels' dream and Adolph Spreckels' money. She wanted a museum devoted to French art, and he spent one million or so to make it happen. WWI interrupted the construction, but Alma kept the momentum going, adding the memorial for Californians killed in the war to her original concept. It opened in 1924, filled with art works that Alma bought and brought back from Europe.

Their permanent collection of ancient and European art spans 4,000 years, with lots of paintings, porcelain, tapestries, and drawings, plus the wonderful Spreckels Rodin sculpture collection, with more than 70 pieces, including "The Thinker," one of five original castings. Along with Rodin, there are works by Degas, Renoir, Monet, El Greco, Rembrandt, Seurat, and lots more. Everything about the place is lovely, and it's well worth a visit.

If you want to see more of what old San Francisco money wrought, go east a few blocks to the small, elite **Seacliff** neighborhood. Located by the water between what would be 28th and 30th Avenues (if they extended that far north), these quiet, shaded streets hold a fabulous number of palatial abodes, including the mansion Robin Williams and family live in. A section just gave way into a massive sink hole during a winter storm, but reparations are nearly completed.

Stretching along the west coast from Lincoln Park south is **Ocean Beach**. It isn't the nicest of beaches (pristine it is not, and it's rarely very warm), but it is the most accessible. You can get there by public transport, and it's pleasant to walk along the embankment or on the beach. There are always wet-suited surfers braving the cold and riding the pathetic swells, and the vast vista of the Pacific never fails to be grand. If you have a car and want beautiful dunes, head south up **The Great Highway** to **Fort Funston** (near Lake Merced) to the big parking lot. It's a huge area where dogs can run free. You can picnic in the ice plant-festooned dunes, and watch the hang-gliders launch themselves from the cliff.

RUSSIAN HILL

Named after an old Russian seal hunting colony and their burial ground on its slopes, the hill is 294 feet high, with swell views of the bay, the bridges, and the rest of the city. The peak is up on Jones and Vallejo, but the neighborhood loosely encompasses the area between Taylor to the east and Van Ness to the west, Bay to the north and Jackson to the south. It's an attractive, steeply hilly place, with lots of homes and apartment buildings, and not a lot going on.

The tip top of Russian Hill (along Green and Vallejo between Jones and Leavenworth, for example) has some gorgeous mansions, and there are lots of small lanes criss-crossing the main streets. The residents are an eclectic mix of old money and new immigrants, of mostly Anglo-Saxon or Chinese background, with a healthy sprinkling of lawyers, stockbrokers, and advertising executives, but Russian Hill had been home to writers, artists, and singers for a long time, and it still is. In the 1890s, bohemian writers and artists such as Charles Norris, Maynard Dixon, and George Sterling lived here, and later on, Fanny Osbourne Stevenson, the beloved widow of Robert Louis Stevenson, returned to San Francisco after her husband's death, and had architect Willis Polk build her a house at 1100 Lombard (at the top of the crooked street) in 1900 (a dedicated group managed to save it from the fire in 1906).

Some buses come through Russian Hill (the 19, 27, 12, 83, and 45) but the Hyde Street cable car is probably the most popular route, taking you from Union Square to Aquatic Park via Russian Hill. If you're driving, be aware that Russian Hill parking is horrendous, and the steep descents over sharp precipices are fine on your car (if the brakes are good) but they turn brave tourists' knees to jelly. Leavenworth is one way going north and Jones is one way going south, and Union and Pacific are the best streets to take if you're driving east or west (many of the others dead-end in stairways if you're going east to North Beach). If you're on foot, the descents are no less steep, but you can take it any speed you want.

Two stairways link Russian Hill and North Beach, steep and beautiful routes that pass through terraced green gardens. The **Green Street Steps** number 127; they connect Taylor to Jones and are the easier of the two. The **Vallejo Steps** have 250 to their credit, with a few stepless inclines thrown in; they go from Jones to halfway between Taylor and Mason (they're in two segments, and you have to cross Taylor to continue), are by far the more strenuous, and also the lusher and more beautiful, going as they do via **Ina Coolbrith Park** (named after the fascinating woman who worked on the newspaper with Bret Harte and Mark Twain, and later, as Oakland librarian, introduced both Jack London and Isadora Duncan to the world of books). They are, however, just as lovely coming down as going up if you don't feel your legs are in shape for a major haul.

Polk Street is the main commercial strip, and it's chock-a-block with coffee houses and video rentals, organic produce markets and a multitude of ethnic eateries. There are also a number of singles bars that get jam packed nightly. It's a great place to go for picnic supplies, what with the Real Food Deli on Polk and Vallejo, the Cheese store on Polk and Pacific, and the Jug Shop on Pacific on the other side of Polk.

The most popular site in Russian Hill (if not the whole city) is the zig-zagging block of **Lombard**, *between Hyde and Leavenworth*, called "the crookedest street in the world" (incorrectly - there's a more crooked one, Vermont Street between 20th and 22nd in Potrero Hill). It must be a nightmare to live there, what with the non-stop traffic that daily clogs the wiggly lane. The terraced gardens and well-kept buildings are beautiful, as are the views, but we recommend a walk rather than a drive down.

For a less populated walk, find **Macondray Lane**, *off Leavenworth between Union and Green*. It's a lovely cobbled pedestrian path through gardens and Edwardian homes that ends in a stairway heading down to Taylor. It's just about as romantic and pretty as a public lane can be.

The S. F. Art Institute, *800 Chestnut near Jones, 415-771-7020*, is a fine art school with a striking tower, a steep hill to climb, Italianate architecture, Diego Rivera murals, a nice cafe, and fantastic views. There are no tours or fees, and you're free to wander and enjoy. The Russian Hill campus was built after their Nob Hill Mark Hopkins mansion was burned in 1906, but they got their start as an art institute in 1871, and they have figured strongly in the art scene ever since.

SOUTH OF MARKET - SOMA

Known as **SoMa** for short, it's the sprawling, industrial region stretching from the Bay to the Mission, full of warehouses and lofts, discount outlets and convention centers, museums and trendy restaurants, gay bars, and a zillion dance clubs. This is one area that's not very pleasant to walk around in. There are no hills with great views, few charming Victorians, and no quiet, tree-lined residential streets. What you've got are a lot of four-lane avenues loud with fast traffic, smelly with exhaust fumes, as cars whiz off the freeway ramps. Center for the Arts provides a welcome respite with its landscaped gardens, waterfalls, and lawns, the museums are worth exploring, and the restaurants are worth the special trip, but it's best to come by car, bus, or taxi, and plan your route so you don't need to travel far by foot. At night, if you want to dance this is the liveliest district in town, but it's not the safest. It's best to take a cab, drive, or go with a group.

Its tone has changed over the years. In the early days of the Gold Rush, miners set up tent communities that lasted for years. There were posh pockets (Rincon Hill, South Park) where the newly rich lived in the mid

1800s, but these went out of style when the cable cars made Nob Hill accessible and popular. There used to be farms and tanneries, and lots of new immigrants, till the quake and fire of 1906 obliterated the place. Industry built up from the rubble and ash, and the space was home to factories and warehouses into the 1950s.

Then, as in New York and London, artists and poor college grads were attracted to the cheap rents and loft appeal, and a new element began to grow. South of Market now, residentially speaking, is an interesting mix of artists, architects, Asian immigrants (there are large Vietnamese and Filipino communities here), prostitutes, and homeless. To the west, the streets have a slum-like feel, and the area around Sixth and Seventh near Market is decidedly trashy, while the further east you go, toward the Bay, the more the Financial District begins to assert its voice.

Full of good places to eat, and a growing museum neighborhood, South of Market provides a window on the cutting edge of San Francisco trends and art scene.

Center for the Arts, *701 Mission near Third, 415-978-2787*, in **Yerba Buena Gardens**, is a beauty. A peaceful haven from the traffic and noise, the five and a half acre park that opened in 1993 to rave reviews has lovely gardens, slick fountains, cafes, and lots of museums, film, theaters (for film, dance, and plays), galleries, lectures, and musical performances. There is also plenty of garage parking nearby, though it's an easy walk from bus and BART depots. Center for the Arts attracts new exhibits, multi-cultural productions, and modern dance, as well as more traditional entertainment like chamber music and the San Francisco ballet.

There are also dance festivals, such as the **Edge Festival** in March exhibiting what's new in choreography, and the **Ethnic Dance Festival** in early June. The program is varied, interesting, and it changes all the time. Your best bet is to call ahead for their bi-monthly program, or when you arrive for their current shows (or, if you have on-line access, you can email them at: yerbabuena@aol.com or check the web page at: http://www.hia.com/hia/yerbabuena).

Moscone Convention Center, *747 Howard between Third and Fourth, 415-974-4000*, was the first part of the Yerba Buena complex to be completed, but it holds most interest for convention groups. It's immense - the largest site of the kind in the city - and it attracts all sorts of large gatherings. The Democratic convention was held here in 1984, and MacWorld hosts its computer extravaganza here yearly. If you're just seeing the sights, however, there's no reason to visit Moscone, unless there's a convention to your liking.

The **San Francisco Museum of Modern Art**, *151 Third near Mission, 415-357-4000*, better known as SFMOMA, is new and sleek and a fine addition to the Center for the Arts. It's open daily 11am-6pm, and it stays

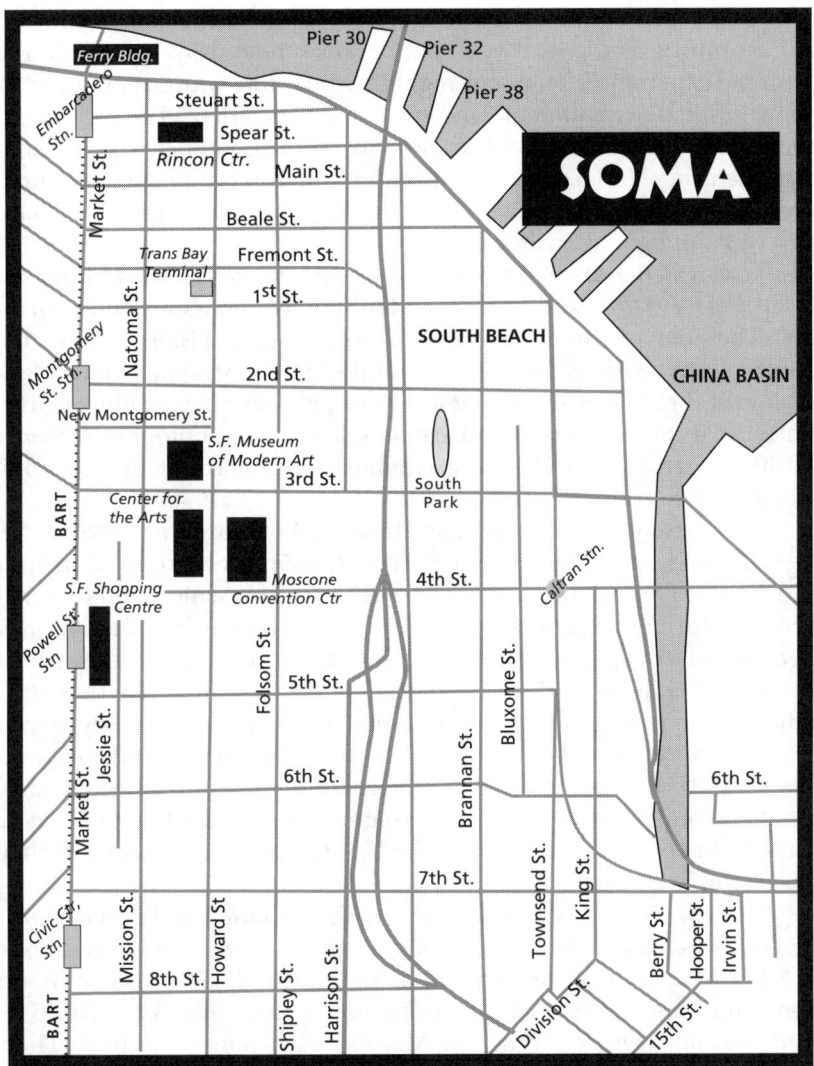

open Thursdays till 9pm. Admission is $7 for adults, $3.50 for senior citizens and students over 12; it's free to all the first Tuesday of each month, and half-priced the third Thursday of the month from 6-9pm. There are parking garages all around, but it's easy to get to from the Powell BART station and a multitude of bus lines. In the fine tradition of San Francisco buildings, the new site for SFMOMA is controversial.

Designed by Mario Botta and completed in January of 1995, some love the Modernist lines, brick facade, and interior atrium, while others complain it's the ugliest monolith ever. Go, enjoy, and decide for yourself, but avoid free Tuesday, if you can, because the crowds greatly detract from the experience. Thursday nights are busy too, with a reputation for being a fine place to mingle and meet and find a date. The exhibits, of course, change all the time, but they have some good permanent shows like "Picturing Modernity: Photographs From the Permanent Collection" and "From Matisse to Diebenkorn: Works From the Permanent Collection of Painting and Sculpture."

Nearby is the **Ansel Adams Center**, *250 Fourth between Howard and Folsom, 415-495-7000.* It's open Tuesday-Sunday 11am-5pm, and 8pm the first Thursday of the month, and on Saturdays at 11:30am they offer docent tours. Admission is $4 for adults, $3 for students, and $2 for seniors and children 13-17. Dedicated to photography, exhibits feature Ansel Adams memorabilia and artifacts, landscape photography from a wealth of artists, and changing exhibits on all sorts of photographic themes.

Not far away is the **Cartoon Art Museum**, *814 Mission near 4th and 5th, 415-227-8666.* Open Wednesday-Friday 11am-5pm, Saturday 10am-5pm, and Sunday 1-5pm, admission is $4 for adults, $3 for seniors and students, $2 for children 6-12, and free for all the first Wednesday of the month. Dedicated to the preservation of cartoon art in all its forms, they have a permanent collection with 11,000 original pieces from which they stage exhibits that change every few months. Starting in 1984, they were a "museum without walls," finding space in local museums and corporate lots. In 1987, Charles M. Schulz (of *Peanuts* fame) set up an endowment for them, and they set up their museum in the Yerba Buena Gardens center. One of three museums in the U.S. focusing on cartoon art, their five rooms are worth viewing.

Close to the foot of Market, the **Jewish Museum San Francisco**, *121 Steuart, between Mission and Howard, and near the Embarcadero Bart station, 415-543-8880,* is open Sunday 11am-6pm, Monday-Wednesday noon-6pm, and Thursday noon-8pm . Admission is $3 for adults and $1.50 for students and seniors, but the first Monday of each month is free. There are docent tours each Sunday at 2pm and Thursday at 6:30pm, and the gift shop is open during gallery hours.

The museum's exhibits are always changing, but the theme is always Jewish, and they're generally very interesting, and well-displayed. They have shown a photographic history of the Warsaw Ghetto, a collection of Hanukkah menorahs from around the world, and paintings from modern Bay Area artists, to name a few. Give them a call to see what's on during your visit.

Aside from Museum Central, most people visit SoMa for the restaurants and clubs, so check the *Where To Eat* and *Nightlife* chapters for the descriptions and reviews.

SUNSET

This massive residential sector of San Francisco goes from Stanyan in the east to the Pacific in the west, from Golden Gate Park in the north to Daly City in the south. Mostly quiet, fog-bound streets with one and two family homes, there's not that much here to interest a tourist. There's a lively section in the northeast, known as the Inner Sunset, near the UCSF campus, the park, and Haight Ashbury, that can be fun to wander. Full of cafes and shops and restaurants, it caters to the medical staff, and the young families and professionals that live nearby. The Outer Sunset, however, is less intriguing, aside from the zoo and Stern Grove.

The **San Francisco Zoo**, *on Sloat near 45th Avenue (not far from the ocean), 415-753-7061 for information, 415-753-7083 for recording*, is open daily from 10m-5pm, 365 days a year. Adult admission is $7, it's $3.50 for youth aged 12-15 and for seniors, and $1.50 for children aged 3-11. If you want to be there for the feedings, come mid-day. The big cats are fed Tuesday-Sunday at 2pm in the Lion House, and the penguins are fed daily at 3pm. This is a lovely zoo, especially on rare days when the sun is shining in the Outer Sunset. It was first opened in 1929, and was gradually developed with WPA funds. After going mostly private a few years ago, the zoo finally had enough money to renovate, and new animal structures have been built to simulate the natural habitat as much as possible, making it more pleasant for the animals, and more interesting for the visitor, too.

The **Children's Zoo** (open 10am-4pm) has a number of programs to get up-close and personal with the animals. There's the Insect Zoo (with great hissing cockroaches), the Barnyard (where you can touch and feed the domesticated farm animals), The Animal Nursery (with viewing windows through which you can see the zoo staff tend the zoo babies), and the Carousel (a beautifully carved wooden carousel that was built in 1921). There's also a Zebra Zephyr Train that takes you around the zoo for $2.50 an adult, and $1.50 a senior or child. There are snack stands throughout, offering burgers, hot dogs, fries, and more, and the Terrace Cafe with indoor and terrace dining.

The quality and options are certainly better than standard, with sandwiches, soups, and salads. However, if you're hungry and don't want to dine chez zoo, Taraval Avenue isn't far. It's the commercial boulevard of the Outer Sunset, and it's crammed with every type of restaurant and cafe.

> ## NATURAL HABITATS AT THE ZOO
>
> *A new wart hog exhibit has just opened, filled with mud banks and wallows and two very dirty, happy wart hogs. There's a 2.2 acre multi-species Australian WalkAbout, with kangaroos, wallabies, emus, and such all mingling in an open, grassy environment. Gorilla World and the Primate Discovery Center are amazing. The gorillas are in a lush expanse of trees and rocky outcroppings in one of the world's largest natural gorilla exhibits, and the Discovery Center houses 15 rare and endangered species in green meadows and soaring outdoor atriums.*
>
> *The Feline Conservation Center, just opened in '94, houses the Big Cats (snow leopards, puma, black leopard, and more) in an unusual natural setting. There are climbing logs and lots of plant life, plus a video system to help you observe the shy creatures. There's also Otter River, Penguin Island, a wading pool for the Greater One-Horned Rhinoceros, a large forest habitat for the African Wild Dogs, and the 2.6 acre Musk Ox Meadow.*

Stern Grove, *Sloat and 19th, 415-252-6252*, is a big park full of eucalyptus groves and grassy hills. Generally speaking, it's not worth your while to make a special trip out here, but on summer weekends, the quiet glade gets packed, thanks to the free Sunday afternoon concerts June-August. Ranging from big band to opera to symphony, the mostly classical music floats over the lawn as families dive into big picnics, and enjoy. Take a look at the weather before heading out, though, because summer afternoons often bring heavy fog to the Sunset. Bring some warm clothes just in case.

The other nice Sunset feature is the **beach**. But while the Zoo and Stern Grove are fairly accessible by bus, you need a car to get to the good beaches. Fort Funston is south of the Zoo along the Great Highway, with hang gliders, happy leash-free dogs, and beautiful sand dunes. See Ocean Beach in the Richmond section for more details.

TELEGRAPH HILL

Also known previously as Loma Alta, Windmill Hill, and Signal Hill, Telegraph rises up 284 feet to the east of North Beach, before plummeting down to Levi Plaza and the Embarcadero. The hill gets its name from the semaphore station built in 1849 to alert the populace of arriving ships. Today the hill is home to people wealthy enough to afford the gorgeous houses with their even more stunning bay views, but in 1849, the only folks who regularly climbed the hill were the spotters who from that high vantage could easily see ships sailing through the Golden Gate. They'd relay semaphore to downtown merchants, so they could set up shop, and get ready for the incoming cargo. Everyone knew the signals by heart, and could tell in an instant if the ship was carrying cargo from around the horn or mail from up the coast. So the story goes that one evening during some amateur Shakespearean entertainment, one of the actors spread wide his arms while asking "What means this, my lord?" To which a comedian in the audience roared "Sidewheel steamer!" But fog sometimes obscured the signal flags, and in 1853 an electric telegraph was installed (changing the name from Signal to Telegraph Hill).

Aside from the pretty houses and muscle-searing exercise, the reason to climb the hill today is for the Coit Tower view. Even in 1914, before the tower was built, Frank Morton Todd wrote: "The counterpart of Telegraph Hill exists in no other large city in the United States. No one can begin to know San Francisco until he has climbed it." And no matter whether you come from North Beach or the Embarcadero, you have an ascent and a half. From North Beach up Filbert to Coit Tower is the less hilly of the two, with 110 steps and a lot of stepless inclines. From Coit down to Montgomery it's 178 steps, then there are the Greenwich Street Steps from Montgomery down to Sansome, which number 210. The Greenwich Street Steps are plenty steep, but they are glorious, going through a jungle of green foliage and bright flowers all the way down, with the bay to look at while you catch your breath.

Coit Tower, *on top of Telegraph Hill*, is a 180-foot land mark that can be seen for miles. It was built in 1933 with money ($125,000) left by Lillie Hitchcock Coit (1843-1929) "for the purpose of adding beauty to the city which I have always loved." Lillie was quite a character. She came from a well-to-do and socially prominent family (that happened to be Confederate sympathizers in a Union state), and she was notorious for dressing as a man the better to drink, gamble, and smoke cigars in the North Beach saloons. She was friends with many firemen, she became the official mascot to the Knickerbocker Hose Company #5 in 1863, and she rarely missed a fire.

Still, Coit Tower, built in her honor, was never intended to look like a firehose nozzle or fire plug, as the story often goes. It was merely meant to be distinctive and tall, and this it accomplishes. Though H. A. Haskell in 1934 said "I consider it [Coit Tower] a blemish, without the remotest artistic significance; a defacement of a natural formation that ever delighted the eye of those approaching the city by water," it's now a beloved landmark and popular destination.

You can visit the tower and see the swell views of the bay any old time, but if you want to ascend to the viewing platform, you need to get there between 10am-6pm, and pay $3 for adults, $2 for seniors, and $1 for children under 12 for the elevator ride up. The Coit shlock shop (where you buy the elevator tickets) is very tiny, but the lower level (open to the public from 10-6) is full of wonderful frescos that can be seen for free, expressing the social realism of the times. All the walls are covered with scenes of American laborers - including all races and most occupations.

There are folks working in bakeries, factories, and soda fountains, picking oranges, sorting apricots, and shelving books in a library. The murals are the work of 26 artists, as commissioned by the government's Public Works of Art Project, which paid $38 a week. The artists, inspired by the renowned Mexican muralist Diego Rivera, as well as by the social troubles, optimism and humanistic concerns of the times, painted a series of vibrant and beautiful murals showcasing the history, politics, and human and natural wealth of California. The Rivera style and colors are lovely, while the loving attention and respect accorded the worker are clearly and poignantly dated. The view of the bay is very fine, and the walk is invigorating, but the murals are really special.

TENDERLOIN

This is a residential and commercial neighborhood west of Union Square and south of Nob Hill, mingling with the Civic Center sprawl. It's a very cheap district, and not very safe. New immigrants (mostly Asian) crowd old apartments with large families, and the poverty is everywhere. There are wonderful ethnic restaurants on every street, where a couple dollars will fill you with good food, as well as prostitutes and drugs clogging the night-time corners. During the day you generally have nothing more intimidating than panhandling and shabby surroundings to face, but at night there's a high rate of crime.

It was one of the first areas built up after the 1906 fire and quake, with hotels erected round the clock for the new homeless. More hotels were built for the 1915 Panama Pacific International Exposition, and the result was lots of hotels, more than was needed by the tourist boom. Many became brothels, and the district's whoring tradition got its start.

TWIN PEAKS

Towering west of Noe Valley, they stand tall at 904 and 911 feet high, not counting the TV towers on top. The view is lovely from there, and it's as windy and chilly as it is lovely. It's a workout to walk up there, and lovely to wander the winding small streets (you can take the 36 bus near to the top if you don't want to walk).

While the English name is fairly self-explanatory, the old Spanish name of *Los Pechos de la Choca* (Breasts of the Indian Maiden) comes from an old legend in which the daughters of the Chief, beautiful twins, saved their people from the invading enemy. After plucking special flowers, they prayed to the Great Spirit to first bring on a mighty fog to confuse the enemy, and then second to change them into barking seals. They then prayed for the Great Spirit to evermore guard the welfare of their people. The Great Spirit was so well pleased with the prayer that the wish was granted. The twins were turned into Twin Peaks so they could watch over all the land and guard those sleeping at their feet.

Be that as it may, the Peaks now are residential slopes offering views of the city spread out below.

UNION SQUARE

Union Square is a pretty 2.6 acre bit of green between Geary, Powell, Stockton, and Post, surrounded and superseded by Saks, Macy's, and Neiman Marcus. There are more hotels here than anywhere else in the city, and the surrounding blocks hold fashion boutiques, restaurants, jewelry stores, and the theater district. Its origins, however, were far more modest. John Geary decided in 1852 that he'd had enough of San Francisco and was going back home to Pennsylvania. As a good-bye gift, he gave the city some land downtown, and the city made it public. In the late 1850s, the square was a favorite meeting and speechifying spot for pro-Union rallies, as the state tried to decide its stance. In 1861, California opted not to secede, and Union Square was named for that decision.

The square itself is not why most come here these days, and few ever notice the graceful palms and the **Victory Monument**, designed by Robert Ingersoll Aitken in 1903 to celebrate Commodore George Dewey's 1898 victory over the Spanish fleet during the Spanish American War in Manila. People come here, not to bone up on history, but to shop. Along with the major department stores (Macy's, Saks, Neiman Marcus), there's Laura Ashley, Loehmans, Brooks Brothers, Banana Republic, Gap, Gumps, Hermes, FAO Schwarz, Tiffany, and nearby Nordstrom's in the San Francisco Center.

This is also the site of the **Powell cable car terminus**, and lines of tourists wrap around the curve, waiting their turn (there's usually less of a wait for the California line). Also on Powell and Market is the **Powell BART station**, and the **San Francisco Visitor Information Center**, *lower level of Hallidie Plaza, 415-391-2000.*

The **TIX Bay Area** office, *on the Stockton side of the square, 415-433-7827,* sells half-priced theater tickets, and you can buy the $10 Golden Gate Cultural Passes here, too. **Maiden Lane** is directly across from TIX, and its name is a bit ironic, given its sordid history. It was once a nasty Barbary coast alley (back when it was called Morton Street), but the 1906 fire finally did what the police couldn't, and rid the area of its vice. The street is now a very chic lane with expensive restaurants, galleries, and boutiques. If you take a stroll there, check out #140 Maiden Lane, which was built by **Frank Lloyd Wright**, and is said to have been a model for his designs for the New York Guggenheim.

WESTERN ADDITION

Most of this neighborhood below Pacific Heights and west of Van Ness is down in the dumps, economically, developmentally, and morally speaking. Sad housing projects are filled with struggling families and angry youth. Some atrocious violent crimes have been perpetrated lately on victims who just so happened to be in the wrong place at the wrong time, and you are advised to take care at night, especially.

That said, there are some fine places to visit here, and there's a lot that can be seen and enjoyed in safety during the day. The district was added to the city grid in 1858, and it was first popular in the late 1800s. It really began to be built up, however, after the 1906 fire wiped out downtown, and the stunning Victorians attest to the prosperity this area once enjoyed.

Alamo Square Park is up on a hill, *bound by Steiner, Hayes, Fulton, and Scott*. Nearby are both the projects and yesteryear's beautiful mansions, plus the stretch of colorfully refurbished Victorians that have been photographed so often on their hilly perch that they're now known as **Postcard Row**. Beginning at Fulton and Steiner, there are plenty of "Painted Ladies" (the houses, that is) to frame in your camera lens. The park is just a couple of square blocks, but it's lovely and green. Sitting pretty on a knoll atop a hill, there are panoramic views of the city, benches, picnic lawns, and the smell of eucalyptus. You can see from Twin Peaks to the Bay waters, birds twitter, and life is good.

Japantown is probably the second most popular Western Addition destination, following Postcard Row. *Centered around the Japan Center Mall between Geary and Post, Laguna and Fillmore*, Japanese Americans have been living here since the 1860s. By the 1930s there were Japanese shops, restaurants, markets, and temples (both Shinto and Buddhist), but the place was a ghost town during World War II, while its residents were forcibly relocated to internment camps. The district began to flourish again following the war, and in 1968 the multimillion-dollar, five acre **Japan Center** designed by Minoru Yamasaki opened with a three-day folk festival shebang.

The Center buildings, with their restaurants and shops, are connected with covered bridges crossing Webster and Buchanan streets. **Peace Plaza and Pagoda**, *located between the Tasamak Plaza and Kintetsu buildings*, is the center of the annual Cherry Blossom Festival. Also in the area is an outside pedestrian mall on Buchanan between Post and Sutter, that's nicely cobbled, with good restaurants. There's validated parking in the garage (the entrance is on Geary), and bus service from the 38, 2, 3, 4, and 22 lines.

For relaxation, there are two Kabuki venues. The **AMC Kabuki 8 Theaters**, *1881 Post near Fillmore, 415-931-9800*, has six screens showing first run films, and a sunset discount for the film closest to when the sun goes down. And next door is **Kabuki Hot Springs**, *1750 Geary, 415-922-6000 for recorded info, and 922-6002 for reservations*, with magnificent hot tubs and Japanese shiatsu massage, and they're open 10am-10pm on weekdays, and 9am-10pm on weekends. They have a communal bath for men open Monday, Tuesday, Thursday and Saturday, while the women's communal days are Wednesday, Friday, and Sunday, but you can rent a private bath with sauna any day. Plan prices vary from $10 to $65, depending on if you prefer a public or private soak, if you want massage, and for how long.

The **Fillmore**, sometimes called the Mo (after Detroit's Motown), is a section of the Western Addition that is centered along Fillmore Street, roughly within the confines of Bush, Webster, Turk, and Steiner. A lively and thriving African American neighborhood in the 40's when the workers were pouring in to the city to assist in the war effort, this was the hub of San Francisco's jazz scene at one time. The district became quite run down over the decades, however, with turf wars (toughs from the Mo were not welcome in Hunter's Point, and vice versa), drug activity, and general rough times. Revitalization, however, is in the air.

The lines between posh Pacific Heights and seedy Fillmore are getting more and more blurred, as fine restaurants and shops open on Fillmore, but there's more to it than that. The residents want to bring back the glory days when Fillmore meant good music; some fine jazz clubs have opened, and more are being planned. The Blue Note, the hot music club from New York, has been talking about opening a branch in the Fillmore, and it looks like the deal is just about done. Exciting as all this is, most of the district is still bleak, financially distressed, and not that safe for casual night strolling. You're better off driving or taking a cab.

LESS VISITED NEIGHBORHOODS

Bayview

South of Potrero Hill and sprawling out to India Basin and Hunter's Point, this is an economically distressed, crime-ridden neighborhood that's not on the regular tourist beat. It was settled in the 1940s by African Americans manning the Hunter's Point Naval Shipyard, but the district lost its edge when the shipping industry bottomed out.

Bernal Heights

Bernal Heights is a 325 foot hill south of the Mission and west of Bayview. Quiet and residential, it's becoming popular with young families who can't afford to buy homes in more prestigious neighborhoods. It's pleasant to live there and tend your garden, but there's not much cause to visit.

Potrero Hill

Located east of the Mission, south of the SoMa district, and west of the Bay, this 300 foot high neighborhood is not a big tourist draw. It's a residential community, part black, part Latino, and part multicultural artist, with rough projects and artsy lofts, plus some very cordial restaurants.

The **Anchor Brewing Company**, *1705 Mariposa near DeHaro, 415-863-8350*, churns out its superlative Anchor Steam Beer as they have been for over a century. It is now owned by Mr. Maytag (of dishwasher fame), and you can have a tour of the brewery Monday-Friday, 2pm, free of charge, but you need to call ahead to reserve.

15. NIGHTLIFE

"San Francisco has a tradition of sin which began in the Roaring forties, when men rooted in the earth for gold," said Beniamino Bufano, and while not all the entertainment today is sinful, San Francisco still kicks up her heels and shows you a good time.

CLUBS, PUBS, & BARS - POSH

From cabaret to dance floor to sky-scraping jazz lounge, these watering holes cater to an exclusive set who don't mind paying $6 a drink for the sake of sipping it in a stunning room, be it traditional or designer chic, to celebrate a special evening or merely to enjoy the fun.

DOWNTOWN

THE PIED PIPER LOUNGE, *Sheraton Palace Hotel at Market and New Montgomery, 415-392-8600*, serves lunch daily 11:30am-2pm, and a bar menu after. The atmosphere is warm and clubby, with richly dark wood paneled walls, crystal chandeliers, lovely sky light stained glass, and the magnificent Maxfield Parrish painting over the bar. It's a classy place for a drink (though not everyone imbibing there is a class act), and there's enjoyable '40s style jazz, with a singer and band, Thursdays and Fridays from 7-10pm.

NOB HILL

NEW ORLEANS ROOM, *Fairmont Hotel at 950 Mason near California, 415-772-5259*, features cabaret performances at 8 and 10pm, reservations strongly advised. Tickets are $15 midweek and $20 on weekends (with a one drink minimum), and there's an additional $5 charge if you buy your ticket at the door. Inside it's all a nightclub ought to be, with dim lights, small round tables, and a stage; slender brass hurricane lamps on the tables provide just a bit more mood and light. People stream in when the doors open, dressed to the nines and looking for the best seats. Orders are taken for drinks and appetizers (you can skip the $12 Tour de France described as a "canapé travel through the nuances of French cuisine"), and the show begins. The talent is dependable, the quality high, and the style is cabaret (no dancing, you just sit and enjoy) but the theme and content vary.

TONGA ROOM, *Fairmont at 950 Mason, 415-772-5278*, is a fun bit of tropical paradise gone campy. The Polynesian bar sports bamboo, draping flowers, and nautical nets, plus a pool-side dance floor on which Tonga patrons shake and shimmy to the dance hits performed live by a cheesy band that floats on a covered raft. Every 40 minutes or so a simulated tropical thunder and lightning squall strikes, with water whooshing down in the pool (this is why the raft is covered), the thunder roars, and the lights sputter to make like lightning. Rum-filled riki riki drinks come in coconut bowls with long straws and the requisite paper umbrella, and a good time is had by all.

UNION SQUARE

CAMPTON PLACE, *340 Stockton, 415-781-5555*, has Martini Night in their bar on Wednesdays 5:30-7:30pm, featuring music from the '30s and '40s played by the Martini Brothers, and special Sky Vodka drinks for $4 (all other drinks start at $6).

CLUB 36, *345 Stockton up on the 36th floor of the Grand Hyatt, 415-398-1234*, has no cover charge and no drink minimum, and is open Monday-Friday 4pm-2am and Saturday-Sunday 2pm-2am. What it does have is a very swell view of the city, and jazz piano Tuesday-Saturday 9pm-2am. The drinks are a bit pricy ($6 and up), and the clientele is usually business travelers staying at the Hyatt, though San Francisco locals sometimes stop by as well. Midnight on a Saturday evening will find the place packed and most of the clubby, deliciously comfortable chairs may well be taken. People munch on the little party snacks each table is supplied with, watch the spectacular view of the city at night, and talk about shoes and traffic and local politics. It's not an exciting place to be, despite the views, and despite the posh decor. Larry Vuckovich (the piano player) is quite adorable in his black beret, and he plays some fine jazz, with just enough swing and jaunt in to be interesting, but not intrusive enough to drown out your conversation.

THE COMPASS ROSE, *335 Powell in the Westin St. Francis, 415-774-0167*, promises a sumptuous evening of sparkle and swing, week nights 8-11pm (no cover) and weekends 9pm-1am ($5 cover after 9pm). Up a few steps but a world away from the lobby, the towering polished columns rise to the ornately carved ceiling, the carpets are plushly oriental, and there's a magnificent painted screen behind the band. For the full story of the room you can read the High Tea description, but an evening at the

Compass Rose has more to do with ambiance than history. You can have a cocktail, take coffee and dessert, or dine from 5-10pm off their dinner menu for $17-$25 an entree. The richness of colors and textures and food grows over an evening, creating a languid yet formal atmosphere that is not for every night nor for everyone. If your tastes run to excellence and style (dash the cost), if you love refined swing and want a wine of the best caliber, the Compass Rose does it right.

THE COMPASS EXPERIENCE

The Compass Rose is an interesting place. A few steps above and overlooking the lobby, you get to sit back and watch the people below meet and talk and stroll, but you don't really get the intimate, private sense of an enclosed room. The elegant couches aren't quite as comfy as they look, and though you're neatly tucked in with napkins by an attentive staff, it's not that convenient for dining. The jazz trio plays swing sets throughout the evening, and generally couples dance on the small marble floor. Sophisticated folk glide and dip, nattily dressed wooers press close and surreptitiously grope. Even if you don't dance, the jazz makes nice background music and it's entertaining to watch the dramas play out on the floor.

Should you chose to eat here, prepare to dine magnificently and spend a lot. The starters run $7.50-$12.50 and are sensational. The Dungeness crab cakes are perfect, as are the ginger roasted prawns with pineapple sauce, and the unusually fine pot stickers. Main dishes are more substantial and cost $17-$25. For this you can get large and succulent plates of baked monkfish, Sonoma lamb chops, Black Angus tenderloin of beef, or grilled Ahi tuna Nicoise. The wine, cocktail, and cordial lists are just as fine and equally expensive (ports, for example, go from the standard Ficklin at $7 a glass to the sumptuous Dow's thirty–three year old port at $32 a glass). But in all the excitement, don't neglect the desserts. The Truffle Slice ($5.75) is dangerously chocolatey and sublime. So intensely rich is the chocolate (in its raspberry and Frangelico drizzled sauces) that we advise you not to eat it too close to bed-time, lest your heart race all night from its intensity.

HARRY'S STARLIGHT ROOM, *Powell and Sutter on the 21st floor of the Sir Francis Drake, 415-392-7755*, is an amazing place open 9pm-1am Tuesday-Saturday, with $5 cover charges Wednesday-Thursday and $10 Friday-Saturday. Draped in yards of rose-tinted silks that scallop along the windows and billow on the ceiling, crystal chandeliers reflect the minimal light off the gold fabric of the wallpaper for an almost campy, romantically sumptuous look. The 400 yards of tassels (imported from France) adorn the curtains, and the low light, mirrors, velvet booths and dark wood bring to mind the luxury Pullman cars of another time, with just a touch of the bordello to it. Dressy and glittery and sinful, you can munch on caviar, oysters, or carpaccio ($7-$35), go for cocktails ($5.50-$7.50), or just dance. Men and women dress up, come in couples, in parties, or single and on the prowl, and the Harry Denton Starlight Orchestra plays very danceable Motown, swing, and blues.

If you like to dance but don't have a dance partner in ready supply, the Starlight Room is a safe place to mix, mingle, and dance without the meat market aura that taints some other night spots. The view is all a 21st floor view should be, and the decadent opulence creates a fun mood.

PLUSH ROOM CABARET, *940 Sutter between Leavenworth and Hyde, 415-885-2800*, has entertainment most nights around 8pm for $10-$15 a show (plus a pricy two drink minimum). This in an intermediate sort of cabaret, one where you could show up in jeans or formal evening garb and feel at home. The stained glass ceiling is colorful without being lovely, and the furnishings follow suite - adequate but not elegant. And as evening entertainment goes, it all depends on the line-up for the night. The room is intimate, and most tables are fairly near the stage, but the acts aren't very sophisticated. There are some cute numbers and sassy songs, but they don't usually get the same level of talent that the New Orleans room books.

THE RED ROOM, *in the Commodore at 825 Sutter near Jones, 415-346-7666*, is open nightly 5pm-2am. It's the new place to be in San Francisco, designed by the Commodore Hotel, and attracting the city's artists, architects, and other assorted cool denizens. The atmosphere, though contemporary, recreates the decadence of bygone eras. It's red, very red, and sensual and dusky and dissolutely appealing.

THE REDWOOD ROOM, *in the Clift Hotel at 495 Geary near Taylor, 415-775-4700*, glows with class, history, and the deep timbre of the single 2,000 year-old redwood tree, cut to size in 1933. The classic art deco lights and Gustav Klimt pictures have been awarded every design rave imaginable, but it's not overwhelming; the Redwood Room, which was the hottest spot to hit San Francisco in the '30s, is still a comfortable and lovely place to sit, chat, and spend some time. There's jazz scheduled Friday and Saturday 9pm-1am, but there are often spontaneous jam sessions from famous guests who can't resist, as well.

There's a Redwood Room tradition of cigars here, and they are sold at the bar, but the soaring ceilings and good ventilation make it comfortably odor-free for those not so inclined. You can go with just cocktails ($6 or so per drink), or dine here as well. Either way, you'll spend a bit but reap a lot of the inimitable atmosphere and style.

BLUES & JAZZ

FINANCIAL DISTRICT

BIX, *56 Gold Street near Jackson, 415-433-6300,* is open for lunch on weekdays and nightly for dinner. It's a gorgeous '20s style supper club with stylish American food and live jazz entertainment. The columns soar, the martinis clink, and the culinary specialties like caviar, steak tartare with grilled olive bread, and grilled pork chop cost $14-$25. Folks, mostly from the Financial District crowd, get all dressed up in their retro chic to enjoy a fashionable night out.

CAFE BASTILLE, *22 Belden off Bush between Kearny and Montgomery, 415-986-5673,* has jazz or blues every night but Monday from 7:30-11pm. The food here is okay rather than special, but the music is often quite nice.

CAFE CLAUDE, *7 Claude Lane (a small lane between Grant and Kearny off Bush), 415-392-3505,* is a French Restaurant with evening jazz Tuesday, Thursday, Friday, and Saturday starting around 7 or 8pm and lasting till 10 or 11pm. There's no cover, it's cozy, and the food is quite good, but the acoustics are such that with the close seating and all, it's not a place for an easy conversation once the music starts.

FISHERMAN'S WHARF

LOU'S PIER 47, *300 Jefferson in Fisherman's Wharf, 415-771-0377,* is a rocking place with live rhythm and blues every night of the week. The covers range from $4-$8, and the bands start up around noon on weekends and 8pm weekdays, and play till 2am. They have pretty good food, too.

MARINA

BLUES, *2125 Lombard near Fillmore, 415-771-2583,* is open nightly 8pm-1:30am, and the music starts at 9pm. Thursday-Saturday there's a $5 cover. This is a popular, crowded music club with a terrible attitude. Try to get in on a Saturday night and the staff dishes out sneers and ooze self-satisfaction, while playing favorites with who gets in when. And let's say you persevere and gain admission, you haven't really gained that much. Leopard print booths and pictures on the wall of naked, sprawling women lend a sleazy tone that is just sleazy, not chic. There's a small, steamy postage-sized dance floor, and the rest is packed with smug twits, slopping beer and filling the place with smoke. Gross in a gentrified sort of way, $5 gets you in, but it's worth ten times that to get back out.

PARAGON, *3521 Scott between Chestnut and Lombard, 415-922-2456.* The bar opens at 4:30pm daily, dinner is served 5-10pm, and there's live music Sunday-Wednesday nights (no cover charge), featuring jazz, blues, or rock and roll. A favorite weekend hang-out for singles in their 20's and 30's, they stand around eyeing the crowd and don't mind talking over the ear-splitting music. Yuppie sardines are packed in so tight it takes a miracle and very sharp elbows to go the length of the bar gauntlet on a weekend night. In the back, however, is a dining area with nicely set tables, serving food that attends to no particular theme, including a risotto, a paella, some rosemary lemon chicken, and a sirloin steak, for $10-$14 a dish.

PASAND LOUNGE, *1875 Union near Laguna, 415-922-4498*, has live jazz nightly 8pm-1am, while the restaurant serves Indian food from 11:30am on. The atmosphere isn't much: there are lots of glass-topped tables with Pasand Restaurant advertisements tackily pressed beneath, and a heated patio in back that is steamy and not appealing. The jazz is oppressively loud, so you'd better decide you like it before sitting down, because that's all you'll be hearing; you sure won't be able to talk over it.

MISSION

ALBION CLUB, *3139 16th near Valencia, 415-552-8558*, has music (jazzy, bluesy, acoustic) on Sunday evenings 5-8pm, no cover. A neon sign above the bar proudly and pinkly proclaims "Service For The Sick," but in fact the Albion is a bit mellower than Dalva next door. The sound system pours out varied tunes, and a real mix of folks hunker about. It's kind of a cool place for a drink, trendy enough to be part of the scene, but without the claustrophobia of Dalva.

BLONDIES' BAR & NO GRILL, *540 Valencia near 17th, 415-864-2419*, is one of the coolest local gems on Valencia, a small and likable bar with a slightly scuffed but serviceable pool table. Saturdays is their live jazz night (from ragtime to fusion), showcasing some of the best local and out-of-state talent around; the music starts around 9:30pm and there's no cover. Ricci Cornell and Clarice Lacau (Blondies' owners) opened seven years ago, and the bar now is one of the most popular best-kept secrets in the city, with intriguing art on the wall, and an interesting crowd that's nice to look at, and doesn't feel sleazy.

Those in the know crowd the small room, hang out, take in the excellent music, and the stellar martinis too. Featuring vodkas and olive stuffers from the world over, the most popular by far is the Russian Vodka martini (Stoli up with an olive stuffed with house-smoked salmon), but the Danish Fris with bleu cheese stuffed-olives is no slouch either. The newest entry celebrates the inauguration of San Francisco's new mayor, Willie Brown. The Wild Willie is a classic vodka martini with black Sambucca and three coffee beans to conjure up the health, prosperity, and happiness the number three represents according to Ricci's Sicilian background. But whatever your background or politics, Blondies' is a swell bar. Club Red is a Sunday evening event from 7pm-midnight, with DJ hip-hop, house, and salsa for all women and their friends. Jazz on the Line is a very talented group that's booked here every fourth Saturday of the month, or see who's lined up for the rest of the month.

BRUNO'S, *2389 Mission and 20th, 415-550-7455*, is another new and happening place. The lounge is open nightly from 6pm-2am, while dining room service is on Tuesday-Sunday 6:30pm-1am. They have live music (bebop, straight-ahead jazz, swing, Latin jazz, Dean Martinesque lounge music, and Felliniesque Italian film soundtrack music, though jazz dominates) in the bar lounge and the smaller Cork Room on Tuesday-Saturday starting at 10pm for $3.

Each night there are two bands (one in each room) that play while the other is on break, keeping the energy up and the momentum going. There's also good food in the dining room, but the two experiences are kept quite separate. It's sort of a chic place in a retro '50s, not-so-classy way, attracting swarms of 90s folk who sip martinis and feel swell. It's in and hot because it's in and hot, and that's the way popularity works. The lounge, smoky with dim, red light, gets packed when a band's playing, then people move on to the Cork Room for the next group, and the hostess sashays about in a black flapper cocktail dress while the patrons lounge in jeans and soak up the scene.

ELBO ROOM, *647 Valencia between 17th and 18th, 415-552-7788,* is a stand-up rather than sit-down jazz place, catering to a diverse 21-24 year old crowd. The live music, mostly new or acid jazz, goes from 10pm-1:30pm, the covers vary from $3-$5, and Thursday they have a Soulvation DJ dance night. Dog Slide is a good band that plays here frequently. There are two floors, three pool tables, 15 draft beers, an indoor ATM machine, and a 1963 black & white photo booth that works great and churns out a strip of four shots for just $2.

RADIO VALENCIA, *1199 Valencia near 23rd, 415-826-1199*, has re-emerged like the phoenix from the traumatic incident last year when a fire truck accidentally visited them through their plate-glass window. But they're repaired and reopened, much to the community's relief. They're open weekdays at 5pm, weekends at noon, and stay open nightly till midnight, but the musical entertainment is just on weekend nights 7-10pm. There's swing jazz on Friday, improvisational jazz on Saturday (with a $5 cover), and bluegrass on Sunday nights. The kitchen cooks up big batches of homemade soup, salads, pizzas, and focaccia sandwiches for about $5 a plate, and it's pretty good. Radio Valencia is one of those genuinely friendly, relaxed and relaxing places to hang out, eat good food, and listen to music; it's a fine place to pass the evening with friends.

NORTH BEACH

GATHERING CAFFE, *1326 Grant near Green, 415-433-4247*, is open Monday-Friday 7pm-2am and on the weekends 11am-2pm. There's live jazz nightly, and never any cover in this smallish, friendly, good-vibes place, and no drink minimum, either. There are small marble-topped tables, a small bar, and straight-ahead jazz. The volume's pretty high, however, so you need to be into the music, because it's too loud to talk.

GRANT & GREEN, *1371 Grant by Green, 415-956-9605*, is a small, dingy neighborhood blues dive with a bar, some small tables, and a little dance floor that gets a lot of use. There's usually no cover charge Sunday-Tuesday, and later in the week the cover hovers around $3. Yes, it's smoky, and lacking in any of the finer amenities, but the music is often quite good (they book rockin' good local blues bands). The drinks are not expensive, you won't get hassled, and you can let your hair down and have a good time.

HI-BALL LOUNGE, *473 Broadway near Kearny, 415-397-9464*, once the Jazz Workshop where Miles Davis and John Coltrane used to play, has just recently reopened in North Beach. It opens nightly at 7-9pm, depending, and the cover charge varies as well, depending on the performers, from $5-$10. Tuesday nights they offer swing dance lessons. There's a full bar (Martini Happy Hour is Thursday-Friday 5-9pm), and snacks are coming soon. Inside, the walls have a new zebra look, there are candle-lit tables and round booths up front, and a bar near the entrance that gets fully packed. The small dance floor by the stage is where those in the know cut their rugs to the jazzy, swing-style music under the dim red lights. The Hi-Ball brings back a chic sort of entertainment, the dance jazz club, that is fun and stylish, and at a price that isn't prohibitive. It gets a bit smoky inside sometimes, but the upbeat mood, casual class, good quality music, and genial air all combine to make this an unusually appealing night club.

JAZZ AT PEARL'S, *256 Columbus near Broadway, 415-291-8255*, has music 9pm-1am Monday-Thursday and 9:30pm-1am Friday-Saturday. They get all sorts of groups, from big 20-piece bands to trios and quartets, and there's never any cover charge, though there is a two-drink minimum. Inside, the bar ledge and little tables facing the stage have candles but no great appeal. It's nice enough inside, but not enough to want to stay when the music's done. Because they don't charge covers, the quality of the jazz they book doesn't seem as good as some of the other jazz spots in town, but it doesn't hurt to check them out if you're in the neighborhood. Just walk by on Columbus, and decide for yourself if the music make you want to stay.

THE SALOON, *1232 Grant near Columbus, 415-989-7666*, is open nightly with live rhythm and blues. There's no cover during the week, and on weekends it'll cost you $4-$5 to get in. The Saloon attracts a roughish denim-clad crowd, the sort who want some cheap beer, a bar stool, and a thumping good time, though on occasion some beer-soaked knucklehead causes trouble. But in general, this is just an unpretentious, bare-bones bar with no-frills music, a small dance floor that gets a lot of action, and air that hangs heavy with smoke.

PACIFIC HEIGHTS

RASSELAS JAZZ CLUB, *2801 California, 415-567-5010*, near Divisadero, with live music nightly, 8pm-midnight weekdays and 9pm-1am weekends. There's no cover, but there is a two-drink minimum per set. Unfortunately, the tables and chairs are uncomfortably close together, making passage difficult, and conversation impossible. The music is very loud, so that better be the reason you're here, because you'll ruin your voice if you try to talk with your friends. As for the music, it varies, depending on the performer. Sometimes it's pretty good, but often it's just awful and tacky. Take a listen at the door before you make Rasselas a part of your evening plans.

POLK GULCH

COCONUT GROVE, *1415 Van Ness between Bush and Pine, 415-776-1616*, has shows nightly from 7pm on for $5-$55, depending on the act, but Tuesdays and Wednesdays are often reserved for private parties. Once past the doormen in tuxes, you have a choice of dinner or drinks. If you go for the whole dinner experience (about $40 per person), you get a beautifully set, candle lit table in the dining room, facing the stage, and you should reserve in advance. Diners typically get dressed in their best finery, trotting out their most elegant, retro threads. There's no dancing, no matter how hot the music, but along with their meal, diners get a whole evening's entertainment in the best tradition of the supper club.

But there is another, less expensive option – the bar. It's a little further from the stage, but all the stools give a clear view of the stage. There you can have a drink, socialize, and enjoy the act for a less substantial investment. But no matter where you sit, the music is generally top notch. They book good singers, and while it depends, of course, on the night, they do a good job bringing in quality jazz and blues cabaret style entertainment. That's all on the plus side. The decor, however, is a bit foolish. Tall plastic stylized palms have amber glowing coconut lights, and all the exposed pipes on the ceiling don't match the mood. Still and all, if you want to dress up, sit down, and be entertained, the silly palms hardly matter.

JULIE RING'S HEART AND SOUL, *1695 Polk near Clay, 415-673-7100,* is a 1930s style jazz supper club. The club is open Tuesday-Saturday with shows at 6pm and 9pm, dinner is served 6pm-midnight, and cover charges range from $4-$8. The food items are mostly Latin in flavor, they cost $5-$8 for snacks (the large bowl of steamed mussels is especially popular), the entrees are $14-$19 (and they're pretty good), and the bartender pours a good drink behind his black bar. But the food is secondary to the club aura and entertainment quality, both of which get high marks.

While from the outside the club doesn't look like much, inside there is a lot to like. The lighting is just right for a romantic evening out, and the lamps of wrought iron and parchment are very cool. There are textures and colors, and no clouds of smoke hovering in the air. People sit at linen-covered tables or recessed on tan banquettes, while upstairs behind the wrought iron rail is another line of intimate little tables against the red drapes. And best yet, they book some really class talent, too (listen in when Kelly Gray performs, for a real jazz treat). While the Julie of Julie Ring's is the same Julie who owns Julie's Supper Club, this place is far classier and sophisticated. It's an extremely pleasant club in which to pass the evening with friends and listen to some good music.

RICHMOND

OROCCO, *3565 Geary between Stanyan and Arguello, 415-387-8788*, calls itself an East-West Supper Club, and is open nightly 6-10pm, with late night suppers Friday-Saturday 10pm-midnight. The focus is on the food; there's no cover charge, and the music is atmospheric background (all jazz - straight-ahead, soul) during dinner, slightly more beefed up later, but people don't dance (there's no dance floor). The East/West aspect comes from the owners, the design, the neighborhood, and the menu. After the live music there's a late night DJ listening set that might include newer acid jazz and funk.

SOUTH OF MARKET

ELEVEN, *374 11th near Harrison, 415-431-3337*, has atmosphere, style, and Monday-Saturday they have live jazz, too. Dinner jazz plays 7-10pm, followed by hip, funky jazz for the night crowd (till 11pm or 12am week nights, till 1:15 weekends). Wednesday-Saturday, bar customers who aren't dining are charged a $5 cover from 9:30pm on, but that's where the scene is. And parking is free at nearby Costco.

They serve dinner till 11pm, and the Italian food ($6.75-$15) ranges from mediocre to good. There are pizzas with toppings like rock shrimp or gorgonzola, pastas with a variety of vegetables and seafood, and meaty entrees featuring chicken, pork, steak, and fish. Wrought-iron cushioned chairs are set off nicely by the white linen and candlelight, and the walls, adorned by iron trellises, are subtly imprinted with Mediterranean images of pottery and grape clusters. The bar area, done up with lots of mahogany, is romantic, cool, and popular with the with-it San Francisco 20s and 30s crowd, and the cocktail and liquor list is quite capacious. The jazz group is up on a ledge in back, and you can sit below or dine upstairs, eye level with the musicians. Unlike at Slim's and DNA across the street, Eleven's sophisticated guests are dressed in their SoMa best - meaning jeans or leather or blazers or minis or whatever makes folks feel most cool.

42 DEGREES, *235 16th Street off Third, 415-777-5558*, is a new chic supper club with excellent Mediterranean food. Jim Moffat (owner and chef) started this place in April of '85, in the space previously occupied by Caffe Esprit, with its 20-foot ceilings and curving staircase up to the mezzanine. It's open for lunch weekdays 11:30am-3pm (but they don't take lunch reservations) and dinner (for which reservations are taken and suggested) Wednesday-Thursday 7-11pm and Friday-Saturday till midnight. There's jazz nightly at 8:30 (easy and mellow to go with dinner), and entrees ($12-$20) like seared duck breast with wilted escarole.

HARRY DENTON'S BAR & GRILL, *161 Steuart near Howard, 415-882-1333*, has live jazz, motown, or rhythm & blues Monday-Saturday starting 9-9:30pm with a $3-$10 cover Wednesday-Saturday, and a weekend disco that goes from 10:30pm-1:30am on weekends in back. They are also a restaurant, and serve food daily 11:30am -10pm. At night it's quite the scene. It's a partying, cocktail-swilling, power-suited, mostly single, yuppified crowd. Well, not everyone's in a suit; plenty of folks are quite casually dressed, but the tone is definitely financial district after hours plush. The whole place buzzes with the sound of noisy, cheerful chatter.

Red velvet, dark woods, street lamp lights and a jungle motif on the ceiling decorate the room, while musical instruments line the mantel, and if the cocktail waitresses' little black skirts were any shorter, they'd cease to exist. There are tables and booths near the small stage, but the bar gauntlet is so crowded (even early on a Thursday) that you need sharp elbows and no manners to worm your way through. Up the stairs is the calmer dining room, set up with a bistro air, palms trees, and walls full of colorful European posters. Here you can dine on jazzed up American food for $8-$16 an entree. Back in the bar, the music is okay. It's certainly not awful, but nor should it be the main reason you choose to go to Denton's.

JULIE'S SUPPER CLUB, *1123 Folsom near 7th, 415-861-0707*, serves up live bands with your supper Thursday-Saturday, ranging from soul to rock-a-billy to rhythm & blues. Thursday the music plays 9pm-12:30am and there's no cover, while Friday-Saturday a cover of $5 starts at 10:30pm when the music starts, and the band plays till 1:30am. Inside there's a formica bar with white bar stools, and a row of white linened, candle-lit tables against the wall, the decor isn't really cozy nor full art deco, either.

They serve all the trendy dishes ($7.50-$15) like grilled Ahi tuna and braised Sonoma rabbit, but it doesn't seem to be what's hot in the music or social scene. People come in looking like they want to be where the action is, and though this once was the place, it isn't anymore.

UP & DOWN CLUB, *1151 Folsom near 8th, 415-626-2388,* has jive samba on Wednesday, and a variety of classic jazz, acid jazz, and jazzy hip hop the other nights from 9:30pm-12:45am, for $3-$5 a cover. Inside, it's a very cool place, from the hip design to the people who hang here. There's a downstairs and an upstairs (hence the name), using separate entrances from outside, but both of which are accessible for the same cover.

Downstairs is where the live music is, and the curvy bar and wavy lines, and the tables topped with linen and candles and tulips. Dinner ($11.50-$15.50 for entrees, $4-$7 for starters) is served Wednesday-Saturday from 8-10pm, reservations are needed, and the feijao cum camaro (Portuguese black beans with prawns), peppered ribeye, and roasted chicken are all pretty good. People mill about, dressed in everything from cocktail outfits to jeans and singlets, drinking or eating or just listening to the band perform what's hot and interesting in the jazz world. Artistic and designed to the hilt, the textures and decorations are as sophisticated and savvy as the people who know to come here, from the professional yuppies to the young hipster crowd to the Bay Area suburbanites going out on the town for the night. Upstairs is more for the dancing crowd, with DJ hip-hop and rap fueling a racially mixed San Francisco crowd on a small dance floor. There's a bar and some stools, a few booths, and pictures of jazz greats lining the walls, offering a subtle reminder that while cool is good, it's the music that counts.

UNION SQUARE

BISCUITS & BLUES, *401 Mason near Geary, 415-292-2583,* a new-comer that started February of '95, is open Tuesday-Saturday 6pm-1am. The music goes 9pm-1am, and the kitchen is open 6:30pm-midnight, serving simple southern cuisine at $8-$10 an entree. You pay your cover ($5-$20, depending on the act) and go downstairs, where the music and food is happening. The music's so loud you need to shout in the waitress' ear to order, and you can just forget about conversation, but it's usually pretty good blues, and the dance floor is waiting, under the banner reading "dedicated to the preservation of the blues." People really work up a sweat there, mixing with the faint odor of candle wax emanating from the tall, colorful, glass-sheathed table tapers. The tables also sport galvanized buckets of flatware and napkins, reminding you of the jambalaya, fried chicken, and catfish po' boys that can be yours.

THE BLUE LAMP, *561 Geary between Taylor and Jones, 415-885-1464*, is the epitome of the blues dive. It's a great, funky place booking local, cheesy blues bands. Weird and wonderful fabric, scalloped and tucked and buttoned, gives texture and unique personality to the walls and ceiling, while locals and out-of-towners crowd the tables, and dance in the aisle, listening to the low-down, no-frills dive blues. This funky blues bar has authenticity and character, and a lovely crystal chandelier that hasn't been cleaned for a good 20 years. Talk to Patrick Archer (5-8pm Monday and Thursday) for cover info.

LES JOULINS JAZZ CLUB, *44 Ellis between Powell and Stockton, 415-397-5397*, is a French Restaurant that has jazz every night from 8:30-10:30 or so, and a fairly brusque staff. You can come for dinner or just for cocktails or dessert if it's mainly the jazz you're after, and there's no cover. They play jazz standards, but with different accents on different nights. Sunday-Tuesday the jazz has a blues tone, Wednesday and Friday it's Latin style, Thursdays it's bebop, and Saturdays they have a quartet doing '30s style jazz.

MASON STREET WINE BAR, *342 Mason, 415-391-3454*, has been around since 1987, offering that classic combination of good wine and jazz. Open Sunday-Thursday 8pm-midnight (no cover) and Friday-Saturday 9pm-1am ($5 cover), there's no minimum drink requirement though they'd prefer you to order something. Large menus list scads of wines, champagnes, ports, and beer (no hard liquor here), and folks listen to the casual jazz while they sip their Clos du Bois or Stag's Leap. It's a pleasant spot, with no cover charge.

There's a nice sitting area with tables and chairs up by the band, and a wine bar and sofa lounge in back. Colorful artwork decorates the tiled walls, and you can snack on a cheese plate ($5 for small, $10 for large) while you sit back and enjoy.

WESTERN ADDITION

STORYVILLE CLASSIC JAZZ CLUB, *1751 Fulton near Masonic, 415-441-1751*, does classic jazz and serves New Orleans food daily 5pm-1am, with weekend covers of $5 (except when special visiting groups jack the price up to $15), and parking is available ($3 during the week and $5 on weekends). This is a place that takes music, people, and food seriously, and lets you enjoy them all, according to your tastes.

There are two rooms to Storyville, the first being the lounge bar (smokers welcome) and the inside room (smoke-free) has the music and stage. The room is draped in red and accented black, glowing dimly with table candles and hearth fire. Each room has its own warm hearth spot, with fireplace and soft sofa alcoves. Grab one if you can, because they go fast. People filter in on their own and in groups, dressed in jeans and sweaters, clearly an educated, diverse crowd of all ages and colors. Some are here for the music, and it's loud enough for them to focus intently as Don Pender pours it on, but the music is soft enough to let you chat without having to shout and strain. Others enjoy the music in the background, but have come for the food. Vast plates of gumbo and Cajun fried oysters, barbecued pork ribs with collard greens, fried chicken with mashed potato and 'slaw ($9-$14) take over, and momentarily distract the sweethearts nearby. Whatever your passion, be it food, drink, or jazz, Storyville delivers.

The name comes from New Orleans Storyville district (dating from 1895) which was the red-light district; it's where Jelly Roll Morton helped give birth to jazz, and Louis Armstrong grew up and learned up to play jazz there as well. George Wayne (Newport Jazz Festival's promoter) had a Boston Storyville Club for a while, but he sold the name rights to Don Pender (a jazz artist in his own right, with 8 CDs to his name), and now Pender has set up a classic jazz venue again, something San Francisco hasn't had since Keystone Corner in North Beach closed some 15 years ago, and has truly needed. It's a place you could come on your own, bring a date, your friends, your mother, or the visiting friend you haven't seen for years.

ROCK & PUNK

MISSION

KILOWAT, *16th Street near Valencia, 415-861-2592*, is a punk rock club, complete with young barely-out-of-college kids and the ubiquitous tall red plastic cups full of keg beer. There are great copper pipe sculptures of an octopus and sharks hanging from the ceiling created by a local genius plumber, but you really need to like punk to want to be a part of this hurly burly set.

They stage shows from local and national groups such as the Mommyheads, Dirt Cousin, Steel Pole Bathtub, and the Demolition Dollrods for $5-$7 cover. If these names are meaningful to you, the Kilowat is your scene.

RICHMOND

LAST DAY SALOON, *406 Clement between Fifth and Sixth Avenues, 415-387-6343*, plays mostly rock & roll for between $3-$5. The doors open at 9pm and they close at 2am.

WORLD MUSIC

FISHERMAN'S WHARF

FIDDLER'S GREEN, *1333 Columbus, 415-441-9758*, is an Irish pub with Guinness, Irish Coffee, live music nightly except for Saturday, and a disco upstairs on the weekends (the disco times will be expanding soon to Thursday-Sunday, at least). Downstairs, Sundays and Thursdays the music is basic rock & roll, but the other nights feature Irish, usually a ballad singer doing traditional and folk. There's no cover, and the live music goes from 9:30pm-1:30am, though the pub stays open till 2am.

NORTH BEACH

O'REILLY'S IRISH PUB, *622 Green near Columbus, 415-989-6222*, plays Irish music Wednesday, Thursday, and Sunday nights from 9:30pm-12:30am or so, and on Tuesday there's live rock and roll, at least for now (the schedule is still in flux). They are trying to get Irish set dancing going on Sunday afternoons from 4pm on, and you don't need to know what you're doing to join in, because people there will instruct.

There is also a restaurant attached (see *Where To Eat* chapter) serving traditional Irish dishes. The bar is impressive, and seems to have established a large regular clientele in just a few short months. There are dark wood columns imported from Ireland, and stained glass insets. In back, the whole wall is taken up with a colorful mural of larger-than-life literary greats such as Shaw, Beckett, Yeats, and Joyce, cavorting and glowering and slugging back beer, looking like Toulouse-Lautrec had taken these eccentric iconoclasts and set them in a trendy cafe. The artists portrayed there would scream in their graves at their likenesses being used to decorate the background and to authenticate the good Irish taste of the bar owners. There are also a goodly number of black & white photos (both of the writers and of candid Irish scenes) that are well-done and interesting.

The juke box is fairly Irish, too, with traditional and modern groups (Clannad, Planxty, The Bothy Band, Pogue, and Van Morrison) joining the Kinks, Muddy Waters, and Leonard Cohen. Inside, the bar has a *Cheers* type feeling, but it's definitely a drinking person's social bar, not a place to nurse a beer and read the paper. Even the music plays second fiddle to the more absorbing entertainment of drinking and milling and talking. Few stop to listen when the fiddlers (squeezed into a corner under Shaw's bushy brows and disdainful glower) set to playing.

RICHMOND

PLOUGH AND STARS, *116 Clement, 415-751-1122*, is an Irish pub with Guinness on tap, Irish music on stage, a pool table, and a cordial if smoky air. The music starts up nightly around 9:15, and the cover of $3 is weekends only. The quality varies, depending on the group, but if you can make it when Tipsy House is playing you should hear a good set.

SOUTH OF MARKET

JELLY'S, *Pier 50, 415-495-3099*, has Argentinean tango music out on the patio during the summer. Why Jelly's? Ricci Cornell, co-owner of Blondies' Bar & No Grill as well, says 'cause jam don't shake like that. If the proposed new ball park makes it in China Basin, Jelly's will be well placed as the perfect place to go after the game.

ECLECTIC

FINANCIAL DISTRICT

PIER 23 CAFE, *Pier 23 near Battery, 415-362-5125*, is open Tuesday-Saturday from 11:30am on, with nightly music ranging from New Orleans style to reggae to salsa to blues. On weekdays, admission is free and the music plays 5-8pm and 9:30-midnight, while on weekends, the music goes 10pm-2am and the cover is $5.

HAYES VALLEY

PLACE PIGALLE, *520 Hayes near Octavia, 415-552-2671*, has various events, some jazzy and some spoken, and inside, the comfy leather sofas help provide a welcoming ambiance. Tuesday is poetry, but other nights range from swing to jazz improv to anything else. The doors open at 4pm and events usually start around 8pm, and while there's no cover charge, they appreciate donations.

MISSION

CHAMELEON, *853 Valencia between 19th and 20th Streets, 415-821-1891*, has live music varying from blues to punk rock, and the cover varies too. Inside it's dim with red lights, while from the exposed beams of the ceiling hang glittery stars that look like the ones you made in third grade. The music is loud and the crowd is young; you know best if that's you or not.

EL RIO, *3158 Mission near Army, 415-282-3325*, has rock & roll Saturday night from 10pm, and salsa Sunday afternoon from 4pm. The cover is $5, though it could be climbing to $7 soon.

NORTH BEACH

BIMBO'S, *1025 Columbus near Chestnut, 415-474-0365*, is a large nightclub booking acts that range from blues to cabaret to alternative rock to jazz. They're usually open on the weekends, and sometimes during the week as well, and the cover ($7-$30) depends on who's appearing. Call them or check the paper to see what's on. Inside, it's very dark and can accommodate a lot of people and a lot of styles. The stage is big, as is the dance floor in front of it. There are plenty of tables for the sit-down cocktail drinkers, and a separate bar room with stylish decor and plenty of room in which to socialize and mill about. They tend to get enthusiastic crowds, but the expression depends on the performance. For a rock concert, crowds get in gear and dance till dawn, and for some of the swing bands, the fedoras and retro gowns get dusted off, and Bimbo's looks like it just stepped out of the 40s.

COCODRIE, *1024 Kearny near Broadway, 415-986-6678*, has live music nightly (starting 9-10pm)ranging from zydeco to alternative rock to reggae. Admission is $3 during and week and $5 on the weekends, and you need to be 21 or over (they used to welcome the 18-20 crowd, but no longer). Wednesday is zydeco night, otherwise you need to check the paper or call to see who's playing. Inside, there are a couple of tables, some pinball machines and pool tables, and a dance floor. It's not fancy, but neither is it sleazy. It's just a local bar with music, and the people who come do so because they want to hear that particular band. The customers change from night to night, but the music focus remains the same.

POTRERO HILL

BOTTOM OF THE HILL, *1235 17th between Texas and Missouri, 415-621-4455*, is a casual, friendly place with a wide variety of live music nightly. Bands range from alternative rock (that's the main kind) to punk to fusion jazz to hip hop. Covers are $3-$7, and every Sunday there's a barbecue – $3 for admission to the Sunday band plus all-you-can-eat barbecue. Call for the schedule, or check the newspapers.

SOUTH OF MARKET

SLIM'S, *333 Eleventh between Folsom and Harrison, 415-522-0333*, is Boz Scaggs' club, and he even puts in a surprise appearance on occasion. Their schedule changes from week to week, but they usually have a show nightly, hosting name bands that include but are not limited to blues, rock, alternative, and reggae, with covers ranging from free to $20, but averaging $10-$12 (sometimes advance purchased tickets are a little less, and often they're a very good idea - lots of shows sell out). The doors open an hour before the show, and people usually start lining up way before that. You can park on the street for free (it's rarely a problem) or at nearby Costco for $5. Unlike other music clubs in SoMa, people come to Slim's for the music first and foremost. They don't worry what to wear because no one cares, and it's not a place to meet people. It's all about the show.

Inside there are tables and chairs on the main floor (get there early to grab one), and more upstairs in back. Down in front up by the stage is the dance floor, and it typically sees a lot of action. Get a good group up on stage and you can dance your fool heart away all night, or listen from the comfort of your seat and leave the sweating to someone else. Either way, Slim's is a good venue to enjoy the bands you want to hear and see live. Call their info line for the week's line-up, and instructions on how to get tickets.

TENDERLOIN

GREAT AMERICAN MUSIC HALL, *859 O'Farrell, 415-885-0750*, is a wonderful setting for a wide variety of musical concerts and performances. It was once a bordello, as evinced by the ornate rococo interior, complete with mirrors, red paint, and gilt trim, but now the fancy box seat balconies and seats around tables below are filled with music lovers. Prices range from around $8-$16, you can see their listings in the free *San Francisco Weekly* or call them, and tickets are available from their box office or from BASS for an additional $1 per ticket surcharge. Drinks and so-so food are served, but stay away from the horrid nachos.

UPPER MARKET

CAFE DU NORD, *2170 Market near Church and Sanchez, 415-861-5016,* has an eclectic range of music entertainment, most of which is jazz-based, evenings from 10pm or so till 12:30 or 1am, with a cover of $3-$5 after 10pm. Wednesday-Saturday they serve dinner and feature jazz groups. Sunday is swing night, and the dance floor is cleared of dinner tables, while Tuesday the floor's cleared for salsa. Mondays the options vary. Right now it's a cabaret night, but it might change again.

Whatever's going on, the cavelike downstairs is full of ambiance, with a good bar and room to dance.

NOTABLE BARS

CHINATOWN

BUDDHA LOUNGE, *901 Grant near Washington, 415-362-1792*, is a weirdly wonderful bar, tacky to the max, with red vinyl booths, a five-foot Buddha, plenty of incense, and an excellent selection of Chinese beers.

LI-PO, *916 Grant is just across the street from the Buddha Lounge, 415-982-0072.* It exudes its own red-tented, gaudily sleazy ambiance, and can be fun or a bit depressing, depending on your mood and how empty they are.

FINANCIAL DISTRICT

EQUINOX, *atop the Hyatt Regency in Embarcadero 5, 415-788-1234, ext. 30*, is notable because it revolves, providing magnificent city views every which way.

HAIGHT ASHBURY

PERSIAN AUB ZAM ZAM, *1633 Haight near Cole, 415-861-2545*, is run by the finicky Bruno, as it has been for a long time (and was since prohibition days and before by his father), and he opens it when he feels like it. The bar is most famous for Bruno's irascible tendencies to chuck people out of there and direct them "to the very nice bar on the corner," assuring them with no great friendliness that they'll like it there much better. An odd business tactic, Bruno is getting old (probably in his 70s, but don't ask or you'll be sipping suds at Achilles Heel down the street faster than you can say Persian Aub Zam Zam), and he has less and less tolerance for what feels to him like a crowded bar or ogling spectators.

All that said, if Bruno lets you actually add money to his coffers and imbibe in his establishment, it's a very delightful experience. Bruno's martinis are part of the Aub Zam Zam mythology, and they are truly wonderful. He's a martini master, and while it pleases him to be asked to do what he does best (gin, up and dry, with an olive), it'll be a pleasure for you, too. Inside it's like another world. Dimly lit and decked out with a wonderful array of Middle Eastern treasures, it's a decadent but soothing experience to perch on a stool at Bruno's handsome, curving bar (don't ask for a table, it'll only irk the daylights out of Bruno to have you take your drink to what he terms the "horrible room" in back) and take in the peaceful atmosphere he works so hard to maintain, while Haight Street goes on about its mad rush just outside. Neither Bruno nor the Aub Zam Zam can last forever, and they'll be missed sorely when Bruno's testy tirades are heard no more.

MISSION

CAFE BABAR, *994 Guerrero, 415-282-6789*, is a low-keyed bar with your basic tables and chairs, a good selection of wines and sake, and a very nice crowd of regulars.

DALVA, *3121 16th near Valencia, 415-252-7740*, has a DJ on Saturday starting around 10, no cover, and scads of trendy faces packed in like chic sardines. Saturday night at Dalva takes a lot of initiative to elbow through the happening crowd along the narrow strip past the bar. Too noisy for easy conversation, if you come early enough to get a table it's a fun place to watch everyone watching everyone else. Week nights it's a little less of a scene and easier to grab a table and talk.

LA RONDALLA, *901 Valencia near 20th, 415-647-7474,* is a great place that lives its Mexican tradition to the hilt. Open from 11:30am-3:30am Tuesday-Sunday, it's the bar that's the main attraction. Gold tinsel streams from the ceiling, bouncing light from the revolving mirror ball, and red-gold foil hangs in festive bunches. It's that sort of place. With the red lights, roving mariachi bands, and devil margaritas, it's hard to lose. Though the bar dishes up the most atmosphere and entertainment, they also have a kitchen that keeps the Mexican food ($6.50-$9.50) coming till the wee hours. It's good enough, though not superlative, and is especially welcome if you get a late-night surge of hunger. Then you can always go back to the bar.

LATIN-AMERICAN CLUB, *3286 22nd near Guererro, 415-647-2732,* is a trendy bohemian slacker hangout, attracting the twenties crowd (and on occasion the Redman, a local legend who paints himself red). They have a pool table, a juke box, a friendly bar, and a decadent voodoo-esque decor with local art on the walls and a touch of Santeria throughout the club.

LONE PALM, *3394 22nd Street, 415-648-0109,* is a popular bar with a nice crowd, a piano, and little tables draped in white linen and candle-topped. Cozy and lively, there are green palms, of course, everywhere.

MAKE-OUT ROOM, *3225 22nd near Valencia, 415-647-2888,* is another new and trendy Mission bar that appeals to a different youthful substrata. This is the place to go to proudly display your new tattoo or pierced navel, your tongue stud or leather ensemble. It's not a biker hangout, however. Most of the Make-Out Room faithful are middle class whites following the latest in body piercing fashion, and this is the place to show it off.

RITE SPOT CAFE, *2099 Folsom, 415-552-6066,* is a friendly bar, not at all pretentious, but with linen covered tables and ambiance-adding candles. It's not worth a special trip, but if you're in the neighborhood it's a really nice place to hang your hat and have a drink. They have a piano player from 9pm-midnight week nights and 10pm-1pm on weekends, and a pretty good, reasonable menu if you're hungry. There are appetizers ($3-$4.50) like onion rings, bruschetta, and spicy calamari, and entrees ($5-$9) like burgers, sandwiches, various pastas, and veal meals.

UPTOWN, *200 Capp near 17th, 415-861-8231,* is a comfy and conge-nial neighborhood drinking establishment. They have a sofa area in back, booths and a bar up front, a pool table round the corner, and an easy, relaxed air. Rotating fans disperse the smoke, Tiffany-style lamps spread an amber glow, and jazzy music fills the background. Once a local lesbian hang-out, you'll find most anyone there now.

NORTH BEACH

FRANKIE'S BOHEMIAN, *443 Broadway near Kearny, 415-788-7936*, is a large space with a prime Broadway location, devoted to young people looking for action and diverse beers. The brick walls, and red, arched colonnade gives atmosphere, and the loud music provides a challenge if you want to hold a conversation. On a weekend night, you'll find lots of beer lovers, mostly in the 21-35 age range, mostly white, mostly looking for the thrill that comes from drinking in an establishment with the word "bohemian" in its title. There is food here as well (burgers, salads, pasta, seafood, and chicken for $7-$10) from 11am-11pm daily, but the main draw appears to be the beer and the frat-party energy.

SPEC'S MUSEUM CAFE, *12 Saroyan off Columbus (half a block down from Broadway and next to Jazz at Pearls), 415-420-8556*, is a North Beach neighborhood diamond in the rough. The worn wood tables are whisky-stained, and the old dented ashtrays are probably cleaned occasionally, though you'd never notice. But if the furniture is the worse for wear, the vast collection of historic signs, objects, and stuff that lines the walls and hangs from the rafters makes Spec's like no other bar. There are posters from WWII warning "If you talk too much this man may die," there's a blow fish, a stuffed armadillo, a sign saying "Men aloft energize," an oosik, and a sculpture of a mongoose fighting a cobra. There's plenty more there, besides. It's a swell place that's completely unpretentious.

TOSCA CAFE, *242 Columbus between Broadway and Pacific, 415-391-1244*, is a traditional piece of North Beach nightlife, and it's open nightly from 5pm. The cafe looks like it hasn't changed its red-vinyl booths, murky oil paintings, and lamp chandeliers in the nearly 80 years since it opened in 1919, and the jukebox certainly harks back to some old favorites. There's Enrico Caruso and Nat King Cole, *Addio Di Mimi* from La Boheme and Duke Ellington's *Satin Doll*, but on the weekends, it's a waste of time and money, because the thumping beat from the Palladium disco reverberates annoyingly throughout. Plenty of people put up with it for the pleasure of sipping one of their House Cappuccinos (chocolate, cappuccino, and brandy), and happily the Palladium only operates Thursday-Sunday on a regular basis.

A real North Beach crowd squeezes into the old booths or takes cocktails at the bar, and the atmosphere is lively and festive. But if you want to play with the juke box and enjoy the aura without the thump thump thump of the disco, stop by during the week.

VESUVIO CAFE, *255 Columbus near Broadway, 415-362-3370*, is an interesting bar that opens daily at 6am. It's also best during the week nights, but for different reasons. While the niches and corners, upstairs rail tables and views into Kerouac Alley remain the same, you're far more likely to get a seat under the picture of James Joyce or to enjoy the Booth for Lady Psychiatrists on a Tuesday eve than a Saturday, when the place is too packed to enjoy the quirky decor and old North Beach ambiance.

They have been serving suds since 1948, and in the 1989 earthquake, Vesuvio was the only neighborhood place that stayed open. They lit the bar with candles in the overhead chandelier, and served as a meeting and bonding place for the locals who felt wigged out by the 7.0 earthquake. On your average, less traumatic night, Vesuvio has a lot of character, but as the whole neighborhood gets overrun with Bay Area suburbanites going out on the town Friday and Saturday nights, the weekend isn't the best time to appreciate its charms.

SOUTH OF MARKET

CAFE MARS, *798 Brannan near 7th, Street, 415-621-6277*, never has a cover, despite their varied DJ entertainment that usually starts around 10pm. Tuesday night is soul night and Wednesday is acid jazz, but the rest of the nights rely on their eclectic CD collection, ranging from Monkees to acid jazz to Bachman Turner Overdrive. The crowd changes with the night, but weekdays usually see a San Francisco crowd. Tuesday gets a young 25-30 group, Wednesday the ages inch up to 25-35, Thursday the trend continues with 35-40, and the weekends are for everyone, with ages 25-40, all races, and lots more bridge and tunnel people (yuppies from the suburbs over the bay) mixing in and overflowing the place, sipping cosmopolitans and managing to talk over the very loud music. The decor is trendy funk, there's a pool table covered with cherry-red felt, and while this isn't generally a dance club, it's not unprecedented for a group to burst into spontaneous dance. They have been going strong for two years now, and don't know what exactly is the key to their great success, but they certainly appeal to a lot of people.

TWENTY TANK BREWERY, *316 Eleventh near Folsom, 415-255-9455*, is open daily from 11:30am-1:30am. At night, this big warehouse of dark wood and cement blocks is filled with wooden tables and a crowd of twenty and thirty somethings milling about drinking up pints of beer. They serve pizza , sandwiches, and finger food to be washed down, but the emphasis here is on the many varied brews, which range from Martin's Mello-glow Pale to their flagship Kinnikinick "Club" Standard to the brownish-black drink called Pollywanna Porter, plus many more. The bar area gets very busy, and the bar shuffleboard game near the wall seems to be a very happening activity, while the quieter tables are upstairs with a view of the action below.

TENDERLOIN

EDINBURGH CASTLE, *950 Geary between Larkin and Polk, 415-885-4074*, is open 5pm-2am, with parking and fish and chips. Wednesday-Saturday 10:30pm-12:30am there's music (alternative rock, country, rock & roll) and when there's a cover it's $3-$4. The Castle is an endearing place. Underneath the dim, smoky light and grungy tartan carpet, this is an easy-going pub. Lots of Welsh ale, Guinness, and Blackthorn cider flows on tap, and a bulletin board keeps the Scottish contingent abreast of local Scottish events.

People hang out in jeans and comfort clothes. They sit over pints in booths, or play darts and pool in back. Upstairs are a few more booths, dimly lit and perfect for that romantic date, and further on is the music room, complete with stage and unpretentious band: noisy and energetic, lacking polish but banging out the rock with the best of intentions. As smoky bars go, this is a likable pub and a fine place to knock back some beers with your mates.

LATIN DANCE CLUBS

FINANCIAL DISTRICT

SOL Y LUNA, *475 Sacramento between Battery and Sansome, 415-296-8191*, is a Latin Supper Club in a sleek, industrial setting with a patio. They have live music nightly Monday-Saturday (Flamenco jazz, rumba, salsa, and Latin jazz) but times vary from night to night, so you should call for the week's schedule. There's no cover charge Monday and Tuesday, but Wednesday-Saturday it's $5-$10 to enter, and there's free parking after 5pm. The Spanish tapas style food is okay, though not as good as the menu makes it sound, and a DJ spins a variety of sounds after the live groups finish.

MISSION

CESAR'S LATIN PALACE, *3140 Mission, 415-648-6611*, is a San Francisco tradition. Way out in the Mission near Cesar Chavez Street, they are open on the weekends only with live salsa orchestras, local and international. The music starts at 9pm and goes till 5am, the cover is $8-$10, and the parking is in the Kelly Moore Paint Store. The dance floor is hot here, and so is the action. Folks get all dressed up (but you don't have to) and come on hot dates, or else they're looking for one. Guys cruise the tables looking for stray women to dance with, and the dance floor is full of swishing hips till the early morning hours. Come prepared to practice your Spanish, and swivel to the music.

UPPER MARKET

BAHIA CABANA, *1600 Market near Franklin, 415-626-3306*, plays live salsa Thursday, Friday, and Sunday, while on Saturday they have a samba band. The music starts around 9:30-10pm, dinner is served 5-10pm, and cover charges are $5-$10. People get dressed up and come to dance, but you'll need to know the steps to really enjoy.

> ## DANCE CLUBS, DISCOS, & BARS - FROM TRENDY TO CHEESY

FISHERMAN'S WHARF

SILHOUETTES, *155 Jefferson between Taylor and Mason, 415-673-1954*, is a bar with music and dancing Tuesday-Sunday from noon-2am, though the place doesn't get hopping till 10ish on the weekends. The music, DJ operated, is mostly 70s and 80s fare, and there's a cover of $5 Friday and Saturday after 9pm.

HAIGHT ASHBURY

BOOMERANG, *1840 Haight near Stanyan, 415-387-2996*, is a smoky dive with a pool table and live music six nights a week. The music starts 9 or 9:30pm with a cover of $3-$7 and goes from folk to techno to hard rock & roll (featuring such headliners like Super Stooges and Torn Dog Lips). It's something to do if you're in the neighborhood, but not worth going out of your way for.

LOWER HAIGHT

NICKIE'S BBQ, *460 Haight near Fillmore, 415-621-6508*, is open Monday-Saturday 9pm-2am, and Sunday from 4pm-2am. The music features Grateful Dead jams, African, hip-hop, groove jazz, funk and soul, 70s funk, and Irish alternative, depending on the night, the cover is usually around $5, and the dance floor gets so packed on a weekend all you can do is wriggle and squirm and get steamy.

MARINA

VOX, *2001 Union near Buchanan, 415-567-3121*, is a new nightclub and sports bar combo that opened New Years of '96, replacing the beer-swilling Cal's that used to occupy this space. It's off the street in Union Plaza, in the back and up some stairs (just follow the signs). There's a lovely patio with lots of terra cotta and a balcony looking over the street, an inside room with bar, pool table, darts, and foosball, and downstairs is the polished-wood dance floor, with its own bar, flashing, swirling lights, and huge video screen. There's music (all sorts, all sounds, with techno, hip-hop, and 70s-80s mix) all week 8pm-2am, but a DJ takes charge Thursday-Saturday with a $5 cover (for now).

NORTH BEACH

THE PALLADIUM, *1031 Kearny near Broadway, 415-434-1308*, is one of few places the 18-20 year-olds can go to dance. Thursday and Sunday it's open 9pm-4am and the cover is $7, while Friday-Saturday they're open 9am-6am, and the cover is $10. There are an impressive number of security men about, keeping the rowdies under control so the others can dance and mill about to their hearts' content. There's the usual dim lighting and bass-thumping beat that young folks love and old folks detest, but the genre varies.

Thursday they play modern rock, Friday and Saturday is for high energy techno house, and Sunday it's megadance, with the top ten from the past ten years. Along with the black lights, there's also pinball and video games, if you want to take a break from dancing. And while anyone's welcome, the 18-and-over factor means the median age is pretty young.

RUSSIAN HILL

BABLYON, *2260 Van Ness, 415-567-1222*, is a place to be avoided. The weekend cover is $8 before 11pm (when the music starts) and $10 after. The attractive interior with marble pillars and terra cotta-hued arches doesn't help overcome its serious attitude problem. A disco mirrored ball endows the dance floor with speckled light, and dressed up youths trying to look way cool sit at candle-lit tables, waiting for action. The owner (who often stands at the door the better to curl his lip at the world) is a surly man, and his aura fills his place, along with smoke, perfume, and young made-up, lusting kids.

JOHNNY LOVE'S, *1500 Broadway near Polk, 415-931-8021*, is one of those places people love or despise, with no middle ground. There's a live band Thursday-Saturday, and the cover ranges from $2-$9, depending on the night. Go there on a weekend night and you'll find oodles of twenty and thirty somethings, shaking it all over the dance floor to the loud, driving beat. Couples go there, groups have parties, and single sharks cruise for strays, and by 11pm every bit of bar space is three-person deep. Folks stand about, all dressed up and showing it off, while others sit in booths eating and watching the human parade. There are two bar areas, one with TVs and the other with the band, and lots of bar ledges and stools. During the week, they have themes and incentives to keep business up. Tuesdays is stewardess night, Wednesdays has a 70s theme, etc. Some of those who think it's the most, love it for the great hip-hop music, while people walk by outside muttering about the awful music. It's safe to say that if you don't like hip-hop, you won't care for Johnny Love's. It certainly is a social, genuinely friendly place, and far less sleazy than you'd expect a reputed pick-up joint to be.

SOUTH OF MARKET

CITY NIGHTS, *715 Harrison near Third, 415-979-8686*, holds court Saturday nights, only. They say they're the largest night club in San Francisco, and with 15,000 square feet of multi-tiered dance space, it sounds plausible. The DJ-spun music is house, ages 18 and over are welcome, but there is a dress code requiring no athletic shorts, and collared shirts for the men. Inside, it's a well-made, finished warehouse look, with brick floors, painted walls, arches, and colored lights, and a bit more design sophistication than the other warehouse dance clubs. Youths mill about, dance, and watch the show. The beat is all house music, and there are lots of rooms and corridors, upstairs and down, in which to hear it in this big, sprawling place.

DNA LOUNGE, *375 Eleventh near Harrison, 415-626-1409*, has live bands and dancing, with covers ranging from $5-$10. On Fridays they often feature a 70s disco band, while Saturday and Sundays are for 80s nostalgia music. Call the info number for their weekly line-up and a taste of their particular (infantile?) brand of humor. Inside, it's a 20s and 30s crowd, having a bash in the neo-trendy, exposed pipes warehouse, despite the sticky wood floor. Jeans predominate, though flip little dresses aren't out of place, either. Downstairs you have the band stage, the dance floor, and the bar. Upstairs are the railings so you can lean over and watch the show below, plus some beat-up couches in which to sit back and take a break. Your call.

DV 8, *55 Natoma near Mission between First and Second Street, 415-957-1730*, is a super-huge warehouse warren of rooms all devoted to dance and revelry, that's open 11pm-5am on Thursday and Sunday, 10pm-5am Friday-Saturday. It's owned by the same folks who run the Caribbean Zone, and the entrance is around the back of the restaurant. As with many SoMa clubs, each night hosts a different theme, crowd, and name, and the covers range from $5-$10, and ladies are often free before 11pm. Thursdays it's Club Lift, which attracts the local, alternative crowd, mostly gay, who come to hear the music and dance like crazy. Friday night's *Wild 107.7 In the House* gets people from all over the Bay Area, mostly straight. Saturday's Club Eden, done up with apples and the works, is really popular with everyone. Sunday night, the techno and house night, is called Spundae, and the crowd really bounces.

But whatever night you choose to go, the rooms and decorations are just amazing, if you can see them through the flashing lights and past the steamy hordes (DV8 holds 2,500 people, easy). There are pool tables and inviting sofas in one room, white gauzy curtains and eerily wonderful white papiermache human figures attached to the ceiling in another, raw cement pillars for the rough look downstairs, and a psychedelic funk room with cool designs and wild murals. All in all, there are six dance areas (each with their own DJ spot, playing anything from house to hiphop to funky underground house), plus tons of bar areas ready to go. The music blasts, so don't count on conversations of any kind, and when the place is hopping it's easy to wander forever, lost and disoriented, so bring a compass or a friend with a good sense of direction.

HOLY COW, *1535 Folsom is just down the street from the Paradise Lounge, 415-621-6087,* and there's never a cover charge. You can't miss it, thanks to the big black & white papiermache cow dangling its udders outside. Inside the club, the music throbs and young bodies gyrate on the crowded dance floor. It's a happy place, in a noisy sort of way. The DJ spins lousy 70s disco, but folks drink, manage to talk, and dance, and the atmosphere remains genial, no slimy pick-up joint flavor to it at all (though people do meet people they like, it just doesn't feel sleazy). The walls are of wood, decorated with interesting pictures and old signs, and the crowd (made up of locals and European tourists) are usually from 21-35. What makes this place popular is the pleasant attitude of the people who keep coming, so it's a self-perpetuating cycle of the most positive sort.

HOTEL UTAH, *500 Fourth near Bryant, 415-421-8308,* is a refreshing change of pace from the usual warehouse dance space in SoMa. They have varied live bands nightly, with open mike Mondays starting at 8pm, improv jazz on Tuesdays, and Wednesday-Sunday local bands playing acoustic folk to hard core punk, blues and rock & roll to reggae. Covers range from 0-$7 (starting around 8pm) and the music starts anywhere from 7:30-10:30 and lasts till 1am.

This place is popular with the professional crowd (computer analysts, teachers, judges, architects), and it's a place where regulars come in casual, comfortable clothes to hang out in the narrow bar area under one of the mounted deer heads, listen to the music, and have a few drinks, but it's also a place where folks come to make new acquaintances and flirt by the long wood bar with the carved mahogany pillars in back. They have good beers on tap, and a congenial air. However, depending on the band of the night, the music may take priority, in which case you'd head down a few steps to join the throng, or up above to hunt for seats in the little alcoves, and get a great view of band and bar. It's too loud to talk easily up there, but you can manage to have a conversation down near the bar.

THE PARADISE LOUNGE, *1515 Folsom near Eleventh, 415-861-5121,* is a bar with live bands that play all sorts of music, generally starting at 9pm or so, for $3-$7 a cover. Inside it's quite dim, with your standard tables and settees, pinball and bar. Then there's the room with the band,

and it's filled with sound and endless bodies packed tightly together. Or go upstairs to take it all in from the voyeur's perch. Check the Sunday Datebook section of the *San Francisco Chronicle* or *Bay Guardian* to see what's on for the week, or call them in the evening.

SOUND FACTORY, *525 Harrison between First and Second, 415-543-1300*, opens at 9:30pm, admission is free till 10pm, when the cover's $10, and there's a mild dress code that rules out sneakers, hooded sweatshirts, or caps. Most of the music is house, but it varies from room to room (the Blue, the Red, or the Loft), featuring sounds such as Latin salsa, retro funk and disco, and underground house. The massive place is done up in neo-tech, with design sculpture, big art video screens, a curvy bar and blue lights. There's a pounding DJ mix and swirling lights covering a dance floor and stage, plus a room with pool tables and couches. And there's an upstairs, too, with more pool tables and more passages in which to get lost.

1015 CLUB, *1015 Folsom near Sixth, 415-431-1200*, their events change all the time (as do the covers, but they're usually around $10), so the best thing to do is to call their number for a recording of what's happening that week. Though some DJs and happenings bring bigger crowds than others, in general, this is one popular place, with long, long crowds waiting to get into the jammed, steamy interior. There you'll find lots of bodies of many races and types, mostly in their 20s, a very packed dance floor, and flashing lights. There's an upstairs, too, which sometimes gets rented out for private parties. It's posher and less crowded up there, with sofas and booths, fake leopard skin settees, and more socializing than dancing. It may not be easy to get in, but it's harder to get out. Trying to find the exit through the mass of flesh can be a frustrating, suffocating experience whose final reward is the sweet, fresh air of Folsom Street.

330 RITCH, *330 Ritch off Townsend between Third and Fourth, 415-541-9574*, is open Monday-Saturday, the music starts at 10pm and the cover is $5-$15. They have live jazz Mondays and Wednesday, and live salsa on Saturday (with free lessons at 8:30pm), while the other nights a DJ plays stuff from acid jazz to dance hall reggae and house. Tuesdays is usually soul and hip-hop night, and Fridays they offer free parking before 10pm, and they have a happy hour from 6-8pm.

This is a more upscale spot, with stylishly exposed brick walls, and a busy dance floor surrounded by tables of cocktail sippers all done up in their SoMa best. Behind this scene is another room that's a little quieter, with a pool table and booths. It's a lively nightclub, with people endlessly queued up outside, waiting to get in.

TENDERLOIN

MISS PEARL'S JAM HOUSE, *610 Eddy between Polk and Larkin in the Tenderloin, 415-775-5267*, serves dinner Wednesday-Sunday (6-10pm

Wednesday-Thursday, 6-11pm Friday-Saturday, 5:30-9:30pm Sunday), they have live reggae Friday-Saturday, and valet parking Friday-Saturday. Got all that? They're also instituting a Sunday Brunch 11am-2:30pm starting after Easter. Best known for their weekend dance parties, the cover is $5 and they get very crowded.

UNION SQUARE

CLUB OZ, *Powell and Geary on the 32nd floor of the Westin St. Francis, 415-774-0116,* is an upscale version of your basic disco. If you enjoy the pulse and throb of the disco beat, the razzmatazz of blinking lights and video screen, Club Oz does it up in style. It has a $5 admission on Sunday, $8 Monday-Thursday, $15 on weekends, and should you want drinks as well, that's another $15 for two. Opening at 9pm but not really hopping till 11pm or so, the mix is Euro House, and the style is sleek. The view of the city at night through their enormous bay windows is unbeatable, and the cozy little seating nooks give you privacy with your honey. The place is full of faux rocks, mirrors, glass, and trees strung with lights. There's a central dance floor where you can strut your stuff or watch others do the same.

LENNON REVOLUTION IN THE MAKING

Julian Lennon - singer, John Lennon's son, and now restaurant and club man - has laid plans for a dance club, lounge, and restaurant on prime Union Square property. "Revolution" is the name, and it's to be on Maiden Lane (between Grant and Stockton), and fronting on Geary. It'll do lunch, it'll do dinner, it'll have a basement dance club and a mezzanine level jazz, rhythm, and blues lounge. The Revolution (a reference to the healers of humanity rather than the Beatles song of the same name) will honor heroes of change in a gallery of artwork, proceeds of which will benefit the artist's preferred charities as well as the local arts community. If all has gone according to plan, this should be one of the hottest new venues on the club scene by November 1996.

CLUB 181, *181 Eddy is near Union Square, but that one extra block west puts you into the Tenderloin, 415-673-8181.* If you walk, you'll notice the shift, pass the street life, and feel the sleazy atmosphere. The club, however, is safe, and the dress code (no tennis shoes, torn jeans, or athletic wear) keeps the street element on the street, as does the $7 cover charge ($5 during the week). Se Padilla, the man who started it all four years ago, wanted to create a lounge feel that was comfortable, a nightclub with energy and style, with elegance but no attitude. The walls are curvy, with hardly a straight line to the place, and the music is funk for now, but it's liable to change with times (it started out as acid jazz, but now has more of a '70s feel, with lots of brass).

The evolution of the music here is just a continuation of this location's entertainment history. The bar dates back to the '30s, and in the '40s this was known as a breakfast club (one of those illegal after hours spots serving booze from 2am-6pm); in the '50s they went legit as a jazz club (Ray Charles played here), and that was replaced by a burlesque show in the '60s. It was closed down for years, but has been brought back to life in its present dance club format.

They have a loyal local following with a real San Francisco mix of races and colors, dancing as the mirror disco ball spins light spots on the floor, and disco jazz fills the room. You can dance, you can attempt to converse over the loud music, hang out in the pool room, or visit the new attached DJ dance room. It's not a scene for everyone, but it's an interesting place to dance, and the bouncers keep it safe.

GAY DANCE CLUBS

THE ENDUP, *4016 Sixth near Harrison, 415-896-1075*, is generally open Thursday-Monday 10pm-2am, plus additional Saturday and Sunday hours 6am-9pm. However, the EndUp is one of five clubs in the city to obtain the precious round-the-clock license (allowing them those 2-6am hours), and they will stay open to take in the spillover from closing bars when the situation warrants. The idea is that after a busy evening of club-hopping or whatever, this is where you *end up* to polish off the night. They offer a wide variety of entertainment, with covers ranging from $4-$8, and different themes attracting different clientele on different days.

It's quite the place, with enough visual stimuli to send you running to the central bar for another stiff one, but the style and content depend on the theme of the night (or day). Saturday night is Club Vertigo, attracting a young, gay crowd (but daytime Saturday, called Otherwhirled, sees a mixed but mostly straight group). At night, go-go dancers in drag strut their stuff on platforms, while psychedelic swirls left over from the 60s decorate the walls and swiveling mannequin legs hang from the ceiling. Video screens flash more food for the eyes, ultraviolet light makes all your whites turn purple, and the dance floor throbs with the DJ's house mix. Sunday from 6am-evening is T-Dance, the busiest of events that's been around for 20 years and appeals to a mixed crew, while the night belongs to Mother's Milk, a gay venue. Monday is a reggae theme with Club Dread, and Thursday's Bedlam has a gothic flavor, attracts a straight crowd, and plays industrial house music. Friday night is The Scene, going after a mixed population, but it hasn't been too popular and may be changing.

RAWHIDE II, *298 Seventh, 415-621-1192*, is the place to go for country music and square dancing. It attracts a youngish crowd, and everyone there is into the music and the dance.

THE STUD, *399 Ninth near Harrison, 415-252-7883*, plays a range of music to a range of people. The dim lights mostly hide the bare floor, while the dancing goes on in back, past the smoky, unremarkable bar. Sunday the DJ spins 80s music, and Monday is house-funk night, a popular evening which tends to attract a largely black crowd. Wednesday it gets packed out for oldies night, attracting a mixed group, and Fridays-Saturdays usually has '70s and '80s tunes. There is entertainment Tuesday and Thursday as well, but it varies. The cover ranges from $1-$4, and while the bar is predominantly gay, it attracts a sizable straight crowd some nights as well.

TROCADERO NIGHT CLUB, *520 Fourth near Bryant, 415-495-6620*, has varied clubs and live bands with covers from free-$20. Monday is Deathguild night, a gothic evening, Wednesday they have Bondage A-Go-Go ($5), an erotic fetish dance club with a bondage pit upstairs and flaming go-go cages. Friday it's Terminator, with rock & roll and alternative music, set up like a circus side show with tattoo artists and body-piercers, Armenian rubber men and sword swallowers, and admission is $18 before midnight, $10 after. Saturday they host live shows of various sorts, from ska to 80s new wave, and some Sundays they have punk, no cover.

On club nights, entrance is for those 18 and over, but all ages are welcome for the live shows, and while the bar is active, so is the kitchen, serving up southwestern dishes and tapas. Inside, it's dark, jammed-full, and steamy, with a revolving disco ball and colored lights. There's a lot of roaming around and it's easy to get lost in the densely packed rooms. This is not the place for claustrophobics.

TOWNSEND NIGHTCLUB, *177 Townsend near Third, 415-974-6020*, is a vast, 10,000 square foot dance complex, and while it features different music styles that appeal to varied segments of society on different nights of the week for a cover of $5-$15, there are almost always lines of people outside, waiting to get in. Once inside, there's the pounding beat provided by the excellently maintained Richard Long sound system, the foggy colored lights, a circular central bar, and a big cement dance floor under circus lights up front where the action is. The first Friday of each month, this is Club Q, with house music drawing an exclusively female (mostly but not all lesbian) crowd, with go-go girls dancing on side scaffolding. Saturday nights are for Club Universe, which stays open till 7am, has a DJ spinning house music, and attracts a group that's about 75% gay. The decor changes from week to week, so the warehouse space may be done up in a Roman theme one night, with columns and statues and grimacing emperor friezes, while another week there might be a jungle motif. And Pleasuredome (each Sunday), is one of the best-known disco nights in the gay community.

Around the back is the **KING STREET GARAGE**, another dance space with its own venue, but under the same management. It's darker and smaller than the Townsend space, with the dance floor on the main level and an upstairs area with tables and snacks, and a rail over which to view the throng below. The first Friday of each month they host Informal Nation, which plays house and hip-hop, and raises money for all sorts of worthy causes, while the second and fourth Fridays see Asia, a dance club for gay Asian males. The first Saturday there's Wicked, one of the longest running raves, attracting famous rave DJs, and the second and fourth Saturdays host Futora for the gay Latino community. Then there's the Mothership Connection (the third Saturday) playing all types of music for a very diverse (whites, blacks, yuppies, college kids, you name it) crowd. And there are special nights too, like DUI (dancing under the influence) which is a straight Asian club, and Cream of Beat, a big rap bash with a strong black following that takes place the nights before major holidays.

HOLE IN THE WALL SALOON, *289 Eighth Street, 415-431-4695*, is a roughish gay bar. Outside you'll find a line of motorcycles, and inside it's dark and smoky, with a pool table, a cigarette machine, and lots of tinsel hanging from the ceiling. It's not for everybody.

DRAG SHOWS

NORTH BEACH

FINOCCHIO CLUB, *506 Broadway near Kearny, 415-982-9388*, is open Thursday-Saturday, and the doors open at 7:45. Shows start at 8:30, 10, and 11:30pm, but the $14.50 admission ticket is good all night. You can enter whenever you'd like, leave, and come on back during another show, if you so choose. Finocchio's has been doing female impersonations since 1936, and they do a very professional show, unlike Kimo's. There are lots of linen-covered, candle-lit tables, and a big stage for the performers to do their thing. There's dancing, lip-synching, and singing, there's camp and Broadway show-tunes, but whatever the number, the good-natured performance has a nice mix of wit and warmth. This is a comfortable place for gay, straight, local, and tourist to come for a show, and get some old-fashioned, traditional entertainment served up in drag.

POLK GULCH

KIMO'S, *1351 Polk near Pine, 415-885-4535*, has a bar upstairs and down, but their specialty is drag shows. They go on Friday and Saturday nights (sometimes other nights as well) from 9 or 10pm-1am, admission is $5-$10, and there's a two-drink minimum. Downstairs it looks like just another seedy bar, but it's quite the drag scene upstairs. There are tables with red candles, windows over Polk Street, and a tolerant attitude that accepts whoever walks in, whether you're in drag or not, male or female, gay or straight.

It's a low-budget, friendly sort of place where everyone seems to know one another, and no one gets upset if the show is delayed 30 minutes because Tiger Lily isn't ready yet. Decor is not the strong suit here, and a few spider plants and floral table cloths is as far as it goes. That's not why the guys come here. It's a place to get all dressed up with wigs and the works, josh around, and watch the dance and lip-sync show.

KARAOKE

FISHERMAN'S WHARF

CLUB BIEN BIEN, *383 Bay near Mason*, is a karaoke club done up in Hong Kong style and is open nightly from 9pm-2am, but their disco downstairs is only open Friday and Saturday nights. It's free before 10:30, but after that it costs $10 to get in to the disco (but remains free to go upstairs to the karaoke lounge). There are special karaoke rooms with themes (Japanese, ancient Egypt, the Harley room, etc.) that you can rent, a general karaoke bar, plus video games, and pool tables.

JAPANTOWN

There are a good number of karaoke bars in **Japan Center** and in the surrounding neighborhood.

STRIP SHOWS

NORTH BEACH

There are a ton of strip joints along Broadway between Columbus and Kearny, and a couple on Kearny as well.

SOUTH OF MARKET

GOLD CLUB, *650 Howard near New Montgomery, 415-536-0300*, calls itself a gentleman's supper club, which are all nice words for a girlie strip joint. To be sure, it's more refined and less sleazy than Mitchell Brothers, and there is a dinner buffet that's included in the $20 entrance fee, but still, the entertainment here comes from the svelte and buxom lovelies who dance and strip on stage. It's appropriately dark in here, so you won't be easily recognized, and it's a very mixed clientele. There are couples, groups and lone wolves, men and women, and a fairly even mix of white and Asian all ogling the show. Actually, the stage strip is just the general show; there are private gyrations going on all through the club, called Table Dances.

There's no actual physical contact or G-string removal, but for $10 you can have one of the women swivel her parts and stroke her own limbs just inches from your face. Or, pay the extra $10 for VIP privileges, which consist mostly of going upstairs to the VIP lounge. There are softer chairs up there, you can invite one of the girls to join you for a drink, or get one of the VIP $20 Table Dances - a more involved display that gives you your extra ten dollars worth.

TENDERLOIN

MITCHELL BROTHERS, *895 O'Farrell near Polk, 415-776-6686*, is the oldest, best-known sex show in town, open daily 11:30am-2am. It costs $30 to get in, and that gives you access to the strip show room, where lap dancers strut about in G-strings, ready to "dance" and wiggle in your lap for $20 or so, with additional money prolonging the dance. There's the Ultra Room and the Green Door Room where you get a private booth with a window on the show inside, and theaters showing sex films, too.

To add to the fun is the scandal of a few years ago, where one of the Mitchell Brothers was found guilty of murdering the other Mitchell Brother. Despite the fraternal discord, the show still goes on; it's a bit of a seedy place, but they have been around for a long time.

NIGHTLIFE BY NEIGHBORHOOD

Chinatown
> **Buddha Lounge**, *901 Grant, 415-362-1792*, bar
> **Li-Po**, *916 Grant, 415-982-0072*, bar

Hayes Valley
> **Place Pigalle**, *520 Hayes, 415-552-2671*, eclectic

Fisherman's Wharf
> **Club Bien Bien**, *383 Bay, 415-399-9555*, karaoke
> **Fiddler's Green**, *1333 Columbus, 415-441-9758*, Irish
> **Lou's Pier 47**, *300 Jefferson, 415-771-0377*, blues
> **Silhouettes**, *155 Jefferson, 415-673-1954*, dance club

Financial District/Downtown
> **Bix**, *56 Gold Street, 415-433-6300*, jazz supper club
> **Cafe Bastille**, *22 Belden, 415-986-5673*, jazz
> **Cafe Claude**, *7 Claude Lane, 415-392-3505*, jazz
> **Equinox**, *atop the Hyatt Regency in Embarcadero 5, 415-788-1234, ext. 30,*
> bar

The Pied Piper Lounge, *Sheraton Palace Hotel at Market and New Montgomery, 415-392-8600,* bar
Pier 23 Cafe, *Pier 23, 415-362-5125,* eclectic music
Sol y Luna, *475 Sacramento, 415-296-8191,* Latin nightclub
Haight Ashbury
Boomerang, *1840 Haight, 415-387-2996,* dance club
Persian Aub Zam Zam, *1633 Haight, 415-861-2545,* bar
Lower Haight
Nickie's BBQ, *460 Haight, 415-621-6508,* dance club
Marina
Blues, *2125 Lombard, 415-771-2583,* blues
Paragon, *3521 Scott, 415-922-2456,* jazz and rock
Pasand Lounge, *1875 Union, 415-922-4498,* jazz
Vox, *2001 Union, 415-567-3121,* dance club
Mission
Albion Club, *3139 16th, 415-552-8558,* blues and jazz
Blondies' Bar & No Grill, *540 Valencia near 17th, 415-864-2419,* jazz
Bruno's, *2389 Mission, 415-550-7455,* jazz
Cesar's Latin Palace, *3140 Mission, 415-648-6611,* Latin nightclub
Cafe Babar, *994 Guerrero, 415-282-6789,* bar
Chameleon, *853 Valencia, 415-821-1891,* eclectic
Dalva, *3121 16th, 415-252-7740,* bar
Elbo Room, *647 Valencia, 415-552-7788,* jazz
El Rio, *3158 Mission, 415-282-3325,* eclectic
Kilowat, *3160 16th, 415-861-2595,* punk
Latin-American Club, *3286 22nd, 415-647-2732,* bar
La Rondalla, *901 Valencia, 415-647-7474,* bar
Lone Palm, *3394 22nd, 415-648-0109,* bar
Make-Out Room, *3225 22nd, 415-647-2888,* bar
Radio Valencia, *1199 Valencia, 415-826-1199,* jazz and bluegrass
Rite Spot Cafe, *2099 Folsom, 415-552-6066,* bar
Uptown, *200 Capp near 17th, 415-861-8231,* bar
Nob Hill
New Orleans Room, *in the Fairmont at 950 Mason, 415-772-5259,* cabaret
Tonga Room, *in the Fairmont at 950 Mason, 415-772-5278,* bar
North Beach
Bimbo's,*1025 Columbus, 415-474-0365,* eclectic
Cocodrie, *1024 Kearny, 415-986-6678,* eclectic
Finocchio Club, *506 Broadway, 415-982-9388,* drag show
Frankie's Bohemian, *433 Broadway, 415-788-7936,* bar
Gathering Caffe, *1326 Grant, 415-433-4247,* jazz
Grant & Green, *1371 Grant, 415-956-9605,* blues

Hi-Ball Lounge, *473 Broadway, 415-397-9464*, jazz
Jazz at Pearl's, *256 Columbus, 415-291-8255*, jazz
O'Reilly's Irish Pub, *622 Green, 415-989-6222*, Irish
The Palladium, *1031 Kearny, 415-434-1308*, dance club
The Saloon, *1232 Grant, 415-989-7666*, blues
Spec's Twelve Adler Museum Cafe, *12 Adler, 415-420-8556*, bar
Tosca Cafe, *242 Columbus, 415-391-1244*, bar
Vesuvio Cafe, *255 Columbus, 415-362-3370*, bar

Pacific Heights

Rasselas Jazz Club, *2801 California, 415-567-5010*, jazz

Polk/Russian Hill

Bablyon, *2260 Van Ness, 415-567-1222*, dance club
Coconut Grove, *1415 Van Ness, 415-776-1616*, jazz supper club
Johnny Love's, *1500 Broadway, 415-931-8021*, dance club
Julie Ring's Heart and Soul, *1695 Polk, 415-673-7100*, jazz supper club
Kimo's, *1351 Polk, 415-885-4535*, drag show

Potrero Hill

Bottom of the Hill, *1233 17th Street, 415-621-4455*, eclectic music

Richmond

Last Day Saloon, *406 Clement, 415-387-6343*, rock & roll
Orocco, *3565 Geary, 415-387-8788*, jazz supper club
Plough and Stars, *116 Clement, 415-751-1122*, Irish

SoMa (South of Market)

Cafe Mars, *798 Brannan, 415-621-6277*, bar
City Nights, *715 Harris, 415-979-8686*, dance club
DNA, *375 Eleventh Street, 415-626-1409*, dance club
DV 8, *55 Natoma, 415-957-1730*, dance club
Eleven, *374 11th Street, 415-431-3337*, jazz
The EndUp, *4016 Sixth Street, 415-896-1075*, gay dance club
42 Degrees, *235 16th Street, 415-777-5558*, jazz supper club
Gold Club, *650 Howard, 415-536-0300*, sex show
Harry Denton's Bar & Grill, *161 Steuart, 415-882-1333*, blues
Hole In The Wall Saloon, *289 Eighth Street, 415-431-4695*, gay bar
Holy Cow, *1535 Folsom, 415-621-6087*, dance club
Hotel Utah, *500 Fourth, 415-421-8308*, dance club
Julie's Supper Club, *1123 Folsom, 415-861-0707*, blues supper club
Jelly's, *Pier 50, 415-495-3099*, Argentinean
The Paradise Lounge, *1515 Folsom, 415-861-5121*, dance club
Rawhide II, *298 Seventh, 415-621-1192*, gay dance club
Slim's, *333 Eleventh, 415-621-3330*, eclectic music
Sound Factory, *525 Harrison, 415-543-1300*, dance club
The Stud, *399 Ninth, 415-252-7883*, gay dance club

Ten 15, *1015 Folsom, 415-431-0700,* dance club
330 Ritch, *360 Ritch, 415-541-9574,* dance club
Townsend Nightclub, *177 Townsend, 415-974-6020,* gay dance club
Trocadero Night Club, *520 Fourth, 415-495-6620,* gay dance club
Twenty Tank Brewery, *316 Eleventh, 415-255-9455,* bar
Up & Down Club, *1151 Folsom, 415-626-2388,* jazz
Tenderloin
Edinburgh Castle, *950 Geary, 415-885-4074,* bar
Great American Music Hall, *859 O'Farrell, 415-885-0750,* eclectic
music
Miss Pearl's Jam House, *610 Eddy, 415-775-5267,* reggae dance club
Mitchell Brothers, *895 O'Farrell, 415-776-6686,* sex show
Union Square
Biscuits & Blues, *401 Mason, 415-292-2583,* blues
The Blue Lamp, *561 Geary, 415-885-1464,* blues
Campton Place, *340 Stockton, 415-781-5555,* bar/jazz
The Compass Rose, *335 Powell, 415-774-0167,* jazz
Club 181, *181 Eddy, 415-673-8181,* dance club
Club Oz, *in the Westin St. Francis at Powell and Geary, 415-774-0116,*
dance club
Club 36, *345 Stockton, 415-398-1234,* bar
Harry's Starlight Room, *in the Sir Francis Drake, Powell and Sutter, 415-392-7755,* bar
Les Joulins Jazz Club, *44 Ellis, 415-397-5397,* jazz
Mason Street Wine Bar, *342 Mason, 415-391-3454,* jazz
Plush Room Cabaret, *940 Sutter, 415-885-2800,* cabaret
The Red Room, *825 Sutter, 415-923-6800,* bar
The Redwood Room, *495 Geary, 415-775-4700,* bar
Upper Market
Bahia Cabana, *1600 Market, 415-626-3306,* Latin nightclub
Cafe du Nord, *2170 Market, 415-861-5016,* eclectic music
Western Addition
Storyville Classic Jazz Club, *1751 Fulton, 415-441-1751,* jazz

16. CULTURE

DANCE

San Francisco Ballet, *415-865-2000,* usually performs in the Opera House, but while it's being retrofitted to repair damage incurred in the 1989 quake, the ballet will go on in a number of locations around the Bay Area, such as Yerba Buena Gardens south of Market, the Palace of Fine Arts in the Marina, and Zellerbach Hall at UC Berkeley.

Center for the Arts, *Yerba Buena Gardens, 415-978-2787*, has fine art, popular culture, and changing dance and musical performances. There are also lovely gardens, spiffy fountains, and a general respite from the noisy, busy hum of downtown.

There are also dance festivals, such as the **Edge Festival** in March exhibiting what's new in choreography, and the **Ethnic Dance Festival** in early June.

FILM

There are movie theaters throughout the city, from first-run complexes like the Kabuki in Japantown to art film and oldies theaters like the Castro. If you want to see a film, check the papers for the day's listings, but there are a few things to keep in mind. **The Castro** is a beautiful old theater with an organ that gets played before films, and the **Red Vic** is a Haight Street tradition, with couches as well as chairs, good popcorn and coffee served in real bowls and mugs, and an old group of film-buff friends that formed the co-op, choose the films, and run the show.

Some theaters (but not all) have matinee bargains, the **ACM Kabuki 8 Theater** has a dusk special (the show closest to sunset is half-price), and there are great film festivals here in the spring (The **Asian Film Festival** is in March and the **International Film Festival** starts late April or early May). In the spring there's the **Asian American International Festival**, the **San Francisco International**, and **Spike and Mike's Festival of Animation**. In June, there's the **San Francisco International Lesbian and Gay Film Festival**, and in November the **Roxie Cinema** hosts the **Film**

Arts Festival, celebrating low-budget features, documentaries, and experimental short films from Bay Area film makers.

CLASSICAL MUSIC

There are plenty of seasonal concerts and series, so check the papers for a full listing.

San Francisco Opera, *301 Van Ness near Grove, 415-864-3330*, will start off their fall opera season in the newly refurbished Opera House.

San Francisco Symphony, *201 Van Ness near Grove, 415-431-5400*, is now under the baton of Michael Tilson Thomas. Inside, it's beautiful in a light and modern way. There is a symmetry and grace of lines, the bright wood of the stage sets off the black-clad musicians, the box seats' scrolled white prows resemble the stylized bow of a ship. More importantly, though, the sound is superb. The work of a few years ago has paid off, and the many hanging glass panels and cloth drops (easily adjustable for continued sound tinkering) ensure that the sound is pristinely pure, reflected cleanly and distinctly so you can hear the individual sections as well as the glorious whole.

Grace Cathedral Concerts, *Grace Cathedral at 1051 Taylor on Nob Hill, 415-776-6611*, hosts concerts from time to time. Some of the concerts are free to the public, while others charge an entrance fee, but the concert information line can give you all the details.

Old First Concerts, *Old First Presbyterian Church at Van Ness and Sacramento, 415-474-1608*, tends towards solo performances and chamber music. There's at least one concert a week, costing $7-$9, but you should call for the exact details.

Noontime Concerts, *Old St. Mary's Church at 660 California in Chinatown, 415-288-3840*, hosts free midday (12:30pm) concerts each Tuesday.

OTHER MUSIC

Golden Gate Park Band, *415-666-7107*, performs Sundays at 1pm from April-December in the Music Concourse in Golden Gate Park between the de Young Museum and the California Academy of Sciences. It's free, and it's a fine place for a picnic.

Stern Grove Midsummer Music Festival, *415-252-6252*, runs yearly from mid-June to mid-August, with wonderful free performances, from jazz to opera, in Stern Grove's beautiful (if sometimes foggy) outdoor setting in the Sunset.

Audium, *1616 Bush near Franklin, 415-771-1616*, performs its "Sound Sculptures" weekends at 8:30pm. With 136 speakers projecting sounds in total darkness, the Audium experience is 75 minutes of aural exploration.

THEATERS

San Francisco stages a lot of plays, from old repertory standards to new playwrights' cutting edge plays. *The Chronicle* or *Examiner* newspaper Datebook sections will list what's on in the city, as will the free *Bay Guardian* weekly.

ACCORDING TO THE STARS

Walter Pidgeon: "From vaudeville days to today, I've always looked forward to visits to San Francisco. It's one of the best 'show towns' in the world ... It's like New York with a California climate. It's a city that's smart, without being 'upstage' as we actors call it."

Richard Burton: "San Francisco audiences are like litmus paper, fast as light. Even at the matinee this afternoon they got everything. They're so intelligent and witty, and I am not being fulsome, I mean it, they encourage you."

Luisa Tetrazzini: "I like San Francisco better than any other city in the world ... Where else could I sing outdoors on Christmas Eve!

Katherine F. Gerould: "San Francisco is the most sophisticated city in the country. From prize-fights to grand opera, it is nearly always in good taste, yes and has delicacy. A San Francisco audience is a test of a good play. As a matter of fact, a New York audience is no test at all."

Mainstream Theaters

American Conservatory Theater-ACT, *415-749-2228,* stages plays at the **Stage Door**, *420 Mason,* and their newly renovated, beautiful **Geary Theater**, *415 Geary.*

The Curran, *445 Geary, 415-776-1999,* has been showcasing The *Phantom of the Opera* forever, and there's no final date in sight.

Golden Gate Theater, *at 1 Taylor near Golden Gate and Market,* and **The Orpheum**, *at 1192 Market near the Civic Center,* can be reached at *415-776-1999 or 800-225-2277* for tickets.

Lorraine Hansberry Theater, *620 Sutter, 415-474-8800*

THE GEARY THEATER

The Geary was first built in 1910, and has provided a stage for great performers over the years, such as Fanny Brice and Sarah Bernhardt. Helen Hayes made her 17-year-old debut here, Laurence Olivier played opposite Vivien Leigh as Romeo and Juliet, and Ethel Waters, Edith Piaf, and Josephine Baker have all performed here. The 1989 earthquake closed the Geary in a shower of plaster, but it finally reopened $27.5 million later in 1996, newly beautiful and ready for more shows to go on.

Marine Memorial Theater, *609 Sutter, 415-771-6900*
Theater on the Square, *450 Post, 415-433-9500*
The 450 Geary Studio Theater, *450 Geary, 415-673-1172*

DISCOUNT TICKETS

TIX Bay Area, 251 Stockton on Union Square, 415-433-7827, sells half-price theater tickets the day of the performance and advance tickets for theater, dance, music, and opera. It's open Tuesday-Thursday 11am-6pm and Saturday 11am-7pm, and you can call to see what they have got.

Berkeley Repertory Theater, *2025 Addison in Berkeley, 510-845-4700*
Free Shakespeare in the Park Festival, *415-666-2221,* does its outdoor performances in Golden Gate Park through September (once most of the summer fog's burned off). It's free, though they pass a hat around, and it's a swell opportunity for a picnic.

BEACH BLANKET BABLYON

Beach Blanket Bablyon, at Club Fugazi, 678 Green near Powell, 415-421-4222, costs $18-$45, depending on day and seat. This has been a kitchy San Francisco institution since 1974, when Steve Silver first started with the campy songs and enormous hats. It is everlastingly popular, but that doesn't mean necessarily that you'll like it. The show themes change all the time, but they all involve song and dance routines that paint the world with a very broad, silly style of humor that will either make you laugh like a loon or cringe with pain.

Theater – Fringe
Asian American Theater, *403 Arguello, 415-751-2600*
Intersection for the Arts, *446 Valencia, 415-626-3311*
Cowell Theater, *at Fort Mason, 415-441-3400*
Magic Theater, *at Fort Mason, 415-441-8822*
Marsh, *1062 Valencia, 415-641-0235,* hosts a lot of up-and-coming, very clever monologists (like Josh Kornbluth) and plays that are worth checking out.
The Phoenix, *301 Eighth, 415-621-4423*
Theater Artaud, *450 Florida, 415-621-7797*
Theater Rhinoceros, *2926 16th, 415-861-7933*
San Francisco Fringe Festival, *415-931-1094,* features experimental theater throughout the downtown area.

COMEDY

Climate Theater, *252 Ninth, 415-978-2345*
Cobb's Comedy Club, *2801 Leavenworth in The Cannery, 415-928-4320*
Punch Line, *444 Battery, 415-397-7573*

THEATER SPORTS

BATS at Bayfront Theater in Building B, on the third floor of Fort Mason Center, 415-824-8220, stands for Bay Area Theater Sports. They do an innovative, fun version of improvisation, using teams that perform and compete on given topics and themes according to various rules. The skits aren't prepared, so what you get ranges from mildly amusing to hilarious, but it almost always makes for an entertaining evening. They're on Mondays at 8pm, tickets are $8 (general seating, and $2 off for students and seniors), and parking is free.

17. SHOPPING

BOOKSTORES

Acorn Books, *740 Polk near Ellis, 415-563-1736*, is a clean, well-organized museum of used, rare, and out-of-print books that's great for browsing.

A Clean Well Lighted Place for Books, *601 Van Ness between Turk and Golden Gate, 415-441-6670*, is an excellent store with a large selection, and they have interesting readings and author talks at night.

A Different Light Bookstore, *489 Castro near 18th, 415-431-0891*, is the best Gay and Lesbian bookstore in San Francisco, and it's run by a very nice staff.

Barnes and Noble, *2552 Taylor near Bay (next to Cost Plus), 415-292-6762*, has two floors full of a fine selection of new books of all sorts, and they have a very nice cafe area, too.

Borders Books and Music, *400 Post near Powell, 415-399-1633*, is a lovely and conveniently located full-service book store with two floors of books plus an espresso bar and cafe tables.

City Lights, *261 Columbus near Broadway in the heart of North Beach, 415-362-8193*, is a wonderful book store as well as a bit of San Francisco history. Opened by Beat poet Laurence Ferlinghetti in 1953, they have got fine collections of fiction (both local and worldwide), drama, poetry, and alternative-political analyses and histories. They also have a good travel and cookbook section, and it's a friendly, interesting place to browse or buy. They're open till midnight, and they often have events like readings or mountain music.

Columbus Books, *540 Broadway, 415-986-3872*, is an excellent discount book store of new and used books that has been a favorite for years. Sandwiched between a strip joint and an adult sex toy store, Columbus Books is a welcome haven for the perusal of literature. And now they're expanding. A space has been cleared up front by the window, nice tables have appeared, and fine coffee brought in. Now you can thumb through the texts seated comfortably at a table while sipping your choice of espresso, cappuccino, latte, or coffee. Life doesn't get much better.

Discount Medical Books, *345 Judah near 9th in the Inner Sunset, 415-664-5555* and **Discount Textbooks**, *3950 19th near Junipero Serra in the Sunset, 415-585-2665*, are owned by the same people who run Columbus Books with such flair.

Green Apple, *506 Clement near 6th in the Richmond, 415-387-2272*, has been a local favorite for more than 25 years. They have aisles full of used books of all sorts, and a healthy new book section, too. If you like books, it's hard to resist browsing there.

Modern Times Bookstore, *888 Valencia, 415-282-9246*, has a well-stocked leftist selection.

Old Wives' Tales Bookstore, *1009 Valencia, 415-821-4675*, is a treasure of feminist literature.

Rand McNally Map & Travel Store, *595 Market near 2nd, 415-777-3131*, is the largest store in the city dedicated solely to travel books and paraphernalia.

Stacey's, *581 Market just next door to Rand McNally, 415-421-4687*, has two floors of books about everything, with one of the best and most comprehensive selections in the city.

Thomas Bros. Maps, *550 Jackson near Columbus, 415-421-4687*, is an excellent small travel book store with local and international books and maps, and a conscientious, friendly staff.

William K. Stout Architectural Books, *804 Montgomery near Jackson, 415-391-6757*, is the best place to go for new, used, and rare books on architecture.

CANDY

The Candy Jar, *210 Grant near Post in North Beach, 415-939-5508*, has jars full of all sorts of chocolate covered, fruit-filled, truffled goodies.

Chocolate Heaven, *Pier 39 at Fisherman's Wharf, 415-421-1789*, has over 1,200 chocolate items, lending credence to their motto "the greatest chocolate store in the world."

The Fudge House, *also on Pier 39, 415-986-4240* – they make all their own candy by hand on large marble tables.

Ghirardelli Chocolate Manufactory, *900 North Point in Ghirardelli Square near Fisherman's Wharf, 415-474-3938*, has been churning out the chocolate since 1852.

Nuts About You , *325 Hayes Street, 415-864-6887 and at 2 Embarcadero, 421-7990*, are old-fashioned stores with candies, nuts, and dried fruit.

See's Candies, *542 Market, 415-362-1593 and at 3 Embarcadero, 391-1622*, have been supplying San Francisco with quality candy for 75 years.

CHILDREN'S CLOTHES

Choice$, *899 Howard near Yerba Buena Square, 415-495-2628*
San Francisco Fashion "Baby & Me," *958 Market, 415-771-2035*
Small Frys, *4066 24th Street in Noe Valley, 415-648-3954*

CLOTHES BOUTIQUES

Ambiance, *1458 Haight near Ashbury, 415-552-5095*, is open Monday-Friday 11am-7pm and weekends 10am-7pm. They are the best women's clothing boutique in San Francisco. Their stock changes frequently, but they can always be counted on to have beautiful, interesting, unique clothing, plus jewelry and handbags. Their prices are average for a nice boutique, though they often have a sales rack or two with discounts.

Avant Premiere, *1942 Fillmore near Pine in Pacific Heights, 415-673-8875*, is open Friday-Wednesday 11am-6:30pm and Thursday till 7pm. They carry very lovely clothes and boutique designs made out of fine materials.

Earthly Goods, *1981 Union near Buchanan in the Marina, 415-922-0606*, is open Monday-Saturday 10am-8pm and Sunday noon-5pm. They have beautiful styles in natural fibers, though they also now carry acetates and such, with clothes for comfort and clothes for dress-up.

Dantone, *1796 Union near Octavia in the Marina, 415-776-7008*, carries very good quality dresses, suits, slacks, shoes, and etcetera, and they're open Monday-Saturday 10am-7pm, and Sunday 11am-6pm.

Firuzé, *2001 Union up the street near Buchanan in the Marina, 415-921-5809*, carries high fashion European women's clothing and is open 10:30am-7pm daily.

Obiko, *794 Sutter near Jones (not far from Union Square), 415-775-2882*, is open Monday-Saturday 10am-6pm. Small and personal, Obiko retails custom, one-of-a-kind clothing made from an interesting assortment of fabrics and textures. The styles are gorgeous, elegant, and unique, and with price tags to match. It's a fun place to poke around in, and you will definitely find items that no one else at the party is wearing. They have some unusual and lovely jewelry as well.

Union Square is full of clothing shops, including The Chanel Boutique, Celine Paris Boutique, Georgiou, Jaeger, Marimekko, Talbots, Wilkes Bashford, Patrick James, Bullock & Jones, Gianni Versace, the Scottish Tartan Shop, and many more.

CLOTHES FACTORY OUTLETS

Burlington Coat Factory, *899 Howard near 5th, 415-495-7234*, has famous-make coats and shoes at 25%-60% off.

Georgiou Outlet, *925 Bryant*, *415-554-0150*, cuts 50% to 70% off the regular prices.

Marguerite Rubel Factory Outlet, *543 Howard South of Market*, *415-362-2626*, has been selling women's wear at factory prices for 50 years.

CONVENIENCE

Woolworth, *880 Market*, *415-986-2164*, has just about everything.

Walgreens and **Merrills** branches throughout the city carry most items, too.

DEPARTMENT STORES

Macy's, *Stockton and O'Farrell*, *415-397-3333*

Neiman Marcus, *150 Stockton near Geary*, *415-362-3900*

Nordstrom, *865 Market in the San Francisco Shopping Center*, *415-243-8500*

GIFT ITEMS

Cost Plus, *2552 Taylor near Bay in Fisherman's Wharf*, *415-928-6200*, has an enormous selection of imported gifts, jewelry, furniture, coffee & tea, food, and wine.

The Exploratorium Gift Shop, *in the Exploratorium*, *415-561-0360*, has some of the neatest gadgets, books, toys, and things anywhere.

FAO Schwarz, *48 Stockton by O'Farrell*, *415-394-8700*, has three stories of the world's best toys.

F. Dorian, *388 Hayes*, *415-861-3191*, has hand-crafted items from around the world, with interesting jewelry and home accessories.

Flax Art & Design, *1699 Market near Valencia*, *415-552-2355*, sells the new Play San Francisco trivia game.

Gumps, *135 Post*, *415-982-1616*, is an integral part of San Francisco, as a purveyor of the elegant and the exotic since 1861.

Main Line, *1928 Fillmore between Pine and Bush in Pacific Heights*, *415-563-4438*, has an eclectic mix of gift items, with especially wonderful hand-blown glass vases, some unique clocks and watches, artistic objects, and more. They also have a Castro branch, *516 Castro*, *415-863-7811*.

Perestroika Store, *Pier 39*, *415-788-7043*, has authentically Russian merchandise such as art, lacquer boxes, jewelry, amber, and matrioshka dolls.

TT Globe Trotter USA, *418 Sutter near Powell*, *415-434-1120*, has just opened its doors and is devoted to *Tintin* merchandise.

INTERNATIONAL NEWSPAPERS & PERIODICALS

Harolds International Newsstand, *524 Geary Street at Jones, 415-441-2665*, is open daily 7am-11pm and has just about any newspaper or magazine you might care to peruse.

International Deli, *587 Post near Taylor, 415-771-1558*, is open daily 9am-9pm. They have a full rack of international and out-of-state newspapers, as well as a salad and deli counter and a few tables.

Café de la Presse, *352 Grant near Bush, 415-398-2680*, is open daily 7am-11pm. They have international and out-of-state newspapers plus an espresso counter, wine and beer, and a good selection of pastries.

A. Cavalli & Co., *1441 Stockton near Vallejo, 415-421-4219*, is open Monday-Saturday 9am-5:30pm. They sell newspapers from Europe and the U.S., as well as Italian books, records, and videos.

Snack Attack, *734 Market between Grant and Kearny, 415-291-0668*, sells newspapers from all over (plus assorted snacks and drinks) Monday-Friday 6am-6pm and Saturday 8am-5pm.

MISCELLANY

Jim Mate Pipe Shop, *575 Geary between Taylor and Jones, 415-775-6634*, sells the finest of pipes, cigars, lighters, and tobaccos, and has done for 47 years. They're open 9am-5:30pm Monday-Saturday for all your tobacco needs.

MUSIC

Star Classics, *425 Hayes near Gough, 415-552-1110*, is open Monday-Saturday 10am-8pm, and Sunday 11am-6pm, and they specialize in jazz, classical, opera, Broadway, and film scores.

Streetlight Records, *3979 24th Street near Sanchez in Noe Valley, 415-282-3550*, and *2350 Market near Castro, 415-282-8000*, has an enormous selection of new and used CDs, LPs, and cassettes.

Tower Records, *on the corner of Bay and Columbus (near Fisherman's Wharf), 415-885-0500*, is open 9am-midnight daily, and they have got a huge selection of pop, classical, jazz, blues, world, rap, and any other category you can think of. They also have listening stations for the selected CDs of the week.

Virgin Megastore, *2 Stockton near Union Square, 415-397-4525*, has more than 150,000 music titles to chose from, with multimedia and software products as well.

Wherehouse Entertainment, *30 Powell near Union Square, 415-951-8612*, is another music giant.

PHOTOGRAPHIC EQUIPMENT

Adolph Gasser, *181 Second Street is downtown, south of Market, 415-495-3852.* They have been selling quality new and used photographic equipment since 1950. Trade-ins accepted, and they rent camcorders, too.

Camera Boutique, *downtown at 342 Kearny, 415-982-4946*, is another fine camera store with helpful, knowledgeable staff, a good selection of cameras, and video rentals.

SEX PARAPHERNALIA

Good Vibrations, *1210 Valencia 415-974-8980*, is a feminist sex store with a modern approach.

SHOPPING CENTERS

The Anchorage is a square block of shops in Fisherman's Wharf, bounded by Leavenworth, Jefferson, Beach, and Jones. There's validated parking, and an ATM.

The Cannery is in the old 1906 Del Monte peach cannery. It's now a mall, and is at the corner of Leavenworth and Beach near Fisherman's Wharf.

Crocker Galleria is near Union Square on the block bounded by Post, Kearny, Sutter, and Montgomery. There are more than 50 shops and restaurants in the glass-domed, airy mall.

The Embarcadero Center is at the foot of Sacramento near the Financial District. Made up of five buildings, there are over 125 shops and restaurants.

Ghiradelli Square on North Point, Polk, Beach, and Larkin has more than 70 shops and restaurants in the complex, part of which is in the Woolen Mill dating back to 1864.

Pier 39 has more than 100 shops catering to the millions of tourists who visit each year.

San Francisco Shopping Center downtown at Market and Fifth has four tiers of shops plus Nordstroms under a 150-foot atrium of glass, green granite, and Italian marble.

Stonestown Galleria is off in the Sunset on 19th and Winston. It's a large mall with a mix of department stores, smaller specialty shops, and restaurants.

Union Square is a small park, but the streets surrounding it are really an unbound shopping center, full of every type of store possible, but concentrating on fine clothing for men and women.

WINE

California Wine Merchant, *3237 Pierce near Lombard in the Marina,* *415-567-0646*, features top-notch and hard-to-find wines from California and Oregon.

Caruso's, *4011 24th near Noe in Noe Valley, 415-282-3841*, has a good selection for very reasonable prices.

Coit Liquors, *585 Columbus on the corner of Union in North Beach, 415-986-4036*, has a good selection of wines and a helpful staff.

Cost Plus, *2552 Taylor near Bay in Fisherman's Wharf, 415-928-6200*, has an enormous discounted wine department along with their other gift, furniture, coffee & tea, and food sections.

Jug Shop, *1567 Pacific near Polk in Russian Hill, 415-885-2922*, has a vast array of wines, a nice staff, and a parking lot.

Wine Impression, *3461 California near Laurel in the Richmond, 415-221-9463*, has fine wines at discount prices.

18♦ SPORTS & RECREATION

BASEBALL

Oakland Athletics, *510-638-0500*, play in the Oakland Coliseum April-September, and you can get there easily on BART.

San Francisco Giants, *800-734-4268*, play in Candlestick Park (recently renamed 3Com Park) from April-September. You can buy tickets at the game, or at the **Giants Dugout**, *170 Grant near Union Square, 415-982-9400*. Muni runs special buses there, from California just west of Van Ness, as well as a number of other city locations. Call Muni, *415-673-6864*, for details.

BEACHES

Baker's Beach is to the west of the Presidio.

Fort Funston Beach is south of Ocean Beach near Lake Merced.

Ocean Beach is as far west as you can get, from the Cliff House and on south.

Stinson Beach is up north an hour or so in Marin County.

Tennessee Valley Beach is also in Marin County in Mill Valley.

BICYCLING

To rent a bike, you'll need a drivers license, passport, or credit card.

Avenue Cyclery, *756 Stanyan near Waller and Golden Gate Park, 415-387-3155*, is open 10am-6pm daily, and they charge $5-$6 an hour.

San Francisco Wheels Bike & Scooter Rentals, *2715 Hyde on Fisherman's Wharf, 415-931-0234*, rents 2-passenger scooters and 21-speed mountain bikes, along with free maps, locks, and helmets. The bike rates are $5 an hour, $25 a day (24 hours), and $90 a week, while the scooters are $35-$100 a day and $150-$425 a week, depending on the power and model. They also rent motorcycles ($150-$170 a day, $700-$825 a week). Insurance, helmets, saddlebags, and mileage is included in all scooter and motorcycle rentals, and attachments for children are available for the bicycles. They are conveniently located if you want to take the ferry over to Sausalito, or you can zip over the bridge as well.

Lincoln Cyclery, *772 Stanyan near Waller, 415-221-2415*, is by the eastern entrance to Golden Gate Park. They're open Sunday 11:30-5pm, and all other days 9am-5pm, except for Tuesday, when they're closed. Rentals cost $5 an hour or $25 all day.

Start to Finish Bicycles, *672 Stanyan near Haight, 415-750-4760*, is open daily 10am-7pm and rentals are $14 for two hours or $25 a day.

San Francisco Bicycle Tours, *415-351-2453*, runs two bike tours daily, one from 10am-12:30pm and the other from 1-3:30pm. They leave from *2715 Hyde Street* (at American Rentals), and it costs $30, which includes the bike rental and a granola bar snack.

BOATING

Cass' Charters and Sailing School, *415-332-6789, 800-472-4595*, runs a sailing school, and rents bareboat and skippered charters on 22-75 foot boats.

Capt. Case Powerboat and Waterbike Rental, *in Schoonmaker Point Marina in Sausalito, 415-331-0444*. There you can rent Boston Whaler powerboats and zippy waterbikes.

Let's Go Sailing, *979 Bush, Suite 503, 415-788-4920*, takes you for a one and a half hour sailboat ride on the Bay in their 65-foot MacGregor for $20 per person.

Model yachts are sailed at Spreckels Lake near 36th in Golden Gate Park.

Opening Day of Yachting Season is on the last Sunday of April. And if you don't have your own boat, or friends with boats, you can climb a tall hill and watch the bay fill up with sails.

Sausalito Jet Ski, *1385 East Francisco, Sausalito, 415-753-8754*, rents jet skis for $40 an hour and $175 a day, and they're open Tuesday-Saturday 10am-6pm.

Sea Trek Ocean Kayaking Center, *in Schoonmaker Point Marina in Sausalito, 415-488-1000*. To get there, head down Bridgeway, and when you see Margaritaville Restaurant, turn right at the next light. Turn right again at the bottom of the hill, then just follow the road till you reach them under the palm trees on the beach. They rent single kayaks for $20 for 2 hours, $35, for 4, and $45 for a full day, while double and triple person kayaks are $35 for 2 hours, $45 for 4, and $65 for a full day. Open deck boats require no experience but to paddle the traditional closed kayaks, you need to have had some experience, or take their introductory class, which is 7 hours on Fridays-Sundays for $90. They are very nice people there, and paddling about in Richardson Bay, to Angel Island, or on through the Golden Gate on a sunny day is great fun.

Stow Lake, *in Golden Gate Park, 415-752-0347*, rents row boats and paddle boats. The rates start at $9.50 an hour for the row boats, and the paddle boats start at $10.50 an hour (the rates go up for more than two people).

Yukon Jack, *Pier 40 in the South Beach Harbor, 415-241-1803*, takes you on a sleek, 52-foot 1992 ocean race winner for a two hour sail, leaving at noon, 2:30pm, and 5pm.

CAMPING

There is delightful environmental camping available courtesy of the Department of Parks & Recreation. Call *800-444-7275*, as early as you can to reserve a spot nearby on **Angel Island**, or **Mt. Tamalpais**, or further up north at **Salt Point** or the **Sonoma Coast**.

ELECTRONIC AMUSEMENT

Q-Zar, *2801 in the Cannery, 415-775-6700*, is an amazing laser game. Open 10am-midnight Sunday-Thursday and 10am-1am Friday-Saturday, it costs $7 an experience, and 2-hour parking is validated nearby. You suit up in vest and phaser, then you're off to the 4,000 square foot arena of fog, mazes, and music to try to zap the opposing team with visible laser fire. 100% interactive games start every 20 minutes and the game lasts for 15 minutes, but the whole deal takes 30 minutes to suit up, get instructions, and play. Mornings and afternoons see more kids (5 years and up is the general rule, but the limit is flexible and depends more on the child and whether he or she likes it), and in the evenings there tend to be more adults.

Cyber Mind *in the Embarcadero, 415-693-0348,* is a virtual reality center. Open Monday-Thursday 10am-8pm, Friday-Saturday 10am-11pm, and Sunday 11am-7pm, this is a wild and highly entertaining place. In virtual reality, you play with or against other people (friends, family, corporate colleagues, etc.) to blow them away, shoot 'em up, or play pool where you are the cue ball.

FISHING

Fishing charters leave Fisherman's Wharf, and are coordinated by Jacky Douglas, *415-586-9800*. They take 15-25 passengers, cost about $45 per person, and go for salmon, bass, sturgeon, halibut, or shark.

Saint-James Fishing Center, *800-245-8532,* arranges charters for salmon fishing and whale watching.

FOOTBALL

The **San Francisco 49ers'** Football Season in Candlestick Park (recently renamed 3Com Park), *408-562-4949,* begins in August, lasting into December.

FLY-CASTING

There's a **fly-casting pool** *in Golden Gate Park (roughly near Sunset Blvd.), 415-386-2630*. It's a public facility and it's always open, but the equipment there belongs to the club members, so you'll need to bring your own. However, there are usually experienced folks around to give you a few pointers, if you want them.

GLIDERS

Calistoga Gliders, *1546 Lincoln in Calistoga, 707-942-5000*, offers an easy way to see the area with rides over Napa Valley. Gliders start at $79, and antique biplane rides start at $100.

GOLF

Golden Gate Park Golf Course, *415-751-8987*, is a nine-hole course near 47th and Fulton. It's open daily 6am-8pm, and it costs $10 during the week and $13 on weekends. No reservations necessary.

The **Arnold Palmer Presidio Golf Course**, *415-561-4653*, is now open, for the first time ever, to the public. It was built in 1895, and is the second oldest course west of the Mississippi. The views of city and ocean are unbeatable, and course itself is beautiful, with 160 acres full of cypress and eucalyptus and green, rolling hills. The course has just been renovated, and a new club house has just been built. It's a good idea to call and reserve, and the 18-hole green rates are $25 on weekdays, and $35 on the weekend. To get there by car, drive down Arguello, into the Presidio, to the golf course.

HIKING, WALKING, & RUNNING

Examiner Bay to Breakers, *415-808-5000, ext. 222, or 777-7770*, is San Francisco's annual spring race, the world's largest. More than 100,000 contestants, many of whom are dressed in incredible costumes, run or walk their way from the Bay to the Pacific Ocean. For a small subset it's a very serious race, attracting the fleetest runners from around the world. For the rest, it's a party, a spring version of Halloween, a goofy lark, and a chance to dress up in the most ridiculous outfit you can think of. Early registration will be about $15, otherwise it'll cost you $20 to run. Usually in May, the exact date changes each year, so call for details.

San Francisco Hillstride, *415-668-2243*, starts a seven mile stroll up and down the city hills, starting on the Marina Green.

The Bridge to Bridge Run, *415-974-6800*, is similar in concept to Bay to Breakers, and runs a 12 kilometer course, starting at 9am at the Golden Gate Bridge, making its way east to the Bay Bridge.

Free City Walking Tours

City Guides free walking tours, courtesy of Friends of the Library, 415-557-4266, last one to two hours and take place rain or shine. What follows is a sampler of the 21 walks they offer. For more details call (especially if you'll be part of a large group), and have them mail you a schedule.

Brothels, Boardinghouses, and Bawds - For a glimpse into the world's oldest profession, meet at Maiden Lane Gate (Kearny between Post and Geary) the second and fourth Monday of each month at noon.

Chinatown - To explore the side streets and alleys, meet at Portsmouth Square (Kearny and Clay) Saturday at 10 am.

THE STEPS OF SAN FRANCISCO

*Two stairways link **Russian Hill** and **North Beach**, steep and beautiful routes that pass through terraced green gardens. The **Green Street Steps** number 127; they connect Taylor to Jones and are the easier of the two. The **Vallejo Steps** have 250 to their credit, with a few stepless inclines thrown in; they go from Jones to halfway between Taylor and Mason (they're in two segments, and you have to cross Taylor to continue), are by far the more strenuous, and also the lusher and more beautiful. They are, however, just as lovely coming down as going up if you don't feel your legs are in shape for a major haul.*

***Nob Hill** also has steps to ease the steep incline. Going down the **Taylor Street** hill between California and Pine, 192 half-steps parallel the sloping sidewalk. The steps are awkwardly built, and people frequently just stride along on the sidewalk, unless those people happen to be wearing high heels, in which case they deeply appreciate the shallow stairs.*

*Then there are the steps from Telegraph Hill down to Sansome near Levi Plaza and the Embarcadero. From North Beach up Greenwich Street to **Coit Tower**, there are 110 steps and a lot up unquantifiable inclines. From Coit down to Montgomery it's 178 steps (with 18 steps up to Julius Castle, if you're stopping off there), then there are the **Greenwich Street Steps** from Montgomery down to Sansome, which number 210. This last part, while it's the steepest, is also the most beautiful, as the stairway winds along through lush foliage with amazing garden and endless bay views.*

City Scapes and Roof Gardens - To see some of San Francisco's hidden treasures and breathtaking views, meet at the Native Sons monument (Montgomery at Market) on Wednesday at 10am.

Gold Rush City - To examine the lives of those who traveled across the continent to make their fortunes, meet at the corner of the Transamerica pyramid, near the flower stand (Clay and Montgomery) Wednesday at noon and Sunday at 2pm.

Haight-Ashbury - This mildly strenuous walk relives the '60s and '70s on the first, second, and third Sunday at 11am from the Park Branch Library, 1833 Page.

Mission Murals - To tour the beautiful artwork that decorates the Latino neighborhood streets, meet behind Flynn Elementary School (Precita and Harrison) the second and fourth Saturday of each month at 11am.

Pacific Heights Mansions - To tour the neighborhood's finest, meet at the top of the steps in Alta Plaza Park (Pierce and Clay) Saturday at 11am.

Telegraph Hill Hike entails many stairs, but the picturesque view and exquisite gardens make the climb worthwhile. Meet at the Marconi Monument in the tiny park where Lombard becomes Telegraph Hill the first and third Thursday at 5:30pm.

Victorian San Francisco - To see the early mansions and classic Victorians that surround Lafayette Square, meet Sunday at 2pm at 1801 Bush at Octavia.

Hiking Outside the City

East Bay's **Redwood Regional Park**, *510-635-0135, ext. 2578,* is another redwood option, open daily 5am-10pm. To get there from I-80, take Highway 24 east to Skyline Boulevard South, and the Skyline Gate entrance is on the left. It's an alternative to Muir Woods with redwood groves (still impressive though they aren't old-growth) and without tourists . Visitors to Redwood Park tend to stick to the main paths, leaving the single-track trails tranquil. For a 7.5 mile loop that takes you through groves of redwoods and returns along the park's stream, start at the Skyline Gate entrance, and follow the West Ridge Trail for about half a mile to the French Trail. Many other trails cross the French Trail before it dead-ends at the Orchard Trail; turn downhill toward the canyon floor on any of them and go left on the Stream Trail to get back to where you started.

San Pedro Valley Park, *415-355-8289,* is open daily 8am-7pm, is less than 15 miles from San Francisco, and offers well-tended and varied hiking trails. Take Highway 1 into Pacifica, turn east on Linda Mar Boulevard, then right on Oddstead Boulevard. They have a number of paths, most less than four miles long, that wend through eucalyptus, cypress, redwoods, chaparral, meadows, creeks, and patches of wildflowers. Sometimes you get to see deer or chipmunks, too. Brooks Falls Trail is a nice 3-mile loop, and Montara Mountain Trail (which takes you to Montara State Beach) is full of lovely flowers like gold chinquapin, yerba santa, and monkeyflower.

See Chapter 19, *Day Trips & Excursions,* **Marin County** section, for hikes in the Headlands, Muir Woods, and Point Reyes.

HOCKEY

Bladium In-Line Hockey Rink, *1050 3rd Street, 415-442-5060*, is open 11am-midnight Monday-Friday, and 9am-midnight Saturday-Sunday.

Holiday Ice Skating *at the Embarcadero Center, 800-733-6318*, starts in November and lasts through January.

The **San Francisco Spiders** Hockey Season, *510-762-BASS*, starts its season in the Cow Palace in October and runs through April.

HORSEBACK RIDING

Golden Gate Stables, *415-668-7360, located in the center of the park*, and they're available for lessons and rentals. They do guided hour tours (call in advance to reserve) for $20 per person.

HOT TUBS & MASSAGE

Hot Tubs, *2200 Van Ness near Vallejo, 415-441-8827*, is open daily from 11am-midnight. They have private suites with tiled hot tubs, redwood saunas, available first come first served, for $11.50 per person per hour. They also offer massage daily noon-9pm, for $35-$62.50 (for 45 minutes to 90 minutes) with half an hour of sauna free. Reservations are required.

Kabuki Hot Springs, *1750 Geary, 415-922-6000 for recorded info and 922-6002 for reservations*, has magnificent hot tubs and Japanese shiatsu massage, and they're open 10am-10pm on weekdays, and 9am-10pm on weekends. They have a communal bath for men Monday, Tuesday, Thursday and Saturday, while women can go Wednesday, Friday, and Sunday, but you can rent a private bath with sauna any day. Plan prices vary from $10 to $65, depending on if you prefer a public or private soak, if you want massage, and for how long.

Osento, *955 Valencia 20th, 415-282-6333*, a women's bathhouse with steam rooms, hot tubs, and massage. They're open 1pm-1am daily (midnight is the latest you can enter), and a hot tub soak costs $8-$13, on a sliding scale (towels rent for $1, or bring your own), and they accept cash only. Massages also operate on a sliding scale, with half an hour for $25-$35, an hour for $45-$65, and 90 minutes for $70-$90.

POOL & BILLIARDS

Chalkers, *Rincon Center at Spear and Mission, 415-512-0450*, is a big, beautiful pool hall, clean and very likable. Open Monday-Friday 11:30-2am, Saturday 3pm-2am, and Sunday 3-11pm, they have a full menu of soups, sandwiches, and pastas (about $6 each), lots of ales and wines, and a comfortable area to dine and watch. Generally speaking, you must be 21 or older (with I.D.) to enter, but Saturday and Sunday before 7pm kids are allowed so long as they're accompanied by an adult. Parchment lamp shades light each pool table, exposed pipes line the ceiling, and groovy tunes (reggae, rock, etc.) play softly in the background.

There are miles of clean green felt, racks of straight cues, warm wood tones, and rooms full of tables (31 to be exact). Prices vary according to time of day and week (weekday rates are lower, say, than weekend nights), and by the number of people per table. On a week night, the rates are $5 an hour per person, with discounts if you're more than two to the table. They also have tournaments from time to time, for juniors and adults, often on weekends.

The Great Entertainer, *975 Bryant South of Market, 415- 861-8833*, is a large center with billiards, snooker, shuffleboard, table tennis, darts, foosfall, and a video arcade. They're open Sunday-Thursday 11am-2am and Friday-Saturday 11am-3am.

Hollywood Billiards, *61 Golden Gate, downtown, 415-252-9643*, is San Francisco's oldest pool room. They have 37 antique tables and the longest bar in the city. They're open 24 hours a day with security parking, and they have got a more traditional, authentic pool room ambiance that's different from the more upscale Chalkers or Great Entertainer.

South Beach Billiards, *270 Brannan, 415-495-5939*, is another South of Market pool hall. They have got 37 pool tables just like Hollywood Billiards, but with indoor boccé ball and a cafe as well. It's open Monday-Friday noon-2am and 2pm-2am on the weekend.

RIVER RAFTING

Ahwahnee Whitewater, *800-359-9790*, leads river trips in Yosemite and Lake Tahoe.

California River Trips *(800-773-0066)* leads whitewater trips in Gold Country.

ROCK-CLIMBING

Mission Cliffs Rock Climbing Center, *2295 Harrison near 19th, 415-550-0515, or check online at http://www.mission-cliffs.com/mission-cliffs/*, at has a basic techniques class every Monday and Wednesday at 6:30pm for $27 (including all equipment as well as instruction), and advanced techniques classes ($37) as well. They put out a calendar each month with special classes (like yoga), events (like kids belay), and celebrations.

ROLLER BLADING

Golden Gate Park Skate & Bike, *3038 Fulton near Sixth, 415-668-1117*, is open 10am-6pm Monday-Saturday and 9am-6pm on Sunday. Rentals are $6-$7 an hour and $24-$28 a day.

Mikes Bikes & Blades, *Stow Lake in Golden Gate Park, 415-668-6699*, is open weekdays 10M-5pm, and weekends 10am-6pm, and the blades rent for $5 an hour or $12 for a four-hour half day.

Skate Pro Sports, *27th and Irving near Golden Gate Park, 415-752-8776*, is open weekdays 11am-7pm, Saturdays 10am-5pm, and Sundays 11am-4pm. They rent for $5 an hour, (and a free half hour to get accustomed), or $20 for the day (and bring them back the following day).

Skates On Haight, *1818 Haight near Golden Gate Park, 415-752-8375*, is open weekdays 11:30am-6:30pm (except Tuesdays when they're closed) and 10am-6pm on weekends. They have been there since 1975, but their prices have gone up a bit, and are now $7 an hour or $28 all day.

SEAPLANES

Commodore Seaplanes, *415-332-4843*, has 30 minute and 45 minute tours out of Sausalito ($74-$89) and 30 minute tours from Pier 39 in Fisherman's Wharf for $89. They'll take you up and over Marin and San Francisco for a different perspective.

SWIMMING

This is not a real swimming town. The days are rarely hot enough and the ocean and lake waters are rarely warm enough for outdoor swimming, so most swimmers turn to indoor pools. A number of hotels have pools, otherwise there are the municipal pools (in the phone book, and not all that pleasant) or private clubs. The following clubs sell day passes (generally around $8-$12 a day) which will admit you to their pool as well as the **fitness** and **racquetball** facilities.

The Bay Club, *1 Lombard, 415-433-2550*

Cathedral Hill Plaza Athletic Club, *1333 Gough, 415-292-1741*

Golden Gateway Tennis & Swim Club, *370 Drumm, 415-616-8800*

Koret Center, *Turk and Stanyan, 415-666-6820*

Sheehan Hotel, *620 Sutter near Mason, 415-775-6500*

YMCA Embarcadero, *169 Steuart, 415-957-9622*

TENNIS

San Francisco Recreation and Park Department, *415-753-7001*, has more than 100 free tennis courts, available on a first come, first served basis. Call for exact locations. You can make reservations on weekends, *415-753-7101*, but there is a fee.

19. DAY TRIPS & EXCURSIONS

ALCATRAZ

Just east a tad from the Golden Gate Bridge, the rocky island of **Alcatraz**, *415-705-1042*, worms its way into the majority of San Francisco post cards and pictures, and it takes a firm grip on our imaginations, too. It hasn't incarcerated a hardened criminal since 1963, but in our minds, Alcatraz still conjures up images of Al Capone and Robert Stroud "Bird Doctor of Leavenworth," or Clint Eastwood trying tenaciously to escape.

There is something intriguing about a maximum security island prison for society's incorrigibles, and a trip out to "The Rock" just builds on our morbid fascination. Add to that a pleasant ferry trip (the only legitimate way there), stunning bay views, and low expense, and it's no wonder the island receives close to four million visitors a year. And while mass appeal doesn't always insure a good time (the strictly regulated single file line-up and parade through the winding red cattle rail, herding tourists in controlled single file seems an apt introduction to the Alcatraz experience), Alcatraz appeals to all ages, and it makes for a great morning or afternoon.

The **Red & White Fleet**, *at Pier 41 (just west of Pier 39), 415-546-2700*, has a corner on the Alcatraz ferry market, with ferries leaving ten times daily from 9:30am-2:15pm, and returning 13 times a day from 9:50am-4:30pm (the boarding takes about 20 minutes, the trip itself is about five minutes, and you should reserve your tickets in advance - plan on a few hours from start to finish). The fares are $6.75 for adults, $5 for seniors, and $3.50 for children 5-11, and they include everything but the audio tours. If you want an audio tour (this entails you wearing a cassette player and following the recorded instructions around the cell block while information, anecdotes, and convict interviews play at the appropriate spots), you can pay an extra $3.25 (for adults and seniors) or $1.25 (for children under 12) on your ferry ticket, but you can also rent the equipment on the island for exactly the same price, so if you want to look into the other tour options, you lose nothing by holding off.

The rangers lead tours for free, usually three to five times a day. Approximate start times are 10:15am, 11:30am, 1:15pm, and 2:15pm, but it varies from day to day, depending on staff availability (the 30 or so National Park island rangers have been reduced by budget cuts to a mere six or seven, and they do the best they can). The topics of the walks vary too, including topics like the Natural History of the Island, Fortifications, Doing Time, Escape Attempts, Indian Occupation, and Hollywood Alcatraz.

They last 45 minutes to an hour, and go around the island, and sometimes inside the cell block, too (while you can walk inside the infamous "hole" or seclusion unit, you can no longer thrill to the experience of being closed up in the dark, due to safety regulations - the doors were getting sticky and unreliable). The rangers are wonderfully well-informed about everything you have ever wondered about Alcatraz, and they seem to love leading the tours.

Initially, the audio tour may seem like more of an individual pursuit, avoiding that group glut feeling, but in fact the audio tours end up making everyone cluster about the same spots as well, although you do get the extra sound effects of doors clanging shut, and interviewed convicts saying "Well, a lotta duh, duh, hoods that were still on the island when I was dere—ya know, dey didn't mean nothin' to me." The rangers tell all the same information, include interesting details the tapes omit (like the fact that Shirley Temple was a convict favorite, or that Al Capone ended up with a job in the laundry washing uniforms for guards and military personnel), they answer questions, and share their warmth and sense of drama as well.

Because there's no set schedule, it's hard to plan how to attend a ranger tour, but their best advice is to go to the island in the morning (thereby avoiding the late afternoon crowds, too). And if there isn't a group leaving when you are there, or they aren't covering your favorite topic, ask a ranger if he or she has some spare time. They're willing (in fact, they really like to, if they are free) to take a small group of 20 or fewer on a behind the scenes tour (to the roof or other off-limits areas), if you ask.

The one other option is a self-led tour. You can purchase a guide pamphlet for 50 cents that tells the history and directs your feet to notable points, but you miss the flair and drama of the story tellers with this approach. There is also a short *Secrets of Alcatraz* video that is shown at regular intervals, but it's pretty much a waste of time. It makes better sense to do whatever tour option you prefer and see the island, then see how much energy and curiosity you still have before hopping the ferry home.

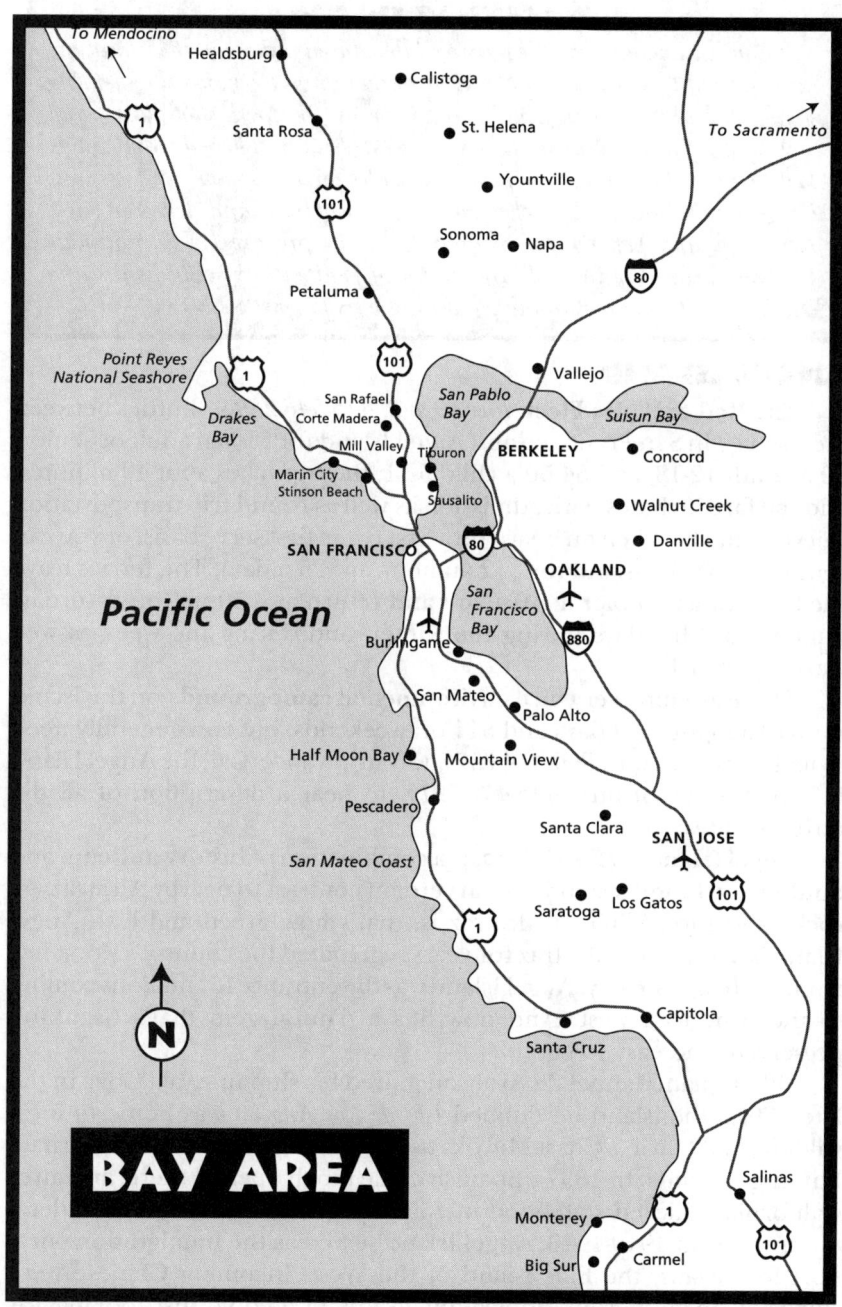

ALCATRAZ SHLOCK

Souvenir shops near the ferry and the museum shop on the island are thronged with every imaginable Alcatraz memento. If you want something saying "property of Alcatraz," there are mugs, tee shirts, shot glasses and socks, yours for $2-$16, but there's lots more, besides. There are amazingly tacky stuffed dolls in jail stripe and shackles for $6, or you can bust your budget on the $80 denim jacket with a picture of the island etched on back. Key rings and pencils are in abundance, or prepare for the ultimate Christmas card, and get all dressed up in penitentiary striped suits and caps, and get your pictures taken behind bars for just $2.80.

ANGEL ISLAND

The Red & White Fleet, *Pier 43 1/2, 415-546-2896*, shuttles between Pier 43 1/2 in San Francisco and Angel Island for $10 an adult or senior, $9 a youth 12-18, and $4.50 a child 5-11; the trip takes abut 40 minutes, and the fare includes park admission as well as round-trip transportation (bicycles can be taken on board on a first come first serve basis, or you can rent bikes on the island for $12 an hour or $25 a day). The ferries leave the San Francisco pier at 10:40am and return at 4:50pm (on Saturday, Sunday, and holidays during the winter, and during the week as well starting April 1).

There are nine very nice environmental **campgrounds** on the island for $10 a night weekdays and $11 on weekends, but you generally need to make reservations, *800-444-7275*, way in advance. Call the Angel Island information recording, *415-435-1915*, to hear a description of all the different sites.

Angel Island, *415-435-1915*, is a combination of history museum and outdoor park, and it stands out in verdant contrast to nearby Alcatraz. As rocky and forbidding as Alcatraz is, that's how green and lush Angel Island is. And while Alcatraz for years segregated the country's worst few from the rest of society, Angel Island was the entrance for millions coming to the American west. And now, it's a natural gem that's beautiful, preserved, and easy to get to.

When Juan Manuel de Ayala anchored his ship in Ayala Cove in the late 1700s, the island he dubbed *Isla de Los Angeles* was home to local wildlife, and Marin's Coast Miwoks used to paddle out there for alternate hunting grounds. In 1837 a Spanish cattle ranch opened there, and after California achieved statehood in 1850, Angel Island became a Federal outpost. From 1910-1940, Angel Island served as the immigration entry port for Asians, the Ellis Island of the West. Incoming Chinese were subjected to numerous unpleasant exams by people just looking for reasons to deny entrance, thanks to the Chinese Exclusion Act, while

Europeans and other Asians were admitted with little hassle. A museum now commemorates those days, and you can see the scores of Chinese poems inscribed on the old immigration walls. The poems have been collected and translated in the book *Island* by Him Mark Lai, Genny Lim, and Judy Yung, giving voice to the fears and distress foisted upon the newcomers.

However, most people take the ferry to Angel Island to hike and picnic and lounge on the beach, with perhaps a nod toward the historic buildings in passing. There are lots of picnic tables and barbecue grills near the ferry, but you'll need to bring charcoal, because wood fires aren't allowed. The island has over 13 miles of trails and roadway for hiking, and 8 miles of roadway for biking. Beware the poison oak that lurks off the trail: stick to the beaten paths and beaches and you've nothing to fear.

SOUTH SAN FRANCISCO

Acres of Orchids, *1450 El Camino Real in South San Francisco, 415-737-2452*, is open daily from 9am-6pm and offers free tours daily at 10:30am and 1:30pm. The Acres (35 of them) hold tons of greenhouses growing gardenias, eucalyptus, cut flowers, and many varieties of orchids. Rod McLellan's flower emporium started back in 1859 when his grandfather ditched his gold prospecting plans and decided to make money selling vegetables to miners instead. The business blossomed, as it were, into flowers, and the gardenia corsage was invented here.

THE EAST BAY

BERKELEY

Twelve miles northeast of San Francisco, **Berkeley** is a city with 102,724 residents, a hot-bed of revolution, a platform of political correctness, and the home of the University of California's first and most prestigious campus. But Berkeley changed hands and names a few times before it came to be the outspoken land of civic rights it is today. The land had been granted by the Spanish crown to the Peralta family in 1820, then purchased in 1853 by Americans who settled there and renamed it Ocean View.

It wasn't till 1866 that the town was renamed after George Berkeley (1685-1753), the Irish philosopher who worked hard to promote higher education for the colonists, and the university was created in 1868. One of the British empiricists, Berkeley's characteristic doctrine was expressed by the Latin phrase *esse est percipi* ("to be is to be perceived"). A twist on this philosophy was taken by the Berkeley university students in the 1960s. Angry at the U.S. involvement in Vietnam, the students felt that just being was not enough to be properly perceived, so they held some major demonstrations to get national attention. Nowadays, people visit Berkeley to see the grand campus, to hear that rare sound of people proudly proclaiming their liberalism, and to escape from the July fog of San Francisco into the reliably hot and sunny Berkeley summer.

Where to Eat
EXPENSIVE
Nouvelle California Cuisine
    CHEZ PANISSE, *1517 Shattuck near University, 510-548-5049, has the restaurant downstairs which serves dinner only Monday-Saturday, and reservations are absolutely required (with dinner seatings of 6-7:15pm and 8:30-9:15pm). The meals there are fixed price, starting at $35 on Mondays up to $65 on the weekend. Upstairs there's the cafe, which is open Monday-Saturday for lunch 11:30-4pm, and dinner 5-11:30pm. Lunch time reservations can be made for the same day (call in the morning for a lunch seating), but they don't take dinner reservations at all.*

    The menu changes daily, but the a la carte entrees cost about $13-$17, and the extraordinary quality of fresh ingredients and unique combinations as pioneered by Alice Waters never waivers.

Seafood
    SPENGER'S FISH GROTTO, *1919 Fourth near University, 510-845-7771, a Berkeley fish tradition since 1890, is open Sunday-Thursday 7am-11pm, and on weekends 7am-midnight.*

    They have lots of fish and seafood platters from $11-$20, depending on whether you go for the sand dabs, the crab meat, oysters hangtown fry, or broiled lobster tail. There are also seafood sandwiches, and a variety of salads, both with seafood and without. Whatever you choose, there's a rollicking good spirit there, big tables full of good food, and a long wait if you didn't make reservations beforehand.

MODERATE
Italian
    VENEZIA CAFFE AND RISTORANTE, *1799 University near Grant, 510-849-4681 is open for lunch Monday-Friday 11:30am-2:30pm and for dinner Monday-Saturday 5-10pm, and Sunday 5:30-9:30pm.*

    Children get their own menu with black & white drawings for them to color with the Venezia gift of free crayons, and they get a small free plate of antipasti too, making dining here with the kids a real pleasure. Inside, it's decorated like an outdoor piazza, with a central fountain that is used as a wishing well, a clothes line strung with clothes, and ceiling to floor murals painted with Italian storefronts, houses, etc. The atmosphere is delightful, and the food is terrific. The pasta is made fresh daily, and the plates ($9.25-$14.50) come with your choice of soup or salad. There's fettuccine al pesto, spinach and ricotta ravioli in a variety of sauces, daily cannelloni, and wonderful malfatti con funghi.

There are meat and vegetarian sauces, and lots of choices from spicy Italian sausage with eggplant to prawns on linguine in a garlicky olive oil base. Or, if you prefer, there are non-pasta dishes ($11.50-$14) like roast chicken, grilled chicken sausage with polenta, or oven roasted eggplant with garlicky farfelle. But the bottom line is the food is good and you really can't go wrong.

Japanese

KIRALA, *2100 Ward street on the corner with Shattuck, 510-549-3486, is open for lunch Tuesday-Friday 11:30am-1:45pm, and for dinner Monday-Saturday 5:30-9:30pm, and Sunday 5-9pm.*

The atmosphere is very open and casual, but the food is all traditional Japanese. The main item here is sushi, and it's delicious. You can order combination plates ($12.50-$16) or a la carte, but however you order, the fish is fresh and exceedingly tasty. During lunch, they also serve udon and donburi bowls of warmth and goodness for $5.25-$7.75, depending on whether they're topped with vegetables, beef, or seafood. At night the noodles are put away, and the specialty is robata (skewered items done on the grill). They cost $1.50-$7.50 a skewer, and come lightly flavored with teriyaki or garlic cream. A smorgasbord of a la carte sushi and robata skewers makes for a varied and delicious meal.

Thai

PLEARN THAI, *2050 University near Shattuck University, 510-841-2148, is open daily from 11:30am-10pm .*

If you prefer Thai food, Plearn has lunches for $4.50 and dinners from $5-$11. There are the usual assortments of curries and soups, dishes with fried cashews and chili, dishes with bean curd and black bean sauce, and vegetarian pad thai, but they are prepared with good ingredients, and come out very nicely.

INEXPENSIVE
American

BRICK HUT, *2512 San Pablo near Dwight Way, 510-486-1124 is open daily 8am-3pm for breakfast and lunch, and Wednesday-Sat. for dinner 5:30-10.*

Run by stridently feminist, down-to-earth women who know good food, the breakfast ($4.75-$7.75) is great. Much of it is typical breakfast fare of eggs and homefries, omelets with special names, waffles, pancakes, and french toast but they're all done marvelously well, and the pancakes and waffles (made of whole wheat or corn) as well as the french toast can all be topped with fruit, as well. Or watch your cholesterol and get the extremely popular tofu sauté. Breakfast goes till 3 but lunch ($4.50-$6) starts at 11am, with burgers of all sorts, sandwiches, french fries and onion rings, and great salads. Dinner ($6-$9) is good, too, with the burgers, panini sandwich with pesto and grilled veggies, pizzas, fine pasta, and Consuela's famous meatloaf. How can you go wrong?

THE COUNTER, *next door at 1901 University, 510-849-4165, is the American equivalent of ¡Ay Caramba!, and they're open Sunday 8am-9pm, Monday-Thursday 11:30am-10pm, Friday 11:30am-midnight, and Saturday 8am-midnight.*

You can come here for your burgers and sandwiches, salads and soups ($4-$7); it's all fresh and full of quality ingredients. Some of the salads are quite substantial, like the grilled chicken or seafood salad, and the bowls of gumbo, chili con carne, polenta, and vegetarian onion soup are hearty and warm. Or there are burgers that run the gamut from your basic third-of-a-pound of beef to the turkey burger, veggie, or tofu. Sandwiches come in all denominations, too, with chipotle chile barbe-cued chicken breast, grilled eggplant with pesto, polish sausage, crabmeat, or vegan. In case that's not enough there's a selection of potato chips (homemade), fries, slaw, and corn bread, too, just to make sure you don't leave hungry.

CHEAP CAFES

*Telegraph Avenue is lined with cafes, offering every type of coffee and tea drink known to man, a place to hang out and solve the world's problems, plus lots of inexpensive food. **The Blue Nile**, 2525 Telegraph, 510-540-6777, has Ethiopian food, **Blondie's Pizza**, down the street at 2340 Telegraph, 510-548-1129, has good pizza by the slice, and **Mario's La Fiesta**, 2444 Telegraph, 510-540-9123, has very fine Mexican cuisine. **Caffe Mediterranean**, 2475 Telegraph, 510-841-5634, is the epitome of the Berkeley cafe culture, but **Cafe Milano**, 2522 Bancroft, 510-644-3100, and **Espresso Strada**, 2300 College, 510-843-5282, are close runners up.*

Mexican
¡AY CARAMBA!, *1903 University by M. L. King Way, 510-843-1298, is open daily from 11:30am-9:30pm, except Sunday when they close at 9pm.*

They're owned by the same folks who run Venezia, but here the cuisine is Mexican instead of Italian. There are burritos, soft tacos, quesadillas, tostadas, and platos with entrees, salad, rice, and black beans ($2.75-$6.75), plus the nice addition of children's plates (for 12 and under) that are a bit smaller and cheaper ($1-$4). The burritos have the usual, as well as less common fillings such as charbroiled mahi-mahi or marinated squid, and the sauces (tomatillo for the pork and garlic for the chicken) are excellent. The platos include mole, flautas, enchiladas, and tamales, and it's all fresh and well-done.

Seeing the Sights

The actual **UC Berkeley campus**, known as Cal by its friends and alum, spans 178 acres on the beautiful 1,282 acre property, and the university has more than 30,000 students enrolled. It's easy to get there (drive over the Bay Bridge or better yet, take BART). Parking is difficult in Berkeley, but the Berkeley BART station on Shattuck is just a few blocks from the campus. You can wander around, or drop by the **Visitors Center**, *University Hall at University and Oxford, 510-642-5215*, which is open weekdays 8am-5pm and has maps, self-guided tour brochures, and student-led tours 10am and 1pm Mondays, Wednesdays, and Fridays. Unfortunately, the center is half a mile from the campus, and if all you want is a map, you can get one from the Student Center at Sproul Hall.

Sproul Plaza inside the campus at Telegraph and Bancroft is a lively hub, full of students reading, debating, flirting, rhapsodizing, or going to and from class. Another landmark is **Sather Tower** (307 feet tall and modeled on the St. Mark's tower in Venice) that's better known as the Camponile. Its carillon plays three times a day, and the elevator will take you 175 feet up to an observation deck for $1. Across from the tower is **Bancroft Library**, with the gold nugget that started the rush, and more than 7,000,000 books.

The **University Art Museum**, *2626 Bancroft Way, 510-642-0808*, fans out with its ramps and balconies in the 1970 cubist structure designed by Mario Ciampi, and it has a good collection of Asian and twentieth-century Western art. It's open Wednesday-Sunday and costs $5 for adults and $4 for seniors. **The Phoebe Apperson Hearst Museum of Anthropology**, *Kroeber Hall at Bancroft Way and College, 510-642-3681*, is open Wednesday-Friday 10am-4:30pm and Saturday-Sunday noon-4:30pm. Admission is $2 for adults, $1 for students and seniors, and 50 cents for children under 16. There are over 400,000 anthropological treasures rotated on display, but you can call to hear their current exhibits.

And then there's **Lawrence Hall of Science**, *on Centennial Drive, 510-642-5132*. The Radiation Laboratory at Berkeley, headed by Ernest Lawrence, was the scene of early experiments in atomic fission and a key center in US development of the atomic bomb during World War II; the laboratory continues to provide facilities for research in high-energy physics and nuclear chemistry, and the museum, which is excellent, is open daily 10am-5pm, and costs $6 per adult, $4 for youth 7-18, seniors, and students, and $2 for children 3-6.

Beyond the campus, Telegraph Avenue is a crowded street full of cafes, vendors, crafts, and panhandlers. The aura has changed from its time in the 60s limelight, and the spirit of free love is no more. Some things don't change, however, and **Cody's Books**, *2454 Telegraph*, is still one of the best book stores in the Bay Area, and **Moe's**, *2476 Telegraph*, next door is equally good for used books. Just east of Telegraph *between Haste and Dwight Way* is **People's Park**, the plot of dirt that inspired so many angry demonstrations and led to one student's death in the 1960s. It hasn't aged gracefully, but it's a significant part of Berkeley's history all the same.

Takara Sake USA Inc., *708 Addison Street near University (just off Highway 80), 510-540-8250*, has free daily tastings noon-6pm, and is a change of pace from the campus. It's educational and tasty, and the tasting room is designed in traditional Japanese style, with low wooden benches, and large lanterns hanging from the ceiling.

Tilden Regional Park, *in the Berkeley Hills (follow signs from Grizzly Peak Blvd.), 510-525-2233*, is beautiful, and free. It's great for families with little children, for nature lovers, hikers, and picnickers. There's even a miniature steam train (open Saturday, Sunday, and holidays 11am-6m all year, and Monday-Friday noon-5pm during spring and summer vacations). It's $1.50 per ride, and children generally love it. There's also a beautiful old merry-go-round built in 1911, one of the few "menagerie-type" Herschell-Spillman carousels still around, with rides for $1. Also popular with kids is the Little Farm, with a diminutive red barn and windmill, and normal-sized cows, sheep, pigs and more. It's all on a 740 acre nature study area, and there are several half-mile to full-mile trails to choose from.

OAKLAND

Just across the Bay Bridge from San Francisco and south of Berkeley is Oakland. A large and busy city with a population of 372,242 and a rejuvenating economy, they have lovely residential streets, beautiful houses in the hills, an airport, a baseball team. Still, there's not really much draw for a tourist, though it's not like there's a dearth of things to do once you get there.

You could visit the **Oakland Museum**, *510-834-2413*, or the very beautiful 155 acres of **Lake Merritt** parkland nearby. The **Natural Science Center and Waterfowl Refuge**, *510-238-3739*, attracts hundreds of birds in winter, and **Childrens Fairylands**, *510-832-3609*, is a small amusement park with a puppet theater and merry-go-round. And there's the bizarre **Housewives' Market** downtown *by Fourth and Clay*. If you enjoy the gory, you'll love seeing counters full of hogs' heads and other various animal parts being sold to eager customers. Less perverse, there's always **Jack London Square**, *by the waterfront*, a collection of shops and restaurants named after the author who used to work the boats and down his ale there. It's a little less tacky than Fisherman's Wharf in San Francisco, but it's no reason to cross the bridge to Oakland.

More tempting is the **Paramount Theater**, *on Broadway between 20th and 21st (near the 19th BART station), 510-465-6400*. Built in 1929 by Timothy Fluger, it's a stunningly beautiful place, worth it just for its own sake, let alone whatever show is being hosted, with a bar downstairs. It was closed to the public during WWII, but stayed open round the clock showing movies to soldiers as its contribution to the war effort. Now they do various events, like the Oakland Symphony, performances from the likes of k. d. lang, talks by various celebrities, and occasional Hollywood Classic movies. When it's a movie night, the show starts half an hour early, with organ music and old newsreels. They also do tours of the building the first and third Saturday of each month.

Gertrude Stein made a crack in 1937 when she wrote of Oakland "There's no there there," and Oakland is still smarting from it. They even put up a sculpture to "There" downtown on City Square, which is a little pathetic, when you think of it. There are certainly qualities in Oakland's favor, and *Money* magazine ranked it 20th in their 1990 Best Place to Live survey, but it's not winning any awards as Tourists' Choice.

THE NORTH BAY - MARIN

Over the Golden Gate Bridge just north of San Francisco lies **Marin**, the county of bucolic splendor, tolerance, environmental passion, redwood trees, New Age rites, and beautiful beaches. It is both the butt of San Franciscans' silly jokes (mostly beginning with "How many Marin residents does it take to screw in a light bulb?") and the natural gem of which Northern California is most proud. Marin takes a lot of guff from more cynical types about its aromatherapy and hot tub culture, but few deny their wisdom in preserving the regions great natural assets.

There are the bluffs of the **Marin Headlands** and the redwood trees in **Muir Woods**, the coastal trails in **Tennessee Valley** and the views from atop **Mt. Tam**. **Muir** and **Stinson beaches** are lovely, **Bolinas** is great for bird watchers, and **Point Reyes** takes your breath away each time you visit. The twisting route along Highway 1 might make you weary or car-sick, but the views are sensational.

THE MARIN HEADLANDS

The **Headlands** of the **Golden Gate National Recreation Area** (**GGNRA**) are on the southwestern tip of the Marin Peninsula, and they are fantastically beautiful, with their grassy knolls and poppy-strewn hills, craggy rocks and pebbled beaches. When San Franciscans get to feel edgy and stressed, when their city begins to feel too urban, they head over the bridge and rejuvenate their souls in the headlands. It's easy to feel cold when the fog and wind sweep off the bay, but the soul leaps and thrills and does all those cliché-happy things when confronted with so much sublime loveliness. Take a sweatshirt or sweater, and enjoy.

Arrivals & Departures
By Car

The Marin Headlands are wild and open, wind-swept and shrubby, and very easy to get to from San Francisco by car. Just take 101 North over the Golden Gate Bridge and get off almost immediately on the Alexander Exit. Don't go into Sausalito, but follow the Golden Gate National Recreation Area (GGNRA) signs to a tunnel under the freeway, then on up the GGNRA road to your right, following signs to Fort Barry and Fort Cronkhite.

By Bus

The Muni 76 goes across the bridge and all the way to Fort Cronkhite, but only on Saturday, Sunday, and Holidays. It starts downtown at Fourth and Townsend and continues west to Lombard. Check a Muni map to find the most convenient bus stop on its route.

Seeing the Sights

Begin with the **Marin Headlands Visitors Center**, *Fort Cronkhite, 415-331-1540*, open daily from 9:30am-4:30pm. There are trails to wander on, old military bunkers to poke around in, and grassy hills that were made for picnics looking over the bay towards San Francisco. **Conzelman Road** is the one closest to the bluffs overlooking the bay, and it has turnouts with fantastic views, while **Bunker Road** is further inland, and leads to Fort Cronkhite, the Visitors Center, and a beach full of wind-and-waves polished, multi-colored pretty stones.

The **California Marine Mammal Center**, *is also at Fort Cronkhite, 415-289-7325*. They rescue and rehabilitate sick and orphaned sea lions and seals, and they're open from 10am-4pm daily. The population fluctuates, but they usually have close to 30 on site, with eight or so elephant seals that the public can actually see. They do a good service, and it's run by nice folks.

The **Point Bonita Lighthouse**, *415-331-1540*, is now open to the public. The trail is open 12:30-3:30pm Saturdays and Sundays. It's at the end of Conzelman, and there are signs pointing you there. There's parking by Point Bonita, and trails originate there and go to the Lighthouse. There are docents there to answer questions, and they'll lead a tour if there are enough people gathered. You can also reserve a spot on their

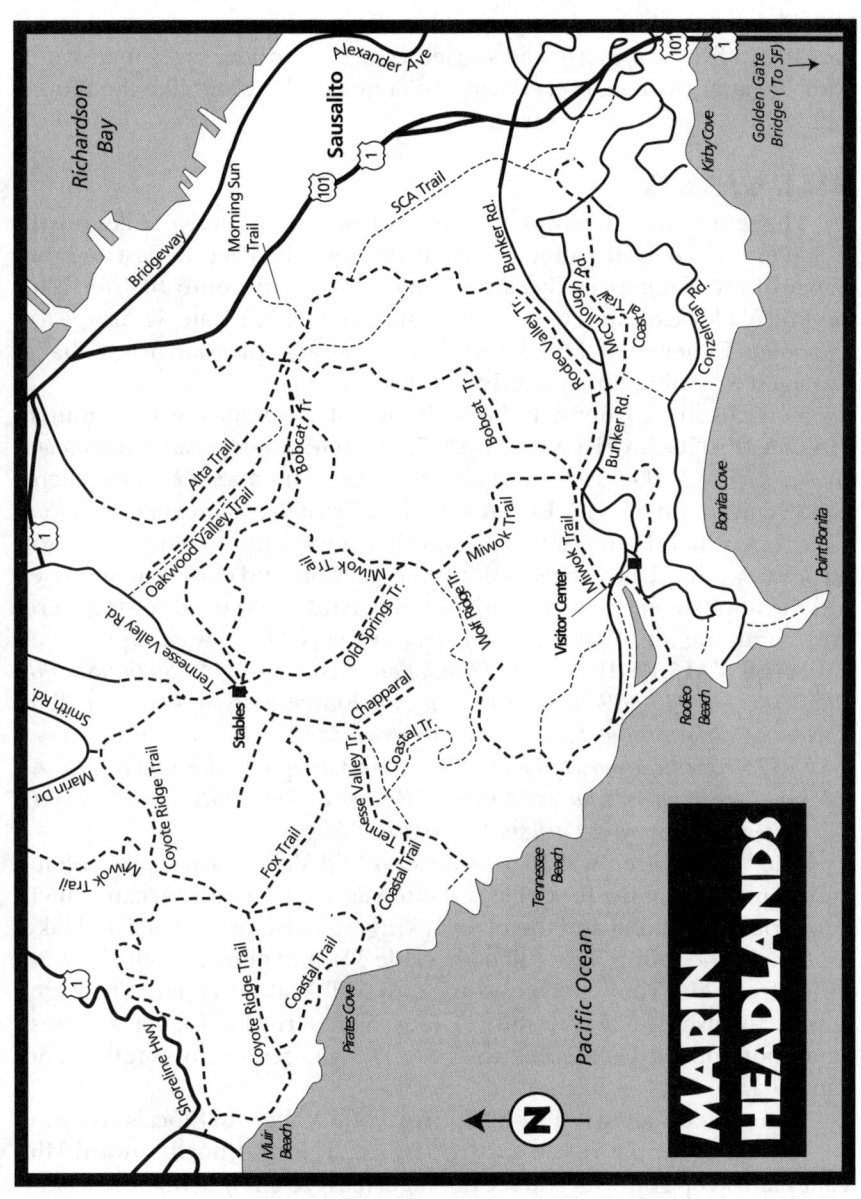

full-moon tours through the Marin Headlands Visitor Center, but book as much in advance as you can. The reservation system now follows their quarterly calendar, so February 15th is the opening date to reserve for March, April, and May dates, and so on. They take up to 45 people and they fill up fast. They also lead sunset tours (depending on demand and available staff), you can reserve at the same number, and like the moon walks, the sunset tours are free.

MILL VALLEY

There are other lovely places further north, too. Twelve miles north of San Francisco, **Mill Valley** sits pretty between the Pacific coast and the slopes of Mt. Tamalpais. By car, it's an easy drive on route 101 north to the Mill Valley exit, and by bus, you can take Golden Gate Transit, *415-332-6600*. Either way, Mill Valley is a small and pleasant town that's managed to avoid getting overly cute or stuck-up.

You can stroll around and dine in one of their cafes or restaurants. **PIAZZA D'ANGELO RESTAURANT**, *22 Miller across from the downtown square, 415-388-2000*, is open daily 10:30am-11pm and serves excellent Italian cuisine for $7-$17. **EL PASEO**, *7 El Paseo near Sunnyside, 415-388-0741*, open nightly for dinner, is another good option. They have got great French food like snails, onion soup, salmon, and chocolate mousse, and the atmosphere is warm and intimate. And if you need to stay there over night, the Mill Valley Inn is lovely in a very Marin way.

MILL VALLEY INN, *165 Throckmorton Avenue. 415-389-6608, 800-595-2100, fax 415-389-5051. This inn is a European-style pensione with a Northern Californian look. They have 16 rooms ($125-$165) and two cottages ($155-$165), with a variety of amenities (depending on price range) such as balcony, French doors, and wood stove. All rates include continental breakfast and espresso bar, morning newspaper, and parking.*

The Inn is within walking distance of Mill Valley's cafes and restaurants, but it's set at the foot of Mt. Tamalpais, from where you can launch into mountain biking and the many hiking trails, or just sit back and take it all in. All the rooms have full bath, cable TV, and phone, while the view varies from Mt. Tam's redwood trees to Mill Valley proper. The ergonomic furnishings are unique, using Northern California artisans' handcrafts of local materials to create a style geared to comfort and natural appeal.

Tennessee Valley is a side trip from Mill Valley that locals treasure but few visitors know. It's an easy trip by car. Take 101 north toward Mill Valley and keep going till you see the small (easy to miss) Tennessee Valley Road sign to your left, by the fruit stand and church. Turn left on Tennessee Valley Road and drive till you get to the parking lot, and you're there. From the parking lot, you can walk down the mile-long path to

Tennessee Beach or take one of the trails that head up, up, up into the coastal hills. The views from the peaks are just as nice as can be, and it's a great place for a picnic (there's fresh fruit and nuts available at that fruit stand where you turn off the main road).

You can watch the hawks play in the air streams, hike along the old fire road, or down the Coastal Trail to the beach. In spring the place is always alive with wild flowers, and in summer it's burnt golden brown, but it's a special place no matter what season.

MOUNT TAMALPAIS STATE PARK

Mount Tamalpais State Park, *415-388-2070*, is open daily 8am-sunset, and is better known as **Mt. Tam**. To get here, take Hwy. 1 to the Panoramic Hwy. Keep going up past Pan Toll Ranger Station and park headquarters, *801 Panoramic Highway*, where you can get maps of hiking trails, to the parking lot a quarter of a mile from the summit (which is 2,600 feet high). It's a wonderful place to go for hiking or biking, as its 6,400 acres of park has over 50 miles of trails.

There are leisurely strolls through grassy meadows and arduous treks up steep peaks, picnic spots, beaches and streams, and all sorts of vegetation along the way. There are redwoods and ferns, and in spring the place is crazy with wild flowers. The **Mountain Theater**, *415-383-0155, on Ridgecrest Blvd.* is a natural Greek-style amphitheater with terraced stone seats used for summer productions and a pagan celebration of the summer solstice. Dress in layers to accommodate the wild-card weather. The fog rolls in on Mt. Tam like nobody's business, and can change a hot hike to a miserable chill in mere minutes. With proper clothing, however, the views from the top while the fog swirls all around are absolutely wonderful.

If you want to stay overnight, there are **environmental campsites** for $10 a night, and rustic **Steep Ravine Environmental Cabins** on Rocky Point for $30 a cabin. The cabins are an especially good deal. They're wonderful redwood houses with wood stoves, separate pit toilet restrooms, and platform beds (you bring your own sleeping bag and pad) that can sleep five. To reserve a cabin or campsite, call **Mistix** at *800-444-7275* as far in advance as you can.

MUIR WOODS

Muir Woods, *on route 1 just 17 miles north of San Francisco, 415-388-2595*, is beautiful no matter what the weather's doing, and it's open daily from 8am-sunset. It's a hike-through park, and no cars are allowed past the visitor center. The impressive redwoods in this 550 acre park shoot so high, you could get a crick in your neck looking at them all. Some of the oldest (close to 1,000 years old and still growing) are nearly 250 feet tall; this is what all the environmentalists mean when they talk about old-growth forests. There are 25 miles of lovely paths over streams and through stands of famous redwoods such as Bohemian Grove and Cathedral Grove, with paths ranging from the very easy to the exhaustingly strenuous. There's no picnicking or camping, nor are pets allowed.

The dense forest canopy keeps out most weather, and the drippy moss and ferns create great atmosphere. It's majestic and serene, and no wonder dentists tack pictures of Muir Woods scenes to their ceilings to soothe and calm their patients. The trip there, however, can be anything but soothing. The lanes of Route 1 are narrow and winding, and when there's a lot of traffic, it just crawls along impatiently behind the slow one at the front. Good intentions are rarely easy to keep, but if you're going to visit on a weekend, you'd be best off heading out early, like before 10am.

If you want the redwoods without the hassle, **Red & White Fleet**, *415-546-2700*, runs an all-day (5 hour) tour for $24 an adult and $12 per child. They take care of all the driving and parking, you get plenty of quality redwood time, plus a visit to Tiburon.

STINSON BEACH

Keep going up Hwy. 1 and you'll get to **Stinson Beach**, nestled down in the dip between two ridges. It is, indeed, a lovely beach, but not necessarily worth the weekend trek. On a hot summer Saturday or Sunday, you and your car may well overheat as you sit in traffic and inch along the coastal highway, cursing yourself for not just taking the Tennessee or Muir or Moss beach turnoff. On a weekday you stand a better chance of making good time; otherwise get yourself on the road nice and early. There are a couple other things to consider as well. This being Northern California, it's unlikely the water will be warmer than 60°, so swimming isn't that appealing unless you visit during a rare heat wave, and during the summer, the fog is as likely to swamp the coast up north as it is in San Francisco.

All that said, the three-mile stretch of clean (though not white) sand is beautiful and all a beach should be. The little town puts up with carloads of intruders with good grace, and lots of good picnic food is readily available. And for the surfers, *415-868-1922* will get you a surfing report.

BOLINAS LAGOON PRESERVE

Bolinas Lagoon Preserve, *415-868-9244*, a small, lush canyon with eight miles of trails, is the spring nesting site for flocks of great egrets and great blue herons, and it's just three miles north of Stinson Beach. It's a part of **Audubon Canyon Ranch** in Marin County, and is open to the public weekends and holidays, 10am-4pm, March 18-July 16. Around the end of March and early April, the egrets perform an elaborate courtship dance, which involves posturing, ritual twig presentations, and feather displays, while the herons, who arrive earlier than the egrets, are about ready to hatch their chicks.

POINT REYES NATIONAL SEASHORE

Point Reyes, *about 25 miles north of San Francisco, 415-663-1092*, is a vast, verdant land of flowers, trails, beaches, birds, shrubby terrains, and salty breezes. Take Highway 1 to the Bear Valley Road exit (just west of the village of Olema, and a ways past Stinson), turn left at the stop sign on Sir Francis Drake Boulevard, then bear right at Pierce Point Road, which ends at the historic Pierce Point Ranch and the Tomales Point trailhead.

Point Reyes is no secret, and lots of folks head up there on weekends to escape the city, but the 65,000 acres of lagoons, marshes, beaches, dunes, and forests are big enough for solitude if that's what you're after, and a weekday should virtually ensure seclusion. **Tomales Point** (the northernmost spot) makes for a gorgeous peninsula hike down a mildly sloping trail, with the Pacific pounding on one side of you and **Tomales Bay** idly lapping the other. The grasslands are dizzy with yellow wildflowers, lupines, poppies, and fiddleneck buttercups, and if you go in March, you might see some gray whales migrating north, call *415663-1092* for special programs.

There's a **lighthouse** out there that really isn't as exciting as it might seem, though it makes for good whale watching; the real wealth lies in the meadows and coastline. The weather, however, is very unpredictable, so bring a wind-breaker and sweater as back-up even on a sunny day.

The map on the following page will help you get oriented for a beautiful, relaxing excursion to Point Reyes.

SAUSALITO

Before the Europeans came colonizing, **Sausalito** was home to a group of Miwoks, but the 1775 exploratory travels of Juan Manual de Ayala, the man who named the place *Saucelito* ("little willow" in Spanish) put change in motion. For much of the 19th century, Sausalito was just a whaling port, but railroads connected Sausalito to the north, and ferries eased transportation to San Francisco, and the people began to visit just for fun, but it was a different kind of fun than they go for today.

In the 1900s, instead of boutiques, restaurants, and craft stores, you'd more likely find saloons, whorehouses, and gambling. Bootleggers did well there in the 1920s, and an influx of shipyard workers swelled the

population in the 1940s, dividing Sausalito residents into "hill snobs" and "wharf rats." The first element will always remain, because the hills of Sausalito are topped with lovely homes that afford stunning views which can be afforded by few. The wharf rats, however, have evolved with the times into an artist colony Sausalito generally views as a feather in its cap, and a houseboat community the town often feels is poking a finger in its eye. They live to the north in Richardson Bay, and for pennies a month they share the town with those who pay thousands for the privilege.

Sausalito today is a pretty town, charming and lovely and small enough to easily visit in a day. Sausalito also earns most of its baguette and butter from the tourist trade, and the flavor of downtown is mostly that of a tourist village. A little too small to handle its popularity without losing some of its original personality, a sunny summer weekend jaunt can take on sheep herd characteristics. If you have the flexibility and want to visit, try a day midweek, or in the thick of blustery winter.

Orientation

This bayside town is just eight miles north of San Francisco, on the southern end of the Marin County peninsula. Bridgeway is the main strip in Sausalito. It parallels the coast, it is the street the Route 101 ramp deposits you on if you're driving, and it's just half a block up from the ferry dock. It is also the location of most of Sausalito's boutiques, restaurants, and action. Caledonia is one block up and parallel to Bridgeway. It's a quieter street, and it's where you'll find markets and less-touristed cafes.

Arrivals & Departures

By Car

Sausalito is an easy jaunt by car. Just head north from San Francisco over the Golden Gate Bridge and take the Alexander Avenue exit to your right shortly after you get off the bridge. The ramp will take you down a long hill and deposit you on Bridgeway, the main street in town. On sunny weekends, however, this road can get severely jammed.

By Ferry

The Red & White Fleet, shuttles between Pier 43 1/2 in San Francisco and the dock in Sausalito, *415-546-2896*, for $5.50 each way. The ferry takes 20-40 minutes, and they leave San Francisco Monday-Friday 11am, 12:15pm, 1:35pm, 3pm, and 4:50pm and return 11:50am, 1:05pm, 2:20pm, 3:40pm, 5:45pm, and 8:20pm. On Saturday, Sunday, and holidays, the ferries from San Francisco leave 10:40am, 12:35pm, 2:10pm, 3:45pm, and 5:50pm, and return 11:15am, 1:10pm 2:45pm, 4:20pm, and 6:25pm. These ferries tend to be more crowded than the less expensive Golden Gate boats.

The **Golden Gate Ferry**, goes between Sausalito and the Ferry Building at the foot of Market Street in San Francisco, *415-332-6600*, for $4.25 each way.

TAKE THE FERRY!

The ferry is a very civilized method of transportation, especially on a fine, sunny day. The sky and bay are blue, the passengers lounge on deck benches and the motors make the boat throb appealingly. Turn around so the Ferry Building clock is astern, and you're off at a good clip through the incredible beauty of San Francisco Bay, as white seagulls cavort above. It's windy up on the top deck, and on the foredeck as well, where the view is better. Inside are tables (with protective ridges), and refreshments as well.

There's coffee and tea, fruit juices and sodas, beer, wine, and hard liquor, and an assortment of pastries, pizzas, and snacks. Or just sit there out of the wind and enjoy the view. And there's no smoking anywhere, inside or out.

By Bus

Golden Gate Transit, *415-923-2000*, #10 goes between San Francisco and Sausalito twice hourly from 6am-6:12pm, while the #20 keeps running once hourly till 1am. Fare is $2 each way (have exact change ready). There are a number of Golden Gate Transit bus stops throughout the city (especially along Van Ness Avenue and Lombard), but you can call the number for advice on the stop closest to where you are.

By Bicycle

Cycling to Sausalito is a popular trip for those with a few muscles in their calves. You can rent bikes at Fisherman's Wharf and you can cycle both ways over the Golden Gate Bridge, or you can opt to take the ferry one way (or both ways, for that matter).

Getting Around Town

By Foot

One of the pleasures of Sausalito is wandering about on foot, and most of the town is central and as compact as the steep hills allow. This allows you to come by ferry and not feel stranded. There are some severe inclines to get to, say, Alta Mira Hotel, and it is exhilarating to climb the stairs on foot.

By Car

It is, of course, easier and less strenuous to go by car. The downtown area gets clogged with automobiles very easily, especially on weekends, since the small lanes weren't really built for heavy traffic, and sitting in a traffic jam may not be your idea of fun.

By Bicycle

Bicycle travel is a good alternative. You can whiz a long the bike lanes on Bridgeway with no problem, though the hills are still pretty daunting if you want to go inland off the main drag.

By Bus

The **Sausalito Shuttle**, *415-331-7262*, plies Bridgewater, but in April-October only.

Where to Stay

HOTEL SAUSALITO, *16 El Portal. 415-332-4900. Located just up from the ferry dock, this hotel has 16 rooms under major renovations, and priced around $135-$165. The hotel should be open for business again by fall, 1996, but you should call first and check.*

The total overhaul is changing the former Victorian aura to a Northern Californian style (similar to their Mill Valley Inn), with the major emphasis on accommodating the business traveler. Special furniture (hand-crafted by northern Californian artisans) were fashioned for beauty, ergonomic comfort, and laptop function. Everything from the desks to the lighting, in contrast with the Alta Mira, use the best of what's modern, making it easier to work from a hotel room while enjoying the natural fibers and local woodwork with a chic California feel.

ALTA MIRA, *125 Bulkley Avenue. 415-332-1350, fax 415-331-3862. The Alta Mira is a beautiful old hotel, very charming and lovely, with 34 rooms that range in price from $70-$170, depending on size and view.*

The name *alta mira* means high view, and it's most appropriate. The hotel is set way up the hill, and the views are indeed worth the climb up the 52 steps and longish pedestrian incline of Exelsior Lane (the route by foot from Bridgeway) to the entrance steps of the Alta Mira. They have a variety of accommodations, from small, lovely rooms featuring old world charm, antiques, and a beautiful deck with fantastic view of the bay and San Francisco that start at $95 to cottages that are perfect for families that cost $105-$170.

Room sizes range from a single room with shower to a 3-bedroom suite with full bath. The views vary from bay to garden, and while some rooms have patios, others come with their own fireplaces. Everything's possible here, and it's all charming. Originally built in the 1880s as a private residence, and later converted to hotel, it burnt to the ground in 1926, was rebuilt, and has gradually been expanded a bit here and there to the Alta Mira of today. Pink wash on wood and stucco, graceful terraces and gracious staff make this a very special place to stay.

CASA MADRONA HOTEL, *801 Bridgeway. 415-332-0502, 800-567-9524, fax 415-332-2537. This lovely hotel has 32 rooms, suites, and cottages. Room rates run $105-$185, and the suite, which is stunning, is $245.*

Tucked away on Sausalito's slope, the Casa Madrona rooms are imbued with a Victorian feel along with modern amenities and pampering touches. Rooms are cozy with nice views of garden or bay, and the higher the rates, the more elegant and luxurious they become. Each room has its own personality, however, and no two are alike. There's the white wicker look, the country French, the Southwest feel, canopied beds, fireplaces, private decks, and more. Just choose what you want when you make your reservations. It's a lovely place that is relaxing and engenders the easy contentment of another time. The rates include breakfast, and a social hour every evening with wine and cheese. There's an outdoor jacuzzi, a massage room, and a very fine, gourmet restaurant as well.

THE INN ABOVE TIDE, *30 El Portal. 415-332-9535, 800-893-8433, fax 415-332-6714. Located right over the bay, this inn has 30 rooms and suites, costing $185-$250 for rooms and $400 for suites.*

Not overly attractive on the outside, the rooms themselves are very modern and comfortable, with spare lines and spectacular views. The hotel just opened in August of '95, so everything is new and swell and all non-smoking. There are private decks and fireplaces, data ports and terry robes, hair dryers and binoculars. The hotel provides continental breakfast and evening wine, and other services like dry-cleaning and massage are available.

Where to Eat

There are plenty of places to eat in Sausalito. A town that thrives on tourism like Sausalito doesn't stint on restaurants. The selections below are some of the best.

EXPENSIVE
Basque

RESTAURANT GUERNICA, *2009 Bridgeway. 415-332-1512. Guernica is quite a ways from the main drag, just across the street from the Bay Model. It's open Sunday-Thursday 5-10:30pm, Friday-Saturday 5-11pm, so it's only an option if you're staying overnight or come by car (there's parking in back).*

The interior is Basque, with lots of stone, dark wood, stained glass, and yellow leather. The tables are set formally with white linen and slim vases of red carnations. Dinners starts with choices like steamed clams or mussels, pate maison, or escargots Bordelaise ($4.50-$6.75), and the entrees ($9.50-$15) provide a lot of seafood and meat dishes like paella

San Sebastian, prawns in a Basquaise sauce, chicken Guernica, lamb shank sheepherder style, or veal picatta. Guernica offers a vegetarian paella as well, and a pasta of the day.

There's also a children's dinner for $6.50 and special meals for two of Paella Valenciana or rack of lamb Guernica for $36-$40. If you like garlic you should love it here, as the Basque cuisine is founded on the virtues of the garlic clove.

Continental

ALTA MIRA, *125 Bulkley Avenue (see hotel lisitng for directions). 415-332-1350, fax 415-331-3862. Alta Mira is a gorgeous, lofty setting for Mediterranean meals rich in seafood.*

Breakfasts feature lots of eggs, salmon, and crab ($9-$19), and they serve elegant gin fizz and mimosa cocktails to go with them. Dinner starters like ceviche, smoked trout, or jumbo prawns on a pastry shell are followed by a variety of meats (chicken, roast duck, seafood, veal, filet mignon, lamb) in a wealth of rich sauces for $14-$19. The food is good, but it's really the Alta Mira ambiance for which people ascend the heights.

Italian

ANGELINO'S, *621 Bridgeway. 415-331-5225. Fabulous Italian food is served daily from 11am-9:30pm in the summer, but they're closed Tuesday in winter.*

Angelino's lunch and dinner menus are fairly similar save for the prices, which run $8.25-$19 for lunch and $11-$21 for dinner. There are plenty of pizza (plus panini during lunch, and calzone during dinner) preceding a full menu of homemade pasta with ravioli stuffed with ricotta, gnocchi in tomato or pesto sauce, fettuccine alla Carbonara, and great linguini and clams. They also specialize in seafood dishes, with lots of prawns, salmon, clams, and calamari in various lemon, olive oil, and garlic sauces. And there are a few chicken, veal chop, and New York steak plates as well. All the food is expertly prepared, fresh, and very delicious.

MODERATE
Seafood

THE SPINNAKER RESTAURANT, *100 Spinnaker Drive. 415-332-1500. Located north of the ferry landing and open daily 11am-11pm.*

The Spinnaker has been serving fresh seafood since 1962, and they are still a popular place. While chicken and red meat dishes are available, the bulk of the menu offers seafood - in soup or sauce, off the grill, with pasta, or chilled on the half shell. The fish, prawns, and bivalves ($12-$17) are fresh, and the water view is always a pleasure. The Jerk Chicken is also good, as are the massive slabs of steaks. Be forewarned, however, that they have an extensive dessert menu as well, so leave room for the mousse. They do a fine Sunday Brunch as well.

INEXPENSIVE
American
THE LIGHTHOUSE CAFE, *1311 Bridgeway, 415-331-3034. The cafe is a popular breakfast and lunch spot that's a bit off the main drag. Open daily 7am-3pm.*

The Lighthouse (a Sausalito institution for 30 or so years) was bought 4 years ago by a Danish family, and that is why, in addition to the omelets, pancakes, burgers, and sandwiches, the Lighthouse Cafe offers a number of Danish specials (Danish meatballs, herring, etc.), along with the otherwise standard American fare.

The meals here range from $4.75 (two eggs with home fries) to $7.50 for the Danish lunch plate. The interior is informal in a roadside diner sort of way, with naugahyde booths and bustling waitresses bearing huge platters of standard grub.

Sandwiches, Salads, & Deli
THE CALEDONIA KITCHEN, *400 Caledonia. 415-331-0220, fax 331-0223. Located by the corner of Litho, this is a bright, very pleasant market and cafe, open Sunday-Thursday 8am-8pm and Friday-Saturday 8am-9pm with fresh and original salads, and excellent sandwiches for very reasonable prices.*

The food is the main thing, but the atmosphere is another reason to come here. The ochre and salmon colors are muted, just like the background music which stays in the background, and the tables inside and out have views of the park. The tile floor, slanted ceiling, plants and flowers finish off the decor. You order your food at the counter, and both the goat cheese baguette and roasted turkey focaccia sandwiches are sensational, and there are 8-10 innovative salads daily. A satisfying lunch costs $4-$6.25, there are great desserts, too, and the ambiance is much more agreeable and airy than the Lighthouse.

Picnic Supplies
Sausalito Market *on Caledonia is at the corner of Pine.* It's a grocery store with cold drinks and fresh produce, and they're open daily 8:30am-8pm.

One block further *on Caledonia at the corner with Turney* is the **Real Food Company**. It's an organic produce market, open daily 9am-9pm, with a counter of vegan rolls and veggie sandwiches and salads.

The Caledonia Kitchen described above is also a good picnic supply option.

Seeing the Sights

Bay Area Discovery Museum, *on East Fort Baker, 415-331-2129 or 415-487-4398 for taped information*. While not located downtown, it's easy to get to by car. From San Francisco, get off at the Alexander exit (the 2nd exit after the bridge), bear right, and take the first left, then follow the small museum signs. The museum is open Tuesday-Thursday 9am-4pm, Friday-Sunday 10am-5pm, and it costs $6 for children and $7 for adults.

This museum is geared for children, and its hands-on. In the Science Lab you can touch a snake or make a plaster cast of a paw print. The Media Center has all sorts of CD ROM disks to view and internet access to play with, and there's a Tot Spot especially for the young, with a Bat Bungalow, a place to float with the fish, and a chance to dress up in wonderful costumes. There are also a plethora of outdoor activities such as nature hikes, science experiments, art projects, crab fishing off the pier, and more. The headlands weather tends to change very swiftly, so multiple layers is wise. They do have a cafe, and all buildings are wheelchair accessible.

Bay Model, *2100 Bridgeway. 415-332-3870*. Bay Model is open Tuesday-Saturday 9am-4pm in winter, Tuesday-Friday 9am-4pm, weekends and holidays 10am-6pm in summer, and admission is free. Designed and operated by the US Army Corps of Engineers, spreading out over 1.5 acres, and using 286 five-ton concrete slabs, the Bay Model is a three-dimensional representation of the San Francisco Bay and Delta, complete with interactive gadgets to simulate the tides and currents. This is the bay bottom-up, without all that messy water in the way, and it's been used to help understand the bay ecosystem, maintain the ecological balance, and prepare for earthquakes.

In addition to some videos, computers, and other interactive displays, there are guided tours available for ten or more per group *(call 415-332-3871 to arrange)*. Marinship 1942-1945 in the Visitor Center (the old shipyard warehouse) is an exhibit to commemorate the 20,000 men and women who worked the three shifts to build the Liberty cargo ships, tankers, and oilers demanded by the war effort. To get there from downtown Sausalito, take Bridgeway Boulevard northwest to Harbor Drive. Turn left, then turn right on Marinship Way and follow the signs.

Sausalito Annual Art Festival takes place Labor Day Weekend from August 31-September 2.

Shopping

Downtown Sausalito along Bridgeway is lined with shops and boutiques of every kind. If shopping is your pleasure, you've come to the right town.

Sports & Recreation

Sea Trek Ocean Kayaking Center, *in Schoonmaker Point Marina, 415-488-1000*. To get there, head down Bridgeway, and when you see Margaritaville Restaurant, turn right at the next light. Turn right again at the bottom of the hill, then just follow the road till you reach them under the palm trees on the beach. They rent single kayaks for $20 for 2 hours, $35 for 4 hours, and $45 for a full day, while double and triple person kayaks are $35 for 2 hours, $45 for 4 hours, and $65 for a full day. Open deck boats require no experience, but to paddle the traditional closed kayaks, you need to have had some experience, or take their introductory class, which is 7 hours on Fridays-Sundays for $90. They are very nice people there, and paddling about in Richardson Bay, to Angel Island, or on through the Golden Gate on a sunny day is great fun.

Sausalito Jet Ski, *1385 East Francisco in Sausalito, 415-753-8754*, rents jet skis for $40 an hour and $175 a day, and they're open Tuesday-Saturday 10am-6pm.

Wheel Escapes, *30 Liberty Ship Way, #210, 415-332-0218*, is open for bicycle rentals weekdays (except Tuesday when they're closed) 10am-6pm and weekends 9am-7pm. You can rent hourly ($5-$8) and daily ($21-$35), depending on the bike type, and they have bicycle trailers to tote children ($3 an hour, $15 a day) as well. To get there from downtown Sausalito, head up Bridgeway till just before the Bay Model, and turn right towards the water onto Liberty Ship Way.

Hawaiian Chieftain, *415-331-3214*, is a 103 foot replica of a 1790s tallship, and they offer three-hour sunset bay sails every Wednesday and Friday 6-9pm for $25-$30 as well as Sunday jazz and reggae brunch cruises 11am-2pm for $45.

Practical Information

There's a **Visitor Information Kiosk** *right near the ferry dock* that's open daily 11am-5pm, and a **Visitor & Historical Center**, *777 Bridgeway, 415-332-0505*, open Tuesday-Sunday 11:30am-4pm, but good luck ever reaching someone on the phone.

THE WINE COUNTRY - SONOMA & NAPA VALLEYS

Travel northeast from San Francisco for an hour or so and you'll reach the **Wine Country**, with some of the most beautiful landscapes, charming inns, gourmet dining, and spectacular wines this side of the Atlantic. It's one of the most popular destinations for San Francisco residents and out-of-state visitors alike, and that many suave and sophisticated people can't be wrong. It's an easy trip by car (and possible but much less convenient by Greyhound Bus), and it is genuinely lovely (though in different ways) during each season of the year.

Sonoma County runs about 60 miles from its southeastern tip on San Pablo Bay to its northwestern Pacific coast town of Annapoulis. It's about 35 miles at its widest stretch from the Pacific Ocean to its eastern border with Napa County, but the narrow strip of Sonoma Valley is just 17 miles long. To the south there's Petaluma, a pleasant rural town known for its poultry farms ("chicken capital of the world") and the filming site of *American Graffiti* and *Peggy Sue Got Married*. **Sonoma** itself is a pretty, Spanish-style town with a central plaza, the Sonoma Mission, preserved old adobe buildings, and lots of Bear Revolt history. **Santa Rosa**, its largest city, is pretty close to the center of the county.

Along with **Bodega Bay** (a beautiful fishing town most famous as the location where Hitchcock's *The Birds* was shot), **Jenner** (another small fishing town), the **Sonoma Coast State Beach**, **Jack London Park**, and **Sugar Loaf Ridge State Park**, Sonoma boasts **Sebastopol** (Mecca for Gravenstein apples), the **Russian River** resort area, the **Lake Sonoma Recreation Area**, **Healdsburg** (a pleasant town that's centrally located near Russian River and the three Sonoma valleys), **Cloverdale** (jump off point for river rafting), and of course some great **wineries**. Sonoma is less densely planted than Napa, but this is where the California wine industry started in 1824, and they have around 100 wineries in their narrow valley, with big names such as Kenwood, Glen Ellen, Ravenswood, Sebastiani, Smothers Brothers, Clos du Bois, and Korbel Champagne Cellars.

Napa County, the principal part of the Wine Country, is to the east of Sonoma, and is substantially smaller. At its longest from north to south, Napa stretches about 35 miles, and the county's width is more like 22 miles. **Calistoga**, its best-known town, lies on Napa's western border near Sonoma. The blue-collar town of **Napa** is towards the southern end of the county, with small boutique towns **Yountville** and **St. Helena** nearby, and **Lake Berryessa** (a beautiful and popular reservoir with all the usual lake activities: fishing, swimming, sailing, water skiing, and camping) is off to the east. Grape vines are everywhere here, with about 200 wineries within the small county. Napa has some of California's premier wineries, including Sterling, Stag's Leap, Clos Pégase, Domaine Chandon, Stonegate, Robert Mondavi, Beringer, and Rutherford.

For more information on Napa and Sonoma attractions, lodgings, and their various annual festivals and events, you can call the **Sonoma Valley Visitors Bureau**, *707-996-1090*; **Sebastopol's Chamber of Commerce**, *707-823-3032*; the **Russian River Chamber of Commerce**, *707-869-9009*; **Healdsburg Chamber of Commerce**, *707-433-6935*; **Lake Sonoma Recreation Area**, *707-433-9483*; **Cloverdale Chamber of Com-**

merce, *707-894-4470*; **Napa Valley Conference and Visitors Bureau**, *707-226-7459*, or **Napa Tourist Information Office**, *707-253-2929*; **Lake Berryessa Information**, *707-966-2111*; **Yountville Chamber of Commerce**, *707-944-2929*, and **Calistoga Chamber of Commerce**, *707-942-6333*.

Finally, see *California Wine Country Guide* by Nicole O'Hay, Open Road Publishing, for the best of the wine country, including wineries, tips on wine, great inns and restaurants, and annual events.

THE WINE TASTING TOUR

If you want to really explore Wine Country, and enjoy visiting lots of wineries and tasting their wares, you should consider the V.I.T. (Very Important Taster) package. They offer a 100-page guide to all the 95 participating wineries, a map of both Napa and Sonoma wine regions, a reference chart showing which wineries have which varietals, and a V.I.T. card that assures waived tasting fees and 5%-35% off wine purchases from the 95 wineries. The cost for one person is $20, but it's just $25 for two. Given that most of the wineries charge $3 or so a tasting, it works out to be a convenience and a savings for a couple planning to visit five or more wineries.

For more information, or to order, call 707-255-1639, write to V.I.T. Wine Marketing, POB 174, Napa, CA 94559, or e-mail at vitwine@aol.com).

All these towns have places to stay, but for sheer number, diversity, and range of rates, Calistoga surpasses all. Calistoga also has some nightlife, a variety of activities beyond wine-tasting, it's centrally located on the border of Sonoma and Napa, and you can reach it without having to drive on Route 29, which gets so clogged with weekend traffic it begins to make coastal Highway 1 look good. All these attributes make Calistoga an excellent home base if you want to do more than a day trip and really explore the Wine Country.

CALISTOGA

Sam Brannan, the 19th century Mormon millionaire entrepreneur, founded the upper Napa Valley hot springs spa of **Calistoga** in 1859. He wanted to start a "Saratoga of California" like the well-known spa in New York, but he stepped on his tongue and came up with "Calistoga of Saratina" instead. He set up a spa resort community at the foot of Mt. St. Helena and now it's an attractive and successful town of 4,000 (fewer in winter, and crowded with tourists in the summer) that's still supported mainly by Calistoga bottled mineral water and the ceaseless flow of money guaranteed by the hot springs spa tourist trade. Most visitors come for some spa pampering or to tour the wineries nearby, and it's also popular for get-away-from-it-all weekends.

To the uninitiated, it looks like a charming, one-horse town, worth a stroll before moving on through Napa's wine country. Go beyond the doors of the main street establishments, however, and you'll find mud baths, aromatherapy whirlpools, a legion of massage experts, and some of the best eating in California; it's a town well prepared to coddle and pamper your body, spirit, and gastronomic needs.

Part of what is great about Calistoga, however, is that it's not been boutiqued and cutesied beyond recognition like, for example, the main street in nearby St. Helena. Though the tourist trade is clearly important in Calistoga, it doesn't set the tone of the town.

Orientation

It is hot here in the summer, not surprising considering Brannan set his town on a site the Wappo Indians named "Colaynomo," their word for "hot oven." Autumn is a great time to come; it's a little cooler and the wineries are in mid-harvest. Lincoln Avenue, the main street, runs east to west through Calistoga, and most of the places to eat, stay, soak, or do business are right on Lincoln, including Tourist Information.

Arrivals & Departures

By Car

Driving from San Francisco shouldn't take more than 1.5 hours, assuming no traffic or other hindrances. Go north up 101 till a little past Santa Rosa, where you take the Mark West Springs Road exit (the sign also says Calistoga).

Turn left on Petrified Forest Road and then right at Routes 128 & 29. A left at the light puts you on Lincoln, Calistoga's main street.

By Bus

Greyhound, *800-231-2222*, connects to most locations, departing once daily. Round trip to San Francisco (3.5 hours) is $29. **Napa Valley Transit**, *800-696-6443*, has buses many times daily to Vallejo for $2.50.

Getting Around Town

It's easy to navigate town on foot, but to see the sights nearby you'll need a car or a bicycle.

Where to Stay

There are hotels, inns, small bed & breakfasts, camp sites, and spas. If you stay at a spa, you don't have to ruin the relaxation by trudging back to your hotel, but in most cases, you give up in atmosphere what you gain in convenience. The following places to stay are listed from most to least expensive, not by recommendation or type. There are wonderful places to stay in Calistoga; all you need to do is read the descriptions and choose the budget and atmosphere that suits you.

THE ELMS, *1300 Cedar. 707-942-9476, is a B&B in a 1871 home, with prices from $110 to $185 (off-season discounts available).*

The rooms are elegant and lovely, the bathrooms are enormous, and the restored house is kept up in beautiful style.

LA CHUMIÈRE, *1301 Cedar, 707-942-5139, has two distinctive guest rooms with elaborate bathrooms for $125 ($135 on weekends) in a restored 1932 Cotswald Cottage, and a private cottage for $150 ($175 on weekends), with some off-season discounts.*

This is another small and well-maintained B&B. The rooms are lovely, and there are interesting extras, too. There's a hot tub, a tree house deck, a flourishing garden, and room-service massage service that'll do you in your room or up in the tree house.

MOUNT VIEW SPA AND HOTEL, *1457 Lincoln, 707-942-6877 has doubles from $85 to cottages with hot tub and deck for $190. All are elegantly furnished and comfortable with bath, phone, and air-conditioning.*

This hotel is in a restored 1917 historic landmark that's wonderfully renovated, and it's very centrally located on Lincoln, right near all the best restaurants and night spots. They also have a spa that does Fango mud, a nice pool to lounge by, plus an award-winning restaurant and saloon.

INDIAN SPRINGS, *1712 Lincoln, 707-942-4913, has individual cottages for $95-$150 (depending on size, season, and day of week) equipped with kitchenettes, barbecue set-ups, and lawn furniture.*

The cottages are lovely, with thick terry robes, pleasant furnishings, and your own spot of lawn. To the east of town, it's not in the thick of things, like the Mount View. Along with their mud spa service, they have tennis courts, adorable bicycle surreys, and sweet-smelling oleander bushes that line the driveway. They also have a magnificent Olympic-sized pool that was built in 1913.

SCOTT COURTYARD, *1443 Second, 707-942-0948, is a B&B with attractive, spacious suites (some with kitchenettes) for $125 a room.*

It is a secluded inn off the main drag, with a private pool, beautiful garden, a hot tub, and festive tropical art deco decor.

BRANNAN COTTAGE INN, *109 Wapoo, 707-942-4200, was one of the original Brannan guest houses and it's now a B&B with rates from $105 to $140.*

With white picket fence and porch rockers, it looks authentic. The rooms are done up with period charm, and they retain the gracious, leisurely pace of the old spa days.

ROMAN SPA MOTEL, *1300 Washington, 707-942-4441, has rooms from $66 to $136, depending on season, day of week, and kitchen facilities.*

All rooms have private bath, air-conditioning, and TV, but no charm. There is a nice garden, and a pool, and while they don't actually have their own spa facilities, International Spa is just next door.

PINE STREET INN AND EUROSPA, *1202 Pine, 707-942-682, is an inn has comfortable, attractive rooms for $85-$95. There are often some weekday specials, and continental breakfast is included.*

In addition, they give Fango mud baths, and have a small pool. It's a nice option that is quiet (a few blocks off the main street), peaceful, and well-run.

BRANNAN'S LOFT, *is located at 1436 Lincoln, 707-963-2181, but you need to make inquiries and reservations by phone. Their rooms are $65 midweek, $95-$125 on weekends, and include kitchen, bath, air-conditioning, and TV.*

They also offer access to pool and jacuzzi, and a central Lincoln Street locale.

GOLDEN HAVEN SPA, *1713 Lake, 707-942-6793, has standard, cheerless motel rooms (with air-conditioning and refrigerator) for $49-$115.*

This place also features a swimming pool and mud bath spa.

HIDEAWAY COTTAGES, *1412 Fairway, 707-942-4108, is located two blocks up from Lincoln, with cottages $40-$150, depending on size and kitchen facilities.* The key here is quiet. When they say it's for adults only, they don't mean it's a swinging joint, they mean no noise, and it's popular with senior citizens staying a month or more, and with some honeymooners.

DR. WILKENSON'S HOT SPRINGS, *1507 Lincoln, 707-942-4102, is a better bargain off-season ($49-$79) than in the summer ($69-$99).*

In the motel, the rooms are decorated in cinder block and green carpet, though their Victorian rooms are more elegant. They have earned a strong reputation from their mud baths, but the hotel aspect is not very special.

NANCE'S HOT SPRINGS, *1614 Lincoln, 707-942-6211, has drab, slightly run-down but clean motel rooms for $50-$75.*

The rooms all have a TV, phone, kitchenette, and air-conditioning, and they have a small pool as well as mud facilities.

CALISTOGA HOT SPRINGS SPA, *1066 Washington (south of Lincoln), 707-942-6269, has off-season rates from $64, summer rates from $71, and discounts for longer stays.*

The rooms are pretty standard, with kitchenette, phone, TV, and air-conditioning. They also offers the usual mud baths, and have an exercise room with Universal machines, weights, aerobic dance classes, and pools.

CALISTOGA INN, *1250 Lincoln, 707-942-4101, is a comfortable old hotel with personality, continental breakfast, a garden patio restaurant and a brew pub. The rooms (all share hall baths) are $49 Sunday-Thursday and $60 on weekends, and continental breakfast is included.*

At the eastern end of town by the river, this old hotel exudes charm and personality, and it's easily affordable. While the towels are awful and the rooms have no phones, TV, or private baths, they're comfortable and pretty, and retain much of their turn-of-the-century flavor; the front ones even have balconies overlooking the main street (though the rear ones are quieter). White paint, floral curtains, a sink, and a big comfortable bed with feather pillows make the room pleasing to the eye and body after a hard day's lounging in the spas.

In the morning the breakfast starts you off with cereals, cakes, and fruit, and in the evening you can hang out in the Inn's brew pub, which sometimes books music as well. And it's just minutes from anywhere in Calistoga. Of the dozens of places to stay in Calistoga our favorite place by far is the Calistoga Inn.

TRIPLE S RANCH, *4600 Mountain Home Ranch Road, 707-942-6730, is a family-run mountain ranch. Five miles from Calistoga, it is west on Petrified Forest and north on Mountain Home Ranch. April through December, they offer eight homey redwood cabins for $42 a single and $54 a double.*

The Triple S Ranch, in business since 1960, offers another inexpensive place to stay. A few miles from town, their cabins are more remote, which can be an advantage or a drawback, depending on your inclination. The redwood cabins are cute in a basic, undecorated way; it's just a shame that the lovely wood is partly hidden inside by pale, awful paneling. The porches, on the other hand, are swell for sitting out, digesting your meal, and watching the stars appear.

If you want to be away from the action, or if you are coming with kids, the Triple S can be a good option. The cabins hold up to 4 people easily, and have their own private bathrooms. And the people who run the ranch are down-to-earth and genuinely nice. They have a pool, a restaurant renowned for its onion rings, and a great, welcoming attitude.

NAPA COUNTY FAIRGROUNDS, *1435 Oak, 707-942-5111, has tent sites with hot showers for $10 and camper hook-ups (with electricity) for $15.*

It's a fairly central place to be that's just a five-minute walk from Lincoln Street, but it's as bucolic as the state park.

BOTHE-NAPA STATE PARK, *3801 St. Helena Hwy. N., 707-942-4575, has camp sites with hot showers for $14 ($3 for swimming pool). Call 800-444-PARK for reservations.*

This is a very beautiful site to camp.

Where to Eat

The food in Calistoga is incredible. It's superb. They have top-notch chefs from all around Northern California, not surprising really since Calistoga attracts lots of tourists with well-developed, discerning palates. Food in Calistoga is one of the pleasures that can be enjoyed and lingered over no matter what the weather's doing.

EXPENSIVE
Creole

CATAHOULA RESTAURANT, *in the Mount View Hotel at 1457 Lincoln, 707-942-2275, opened recently and does very popular Cajun cuisine at hotel prices.*

The spicy, pricy, gourmet Louisiana dishes from the Catahoula Restaurant (run by Jan Birnbaum, who used to be chef in Campton Place) are exceptional, and the Catahoula Saloon next door, with all the swell Catahoula dog photos, is great for cocktails.

MODERATE
American

TRIPLE S RANCH, *4600 Mountain Home Ranch Road, 707-942-6730, has American food that's popular with the locals. Five miles from Calistoga, it is west on Petrified Forest and north on Mountain Home Ranch.*

Dinner at the Triple S Ranch is a special experience, but not quite as enjoyable as you might hope. Surrounded by tables of white-haired old ladies in track suits, this is clearly where the locals come to escape the healthy gourmet goat cheese salads and arugula pizzas that have taken over Calistoga, and revel in good old-fashioned fat. The deep-fried onion rings, the pride of the Triple S Ranch, live up to their reputation, but the rest is pretty disappointing.

Italian

BOSKO'S RISTORANTE, *1403 Lincoln. 707-942-9088.*

Bland and doughy pizza and fresh but unoriginal pasta. It's homey and a popular place, especially with families, and it gets very full on the weekends, but there are far better establishments in which to spend your money.

Mexican

CAFE PACIFICO, *1237 Lincoln. 707-942-9088.*

Bland, overpriced Mexican food and a margarita hour.

LAS BRASAS, *1350 Lincoln. 707-942-4056.*

Tastier over-priced Mexican food, and a mesquite grill.

Nouvelle California Cuisine

WAPPO BAR & BISTRO, *1226B Washington. 707-942-4712.*

This is a new restaurant that does everything right. From their great summer gazpacho to their beautiful patio, it's a special place to eat. Lunch for two costs around $20, though dinner with wine, appetizers, and dessert might run closer to $50. There are many truly fine places to eat here, but our favorite has got to be Wappo Bar & Bistro. The food is not only spectacular, it's creative and unusual as well. If the chile rellenos in pomegranate sauce is on the menu, you'll be extraordinarily lucky. Their pork sandwich with garlic aioli is also an amazing repast, and makes me a bit hungry just to think of it.

The grape arbor patio is just as romantic and lovely as could be, but if it's blustering and stormy out, their two dining rooms (in buildings next door to one another) do quite nicely. Wappo's is a reason in and of itself to go up to Calistoga.

ALL SEASONS CAFE AND WINE SHOP, *1400 Lincoln, 707-942-9111, has innovative sandwiches & salads from $5.95, and an enormous wine list.*

This is a pleasant place to dine, and the food's good. Their salads are magnificent, and can easily make a nice lunch for two, and their sandwiches are imaginative and very fine as well. With marble-top tables, checkered tile floor, and wine-savvy waiters, it's a very pleasant place to dine, sip, and watch the world stroll by.

CALISTOGA INN, *1250 Lincoln. 707-942-4101.*

There's a restaurant inside and out. Dinners aren't cheap, but the food is fresh and tasty, and the garden patio provides a nice setting. Their garden patio restaurant is more of an attraction in fair weather, but the food remains great whether it's eaten out of doors or in their formal dining room.

INEXPENSIVE

American

BIG DADDY'S, *1522 Lincoln.*

The central spot for burgers, fries, and shakes, as well as the meet-up point for classic car aficionados.

FELLION'S DELICATESSEN, *1359 Lincoln. 707-942-6144.*

Serves breakfast and sandwiches. The atmosphere is unappealing for a sit-down meal, but it's a good, inexpensive place for picnic supplies.

THE HOME PLATE, *on Hwy. 128 & Petrified Forest Road.*

Not well located; the burgers are a cut above McDonald's, but not by much.

Chinese
SOO YUAN, *1354 Lincoln. 707-942-9404.*
The one Chinese restaurant in town, serving reasonable Mandarin and Szechwan food.

Mexican
CALISTOGA DRIVE-IN TAQUERIA, *1207 Foothill Boulevard by the west end of Lincoln. 707-942-0543.*
Good, cheap Mexican food with plastic picnic tables outside.

COFFEE JOINTS IN CALISTOGA

Calistoga Roastery, 1631 Lincoln, with an outside deck roasts their own, and serves a great cup of coffee. It's a very pleasant place to hang out and watch the world go by.

Cafe San Marco, 1336 Lincoln, is pleasant and friendly, and serves strong coffee.

Hydros, 1403 Lincoln, in the old 1902 Armstrong Building, is the most central, and will do if you can't haul yourself a couple blocks left or right to one of the others.

Seeing the Sights
Old Faithful Geyser *is two miles north of Calistoga on Tubbs Lane, off Hwy. 128,* and it shoots a blast of boiling water 60 feet up in the air, surrounded by steam and camera-clicking tourists. The average interval between eruptions is now 1 hour, 50 minutes, but it varies depending on seismic activity and drought conditions. The site is open 9am-5pm, and costs $5 per person.

The Petrified Forest *is five miles west of Calistoga on Petrified Forest Road,* and is open 10am-5pm for $3 per person. Mt. St. Helena erupted over 3 million years ago, covering the area in lava and ash. The site now is a redwood forest, with petrified trees interspersed. It is a pleasant and interesting place for a walk, but it's not a big deal. They have a small museum that does a credible job on the geology, and a gift shop with polished semi-precious stones that promise a variety of emotional benefits from softening stubbornness to relieving stress.

The Sharpsteen Museum and Sam Brannan Cottage, *1311 Washington, 707-942-5911,* is open daily from 10am-5pm and is free. The museum celebrates the work of Walt Disney animator (and museum donator) Ben Sharpsteen and the life and times of Sam Brannan, Calistoga's founder.

Nightlife
The Surfwood, *1410 Lincoln,* with a band and dancing, is the place to be on Friday night. The whole town and surrounding communities turn

out and dance it up. On Saturdays they have either jukebox or live music, but the Friday hoopla is missing.

La Vista Restaurant, *1330 Lincoln*, serves Mexican food, and has music Friday (sometimes poorly attended), but their Saturday Spanish music is more popular.

Catahoula Saloon, *1457 Lincoln*, is a great bar, and the drinks are sensational. You can order from the restaurant menu while you work on their outstanding home-made Bloody Mary (with hot pepper swizzle), and take in the canine decor motif. They sometimes speak of plans to start up jazz on the weekends, but it's not a reliable music venue for now.

The Calistoga Inn Brew Pub, *1250 Lincoln, 707-942-4101*, offers a fine selection of wine, their own beer, and live music most nights. The bands change, but they often book acoustic folk or pop, of moderately entertaining quality.

You can also check out **The Abby Restaurant**, *3022 N. St. Helena Highway, 707-942-6725*, for weekend jazz.

Shopping

The Calistoga Depot, *1458 Lincoln*, built in 1868 for the trains that used to run, has retained its classic shape but not its function. The Depot now contains oodles of gift shops and boutiques, and better still, the Chamber of Commerce in back.

Other than that, people generally buy wine from the wineries or mud treatments from their favorite spa.

Sports & Recreation

Spas & Mud Baths

Calistoga is bursting at the seams with mud bath and massage facilities. All the spas offer mineral baths and massages along with their featured treatments, and some have lodgings as well, but mud baths are the signature recreation in Calistoga. If your body stores any tensions from your daily grind, a treatment package with mud, steam, and massage (around $60-$80) can be a great release. Lying stretched out in hot mud imparts a buoyant, warm, weightless feeling from the combined density of the mud and heat of the hot springs water, the steam wrap that follows relaxes you just a bit more, and the massage polishes you off. After a couple hours of warm pampering attention to your body, you ooze well-being, dig a few dregs of mud from under your nails, and try to remember what tension felt like.

While the spas that are hotels as well are described in the *Where To Stay* section of this chapter, here are the ones that just attend to your body (note: the prices here are for the whole treatment package, but you can get a la carte treatments for less).

Lincoln Avenue Spa, *1339 Lincoln, 707-942-5296*, is an old bank that's been transformed. They offer body mud applications in attractive red-bricked and green-tiled old bank vault rooms for $55.

International Spa, *1300 Washington, 707-942-6122*, is known for its New Age music and aroma-therapeutic aura, and does classic mud baths for $65.

The Calistoga Massage Center, *1219 Washington, 707-942-6193*, offers massages only for $25 and up.

Lavender Hill Spa, *1015 Foothill Boulevard, 707-942-4495*, is into aromatherapy and reflexology as well as Fango mud baths, and they charge $60.

Mount View Spa and Hotel, *1457 Lincoln, 707-942-6877*, offers Fango mud and a fancy Jacuzzi with waterfalls, jets, etc. for $60, and includes a nice pool to lounge by.

Indian Springs, *1712 Lincoln, 707-942-4913*, has a full mud treatment for $85, featuring 100% ash (they claim this is better than peat). They also have a beautiful, Olympic-sized pool that was built in 1913, with sensational decoration.

Pine Street Inn And Eurospa, *1202 Pine, 707-942-6829*, gives Fango mud baths for $49, and has a small pool.

Golden Haven Spa, *1713 Lake, 707-942-6793*, has friendly staff that administer traditional mud in cement tubs for $60, and a swimming pool too.

Dr. Wilkenson's Hot Springs, *1507 Lincoln, 707-942-4102*, has mud baths in tile tubs for $69, and full facial treatments too, and you'll need reservations for either (bear in mind their last treatments are at 3:30). It's a popular place, with great postcards of shriveled Dr. Wilkenson immersed in mud, but their fame has gone to their heads and they're not very friendly.

Nance's Hot Springs, *1614 Lincoln, 707-942-6211*, does mud for $62, and has a pool.

Calistoga Hot Springs Spa, *1066 Washington, south of Lincoln, 707-942-6269*, offers the usual mud baths, plus an exercise room with Universal machines, weights, aerobic dance classes, many pools, and treatments for $57.

SPA TREATMENTS EXPLAINED

Mud Bath – *You immerse yourself for 10 minutes in a tub of "thermally active" (i.e. hot) mud. The heat relaxes your muscles, and the sweat detoxifies the skin.*

Fango Mud – *Special "dehydrated volcanic mud" with pine oil and herbs added to a whirlpool bath. Detoxifies and relaxes, while anaspirin additive soothes aches.*

Seaweed Bath – *Here you soak in a blend of French seaweed and cucumber gel. Meant to be invigorating.*

Milk-Whey Bath – *Powdered milk whey in a tub creates a soothing florescent green soak. Moisturizes skin, helps psoriasis.*

Aromatherapy – *You choose from a vast array of aromatic oils, such as Anti-stress, Citrus, or Eros to scent your steam, whirlpool, or massage. This works on the nervous system, so they say, to neutralize positive ions.*

Body Mud Treatment – *You slather your body in a thin layer of mud (Herbal Mineral, Sea, or Mint), painting all save your face and the soles of your feet, then climb carefully onto the sauna table to steam. Cleanses and softens your skin while soothing muscles.*

Herbal Wrap – *A mud alternative, you're wrapped in steaming linens that have been steeped in various herbs. Detoxifies and purifies your system.*

Seaweed Wrap – *You are coated with warm Mediterranean seaweed. Cleans, rehydrates, and tones your skin.*

Reflexology – *This technique applies pressure to the nerves in your feet. Strengthens "deep organ incirculation" and your immune system.*

Acupressure Facelift – *Gentle acupressure is applied to specific points, followed by warm herbal compresses. Helps remove wrinkles, aids circulation, restores skin tone.*

THE WINERIES

If the weather is clear and the sun is shining, there are some great outdoor activities. **Napa Valley** is rightfully known for its wineries, and there are many fine ones within cycling distance (you can do a driving tour, too, but cycling is a little safer if you'll be wine tasting). Pedaling around is fun and easy, even if you're not an accomplished cyclist.

In fact, if it's been a long time since you straddled a bike, you'll be amazed at how easy it all is now. Gone are the three-speed banana seats and such. Calistoga rents hybrids - a cross between a street bike and a mountain bike. It's easy to shift the 21 gears, easy to pedal, and delightful to explore the back streets and rural lanes in the stunning countryside around Calistoga. And while it's tough to carry a case of wine back in the handle bar basket, it's easy to make a few stops on your drive back home.

This area is, of course, floating in wineries. As mentioned earlier, you can consult Open Road's *California Wine Country Guide* ($11.95). There is also a free *Wine Country Guide* at the Chamber of Commerce that shows where they all are, and Mattioli's *In Your Pocket Guide* ($1.50 at the Calistoga Book Store) which shows bike routes.

A few of my favorite wineries include the following: **Vincent Arroyo Winery**, *2361 Greenwood Avenue*, is a small family operation. They feature really nice people, good and affordable wine, and a personal touch. **Clos Pégase**, *1060 Dunaweal Lane*, is a remarkable place to visit if you like art. They have wine tasting ($3 for four samples) and magnificent sculpture, including a six-foot thumb by French sculptor Cesar, and a terrific, leering Bacchus. **Dutch Henry Winery**, *4310 Silverado Trail*, is another small family-owned operation with free tastings and reasonable rates. In contrast, Coca Cola's **Sterling Vineyards**, *1111 Dunaweal Lane*, is a big corporate production. For $6 you get a 30-second gondola-car ride up the mountain for valley views and mediocre wine.

If you want to enjoy the scenery without imbibing, there is hiking at **Bothe-Napa State Park**, *three miles south at 3801 N. St. Helena Highway*, as well as in **Robert Louis Stevenson State Park**, *three miles northeast of Calistoga on Highway 53*, which is where Robert Louis Stevenson honeymooned, got his inspiration for "Silverado Squatters," plus some settings for *Treasure Island* as well. You can hike up to his cabin site or amble along the Mount St. Helena Trail.

Calistoga Gliders, *1546 Lincoln, 707-942-5000*, offers a less athletic way to see the area with rides over Napa Valley. Gliders start at $79, and antique biplane rides start at $100.

And **Wild Horse Valley Ranch**, *on Wild Horse Valley Road near Napa, 707-224-0727*, offers horseback riding. It's a bit of a drive from Calistoga, but no more than a half hour away.

Practical Information

Annual Events: February-Mustard Festival; March-Napa Valley Marathon; July-Napa Horse Show; Wine Country Film Festival; September-Bike tour; October-Beer & Sausage Festival - call *707-942-6333* for details.

Bank of America: *1429 Lincoln*, open 9am-6pm Monday-Thursday, and 9am-7pm Friday, is the only bank that cashes foreign and US traveler checks, though plenty of other banks have ATMs.

Bicycle Rentals: You can rent bikes from Jules Culver Bicycles, *1227 Lincoln, 707-942-0421*, for $6 an hour and $19 a day, or from Palisades Bike Shop, *1330B Gerard, 707-942-9687*, for $8 an hour, $15 for 4 hours, and $30 a day, and they'll both be happy to suggest some routes.

Tourist Information: *1458 Lincoln behind the Depot building, 707-942-6333)* and pamphlets can be found at the friendly Chamber of Commerce. The office is open daily 10am-5pm, or you can look up their online web page at http://www.napavalley.com/calistoga.html

GUIDED TOURS OF THE CITY & THE GREATER BAY AREA

Limo's Limited, *415-986-5436*, provides comfortable and personal tours to the Wine Country, Muir Woods, or wherever. They also do airport shuttle service for $30.

Great Pacific Tours, *415-626-4499*, runs mini van tours of San Francisco, the Wine Country, Muir Woods, Sausalito, Carmel, and Monterey, for $27-$59.

Highlights Tours, *1398 Bryant, 415-697-2529*, has tours of the city, Muir Woods, and Sausalito for $33.

Tower Tours, *77 Jefferson, 415-434-8687*, offers city tours, Alcatraz and bay cruises, Muir Woods and Sausalito, Wine Country, Monterey and Carmel, or Yosemite in a day for $25-$95.

Wine Train, *707-253-2111 or 800-427-4124,* provides a Wine Country tour, of sorts, but it's a tour where you never leave the train. It's more of a meal on wheels, where you eat very fine food, do a lot of tastings, and look at the pretty scenery going by. It costs $60 for the lunch 'tour' and $70 for dinner, and while the 1917 restored train is quite elegant, you won't really see that much of Napa Valley.

Cable Car Fun tours, *415-922-2425, 800-562-7383*, offer motorized cable car tours of San Francisco leaving from Taylor at Jefferson near Fisherman's Wharf (there's also a shuttle leaving from Macy's on Geary in Union Square that'll take you to the Wharf). The tour lasts 1 hour, costs $12 for adults and $5 for children 12 and under, and hits the major downtown sites of Nob Hill, Union Square, and Fisherman's Wharf. Visitors tend to like it because of its cable car shape, but San Francisco locals sneer profusely and heap scorn on the faux cable cars and their naïve patrons.

Cruisin' the Castro, *415-550-8110*, is a walking tour of the Castro, San Francisco's gay neighborhood. Trevor Hailey knows her community and her history, so her 3.5 hour tour (brunch included, $30) provides an excellent introduction to SF's gay community. The tours start at 10am at the Harvey Milk Plaza by Castro's Muni station, Tuesday-Saturday, and you'll need to make reservations in advance.

Carriage Charter, *at the Carriage House on Powell and Jefferson, 415-398-0857,* provides horse-drawn carriage tours of North Beach, Aquatic Park, and the waterfront. Usually available daily at Pier 41 from 3-11pm, in winter operations are scaled back to Thursday-Sunday evenings only. There are mini-wharf tours (20 minutes for $25), wharf tours (35 minutes for $45), and deluxe wharf tours (50 minutes for $65), and the rates are for the whole carriage, not per person. They also rent carriages for special events like weddings and mayoral inaugurations (Willie Brown rode down the wharf in a horse-drawn carriage to start the inauguration festivities in January '96).

Hunting Bargains, *415-892-1088*, takes you on a guided outlet shopping tour for $36 per person. Reservations required, the tour takes about five hours, and leaves from Fisherman's Wharf at 9:45am, or from Union Square at 10am.

Wine Country Carriages, *Office-Farm, 3325 Gravenstein Highway N., Sebastopol, Sonoma County, 707-823-7083, 800-500-7083*. To get there from San Francisco takes a little over an hour. Drive over the Golden Gate Bridge and take 101 North to the Guerneville Road exit just north of Santa Rosa. Go west on Guerneville Road for eight miles to Hwy. 116. Go left and 3/4 mile down Hwy. 116 the farm is on the left.

A one hour trip can cost $50-$300, four hours ranges from $150-$600, and a six-hour jaunt costs $200-$800. They stop at a number of sites, including wineries, farms, and woods, and they'll prepare a gourmet picnic lunch as well for $25 per couple (or you can bring your own and use their picnic tables). There are also horse-drawn tours of Calistoga (off Lincoln Avenue, just behind the small airport) from a 15-minute flit ($20-$30) to a two-hour wine tasting tour ($100-$550). Carriage transport is a fun treat in the city, but it lends itself to country travel even more, especially with a picnic and a few wine-tastings to complete the picture. All prices include a properly attired coachman, and they suggest you get into the spirit of the event with your own attire.

CARRIAGES FOR ALL OCCASIONS

Wine Country Carriages keeps a fine stable of Standardbred trotters and a barn full of antique and fully functional carriages of sizes and styles to fit various needs. The Concord stage coach from 1868 works well for a big group of up to 20, the 19th century fringe-topped surrey is more the thing for a romantic tryst, the Dray Wagon does a fine hay ride, and the distinctive Victoria & Pair is often chosen for wedding couples, guests of honor, and any of those events that call for horse-drawn elegance. There are 13 different original, authentic carriages in all, and wine country tour prices vary according to length (1-6 hours) and capacity (2-20 people, depending on the carriage model).

San Francisco Pedicabs, *415-673-7203*, is run by the same company who rents the carriages. Steel-calved operators, wise in the ways and the lore of the city, provide you with transportation and information. They're available at Pier 41 and will take you to the cable cars ($4), Ghirardelli Square ($5), on a Wharf tour or around Chinatown ($12.50), or to all of the above ($25). The cabs take up to 3 passengers, and prices are negotiable. The rates listed above are per passenger and one way.

Hornblower Dining Yachts, *Pier 33 on the Embarcadero (at the foot of Bay), 415-788-8866,* offer a number of excursions that combine bay cruises with dancing and dining. Hornblower Cruises include dinner cruises (7:30-10:30pm) for $54.50-$66.50 (depending on the night), Friday lunch cruises (12:30-2pm) for $26.50, and weekend brunches (11am-1pm) for $32.50-$36.50. There are discounts for seniors and military, and children under 13 get 50% off. There are also Monte Carlo Cruises which features a casino on board, laser karaoke, and a DJ dance hall as well as the lunch or dinner, and those trips are $26.50-$49, depending on day and time. You board half an hour before departure, and attire is dressy to semi-formal for dinner cruises but more casual for lunch or brunch. A bay cruise is always fun, but Hornblower doesn't give you quality for your money. It's a somewhat tacky experience, with mediocre food.

Pacific Marine Yachts, *Pier 39, 415-788-9100,* offers the same sort of cruises that Hornblower does, but of far greater quality. Their Sunday brunch cruise (11:30am-1:30pm) aboard the San Francisco Spirit for $40 has much better food, and the experience is classier and geared to higher standards.

The Oceanic Society, *415-474-3385,* offers a different kind of trip, out to the Farallon Islands to see the whales, dolphins, sea turtles and birds. It costs $48 for the January-April six-hour whale watching trips, and $62 for the June-November eight-hour Farallon Island natural history expeditions. They leave every Saturday-Sunday, and some Fridays, passengers must be at least 10 years old, and advance reservations are necessary.

20. CALENDAR OF ANNUAL EVENTS

JANUARY

Whale Watching is in season all winter till April, as the gray whales migrate along the Pacific coast.

FEBRUARY

Chinese New Year goes by the Chinese lunar calendar (it's the first full moon after January 19th), so the dates are different each year. In 1997, New Year's Day is February 7th, and the elaborate night-time Golden Dragon Parade is February 22nd. Fire-crackers pop for weeks in Chinatown, lion dancers strut their stuff, and the new Miss Chinatown USA is crowned. Call *415-391-9680* for details.

San Francisco Tribal, Folk, and Textile Art Show, *Fort Mason, 310-455-2886*, has over 100 folk and ethnic art dealers selling North American pottery, baskets, textiles, and jewelry.

San Francisco Orchid Society's Pacific Orchid Exposition, *415-546-9608*, takes place in Fort Mason towards the end of February with a blaze of color beauty.

MARCH

TulipMania, *415-705-5500*, is an annual festival of tulips that is generally the first week of March. Over 40,000 colorful tulips from around the world are on show, and there are free guided tours.

Asian American International Film Showcase is held each year at the Kabuki 8 Theater in Japantown, *415-863-0814*, usually in the first or second week of March. Call for details and screening times.

Celtic Music & Arts Festival, *415-392-4400*, in early March precedes St. Patrick's day with a celebration of Irish dancing, food, and crafts.

The St. Patrick's Day Parade takes place the weekend closest to March 17th, though it doesn't compare to the east coast celebrations.

The Edge Festival, *415-824-5044*, showcases cutting-edge choreography, and charts the directions dance may take. It's held around the city, so you'll need to call for details.

APRIL

The Saint Stupid Parade runs every April 1st down Market Street in honor of April Fools Day and dupes everywhere.

Cherry Blossom Festival, *415-563-2313*, is Japantown's annual mid-April spring rite. Along with the pink blossoms, the festival features taiko drumming, martial arts, crafts, music, dance, plenty of Japanese food, and a parade from Civic Center to Japantown.

San Francisco International Film Festival, *415-929-5000*, is a great annual event. The exact starting date changes yearly, but it usually begins in the second or third week of April, and runs two or so weeks into the beginning of May. All the new films get showcased there, and it's worth looking through the schedule and film descriptions.

Spike and Mike's Festival of Animation, *415-567-6642*, usually starts in April but lasts into May. It's held in the Palace of Fine Arts Theater, showing animated films of all sorts.

San Francisco Giant's Baseball Season, *800-734-4268*, in Candlestick Park from April-September.

Opening Day of Yachting Season is on the last Sunday of April. And if you don't have your own boat, or friends with boats, you can climb a tall hill and watch the bay fill up with sails.

MAY

Cinco de Mayo Celebration, *415-826-1401*, is a gala celebration in the Mission. There's a parade, dancing and music, great food, and lots of festive spirit. It's held annually on the weekend closest to May 5th, and it's a good time.

San Francisco Youth Arts Festival, *415-759-2916*, celebrates San Francisco students with music, theater, and art in Golden Gate Park.

KFOG Sky Concert, *800-733-6318*, in Justin Herman Plaza down by the foot of Market Street hosts an evening concert and lots of fireworks.

Examiner Bay to Breakers, *415-808-5000, ext. 222, or 777-7770*, is San Francisco's annual spring race, the world's largest. More than 100,000 contestants, many of whom are dressed in incredible costumes, run or walk their way from the Bay to the Pacific Ocean. For a small subset it's a very serious race, attracting the fleetest runners from around the world. For the rest, it's a party, a spring version of Halloween, a goofy lark, and a chance to dress up in the most ridiculous outfit you can think of. Early registration will be about $15, otherwise it'll cost you $20 to run. Usually in May, the exact date changes each year, so call for details.

Carnaval, *415-826-1401*, is SF's interpretation of **Mardi Gras**. Even though it's traditionally held in February in Rio and New Orleans, the weather's nicer here in May, so San Francisco holds its version in late May. There's a parade with lots of samba dancers and music, and loads of food.

JUNE

Ethnic Dance Festival, *415-474-3914*, in the Palace of Fine Arts in early June features performances by more than 900 dancers and musicians.

Haight Street Fair, *415-661-8025*, puts on an annual bang-up neighborhood celebration with food stands and craft stalls, music and dancing and partying in the street till nightfall.

Great San Francisco Bike Adventure, *415-668-2243*, in Moscone Field starts California's largest annual bike tour, covering 15 miles of San Francisco sites.

Make-A-Circus, *415-776-8470*, invites audience members to participate in these free musical comedies in San Francisco parks from mid-June to late September. Call to find out the where and when.

North Beach Fair, *415-403-0666*, turns North Beach into an amusement park of great food, craft stalls, music, and festivities.

Stern Grove Midsummer Music Festival, *415-252-6252*, runs yearly from mid-June to mid-August, with wonderful free performances, from jazz to opera, in Stern Grove's beautiful (if sometimes foggy) outdoor setting in the Sunset.

San Francisco Music Day, *415-391-0370*, has various bands playing all sorts of music all over San Francisco.

San Francisco International Lesbian and Gay Film Festival, *415-703-8650*, showcases more than 350 films, most of which play at the Castro Theater.

Lesbian, Gay, Bisexual, Transgender Pride Celebration Parade, *415-864-3733*, goes from the Civic Center to the Embarcadero in an annual celebration of pride.

JULY

Independence Day, *415-777-8498*, celebrations always includes magnificent fireworks over the bay, they start at 9pm, and a boat or roof-top is a great place to watch the show.

Jazz and All That on Fillmore, *415-346-9162*, is a celebration of Fillmore Street and its jazz roots, with lots of music, food, wine, and art.

Cable Car Bell-Ringing Championship, *415-923-6202*, in Union Square has gripmen competing on the National Landmark's bell.

The San Francisco Symphony POPS, *415-431-5400*, series starts in mid-July and goes for a few weeks into the start of August.

Blues and Art on Polk, *415-346-9162*, converts Polk Street into a music, crafts, and food fest.

AUGUST

The San Francisco 49ers' Football Season, *408-562-4949*, begins in August, lasting into December.

Nihonmachi Street Fair, *415-771-9861*, in Japan Center has lion dancers and taiko drummers, arts and crafts, food, and children's events.

Filipino American Arts Exposition, *415-436-9711*, in the Center for the Arts at Yerba Buena Gardens is an outdoor fair with folk art, films, and a parade down Market Street.

Ringling Brothers and Barnum & Bailey Circus, *415-469-6065*, usually makes its San Francisco stop at the Cow Palace at the end of August or the beginning of September.

SEPTEMBER

Absolut a la Park, *415-383-9378*, in Golden Gate Park makes its appearance on Labor Day weekend, with food stalls from 50 restaurants and 40 wineries and breweries, plus a varied schedule of music and other entertainment. Folks spread out blankets and make it a day.

San Francisco Fair, *415-703-2729*, also takes place during Labor Day weekend down at the Civic Center. They have got lots of competitions like the Impossible Parking Space Race, and Fog Calling, plus food and music.

Renaissance Pleasure Fair, *415-892-0937*, is usually in Marin on Labor Day, but you'll need to call to get an exact place. What they have is an elaborate and enthusiastic event filled with costumes, music, food, and revelry to bring you back to ye merry olde England.

Free Shakespeare in the Park Festival, *415-666-2221*, does its outdoor performances in Golden Gate Park through September (once most of the summer fog has burned off). It's free, though they pass a hat around, and it's a swell opportunity for a picnic.

San Francisco Fringe Festival, *415-931-1094*, features experimental theater throughout the downtown area.

Opera in the Park, *415-864-3330*, is a day of free opera arias in Golden Gate Park.

Viva Mexico!, *415-292-0202*, celebrates Mexican Independence Day on Pier 39.

Chinatown Autumn Moon Festival, *415-982-6306*, on Grant Avenue celebrates with lion dancing, martial arts, and plenty of firecrackers.

San Francisco Hillstride, *415-668-2243*, a seven mile stroll up and down the city hills, starting on the Marina Green.

San Francisco Blues Festival, *415-979-5588*, is held the end of every September in the Great Meadow of Fort Mason. It's the oldest blues festival in America, and it usually gets a good line-up.

Sukkot, *415-346-9162*, is celebrated according to the Hebrew calendar, so it could be late September or early October. The Festival of the Booths is celebrated on Sacramento and Lake with harvest foods, wine, music, and crafts.

OCTOBER

The San Francisco Spiders Hockey Season, *510-762-BASS*, starts its season in the Cow Palace in October and runs through April.

The World Pumpkin Weigh-Off, *415-346-4561*, takes place every October, though the location changes.

The Bridge to Bridge Run, *415-974-6800*, is similar in concept to Bay to Breakers, and runs a 12 kilometer course, starting at 9am at the Golden Gate Bridge, making its way east to the Bay Bridge.

The Castro Street Fair, *415-467-3354*, fills the Castro full of food, arts, music, and revelers.

Fleet Week Celebration, *415-705-5500*, is a week full of Navy men and Blue Angels air shows. North Beach still draws the sailors at night, there are aquatic activities during the day, and the Blue Angels (precision formation flyers) drone over the city to the delight of some and the irritation of others.

Italian Heritage Day Parade, *415-434-1492*, celebrates Columbus and the Italian community with a weekend of Italian music and food, and a parade from Fisherman's Wharf to North Beach on the weekend closest to Columbus Day.

Great Halloween and Pumpkin Festival, *415-346-9162*, takes place the week before Halloween, with a costume parade, pony rides, and contests for pumpkin-carving and pie-eating.

San Francisco International Accordion Festival, *415-775-6000*, in the Anchorage Shopping Center near Leavenworth and Beach has accordion music of all sorts, including the "I'm San Francisco's Main Squeeze" contest.

Grand National Livestock Exposition, Rodeo, and Horse Show, *415-469-6065*, is a world class competition with thousands of cattle and horses, held annually in San Francisco's Cow Palace toward the end of October.

The Exotic Erotic Halloween Ball, *415-864-1500*, is an annual San Francisco lalapalooza that used to be a lot racier than now, though it's still not a sedate afternoon tea.

NOVEMBER

Dia de los Muertos (Day of the Dead), *415-826-8009*, is commemorated November 1st and 2nd in the Mission. This pre-Columbian holiday was revived in 1972 by Galeria de la Raza Studio, and celebrates the dead with costumed processions, window displays, and special foods such as the bread of the dead, and sugar skulls. You'll find windows and crafts in the Mission honoring the holiday during the last weeks of October as well.

Film Arts Festival, *415-552-3456*, is held in the beginning of November at the Roxie Cinema to celebrate low-budget features, documentaries, and experimental short films from Bay Area filmmakers.

Holiday Ice Skating *at the Embarcadero Center, 800-733-6318*, starts in November and lasts through January.

DECEMBER

The New Pickle Circus, *415-826-0747*, always starts off the holiday season with entertainment that's as appealing to adults as to children.

Lighting of Hanukkah Menorah takes place in Union Square during Hanukkah.

Christmas Season in Union Square offers shopping and lights, department store decorations, and the annual ballet performance of *The Nutcracker*.

New Year's Eve is a vast San Francisco party, with most restaurants putting on special dinners and shows, bars crowded to bursting, and revelry in the streets till late.

21. PRACTICAL INFORMATION

Better Business Bureau, *415-243-9999*

Bus Companies
• **AC Transit,** *415-839-2882*
• **Golden Gate Transit,** *415-923-2000*
• **Greyhound,** *415-558-6789*
• **Muni** (also known as San Francisco Municipal Railway), *415-673-6864*
• **SamTrans,** *800-660-4287*

California Road Conditions, *415-557-3755*

Car Rentals
• **Ace,** *415 Taylor, 800-709-8200*
• **Alamo,** *687 Folsom, 415-882-9940*
• **A-One,** *434 O'Farrell, 800-287-3978*
• **Avis,** *675 Post and San Francisco Airport, 800-331-1212*
• **Bay Area Rentals,** *229 Seventh Street, 415-621-8989*
• **Budget,** *321 Mason, 800-601-5385*
• **California Compacts,** *254 South Airport Boulevard, 800-954-7368*
• **Continental,** *404 O'Farrell, 800-851-3515*
• **Dollar,** *a number of city locations, 415-771-5300*
• **Enterprise,** *1133 Van Ness, 800-325-8007*
• **Hayat,** *1409 Rollins, Burlingame, 800-922-7748*
• **Hertz,** *at a number of city locations, 415-775-2002*
• **National,** *550 O'Farrell, 800-227-7368*
• **Payless,** *734 East San Bruno, San Bruno, 800-729-5377*
• **Reliable,** *349 Mason, 415-928-4414*
• **STLB,** *830 Huntingon, San Bruno, 800-433-3058*
• **Sunbelt Sports Cars,** *320 O'Farrell, 415-771-9191*
• **Thrifty Car Rental,** *520 Mason and San Francisco Airport, 800-367-2277*

Disabled Resources
- **Independent Living Resources Council** of San Francisco, *415-863-0381*
- **The Center for Independent Living**, *510-841-4776, in* Berkeley

For further travel plans, try the **Bay Area Outreach Recreation Program**, *415-510-849-4663*, or **Escape Artists Travel**, *510-652-1700*.

Emergency, call *911*

Ferries
- **Blue & Gold Fleet**, *Pier 39 of Fisherman's Wharf, 415-705-5444*
- **Golden Gate Ferries**, *Ferry Building, 415-923-2000, 415-332-6600*
- **The Red & White Fleet**, *Pier 43 1/2, 415-546-2896*

Fire, *415-861-8020* (or *911* in an emergency)

Information
- **San Francisco Visitor Information Center**, *900 Market near Powell*, *415-391-2000*, open Monday-Friday 9am-5:30pm, Saturday 9am-3pm and Sunday 10am-2pm, is the source for information, multilingual advice, and brochures.
- **AAA California State Automobile Association**, *150 Van Ness, 800-272-2155*, offers a load of services (like free maps) for members Monday-Friday 8:30am-5pm.
- **Senior Citizens' Information**, *415-626-1033*

Medical
- **Ambulance**, *415-931-3900*, in an emergency call *911*
- **Haight-Ashbury Free Clinic**, *558 Clayton near Haight, 415-487-5632* .
- **Saint Francis Memorial Hospital**, *900 Hyde near Pine, 415-353-6000*, provides all major acute care and has 24-hour Emergency Room service.
- **San Francisco General Hospital**, *1001 Potrero Avenue between 22nd and 23rd, 415-206-8000*, has an emergency room open 24 hours a day. This is the county hospital serving the needy San Francisco population, and waits are often long. Come in a genuine emergency, but not for general outpatient needs.
- **San Francisco Medical Society**, *415-561-0853*, will help refer a doctor.
- **University of California at San Francisco** (UCSF) Medical Center, *415-476-1000*.
- **Women's Needs Center**, *1825 Haight Street, 415-221-7371*, has been providing quality, sliding-scale service to women for years. They're a good phone resource, too.

Motor Vehicles Department, *1377 Fell Street near Masonic, 415-557-1191*

Parking Garages
- **Chinatown: 433 Kearny**, *415-956-8106*, between Pine and California is open 24 hours, every day; and **733 Kearny**, *415-982-6353*, between Clay Washington is open round the clock every day.
- **Civic Center: 355 McAllister**, *415-863-1537*, between Polk and Larkin is open till midnight Sunday-Thursday, till 1am Friday-Saturday; **360 Grove**, *415-626-4482*, between Franklin and Gough is open till 10pm Monday-Friday unless there's a performance, in which case they stay open till 12am. They're usually closed on weekends, but stay open for performances.
- **Downtown: 123 O'Farrell**, *415-986-4800*, between Powell and Stockton is open till 1am Sunday-Thursday and till 2:30am on weekends; **444 Stockton**, *415-982-8370*, between Sutter and Bush is open every day, round the clock.
- **Financial District: Embarcadero Center**, *415-398-1878*, in Embarcadero One, Two, Three, and Four are all open daily, round the clock; and **250 Clay**, *415-433-4722*, between Battery and Davis is open Monday-Thursday till midnight, Friday-Saturday till 2am, and Sunday till 10pm.
- **Fisherman's Wharf: 665 Beach**, *415-673-5197*, near Hyde is open till 2am.
- **Japan Center: 1660 Geary**, *415-567-4573*, between Buchanan and Webster is open Monday-Friday till 2:30am, and round the clock on the weekends, and they accept Kabuki Theater validations.
- **Marina: 2055 Lombard**, *415-495-3772*, between Fillmore and Webster is open Tuesday-Wednesday until 1am, Thursday till 2:30am, Friday-Saturday till 3:30am, and Sunday-Monday till midnight.
- **Mission: 90 Bartlett**, *415-565-7357*, near 21st is open till midnight Monday-Thursday, till 2am Friday-Saturday, and till midnight on Sunday; **1660 Mission**, *415-558-6510*, by the corner of 13th Street and South Van Ness is open Monday-Friday till 6pm.
- **North Beach: 766 Vallejo**, *415-558-9147*, between Stockton and Powell is open Monday-Saturday till 2am and Sunday till midnight.
- **South of Market: 255 Third**, *415-777-2782*, between Howard and Folsom is open Monday-Friday till midnight and Saturday-Sunday till 11:30pm; **833 Mission**, *415-982-8522*, between Fourth and Fifth is open 24 hours a day, seven days a week; **Third and Folsom**, *415-543-4533*, stays open Monday-Friday till 11pm, Saturday-Sunday till 6pm, and has a flat rate of $15 for the day; **7th and Harrison**, *415-495-3770*, near the Hall of Justice is open 24 hours a day, 7 days a week, but the attendant is on duty Monday-Friday till 7pm.

• **Union Square**: **333 Post**, *415-397-0631*, near Geary is open daily and hourly.

Pharmacies
• **Walgreens** are located throughout the city, but the branch at **498 Castro**, *415-861-6276*, is open 24 hours, with a pharmacist on duty. There is also a branch conveniently located at **135 Powell**, near the cable car turnaround open 8am-midnight (though the pharmacist leaves at 8pm). Check yellow pages for other locations.

Police
• Call *415-553-0123*, in an emergency call *911*. There are also specialty numbers, like the **Sex Crimes Unit**, *415-553-1361*, and the **Rape Treatment Center** 24-hour hot-line, *415-206-3222*.

Taxis
• **City**, *415-468-7200*
• **De Soto**, *415-673-1414*
• **Luxor**, *415-282-4141*
• **National**, *415-648-4444*
• **Veteran's**, *415-552-1300*
• **Yellow Cab**, *415-626-2345*

Trains
• **Amtrak**, *415-982-8512, 800-872-2745*
• **BART**, *415-788-2278*
• **CalTrain**, *415-495-4546*

INDEX

452 SAN FRANCISCO GUIDE

FROM THE PUBLISHER

Our goal is to provide you with a guide book that is second to none. Please remember, however, that things do change: phone numbers, prices, addresses, quality of food served, value, etc. Should you come across any new information, we'd appreciate hearing from you. No item is too small, so if you have any recommendations or suggested changes, please write to us.

Have a great trip!

Open Road Publishing
P.O. Box 20226
Columbus Circle Station
New York, NY 10023

TRAVEL NOTES

TRAVEL NOTES

TRAVEL NOTES

OPEN ROAD PUBLISHING
Your Passport to Great Travel!

Going abroad? Don't leave home without an Open Road travel guide to one of these great European destinations:
France Guide, $16.95
Italy Guide, $17.95
Paris Guide, $12.95
Portugal Guide, $16.95
Spain Guide, $17.95
London Guide, $13.95
Holland Guide, $15.95
Austria Guide, $15.95
Rome Guide, $13.95
Israel Guide, $16.95

And if you're traveling abroad to Latin America & the Caribbean, Asia, or the Middle East:
Central America Guide, $17.95
Costa Rica Guide, $16.95
Belize Guide, $14.95
Honduras & Bay Islands Guide, $14.95
Guatemala Guide, $16.95
Southern Mexico & Yucatan Guide, $14.95
Bermuda Guide, $14.95
China Guide, $18.95
Hong Kong & Macau Guide, $13.95

Forthcoming 1996-1997 foreign guides: Greek Islands, Turkey, Ireland, Czech & Slovak Republics, Moscow, Vietnam, Japan, Thailand, Philippines, Mexico, Bahamas, Kenya, and more!

Closer to home, check out Open Road's US travel guide series:
Las Vegas, $12.95
Disney World & Orlando Theme Parks, $13.95
America's Most Charming Towns & Villages, $16.95
Florida Golf Guide, $19.95
San Francisco Guide, $14.95

Forthcoming 1996-1997 US guides: Hawaii, Colorado, California Wine Country, New Mexico, Alaska, Arizona, Texas, Boston, and more!

PLEASE USE ORDER FORM ON NEXT PAGE

ORDER FORM

Name and Address: _____

_____

_____

_____ Zip Code: _____

Quantity	Title	Price

Total Before Shipping _____

Shipping/Handling _____

TOTAL _____

Orders must include price of book <u>plus</u> shipping and handling. For shipping and handling, please add $3.00 for the first book, and $1.00 for each book thereafter.

Ask about our discounts for special order bulk purchases.

Order from:

OPEN ROAD PUBLISHING

P.O. Box 20226, Columbus Circle Station, New York, NY 10023